PENGUIN BOOKS

NEAL CASSADY: COLLECTED LETTERS, 1944–1967

NEAL CASSADY was born in Salt Lake City in 1926. When, six years later, his mother parted from her alcoholic husband, the boy was left in the care of his father, with whom he lived in cheap hotels around Denver and took hobo trips across the country. Cassady began stealing cars for joyriding at the age of fourteen and was subsequently arrested several times, culminating in a year's imprisonment at the Colorado State Reformatory, 1944–45. A year after his release, Cassady married his first wife, LuAnne Henderson. The pair traveled to New York City, where a long friendship with Jack Kerouac and Allen Ginsberg, the founders of the Beat generation school of writing, began. In April 1948, Cassady's marriage to LuAnne was annulled; he then married Carolyn Robinson, settling in San Francisco. With Jack Kerouac a regular visitor, their times together and subsequent road trips across the United States were to become the subject matter of Kerouac's novels, in which Cassady is portrayed as Dean Moriarty and Cody Pomeray. Cassady's long, energetic letters inspired Kerouac to develop the spontaneous prose technique he first successfully employed in his 1951 scroll version of *On the Road*. Cassady was arrested in 1958 on a minor drug charge and spent two years in San Quentin Prison. In the 1960s he met the writer Ken Kesey, becoming his muse, fellow Merry Prankster, Acid Test showman, and driver of the psychedelic bus. Neal Cassady died during a trip to Mexico in 1968, a few days before his forty-second birthday.

DAVE MOORE lives in Bristol, England, and is the author of many articles on the Beat writers. Founding editor of *The Kerouac Connection* magazine in 1984, he also writes on mystery and crime fiction as well as jazz and blues. He is currently at work on the definitive guide to the more than six hundred characters in Jack Kerouac's work.

Sept 10, '48

My- Jack;

Again I'm late - gee, sorry I can't rush my replys. Try & forgive - to show I mean business is - all the hundreds of pamphlets to "Ranch" I'm gathered for you - real work - & too abstract & too early now.

You, Jack, are a true "all-american" you present, (just as you told me you once wanted) a perfect all-american growth - (as did Balzac or Voltaire a all-French growth) - to me.

We can write to each other & be full of contradictions - rights & wrongs - up & down, my boy - & still expect each other to understand - it's beyond me how blithe we are - but, it may be we are this way because - our idea of friendship is just that - no more, who can say? - or, think further Jack & No, but, you won't think further & no, don't say you understand see and that part of anger (and I'm showing) - as something excusable, "because he's a friend" — I'm insulting you, Jack - is it because I'm browbeaten by you (unintentionally) into this? - No NAY; (2)

Letter from Neal Cassady to Jack Kerouac

Cassady, Neal.
Collected letters,
1944-1967 /
2004.
33305207717392
sa 03/02/06

ADY

Collected Letters
{1944–1967}

Introduction by Carolyn Cassady

Edited by Dave Moore

PENGUIN BOOKS

SANTA CLARA COUNTY LIBRARY
3 3305 20771 7392

PENGUIN BOOKS
Published by the Penguin Group
Penguin Group (USA) Inc., 375 Hudson Street, New York, New York 10014, U.S.A.
Penguin Group (Canada), 10 Alcorn Avenue, Toronto, Ontario, Canada M4V 3B2
(a division of Pearson Penguin Canada Inc.)
Penguin Books Ltd, 80 Strand, London WC2R 0RL, England
Penguin Ireland, 25 St Stephen's Green, Dublin 2, Ireland
(a division of Penguin Books Ltd)
Penguin Group (Australia), 250 Camberwell Road, Camberwell, Victoria 3124, Australia
(a division of Pearson Australia Group Pty Ltd)
Penguin Books India Pvt Ltd, 11 Community Centre, Panchsheel Park,
New Delhi–110 017, India
Penguin Group (NZ), cnr Airborne and Rosedale Roads, Albany, Auckland 1310,
New Zealand (a division of Pearson New Zealand Ltd)
Penguin Books (South Africa) (Pty) Ltd, 24 Sturdee Avenue, Rosebank,
Johannesburg 2196, South Africa

Penguin Books Ltd, Registered Offices: 80 Strand, London WC2R 0RL, England

First published in Penguin Books 2004

10 9 8 7 6 5 4 3 2 1

Copyright © Carolyn Cassady, 2004
Notes and commentary copyright © Dave Moore, 2004
All rights reserved

Page 468 constitutes an extension of this copyright page.

LIBRARY OF CONGRESS CATALOGING-IN-PUBLICATION DATA
Cassady, Neal.
[Correspondence. Selections]
Collected letters, 1944–1967 / Neal Cassady ; introduction by Carolyn Cassady ; compiled and edited by Dave Moore.
p. cm.
ISBN 0 14 20.0217 8
1. Beat generation. 2. Cassady, Neal—Correspondence. 3. Cassady, Carolyn—Correspondence. 4. Ginsberg, Allen, 1926—Correspondence. 5. Kerouac, Jack, 1922–1969—Correspondence. 6. Authors, American—20th century—Correspondence. I. Moore, Dave, 1941– II. Title.
PS228.B6C37 2004
973.92'092—dc22
[B] 2003061687

Printed in the United States of America
Set in Aldine BT with Memphis
Designed by Ellen Cipriano

Except in the United States of America, this book is sold subject to the condition that it shall not, by way of trade or otherwise, be lent, resold, hired out, or otherwise circulated without the publisher's prior consent in any form of binding or cover other than that in which it is published and without a similar condition including this condition being imposed on the subsequent purchaser.

The scanning, uploading, and distribution of this book via the Internet or via any other means without the permission of the publisher is illegal and punishable by law. Please purchase only authorized electronic editions, and do not participate in or encourage electronic piracy of copyrighted materials. Your support of the author's rights is appreciated.

Acknowledgments

This book could not have appeared without the encouragement, support, and willingness of Carolyn Cassady. I am indebted to her for making her entire archives available to me and answering innumerable questions about her times with Neal. She read the manuscript, correcting my mistakes and adding further illuminations. My greatest thanks are due to Carolyn, not least of all for feeding me so well during my visits to her home.

Neal's son, Curtis Hansen, provided rare copies of the letters Neal wrote to Curtis's mother, Diana Hansen Cassady, and these are published here for the first time. I'd also like to express my gratitude to Curtis for giving his permission for the inclusion of his mother's letters to Neal.

I am also extremely thankful to Neal's bibliographer Michael Powell for his constant support and the provision of elusive items from his collection. Michael read the manuscript in both draft and proof forms and made many valuable suggestions.

Sandra (sloy) Nichols also read the proofs, and her helpful contributions, as well as her constant support, are greatly appreciated.

Neal's biographers David Sandison and Tom Christopher cheerfully answered questions and provided useful information throughout the project, and I'm grateful to Owen Carlson for his specialist knowledge of the U.S. railroad system.

I'd like to thank the staff at various libraries who assisted me in my quest to obtain more of Neal's letters, in particular Tara Wenger at the Harry Ransom Humanities Research Center of the University of Texas, Polly Armstrong at the Department of Special Collections and Archives, Stanford University, and Bernard R. Crystal at the Rare Books and Manuscripts Library, Columbia University.

Thanks are also due to the following people, who helped in

many different ways: Rod Anstee, Jason Arthur, Ken Babbs, Jim Burns, John Cassady, Ann Charters, Faith Evans, Bill Gargan, Eric Mercer, Bill Morgan, Horst Spandler, Gerd Stern, Kathy Van Leeuwen, George Walker, Joan Wilentz, and Seymour Wyse. Special thanks also go to my editors at Penguin, Michael Millman and Bruce Giffords, for their help and guidance.

DAVE MOORE

Contents

1950

1951

1952

Introduction

As William Shakespeare once remarked, "One man in his time plays many parts." Who was Neal Cassady? This book that Dave Moore has put together shows me how many facets there were to this sparkling diamond in the rough, yet I knew only one or two. So for me it is a "book of revelations," and I find I am as guilty as anyone else of promoting myths about him.

My life with him was only one of the many balls he juggled in the air and was able to keep separate from the others. Does this new knowledge, some of which is revolting to me in the extreme, make me love him any less? Somehow this isn't possible with Neal, no matter how much I disapprove of and regret many of his actions. It wasn't what he did, but what he *was* that got under your skin. All the women he knew and/or loved that I still contact feel the same way.

Clairvoyants saw a halo around him; many considered him a saint. His compassion and humane instincts shone through most of his actions. To him it was not cowardice when he ran from an aggressor, just common sense; he didn't want to hurt anyone, and why ask to get hurt? He also had an uncanny gift for defusing impending violence in others. He is known to have hit women, but I'm sure they asked for it, and that it was a sexual turn-on, as some have confessed to me.

He was certainly further advanced than any of us in wisdom of Spirit, although he himself could not find the spark of divinity within himself, so convinced was he of his worthlessness and guilt. In a past-life reading of his "spiritual origins," the teacher could give only bits of actual lives—the whole reading was like one long prayer. The teacher insisted the channel play it back and listen to this reading—a rare request. She said in all the more than two thousand readings she had given, there were no others like this one.

Many of you will scoff at this bit of information, and that's all right. Everyone will judge Neal from his or her own perspective anyway, as we all must. I am giving you my own orientation and that of a few others.

As Neal wrote in a letter to Jack in early January of 1948: "Most events are inexpressible, they happen in a region of the soul into which no word can penetrate; understanding comes thru the soul . . . I have found myself looking to others for the answer to my soul, whereas I know this is slowly gained (if at all) by delving into my own self only." Here is one example of the brilliance of his mind and the depth of his soul, but his intellect, heart, and desires are in another dimension from his Spirit. So many of us could experience this depth while in his presence, but no one can convey its effect adequately in words. Hence, those who admire him, especially other men, do so largely because of his hedonism, boldness, excess energy.

Some of his declarations about me are not purely accurate, prompted by jealousy or suspicion or fantasy—such as the "varicose veins." Where did he get *that*? Then, aside from some claims to sexual practices that I did not perform, in his letter to Diana on September 10, 1950 (page 145), the middle two paragraph are untrue—a fantasy he made up for Diana. The true facts are told in my book. I've now lost any claim to privacy, and it isn't easy to live with. My own letters to him make me cringe—was I really ever that cutesy? I must foster the "*loving* indifference" Edgar Cayce's teachers advised as the proper attitude in life—exceeding Buddha's "detachment."

Another facet of Neal's mind was his photographic memory. Jack is known as "the great rememberer," but people forget he carried a notebook with him. When he didn't make notes, he often got things wrong. Neal, on the other hand, could remember facts, dates, names, numbers, batting averages, etc., on almost any level and from nearly everything he'd ever read, whether in a newspaper or a book. His ability to assimilate three or four subjects or inputs simultaneously has been noted by some already.

I guess it must be obvious how much I loved and admired this man, even though I cried a lot. He taught me how wrong were the reasons for this suffering, its having been imposed blindly by convention and tradition. It was no accident he was born an Aquarian (love everyone equally). Had I succeeded in leaving him, I would only have taken my problems with me, for I was the problem.

Although Neal constantly denigrated his writing ability, he wasn't hesitant about expressing his beliefs with confidence as to how it should be done—see the section of his January 1948 letter to Jack that begins, "I have always held that when one writes . . ." Then again in his serious letter to Allen Ginsberg of May 15, 1951, where he discusses at length and in minute detail his whole writing experience.

Only Jack and Allen considered him a "writer"; the Beat elite disliked him. Yet his book, *The First Third*, has been selling well around the world since 1971; how many can claim such a track record? This isn't a competition, of course, but he was certainly a "man of letters." Two other books of his letters were published but are now out of print.

Dave's work on this collection is simply awesome; the accuracy of names, dates, places, and relevant characters has never been so complete or correct. It should become and remain the definitive reference book for Beat scholars forever; let's hope they use it and not each other's work, compounding errors.

I hope the readers of these letters and the accompanying notes will look beneath the surface of sensational aspects and find some evidence of the unique soul that was Neal Cassady.

CAROLYN CASSADY

Chronology

1926 February 8: Neal Leon Cassady born in Salt Lake City, Utah, where his father was working as a barber at the Deseret Gym.

1928 Business fails due to Neal Sr.'s increasing alcoholism, and family moves to Denver, where father works in a succession of barbershops.

1931 September: Neal begins school at Colfax Elementary.

1932 Mother leaves, and Neal and father move into cheap hotels, like the Metropolitan, in Denver's skid row. Neal takes extended summer hobo trip with father to visit relatives in Missouri, before Neal commences at Ebert Grammar School.

1933 Neal lives with mother and other siblings at the Snowden apartment building, although takes another long summer trip with father to Utah, New Mexico, and California.

1936 Neal's mother dies in May, and he lives with his half brother Jack Daly.

1938 Begins at Cole Junior High School, Denver.

1939 Jack Daly remarries and Neal sent back to live with father.

1940 Neal steals first car. (By his own admission, Neal "borrowed" more than five hundred cars—for joyriding—between 1940 and 1944, and was arrested three times.) Placed in Mullen Home for Boys, but absconds.

1941 Arrested in Denver for speeding and misuse of license plates, but case dismissed. Meets Justin Brierly, who befriends Neal.

1942 Starts at East High School in January, where he meets Ed Uhl. Travels to Los Angeles for summer. Arrested on suspicion of robbery. Released after two days.

1943 To Los Angeles again. On May 2, arrested for joyriding. Sent to juvenile forestry camp for six months, but escapes after two weeks. Reads Dostoyevsky in camp library. Works at automobile service station in L.A.

1944 In January travels with father to Provo, Utah, to help build steel mill. Returns to L.A. and is arrested in March for previous escape. Sent back to Denver. Arrested in July for receiving stolen goods and sentenced to a year in Colorado State Reformatory, Buena Vista. Begins reading classics from prison library.

1945 Paroled from reformatory in June. Meets Jimmy Holmes, Al Hinkle, and Bill Tomson in Denver pool hall. Also meets Hal Chase. Affairs with Mary Freeland and Joan Anderson.

1946 Works at Ed Uhl's family ranch, near Sterling, Colorado. Back in Denver, meets LuAnne Henderson and they marry August 1. They travel to New York in fall and meet Jack Kerouac and Allen Ginsberg.

1947 Returns to Denver in March. Begins long correspondence with Kerouac and Ginsberg. Meets Carolyn Robinson in Denver that spring. Ginsberg and Kerouac travel to visit Neal in Denver that summer. Neal and Ginsberg visit William Burroughs in East Texas in August. Neal drives Burroughs back to New York in October and returns to Carolyn in San Francisco.

1948 Annuls marriage to LuAnne and marries Carolyn, April 1. Begins work on railroad. Daughter Cathy born, September 7. Neal begins work on his autobiography. In December, Neal drives with LuAnne and Al Hinkle to visit Kerouac in Rocky Mount, North Carolina.

1949 January: Neal, Jack, and LuAnne return to San Francisco, visiting William Burroughs in New Orleans on the way. Neal and Carolyn move into 29 Russell Street that spring. When Jack visits Neal there in August, Carolyn throws them out and they ride back to New York together. Neal meets Diana Hansen at a party and begins affair.

1950 January 26: Daughter Melany Jane (Jamie) born in San Francisco. Neal working in New York parking lot. In July travels with Kerouac to Mexico to obtain divorce from Carolyn. Marries Diana, July 10, although Mexican divorce proves invalid, and returns to San Francisco to continue railroad job; living with Carolyn. Writes long letters to Kerouac and Ginsberg, including the much acclaimed "Joan Anderson" letter. Son with Diana—Curtis Neal—born November 7.

1951 January: Neal makes brief visit to New York to see Diana and Curtis. They agree to an annulment. Experiences writer's block. Son John Allen born September 9. Kerouac visits, late December.

1952 Kerouac stays with Cassadys until April, working on *Visions of Cody*. Begins affair with Carolyn. Neal and Carolyn move to San Jose in August. Kerouac visits on return from Mexico.

1953 Spends month of February working railroad in southeast California. Injures leg in railway accident in April.

1954 Discovers works of the mystic Edgar Cayce. Receives compensation for railroad accident. Ginsberg visits in June. Neal and Carolyn move to Los Gatos, August.

1955 Affair with Natalie Jackson. Fraudulent withdrawal of cash for gambling at horse races. Natalie commits suicide, November 30.

1956 May: Ginsberg's *Howl* published. Kerouac visits Cassadys after fire-watch duties in Washington State.

1957 September: Kerouac's *On the Road* published.

1958 April: Neal arrested for marijuana possession. Sentenced to five years—serves two. Sent to San Quentin prison, July.

1960 Released from prison, June 3. Job recapping tires. Kerouac sees Cassadys during his Big Sur trip, July–August.

1961 February: Commences affair with Anne Murphy. August: Vacation to Denver. Begins mixing with Stanford University students.

1962 Meets Ken Kesey and Merry Pranksters in Palo Alto.

1963 Carolyn divorces Neal. Neal's father dies. Neal travels to East Coast with Anne Murphy and Brad Hodgman, visiting Kerouac in Northport, Long Island. Lives with Anne in Gough Street, San Francisco.

1964 Neal's "Joan Anderson" letter published. Drives Pranksters' bus to New York for World's Fair, June. Meets Kerouac with Kesey and Merry Pranksters. Job in Santa Cruz bookstore.

1965 Living at La Honda with Ken Kesey and Merry Pranksters. Trip to New York and back with Don Snyder, August.

1966 In Mexico with Pranksters, staging Acid Tests. Returned to USA in October, giving final Acid Test in San Francisco on Halloween night.

1967 Returns to Mexico in January, meeting Janice Brown in San Miguel. They travel across the United States together that summer.

1968 January 28: Travels to Mexico. Dies in Mexico, February 4.

1944–45

The earliest surviving letters of Neal's are those he wrote to his benefactor, Justin Brierly,[1] while Neal was incarcerated in the Colorado State Reformatory at the age of eighteen. Neal had been arrested on July 8, 1944, for receiving stolen tires and was sentenced on August 18 to twelve months in the reformatory, which he entered on August 23. Brierly was a Denver high-school teacher and lawyer who had become attracted by Neal and befriended the boy when he first met him, aged fifteen, in 1941. Brierly was impressed by Neal's high IQ of 132 and arranged for him to be admitted into high school.

TO JUSTIN BRIERLY

October 8, 1944
Colorado State Reformatory
Buena Vista, Colo.

DEAR JUSTIN;

Since the last time I have written you (3 weeks ago) I have been transferred from the work gangs (7:30 A.M. to 4 P.M.) to the dairy. Here's a typical day: Get up at 4 A.M., milk 8 cows till 6:15. Take the cows to pasture, eat at 6:45, clean cow barn from 7:15 to 9:30, then miscellaneous duties until noon, eat, grind corn or haul hay until 2:30, take a nap until 3:30, go get the cows, eat at 5 P.M., milk cows again from 6:00 to 8:30, carry milk to kitchen, go to bed at 9:30 P.M.

In the dairy I get 5 good days a month, making it possible for me to get out in May instead of June.

These hours, and the fact that I've been reading a good deal are the primary reasons I haven't written each week.

1. Justin W. Brierly (1905–1985) is portrayed in Kerouac's novels as Denver D. Doll *(On the Road)*, Justin G. Mannerly *(Visions of Cody)*, and Manley Mannerly *(Book of Dreams)*.

Received both your letters. Thanks.

Let me know about the 4 books, after all, I'd hate to have to pay for them & your silence about them implies Mr. Werner hasn't got them.

There is absolutely nothing else I want you to send me, of course, the radio is out & in your last letter you mentioned sending some psychological books, no thanks.

I'm glad to hear Bob Adams is at D.U. [Denver University] & to know Gus Stiny's whereabouts.[2]

To whom did John sell his gum route, you?

I read of Phil Baker's program at Central City, interesting. Will they have the opera in '45 if war's over?[3]

Having heard all of Dewey's speeches and Roosevelt's replies, I'm still convinced of Dewey's superiority, in administration at least.[4]

Willkie's death this A.M. came as a surprise to me.[5]

I must thank you for writing 2 letters in 2 weeks; realizing how busy you are I must insist you write not oftener than once a month.

Strangely enough, I don't miss my epicurean life as much as little things, such as Walt Dean's haircuts. I must get 2000 marks to get out. I now have 175, 7 months to go.

NEAL L. CASSADY

TO JUSTIN BRIERLY

October 1944
Colorado State Reformatory
Buena Vista, Colo.

DEAR JUSTIN;

It was 3 years ago this month that I first became aware of the "old professor" (as Bob, Gus and I used to call you). If you'll recall I had lived at John's[6] about a week when I meet you in Oct. 1941. To more

2. Bob Adams and Gus Stiny were high-school friends of Neal's.

3. Central City, Colorado, thirty miles west of Denver, hosted an opera festival each summer. Justin Brierly was one of its main backers.

4. Thomas E. Dewey (1902–1971). Republican presidential nominee, defeated by Democrat Franklin D. Roosevelt in the presidential election of November 7, 1944.

5. Wendell L. Willkie (1892–1944). Corporation lawyer and Republican presidential nominee in 1940, losing to Franklin D. Roosevelt.

6. Neal was living with Justin Brierly's uncle John Walters and his wife, Lucille, in 1941.

or less mark the starting of our 4th year of friendship, I shall devote this letter to analyzing the influence you have had on my mind, character, temperament & in general my attitude & my reaction to life.

To do this I must assume an objective viewpoint to a matter that, by nature, is necessarily subjective, quite difficult however, to enable me to put on 1 sheet of paper a worthy statement of what I think I've gained & lost by association with you. I must speak dogmatically, which, of course, means a certain degree of exaggeration & distortion of the true facts, but remember each statement, positive though it may sound, is the result of much thought, i.e. a psychoanalysis in thought & deeds of the last 3 years, which differ from the years before that. By noting this difference, modifying it & by a process of elimination, I find not only the amount, but also the degree, of influence you've had on me.

For better understanding I've created 3 titles under which I'll enumerate attributes I've either gained or developed under you. Also if I've enough room I shall speak of the negative points of our relationship. To begin:

1) Mind: I believe I've gained only miscellaneous facts although I've developed a good deal in numerous subjects, I also credit you with my introduction to psychology, but my most important knowledge has derived from philosophy, a study to which you have been indifferent, except perhaps indirectly, in fact, I feel you have subtly endeavored to dispersuade me from indulging in it, fearing I'll become overbalanced, already I have a tendency to be intolerant of society, at least its general opinions, which to you, because of your occupations, is quite important.
2) Character: Truly the most necessary of all you've given me. I could easily write an essay on the importance of a sense of character, consequently you can see how aware I am of it & how much & how carefully one should cultivate character.
3) Temperament: My jaunty manner and ready wit, which is so apparent in my conversation can be largely checked back to you, however, any evenness in my outlook must be attributed to philosophy, not to any silly, feminine, innocent optimism.

NEAL L. CASSADY

TO JUSTIN BRIERLY

October 23, 1944
Colorado State Reformatory
Buena Vista, Colo.

DEAR JUSTIN;

At the corner of 15th and Platte streets there's a café called Paul's Place, where my brother Jack used to be a bartender before he joined the army. Because of this I frequented the place occasionally & consequently have a small bill run up. I believe I owe them about 3 or 4 dollars. If you happen to be in that vicinity please drop in and pay it, will you?

I see Philip Wylie[7] has written another book, "Night Unto Night," supposedly as good as "Generation of Vipers;" Peter Arno[8] also has a new collection of cartoons out, "Man in a Shower" it's called.

They have the Harvard Classics up here, the five foot shelf of books; I've read about 2 feet of it, very nice, I especially enjoy Voltaire & Bacon (Francis).

The football season up here has been a flop. We started out with grand plans; the guards told us if we looked good enough we would go to Salida to play & perhaps one or two other games on the out, but no go. However, I understand the basketball team may get to play some local highschools.

Since the days are getting shorter, because of winter's approach, we get up at 5 o'clock now, instead of 4 as we had been; banker's hours, huh?

I've been here 2 months today (the 23rd), how time does fly.

Please excuse the penmanship, as I can only see out of one eye; this morning I took the cows out to pasture, but on the way they ran out of the road into the corn field. The jackass I was riding couldn't run fast enough to head them, so I jumped off & started to tie him to a barbed wire fence so I could chase the cows on foot. Just as I had tied the reins to the wire he jerked so hard it pulled a staple out of the fence

7. Philip Wylie (1902–1971). American essayist and novelist. His *Generation of Vipers* (1942) waged war on all forms of American hypocrisy and introduced the term *momism*.
8. Peter Arno (1904–1968). Cartoonist for *The New Yorker* magazine.

post and into my left eye. It gorged a chunk out of my eyeball, but luckily failed to hit the cornea. I may lose that eye.

NEAL L. CASSADY

TO JUSTIN BRIERLY

[October 30, 1944]
Colorado State Reformatory
Buena Vista, Colo.

DEAR JUSTIN;

I appreciate the interest you have shown in the eye matter and I want to thank you for it, but, although at the moment I wrote the letter I thought it probable that I might lose the eye, I was told later (by an eye doctor) I would regain satisfactory sight in that eye shortly; a week has gone by and I can see well but not as good as before the accident, also, I am still wearing dark glasses.

Thanks also for writing to the warden, however we have had a new warden (Thomas) since July. I'm rather disappointed to note that you, a man of the world, had failed to read in the newspaper that Ed Lindsley died in an auto accident three weeks ago. I know full well you must have purposely overlooked the article, because of the unimportance of the death of an ex-warden of a reformatory.

Speaking of reformatories, I would like to point out at this time that I have been surprised at some of the petty attitudes the guards assume up here, but most of all I'm surprised at the amount of justice that is, on the whole, utilized by most of the officials. After all, in an institution of this size it is hard to be fair with everybody, as is quite apparent to all, consequently I find it rather easy to accept with philosophical calm the winds of dispute that swirl around this place.

We have moved from the bunk house at the dairy to a new building with recreational facilities, and so I cannot sit down to write an intelligent letter, therefore, I'm not going to write oftener than once a month here after.

Sincerely yours
N.L. CASSADY

TO JUSTIN BRIERLY

[c. November 1944]
Colorado State Reformatory
Buena Vista, Colo.

DEAR JUSTIN;

Early this month I received your gift of a delicious box of candy, then came your subtle letter, and lastly, *The Spotlight*; of the 3 I believe I enjoyed the letter most. Thanks & Thanks.

I have read *all* of Dicken's [*sic*] & Twain's popular works; if you'll recall our discussion on this point concerned "Alice in Wonderland" which I had only skimmed thru. Try again.

I'm sure Mrs. Lindsley feels the same way.

Brilliant woman, Mrs. O'Sullivan, except, of course, for her nauseating Christianity, however, that's probably a necessity (in one form or another) for all otherwise intelligent females.

I hope Gus does not get his tail shot off before this is over; if he can stay at Pearl Harbor long enough, he might succeed. You had previously mentioned Bob Adams entering D.U.; let us keep him there; needless to say, I envy him to a degree, not too high a degree though, or evidently I would have completed High School & taken a try at some "higher knowledge." Ah, sweet opportunity, should I have heed thee?—tut, tut—I'm still young.

Recently I have lost some marks for telling a falsehood, (one of principle). An inmate killed a pig & I denied I knew anything of the affair; since another inmate's testimony failed to collaborate with mine, I lied—consequently I shall get out in June instead of May as I had planned, unless I also lose another 500 marks that I'm on probation for now, (same deal) then I will get out in the last days of Sept. '45. How boring.

I can no longer condone the repetition so obvious in your otherwise very good letters, not only of facts and persons, but of phrases. I shall repeat a few:

1. On Sept. 26 and Nov. 16th you became head of Russian war relief. (I know how busy you are, no need to emphasize)

2. On the same dates Gus also B. Adams was at Pearl, (more excusable, but you shouldn't have mentioned Gus in the second letter unless he had changed locale)

3. One phrase repeated twice in one letter & the same mistake in another note.

I suspect this is caused by you having nothing else to write that you think would interest me.

NEAL L. CASSADY

TO JUSTIN BRIERLY

January 8, 1945
Colorado State Reformatory
Buena Vista, Colo.

DEAR JUSTIN;

I received your package the day before Xmas & still have some of the candy & nuts left—you must thank Mina[9] (I believe that's how to spell her name) for me. Altho I enjoy the various delicacies in the gift package, I feel the book that was also enclosed is worth a ton of assorted sweets & thank you accordingly. Really I find it hard not to rave about it, however, to save space to devote to other things I merely say, Thomas Wolfe is great.

I feel gratified to know you have noticed my improvement in letter writing, but it's evidently not a permanent improvement, as is attested to by my last one.

To say I would just as soon be here as in Denver would be a bit awkward at this time, nevertheless, I honestly think that in the not too distant future I will have become as conditioned to this place that that statement might be true. How jolly!

A beard, huh? I'll wager it's to be a Van Dyke.

The Freudian aspects of reformatory life? No, I'm not capable of giving an objective picture; even if I were to write one, it would be distorted immensely.

Cadet school in New York; which one?; what will he study there?

After looking it up in the dictionary, I've decided that's just what I need, please send me your thesaurus.

I see that Bruce Stout died Thursday night, Dec. 21. If you ever happen to see Dorothy, his wife, please give my regards. Perhaps I haven't told you before, but at my last job she was there as secretary for some time and I came to know her well, doubly so, as I had also known Bruce at Jack Calloway's.

Since I have last written you I have lost my job in the dairy barn

9. Mina Walters was the aunt of Justin Brierly.

(for hitting a cow) & since Dec. 10 have been shoveling sheep manure for my keep; on Dec. 21st I received a goose-egg—as they call it—in my case that means losing 100 marks (17 days), so I get out about June 30 now.

The hundred marks would have been my last bonus up here, but as each goose-egg sets the bonus back a month I'll never get them, for they're not due until July & I'll be gone before then, unless, of course, I lose more marks.

Thank Bob Adams for his card & don't fail to inform me of his progress occasionally.

N.L. CASSADY

TO JUSTIN BRIERLY

February 5, 1945
Colorado State Reformatory
Buena Vista, Colo.

DEAR JUSTIN;

Received an *East Spotlight* early last month & another one early this month; very interesting about Sir Oswald your great-grandpa, you had never mentioned him to me before.

It was with mixed surprise & sorrow I read of the death of Mina E. Walters in the *Post*. I recall, when I was living at John and Lucille's, I took her for an airing in city park in the 1932 Buick she had in the garage. All my regrets, Justin.

I rather pride myself on how completely I have become conditioned to reformatory life. Adjustments in my case began in the intellect, which after some months led to control of the passions, then 90% of the battle was over, after that, my psychological pattern ebbed into an objective recognition. I only hope I can retain some degree of the mental ease I have developed up here, when I again plunge into civilian life. I feel certain the only way is thru a study of Philosophy & applying all the gems of wisdom gathered by sages from Socrates[10] to Santayana,[11] while concentrating on the more important (to me) ones.

How is Bob Adams doing? & what's new with you?

There appears to be a slight chance I may be able to obtain my

10. Socrates (469–399 B.C.). Greek philosopher.
11. George Santayana (1863–1952). Philosopher, poet, and literary critic.

youngest sister[12] when I get out. She will be 15 in May & will graduate from the 8th grade at St. Clara's Orphanage, where she has been since she was 8 years old. The usual procedure when a girl finishes the 8th grade at the orphanage is to give her a year's employment as a maid in some people's home who will accept her. I'm working on several angles now, where some close friends of mine will either need a maid or will adopt her in June when Shirley (her name) gets out. Things are moving. I'll be 19 Feb 8th.

N.L. CASSADY

TO JUSTIN BRIERLY

March 26, 1945
Colorado State Reformatory
Buena Vista, Colo.

DEAR JUSTIN;

I have received both of the *Spotlights* that you have sent me this month, I also have the most enjoyable letter you wrote me the first of the month. No need to tell you I appreciate the whole very much.

I failed to write to you the first week I received your letter (that was March 4) because I had to write to a girl who (I presume) was naive enough to wire me asking if I wished her to come; what made her telegram incriminating was that I was in a position to see her illegally and the warden suspected I had written her asking if she would come and—well—see me. Consequently, I wrote to her that week requesting an explanation. That explains March 4, now for March 10. Again, I didn't send you a missive because I was in Walsenburg participating in a basketball tourney the reformatory had been invited to. We lost. The reason I didn't write last week was because I received an important letter from my drunken father, which had to be answered. From now on you may count on a message from me every two weeks instead of each month as has been my previous habit.

I was quite amazed this A.M. to find that I had been given the best job in the place here, "Office Boy" I am now called, which means I merely sit and type all day. That, of course, explains why this letter is being typed.

12. Shirley Jean Cassady (b. May 22, 1930).

I have just under 90 days to do, although I am not inclined to feel I am getting short.

I see Lucius Beebe[13] has been taking up some of your time; from our previous talks together I understand you and he are quite close; I'll wager his visit was interesting.

I too have been bothered by a head cold, however at the moment my chief complaint is a terrific ear ache.

I have several wagers with the boys that the allies will be in Berlin, but will not have taken it, by May 1st. What do you think?

My ear is giving me an awful beating, therefore, I do believe I shall quit for this evening.

NEAL L. CASSADY

When Neal was paroled from Buena Vista on June 2, 1945, Justin Brierly got him a job recapping tires at a Goodyear factory in Denver. That summer Neal met Jimmy Holmes, Al Hinkle, and Bill Tomson in Pederson's pool hall. In the public library he also encountered Hal Chase, another of Brierly's protégés, to whom Neal had written letters while at Buena Vista. Hal was on vacation from Columbia University, New York, and regaled Neal with stories of the colorful friends he'd met there—Allen Ginsberg, Jack Kerouac, and William Burroughs—and introduced him to the habit of swallowing the strips from Benzedrine inhalers. Neal also had brief affairs with two girls at that time, Mary Ann Freeland ("Cherry Mary") and Joan Anderson, which he later wrote about in a long December 1950 letter to Kerouac.

In early 1946, Neal got employment on Ed Uhl's ranch at Padroni, near Sterling, Colorado, some 120 miles northeast of Denver, where he stayed until April. Back in Denver, Neal met up with sixteen-year-old LuAnne Henderson, and on August 1 they married. The following month, after taking a number of temporary jobs around Denver, Neal went with LuAnne to stay briefly with her aunt and uncle in Sidney, Nebraska, where they earned money by potato-picking before Neal worked as a dishwasher in a restaurant and LuAnne found employment as housemaid for a local lawyer and his wife. Neal resented the harsh way that LuAnne was treated, being forced to rise at 5 A.M. and clean the whole house before the family awoke. In October they absconded with the uncle's car, as well as some of the lawyer's cash and a few books from his well-stocked library, driving as far as North Platte, Nebraska, where they left the car outside the bus station and hopped on a Greyhound bus bound for New York.

13. Lucius Beebe (1902–1966). Prolific writer, prankster, and wit, with regular column documenting New York café society in the *New York Herald*.

Arriving at Fiftieth Street, they met up with Hal Chase in a bar near the Columbia campus, and he introduced them to Allen Ginsberg and Jack Kerouac. Neal had been hoping to attend college in New York, but it was not to be. He and LuAnne moved into a cold-water flat on Lexington Avenue in Spanish Harlem belonging to Allan Temko's cousin Bob Malkin, and Neal found work parking cars while LuAnne got a job at a bakery. When LuAnne was caught stealing from her employers, the couple moved to a room in Bayonne, New Jersey, where they spent Christmas.

1947

In January, following a row between LuAnne and Neal, she left him in New York and caught a bus back to her mother in Denver. Neal looked up his new friends again and began staying a couple of nights a week at Kerouac's house in Ozone Park, and also with Allen Ginsberg. Neal eagerly sought the tutelage of both friends, and especially that of Kerouac, whom he asked to teach him to write. With Ginsberg, matters were more complicated, since Allen became infatuated with Neal and initiated a relationship with him. Ginsberg was bitterly disappointed when Neal returned to Denver in March, and vowed to join him there when his university term ended that summer. (Neal's first trip to New York is described by Kerouac in Part One of On the Road.*)*

TO ALLEN GINSBERG

Jan. 17, 1947
[New York City]

DEAR ALLEN;

I really feel quite badly because of the many obligations I feel toward you, however, I can only explain what has happened & hope, *sincerely* hope you can understand—by a sort of instinctive recognition—of my complete (almost shame) humility for my imposition on you; but to get to the point.

LuAnne[1] has failed me—for what reason I don't know—I can, of course, make generalizations but on the surface, at least, she has left me. Therefore, all of your things are not in my possession—they are at Mrs. Cohen's who lives at 91 W. 46th St., Bayonne, N.J.—at first I

1. LuAnne Henderson Cassady, Neal's first wife, appears as Marylou in Kerouac's *On the Road,* and as Joanna Dawson in *Visions of Cody*. In John Clellon Holmes's *Go,* she is represented by Dinah.

had thought of getting them—by mail—& sending them to you, however, I find that impossible, so you must go out there & get them yourself.

I'm really quite sorry,
NEAL

P.S. Bob [Malkin] has a small, brown, cardboard-like suitcase there, *please* pick it up & give it to him.

Thanks,
N.

I almost forgot—your radio, stove & dishes are all there, but I have with me—& need it badly—your suitcase & toilet articles.

Thanks, Sorry,
NEAL

TO ALLEN GINSBERG

March 6, 1947
Kansas City

DEAR ALLEN;

It has just occurred to me the thing I lack is the address, no, just the names of the publishers, not only the New York ones, but, also, *Horizon* in London & any other ones you know; while you're at it, please send me the names of magazines such as *New Directions* etc., that I might dig.

However, the primary purpose of this missive is an urgent request that you go around the corner to where your tailor is & procure for me my only pair of trousers that are any good.

Now, as for the address, send the publishers & magazine information *immediately,* if you please, send that on to me addressed thus:

Neal Cassady
c/o General Delivery
Denver, Colo.

As for the trousers, send them parcel post at the General Post Office, 33rd & 8th Ave., to me at an address I shall send on to you tomorrow, understand?

I am only writing this to you now, here in Kansas City, because of the sense of urgency & rush which I feel, rather than waiting until I arrive in Denver.

I'm quite sorry but the bus is leaving & I must rush, in fact, the entire letter is written in rush.

Don't fail me now, send the letter immediately & get the pants out, so you can send them tomorrow when I send you my address.

Sincerely now, I really mean this,
Love & Kisses,
NEAL

P.S. I'll write tomorrow.

Neal also left with Ginsberg a list of the books he intended to read:

This list is to be read this year. Some are a second reading.

Criticism: Edmund Wilson—*Axel's Castle; The Wound and the Bow*
Wyndham Lewis—*Time and Western Man; Apes of God*

One or two of these are important, none are really good books, but they all have some factual or expoetical [*sic*] notes.

Herbert Read-*Surrealism* (introduction Gopi)
David Daiches—*Poetry and the Modern World*
Lizzie Drew and Sweeney—*Directions in Modern Poetry*
Francis Scarfe—*Auden and After*
Horace Gregory and Marya Zaturenska—*History of American Poetry*
Allen Tate—*Reactionary Essays*
Babette Deutsch—*This Modern Poetry*
Edith Sitwell—*Aspects of Modern Poetry*
Otto Rank—*Art and Artist*
Cyril Connolly—*Condemned Playground* (First few essays)

These books are general reading that I must become better acquainted with.

Djuna Barnes—*Nightwood*
Albert Camus—*The Stranger*

Louis Ferdinand Céline (Destouches)—*Death on the Installment Plan; Journey to the End of the Night*
Denton Welch—*Maiden Voyage; In Youth is Pleasure*
Christopher Isherwood—*Berlin Stories*
Julian Green—*Closed Garden,* etc.

I must also get a hold of some Kafka, Joyce, Mann, Proust, Gide, and Evelyn Waugh.

These three are so important I must buy them:

Spengler—*Decline of the West*
Kardiner—*Psychological Frontiers of Society*
Korzybski—*Science and Sanity*

I should also dig *Poetry, Partisan Review, Kenyan Review, Horizon, Furioso, Chimaera, View* (Surrealistic), *Antioch Review, Sewanne Review, New Directions, New Signatures.*

All of these are not good, in fact, only *Partisan, Kenyan, Poetry, New Directions* are consistently OK. *View* and *Horizon* are usually alright also.

Now for the ones I should know almost by heart:

Baudelaire—Translation of Symons and Millay
Intimate Journals (preface—Eliot)
Flowers of Evil, etc.
Rimbaud—Biographies by Enid Starkie and Edgell Rickword, *Season in Hell; Illuminations,* etc.
St-John Perse—*Anabasis* (translation, Eliot)
Eloges (translation, Louise Varese)
Rainer Maria Rilke—Biography by E.M. Butler,
Duino Elegies, translation S. Spender and J.B. Lehmann
Selected Poems, translation C.F. McIntyre
H. Crane—Biography by P. Horton; *Collected Poems*
T.S. Eliot—*Collected Poems,* and *Achievement of Eliot*, F.O. Matthiessen
Auden—*Collected Poems*
Yeats—Autobiographies; *Collected Poems; A Vision; Last Poem;*
Poor biography by H.B. Hone;
good short one, *Development of W.B. Yeats* by V.K. Narayana Menon

Only after these are assimilated may I become more familiar with these:

Lautréamont (Isadore Ducasse)—*Les Chants de Maldoror,* translation by Wernham (New Directions?)
Mallarmé—translation by Roger Fry
G.C. Ransom—*Selected Poems*
S. Spender—*Poems*
E.Æ. Cummings—*Collected Poems; 1 x 1; 50 Poems*
Dylan Thomas—*Selected Poems* (New Directions, 1946 Edition)
Joyce—*Collected Poems*
Ezra Pound—*Collected Poems* (Faber, 1955, intro by Eliot)
Personae (New Directions, 1946)
Later Cantos
Paterson—Book I (New Directions, 1946)[2]
Selected Poems (Wallace Stevens essay in it)
W. Stevens—*Harmonium*
L. Durrell—*Cities, Plains and People* (Minor but good)
R. Lowell—*Lord Weary's Castle* (1946)
K. Shapiro—*V-Letter; Person, Place and Thing;* maybe *Essay on Rime*
W. Carlos Williams is minor and not often interesting, but try and read him.
Find *Auden and After* by Francis Scarfe for critical Essay (English Publisher)

Some names aren't really important, but, are particularly interesting to me—Such as Barnes, Waugh, Kafka, Gide, and Otto Rank. I feel they personify the decadence I must free myself from and therefore, I shall use the old, but tried and true, method of saturation.

There are other books I have not listed that are more important, however, I must digest these before moving on to an honestly well rounded knowledge.

N. CASSADY—
March 1947

2. These are actually the poems of William Carlos Williams, rather than Ezra Pound.

To Kerouac, Neal wrote of his seduction, during his bus trip back West, of two women passengers, describing his technique in some detail. Kerouac labeled it "The Great Sex Letter."

TO JACK KEROUAC

March 7, 1947
Kansas City, Mo.

DEAR JACK;

I am sitting in a bar on Market St. I'm drunk, well, not quite, but I soon will be. I am here for 2 reasons; I must wait 5 hours for the bus to Denver & lastly but, most importantly, I'm here (drinking) because, of course, because of a woman & *what* a *woman*! To be chronological about it:

I was sitting on the bus when it took on more passengers at Indianapolis, Indiana—a perfectly proportioned beautiful, intellectual, passionate, personification of Venus De Milo asked me if the seat beside me was taken!! I gulped, (I'm drunk) gargled & stammered NO! (Paradox of expression, after all, how can one stammer No!!?) She sat—I sweated—she started to speak, I knew it would be generalities, so to tempt her I remained silent.

She (her name Patricia Lague) got on the bus at 8 P.M. (Dark!) I didn't speak until 10 P.M.—in the intervening 2 hours I not only, of course, determined to make her, but, how to DO IT.

I naturally can't quote the conversation verbally, however, I shall attempt to give you the gist of it from 10 P.M. to 2 A.M.

Without the slightest preliminaries of objective remarks (what's your name? where are you going? etc.) I plunged into a completely *knowing*, completely subjective, personal & so to speak "penetrating her core" way of speech; to be shorter, (since I'm getting unable to write) by 2 A.M. I had her swearing eternal love, complete subjectivity to me & immediate satisfaction. I, anticipating even more pleasure, wouldn't allow her to blow me on the bus, instead we played, as they say, with each other.

Knowing her supremely perfect being was completely mine (when I'm more coherent I'll tell you her complete history & psychological reason for loving me) I could conceive of no obstacle to my satisfaction, well, "the best laid plans of mice & men go astray" & my nemesis was her sister, the bitch. Pat had told me her reason for going to St. Louis was to see her sister; she had wired her to meet her at the depot. So, to get rid of the sister, we *peeked* around the depot when we arrived at St. Louis at 4 A.M. to see if she (her sister) was present. If not, Pat would claim her suitcase, change her clothes in the rest room & she and I proceed to a hotel room for a night (years?) of perfect bliss. The sister was not in sight, so She (note the capital) claimed her bag & retired to the toilet to change——long dash——

This next paragraph must, of necessity, be written completely objectively—

Edith (her sister) & Patricia (my love) walked out of the pisshouse hand in hand (I shan't describe my emotions). It seems Edith (bah) arrived at the bus depot early & while waiting for Patricia, feeling sleepy, retired to the head to sleep on a sofa. That's why Pat & I didn't see her.

My desperate efforts to free Pat from Edith failed, even Pat's terror & slave-like feeling toward her rebelled enough to state she must see "someone" & would meet Edith later, *all* failed. Edith was wise; she saw what was happening between Pat & I.

Well, to summarize: Pat & I stood in the depot (in plain sight of the sister) & pushing up to one another, vowed to never love again & then I took the bus for Kansas City & Pat went home, meekly, with her dominating sister. Alas, alas——

In complete (try & share my feeling) dejection, I sat, as the bus progressed toward Kansas City. At Columbia, Mo. a young (19) completely passive (my meat) *virgin* got on & shared my seat. In my dejection over losing Pat the perfect, I decided to sit on the bus (behind the driver) in broad daylight & seduce her, from 10:30 A.M. to 2:30 P.M. I talked. When I was done she (confused, her entire life upset, metaphysically amazed at me, passionate in her immaturity) called her folks in Kansas City, & went with me to a park (it was just getting dark) & I banged her; I screwed as never before; all my pent up emotion finding release in this young virgin (& she was) who is, by the by, a *school teacher*! Imagine, she's had 2 years of Mo. St. Teacher's College & now teaches Jr. High School. (I'm beyond thinking straightly). I'm going to stop writing.

Oh, yes, to free myself for a moment from my emotions, you must read "Dead Souls"; parts of it (in which Gogol shows his insight) are quite like you.[3]

3. Nikolay Gogol (1809–1852). Russian prose writer and dramatist. The first part of his comic epic *Dead Souls* was published in 1842, but the second part was burnt by Gogol ten days before his death.

I'll elaborate further later (probably?) but at the moment I'm drunk & happy (after all, I'm free of Patricia already, due to the young virgin. I have no name for her). At the happy note of Les Young's "Jumping at Mesners" (which I'm hearing) I close till later.

To my Brother
Carry On!
N.L. CASSADY

P.S. I forgot to mention Patricia's parents live in Ozone Park & of course, Lague being her last name, she's French Canadian just as you.

I'll write soon,
NEAL

P.P.S. Please read this illegible letter as a continuous chain of undisciplined thought, thank you,

N.

P.P.P.S. Postponed, postponed, postponed script, keep working hard, finish your novel & find, thru knowledge, strength in solitude instead of despair. Incidentally I'm starting on a novel also, "believe it or not." Goodbye.

P.P.P.P.S. Here's to women!!!

N.L.C.

TO ALLEN GINSBERG

March 10, '47
Denver

DEAR ALLEN;

Sorry I'm late in writing to you, however, I've been seeking a place to live & as yet have failed, therefore, you must send the trousers on in this fashion:

Bill Barnett[4]
1156 Gaylord
Denver, Colo.

4. Bill Barnett was better known as Bill Tomson, a friend of Neal's in Denver, whom he had first met in 1945. Barnett was the name of Bill's stepfather. Tomson met Carolyn

Address them simply that way & I shall receive them OK. Thanks.

I trust you have received your shirt by now in the mail. Send my pants parcel post also if you will.

I have been unable to see Justin because my suit & overcoat are in the cleaner's. I intend to see him though when I get them out on Tuesday.

Hal[5] I will see Tue. A.M. just before I speak to Justin.

I have seen LuAnne & have been able to convince her of the need to, for the present, stay at her mother's & work so as to save money to pay Haldon back & such.

I am seeking a room, then a job, then a typewriter, then some money, then to leave here in June.

Other than these things nothing else of interest.

I find that due to not being settled yet I can't begin to write to you as I would desire to, so you see, I & you must wait until I'm settled to begin to speak of other things—understand?

Write only after I've sent you a permanent address for I don't wish our correspondence to fall into alien hands, but, do send on the trousers to the Bill Barnett address.

I shall write again in a few days.

How are you & Jack making out on the overcoats?[6] I could sell 2 now if you could send them to me—both of them are my size—one fellow wants brown & the other wants a blue one—

Till later,
Le Enfant,
N.L. CASSADY

Robinson at the University of Denver and introduced her to Neal. Bill Tomson is Roy Johnson in *On the Road,* and Earl Johnson in *Visions of Cody*.

5. Haldon (Hal) Chase, Neal's close friend in Denver in the summer of 1945, and link with Kerouac and Ginsberg in New York. Hal is represented as Chad King in *On the Road,* and Val Hayes and Val King in *Visions of Cody*. He's also Winston Moor in William Burroughs's *Queer*.

6. Ginsberg's junkie friend Bill Garver stole overcoats from restaurants to finance his habit. Neal wanted Allen to send him some to sell.

TO JACK KEROUAC

March 13, 1947
1073 Downing St.
Denver, Colo.

DEAR JACK;

Your eyes tell you I have procured a typewriter, but, they can't tell you how beautiful it is. It's an Underwood, office model, practically new & worth $75.00. Understanding my joy in having it I know you will excuse my using it to type a personal letter, in fact, I'm sure it will even give you joy since you shan't have to decipher my handwriting.

Speaking of handwriting, the letter I wrote to you on the bus was the worst written of any I know. It was just the setting down of a continuous chain of thought reaction. I was so drunk I can hardly recall the gist of it. In case you can't understand it, I here state it was about a girl.

It has taken me almost a week to get settled. I stayed at a hotel the first 3 days & spent my time in seeing people. Then I found a perfect residence, it is the best I've had in 3 years. Privacy, freedom to have friends down, even women, are all included in this wonderful basement room, with nearby bath, at $6.00 a week.

I shall work in a filling station since I feel that is what I want at present, rather than a job in a bookstore or anything Justin might get for me.

I see you have declined the parking lot job, I feared that would happen. Not from a sense of responsibility to the parking lot or even from the feeling I had that you would have almost liked it, but, rather, because I am in need of an overcoat & believe you & Allen will not be able to get any out of hock, either for yourself or me, until you work a week or so.

I have been so busy getting my next 3 months arranged I am not even capable of relaxing long enough to write this letter. As proof of dashing about I offer the fact that I've not even seen Hal, just called him once. Justin I've seen for 20 minutes & the rest of my relationships the same way. LuAnne, however, I've seen several times.

None of this is interesting, yet that's all I've done, so, of necessity, this missive is boring & monotonous, however, the next time I write look for improvement.

On your part I hope for something with more meat in it. Then I shall be shamed into really writing letters to you.

Honestly, Jack, please excuse me this time & perhaps I can fall into a spontaneous groove in not only our correspondence, but, letter writing in general.

Thanks,
Your Brother,
N.L. CASSADY

P.S. The only drawback to this typewriter is that it's only half mine. What a life, I can't move without others.

One consolation, the pardner in this is the best. You remember my speaking of Holmes?[7]

NEAL

During the next few months Ginsberg regularly wrote to Neal, professing his undying love, and hoping that their relationship could continue when they met again in Denver that summer. Neal at first played along with Allen's suggestions, but was getting involved again with LuAnne and other women and so tried to dampen Allen's ardor. Armed with one of Ginsberg's poems, Neal typed it up on his stolen typewriter and signed it with his own name, in an attempt to impress Justin Brierly.

TO ALLEN GINSBERG

March 14, 1947
1073 Downing St.
Denver, Colorado

DEAR ALLEN;

As you can see I have procured a typewriter, the only bad point is that it's only half mine. I feel certain you will excuse me using it to write personal letters to you, since you would have to decipher my juvenile scrawl otherwise.

I have found a wonderful place to live & it only costs $6.00 a week. My meals must still be taken in cafes however. I have not as yet went to work so I am really in debt.

7. Jim Holmes, a friend of Neal's whom he had met in a Denver pool hall shortly after his release from Buena Vista in 1945. Appears as Tom Snark in *On the Road,* and Tom Watson in *Visions of Cody*.

Speaking of debt, send on those overcoats as soon as possible to alleviate my duress.

I am honestly amazed & overwhelmed at the truly great mass of information you have sent on to me concerning the poem. I appreciate it very much. Needless to say, especially now that I have this typewriter, I shall copy the poem & send it to you within the week.

To say that I got "great kicks" out of your recital of what happened at Vicki's[8] after I left that night, would almost be an understatement, I find that the optimistic tone on which your missive ends is so heartening in its implication that I fear I wouldn't be able to bring myself to really think that the "Peace" will last.

Incidentally, I have found no peace at all since arriving. You see, my basic problem has developed into seeking the proper relationship with LuAnne. Due to our separation she has fallen into a complete apathy toward life. Her inability to meet even the most simple obligations is almost terrifying. Her life is a constant march of obsessions. Her attitude toward everyone is so defensive that it constitutes continual lying, yet she still has many fellows who adore her & is, therefore always getting drunk & has become very slipshod. I, as yet, can't solve this dilemma, however, in due course I feel a solution will be found.

My life is, at the moment, so cluttered up I have become incapable of relaxing long enough to even write a decent letter, really, I'm almost unable to think coherently. You must, then, not only forgive, but find it within yourself to understand & in so doing develop a degree of patience until I am able to free myself enough to become truly close to you again.

On your part, you must know that any letdown in your regard for me would upset me so much that, psychologically, I would be in a complete vacuum. At least for the immediate future I must request these things of you. So *please* don't fail me. I need you now more than ever, since I've no one else to turn to. I continually feel I am almost free enough to be a real help to you, but, my love can't flourish in my present position & if I forced it now, both you & I would lose. By God, though, every day I miss you more & more.

8. Vicki Russell, also known as Priscilla Arminger, was a friend of Herbert Huncke's who worked as a prostitute in New York. Responsible for teaching Kerouac and Burroughs how to swallow the wad inside Benzedrine inhalers. Kerouac and Ginsberg had introduced Neal to her in New York, an event that Neal writes about in *The First Third*. Vicki is featured as Dorie in *On the Road,* and Vicki in *Visions of Cody*. In Burroughs's *Junkie* she appears as Lizzie and Mary, and she's Winnie in John Clellon Holmes's *Go*.

Understanding these things I hope, nay, in fact, know you must pour out more affection now than ever, rather than reacting negatively & withering up so that all is loss, or would be, between us.

Let us then find true awareness by realizing that each of us is depending on the other for fulfilment. In that realization lies, I believe, the germ that may grow to the great heights of complete oneness.

I have not seen Haldon yet, just called him once. I saw Justin for 20 minutes & can say that I emerged the victor, however, I merely mentioned "a poem" & let the suit talk for me. So, you see, each new time I converse with him my statute [*sic*] will grow.

I shall find a job tomorrow & perhaps by losing myself in work again I may become more rational & less upset & unnerved by the emotional shock of returning.

Write soon, I need you. I remain, your other self,

NEAL

TO ALLEN GINSBERG

March 20, 1947
1073 Downing St.
Denver, Colorado

DEAR ALLEN;

I have just finished copying the poem; since I am not a typist you will see in it several mistakes that are so glaring as to almost fill me with shame. I have, however, stuck exactly to your punctuation etc. Also, I have sent you the poem in carbon; now, if you need the prime copy or the original don't hesitate to let me know, and I shall send it on to you.

I almost feel guilty about harping on the coats, for I see in your letter that it has given you some concern. Please excuse the seemingly desperate tone that I had unconsciously taken in speaking of them, my only explanation is that I am so conditioned to dealing with people who must be driven on to doing something by my assuming an urgent tone that I fell into that mannerism with you. I will state that if it's convenient enough to be done without too much trouble you might send on one or two that are my size.

One thing that is really important though, is my trousers. I am honestly in need of them.

Your speaking of Bill B[urroughs] only makes me want to meet him more than ever. I trust that in June you will come West & we shall see he and Joan[9] at that time; continue to keep me informed as to his tribulations etc., just as you did in this letter.

I place you in such high regard academically that I merely reacted normally to your amount of information concerning the literary scene. I presupposed that it had all come out of your head without effort, just as I without effort can speak of football, therefore, when I expressed amazement at the knowledge, it was artificial in that I was complimenting you simply as a means of showing appreciation. So you see I was not truly impressed, but, rather accepted it as further proof of your value. In fact, what you pointed out about it in this latest letter was understood, and understood so well that I find a lack in myself in not implying that, rather than using the false complimentary style to show my thanks to you.

I have given much thought to what I am about to say. I must, I fear, become somewhat incoherent near the end of this paragraph, but, bear with me as I am consciously trying to formulate our, no, my feelings. First, realize I am not intellectualizing nor doing anything other than being governed by pure emotion (incidentally, I feel that is the key to whatever awareness you sensed in me) in my effort to state to you what my present position is. Now, I shall tell my fears, desires, feelings of all types, and then, if possible, attempt to analyze them. Allen, this may sound strange, but, the thing that is uppermost in my mind at the moment is a fear. How can I state it? I believe it is almost paranoiac in its intensity, with each of your letters I feel it more. I have difficulty in putting my finger on it, but, it's a real fear of losing you. It's a combination of a knowledge of lack on my part, not only academically, but, in drive as well, also, a sense of outcast that makes me feel at times as if I were really imposing on you for me to try and become closer. I have become more defensive psychologically in direct ratio to my increasing degree of realization of need of you. The thing that is closest to the truth is the simple statement that you are too good for me. I am above feeling envy of you, and don't fall into a sort of loving admiration either, rather, I have a sort of confused sense of loss when I think of you. The whole thing is quite

9. Joan Vollmer Adams (1924–1951) was the common-law wife of William Burroughs. Portrayed as Jane Lee in *On the Road,* June Hubbard in *Visions of Cody,* and June Evans in *Book of Dreams, Desolation Angels,* and *Vanity of Duluoz.*

beyond me at present, yet, somehow this is different than previous times when I felt an inability to cope with our relationship. This time, although, it's negative in its psychological aspect, I find true concern of our need so much that I, in reality, feel stronger than at any other time since I met you. I mean, stronger in desire and ability to struggle to handle our affair, rather than healthy positive drive toward freedom for us. You can see I am now in a position for the first time of being a drain on you insofar as I have become aware of a neurotic negative almost compulsive need of you. I feel as if I were a woman, about to lose her man, primarily because as you become more straight through me, or otherwise, you will need me less, and, also secondarily, because I know as that happens I shall need you more. This is as I say, the uppermost fear. Alongside of that is a remnant of the old feeling I had in NY of a need to free myself of Denver and all it implies before I can progress, at least, with you. Then there are other things which are bothering me, but, they are unimportant compared to the above.

Allen, forgive me, but I must break off now. I have been really busy these last few days and haven't had any rest; right now it's 5 A.M. and I must rise at 9:30 A.M. I am completely beat, causing my fluctuations in thought I think.

Let me end on one line in your wonderful letter—"I will be prepared for you I think, when we meet, but on other terms than those which I'd formerly conceived and which I tried to force on you." I find that statement holds true for me as well as you, Allen, whether for better or worse we must see, but, whichever way it goes, I know I can't help from profiting thereby and perhaps you can also (though, I fear you can't since I no longer have anything to offer, and, therein lies my loneliness).

I leave you in complete weariness and apology.

But, By God, L'enfant or no, whether you think it's mad or not, whether "it's not as we feel or I want to feel," to quote you. I still love (what a weak word) you.

Bah I'm tired,

NEAL

P.S. Speaking of overcoats, don't try and sell them; we'll wait until this fall and get more out of them then, not only that, but, when we set up housekeeping then we'll make a record machine and really get gone and yet be straighter than any 10 psychologists. Use the record machine as an indication of all things fine and the other as a statement of our disciplinarianism.

I'm so tired I can't even type, let alone think.

Please excuse.

N.L.C.

To Jack, Neal explained his current problems and some of his techniques for dealing with people. He urged Jack to complete work on his novel The Town and the City *and mentioned that he intended writing the story of his own life.*

TO JACK KEROUAC

March 27, 1947
1073 Downing St.
Denver, Colorado

DEAR JACK;

I put off writing to you for four days, then wrote a letter, then, on the second day thereafter tore it up, since it was already outdated. So this is my next attempt, let's hope you get it, I'm almost 2 weeks late in writing you as it is and it's given me much concern.

Part of the above laxity in correspondence is due to my emotional upheaval of late, but most of it is my honest feeling of lack in becoming close to you at this time, due to the upheaval, by writing. Having combated this as well as I'm able and not being capable of just dashing off an extemporaneous letter, as you seem able to, and having it include my true feelings, I am at last reaching a state, psychologically, in which I can send this letter, however, I'm not free as yet by any means.

Instead of trying to describe what has been happening to me, I shall just give you the gist of it and pass on:

First I was forced to move by my landlady. Second I was in fear of jail because of LuAnne. Third I was completely fucked up on my job. What happened? Well, after a few days of paranoiac defensiveness, I regained my natural drive and dealt directly with the problems. Problem one the place I live in; after having gotten ready to leave town, removing my hot typewriter etc. I approached the landlady directly, instead of avoiding her as I had been, because of her anger, my bloody and missing bedsheets, girls in my room etc. and with my best con-methods persuaded her to allow me to remain. Now, she loves me again. So, problem one was a complete victory for me. Problem two, my near approach to jail is so complicated I can't tell it here, I shall only state that, here too, I emerged victor and am still free and I feel will remain that way. Problem three, my job, is now almost solved; to prove I could keep it, for character only, I did get it back, then, quit the next day since it was a really terrible job in a filling station. Now, I am competing with a dozen other applicants for a wonderful position at an exclusive restaurant, where, if I succeed in procuring the job I will, of all things, park cars in their parking lot. I shall find out Saturday. So you see Jack, I've been fighting all sorts of negative things, but, I am beyond all the struggle of settling down here again and from here on out will be able to really move on. So let's fall into a potent and true groove in our missives to each other for the next couple of months until I see you. Of course, I'm presupposing you are free enough to move with me in this, I have your first letter as evidence, all I ask is that in our attempt to fall into a closeness again, you remain as sincere as you have been and just because we're writing instead of talking don't let up in what you have to say to me and please, Jack, don't allow yourself to do what I've been guilty of in the past with other people, that is, you are still sincere, but, automatically, the process of writing forces you into a form and therefore, you just say things rather than feel them, and the honest attempt to express these feelings is too much so you just, lazily, dash off a newsy letter, or a pat formal stylized letter, or a wild artificially stimulating one and so on. Those things are for anyone to do, but not us, so to play safe force yourself to think and then write rather than, think what to write about and what to say as you write. Incidentally, I sense just a hint of the above falseness in your letter, but, I know it's just that there was really nothing to write about. That's that, now to answer your letter.

You flatter me unnecessarily about my Kansas City letter, I was just drunk and high.

I don't know what to say after reading your terrific telling of your experience on the parking lot. This is by far the best part of your letter, it personifies the portion of you that I feel closer to than any other, it's very unstraight, complex and really blown all out of proportion, but that's where we shine. As for the negative side, who cares? Just wait till June comes and see whether or not Hal, you and I will latch on to some real fillies. That's what I've spent a good deal of time on since returning and I'm loaded.

It's interesting to read what you say about the coats; for my part you can forget them, use them for yourself. I'm so broke, however, that I've hocked my overcoat and suit, and am now borrowing from everyone in sight just to eat, not having eaten yet today, after finishing this letter I shall go down to a nearby newsstand and steal the change on the papers and go buy some bowery beef stew. That's how sad my material wealth is at the moment, but, somehow, I don't feel worried, in fact, I'm quite happy.

I have not felt up to seeing Haldon as yet, due to all the bullshit I've been going through, it's starting to bother me though, so I'll see him Sunday.

By God! Jack, I sure as hell wish you were here, when I'm with you I somehow feel well rounded, completed, at least at peace with myself, rather than busting my head into a lot of negative goddamned crap that means nothing and just frustrates me and in striking out I become even more involved in the whole imposing mess. What I mean by this is that I am dissatisfied with all my social life. There's no one here, all I do is fuck. Bah!

The next two months I intend to write a simple, chronological, account of my life. This is to be done not, of course, as something to try and publish, but only to help me evaluate all I have done and what to do with it. This task, I hope, will also free me of my background lack of freedom from Denver and all the confused trash I've accumulated here. In fact, I truly think I will no longer need to be concerned about this trash any more and can move on into some healthy knowledge and be not only helping myself, but shall be an aid to you, instead of a fellow condemned one, as we both are until—well, until when, who knows?

I am most anxious to know how you're progressing on the novel, really, if you don't lick the damn thing soon I will be so upset I'll probably bawl, honestly, Jack, *please* get that thing off your chest, all I can think of when I remember you is this crisis you're in and because of that I grieve, rather than find joy when I think of your struggle. If I were just assured that all you needed was time, I'd forget my concern, however, it's been with you so long I fear you must finish it this time, to do you any good, that is to help you grow, so don't become static through the external pressure of time, instead, man, harken back to a while back when you began in the present tense and just wrote, by God! just write Jack, write! forget everything else. Hear me?

How's your mother? what's Fitzgerald doing?[10] and Liberniz?[11] Ed White?[12] etc. Give me all the dope that's new, but don't exhaust yourself on these, what I really want is to know what you're doing and thinking; do you know your letter was just an answer, it didn't include anything about yourself, and that's what I need, not an answer to my letters, understand?

Justin has gone to New York. He left March 20 and is due back the 6th of April. He is lining up the cast from the Met to sing at Central City this summer.

When you get here this summer we'll dig Central and the festival, if only to smirk.

Now, Jack don't feel the rush of time, if you don't get here till July that's OK. Just get the novel by the balls first then think of other things.

Jack, if you have any reason not to it's OK but you know my character, and I've been raving about you to the few guys around here that are important to me, well, it would really be wonderful if you'd send me the Lucien Carr[13] story, if not to show them, at least for me. Please don't feel I'm imposing on you, as I say if you, for any reason don't wish to send me anything it's all right, but, I'd honestly be overwhelmed with joy if you'd send that or, of course, anything you can spare or will allow me to have. Anything you've written I'd love, I'll send it right back, & besides that, truly appreciate it as a gesture of sacrifice & as a symbol of our friendship. Thanks. Here's to us & women.

NEAL

10. Jack Fitzgerald, from Poughkeepsie, New York, was a writer friend of Kerouac's and Ginsberg's from their Columbia University days, appearing as McCarthy in *Visions of Cody.*

11. Probably Neal's attempt at Tom Livornese, a musician friend of Kerouac's in New York. Represented by Tom Calabrese in *Visions of Cody.*

12. Ed White was another Denver student at Columbia University, studying architecture. He was responsible, in October 1951, for introducing to Kerouac the concept of "sketching" with words. Kerouac first employed the technique in *Visions of Cody,* in which the Ed Gray character is based on White. He's also represented by Tim Gray in *On the Road,* and Guy/Al Green in *Book of Dreams.*

13. Lucien Carr, originally from St. Louis, was a friend of Jack Kerouac's whom he met in New York in 1944. David Kammerer, an acquaintance of Carr's in St. Louis, followed him to New York and was so fixated on the younger man that Carr fatally stabbed him during an attempted seduction in August 1944. Kerouac and Burroughs produced a novel about the killing, writing alternate chapters. Its title was "And the Hippos Were Boiled in Their Tanks," and it remains unpublished. Carr appears in Kerouac's novels as Damion in *On the Road,* Julien Love in *Visions of Cody, Desolation Angels,* and *Book of Dreams,* Sam Vedder in *The Subterraneans,* and Claude De Maubris in *Vanity of Duluoz.*

TO ALLEN GINSBERG

March 30, 1947
1073 Downing St.
Denver, Colorado

DEAR ALLEN;

I received the pants and just today got the Van Gogh. I have put the Van G. above my bed & it is just what I wanted, thanks a million.

I think you have the right idea about the coats & we shall try it.

I had already presupposed that I would get a Reichian analysis,[14] but your news has made me even more aware of its advantages.

I don't know how to say this, but you've hit the nail on the head. No more sacrament, no more directing my efforts in the nervous, stupid, neurosis you have outlined so well. I understand perfectly Allen, and by god, you're right! Man, from here on out it'll be a breeze. Really, the formulation you gave is just what I needed. I'm overwhelmed with joy, I feel a sense of relief, I almost know peace again! All of this just thru understanding and agreeing with you.

It's not that I didn't see the "rise I might get out of you" by my last letter, or didn't know you might react by "sacramental sadism" or "sacramental masochism," but I felt I must show my fidelity by that method, since I had little else to offer at the moment and knew you needed a sense of security, however, all that's past now. I had forgotten your insight, your mental straightness of understanding, here, in your last missive you've made me aware again and damn it all, it's perfect! No kidding, this really affects me, you see that's just what I sensed, but couldn't formulate, not only that, but I felt perturbed, not through missing you as much as confused in how I *should* move with you in correspondence, therefore, I fell into a overblown "sacramentalism" toward you . . . Dig?

There's nothing else I can say to you, you have put it all so well anything I could say would be artificial and unnecessary. All I can here state is that I wish you had the letter you wrote so as to keep straight on its implications, you see, I have it and I suspect it will become a bible in that here you have the germ, at least, of what will become to me not only a foundation for our relationship, but almost a

14. Wilhelm Reich (1897–1957), Austrian psychoanalyst, author of the book *The Function of the Orgasm* (1927). William Burroughs introduced the book to his friends and built his first Reichian orgone accumulator box on his South Texas farm in the summer of 1949.

"system" in so far as I know this is what I really am. I too, have destroyed "sacramentalism" in almost everything, but being constantly accused of "brutality"—"con-man" & all that have almost come to feel guilty & forced feeling in some instances.

What you say on "Play" is honestly what I've been doing, or striving for, all my life; therein lies our, or my, confused sense of closeness. Also, I fear, therein lies our strength of tie to each other. I say I fear, for I *really don't* know how much I can be satisfied to love you, I mean bodily, you know I, somehow, dislike pricks & men & before you, had consciously forced myself to be homosexual; now, I'm not sure whether with you I was not just forcing myself unconsciously, that is to say, any falsity on my part was all physical, in fact, any disturbance in our affair was because of this. You meant so much to me, I now feel I was forcing a desire for you bodily as a compensation to you for all you were giving me. This is a sad state and upsets me for I want to become nearer to you than anyone & still I don't want to be unconsciously insincere by passing over my non-queerness to please you. Allen, this is straight, what I truly want is to live with you from Sept. to June, have an apt., a girl, go to college, (just for French to sit in on classes etc.) see all and do all. Under this arrangement we would have each other, a girl, (this is quite similar to you, Joan & Bill) and become truly straight, (thru analysis, awareness of "sacrament" and living together). This, of course, doesn't mean you wouldn't have perfect freedom, in fact, I feel you'd have more freedom than living by yourself, because of the psychological oneness we would obtain. If you grew tired of me, or the arrangement, we could always not see each other, or move, or something. So *Please,* Allen, give this a good deal of thought & even if you're doubtful of its advantages, try & come to accept it, at least temporarily, in the next few months.

I've just reread a portion of your letter and it is really good, my, my, what freedom it gives me toward you. A lot of trash is almost automatically cleared away, I repeat, from here on out, I believe it will be a simple thing for us to come to a better knowledge of ourselves & each other.

Let me leave you with the idea that through this understanding lies our ability to progress together, rather than slide into a sincerity that through "sacrament" will (and has, a bit) become shopworn and false in that, that part of us that is similar would be nullified by the other differences in our individual makeup.

NEAL L.

TO ALLEN GINSBERG

April 1, 1947
1073 Downing St.
Denver, Colorado

DEAR ALLEN;

Received your letter yesterday, I think it's very funny. When I was done chuckling I began to try and figure out what to do. From what you say it appears that Justin has already made up his mind that I didn't write the poem. Be that as it may, I know that I'm going to be as indignant as hell with him, upon his return.

I presumed that Haldon had probably told Justin that it was your work, rather than mine, for I had not even seen Hal since my return and, therefore, he didn't know what we were pulling on J. This was not the case, however, for I saw Hal today and found out he has not even seen J. for at least a month. So now we know that J. was just guessing, unless Ed White had, in answer to J.'s query as to whether I had written anything while in NY, said no I hadn't.

So although J. has inside his own mind decided that I didn't do the work, he has no actual proof. Now, if I really bear down on him when he comes back, i.e., show him all the stuff I have, explain every line, compare your *C[olumbia] Review* stuff with it, rave on for hours, be indignant, etc. I think I can be just capable, not of convincing him, but at least, make him indecisive and unable to reach the honest conviction that it's not my work.

When I believe I've attained as much as I can toward making him truly unable to decide, I tell him to go to hell, reject him completely, demand *my* poem back and stalk away. Thereby freeing myself of the necessity of paying him the money I owe him also, since, after all, he "doubted" me, wasn't deserving of me and all that. Knowing him as I do, I'm certain this will have no effect on him, at least outwardly, but, by going through this I, again outwardly, obtain a degree of freedom, respect, and if I pull it off properly, save "face."

So that is what I'll do, if it fails it's not important anyhow for in reality he and I are so far apart it would all be false and artificial even if it truly were my poem. Incidentally, in our very distance from each other lies most of my strength of argument with him for, in the final analysis, I've not hardly talked to him for two years and he has no way of knowing if I've progressed that much or not. The negative factor therein is that when I did see him I was very monotonous and dull in talking and he has only that to go by, so no wonder he doubts I did the poem. I shall twist this around to where the reason I didn't show enlightenment with him is due to the fullness of my awareness of him and how unimportant, sterile, shallow, base, etc. he is and since I was weary and felt no stimulus with him how could I shine?

Enough of this, as for you, I can't, just as you said, see anything in your postscript. I feel sure the only reason this is so is because I'm trying to read too much into it, so let's not be too concerned since I know that I can only understand, obviously, as much as I see and feel, however, in the p.s. of yours lies so really far gone abstractions, though they're concrete, that I am placing importance on them only in the light of your last letter and its realities. Dig?

Thanks for showing such concern and insight about J. and the poem, of course, I'm so tickled by the humor, just as you, that I can place no objective importance on the whole thing, again, just as you probably don't.

I must dash, I've an important date at 6 P.M. and I want to get this letter off anyhow, so to compensate for the business air of this one, I'll really hit the ball next time, please understand.

Again I urge you, thinking over what I spoke of in my last letter, concerning living together.

Love,
NEAL

P.S. If you've seen Justin again before he left don't fail to tell me all about it. Also, naturally, if you disagree with my plan as to him, or think I should alter it in any way, send the info on right away, since he will be here the 6th, and I should see him right away. I'm going to hold off seeing him until I hear from you though.

How's my boy?

NEAL

Neal continued in his attempt to distance himself emotionally from Ginsberg, emphasizing his essential straightness.

TO ALLEN GINSBERG

April 10, 1947
1073 Downing St.
Denver, Colorado

DEAR ALLEN;

The main anxiety of yours concerning sexual play has, I believe, caused you to presuppose some things, also, I find, there has been a slight exaggeration of all the manifold angles of the entire business; due to this, you instinctively realize there is some lack to your formalization of the problem. This lack comes not only from your overconcern, but, your supposition that we are using the proper method in dealing with this. I, almost unconsciously, think of a picture in which everything is just slightly overdone; the lines are a little thick, the paint is a little heavy, everything is distorted and yet the distortion is so slight that one must really look to know that it is exaggerated. This comparison of a picture and our affair doesn't truly mean, or explain anything but it does show that I sense that we have overdone and overused our concern for each other improperly. Due to this we both are not sure of *exactly* what is to be done.

But, this really, as you know, is not the point. Neither am I trying to excuse or justify myself, for I know that somewhere I have failed to state my feelings and because of this failure to properly commune these "nonverbal" things, I don't feel too badly about your misunderstanding. The thing that concerns me is how am I to get my abstract realizations across to you, not only to prevent things like this crisis to arise, but also to bring us down to a plane where we can both move freely within a groove which includes both of us and yet has no faults in concept. In your "sacrament" letter you brought this out clearly and *that* is why I answered you as I did; where I failed is in using such words as "conning," etc. You may as well forget that you ever received that letter, I know that, in reality, I did not mean what I said; I can't explain it, but somehow, I was being honest with you in New York and yet, again somehow, you were perfectly right in accusing me of artificiality in your recent letter.

I believe, that instead of this being a complex thing it is rather a simple lack of knowledge, i.e. you naturally presume that when I spoke of us living with a woman I meant that I select the woman, whereas, in reality, I meant that *we* find the proper woman. Now, this example shows a simple failure on my part to tell you these things and

I believe also gives the proper slant to an understanding of the whole business.

You suggest that I don't try to alter my emotions to fit yours, or to appeal to yours, also you tell me not to say what I can't feel or deliver. This is not, I fear, really thinking deeply enough, you see, in this sense that is to say, from this approach, I honestly cannot answer you, cannot "really know" what I feel or how I will act. You yourself realize this, for you said that we couldn't tell until we were together again.

I suggest that instead of further, non-progressing, talk in this vein we fall into a mutual groove in which, however false in logic this may sound, we assume a responsibility toward each other (family tie idea), entertain a certain erotic attraction (lover idea) etc., until such time as we do see each other.

Now, as for Brierly:

I shall do exactly as you suggested.

I have been struggling to obtain a job. The latest news is that I will probably drive a taxi here; this is really difficult to fall into and in the process of getting the job I may go to jail on account of a past episode. At any rate, if I talk fast enough I'm in clover, if I fail—I suppose I can get a letter smuggled out to you from the bastille.

Don't fear that Hal and Justin will get together about you, they see each other only by chance (which is so slim that, as yet, they haven't seen each other) and even then would only exchange pleasantries.

Tell me the latest info on tea, if not Norman's[15] connection, then, Bill B[urroughs] and his raising it.

Have you seen Jack or Lou?[16]

In reality, Allen, I'm a simple, straight guy, and in thinking of what I want for the next year I know that without you I'd be lost. I feel a normal brotherly need emotionally for you, just as with Jack or Hal or my own brothers; in fact, my emotional needs are not too strong, for example—I know Hal is the only one in Denver that means anything to me, and yet, I don't even bother to see him. I called him once, briefly, a week after I arrived, and saw him once, briefly, after getting your letter about Justin, and then, only to find out if he'd told Justin. This lack of interest and drive toward projecting myself, or even simply seeing Hal is not through feeling I would be imposing on him, or that he doesn't particularly care to see me or anything of that nature,

15. A friend of Vicki Russell's in New York.
16. Lucien Carr.

quite the contrary, he's similar to Jack in that he urges me to drop around etc., but, I just don't need Hal emotionally enough to do so; I've brought this out so you can see an example of my lack of compulsive, emotional need for anyone. Even women are the same, honestly, I'm pretty independent that way; on one hand it bothers me to think I'm unable to be affected emotionally as much as other people seem to be, on the other hand, this objectivity of emotionality, has, in my life, enabled me to move freely in each groove as it came; therefore, the prime difference of our respective personalities lies in this, and once fully realized, will I hope, tend to weld us together, rather than be a cause for conflict.

Having gotten that out of the way, and knowing that the above difference is our most extreme dissimilarity, I've come to see that, other than that, there is every reason for us to live together next term. I hear you cry "other than that! why, by God, that's all I'm interested in him for!" I know, I know, but, look at me—I've already mentioned I be lost without you from Sept. to next June, as you can see, I mean in *every* way except emotionally, that's why I suggest a woman with us (not only that, you need her more than I)—now, Allen, for christ sake, don't get in an uproar about nothing, you know fucking well that when I say "emotional need" I mean psychologically; I get my nuts off just as you, you rave on about "objectivity" & "sacrament"—I've got that, it's only that I felt unable to live and commune that way with you (or anyone) that has motivated my seemingly false attitude toward you; I repeat, in your "sacrament" letter I thought you saw and understood, my fault laid in assuming this, and being sloppy in my reply, thereby causing this misunderstanding. Beyond that I'm guilty of nothing. So you see, we must understand and move on; if we cannot,—bah don't think of it.

I'm on a spree tonight, I'll tell you exactly what *I* want, giving no thought to you, or any respect or consideration to your feelings.

First, I want to stay here and drive a cab until July; second, go to Texas and see Bill and Joan for a few weeks; third, (perhaps) dig New Orleans with Jack; fourth, be in NY by early Sept, find an apt., go to college (as much as they'll let me), work on a parking lot again, and live with a girl *and* you. Fifth, leave NY in June '48 and go to Europe for the summer.

I don't care what you think, that's what I want. If you are able to understand and can see your way clear to shepherding me around the big city for 9 months, then, perhaps, go to Europe with me next summer that's swell, great and wonderful, exactly what I want; if not—

well, why not? really, damn it, why not? You sense I'm not worthy of you? You think I wouldn't fit in? You presume I'd treat you as badly, or worse? You feel I'm not bright enough? You know I'd be imposing, or demanding, or trying to suck you dry of all you have intellectually? Or is it just that you are, almost unconsciously, aware of enough lack of interest in me, or indifference to my plight and need of you, to believe that all the trouble of helping and living with me, would not be quite compensated for by being with me? I can't promise a darn thing, I know I'm bisexual, but prefer women; there's a slimmer line than you think between my attitude toward love and yours, don't be so concerned, it'll fall into line. Beyond that—who knows? Let's try it & see, huh?

I like your latest poem, in fact, I like most of your poems; through reading more poetry I've become a bit better able to judge and appreciate your work.

Relax, man, think about what I say and try to see yourself moving toward me without any compulsive demands, due to lack of assurance that I love you, or because of lack of belief that I understand you etc.; forget all that and in that forgetfulness see if there isn't more peace of mind and even more physical satisfaction than in your present subjective longing (whether for me, or Lucien, or anybody). I know one cannot alter by this method, but come to me with all you've got, throw your demands in my face, (for I love them) and find a true closeness, not only because what emotionality I have is also distorted by loneliness, but also because I, logically or not, feel I want you more than anyone at this stage.

I'm really beat, off to bed, and a knowledge of relief, for I *know* you must understand and move with me in this; you better not fight against it or any other damn thing, so shut up, relax, find some patience and fit into my mellow plans.

Love & kisses, my boy, oops!, excuse, I'm not Santa Claus, am I? Well then, just—Love & kisses.

NEAL

P.S. I'll keep you informed as to the Brierly business, and do my damnedest to make you a full-fledged myth.

P.P.S. Say, it just occurred to me from out of the blue, probably since I'm in the act of closing, that you meant it when you called me a "dirty, double crossing, faithless bitch"; I've had your letter four days now and I just now suddenly saw that you meant it. Instead of mocking or admonishing you, I excuse you automatically, yet seek a hurt reaction inside myself, failing in this, I realize truly what an unsensitive bastard I really am, here the most important guy in the world calls me that in all earnestness, is honestly hurt and upset by me, and how do I react? do I feel guilty? do I beg forgiveness? hell no! I'm so emotionally shallow I can only worry about my own lack of emotion in not reacting at all. That's my paranoia. ha! ha!

Write soon,

N.

Neal was planning to work at Central City during that summer's opera festival, and he encouraged Allen to try for a job there. The pair also intended to travel to Texas to visit William Burroughs and Joan, who had recently bought a farm in New Waverly, Texas, fifty miles north of Houston.

TO ALLEN GINSBERG

April 15, 1947
1073 Downing St.
Denver, Colorado

DEAR ALLEN;

The taxicab deal has almost fallen through; this has saved me from jail, but is forcing me to get another job—I haven't worked except for one day since arriving here and am really in debt. At any rate, I shall work here until July first, then, go to Central City—35 miles away—on July 6th and work there six weeks as a bellhop in the Teller House. In the middle of August you and I shall go to Bill's, and go to NY near the first of Sept. I feel I, too, can't squeeze in New Orleans this summer.

I will tell you all I know about Justin's ability to get you a job and all I can of Central City: I have, naturally, no idea of what he had in mind when he spoke to you about a job here for you, however, since you mention Central City, I presume you'll work up there in his hotel, either as a bellboy, usher in the opera house, keeper of the books, laborer, bartender's helper, janitor or any other way that he can fit you in. This, although it sounds terrible, need not depress you; it is really unimportant what you do, for, really, all anyone does there is drink, bang & fuck off in general. Now, you can see your official capacity is immaterial except in the amount of money you draw. As for Central itself, the festival starts about July 5th each year; last year it was July 6th, & lasts six weeks. The people are usually in three categories: the prominent, all-agog over music, Denver & New York socialite backers, the arrangers, directors & opera stars themselves (Justin falls in this group)—that's category number one. Number two is made up of all the many who come for one reason or another social, (400), true interest, heard about it, etc.—this group have two things in common: they are outsiders, they spend all the money. The third category is what we'll be in: college guys who fool around at something up there only to satisfy some personal desire—women to prey on, money to filch from someone, prestige to be gained etc., other than this, all other people there live there.

I haven't seen Justin yet, but will do so tomorrow, in school, and arrange some night this week in which to see him at home for the evening. I am putting off any statements until after this interview, then I shall unload in a torrent not only what went on in it, but also all I have to say regarding the whole thing in general; after that it can rest in peace.

Your springtime rebirth seems too much the product of external events to last, but rest assured that I'm with you even though I know that I don't see the reason for it. I fear that in playing with all this business, you have become overinfluenced by Justin. I don't mean he's changed your life by objective guidance, i.e. he can't teach you, but I sense, subjectively i.e. due to your feeling of mastery over him & wanting to continue the egoistical show, he has seduced your basic loneliness into a false hope. To clarify: you've become excited about nothing; Justin is not only holding out psychological fool's gold, but is also so far beneath you that I unconsciously think of a stupid cowmaid luring a Balzac into the barn, of course, it's OK, but, somehow, I had felt you were able to cope with Justin's character & not reeled from the heady wine of victory & allow yourself to fall into this sort of juvenilia. I hope this last paragraph is all off the beam and you are just really looking forward to the West, without any high hopes or artificial thoughts of enthusiasm concerning anything other than a full summer of new experiences, not gain, or worldly profit.

You don't have to answer this if you don't have time, because I'll write again at the end of the week to tell you about Justin's actions & reactions etc.

Love,
NEAL L.

TO JACK KEROUAC

April 15, 1947
1073 Downing St.
[Denver]

DEAR JACK;

What you say about "not to worry about worry"—"not to make an issue of labours" etc. is the one thing I have always had, you can't see that your insistence on believing that the will is all, has, and always will be my basic concept. Since even I am not too sure of what I'm seeking now, you can't say our paths are as seemingly devious as you think. Of course, I know the only reason you have these presumptions is due to my inability to formulate verbally what I feel and failing to pass this on to you, you assume a lack on my part, that is, a failure to really understand you. Because of this I fear you unconsciously are not too damn interested in me, and, although knowing how foolish and unnecessary it is to be that way toward me, you still feel guilty enough to be concerned and yet bored, therefore, fall into false premises about us. Remember, my primary feeling for you lies in just that unconcern & frankness, lack of straightness etc. that you speak of, so don't allow any preconceived ideas of me or my character, or what I'm "seeking" to interfere with that. Just as you outlined Ed White, is just as I think of you & whatever difference there is in our personalities can, should & in my mind is, overcome due only to this knowledge. In other words: sensing a semi-indifference to me, you react just enough to fail to see that in that semi-indifference lies our freedom and any degree of closeness we have. Don't compare me with Allen or Huncke,[17] but rather with someone like Norman or even White.[18] I am similar to Norman in that my native enthusiasm carries me on (just as with you) & similar to White in that I feel only

17. Herbert Huncke (1915–1996). A hustler and heroin addict who hung out around New York's Times Square. He was the Junkey in Kerouac's *The Town and the City,* Elmer Hassel in *On the Road,* and Huck in *Visions of Cody*. He also appears in William Burroughs's *Junkie* as Herman, and in John Clellon Holmes's *Go* as Albert Ancke. Huncke later wrote several books, including *Huncke's Journal* (1965), *The Evening Sun Turned Crimson* (1980), and his autobiography, *Guilty of Everything* (1990).

18. Phil White. A thief and heroin addict friend of Huncke's and Burroughs's. Hung himself while imprisoned in New York's Tombs, 1951. Appears as Phil Blackman in Kerouac's *Visions of Cody,* and in Burroughs's books as Roy *(Junkie)* and Sailor *(Naked Lunch* and *Soft Machine)*.

as much as I'm concerned. This could become involved, all I'm trying to say is, let things fall into their natural order & don't, after really coming on fine, take on a defensive, apologetic air which we both feel only because of a self-imposed sense of obligation, and excuse yourself for something that, in actuality, you are to be commended for. Let's forget all this shit and just scribble to each other what [we] feel, not think.

What you say about the Lucien story strikes me as a little bit overdone, but, nonetheless, right, that is, I feel your decision is justified and I shan't bother you anymore by such requests.[19]

I am leaving town the first week in May, I'll be in Las Vegas, Nevada until sometime in June. I'll go right from Las Vegas to Bill's ranch and stay there until July first, then back to Denver for the Central City festival until August 17th. After that, New York.

I liked your letter very much, that means really that I am desirous of answering it in detail, however, I'm very tired, full of plans for my trip next week & all in all, incapable of being concerned with America and all it means at the moment. Therefore, I must beg off speaking of such things until I am in Nevada and am able to settle down and write to you spontaneously, not, as I am now, because of my compulsive need to.

If you feel up to it, write me just one more time here at this address, I'll be here for two weeks, then I'll send on my Las Vegas address when I get one.

I like your advice most of all and have taken it. I've rejected Justin and feel very little need for anyone at this time, really, I just want to be alone.

I'm closing so soon only because I'm quite fatigued and this letter is five days late as it is.

Have pity and write soon, don't write to say anything, just write.

Your friend,

NEAL L.

P.S. Great! Great! keep going on that novel, man—you're in!

NEAL

19. When Neal had asked, in his letter of March 27, to borrow Jack's story about Lucien Carr and the murder of David Kammerer, Kerouac had apparently declined to send it because of the delicacy of the subject matter.

TO ALLEN GINSBERG

May 8, 1947
1242 Clarkson St.
[Denver]

DEAR ALLEN;

Can you ever forgive me? I mean it, can you? Really, I feel very guilty about my failure to write; of course, I could rationalize myself indefinitely concerning all the lack of time I've had, troubles etc., however, I shan't do that for I should have written anyhow. The real reason I've failed to is, I think, due to my not knowing what would happen next. As I received your last letter I was packing to go to Las Vegas & gamble. Quickly I dashed off a letter telling you so, & the reasons why, then, before I mailed it, I had a minor brush with the police which, incidentally, caused me to move to this address. This change in plans voided my unmailed letter, so I started another, but just then I got a job, and I mean a *job*! Honestly, I work ten hours a day and it's so hard on me that even after ten days at it, I can still hardly drag myself home to fall into bed. I have not done anything, haven't seen Justin, (although I phoned him two weeks ago and made a date), haven't seen Hal, haven't even written to you, man, I've been beat into the ground by this hard work; enough of these excuses, onward.—

Your last letter was a pip, truly the best you've written; insofar as the groove we've been striving for it's perfect. I feel as I reread it that you're right in there, now all we need is for me to fall into it properly. Of course, you've forgotten most of what you wrote but that's not important. You're in!

I must repeat the jobs I suggested as Justin's best are only what I think, as far as I know he might make you vice-president, so try not to feel any drag, and about all remember, he's fallen for you hook, line and whatever else he has; I'm quite convinced that you are, by far, the most important and best loved thing that has happened to him in years, so during the summer really bear down on him and where he'll now eat out of your hand, then he'll even feed you out of his. If it means anything.

I swear I'll see Justin before the week's out and then write to you on the "whole thing in general" whatever I meant by that.

TO ALLEN GINSBERG

May 15, 1947
1242 Clarkson St.
[Denver]

DEAR ALLEN;

The letter I have enclosed dated May 8, is self-explanatory. The reason I must start anew—and this is the fourth time I've begun a letter to you in the last month—is only that I really don't know what will happen next and have been putting off writing until I had something definite to say. Even now I'm indefinite as all hell about what I am to do

May 17, 1947

DEAR ALLEN;

Great news! Here's our plan—please bear with me now. I leave here today to go to Trinidad, Colo. to work; I leave there about June 10th or so and dash right over to Bill and Joan's where I shall meet you and about June 30th or so we come to Denver to work at Central City from July 6 to about August 13th. This is the best and only way for us. After Central we'll be all set. I'll make enough the next three weeks at Trinidad to have a few bucks and we'll save the Central money we make (since I believe our room and board bill will be almost nil up there) to go to NY on. Please Allen steer this course with me this summer.

I know you'll excuse me for all my previous failures in writing the last month when you realize it's only because I've been having trouble with the police, LuAnne etc. You'll see when I arrive at New Waverly the middle of June. You must be there to meet me.

You can write to me at 1242 Clarkson and they'll forward it to me. After you arrive at Bill's write quick and give me precise directions as to how to get there.

Love, Love, Love—write soon, I'll see you in June.

I a poet too.

Love again,
NEAL L.

TO JACK KEROUAC

May 20, 1947
1242 Clarkson
Denver, Colo.

DEAR JACK;

Can you ever forgive me, I mean it, can you? I find it quite difficult to formulate all of the reasons for my failure to answer as quickly as is my custom. When I read your delightful missive over three weeks ago I answered it the same instant, however, the same evening before I had a chance to mail it I had a minor brush with the police which not only canceled my plans for gambling in Las Vegas, but also caused a quick change of address if you'll note. I started a letter informing you of this when I procured a job—and I mean a *job*! I work ten hours a day digging ditches, mixing cement etc.; each night as I arrive home I can barely drag myself upstairs, in consequence, that letter was never finished. Now, something new has come up which makes that letter as invalid as the first of my answers: I leave here Wed. for Trinidad, Colo. I shall work there until June 15th, then off to New Waverly and a sight of Bill and Joan.

What you say of my plans sounding desperate again seems quite true, but in reality, this time I feel no anxious moments of self-doubt as was the case previous to you and NY.

Enough of this boredom—to you—What's this about your wonderful girl, your great vocal artist? You got me so excited about her I must meet her, so damn it all, Jack, don't you go and mess up by splitting up with her before I get a chance to.

Great about the book, great, great! Here's to you, my boy. I'm happy.

God damn it, Jack I miss you I do indeed.

You and Tom [Livornese] have become good and close I see. Good, incidentally, did you ever meet Joe Springer? All you've been doing seems well and unwild, just opposite of my actions of the last few weeks.

Well put, well put—about our letters this season, you are right and have actually relieved a large amount of anxiety I had accumulated. Thanks.

You are of course, wondering just what all the trouble I've been having is, the answer seems presented in one word—friends. For example: I know a lad named Dick Reed, when I was in NY he was in Chicago and evidently shacking up with some gal for just today I had a visitor at one of my previous addresses here and this cop was looking for a Neal Cassady who had made a girl pregnant, stolen money and car and left Chicago. It seems that Dick had done these things under my name—for what reason I have no idea—& then left, so I must clear myself but fear to since the local chief here has arrested me for just the same thing before and wouldn't believe me unless I went to Chicago to be cleared by the girl herself. This sort of thing is a sample of what I've been experiencing since my return, & that's not 1/10th of it.

Write to me at 1242 Clarkson while I'm gone and they'll forward it to me.

Please forgive my hurried and inaccurate typing, I'm aching to fall into bed. If, as you say, you like scribbling, this letter is the acme of perfection between us. Right?

Please, please write and let me know all that is to be done this summer, the period is lost for me, in part, by our distance.

While I'm in Trinidad I'll have lots of time—I hope to try and make up for my letters to you by lots of scribbling.

Your friend

NEAL L.

Shortly after his return from New York, Neal had been introduced by Bill Tomson to Carolyn Robinson, a postgraduate candidate for an MA degree in theater and fine arts at the University of Denver. By June they were living together, and Neal postponed his intended Texas trip. With Allen Ginsberg about to arrive in Denver, anxious to continue their relationship, Neal broke the news to him in a letter to Texas, where Allen had already arrived at William Burroughs's New Waverly farm.

TO ALLEN GINSBERG

[June 1947]
c/o: C. Robinson
Box 1008
Colburn Hotel
980 Grant Street
Denver, Colorado

DEAR ALLEN;

Bill Tomson told me he had just received a letter from you stating that you were now in Texas; he didn't show it to me as he has none of your letters to him—something dark going on—what have you been saying?—I'm kidding.

I haven't written for two reasons: one, I was indecisive whether I would come to Texas for a week or two to meet Bill and Joan or postpone that until the latter part of August and see them just before we went back to NY; two, I didn't think you'd be in Texas until June 15 or so according to a post script in the last letter I received, and I didn't want a dead letter hanging around Bill's house, because it would probably be invalid by the time you arrived due to all of my fluctuating. For example, I've lived with LuAnne a couple of weeks, lived with a couple of old family friends, nurses,[20] a week or so, etc. My work life has been quite similar, so you can see things have been in a fix.

Justin has been hedging, as usual, in fact, I am fearful that whatever commitments he has made to you about procuring you a job may not be fulfilled. The basis of this judgement rests only on my personal experience. Therefore it's probably inaccurate, for you have impressed him enough to force him to go out of his way and find you some beneficial employment. You may suspect by now that he has not done the same for me. As it now stands I shan't be at Central City. I can't say that I'm too sorry for I have found a new interest. I sense Haldon was right in his summary of Central City as being "too gooey."

At any rate, you mustn't remain hanging on a limb in Texas. Although I can promise you nothing in the way of living quarters, work life, even social activity—I still insist that you hurry to Denver so that we can work something out. I am anxious to see you, also whatever you may bring with you; i.e. tea—may I repeat—*tea*.

When you arrive, contact me at 1830 Grant, Apartment 306; phone MA-4493 since I am living day by day and they will know where I am.

Haldon has drifted further away from us, due mostly to his mad preoccupation with his work, so you can't expect too much from him in the way of social contact.

I have met a wonderful girl. Her chief quality, I suspect, lies in the same sort of awareness or intuitive sense of understanding which is our (yours and mine) chief forte. She is getting her Master's at D.U. For some strange reason she came to Denver last year, abandoning the better places, because she could make money at D.U. But she's not really

20. The nurses were the sisters Helen and Ruth Gullion, portrayed by Kerouac as waitresses Rita and Mary Bettencourt in *On the Road,* where Sal Paradise has a brief affair with Rita.

as vulgar as she sounds. Her lack of cynicism, artificial sophistication and sterility in her creative make-up will recommend her to you. She is just a bit too straight for my temperament; however, that is the challenge, just as that is the challenge in our affair. Her basic inhibitions are subtle psychological ones tied up indirectly with conventions, mannerisms and taste; whereas, mine with you are more internal, fearful and stronger. She knows all about the Theatre, draws a fine line, and is quite popular. Don't feel that I am overawed by her, though. I would have a justifiable right in being subjective to that. Somehow, my respect for her seems unimportant. I feel the only reason, really, that she affects me so is the sense of peace which she produces in me when we are together. Secretly, she is the reason I am postponing the trip to Texas until later in the season—wait till you meet her.

Remember, now, I am really at sea here, so when you arrive, I shall almost be dependent on you, rather than vice versa as it should be. But don't let that drag you. We will hit the ball this summer, so barrel on—rush up—hurry to me!

Love,
NEAL

As Neal settled in with Carolyn, he wrote to LuAnne, who was visiting Los Angeles with her Denver girlfriend Lois Williams, urging her not to hurry back. She had, however, returned to Denver by the time Kerouac arrived there that summer, with Neal dividing his time among Carolyn, LuAnne, and Allen.

TO LUANNE CASSADY

July 1947
[Denver]

DEAR LUANNE:

I picked up your amusing postcards as they arrived at general delivery, there daily for one month. I stopped by to see if there was any more news from you, however, as you know, there was none. Finally, [Jim] Holmes gave me your letter to me. Why did you write to him and not general delivery? I know I didn't write to the Glendale address, but, next to the address on the card was the word (hold) which I interpreted as not to write—enough of this, to get on. Delighted to hear you and Lois are getting on so well, let us hope you are becoming more free to live in your own personality and not be too dependent on others—even Lois. I have been working since the day you left at Shoppers Parking Service, have just been fired though and therefore, will leave Denver soon to go East. I have thought of you a good deal lately, but, just as you said in your letter, "realize it can't be"—makes me sad.

I, naturally, desire to see you, but, I realize how impossible it is—so please understand my position and think of me as little as possible so I shall be relieved of my sense of guilt and shame at what I've done to you.

The rational thing for us, then, is really to know how stupidly we've acted and purify our souls by some hard work and non-neurotic thoughts. I, therefore, advise you to live as naturally as possible and obtain satisfaction in knowing you are stronger than I. As far as action is concerned, stay in Long Beach; and struggle to free yourself from all types of subjective emotions—especially toward me—and only then will you be the girl your potentialities indicate. I love you for this time, in the sure knowledge we are, for at least the present, almost completely incompatible due only to my inability to fall in to a proper groove of basic intercourse with you.

On July 17 Jack Kerouac had begun his first trip West, arriving in Denver a week later to meet up again with Neal, LuAnne, and Allen, and to be introduced to Carolyn. When, the following month, Jack traveled on to California to work as a security guard in Marin City with his old school-friend Henri Cru, Neal parted from Carolyn and, in the company of Allen, visited William Burroughs and Joan at their Texas farm. Carolyn, meanwhile, drove to California with other friends. (Part One of Kerouac's On the Road *covers his first trips to Denver and California that summer.) In part of the following letter, Allen addresses Jack as "Jean," the French form of his name.*

TO JACK KEROUAC

August 22, 1947
[Denver]

DEAR JACK;

Received your great little card several days ago, have failed to answer until now because of all the bullshit that's been going on around here.

It appears the possibility of my shipping out is nil, since I can't spend four months in a training camp. As for me and Allen coming out to San Fran., well, what the hell are you doing anyway? You didn't even mention whether you were shipping out or what; so how can I plan?

Due to this Allen and I are going to Texas tomorrow, so write to us there as we'll see what's what. Right?

Helen [Gullion] left Denver a week ago to go to San Francisco; Allen got a card from her asking to know your address, so, Jack, my boy it looks as if you've made a real conquest, since she's not the kind to bother to write to someone asking addresses even when it's really important.

Carolyn and I are having sessions a la LuAnne, enough said.

If you don't write us full of definite plans we won't know what to do, so shall leave Texas in Sept. for NY.

Let me hear all about everything; come on now, one of those big, mad beer-drinking letters.

Really now, I insist, I'm *your* loving brother, not you mine.

Your Pal,

NEAL

DEAR JEAN:

Helen, see, is on vacation (with Ruth?) and can be reached at 914-A Florida St., Frisco itself. You're all set now for a few weeks if all goes well. I hope you get in touch with her. It is a "sweet" turn of fate.

I am sitting at Brierly's desk in the City & County building waiting to make farewell to him. Everything seems so sad and beautiful. It is 3:30 and I had no sleep, sitting up to write *Last Stanzas In Denver,* full of starkness and alas, still all too abstract, but in a way sufficient unto the cause.

ALLEN

Arriving at William Burroughs's farm at New Waverly, Texas, Neal and Allen discovered that another visitor there was their old friend the heroin addict Herbert Huncke, who was assisting Burroughs in tending his crop of marijuana plants. Ginsberg, meanwhile, was making plans to ship out of Houston.

TO JACK KEROUAC

Aug. 31, '47
Bill's Ranch
[New Waverly, Texas]

DEAR JACK,

Just received your letter;[21] quite a real treat to hear from you.

I've just eaten a huge meal; corn on cob, meat, sweet potatoes, peas, peaches, milk, 2 cokes. I'm too full to move or think. I sweat, I smell, I'm dirty.

I'm scribbling away;

Allen & I left Denver 2 A.M. Sunday & arrived here Tuesday dawn. Slept all day & night. Wed. spent in driving the jeep & getting supplies, talking to Bill & Huncke, getting supplies of tea from the garden etc. This is a crazy spot, but I anticipated that & can accept it all & with more kick.[22]

Bill has not received his money from his dad yet & we are unable to buy anything. For the last 3 days poor Joan & Huncke have had very little Benzedrine (2 tubes a day) to skim by on. The money should arrive tomorrow, then I shall drive Huncke & Allen to Houston, 90 miles away. Huncke will go in to restock on Benny & various other stimuli. Allen will go in to see if there may be a ship for him to ship on for a couple of weeks (to NY, say). I am going in to Houston to drive & dig the place.

I'm building Bill a fence, repairing his garage, laying a cement floor, & damming up his creek with cement.

Your letters are really stimulating, but I find them hard to answer. All I can do is ramble on, for to come down to some one subject or . . .

Sept. 2, 7:10 A.M.

Woke up, determined to write; I have several plans in mind, but can't achieve pure certainty on any one of them. Will speak of them when I do, probably in my next letter.

21. Jack Kerouac wrote to Neal Cassady from Marin City on August 26, 1947. See Ann Charters, ed., *Jack Kerouac: Selected Letters, 1940–1956 (SL)*, pp. 113–19.

22. Neal talks about his experiences on Burroughs's farm in the tape section of Kerouac's *Visions of Cody*. Herbert Huncke has also written about these events in *Guilty of Everything* and *The Evening Sun Turned Crimson*.

What are you? A guard in a shipyard? How come? Did Henry[23] set it up for you?

Page 2 of your letter was just right, how I wish I could explain myself to you that well, perhaps I may be able to soon. You're right, great & wonderful. *Please* don't feel I either misunderstand or misunderstand less; even worse—don't think; I seem to detect this, but can't believe it, for a moment I'm not sincere with you or that I enjoy your sadness. The only possible reason you could see me in that poor a light is because I'm confused & incapable, at present, of communing with anyone, even Allen. These things settle themselves if you don't push them. Jack, you must have patience with me.

Sept. 9, '47 8 A.M.

There's a whole week lost, huh? Well, I'm fully qualified to be excused when I tell you where it's gone.

I'll start with Sept. 3. Huncke, Allen & I went to Houston. Huncke went to buy supplies, just as I did, while Allen went to the Union Hall to find a ship. We all met around 4 P.M. Huncke was high & refused to come back here. So we fritted away some time trying to persuade him, but, being unsuccessful, we agreed to meet him at noon the next day.

Allen had gotten a messman's job on a freighter going to France in about 4 days. He decided to report the next day, so he & I came back to New Waverly.

Came dawn Sept. 4, off we rushed to Houston again. We meet Huncke & all 3 of us drove out to the ship to find the steward. Finally found him, he was drunk, so was Allen & Huncke. Allen agreed to come aboard next day & help feed the mess.

We got Huncke to come back with us this time & returned here. The next morning Allen told Bill it was his last day before shipping out, so could Bill give him enough money to rent a hotel room that night.

Huncke, Allen & I would spend that night there (Sept. 5) & at

23. Henri Cru (1921–1992), Kerouac's friend from Horace Mann School, with whom he worked as a security guard in Marin City, August 1947. Portrayed as Remi Boncoeur in *On the Road;* as Deni Bleu in *Visions of Cody, Lonesome Traveler, Desolation Angels,* and *Book of Dreams.*

6 A.M. Allen would depart from us & we would return here by noon the 6th. Bill agreed & off we went.

From the afternoon of the 5th to the morning of the 6th everything was really frantic. First we all got high (on assorted stuff) after an early evening of nigger joints, mad music etc. I told Huncke & Allen I'd see them later & took off in the jeep.

I found a mad woman, drug her back to the hotel room (Huncke & Allen were in the adjoining room) & fucked away. Allen was mad at me, Huncke a bit resentful of my using his room (he had a boy) & the girl was completely bewildered by all this. I passed out cold & didn't come to until 9 A.M. the next day.

The girl was a beauty & had been kicked out by infuriated Allen. Tough. We spent the day in a great hassle. Allen kept postponing going aboard the ship; Huncke kept refusing to leave Houston, & I kept urging more speed or Allen would lose his job; Huncke & I would never get back here in time to bring Bill & Joan ice, etc.

Sure enough, that's what happened; Allen not only lost his job for not showing up, but also was fouled up with the union. All of us returned, dejected, to the downtown area. Huncke still wouldn't come back here & so again Allen & I returned alone & promised to meet H. at noon the next day. That was just the start of more bullshit.

I'm going to cut this short; suffice to say, Bill was angry, (the meat had spoiled), 5 days had been wasted, & we were right back where we started.

The next day I took Allen back to Houston for the last time.

Huncke was met by us & we all sat in the union-hall 4 hrs with Allen hoping to get another ship. Well, he didn't, & the time came for Huncke & I to return here. So, after very tender goodbyes, he & I left Allen in the union hall, waiting to find a ship, reading Henry James & musing on his fate. That was the last we've ever seen or heard of him. Goodbye to Allen for now.

Incidentally, the girl I'd had that night is now in the nut-house, she was picked up, babbling, on the street the next morning. Too bad. Her beautiful body was matched by an idiotic mind. I feel truly sorry & wish I could see her again & perhaps could help her in some way.

Write me here. We leave for NY in a month.

Am I excused for not writing sooner? This won't happen again. So write me, man & watch the answer fly back.

Your pal.

NEAL

P.S. I have a terrible pen, a cardboard box as a stand & a terrible looking handwriting, so please excuse.

N.

"writ by hand" is right

P.P.S. Have you heard from Hal? What's new? Although I know there's little that can be new with Hal.

P.P.P.S. Answer soon & call me down for all my bad habits that prevent me from writing a good letter. Give me pointers, pal.

NEAL

Allen Ginsberg eventually shipped out on the SS John Blais, *to Dakar, Africa. Neal forwarded his letters with an abrupt note.*

TO ALLEN GINSBERG

Sept. 10, '47
[New Waverly, Texas]

DEAR ALLEN;

Here are the letters that have arrived for you.

Will write you later at the other address; must rush to get these away to you.

Glad you like what you're doing (I mean where you're going).

See how much of a rush I'm in.

Love,
NEAL

TO JACK KEROUAC

Sept. 20, '47
[New Waverly, Texas]

DEAR JACK,

Received your letter,[24] great to hear from you again. Went to a Texas football game last night. What a stupid business. The "Sam

24. Kerouac's letter to Neal of September 13, 1947. See *SL*, pp. 125–30.

Houston Bearkats" vs "Louisiana State Wildcats." It was a college game & played at Huntsville, several miles north of here.

The announcer (typical Texan) was completely prejudiced for the home team (the Bearkats). It was not only unfair (his broadcast) but, commanded absolutely *no* knowledge of football.

The fans in the stands were worse (if possible) & so upset me "I'd a 'fit' at the drop of a hat."

Needless to say, the Bearkats outweighed the Wildcats *20* lbs. to a man & won 14 to 0. Enuf—

Friday morning (again) I dashed off to Houston with Huncke. This time we had to get some paregoric for Bill since he's got a slight habit again. Of course, we always pick up Benzedrine for Joan & Huncke.

We arrived about 1 P.M. & Huncke bought some Nembutals (we always use them) & he & I got high.

I dashed about town gunning women shopping & Huncke wandered down Skid Row.

We finally got together—since nothing exciting could happen in the afternoon—& came home, getting here about dark.

Honestly now I can't [remember what I said in my letters to you . . .]

I'm happy to have you say you like them, however. I've improved on the cardboard box, I now use a barrel.

Your coat idea sounds good,[25] as does your anticipation of NY again; however, due to my fluctuating & lack of true knowledge or crystallization of my plans this winter, I can't say for sure I'll be in NY. There are various reasons why this is so. I'll enumerate briefly: 1, Fear of getting busted if I stay with Bill too long. 2, Hardship of getting set up (since I lack the basic drive). 3, Carolyn insists I come to San Francisco to spend the winter with her—she'll make a Hollywood salary by January. 4, Allen's absence—I had counted on him to get the ball rolling academically (or its equivalent). etc. etc.—more of this later, in more concise terms.

Here, tho, are my *exact* plans for the next month. Stay here 'till Oct. 1, drive Bill & Huncke to NY, arrive first week of Oct., stay with Bill at least 2 weeks. After that?—who knows.

Please, Jack, *don't* feel I've lost *any* incentive, I'm just making sure

25. Kerouac had suggested to Neal that they might go into the coat-selling business together.

this time. Understand? I'm just making sure that what I do from here on out is for the best. Thanks.

Apropos of this—Allen. No, he's not fallen out with Bill. He shipped out partially for money. The other reason is me. Don't be bugged at him for kicking the girl out. It was all my fault. I'll explain without delving too far . . .

I understand him & he, I. Finally, it became obvious we must part. It never came up who would leave who or anything on that corny level. So—he shipped out.

Well now, that night when I brought the girl up to the hotel room in Houston, I had promised (since it was his last night) Allen a ball from midnight to 6 A.M.—when he was to leave. Naturally, when I failed to kick the girl out at 12 o'clock he was righteously indignant.

I might add, at this point, the whole thing was completely unknown to me because I *really* passed out about 10 P.M. Boy! was I knocked out!! To cut it short, Allen got rid of the girl & then struggled with my inert & lifeless body all night.

Bill has not reached the tear stage yet, but he's genuinely sorry that circumstances prevent your Plan "B" from working.[26] Here are the circumstances: The jeep is small, so small that there is even talk of making Huncke (this is serious) hitchhike to NY. You see, Bill needs me to drive (Huncke can't) or else I'd hitchhike. There will be all kinds of furniture piled in the back, no room for anyone. Rash as it sounds, one of us may either ride the fender or drag out the rear end. Bill would send Huncke by train (as he is Joan) but, there is just *no* money. Bill has spent all & we'll be lucky (no kiddin') to get there at all. I'm sorry as hell. I've racked my brain to find a way for you to join us, but I have found no way. Bill is so concerned that you understand, he would have added a P.S. explaining to you, but I said I would explain for him. Thereupon he said—"Well, I'm going to write back anyhow. I should have sooner."

So that's the story—no room. Damn it!

I suspect I've read more Balzac than you think, but, his personal life is even more interesting to me. *Lovin'*, yea man!

26. One of Kerouac's plans was to join Neal at New Waverly and drive with him and the others back to New York. Instead he traveled from Marin City to Hollywood, meeting the Mexican girl Bea Franco (Terry in *On the Road*), and spending two weeks with her, picking cotton near Selma, California, before traveling back East by bus.

Your entire letter was very nice, but, I like the last of it best (NY etc.)

Afternoon

Just received another letter from Carolyn. She's written me *20* times since I've been here (18 days). See what a persistent cat she is. There's only one thing wrong with her—too middle class—Ha! Bennington. Oh well.

I got a letter from Allen,—he left Sept. 13 for Dakar, Africa,—stating his intention of being in NY about Nov. 1.

Julie[27] will really be something when she grows up. She's already hep now to many, many things. I want to keep an eye on her & when she's about 8 or 9 see just how far she's gone. It will be quite interesting, I'm sure.

Willie,[28] the baby, is just another kid so far.

Talk about story telling, Huncke gabs in my ear all day & night, he relishes bullshitting with me. We sure whip up a breeze, especially when we're high.

Bill & Huncke & I get high every night on tea & lush. It's "out of this world"—to quote Huncke.

Bill & I spend hours fishing like veterans, although he won't admit it—even to himself—neither of us know a damn thing about it.

I've written LuAnne, requesting a divorce again. She's a fine girl, but not for me. How sad.

Write soon, pal, I like your style. This letter is just like the others—no good. I guess I haven't got it in me.

NEAL

27. Julie Adams (b. 1944), the daughter of Joan Vollmer Adams by a Columbia University student while she was married to Paul Adams.

28. William Seward Burroughs Jr. (1947–1981), the son of William Burroughs and Joan Vollmer Adams; author of the autobiographical novels *Speed* (1970) and *Kentucky Ham* (1973).

TO JACK KEROUAC

[early October 1947]
[c/o] Eugene Brooks
43-31 45th St #5-F
L.I. City, NY

DEAR JACK,

Really sorry I've not written sooner. Bill, Huncke & I left Texas at 8 P.M. Mon. nite (the last of Sept.) & arrived here Thurs. at 6 A.M.[29] Drove 1,860 miles.

Dashed up to Vicki's, washed, shaved, etc. & have spent the rest of my time driving her & everyone else around town.

There's not much news. Bill selling weed, Huncke is not doing anything (just as me) & Joan's getting vicious.

Vicki & I ball & there's a new chick—name Stephanie.[30]

I'm all balled up with all the dashing about I do & yet get nothing done.

I've tried to get my old job back, no go.[31] Other than that—nothing.

I'll wait for you, if I can get some gold—if I can't I'll hitchhike to San Francisco. So that's the score.

How's everything? I've not heard from Allen. *Please,* continue, & always continue, to consider me as your friend. Really, Jack, you're the only guy, except Allen, I give a damn about, understand? So long, Pal, see you soon, I hope.

NEAL

Neal drove Burroughs, Huncke, and their crop of marijuana to New York, arriving October 2. Joan and the children traveled by train. Neal spent several weeks in town and waited there for Kerouac until Monday, October 27, when he caught a bus back to San Francisco, and Carolyn. Jack, hitchhiking the last leg of his journey from Pittsburgh, Pennsylvania, arrived October 29, missing Neal by two days. Allen arrived back from sea shortly afterward, to find a harsh note from Neal, who wanted to finish their relationship. On his return journey,

29. Monday, September 29; Thursday, October 2.

30. Stephanie Stewart, a lesbian jazz pianist, was a friend of Vicki Russell's, and was called Stephanie James in *Visions of Cody,* and Marian in *Junkie*.

31. On his previous visit to New York, Neal had worked at a parking lot.

Neal had briefly stopped off in Denver and, intending to settle down with Carolyn when he returned to San Francisco, visited LuAnne in an attempt to annul their marriage. For financial reasons this was not possible, but Neal obtained a job in a San Francisco car service station and hoped to have enough money to send to LuAnne within a few weeks. Meanwhile Neal and Carolyn had settled into a new apartment in the Richmond district of San Francisco, belonging to a merchant seaman friend, Mike Walton.

TO JACK KEROUAC

[November] 5, 1947
[c/o] Robinson
561 A 24th Ave
San Francisco

DEAR JACK;

I waited for you until Monday night[32] and when you didn't show, since I had to go, I left.

I want you to know, purely and simply, it just could not be helped—in reality, I sense I felt more disappointed than you may have, for you had the pleasure of a reunion with your mother to take the edge off my desertion, but I had no one.

My conviction that Carolyn was enough is, I find, correct—so, don't worry about your boy Neal, he's found what he wants and in her is attaining greater satisfaction than he'd ever known.

Since arriving I have begun to note little thoughts, actions, etc., written them on scratch paper and along with my attempt to recall *all* my past life and record it in a semi-outline, (similar to a diary) is, I'm sure, enough writing to occupy my time this winter.

No work life as yet, but whatever I get will be the same as I always do get, somehow, the job seems to have a tendency to be short on cash and long on ennui, boredom—or, as I used to say (ahem) in my New York period (ahem)—*Drag*.

Please, do be kind-hearted and find the necessary love within yourself to be forgiving; in a typically Kerouacian growl send me a short and gruff note demanding to know "what in the hell I meant by running out of town when *I* was acomin' with new records, ideas *and* addresses, besides, Neal—goddamit—you owed me a ride in that f—kin' jeep" then, Jack, I'll be happy again and we'll *really* carry on.

32. Monday, October 27.

Come on now, give me a new lease on our friendship, and thereby, find one yourself. *You* listen to *me* for awhile; I've made you carry the brunt of the load in our letters, and since you don't have the drive to talk to me (because I've let you down intellectually, and your heart has no warmth anymore, although you like to think it does) to you *I* will talk, yes, even over your protests—I accept the load for awhile.

When I left town Bill and Huncke had sort of fallen out. The main reason seemed to be that Bill had taken up with Garver[33] and, perhaps you didn't know, Huncke dislikes "Mother" Garver. Joan was still leading Bill about and hasn't dropped Bennie[34] either. When I read the portion of the last letter you sent me, to her—Vicki, that is—she said, "are you sure that dream sequence was concerning me, not Stephanie?" and after I reassured her, she continued her Vicki-like bursts of enthusiasm over your impending arrival. This, little kiddies, is the end of our semi-annual, one minute, news and views on the latest NY gossip.

Christ! I'm getting corny.

I've got a lot of old Hampton, Basie, etc.[35] which Stephanie dropped on me as a sort of semi-insult, or to, mistakenly, get back in my good graces (or some such confused thought) to get some junk or tea. The kick comes when one sees her thinking she's killing two birds by giving me the records she didn't want and believing I'm so square I was really knocked-out by her generosity in parting with all these "good" records she'd had for years, etc. etc.—she laid it on thick and I gobbled it up to make her think I was taken in. It was a great scene, especially since she should have been dealing with Bill, but she had just thrown Mr. B. out and had to vamp me so I would "persuade" Bill to think she wasn't so.

What's the latest news from Haldon? I was going to write him, but I feel so pressed with other things and hate to start writing Hal again when I know I'd peter out on him after a couple of letters. Besides he's, I'm sure, much too busy to waste any time on me, since I

33. William Maynard Garver (1896–1957). A heroin addict and overcoat-thief acquaintance of Burroughs, Huncke, Ginsberg, and Kerouac in New York and Mexico City. Garver appears as Bull Gaines in Kerouac's *Desolation Angels, Tristessa,* and *Book of Dreams,* and as Harper in *Visions of Cody*. He also features in William Burroughs's novels *Junkie, Naked Lunch,* and *The Soft Machine* as Bill Gains.

34. Benzedrine.

35. Lionel Hampton, jazz vibraphonist, drummer, and bandleader; William "Count" Basie, jazz pianist and bandleader.

don't stimulate him anyhow. So you give me the word on him. Thanks.

Allen, as you know, was in Africa. The day I left NY I heard from Eugene[36] that he had sent his father a cablegram from aboard his ship saying he'd be in the middle of Nov. Let's hope everything works out for him this season; he really has a rough go.

I am finding it easier to lead a more productive life, having escaped the fixation on my need to write (have you?) I now find I'm relaxed enough to start plugging away at it; this seems to fit my temperament to a greater extent than the old, frantic, unreasoning drive—which, when not let out, started to rot in my gut; sterility followed. I, most certainly, don't wish to force a rehash of all this on you, but really now, Jack, are you healthy? Have you not found yourself at times, dissatisfied with your present—shall we say, Philosophy—toward your Art? I know after 5 years of overbalance—no matter how good the cause—one finds himself cluttered up with so many trite, and otherwise, things that it becomes increasingly difficult for one to function properly or attain to that which they have been striving—this seems, almost always, in direct inverted ratio to the degree of character one has to push with is added the degree of fixation and narrowing—inevitably—of outlook. So, since your great sense of humor prompts you to assume mouth-twisting, cigar-clenching, gruff-voiced mannerisms, it naturally follows that since you've also taken on a semi-stock, reactionary mask—to escape all the mad discussions, etc. which, being overdone in youth have produced therefore in you a strong reaction—you, now, find yourself blocked and two constant thoughts are your bedfellows: The one that has the upper hand now and you cling to is the one you spoke to me of last yr.: "All——

I stop this silly overdone and presumptuous dull shit—sorry, Jack.

November 8

Just got a great letter from Allen; he calls me down plenty & I'm sure he's right. No doubt you agree with him. Well,—I agree with both of you—but, not enough to come back to New York until next year. So, *that's settled*.

36. Eugene Brooks was Allen Ginsberg's older brother, who worked as a lawyer in New York.

Drop me a line & tell me what you & Allen did—in one paragraph he cryptically states, "Jack & I wandered"—I, of course, can imagine what happened (depending on how drunk you got)—up & down the avenues, sitting in bars, etc.—

Your Pal (I hope)
SQUARE JOHN CASSADY

TO ALLEN GINSBERG

Nov. 18, 1947
[c/o] Robinson
561A 24th Ave.
[San Francisco]

MY DEAR, DEAR ALLEN;

My good and lovely boy, please, please, forgive and forget my terribly, terribly, badly done, trite, and illiterate trash, i.e., my last letter.

You show yourself to be your old wonderful self in your letter, your criticisms are delicious, simply great, many thanks.

The above must be the Kingsland[37] influence in me—I wonder if you know how much love I have for him—my god! what am I doing?

I stop the above "inspired sterility" and come down to *you,* (only you)—You, (say I in a presumptuous tone) my a-historical soul-mate, are correct, you are so right, insofar as you go into it and understand the exodus; you are the true genius, but I must accept my role also, and a realllllly think I am doing it the way *I* must!! Damn it, you are almost insolent and overbearing to the point of absurdity in your attack on my overdone and stinking prose, and, I think, delved into that unnecessarily long to the exclusion of the main point of our relationship i.e., my development to maturity, to strength, and grace; since you do have the understanding, Allen, as evidenced by your wonderful, but still partial, knowledge of the reasons for my leave-taking, use that understanding to trust me to my own self, and sense of destiny;

37. John Kingsland was a Columbia University student friend of Ginsberg's and Kerouac's from the mid-1940s. Kerouac characterized him as John Macy in *Visions of Cody*, and as Charles Bernard in *The Subterraneans*.

separate and entirely apart from my straightness, or artistic self, this is a matter of levels, as you know, and I can't allow you to chasten me by using these weapons. Don't think of this duelistically, my friend.

Canton Cheese by Cassady

The above interlude was necessitated by my failure to put 'between n and t in Cant, *so* I made it Canton, then, of course; why not do a take-off on Allen and his "interlude"—*so* I did, *so* I don't like it, *so* I condemn it as not good prose style for its triteness in using Lord Chesterfield, instead of, say, Pete Smith, *so* my interlude is not as good, *so* that still doesn't mean because the artist is no good, neither is the art—look, my boy, see how I write on several confused levels at once, *so* do I think, *so* do I live, *so* what, *so* let me act out my part at the same time I'm straightening it out, *so* as to reach an authentic destiny.

It *Can* Be Done—I'm doing it. What am I saying? I started this letter in good faith and have somewhere gotten side-tracked onto good fun. Let be, let be.

Having solved all this in my "Life with Father," "*Corn*el Blimp" way, I now speak of more serious things; now you take taxation for example, there *is* a problem, or, the degree of pressure at 10,000 ft. in the ocean, it's amazin', says our natural philosophy prof. N. Cass.—Am I mocking myself enough, am I here doing enough penance to suit you for the time being? Answer me, sweet Allen.

On the contrary, I mondify [*sic*] and say I started this letter, not on good faith, but good tea, yep, I met a nigger and bought some; as soon as I got high I sat down to write this, have been at it three hours, have had three thousand separate and distinct thoughts, have written less than three hundred words and, have lost my thoughts, have said nothing, have no regrets, however, for I know, (I repeat) Carolyn is but a step and so is—fuck it. I'm hitler. I mean; I'M HIGH

TO JACK KEROUAC

November 21, 1947
c/o Robinson
561 A 24th Ave.
[San Francisco]

MY DEAR JACK;

You're a great, wonderful guy; thanks Jack.

I'm sitting here listening to Kenton and Musso, Manne, etc. The

Hawk, Illinois Jacquet, and the *really* rococo Dexter Gordon.[38] Music and literature, then other arts, then Philosophy and history; last, science.—First, LOVE, and all that follows: sensatory perception, innate, instinctive knowledge and emotional conceptions that further this knowledge. Your touching of souls; which only "eyes and hands and senses" can do is beautiful and shows the obvious similarity our basic natures have. I must say, however, your "won by reaction" symbol of Ed Whites, Bob Burfords,[39] et al, is, of course, perfect insofar as it goes, but *cannot* contain within itself somehow, the basic certainty of complete truth. I agree the souls of these types are the *correct* ones—after all, you and I are of this blood; but beyond? beyond this? beyond this, etc. sense of self is an objective truth which you, I think, have missed, and I cannot, as yet, formulate. So, let be.

Incidentally, I saw the great, one and only, Thomas Mann[40] day before yesterday. He gave a terrific lecture on "Nietzsche[41] in the light of modern experience," it was not a simple rehash of stock thought and inept handling of our Friedrich, but, rather, pushed into the real "rarefied air" of *True* understanding; not abstract nonsense and trashy, trite inquiries into his motives etc., but, honest dealment with the problem—

Let me proclaim: I am now working, what a business! god, you wouldn't believe it even if you saw it; picture I.B.M. at its worst and double that to receive a faint portrait of the company I work for; McKale's Inc., a gas station outfit, has 12 of these stations and yet, have, with maddening persistency, succeeded in building up a booming business based on "smiling cooperation" and "cheerful service," so these 12 stations now take in more than any other 12 in town. This is maintained by high-pressure selling and all who work for the company take courses and read massive journals full of "the proper method." I can't go on—impossible to describe; much too funny to just tell, you'd have to see it.

38. Stan Kenton, pianist and bandleader; Vido Musso, tenor saxophonist who founded a big band with Stan Kenton in 1936; Shelly Manne, jazz drummer; Coleman Hawkins (The Hawk), Illinois Jacquet, and Dexter Gordon—jazz tenor saxophonists.

39. Bob Burford was a friend of Ed White's who knew Neal Cassady and Jack Kerouac in Denver, 1947. Later became editor of *New Story* magazine in Paris, France. Characterized as Ray Rawlins in *On the Road* and Biff Buferd in *Visions of Cody*.

40. Thomas Mann (1875–1955). German novelist and essayist. Author of *Death in Venice* (1912) and *The Magic Mountain* (1924).

41. Friedrich Wilhelm Nietzsche (1844–1900). German philosopher and poet.

Nov. 24,

I'll never get this off to you.

Nov. 25,

Oh yes I will.

Nov. 26,

Mailed today,—at last.

My letters become more trite daily. Not just here, but everywhere.

Am hot on Spengler,[42] again.—Too, am rereading Joyce[43]—since I'm (ahem), also Irish. (Other half is German, of course). Here's to you.

NEAL

This *is* important. Tell me of your art, your writing,—don't waste your energies; just write of your progress here, *please*. Thanks.

Neal's domestic bliss with Carolyn became complicated when, on December 1, LuAnne arrived in San Francisco with some friends. Neal began liaising secretly with her, anxious that Carolyn remain unaware of his exploits.

42. Oswald Spengler (1880–1936). German philosopher and author whose *The Decline of the West* (1922) was a big influence on Cassady and Kerouac.

43. James Joyce (1882–1941). Irish novelist, author of *Ulysses* (1922) and *Finnegans Wake* (1939).

TO JACK KEROUAC

December 25, 1947
561A 24th Ave.
San Francisco

DEAR JACK;

Hallo, how you?

To me, since first we met, you have always personified an older blood-brother. The prime similarity being, perhaps, our preoccupation with our egos; next, if I may say so, was our mutual overbalanced, and semi-confused, method of logic. This may be attributed to an early extreme; you, with Literature, me, with Philosophy. Despite our deviation from divergent paths, and apparent falling into different patterns, I still find a sense of close understanding between you and I which no other gives to me, and to which I respond by symbolizing you as an—older blood-brother.

On December 1st LuAnne arrived here; she was quite changed, affected a more sophistic air, came on hep and moved with an improved poise. After some preliminary skirmishing we reverted back to an old naturalness of relationship and it was with great difficulty I finally managed to extract the commitment of desire to gain an annulment from her. The process of becoming legally free rests now on money; after the 5th I have some and forward it to her mother in Denver to start the divorce.

Aside from the emotional difficulty there is another and, I feel, more interesting problem—i.e. keeping Lu and Carolyn separated. This game has been going on for a month and is exciting in many ways. I am with both of them at different hours of the same day, daily, I must be on my toes to keep Carolyn from knowing—but, enuf.

I'll see you next fall, after I go to Denver in the spring to get my sister, and live there (or near by) during the summer. I'll be in NY from next Sept. on.

May I falteringly state that I am now starting to write? Both a daily journal and the early recollections of my life are my first task.

I understand from Allen that both Bill and Joan have left town, and that you and he had a couple of serious evenings together—and, he delicately hinted that perhaps the seriousness of the talks were the thing which was keeping you from seeing him more often—'sat so?

How are you writing? good, or not; let me know. Thanks.

Dec. 29

DEAR JACK;

I have great visions, I understand people; I move freely—I know everything.

I am everybody.

Many advisers move me, most are negative, but I'm positive, see?

Dink, oops—drink to Wilde,[44] ugh!

Well then, here's to—ah. Skip it.

May god have mercy on me; the only records I have are not enough, damn it, I think, dear Jack, we've underestimated money, I predict a lucrative year for me, since I'm goin' to make money one object of this year's struggle. Hear me?

So Long,
N.

In an attempt to renew Ginsberg's friendship, Neal told him that he planned to leave Carolyn, who was becoming too serious, and move back to Denver to live with his father and younger sister, Shirley.

TO ALLEN GINSBERG

December 30, 1947
Walton
561A 24th Ave
[San Francisco]

DEAR ALLEN;

The new year is upon us, and with it starts a new season for me. I'm to live by myself from now until spring when I return to Denver. At that time I'll get my sister and my father and we shall live together all summer in Denver; at the finish of this business I'm off to NY.

On December 1st LuAnne came to town and since then has been a constant thorn; she is with an old beau and a girl friend and together they all live in a downtown hotel. Since she doesn't work

44. Oscar Wilde (1854–1900). Irish playwright, satirist, and wit.

(although both of the other two do) and does nothing, even read, she has much time to come by my service station in his car, call on me in the mornings while Carolyn is away and before I go to work; in short, my efforts toward an annulment have been little rewarded, however, now that I've, at last, (during several emotional scenes) made it plain to her that all is finished she has again promised to have her mother gain our legal separation. If this fails this time, when I get to Denver I'll spend the necessary money to get the damn thing.

Helen [Gullion] has gotten married and went to Mexico for the honeymoon; Ruth [Gullion] is all alone and is apparently in need of some companionship so, when you write to 1830 Grant St., apt. 306, be loving.

I am stumbling thru a daily journal and try as I might I am having trouble with the recollection of my early life. This first writing task will be all the more difficult in that I do it daily (everyday thought) and also, in the novel form (my life) just to get started.

I am moving by myself again because Carolyn has practically gotten married to me in the eyes of her family and unless I break quickly things may become drastic. I also can live much more cheaply that way and, needless to say, money has become quite important since I must have some saved by May for Shirley.

I hope to see you next fall, if not, I'll suffer. Goodnight. Started Dickens again.

I love you,
NEAL L.

1948

While living with Carolyn, Neal began making serious attempts at writing, although experiencing some difficulties, as he explained to Kerouac.

TO JACK KEROUAC

Jan. 7, 1948
[San Francisco]

DEAR JACK;

It is not possible to grasp and express things at all as completely as most people, particularly critics, would have us believe. Most events are inexpressible, they happen in a region of the soul into which no word can penetrate; understanding comes thru the soul.

With this introduction I want to say that my prose has no individual style as such, but is rather an unspoken and still unexpressed groping toward the personal. There is something there that wants to come out; something of my own that must be said. Yet, perhaps, words are not the way for me.

I have found myself looking to others for the answer to my soul, whereas I know this is slowly gained (if at all) by delving into my own self only. I am not too sure that the roots of the impulse to write go deep enough, are necessary enough, for me to create on paper.

If, however, I find writing a must (as you've seemed to) then I know I must build my life around this necessity; even my most indifferent and trivial hours must become an expression of this impulse and a testimony to it.

I have always held that when one writes one should forget all rules, literary styles, and other such pretensions as large words, lordly clauses and other phrases as such, i.e., rolling the words around in the mouth as one would wine and proper or not putting them down because they sound so good. Rather, I think, one should write, as nearly as possible, as if he were the first person on earth and was humbly and sincerely putting on paper that which he saw and experienced, loved and lost; what his passing thoughts were and his sorrows and desires; and these things should be said with careful avoidance of common phrases, trite usage of hackneyed words and the like. One must combine Wolfe[1] and Flaubert[2]—and Dickens.

Art is good when it springs from necessity. This kind of origin is the guarantee of its value; there is no other. It follows from this that if I feel the necessity and yet have no talent as such, must I write to compensate?

Oh well, dear Jack, the above shows you, once again, the nonsense, and stupid bugaboos I fight; or do I fight? I'm inclined to think not, and perchance therein lies my flaw.

At any rate I intend to continue grinding out the trash which seems embedded in me. At the same time I fully intend to start playing an instrument; the sax, perhaps. Also, of late, I've become more aware of the theatre as a release; I love to do take-offs on everybody: Chaplin, Barrymore, etc. I feel the urge and jump up and act out, stage, direct, costume and photograph an entire class B movie; all this in a hurried, confused dialogue and pantomime (no dictionary) which is mixed in with frantic rushing from one side of the room to the opposite as I progress with the epic. Scene after scene rolls out; one coming from another, and soon I'm portraying everybody from the script writer to the temperamental star; from the leader who arranges and conducts the music for the sound track, to the stage hands who dash in and out with the sets. Then, falling exhausted, I giggle.

I am being seriously plagued with the hives. It started some weeks ago; my throat swells, breathing is difficult, and great patches of bumps rise on my thighs and buttocks. These start as slight, pimple-looking eruptions and within 30 minutes are huge livid welts the size of a large fried egg; gradually the redness disappears, and the swelling goes down, but, paradoxically, the size increases and the specific area affected spreads, until it, some hours later, again becomes one with the rest of my epidermis. I am quite confident this allergy is directly attributable to the considerable tension both LuAnne and Carolyn

1. Thomas Wolfe (1900–1938). American novelist whose autobiographical *Look Homeward, Angel* (1929) was a major influence on Kerouac's first novel, *The Town and the City*.

2. Gustave Flaubert (1821–1880). French writer best known for his first published novel, *Madame Bovary* (1857).

are causing in me. The doctor feels the same way. A change appears necessary, eh what?

I'm just getting warmed up, so if you please, let me dash on with no regard to dropped letters, misspellings etc.

(Jack, Neal is now gorging himself with the aforementioned Class B movie. This time, he is sprawling on the couch, as usual nude, gazing into cross-eyed space, wheezing "I retreat! I retreat!" to Tibet, that is, accompanying each "retreat" by flailing the arms and legs alternately about. He becomes annoyed at me now.)

Dear Jack, this fiend, Carolyn has just swiped my typewriter for 30 seconds, while I explained *The Razor's Edge*[3] in its entirety.

Jan. 8

DEAR JACK;

Just got your beautiful letter; how I desire to answer as beautifully! Since you wish me to reply exclusively on the subject matter of this latest expression of your wonderful self, I begin the attempt to do so.

Because you have so expertly explained yourself by the logical method of separating the drama into three parts, I shall speak in the same vein. First, the dream: Obviously the dank gloomy basement pertains to your subconscious visual recall of the basement room Allen had in Denver. As far as I know, you haven't been in a basement room since then, so, naturally, I assume your dream mechanism has just simply used that remembered image of Allen's room. The elder cousin and officer may have been literary characters which actually started as Allen and me, yet as you went on, we were forgotten. The idiot and your identification of yourself with him is expected. The idiot is a fabulous symbol. We are both over aware of him thanks to Dostoyevsky,[4] yet in this case, I sense that you've forgotten Dusty[5] in

3. *The Razor's Edge* (1944), a philosophical novel by W. Somerset Maugham (1874–1965), filmed by Edmund Goulding in 1946, starring Tyrone Power.

4. Fyodor Dostoyevsky (1821–1881). Russian prose writer whose novels *Notes from Underground* (1864), *Crime and Punishment* (1866), *The Idiot* (1868), and *The Brothers Karamazov* (1880) were of particular influence on Kerouac, Ginsberg, and Cassady.

5. I.e., Dostoyevsky.

the dream and are in the process of discovering him (the idiot) for yourself, as it were. This process is an extremely interesting one, and one which I've seen nowhere explained properly. It is important here insofar as I mean for you to use the term "discovering him for yourself" to apply to mind, influenced by background knowledge, forgetting that knowledge in the originality and intensity of that very mind's concern with itself, *and* dark will. The idiot symbol appears mixed with your conception of the Faustian enigma.[6] Your exultation, sheer idiotic joy and doing anything you like in the world, manifests the freedom Faust gained; the crime externally forced on you (since you show no guilt) may well be fate as personified by Mephistopheles.[7] The lack of tension up to the last moment before execution could exemplify purposeful unawareness, and this may show the amount of degree that you've reacted against the shallow falsity of not only accepted moral standards, but also your personal disbelief in the position people such as Bill and Allen have (they have different types of soul) placed you. Finally, your simple animal fear of death, unconnected with guilt, is indicative of all true mysticism. I'm sure Dante[8] must have had the same dreams, as surely did Dusty. But *his* dreams were with guilt also. That's the Slavic soul: mysticism plus guilt. But, enough—for I did not mean to confusedly and abstractly write this way. I've said too little and too vaguely. However, suppose the order of events was reversed. Imagine the deed, then the conversation and then the dream. What would one think then? One might say, "If a fellow slept with the thoughts he would have after banging a pal's girl, having a conversation in which he was rejected, and yet reacted by having a positive, happy dream instead of a guilt dream, then it implies that he's reacting in harmony with his soul, which apparently is free from the influence of rebuffs and guilt." But since the dream did happen first, we place value on it, although we cannot say that the dream was verified by reality, we can only say reality reflected the dream.

But, again, enough of the dream, on to the conversation: First let me explain to you what I think of Lucien [Carr], then what I think

6. Faust, the subject of works by Marlowe, Goethe, Thomas Mann, and others, was a legendary wandering magician living in Germany in the fifteenth to early sixteenth centuries.

7. Mephistopheles—the evil spirit to whom Faust is said to have sold his soul in exchange for infinite power.

8. Dante Alighieri (1265–1321). Florentine philosopher and poet whose greatest work was *The Divine Comedy* (1300s).

you think of him, and then my understanding of the conversation. Lucien, to me, is a young fellow who some years ago began a cycle of events in which he was the principal antagonist. Much sought after and sure in his own conviction, he allowed himself the high responsibility of arbitrating life and death. His attributes are distorted by his apparent lack of basic strength. This lack is pragmatically visible. He no longer manifests the things which made you love him, and instead, has a complete servility to jail-begot fears. It is useless to excuse him, or point to his qualities previous to his trials, for subjectively I see him only in relation to his presumptuous act of taking judgement onto himself. Even supposing he had been driven to do it (Dave [Kammerer] was persistent) and due to an incomplete background, (never having been in jail) was totally unprepared to cope with realism. Again, even if we allow him to dry up because of fear of externals, we still cannot allow him to be blind enough to not buy you. Beyond this, he still is not humble. He is humble to fear, to power; he is broken, yet he's a snob! He's a man living in the illusion of the past; he still thinks of himself as a child of the rainbow as of yore. He has not learned that you can't go home again, in your own soul as well as in external relationship. Despite seeing the flaw, in blithely overthrowing the past and relations in it, he persists in the naïve belief that smugly grasping at bourgeois strengths can substitute entirely for Bohemian freedom.

Here's what I think you think of him: You love him, for you remember him as the youth he was; the golden boy. You recall your early impressions of his genius; you think of the dramatic tragedy of Dave's murder (you wrote a story about it) etc., etc. Now, *you* must see Lucien; *you* must force this coy young man to talk with you. You excuse this, yet you're unsatisfied by him, but you rationalize this by saying that you demand too much, or some such thing. You see his faults, but still retain an idealized image because you need it as stimulus.

The conversation: Your disputability and inability to believe in anything you yourself say is caused by and follows from your very genius. Lucien understands this, but cannot bring himself to accept it; just as Prince Hal cannot (but more of Hal later). As Lucien says, you seem to be falling into a terrible pit and becoming completely dishonorable, and, so too am I (I'm happy that you have seen the vision of our basic similarity, as your letter shows). Yet, I seem not to feel a joy from the certainty that people are afraid of me. I, like you, know that some are, but, perhaps because I'm not subjective enough to them, I feel no gladness. But, again, you say you felt low also—strangely, Jack, when I read that and knew exactly how you felt your lowness (through your marvelous description) I saw more clearly than ever how we were different. This difference is my prime concern, so I postpone until another letter my thoughts on it. Until such time, I can think of nothing to say that can equal your idiot.

Why veil the deed? You say it would hurt you to come right out with it. Aha, my boy, you are being ambiguous! Remember, we're idiots! You seduced someone, who? Ginger.[9] And who's the friend in the case? Dear Hal.

Incidentally, you say if he knew, it would shrivel his soul right down to its roots. My God, is he really that bad off now?—oops, I should leave off the "now" from the last sentence, for I know it would be his pride, not his love for Ginger which would shrivel his soul; since I've known his pride all along the "now" is unnecessary.

My terribly stilted style, shallow sounding and intellectual as it is, is perhaps only that way because of the exuberance I feel in hearing about your Wolfean[10] orgy. This Wolfeanism goes beyond poor, pitiful, inadequate Wolfe, so much so that without much study one would not even connect it with Wolfe as a symbol (except as a surface manifestation), however, I—God damn it—there I go again! Really all I wish to do is to have you know that I understand fully; trying to show this to you, I stupidly go on and on trying to clarify it for you and just become more and more confused-sounding to you.

Jack, this letter is full of terribly trite, awful sounding second-hand observations, analyses and other apparently surface-spoken artificialities. This is not so; I mean what I say, and I say them thus poorly, *not* because I get them out of a book, or that I think thusly, but is simply said in this fashion because I've never written and know no other. This, if it's understood, leads to the process that I

9. Ginger Baily was the girlfriend and later the wife of Hal Chase. She performed at New York's Village Vanguard club in 1951, playing folk music with her guitar, and appears as Peaches Martin in Kerouac's *Visions of Cody, On the Road,* and *Book of Dreams*. Kerouac had a brief affair with Ginger the previous fall.

10. Named after the novelist Thomas Wolfe, the "Wolfeans" (Jack and Hal) saw themselves as heterosexual, innocent, unsophisticated Americans, distinct from the "Non-Wolfeans" (Burroughs and Ginsberg), whom they regarded as homosexual, urbane internationalists.

mentioned in the middle of page 2. It is just as if you've never known anything, so you stop and slowly think out how to say what you know from innate, instinctive knowledge—yet, when you put down in terms of what the thought is, the words are inadequate. (This sounds as if I'm troubled with either inadequate vocabulary or am unable to use anything but worn phrases, but this is completely wrong—I mean to say something *entirely* different, but cannot.) To expect words to give one insight into life is like expecting a hog to know astronomy. Look now, how I've stopped and wasted time and paper to say such apparent trash; we all know this—fuckit!

This isn't ten pages, and it hasn't got a mad stamp, and I've explained nothing you did not know, and said nothing that I meant to say, but—by God—I tried my damndest, I said my say and I know you know. That's enough for me and all that I can expect.

I crushed my hand, but it's OK. I took my pills so my hives are OK. I settled LuAnne and Carolyn (inadequately) so that's OK. I guess I'm OK. Twenty years ago General Motors, Chevrolet division, made a car with a 4 cylinder motor. I now own a copy of same. The paint job is original, the motor's original, the upholstery's original, the wheel's original, in fact, the only thing that didn't come with the car when it left the factory in Flint, Michigan is the license plate. Price? Gulp—225 dollars. How much have I paid? 100 dollars. Come to think of it, I'm not OK; I'm broke and in debt up to my ears. God bless the Capitalists.

Now, listen, no fluctuation, no doubts, no bullshit—I'm your brother, see?

Good night,
NEAL
(Sore hand; can't write)
3 hrs. pecking with one hand produced this

At a hectic period in his life, Neal did not write to Kerouac again for six months. In June, while working at Pixley, in the California desert near Bakersfield, he brought Jack up-to-date with events, which included his traveling to Denver to finally annul his marriage to LuAnne, returning to San Francisco to marry Carolyn, who was now pregnant, and commencing work on the railroad.

TO JACK KEROUAC

June 16, '48 P.M.
Pixley, Calif.

DEAR, DEAR JACK; MY GOOD, GOOD FRIEND:

With no preamble I begin by stating, simply—I've nearly gone crazy the last ½ yr—so, please try & understand that fact (tho you know not the cause) & do be good & kind & forgive me.

Your letters to me[11] lay unanswered in my suitcase, each time I'd start a reply I'd have to quit, either because it became a foolish love-note & plea for your sympathy, help, understanding & forgiveness, or because in describing any tortures I'd become too overbalanced or too distastefully, incoherently mad.

Having already tried several times to relate my ache & distorted vision of flesh & latest & most terrified stupidities to you—& failed each time I tried; I quit—instead, comes an unimportant or chronological table of unimportant developments—which are, strangely, entirely removed from my being—almost as if I were telling of another person—I begin:

Jan. 12—Bought a 1941 Packard club coupe, blue, spotlight, heater, radio, overdrive, seat covers, 6 cylinder. 80 top speed, paid $1195 for it, $100 down, $75 a month. Raced 14,000 miles in 85 days—gave it back.

Jan. 20—Quit my job at McKales—was really out of my head at this time—got so saturated with grief would tear across busy blvd. intersections at 50, right thru the stop sign—hoping to get hit.

Feb. 8—My birthday—tried to kill myself again—stole a 38 caliber revolver—several times had it to my temple—tried for 14 hrs.—sweat, nausea, fear—couldn't pull the trigger—drove in a ditch & lay in back seat—tried to cry—couldn't—disgusting.

11. Kerouac wrote to Neal on May 7, 1948 (*SL*, pp. 148–50).

March 1st—Drove to Denver—2894 miles in 33 hrs no sleep—stuck on continental divide 7 hrs at 8 below zero[12]—no anti-freeze in damn radiator—no chains—tried to freeze myself—got too cold & finally stopped a bus & got pushed.

March 5th—Returned to Frisco, made it in 36 hrs thru Wyo. & Utah—picked up young girl—caught crabs from her—drove her from Greeley to San Francisco—left her in hotel—meet her 2 weeks later & drive her (Joy is name) to Sacramento to a whorehouse & she's there now—whoring & eating cock—the bitch.

March 20th—Had wild, wild, wild experience—meet young nigger boy, 25—he has 30 yr old sugar mama—she tells me she loves his beautiful cock—can't do without it—3 times they do it—every other *hour*,—every day. I stay there & get high & dig great music.

March 22—Meet a girl, who, I'd swear, is truly a virgin—or at least, unexperienced—take her to nigger's house—she's really a good girl—I think—3 hrs later she's a little drunk & then, started the greatest show—she does dance for us—she takes off pants—leaves on dress & silk stockings—she stands on head & does splits—she's moaning all the time—mumbling "I love cock, your cock,—eat me, on my food, in my mouth, ease it, feel it, oh." She's always moving, she gets on knees by side of bed & tears open nigger's pants—lifts out long black beauty—jacks & kisses it—moans—then spreads nigger gal's legs—kisses her black, hairy twat—jumps on, beating it, the bed, laying on bed, spreads legs to impossible split, asked to be tied down & raped, nailed, ripped, eaten, bitten—grabs mine & swallows it—try to talk—can't—she's glazed-eyed—lost, spreads her cunt—grabs nigger's ears—forces him down—nigger gal grabs me—4 way orgy—goes on for hours—nigger fucks dog-fashion as she kneels on bed &

12. If this claim is taken at face value, it would appear that Cassady traveled from San Francisco to Denver at an average speed of 111 miles per hour, which, on the roads of 1948 and in the icy conditions Neal describes, would have been near impossible, even considering Neal's driving habits. He may have traveled between the two cities in the times he states, but the mileage of 2,894 is almost certainly that of the round trip, giving an average speed of a more believable 56 mph on the outward journey.

blows me—as I blow nigger gal—etc.—etc.—name is Susie—mad nymph.

March 30th—Drive to Denver again—heartaches. Make it in 37 hrs; get divorce from LuAnne.

March 31st—Drive back—lots of car trouble—go for *46 hrs* straight driving—*without sleep*. Have wreck as I approach Frisco, went to sleep at wheel—lucky, wreck was minor.

April 1st—Marry Carolyn—she becomes my second wife.

April 2nd—Start on railroad—5 days on local, 5 nights on local—trips to Santa Barbara & return.

April 10—Give car back—paid total of $200.00 on it.

April 17th—Finish student trips on railroad—no pay for it.

April 27th—Go to Watsonville—hoping to get started to work—don't.

May 6th—Get tired of sitting in Watsonville, can't get work—railroad not busy enough yet—decide to go to sea—know marine division of Standard Oil Co. boss—see him—he fixes me up.

May 8th—I'm now a full-fledged Ordinary Seaman—papers & all.

May 10th—Start to go to Arabia on "Cheveron," a motorship—get last-minute chance at railroad—decide to work on road until I'm cut-off next January '49—then go to sea until April '49—then return to railroad.

May 17th—Finally will start to work—got call to go to Bakersfield—went.

May 19th—Am in Bakersfield—work for first time in 4 months (except for 2 weeks as book salesman with wild character named Sinex—tell you later).

May 20th to June 6th—Daily routine is this: 15 hrs in Bakersfield—8 hrs on road—10 hrs in Fresno—14 hrs on road—15 hrs in Baker. again, then repeat, repeat.

June 7th—Got call to go to Pixley, Calif. & work on potato-shed local—good job—went.

June 8th to June 16th—Daily routine is this: Up at 8:30 A.M.—work from 9 to 7 P.M.—sleep in outfit car here, eat in café across street—read, write, think & smoke.

That's it, Jack, a brief, partial resumé of my last 6 months—leaving *out* entirely any reference to my *cause* of neurosis. I tell you briefly—it's a girl—not Carolyn, or Susie—you know. Whether you know anything of my lost being or not, I know you are my older blood-brother & feel always better as I realize this. Enuf.

My dear, sweet, great little wife—my perfect Carolyn (she's changed, she's great) is now 7 months along & will present me with my fifth (5) child the last of August. This child, unlike the other 3 boys and a ?—(don't know) I shall keep, raise, & glory in—needless to say, dear Jack—if my baby is a boy—I shall name him after you—& Allen. If it is a girl—I can't, for a name like Jacqueline, or some such thing, is unbearable to think of.

I make no attempt to answer your letters; I'm insisting on a copy—

with autograph—of the great, perfect & loving tome of yours[13]—please believe Jack, I can suspect the sweat you've developed to achieve this thing—I am trying to write too, you know. But, I've new visions I hide—Not the writing so much, as—oh, well,—tell you later, if I can.

You understand, of course, that I want only too much to speak of these things to you, but, you've no idea unless I present a faint semblance of structure & these mad & wild terrors are unworkable as yet—anything I'd say would be presented in my limited vocabulary & become misunderstood by you, & deemed trite, wrong or foolish—I feel like Joyce—a new world of words—Don't feel I believe I need new words to merely translate my private knowledge—I need it to preach a new psychology, a new philosophy, a new morality. That's what we need—a new morality, philosophy & psychology—what a task—how can I expect to speak in a letter?

I'm presumptuous, foolish & very unwise, I feel no need to make demands, or no right to attempt to—all I feel for you stems not from hero-worship (as it used to with Hal, & partially with Allen) but, rather, from a simple feeling of your being an "older blood-brother"—that's all.

This madness has been unlike any I've ever known, *entirely* different—I feel as if I've never had any life before—I do childish things—I think in new, distorted, over-balanced levels. I burn with agony—I sense a loss of most all wisdom I've ever had. When I see a girl I tremble—I spit,—I'm lost.

Don't answer this before June 27th, but, *do* write me before July 13th—for we must move from 561A before July 13. I'll get in Frisco June 27th.

Your ranching[14] is beautiful, if you're serious & want a man who will make $350 to $400 a month on the railroad every year from May to January—& his wife & his child & his knowledge of ranch work & his love for you & your mother—then, take me.

13. Kerouac had only to complete the final chapter of his novel *The Town and the City* and had submitted it to Scribner's.

14. In his May 7 letter, Kerouac told Neal that he intended to become a rancher, spending the money he hoped to make from the sale of his novel on buying a ranch on which to live, with his brother-in-law Paul Blake and boyhood friend Mike Fournier (the Joe Fortier of Kerouac's Lowell novels) as partners. He suggested that Neal might be interested in joining them.

Seriously, now, Jack,—stop & think of it—it's easy really to do. I *know* your mother (you must bring her) & Carolyn would get on together famously—& for us to build a ranch, a great spread, together, would be better than renting rooms for $50 a month the rest of our lives—we had better start right now—we always put off too much—start *now*—bring your buddies—we'll have 7 or 8 rooms—your mother (bless her) & Carolyn (bless her) are exactly alike—Carolyn's a great worker, an interior decorator—I'm convinced it's easy—I'll get the money. A home—to go & come to—to grow old in—to make into a great place—you'll never do it if you don't do it now—please think.

Dropping a line to buddies, "Come down to our place for a week or so" & then, by God, putting them to work as ranch hands. [Jim] Holmes needs it.

NEAL

Ginsberg and Kerouac were relieved to hear from Neal at last, believing that his long silence may have meant that he was in trouble. News of Neal's marriage and the forthcoming child made Ginsberg realize that he was likely to become even more excluded from Neal's life.

TO NEAL CASSADY FROM ALLEN GINSBERG

[c. late June 1948
New York City]

DEAR NEAL,

I spent 30 hours at Jack's—we talked, drank bottles of beer, showed each other the latest manuscripts, and mooned about you—The great event was your letter—we had assumed you were in jail or something—I of course had fantasized you dead, more or less, and even suspected suicide some months back. Myself, this *spring* has been one of madness, much like yours. Frenzy, frenzy, creation that is worthless, drinking, school, etc. I've been working part time and so I had about an even stint of money, and bought a lot of records. What finally pulled me out—to name an external cause since they are the signs by which we mark seasons—was Jack's novel. It is very great, beyond my wildest expectations. I never knew.

But I will let him tell you himself, and then fill in another time; I want to talk to you myself.

Now, I suppose I should congratulate you on your marriage. So OK Pops, everything you do is great. The idea of you with a child and a settled center of affection—shit, I don't like to write prose because you have to say something simple & direct. My mind isn't made up into anything but complete amused enthusiasm for your latest building.

I wish I had your letter here, but it is just as well. I have an image in my mind of the vast realistic vision you spoke of and am struck with a joy at the thought of your possibilities—moving toward realization, toward expression.

When (by implication of ideas or directly) I criticize you, you know and I know I do it out of tension and self justification on obvious levels, obvious ways, and it is hatred showing; so take it as that and if I seem unaware, and you are offended, point it out to me, so there will be no mistake.

However I am slowly coming back or (going forward) to where I can accept you for yourself (whatever that is) without hassles & tension & competition for power; and would be done with my "wrath" toward you and I believe by next season in NY we will be closer than last and I less retiring and arbitrary. Is this not great gentility? Sweet fate.

ALLEN

P.S. I seem to have thrown out Jim Holmes's letters.

Returning from his railroad work at Pixley, Neal moved with Carolyn into a house on San Francisco's Alpine Terrace. In a June 27, 1948, letter to Neal (SL, pp. 154–58), Jack continued to plan for their life together on a ranch. Neal developed the idea by suggesting the addition of other friends, including Allen Ginsberg, Jim Holmes, Bill Tomson, Herbert Huncke, and Jack's boyhood buddy G.J., with visits from William Burroughs and Joan and their two children, a concept that foreshadowed that of a 1960s commune.

TO JACK KEROUAC

July 5 [1948]
New distinguished address:
160 Alpine Terrace
San Francisco

DEAR JACK:

OK, my friend, it's settled then. We'll soon have a place to meet face to face over each morning's grace, and *I'll* set the pace. Gad. Allen had better watch out, as you can plainly see. He's got competition from me.

The words I say here are just simple facts, stated without zest or any degree of artificial enthusiasm; just simple, honest factual planning. Realize this wholly and believe in what I say, like you accept the fact and simply believe that you have two arms or two legs. Rather, actually, I prefer you to accept these statements not as plans as such or vague ideas outlining the future but as an almost inevitable culmination (with, obviously, many modifications, or some modifications or none) of our mutual desires.

Roughly I think it'll take two years to achieve the actuality of living—in the Shakespearean house. Carolyn and I, and soon the child, are living in a three-room apartment (it would be wild in NY) that costs 50 dollars a month. We spend another 50 for food. I spend another 50 for expenses on the road. Miscellaneous we'll figure, takes another 25. I make a minimum of 300 a month; maximum of 350. So add up what I'll save. Of course, this month and next month don't count since I still have to buy all the baby things and the hospital and various other small debts such as a clothing bill for 25, a week's rent still owed on 561A, 24 on my Packard and I'll give Walton whatever balance I can out of these two month's checks for his generosity over the whole period of our relationship and his presentation of a bed, a couch and other household articles. The baby shan't cost too much the first 6 months, but making allowance for that also, we'll figure I'll save exactly 100 a month starting in September. (Or break my neck doing it.)

So, figure 500 dollars clear the first of the year. Now, *count* on this. I get cut off of the railroad through lack of business sometime in January. I go back to work again for the railroad sometime in May. From January to May I can go to sea at over 200 a month or stay in the states and draw a 25 a week unemployment (and work at some job under an alias or not, depending). But, of course, we'll see how things look come January, you understand. I had an opportunity to rent a 5 room house with large place for garden in the rear: all modern for your mother and you and Carolyn and me and the baby. But cost too much. We'd have to live in Richmond. I'd have to work on a poorer division, be away from home etc., etc., so no go. Therefore, our contribution to the cause is for she and I to exist as cheaply as possible and thereby save for the necessary fund our project needs. Needless to say I'm sure you'll do the same.

To fantasize a bit. I envision Holmes, one Bill Tomson, and depending again, one Allen G. grubbing, scrubbing to aid, for they come in as they wish. No hard and fast, naturally, rules or obligations or expectancies or any such bourgeois strains in our veins toward them. The nucleus of our family then is (financially, wholeheartedly) you, your mother, Paul,[15] his wife and child, me, Carolyn and our offspring (*and* your wife?). That totals 8 or 9, figure 9, all living, striving. First cousins to our family then, will be (as they wish from one week to one year) your great GB—George,[16] remember? Allen, Holmes, Tomson—and dear beautiful brother Herbert Huncke. This may seem to be becoming overdone, but, to continue. I don't really mean to include Burroughs (a probable impossibility anyhow) but I do love him and Joan so much you know—pure speculation, but maybe visits at any rate. So, that's another 9 counting Julie and Bill junior. That makes a house that, at one time or another, ought to hold eighteen people. How many rooms is that? Anywhere from ten to thirteen. Kitchen, living room (which must be huge or we'll need two), dining room, figure about 7 or 8 bedrooms, nursery room, or rooms or some such, you understand, Jack. Huge garden—well, I'll stop. I'm sure you have the idea, in fact, better ideas and you decide the limitations if any on our household from guests to residents, locations, etc., etc.

Carolyn has just come up with the obvious points of incompatibility, confusion in management (who'll do the dusting, to be decided over the breakfast table) her conviction that the problem would lie within the personalities of the various women, mostly her own. She fears, you see, Jack, that she couldn't live up to or be enough a part of, and all that womanliness. Carolyn, like most of us, wishes a guarantee as to the outcome of most undertakings, particularly this

15. Paul Blake married Jack's sister Caroline (Nin) in 1945. Their son Paul Jr. was born in May 1948.

16. Neal is probably thinking of G.J., Kerouac's boyhood friend George Apostolos, the G.J. Rigopoulos of Jack's Lowell novels.

one. I have always known of no such guarantee, and, in fact, anticipate none. So what if it doesn't come off well. So what if the household is destroyed by the things she fears—must one always build a house and then have to go down the road apiece to see his friend and share his life? I see a semi-apartment-house, but women have not the love for each other to maintain even that close a relationship for a long period she fears.

This is a dismal ending, but I don't feel dismal: in fact, I think you had better write your opinion of this incompatibility bug which is apparently Carolyn's block. I have no block; I have no fears: I know that this sort of plan or modification will be the ultimate solution for our desires, Jack. Get busy now and write Carolyn a big note reassuring her that everybody is as wonderful to live with as she knows you are. (Just kidding. Don't waste your great genius on Carolyn and me—you've work to do for yourself.)

Strangely, to change the subject, I've been sitting here getting a great big kick, huge kick, out of writing this letter, as dry, dull, flat and boring as it is. It's really fun to sort of purposely seek out and put together choppy, stilted words and sentences such as these have been.

Next letter I answer the rest of your letter. I thought I'd just say a few words concerning the ranch and my willingness and the degree of help that I can give the next six months.

NEAL

P.S. I bought a bicycle. Just shaved off a beautiful Christ-like two month beard and now have a quarter inch crew cut with heavy suntan. Ride my bike to save carfare.

*Kerouac attempted to allay Carolyn's doubts about communal ranch life in a July 10 letter addressed to both Neal and Carolyn (*SL*, pp.158–61). He also asked Neal to investigate possible sites in northern California.*

TO JACK KEROUAC

July 23, 1948
[San Francisco]

DEAR JACK;

I have found a new secret. I could cause the sphinx's doom. I am a beardless Shakespeare. For the first real time in more than three years my soul has faltered in its black, purposeful dash to sick ruin. It's not a cycle. I drink not greedily of sweet sweat and air, nor do I control my mind to stay the stab of fear; no struggle, yet, no peace,—for God has once again touched my seed—it blooms, I blossom.

Platitudes to Joyce, no callow critique, I master the critic soul. Like Schopenhauer,[17] "All my attributes are engulfed by it," woe for the perfectionist who is serious.

Serenity to Wolfe, the overdone, overripe Gulliver. That sad man had the waste of years in his bowels occasioned by stupidly, sterilely beginning in a medium he as little understood as he did his own philosophy—like too many good writers he began with plays, and failed for he felt it unnecessary to know theatre. Subjectively involved, objectively reacting. Result, failure, groggy, ghastly, grovel on the splinters of bamboo earth, final raise of head, then, up, up once again, by the well-known boot straps. Try the novel, he did, success—was it? How did he put it, as he knew glory and found it wanting—perhaps, with my secret, his bowels would have loosed, his genius grow to wisdom. He saw a part, the part, his part, and *told* himself that part—sad fool, and thus, stopped in midstride; *his* own demon entered, willing surrender, ah, the fate of many—even Kerouac?

Neal, you dear fathead, if you honestly think that the last paragraph indicates even a small amount of new secret or, in fact, even partial knowledge of old secret, well, sophomoric thing, either find a better set of secrets, or, cross out that particular paragraph of drivel and try again. Thank you. I shall.

Breath comes quickly, eyes close in squinty anticipation, head lowers until chin point is almost vertical, feet spread as heels raise slightly, hands seek nearest object with fingers quiveringly, tantalizingly caressingly poised, belly tightens, from each buttock twin masses of balled nerves join at base of expectant spine and slowly, then more quickly, tighten, flow, weld, clinch more firmly and at last one explosive spot of sensation travels exotically upwards until spreading like a blush they part at the tensed blades and ripple over the shoulders, slide fadingly into the breast and disappear at the entangled gut's wall. The mind stimulated thus, works with glee, as first thought comes, head is thrown back, mouth strained, cheeks semicircle of cramped muscle, lips, dry, parted in glee. Mad eyes shine with love as they open wide for confirmation of joy from loved one

17. Arthur Schopenhauer (1788–1860), a German philosopher of the pessimistic school.

beside you in bed. Instant glance, greeting good, belly loosens gradually as hands and sensitized fingers begin responding, slowly, more quickly, then, control flung aside, wildly, thumping, masturbating palms on vibrating halfinch panel. Nervously, anxiously, tenderly solicitude flutters outward, wavering, subliminal intelligence grows pensive, then audacity of cogitative ego flashes across in nurtured image, confident, conscious, sane blame is regained, neck swells as goitered atlas of body is pleased. The ride-out begins, taste is not necessary—if flaws are present the claws of tortured talons that burrow at will into the mind's base with their insistence of truth, culture, greatness, art, are placated for just one still moment with surgical bodkin severing turkey-claw tendons and the mind has its still second of trembling relief as the steel, withered, clayed, chicken-claw of fear at the skull's base, being released by the cutting dies sporadically, undirectedly the aged hand loosens its hold and the carbuncle bursts, the boil, reaching a head, pulsates its grey-fear fluid outward and all that remains is the sac scar—for the moment.

The above paragraph is a first, partial attempt at showing one of the many responses I get from playing a phonograph record. The description starts with bated breath as I start the record in motion, I close my eyes as I put the needle in the groove; when the first bars of music begin my ass begins the shuddering nerves reaction. At the end of the first 8 bars my mind begins its function and eyes opening, turn toward the pardner. By the time the bridge is played all my body is in motion, hands drumming, head working, etc. The second chorus brings the intellectual imagining—in this case, conquest of will to death. You get the idea, huh?

I don't mean to waste your time with this trash; here is better talk for you. I have scurried about getting all the dope on ranches, national grazing forests, water rights, land permits, blah, blah, in the form of pamphlets from Sacramento, letters from bureaus, etc.; all this you'll get in the near future as I receive replies. OK?

It is apparent you are at a peak of maturity which has long been my desire to see in you, god grant continuance. Long live Kerouac!

Uncle Haldon[18] has been on my mind lately; would you be so kind as to tell me—

I have fully resolved my San Franco demon; bluntly, in full vigor, with intent, I now turn humbly to Allen. I shan't bother you with it, it's just to let you know.

18. I.e., Hal Chase.

You know I don't mean "waste your time" and "bother you." I, of course, mean simply, these are my problems (joys) and are not to be fumbled away in letters, but,—this is so obvious, I stop.

Ho, man, gee, listen: out of the ether, sterile Frisco airwaves, comes—Chubby Jackson![19] Have *no* radio here, so surprise, as I finish the last paragraph—there's Chubby, but, wait, wait, he's over, what's next? what will they play next—damn, I knew it, "I want to be in loveland," a new release ladies and gents, ugh.

I will write a symphony, a play, a novel, a motion picture. I shall play and lead the orchestra, act in and direct the play, write the critique to my novel, be the director, cameraman and hero of the picture. That's all. Me and Leonardo. Here's the difference: I buy a home movie camera, write, produce, give the dialogue, etc., etc. I stage the play in my kitchen. Allowing Carolyn the honor of making the costumes, scenery, what a tragedy I'll have—and all my own! I compose the symphony with the aid of 5 record players all going at once as I blend the various selections into a great orgasm of sound. The novel is—Stop!!! not frantic, hysterical stop, but, just, stop; how silly to write a parody of myself as it entered my head of how possible it was.

I am working seriously on a short thing about a man digging—oh, well, if I finish it I'll talk about it.

I am starting sax lessons in Sept.; all my money is being directed in such good fashion. Psychoanalysis follows in Oct. I've gotten my appointment and can't start until then. The sax lessons cost 2 bucks an hour, I'd better learn fast.

I have a little thing I've done and if you've time I'd be pleased to send it on to you for any opinion you could give.

The tea I'm smoking now (found great dago I, strangely, hate) I bought last month and is the finest stuff to ever come my way. You (can you?) can have no idea as to how to solve the remnants of your own weed problem (you had one when first we met); if you've forgotten your problem, or solved it, forget I spoke—if you haven't, enclose 10 cents and one boxtop for Dr. Cassady's latest booklet "In defense of Marijuana."

Carolyn is doing a tremendous portrait of me, 4 ft. by 5 ft.; it'll take her 6 months I'm sure. I'll discuss it as art if you wish.

Jack I know you don't know me now, and realizing this (not sadly, but, simply) I'm extended and feel somewhat forced in writing

19. Chubby Jackson, double bass player and songwriter.

to you and thereby am stunted in growth with you. If, perhaps, I heard you speak in other than the "remember" terms I have of you, I could see a way into a new level (not that I need, or feel it necessary, literarily) wherein *I'd* flow better. This means nothing, no lover's demand, no remnants of any hero-worship I might still retain, no youthful looking up, no serious questioning of a Burroughs; just, I ask directly, can you think of a way to make *me* speak more freely to you, and, in doing so, improve my *direct*, *simple* style of writing? Any suggestions of this literary question will be gratefully received. Thank you, Mr. Rilke.[20] I'm home only 8 hrs. in 24, so, see how rushed the RR makes me.

I want to be a cowboy, a rough hombre. I'll grow a beard like "Gabby" Hayes.[21]

NEAL

Upset by the negative tone of Ginsberg's letter of late June, Neal made a final attempt to terminate their relationship.

TO ALLEN GINSBERG

[July 1948]
160 Alpine Terrace
San Franco., Calif.

DEAREST ALLEN;

You and I are now further apart than ever. Only with effort can I recall you; the last half-year has left an indelible print of an utterly different hue, (these are commas—the tail doesn't show, poor ribbon) than that which you are a part of—in fact, to be presumptuous, I honestly doubt if you could feel my sadness,—so, let's skip it.

Since I've not let you see myself of late, you are, of necessity, way, way, way off base in much of your letter. Let's look at it: "Now, I suppose I should congratulate you on your marriage. So, OK Pops, everything you do is great. The idea of you with a child and a settled center of affection—shit, I don't like to write prose because you have to say something simple and direct. My mind isn't made up

20. A reference to the German lyric poet Rainer Maria Rilke (1875–1926).

21. George "Gabby" Hayes (1885–1969), an actor who played a bewhiskered, toothless old-timer in more than two hundred western movies.

into anything but complete amused enthusiasm for your latest building."

You should congratulate me—as you would congratulate me on, say, buying a car, or some such impersonal object. Everything I do is not great. I've never done anything great. I see no greatness in myself—I even have no conception of what is greatness. I'm a simple-minded, child-like, insipid sort of moronic and kind of awkward-feeling adolescent. My mind doesn't function properly. The child and Carolyn are removed from my consciousness and are on a somehow, secondary plane, or, i.e. not what I think of, or dwell on, or am concerned about, except in a secondary way. If you do have complete amused enthusiasm for this latest building, you're being enthused about the wrong thing, at best, the secondary thing.

What I'M trying to say; if you wish to share my intellectual life, or know and deal with what I'm aware of, or concerned about—you're wasting your time and love. Since December I've cared for nothing; of late, as I returned, I came to see only one thing, women—primarily, whores. So, how can we talk of bitches? Do you feel your belly writhe when you pass a woman? Can you see every infinitesimal particle of their soul at a glance? at a sick, loathing glance?—fuck it.

"I have an image in my mind of the vast realistic vision you spoke of and am struck with a joy at the thought of your possibilities—moving toward realization, toward expression."

Oh bullshit, dear Allen, bullshit. I spoke of no vast realistic "vision." What possibilities? I'm ill man, why, why do you speak of realization, expression? I wrote for a month straight—what came out? terrible, awful, stupid, stupid trash—it grew worse each day. Don't tell me it takes years. If I can't write one good sentence in a month of continuous effort—then, obviously, I can't realize, or express.

Three pages of good convincing "art is real" talk, why all this? I've never disputed that, other than the obvious about sterile art. You see, I'm so degenerated I can't even discuss the better parts of your exposition on art. Kerouac, Cézanne, Shakespeare—beyond me.

From what I can understand of them your doldrums are fine. All I can see is the long, continuous doldrum I'm in.

Any amateur psychologist will look at this and pronounce dogmatically: "This young man, Allen, is writing a pronounced defensive letter to you, undoubtedly due to his heavy sense of guilt toward you and his reactionary statements can be attributed to this guilt." See, if you can, thru my defensiveness, the need for a new psychology.

I am aware of one half-possible way out for me—music. Music sends me—I love music, I live music, I become truly unaware of all bullshit of life only when I dig it; I must realize all all all—of music.

No shit, now Allen I can understand more than you can—huh? Not a foolish, sacrificial understanding of the sadness or such vapid—I hate words, they are too much.

Let us stop corresponding—I'm not the N.C. you knew; I'm not N.C. anymore. I more closely resemble Baudelaire.[22]

N.L. CASSADY

When Ginsberg, who had experienced his William Blake vision a couple of weeks earlier, replied to Neal pleading forgiveness and reaffirming his love,[23] Neal sent him a more tender letter in response.

TO ALLEN GINSBERG

August 3, 1948
[San Francisco]

DEAR ALLEN;

The strangely weird peace of utter perfection is surely brewing in my awakened soul's being. I taste the touch of life and pray my mind to preserve its good name. Gone, with cheerful eye, is youth; now I neither fondly preen, nor have restless dream. It seems as though no thing can ever again disturb my breathless beam, the sun; a welding torch has fused, at last, a wholesome one. Yes, now past is the peak of pulsated paste, yet, long till the sadness of evening's fate. Not green, not moulding; wise grace of life my hand is holding.

I am a blithe idiot. In the spirit of a prodigal, sickened son who has wronged his father into a disgusted renunciation, do I write. No foolish pleaded forgiveness, no unfaithful redhead's "I'll never do it again, I love you; honest, I'm sorry" as she twirls her daddy's hair with her finger—no ambiguous lover placating her man—until next time. My guilt, somehow, is not as personalized as it once was; perhaps, Allen,

22. Charles Baudelaire (1821–1867). A French poet whose group of sonnets *Les Fleurs du Mal* (1857) is regarded as one of the greatest collections of French verse.

23. Letter published in *As Ever: The Collected Correspondence of Allen Ginsberg & Neal Cassady*, p. 37.

it's because you are the *Semi*-personification of *truth* to me. I've, long ago, escaped admiration—as such—however, you stimulate whatever degree of hero-worship I've left. But, beyond all this, you stand head and shoulders above any one man I've ever known—that, in itself, is love—calls for love. Again, look at yourself as Prince Myshkin[24]—the idiot—you manifest more of the mystic, the Dostoyevskian religious, the loving Christ, than does anyone else. Or, even, as young Faust, you show more of these supposedly virile, masculine, enigma problems than does, say, Haldon; or, even, especially, Jack (much as I love him). However, off the intellectual now, you are not an abstract symbol to me; nor quite a personal love which I must combat, fear—or flee. Rather, (at last I reach the point) I have a new vision to add to our collection—you are my father. I ask not to begin anew, I ask not to be again to you what I once was. I ask not to have my suffering be offered as compensation to yours. I do ask, as one mature man on this side of the continent speaking to another mature man on the other side, be my father, as Jack is my brother, as Carolyn is my wife. Can you, will you, if not,—

The above paragraph is a beginning of sincerity, and the vision of the father—a good *partial* one—degenerated in the last few lines into a juvenile and overblown triteness which twisted its meaning, left a flat taste, and, finally, petered out completely into a vague, unreal request. Disregard this silliness—let's start again at the line above "I am a blithe idiot."

Of course, we've all been long familiar with Dost.'s work "The Idiot." Personally, I first read it in 1943 in a reform school on the pacific coast,[25] at that time I had never heard of Dost. and that perusal of "The Idiot" was my first introduction to him. The supply of books, and other reading matter, at the institution—Preston is its name—was not too limited in quantity, but, woefully lacking in quality. I can't recall too clearly exactly why I chose the book; I do recall a sense of rush, since the officials allowed the inmates only 10 minutes after lunch once a week to select one book. I recall the title rather repelled me, and I guess I finally chose it, in the last rush of attempt at reaching a decision, because I wondered what kind of stupidities the author would probably state in describing an idiot. Also, I felt a heightened anxiety because if it were no good I'd be stuck for

24. A character in Dostoyevsky's novel *The Idiot*.

25. Neal was arrested for joyriding in Los Angeles in May 1943 (aged seventeen) and sentenced to six months at Forestry Camp 3, from which he absconded after two weeks.

a week with a poor book—as had happened before. At any rate, (to escape this verbosity)

Aug. 4th

ALLEN, OH ALLEN!

I had left this letter unfinished and had gone on a freight train run which took 17 hours, got back this A.M., completely fagged, Carolyn was not here (at the doctor's) and just as I was to fall into bed, I saw your letter perched on top of this sheet in the typewriter.

My eyes were red with fatigue and lack of sleep, my legs ached from pumping my bike home up hill from the depot, my breath came short, I sweated. With hands black from my bicycle's handlebar grips, I opened your letter. It is difficult to describe a tired mind's reaction; a weary emotion's response; a prostrated soul's answer to your sombre note.

Wait, I try to speak simpler; you know I've been wallowing in dark profundities; blackened meanings of things have plagued me, different shades of darkness than I have ever been liable to before. The resultant resolvement entailed much; much thought, much insight, much strength, much love, much wisdom—in a word: much growth. From ennuied hysteria to vibrant sanity in seven months is an experience capable of causing many changes in many ways. Two weeks ago, if one can place a time on such things, I came out of the cauldron cleansed. I'm stronger; better in every way. I enumerate: Looking first at outward manifestations of my activities and interests, I work with zest, function perfectly at it, am not prone to bitching, etc. I get things done; matters of everyday I handle better than ever, no Brierly-like fixation on it, but, simple accomplishment. I utilize time more fully, having only 8–12 hours at home every 24–36 hours I, yet, am more creative than previously. I see all shows worthy, (for example, 6 months ago I didn't deem even theatre worth a block's walk), art museums, concerts, etc. Also, (this is most important) I can, once again, walk into a hip joint, smell hip things, touch hip minds—without crying. As for self-improvement: I'm starting music lessons soon; I'm all set, if necessary, to get psychoanalysis, (got introduction, cut-rate price, at Mt. Sinai; supposedly good) but, perhaps, more interesting to you—I am writing daily; poorly done, poorly executed, woefully weak are words I string together for what I try to say, maybe, only one paragraph, maybe, different subjects each day, maybe, crazy to try (for I seem to get only further embroiled in style) but, I am trying.

I must interrupt here. I just reread the last paragraph—it sounds exactly like Vicki, or Norman, or a resolved Huncke, or any tea-head who is swearing he's cured. Marijuana and psychology seem not to mix well in most cases; the neurosis is first heightened, then fought; any solution becomes intellectual, invalid, and fluctuates for the period of time that each individual's make-up allows involvement. Some never stop, or, perhaps, reach partial alleviation, and then, let things ride. Conversely, marijuana and psychology are necessary if one is to become awakened, i.e. eating your own bitter fruit of knowledge of life, & yourself. It follows, therefore, that why most tea-heads fail is lack of strength with which to temper their insight into their own soul. A Ginsberg soul with a Kerouac spirit is needed. This paragraph is somewhat jumbled and sounds mostly intellectual, or as if I were thinking intellectually; that is not true, I just can't make a point of anything without falling into this style, which is, I believe, a carry-over from the intellectualizations and prose style of my youth (you see, I'm just starting to write again, and I'm beginning where I left off 4 years ago).[26]

I am more concerned with factual problems at present (how to learn music technique, writing technique, and, in general, a return to many of the factual interests—history of clothes; knowledge of flowers, trees, earth; learning to dance (dancing, a peculiar thing I've never told you, is a real inhibition of mine), becoming more learned in art, design etc., reawakened political and economical problems, etc., etc.,) than am I concerned with such non-factual things as we usually deal with. Let me try to elucidate; allow me, please, to try and make myself more clear about this; listen, if you will, as I try to clarify:

In my early years—7–14—I amassed a huge, unassorted storehouse of facts. Related, or unrelated, if it was a fact, I knew it. Important, or unimportant; whether the amount of coffee grown in Brazil last year, or the weight of Trotsky's brain, I dealt with facts. (Psychically, I used this fact-knowledge to impress—I can recall in the third

26. Neal began work on his autobiography, *The First Third,* in 1948, continuing erratically until 1954. Neal (as "Cody") talks of an earlier attempt in the tape section of *Visions of Cody,* explaining that for four years he could not get past his opening sentence: "Cody Pomeray was born on February eighth, ah, [nineteen] 'twenty-six" (pp. 218–19).

grade skipping a half-year because all thru that semester I'd run to the front of the room to ask the teacher if this fact or that fact was not so, return to my seat in triumph as she assured me it was, and, thereby impressed her enough to have her recommend I be promoted more quickly.) When I was 15 years old I discovered Philosophy and a complete flip-flop occurred. By this time I had impressed about as far as one can go and not be too obvious: I had retained my ability to make older people believe me brilliant (witness one Sergeant Thompson who ran the prophylactic . . .[27]

I'd erase the triteness on the latter half of page 2, but, I leave it purposely to show you how my mind wanders shallowly about trying to fix itself on something of worth.

I have periods of semi-consciousness, similar to dozing off or just waking, which are not dreams, nor guilt nightmares, but, are great impressions of things. Often, as I sit on the sand-box of the huge locomotives, I am lulled into a stupor by the drive-wheels' rhythm, and this phenomenon occurs. This is not a new thing to me—I first had dreams of such vividness years ago—but now they are not as they were then. For example: after a year in jail, I'd awaken in a tremble, reliving all the terror, seeing it all again with ten-fold intensity, remembering for days afterwards. Gradually the gratefulness I'd feel at waking each time to find myself free and not in a cell passed into a less intense form of emotional dream and I started a more intellectual type of dream—like this: I stand before crowds, oratory flowing from my lips, moving them to compassion with my tales of prison life, then, having them feeling the tragedy of it all, I'd expound my theories of penal reform, advocate psychiatrists at each city jail with extensive apparatus for immediate and thorough examination of all persons picked up, months—if necessary—of analysis to place them properly; in the gallows, in a whorehouse, in a nut-house, etc., etc. I'd have other types like this: seducing women, confounding senators with my wisdom, etc., etc. I'd also have great, horrid guilt and inferiority dreams—real loathing of myself would result from these; I'd be depressed for days, rationalize myself into humility, or rage, etc. However, today's dreams are not yesterday's, in fact, they are not exactly dreams; the best I can describe them is a sort of coma, or dozing stupor; at any rate, they go something like this:—no, I can't (won't) tell;

27. In *Visions of Cody* (pp. 226–28), Cody talks about his discussions on philosophy with Destry, who ran the army prophylactic station in Los Angeles in the summer of 1942.

suffice to say this, from the material of these visions *alone* I'm writing a play. It's a tragedy; it's close to Shakespeare, close to symbolic modern dance, (Martha Graham?), close to opera. I'm writing it like James Joyce would perhaps have done. I describe the costume, setting, action, dialogue, thoughts, emotions. I have the third act perfectly set up; am only having difficulty with handling it, i.e. I've got the plot, scenes, characters (even to facial expression), perfect, yet, I'm having terrible trouble with making the dialogue good. I get over-long, or condense too much—makes it choppy and stilted. Damn, why is style so hard?

This, I'm sure, is the strangest, poorest, fucking letter I've written in a long time; perhaps it's so poor and weak because of that very fact; I just haven't written a letter in a long time, I don't know.

I must give up this letter, Allen. But for knowing I'd have more difficulty if I started another, I would throw this away and try again. I'm sure, however, you know how I feel: contrite, humble, but, mostly, grateful and thankful for your extreme kindness in offering, once again, your hand to me; no masochistic love is left in me; I'll never bite off your fingers again. It's not as simple as all this, I know, but, if you (or, perhaps I) must wreak your love vengeance on me, do be tender. I stand now in need of much help, but, it would be taunting your love to ask foolishly for technical writing aid, when I came not to your aid, showed no sympathy, flaunted you, like a baby I—you see? You may be thinking "I need his heart, want his love, his soul, yet, what does he want or need of me? does he express a desire for my understanding? does he say he needs and loves me? NO!, ha, he says, oh, so sweetly, I'm so sorry, Allen, for 10 months (almost 2 years) I hurt you, now, in one letter I expect forgiveness, and say, let's start where we left off—oh, yes, by the by Dear Boy, now that you've forgiven and all that and everything's OK now, ahem, ahem, would you be so kind as to aid me in furthering my ability in showing off my nice, sweet, tender little soul—so that people will want to have my autograph, touch my skirt's hemline, gaze at my cute profile and remark hushedly "Neal L. is great"? Well, fuck him, to hell with Neal L., the sterile prick is worthy of nothing. I writhe in agony, I offer myself again and again to him, does he show anything? even one iota of love? NO! the fool, the damn fool that he is, he says, 'Thank you, Allen, I knew I could count on you,' then, blithely goes on sucking me out of all I can give to satisfy his own selfish self." I love, Allen, but, it may take long years to show you how; can you forgive that? Please help me to be worthy to be with you our whole life long. God Bless You my brother. Write soon,

N.

In August, Neal wrote to his Denver friend Bill Tomson, who had married Helen, from Buffalo, Wyoming, and was planning to move to San Francisco. Neal managed to get him a job as a clerk on the Southern Pacific railroad.

TO BILL TOMSON

August 10, 1948
[San Francisco]

DEAR WILLY BOY;

Here, my sweet, at long last, is my much-late latest lyric to my fabulous younger-blood-brother. I do feel most contrite that having been preoccupied with great, growling, purple-pasted, sombre life of late, I had *no* time for you. Instead, like you I'm sure, I've been growing into wisdom. Now, I'm wise; let me speak, once again, to you, my dear Bill. I do fear the natural course of things have had a tendency to deviate us from the mutual direction we once shared. Conversely, however, this sense of loss is good in that I think about, and feel toward, you with much more gleeful fondness; with a glowing awareness of your touch—I say simply; Brother Bill.

Now, listen here, you mustn't start the same foolishness most of the Denver all-bright lads do. Let's have no watered-down "second-youth" spent in wasted effort traveling-big, living-big, acting-big. What I'm saying is: your youthful pure emotion is passed, life tastes jaded, your reactions are sterile, your big-souled desires and big-headed opinions refuse to fuse into reality. You blame all else but yourself: mother, (other stupid peoples), Denver, (other stupid places—that aren't big), women, (no mind; stupid, no soul; more stupid); everything becomes stupid—but you. The one phase of understanding you know does not constitute all understanding, i.e., use insight to *become,* not wallow in prideful insight and just *be*. You must come to see you are nothing, then, grow into something. Ahem, Ahem, for a good example, follow your big brother Neal L. into hell—I used women, tea and psychology—what'll you use?

All kidding aside Bill, I'm leading a great, perfectly pearly life.

How are you coming along? Are you sure of your new gal? Do you have the glee and joy of a rock of Gibraltar in your intelligent guts? (Don't let the huge foolish triteness everywhere about you come to be a cause of frustration and drag to you; sleep with Dante, feel with Shakespeare, work with Eliot and Auden, play with Goethe and Proust, sin with Dostoyevsky and Kafka, suffer with Baudelaire and Rimbaud. Do the same with Art; study and see all Paris 50 years ago, Van Gogh, Cézanne, Gauguin, Lautrec, Matisse, Picasso, etc.) Do the same with music; with your knowledge of Western music, (not hillbilly, of course, but, western swing—big bands, semi-commercial players from [Harry] James to Ziggy Elman, Benny Carter to Johnny Hodges, J[ack] Teagarden to Kai Winding, Gene Krupa to Shelly Manne, Fats Waller to Erroll Garner, Woody Herman to Benny Goodman etc.) You have a natural tendency to dig the half-beat, or off-beat, (witness of old harmonizing on Two O'Clock Jump) now, *forget* this western stuff and convert your rhythm to an intellectual feeling for Eastern Jazz, personified by Dizzy [Gillespie], Howard McGhee, Buck Clayton, Chico Alvarez, Earl Payton, etc., on the trumpets; Lester Young, Coleman Hawkins, Dexter Gordon, Illinois Jacquet, Vido Musso, Wardell Gray, on the tenor saxophones; Charlie Parker, Willie Smith, King Perry, Boots Mussulli, etc., on the alto saxes; Bill Harris (this Harris is the only good Bop trombone player, so, after him the rest of the slush pipes could be played by half a dozen men) is the lead trombone; The clarinet section is difficult also because all the good men are deserting this instrument for the better sounding and more vibrant instrument—the sax, however, a kid named [Matty] Matlock is bopin' good clarinet still; The drums are still being dominated by the great Shelly Manne, although he's modified his style and left Stan Kenton; there is no one on the horizon to beat him, unless we could dig up some of the wild, mad Calypso teahead drummers; Guitar leader is Barney Kessel, next comes Al Harris or even Dave Barbour; Lionel Hampton on the vibes; Eddie Stravinski on the bass; Stan Wrightsman on the piano (he's a greatly underrated French player, who went there a few years ago because nothing good was being done in America), and for arranger: Cameron. This quick, brief resumé of players has left out accidentally such talented men as: Charlie Shavers on trumpet, Harry Carney on sax, Irvin Verret on trombone, Pee Wee Russell on clarinet, [Sid] Catlett, T. Otis, Nick Fatool, etc., on drums.

Once you are in touch and familiar with modern music and its place, its problems, its potentialities etc., you must then dig the classics: Mozart, Beethoven, first; Stravinsky, Mahler, second; then, flit about from one to another; one composer to another, one century to another, past masters to present masters (like Ellington, Kenton, Gillespie) etc. By that time you'll have evolved your own real tastes and desires, and perhaps, do something yourself in furthering today's music.

Just as you are being advised to really dig Literature, Art, Music by me, so too, you must delve into theatre just as fully. The art of drama, dear Bill, is our mutual love, with, perhaps, literature a close second. Of late I find theatre, more and more, looming up as a practical medium for me to work with. Of course, we differ in that you think in terms of acting and picturing acting motifs; you fantasize yourself as a Barrymorian character with overtones of Falstaffian and Don Juanian characteristics; whereas I think more in terms of the play and directing motifs; I fantasize myself into Shakespearean struggles with plot, Andersonian concern with scenes, Hitchcockian methods of capturing Wellesian moments, Joyce-like dialogue, etc. I have envisioned a Maugham-like third act for a great play we could stage in my kitchen; with Carolyn handling the costumes and scenery etc., me directing and producing and casting and writing the play, you would be the lead and portray a Faustian soul lost in the clutches of a negro whore. It's a beautiful thing with everything in it. Faust-like enigma, Human Bondage–like suffering, Wolfe-like scenes of rich social people, Richard Wright–like (with Porgy and Bess overtones) into the negro soul, Martha Graham–like symbolized dance routines, etc., etc.

Please, now Bill, no accusations of verbosity from you, I've just been rattling away in a tone of careless gleeful abstractions to let you know I feel close enough to you, once again, to be allowed to use mixed metaphors, vague foolishness, etc. In my excess fondness and drunken (I'm not) good-fellowship toward you. You warm the cockles of my heart, indeed you do.

More practical now; first, there are no apt's in Frisco at present, at least, none under 70 a month. At best there are some fairly good light housekeeping rooms for 10–15 dollars a week. Of course, as winter approaches things will ease off a bit and a nice apt. for about 50 a month could, with worthy effort, be found. However, the problem of a place to live is secondary and always managed somehow. So, let's consider the prime problem: work. *All* jobs out here are union, with many of them having training periods without pay (Standard Oil, for instance). The grim fact is that even dishwashing is controlled and has no openings. In fact, Frisco has the strange paradox of needing *no* working men, but rather, all openings here are not based on necessary things like industry, commerce etc., instead, jobs are produced by luxury or superfluous needs—salesmen! book, magazines, lingerie, gadgets, brushes, insurance (low-class), drug, etc. Also there are openings for white-collar jobs, banks, offices, department stores IF you have had experience enough to qualify. Thinking now of you as an individual, there are no book stores, no truck driving, no parking lot;—actually, Bill, as I sit here trying to enumerate your skills and job qualifications, I can think of none. Do you realize how little you have worked, and how much this town bases you on references, previous jobs etc.?

Oh, I need no reminding of your willingness to try—to be quite honest, I truly believe you *need* to come out here & do your absolute best toward making your own way. I mean making your own way on *all* levels—work, play, sex, creative outlet, &, in general, making yourself indispensable to as many people & places as is in your power. This means not gadding about in all the hip places, with all the hip people. Rather, I ask you to . . . [ends]

TO ALLEN GINSBERG

August 20, 1948
[San Francisco]

DEAR ALLEN;

All my previous offspring have been boys, but all of Carolyn's family have had girls first; at the beginning I presupposed I'd be content with only a male, however, after a degree of thought, I would be as pleased with a girl. If it is a boy I shall name it: Allen Jack Cassady. I anticipate him always signing his name thus: Allen J. Cassady. Gradually the rather strange sound of Allen Jack will be modified & the middle name, Jack, fall into the oblivion most middle names do fall into & become simply "J."—now that's alright—Allen J. Cassady. All this is external—as for me—I shall (as my brother used to do to me in tender moments) always thruout his life call him: "Jocko." "Now, come here Jocko and I'll share thrills with you of tales of wonder & awe, etc., etc." or: "Climb the tree & get the football, Jocko, etc." Jacques will also be his nickname, a sweeter, all-pure name of real import; Jacques will be used by me to call him to my side to tell of tender things, of life's meaning, of the soul, etc.

So, there you have it—Allen Jack Cassady—Allen J. Cassady he will become—but, to me, he's always Jacques, Jocko, ("Jackie me lad" in an Irish brogue) & at times of anger—"John."

If my child is a female I have decided to name her: Cathleen JoAnne Cassady. This decision required much effort—but, listen on a while yet. I could not call her Jackquline—& there's no good feminine name of Allen. Turning then to the child's (perhaps) wishes I thought that altho Cathleen Cassady is too stock as an Irish type (she would find it difficult to look Irish anyhow with her father only ½ & her mother 1/10 Irish) it would please her vanity in her romantic stage & earlier in life as a young tom-boy (& later in college) she'd be known as simply "Jo."

Among the working friends & about the house others would call her: Cathy. She will sign her name: Cathleen J. Cassady.

As for me (partially since I've always had a hankering to be Joe)—I'll always call her: "Jo." Just as (& for similar reasons) I'll call the boy Jack, I'll also call the girl Joe.

So, again, the girl has many choices: Cathleen JoAnne Cassady, Cathy Jo Cassady, Cathy Cassady, Cathy Anne (at times), Jo Anne (as an alias perhaps), Cathleen J. Cassady, C.J. Cassady, C. JoAnne Cassady, C.J.A.C. (at her initial-happy stage), & finally simply, Jo.

C.C. is her mother's initials & C.C. is her initials. Both the boy and the girl will have J. as a middle initial, & I'll have names starting with J. for them. Enuf.

Too wise to know humility I laid weakly wallowing in fitful fallacies of sickened sadnesses. My tortured tantalized taste was heightened by my body's enfeebled flickered faithlessness. Misread was my mind's diseased sight into my shallow soul's dimmed light.

So I wavered, indecisive on all issues. I considered choices. Fooling myself again.

Love was beyond me—my pretty face denied me its usual right.—How trite.

Above is another of the coma-state thoughts—on the caboose as it comes down the hill into San Jose, Calif. I have a thought in a flash, as I doze, & dash it down—just as it stands—trite style & all.

You're right—you're not my father. I have none. I felt the need for one lately & artificially picked you. In fact, had a recent moment of insight (vision?) & saw what might have been had I had a great Brierly (or I'd not grown beyond him)—but, I fear I've forgotten fathers & can't find one—so, we'll forget it, OK?

How & where is dear, sweet, fine cat Herbert Huncke? Let me have news of that fine friend—(5 times closer to him am I than he would dare believe.)

The acceptance of me—"for what I am & not for what I am not"—is indeed the essence of your love—beautiful, but, heavy with ponderous knowledge. I feel the same great part of olden sorrow of deep darkness of K N O W I N G. The quiet sweetness of life, flower is it?, is in myself I know.

Does the peninsula of paste I traverse daily in toil—have me? nor can the leveled desert of sanden hills claim me as soil, for I fear . . .

Aug. 22 (2 days later)

DEAR ALLEN;

I'll never get this off to you—I can't say anything; is it because there is little to say?—now.

Ah well, I do have moments with you—as perhaps, a semi-symbol; or your sunken soul? Bah—

(This is First Letter, pick up on Sept. 7 one)[28]

Love you, Allen, my mate.

My balls object for today (I fear)

Oh, well, I insist I've dreamed of you, my boy, of you—me too. (any how)

Carolyn gave birth to a daughter, Cathleen JoAnne, in the early minutes of September 7, and Neal rushed to inform his friends.

TO ALLEN GINSBERG

Sept. 7, 1948
[San Francisco]

DEAR ALLEN;

Last night I took Carolyn to the SF Hospital to give birth, at 12:49 this A.M., to a female. Both are well.—7 lbs. 3 ozs.

Life is fine, I awakening again, so sure, so pure.

28. Neal delayed sending his August 20/22 letter, finally enclosing it with the one written on September 7.

Like Rimbaud[29] I've gained, at last, the wisdom of renouncing the literary "sacrament."

I have seen your awareness of my flaw. Thank you.

The hunger hasn't abated, but, my tongue is cloven to my mouth's roof. I can't speak, my thought is sacred now—private knowledge has gone too far. Literature can't answer for me, I must look to my music.

Apropos—I've found my nigger Brierly—name is Leroy "Baby Roy" Johnson—leather goods, short poem writer & pianist. He was great gone hipster on piano from 17 to 27—then, exhausted, contracted T.B.—spent 2 yrs in a sanatorium. Came of this—conversion; yes, like southern Baptist negro he got religion as his reaction.

So, now, renouncing all the hep life he writes spirituals—arranges & plays music for his church.—Finding this refuge because he's no brain—he, nonetheless, is dissatisfied but, can't admit his guilt at knowing religion is not enough to save him.—He condemns himself for not believing enough—no faith, but, enough of his intellectual dealings with his psychic soul.—He's great otherwise. Teaches me piano, & tells me what to do to improve my "mechanics," "reading music" etc., etc.—fine man.

Carolyn is going to Hollywood the second week in October to try out as a beginner at Western Costume Co. She is thrilled at this chance, she's tried so hard to get to crash Hollywood—She begins at $1.11 an hr.—then $1.34 an hr. & if she makes good as a costume designer—$500–$1,000 a week. So, my dear boy—*if* several things break right for me—i.e.—1) the full crew law is retained in the Nov. elections; 2) Carolyn makes Hollywood money; then, you are my guest—forever. See the possibility—one—guaranteed life job—at good pay—on RR for me—two—Carolyn making lots of money—*If* this comes to pass—you are to live *entirely* on my money. You can come to the west, or, if you prefer, stay in the east—(as I would if I could; the west, particularly Calif., has such a Bastardized society) either place you like is OK with me, in the west, or with yourself in the east. The money to live on & allow you to not work is yours. (If this comes thru.)

I had been working on the Brakeman's extra board, liable to call for any train from Sacramento to Wat[sonville] Jct.—Local freight, passenger service, thru freight, etc., but, now I've been assigned a regular run: #201—thru freight between San Francisco & Watsonville Junction 100 miles southward, down the peninsula. So for

29. Arthur Rimbaud (1854–1891). French poet best known for his collections *Les Illuminations* (1872) and *Une Saison en Enfer* (1873).

2½ months I'll go back & forth from here to there & everything's fine in the way of work life, except—in the November elections the people are to favor or disfavor amendment #3, which is the railroad full-crew law. The roads have tried for years to break this law—which states that for every 25 freight cars in a train there must be 1 brakeman—obviously, if the people vote "yes" & the law is broken—I'll lose my job—so, pray they vote "no."

Yesterday, Sunday, I got high on tea & dug the DeYoung Museum in the Golden Gate Park. Great collection there—I thought of you & I at the NY Metro. museum that Sunday long ago.

Bloom was Jewish, Dedalus was Irish, you are not Leopold, nor am I Stephen; but much is told of us by Joyce.[30]

Allen, Dear Allen, the *only* reason you & I can't see (without seeing one another) & speak to each other any more nowadays is because in the last year you & I have both grown into different levels of outward comprehension, & our private terms have changed—so, since we think on unlike levels now, our incomplete letters to each other have not been strong enough to fight (or love) our way thru into changing terms (as our minds have changed) so—dissatisfaction—for both of us;—you are my soul's lighter (not light as my soul's light) but, rather—you are my soul's light-*er*. You illuminate my soul—(God, I'm a lazy little "punk"—look at me Allen, as if I were a "punk" (as a true queer, likened to Wilde's or Gide's boys—in literary terms)—I'm a lazy "punk" at that—to allow my love for you to be stagnated by a use of intellectual masks to allow my elusive cherry to escape from you.—enuf of "punkness," (can't take it, perhaps?))

I, reiterate—it's music—I know (or do I?)—any way, music I'm going to try a while—I need you, my boy for direction of my taste—and love.

Only a soul I give you—la, lay, etc. I love skinny women & strong chinned (queer's ideal) men.—as of this writing, at any rate.

I love all—sex—yes all; all, sex, anyway I can get it I need it, want it, shall *have* it—now. I wanta fuck—In despair I cry "Allen, Allen, will you let me splatter my come at you?" Ect. No, I mean Etc.

N.

30. Leopold Bloom and Stephen Dedalus are characters in James Joyce's novel *Ulysses* (1922).

*Jack Kerouac had written to Neal on September 5 (*SL*, pp. 162–63) and, not having heard from him since late July, urged Neal to reply more rapidly. Jack told Neal that he intended to visit San Francisco during the next few months.*

TO JACK KEROUAC

Sept. 10, '48
[San Francisco]

MY JACK;

Again I'm late—gee, sorry I can't rush my replies. Try & forgive—to show I mean business is—all the hundreds of pamphlets to "Ranch" I've gathered for you—real work, & too abstract & too early now.

You, Jack, are a true "All-American." You present, (just as you told me you once wanted) a perfect all-American growth—(as did Balzac[31] or Voltaire[32] an all-French growth)—to me.

We can write to each other & be full of contradictions—rights & wrongs, up & down, my boy—& still expect each other to understand—it's beyond me how blithe we are—but, it may be we are this way because—*our* idea of friendship is just that—no more, who can say?—or, think further Jack &—no, but, you won't think further—& no, *don't* say you understand me and that part of anger (as I'm showing)—as something excusable, "because he's a friend"—I'm insulting you, Jack—is it because I'm browbeaten by you (unintentionally) into this?—No, nay; I am Shakespeare—not you—you are no more than a semi-fertilized germ of Francis Bacon[33]—you writer of words—you are not souled—you're sold—etc., etc. (I could say more)

Come on, Jack, put up your dukes, (like us brothers will do) "en garde"—take your stance & defend yourself. (Please)

I need that now from you—(incidentally, you did a great, good, brotherly job during the latest "suicide stage"—in your opinion)—I fear you only are capable of thinking in terms of "stages"—so can not grow—a grow is always prerequisited by a soul.

31. Honoré de Balzac (1799–1850). French author of ninety-one interconnected novels known as the *Comédie Humaine*, which Kerouac attempted to emulate with his *Legend of Duluoz*.

32. Voltaire; pseudonym of François-Marie Arouet (1694–1778). French satirist, novelist, dramatist, and poet.

33. Francis Bacon (1561–1626). English philosopher, encyclopedist, and essayist.

My aplomb is spent,—you are a good, understandable boy anyhow—even tho you're not—as you deny—a Wolfe.—that's the last I saw you Jack—I suspected you of being a sterile "Wolfe"—close to me because of sterility—But, since then, you've proven virility & yet, (not seeing each other) allowed me to think of you as a "young Faust"—(who himself personifies sterility) (etc., etc., etc.)

Sept. 22, '48

I have a beautiful baby girl—Cathleen JoAnne Cassady. What a joy she is to me!!—I never knew!

Carolyn is going to Hollywood in two weeks to begin her career at Western Costume Co. as a period costume designer. She starts at $1.11 an hr.—then $1.34 an hr.—then up to $1,000 a week—*If* she can break into a large studio from Western Costume—in 5 yrs or so—if she's lucky. If after 6 weeks there, they tell her she's in for good (this is a trial period—if the boss likes her, etc.) & then (if the November elections don't go against me, & the railroad job is still mine) I go to L.A. to be with her.

So, in the next two months my whole future is to be decided. First, the Nov. 2 voters must vote "no" on amendment #3, or else, I've lost my RR job.[34] Second, Carolyn must make good at Western Costume Co.—that's all. If these two things come to pass for me all else is solved. Money, home, happiness & ability to get our ranch within a much shorter period—say 2 yrs., is then guaranteed. So, pray for me Jack. By Nov. 15 at the latest we'll know whether we've accomplished this great step forward—or lost the fight temporarily. May God be good, by golly, huh?

I was real high on fine gage when I wrote pages 1 & 2—as you could guess I suppose. MAN, & MAN, what fine weed I've got. Only a little left tho.

You remember my mentioning a Denver friend of mine—one Bill Tomson—or Bill Barnett as his step-father's name is—well, he's married a girl named Helen from Buffalo, Wyoming—2300 population, & is now here in Frisco with her. I got them settled on outer Mission

34. As Neal had explained to Ginsberg in his previous letter, Californians were to vote on whether to repeal Southern Pacific's "full crew law," which required railroads to employ up to five extra brakemen on each freight train.

St. & got Bill a job as a Southern Pacific clerk at $200.00 a month. But, he has deteriorated very much, too bad, too sad, but, I still feel him at times—gosh, he's lost all his . . .

Sept. 25

Damn it! Just got word that Carolyn has been turned down in Hollywood—so, Hollywood is out of the question once again. *Fuck it.* We have also been requested to move from here. Glad to, if I can find another place to live.

My only hope is the repeal of amendment #3 on the Nov. ballot.

I wish you could come out here & listen to me talk to you—I hate to write letters lately. *Please,* if you can, come out to Frisco. I'll send money if I still have RR job next month. Love life lately.

Your pal, NEAL

TO JACK KEROUAC

Oct. 7, '48
[San Francisco]

DEAR JACK,

Another great good letter from Jack Kerouac[35]—how I do savor them, & savor the sound of that fine name—JacKerouac.

Of course, I expect the RR job to fall thru in Nov. If, however, it does not, *you* must be here to go to work for the SP—$300 to $400 a month—or more (depends on each working day's breaks) but, even if we don't work (& it's no work—easiest job in the world) on the RR—we will go to work driving buses or street-cars for the municipal RR—at $1.40 an hr. & *all* the time & one-half overtime we want—another job at 3 to 4 hundred a month. Great fine time being a motorman on these trolleys—fine chicks & getting off on Powell or Mason or Grant—some on Market—& late at night, fine fine SF nite, near the end of the run-out at the beach, a girl "walking home" gets on & takes a firm indignant seat & with compressed lips glares ahead,

35. Kerouac wrote to Neal on October 2 & 3, from Rocky Mount, North Carolina (*SL,* pp. 165–68).

then, blocks later, the glare is a glaze & soon she forgets "here & there" & is alone with her soul & regrets as she detrains on 3rd St. & goes home alone to ponder, etc. etc. Come on Jack, let's be big bloated streetcar conductors, & in the chaos & bedlam of morning & evening traffic jams—we'll see & savor all as we rush to maintain our breakneck schedules. We'll chuckle at mad motorists & grin at pretty girls & prove it's untrue that *all* beginners on the SFRR lose 10 to 40 pounds & gets ulcers, nerves & grey hair in the first few months—attempting to be on time & avoid accidents & handle the people—the massive press of smelling humans (it's a fact, Jack, SF has the crushed trolleys of NY subways) (But, only from 6 A.M. to 8 A.M. & 5 to 7 P.M.)—We won't get ulcers or lose weight (I keep the same weight always—haven't varied 5 lbs in 5 yrs) Come on out—we be RR men anyway SP or SF—it's all on rails.

Apropos of Lucien's remark[36] & your good feeling is the blubbering glee I've been gurgling since Cathleen's arrival (& before). Cathleen JoAnne Cassady was born in Stanford Clinic SF Hospital on Sept. 7 at 12:49 A.M. & weighed 7'3" [*sic*] at birth. In perfect shape she came home 7 days later—developed a slight rash—lost it—had feeding troubles—(just interrupted this letter to feed her) & is costing me money. She's a month old today, has gone out into the world 3 times (twice to grocery—once to doctor) & is thriving in general. She's now 21 inches long & weighs 8 lbs 8 ozs. I love her like mad.

Your being blithely mad was *not* at the "rigid-picture" of "real farms" state—it was *started* there; an intellectual seizure of self—I had known your "Job-ian" farmingness before. Still feel it at times. But, your reaction to the shit of sterile intellectuals etc. etc. was not *fixed*—i.e. had no strong "central point" for too long a period at any one time—a girl, a job, a conviction non-idealistic as your's can't "wallow," *naturally*, in darkness of "insanity"—you fluctuate, & fluctuate beautifully—fluctuation is your virtue.

I respected your dignity, heart or such?—I can't say, I only knew a great kick of inward pleasure—lost at times by our own personal picture of the soul, of sad longing, of joy, etc. etc.—we failed at fusion because we were both old enough to have our own—& separate—portraits of knowing; that is—for both of us our "private knowledge" (things we know as innate "truths"—unformulated for the most part—real deep "meaning" which is only gotten across to another

36. Lucien had told Jack that life "gets more and more joyous all the time."

person at rare moments) had gone too far for us to share (at least at that time—since you didn't—deep down—feel up to it) & fuse into welded counterparts. Also, we had gained our "soul" without each other—with others—in different parts of the country etc. etc., in other words we had, after all, never done anything together—stop & think, never have we gone into action as one. However, of course, we need not act, or think of ourselves as one; nay, never do I think in terms of "oneness" or "closeness." We are not "one"—we are just lovers that are somewhat similar in our taste, etc.

Oct. 15, '48

When I think of Chase, I know that I *know* him & much of my desire for him is lost, but, only because I know the (why) etc. of our relationship &, strangely, I'm *not* let down—except, perhaps—but enuf; apathy is a good word for my *care* for Hal—& Temko[37] I never heard of—he's a fat fool.

I can not learn sadness from you—my capacity for it is lost (I know no sadness is to be mine for many years; I think sadness is gone forever for me—ah, how sad).

Indefatigable ways of fighting—you've more than I. I used to be truly indefatigable—sex drove me—now, I like music & am sterile—no cunt is enough for me. Maybe my girl Cathy Jo will continue to make me content & strong thereby.

All the above is just bullshit; thinking along as I write, or writing without thought, just stringing together abstractions that aren't even understandable as gibberish—I live & think so much differently now I can't say anything at all.

Oct. 15—1:43 P.M. o'clock

Jack, just had a *"vision!"*—a real one—yes, & about you—never had one of you before—oh, glimpses now & again, but, this one is whole. I once had a pure one of Allen—now you are there—& *true*!

37. Allan Temko was a friend of Kerouac's from Columbia University who was in Denver during the summer of 1947. Temko is portrayed as Roland Major in *On the Road,* and as Allen Minko in *Visions of Cody*.

Jack, you are great—true, fine, whole—you are right!—God, how beautiful for me to *know* you are not to be doubted—in any way.

Nov. 1, '48 5 P.M.

Just got your last letter; your demands that I write are perfectly just[38]—but, I swear Jack, I've been really busy. 16 hrs on the road then 8 hrs sleep—16 hrs on again, then 8 hrs off—etc., etc.—& for the last two months I had no Sleep—(ah, Sleep,—I must capitalize the word) Of course, I should have written & this is no excuse, however, I don't feel too badly because I've let everything & everyone go—especially you & Allen—because I've been making money—5 hundred in Sept., $625.00 in October,—but I've only saved $700.00. Oh, well—

Tomorrow is the big day—"yes" or "no" on #3. If it's "no"—I'm set—if it's "yes"—I lose this job. I am purposely not sending this letter until Nov. 3, & I'll then know if the election came off good or not. If it's good I'll really celebrate—(I've not seen a show in 3½ months—no nothing, except music in a couple of dives here—incidentally, found great sax man—John, real gone—plays like Flip Phillips & Illinois [Jacquet] & even Coleman Hawkins—He's great—mostly like Flip (whom I've come to love). I'm starting sax lessons at last,—1 buck an hour,—only of course, I'm taking clarinet—& after proficiency on a clarinet I can blow rings around the ordinary sax man.)

Heard Steve Spender[39] speak on Poet In Society recently—good. Running with Jose Garcia Villa,[40] huh?—Who's decadent now? I like the thought of you, probably in a bar, confounding this Villa fellow—he sitting & thinking—("where's this guy Kerouac anyhow!—once in a while he says something good, but usually just listens to me & sometimes grunts approval; at others asks something stupid—oh well, he's fun enough I guess & he does listen good, but, of course, I'm bored, etc., etc.")

38. Kerouac's letter of October 18 demanded that Neal write to him more often. (This letter is reproduced in the *Kerouac ROMnibus*.)

39. Stephen Spender (1909–1995). English poet and critic, friend of Auden, MacNeice, and Isherwood.

40. Jose Garcia Villa (1908–1997). Filipino poet, critic, and short-story writer whom Kerouac knew in New York in the late 1940s and 1950s. Portrayed as Angel Luz Garcia in *On the Road*.

This conception of Garcia Villa is what he used to be—but, I know if he's anywhere at all now, he *must* have lost this sophisticate shitty mind & regained the love of things he had once replaced by tolerance of things. Speak of Villa, if you like.

I must write you a big letter about my "going blank" as you saw so clearly in the superficiality of my letters—this is no better, that is, no clearer or deeper than my last 5 letters. I'll get a good explanation of recent superficialness on my part off to you soon. Don't fear my "going blank" tho, I find it resting at times.

Your Whitman[41] & love ideas are wonderful—but, you know, funny thing—for the first time I was not enthralled & got no erection at this beautiful prose—great prose, geez I like it, but as I read, my inner self felt—somehow,—satisfied that things like your letter are written—I need not write them—struggle thus to capture it on paper—I thought wholly in terms of music as I felt the jump & power of the words. Also as you describe loving, I feel sterile—I'm no horse any more—my bull has turned into a hare—I am not strong—my penis is sore from blowing & masturbating—I'm a nymph, but, talk my sex—speak mad things in my orgasms, I groan & bellow "take my big cock" etc.—enuf.

Look on the outside of the envelope for "yes" or "no" on #3.

P.S. If it says "no" on the envelope—we're in—& you come out here at once—come to SF Jack.

In fact, the vote was yes—to repeal Southern Pacific's "full crew law" and limit the number of brakemen required on each freight train to two, and Neal, as a new employee, lost his first winter's work. He was laid off in the first week of December and was not to work on the railroad again until 1950.

The following week, Neal's friend Al Hinkle[42] *married Helen, a woman he'd met just a few days before. Neal offered to drive them on their honeymoon to New York in a new car he'd bought, a 1949 Hudson, bringing Kerouac back to San Francisco on his return. Much to Carolyn's distress, the group drove off,*

41. Walt Whitman (1819–1892). American poet famous for his epic *Leaves of Grass* (1855). Kerouac had told Neal that he considered Whitman to be a greater writer than Herman Melville.

42. Al Hinkle was a friend of Neal's from Denver pool hall days. Al and Helen are the Ed and Galatea Dunkel of *On the Road,* and the Slim and Helen Buckle of *Visions of Cody*. Al was also portrayed as Ed Schindel in John Clellon Holmes's *Go*.

leaving her alone with a young baby. By the time they reached Tucson, Arizona, Helen had had enough of Neal's driving and demanded to get out of the car. Using Al's railroad pass, she would travel on to William Burroughs's new home in Algiers, outside New Orleans, and await the return of Neal, Al, and Jack there. Meanwhile, the two men journeyed north to Denver, where Neal picked up LuAnne, who was now engaged to be married again. The three of them sped eastward, arriving on Christmas Day at Kerouac's sister's home in Rocky Mount, North Carolina, where Jack and his mother were spending the festive season. After sharing the Christmas turkey, Neal, Al, and LuAnne drove to Jack's home in Ozone Park, New York, pleasing Jack's mother, Gabrielle, by transporting some of Nin's furniture there. With Al and LuAnne established in Ozone Park, Neal and Jack returned to Rocky Mount, picked up Gabrielle, and took her back home to New York. In three days they had traveled two thousand miles.

1949

Neal, LuAnne, and Al moved into Allen Ginsberg's York Avenue apartment and on New Year's Eve attended a series of large parties where, among others, they met Lucien Carr and John Clellon Holmes.[1] At New York's Birdland club, Neal and Jack raved over the performance of blind jazz pianist George Shearing. When it appeared that they would not be arriving in New Orleans to pick up Helen Hinkle as soon as expected, Neal wrote a letter to her on behalf of Al, urging her to catch a bus to New York. Neal also wrote to William Burroughs on behalf of Ginsberg, telling him of their plans.

TO HELEN HINKLE

Jan. 10, 1949
[New York]

DEAR WIFE;

At last everything is solved. I am certain we must stay in NY for, at least, one month.

Actingon this certainty I herein enclose $15.00 for you to come to NY at once. I give you only $15.00 because that's all I have to send to you. Your immediate concern is to supplement this $15.00 with another $15.00 to enable you to buy a bus ticket.

So do this atonce: board a bus, get offon 50th St. (the last station; the bus stops at 34th St. also) & call this number on the phone:

1. John Clellon Holmes (1926–1988) was a writer whom Kerouac first met in July 1948. Holmes fictionalized his encounter with Neal Cassady (who appears as Hart Kennedy) over the New Year period in his novel *Go*. Holmes is portrayed in Kerouac's work as Ian MacArthur *(On the Road)*, John Watson *(Visions of Cody)*, and Balliol MacJones *(The Subterraneans)*.

Pl. 8-0425. After that your worries are over. Just get to NY and call that no. on the phone. After that I'll take care of everything. Understand?

Come to New York at once & call Pl. 8-0425.

Love,
AL

TO WILLIAM BURROUGHS

Jan. 10, 1949
[New York]

DEAR BILL;

Allen has entrusted me to write to you. (He is in Paterson today & I want to get this letter off to you.) He is of the opinion all of us should stay here until we've accumulated some money (otherwise we would burden you with our hungry mouths when we visit you). Therefore, don't expect us until Feb. 15th or so. (Jack K. finishes school by then,[2] etc.)

This is important; Quote from Allen: "Dear Bill; I beg more oolong tea.[3] Send it up with Helen (Al's wife) as she comes, thereby saving mailing. I will pay for it later. Please." Do please send a small portion of tea. Thanks.

To raise money, Al Hinkle sold his leather jacket and pawned his railroad watch. LuAnne pawned her diamond engagement ring, and Jack withdrew the last of his GI benefits. Neal wrote to Carolyn that he hoped to find work in New York.

TO CAROLYN CASSADY

Jan. 11, 1949 1 A.M.
[New York]

DEAR WIFE;

At last! Some money is coming to you! Expect $20.00 on Fri. morning's mail, & another $20.00 Sat. or Sun. or Mon. This $40.00

2. Kerouac had been attending the New School for Social Research, in New York City, since October 1948.

3. Marijuana.

will be supplemented later in the week with another small sum. I do pray it helps a bit.

Take heart, little by little, day by day, driblets of money. I hope to increase the amount to a veritable flood of 10's & 20's—even a princely sum like $35.00 (or more) a week. Soon, dear Carolyn, SOON.

I have not a job yet. Maybe tomorrow will be the bearer of success. I plan 2 jobs. One from 8 to 5 & I also expect to find one from 6 to midnight. I can do it.

Things are looking up. I plan to give *all* my money to you (except 10 a week) & I also am sure of taking care of my car payments.

My heart is heavy. As I reread your letters I feel heavy depression; I can't describe it. I'll tell you what's my plan. This is the result of thought—take it straight: I would lose valuable time getting back to SF. I must stay in NY until *you've* got enough money to be secure. Therefore, I'm going to salvage all my strength & work straight thru until you write & say you're settled as you want to be settled. I estimate these money totals: $20.00 on Fri., $20.00 on Mon. (or before), $35.00 around Jan. 20th & regularly thereafter about 45 or 60 a week, until you are out of debt & living where you want to live. I pray you can last until regular aid is on its way to you.

I tried to sell the car, $2000.00 was the most I could get (not even that) & out of the $2000.00—$1986.81 would go for the installments & I'd get $13.19 for myself. I'm stuck with the car (unless I find a fool who would give me 22 or 23 hundred for it). (You can buy a new Hudson sedan here in NY for 2389 dollars.) So I'll take care of car & you too. I wound all the people I love—why?

NEAL

It appears that Helen Hinkle and William Burroughs did not receive the letters from New York, and so Helen did not catch a bus to New York, but remained at Burroughs's house outside New Orleans. Burroughs wrote to Ginsberg demanding that Al Hinkle collect his wife as soon as possible.[4] *Accordingly, on January 19, Neal, LuAnne, and Jack left in the Hudson for Louisiana. After spending some time with Burroughs and his family, Al and Helen found themselves an apartment on Rampart Street, New Orleans, while the other threesome drove on to San Francisco, arriving there the last week of January. Back with Carolyn, Neal found a job as a cookware salesman, and Kerouac stayed*

4. Letter from William Burroughs to Allen Ginsberg, January 16, 1949. Published in *The Letters of William S. Burroughs, 1945–1959* (pp. 35–36).

with them for a few days. Together they visited the San Francisco jazz clubs and saw Slim Gaillard. When LuAnne appeared on the scene, Jack escaped the fraught atmosphere in the Cassady household, eventually returning home to New York by bus via the Northwest, in the second week of February. (Kerouac writes of his experiences with Neal that winter in Part Two of On the Road.*)*

TO ALLEN GINSBERG

Feb. 3, 1949
[San Francisco]

DEAR ALLEN;

I've arrived and have a good job, but since all I sell is on a commission basis I'm not sure of any money, in fact, I've made no money yet, just laid out almost 10 dollars to get started.

I *must* have the car registration slips at once. The new plates etc. are now due and the letter I got from Carolyn had my car slips enclosed for me to use to prevent losing the car. I forgot this letter at your place and you'll find it in your desk somewhere I believe. Tear the place up if need be, but, please find it for I not only know that I can't get any new ones but—you know, it must be done.

NEAL

Matters came to a peak with LuAnne when Neal struck her on the head, breaking the thumb of his left hand.

TO ALLEN GINSBERG

March 15, 1949
[San Francisco]

DEAR ALLEN;

The Ides of March and your punk, puny Caesar Cassady, is at another of his phoney Rubicons. Let no die be cast, I am purple paste without will or way to cast it; I broke my hand. I'm a southpaw so I hit LuAnne with a left thumb to the forehead, caused an incomplete fracture of four bones about the base of the thumb. This particular "Bennet's Fracture" took three different settings, plus x-rays etc., which included an awful total of 21 hours on hard benches over a 3 day period. I ended up with an operation wherein the stupid Slavic doctor shoved a steel pin thru my thumb under the nail and thereby created enough traction so that, with the aid of a large wire extending over the cast, the bones could be stretched sufficiently to allow it to heal without deformity. This happened a month ago, so the cast will come off next week; let us hope it leaves no stiffness for I fear with the already enlarged fingers and joints I have by nature this further bullshit of the thumb will interfere even more with any sax playing I may attain.

Your pleasant little note came at an opportune time; you see, I am now formulating plans for the current year and your poignant offer of refuge to me was touching. My gratitude is much heightened by the lonely manner of my present existence. I'm lonely and restless in that the conviction of action seems not to stay with me. Action in the sense of continuity of purpose is now quite impossible. I lead a shallow simpleton life, little agreements of mind and emotion escape my endeavors. Long or involved speech, coherence of logic, literate leadership of conversation; all quite beyond me. I'm listless without reason. I sit as would Rodin's statue were his left arm dangling, (The Thinker's brow is false) I sigh with looking out the window over the city—to the east—and north, horizons, clouds, the streets below me. I'm as far west as one can go; at a sloppy ebb-tide.

Joan is brittle, blasé brittleness is her forte. With sharpened laughs and dainty oblique statements she fashions the topic at hand. You know these things, I need not elaborate. But, you ask for an angle, well, Julie's hair is matted with dirt I am told; oh fuck it, normal disintegration of continued habit patterns (child raising here) has Joan laboring in a bastardized world wherein the supply of benzedrine completely conditions her reaction to everyday life. ETC. I love her.

March 17, 1949

DEAR ALLEN;

St. Patrick's day; I drive my snakes out, let it be a present peace or no: I like it.

I'm free of LuAnne, my friends are my friends; but, I have a child. My life's blood she is, lovely and perfect—she wakes at this very moment, I stop to kiss her. SO. I live in the child for as long as is possible, that's my stand; after that: the world, you, saxophones, and harden struggle to succeed. You see, it's all very clear to me: I will take care of Cathy as long as Carolyn will allow me, which may be, I hope, forever; where she severs relations I will lead other lives; until that time—Cathleen Jo Anne is my charge.

Ah Huncke my dear, dearest, alter ego, you alone might not . . . [ends]

At the end of March, Harcourt Brace agreed to publish Kerouac's The Town and the City, *and Jack received a $1,000 advance. On April 22, Allen Ginsberg, Herbert Huncke, Vicki Russell, and Little Jack Melody*[5] *were arrested for handling stolen goods. Ginsberg was sent to the Psychiatric Institute of Columbia Presbyterian Hospital, and the others to prison. Two weeks earlier, William Burroughs had been arrested in New Orleans for possession of narcotics and guns, but escaped imprisonment on a technicality. After a week in a private sanitarium taking a cure, he moved his family to a farm at Pharr, Texas, near the Mexican border. In May, Kerouac moved with his mother to Denver for the summer and began editing* The Town and the City *for publication under the guidance of editor Robert Giroux.*

In a long letter that had taken him three weeks to complete, Neal kept Jack abreast of the latest events in his life. Kerouac was to use extensive parts of this letter verbatim in the published version of On the Road, *including the sections concerning Neal's broken thumb and his daughter Cathy (Part Three, chapter 2), and his reminiscences about stealing license plates for his first car (Part Three, chapter 9).*

TO JACK KEROUAC

July 3, 1949
29 Russell St.
[San Francisco]

DEAR JACK;

In a way it is too bad you left NY, you see, when Al Hinkle and Jim Holmes left here some weeks ago on their way to Maine, they promised to stop over in NY and give you all the carefully worded apologies I'd prepared.

I hit LuAnne on the forehead on Feb. 2nd and broke my left thumb just above the wrist. The setting of the bones was difficult and

5. Jack Melodias (Little Jack Melody) was a hoodlum boyfriend of Vicki Russell's. He appears as Little Zagg in *Visions of Cody* and as Rocco Harmonia (Little Rock Harmony) in John Clellon Holmes's *Go.*

took three separate castings, 23 combined hours of sitting on hard benches waiting etc. The final cast had a traction pin stuck thru the tip of my left thumb. In April when they took the cast off the pin infected my bone and I developed osteomyelitis which has become chronic and tomorrow I have another operation which, if it fails (one month in an immobile cast) will result in the amputation of my left thumb.

I took care of the baby, while Carolyn worked, from Feb. to June. Near the end of May I thought my thumb was healed enough for me to work. Carolyn quit her job and on June 1st I went to work for Goodyear as a mold man curing recapped tires. Very hard and hot work but I liked it. Now it seems I will lose my job Tuesday when I show up with my hand in a cast again. This leaves Goodyear in a hell of a hole, since there is no one to take my place. Of course Carolyn has found no other job so there is no income and, when the fifty bucks I've got is gone—

LuAnne has married Ray Murphy who has sharpened a sword and is dashing about town trying to find me so he can cut my throat. I've had two narrow escapes; he got to Liberty Street soon after I moved, and three days ago he finally got my phone number here and called to try and find the address. If the prick does manage to find this house and is foolish enough to attack me I'll kill the bastard.

The general labor situation in Frisco is very bad, however, I'll call various shoe factories and the union to see what chances your mother might have. I'll send on this info soon.

Don't go to China. There is a man at Goodyear who has just come to this country after 25 years there. Everything's tough in China; he really knows. Business, the weather, land, and the whores are terrible.

My terrific, darling, beautiful daughter can now stand alone for 30 seconds at a time. She weighs 22 lbs. and is 29 inches long. I've just figured out she is 31¼ percent English, 27½ percent Irish, 25 percent German, 8¾ percent Dutch, 7½ percent Scotch. 100 percent wonderful.

Try Five-Points in Denver for bop, the Rossonian Hotel; and a couple of places across the street on Welton between 26th and 27th Sts. There may be a spot or two downtown or on the north side where the Dagos live. Other than that I just look for good juke boxes.

Strangely, last nite, big dream about Slim Gaillard. He met me at the hospital. (Spend so much time in Hospitals I dreams of them.) I was sickened by the huge bloated women on the beds with their red meated bellies exposed to the air. There was no skin just raw infected meat like rotten beef. I went across the corridor and made it to a tree outside to puke. The lawn was polluted all about from the green shit I brought up. I didn't want my clothes dirtied and just managed to stagger across a sidewalk to lie down. It was a county hospital and there were poor people standing all around the entrance waiting, and watching me. A group of black men were squatted near where I fell. As I regained my strength I laid there watching them. They were talking in quiet tones. I remember I knew it was Slim only in that his gestures were less animated than the others, and from the wry expression on his face. When I approached him he said that he'd been waiting for me. Perhaps you might know the mixed feelings of admiration and inability to be close to him I felt. I was unable to tell him how dumb I felt not to be coherent about my admiration. That's how the dream ended, with me just sitting there watching his face and wishing I could speak.

Monday, the 4th.

Good news! I saw the doctor this morning and he said I could work while the hand was in the cast.

Sat. midnite, the 16th.

God, just heard that great George Shearing, remember God Shearing, Jack? God Shearing and Devil Gaillard. That's us Jack, a mixture of George and Slim. The images we struck of George, a sightless God; of Slim, an all-seeing being—

My hand stinks. A rotten odor permeates the atmosphere for several feet all about it. The cast weighs heavy. Sweating makes the thumb gooey and it sticks to the plaster-of-P. I do an *impossible* task; my job is so difficult it saps everything from strong, two-fisted men; yet, with one hand I throw the heavy truck tires in a real frenzy of accomplishment. I'm amazed.

Your second letter, a note, a tone of madness consciously expressed; but more, consciously maintained; had the sheet of paper been smaller the sustained note would not have been. Consciously sustained notes may be poor, but, as in music, by far the most difficult, and interesting.

I have a million images, all personal and torn they last but an intense moment, but reoccurring the second time they lead to new ones. And so I rush on from one new discovery to the next, telling myself I'll return and play with this or that. Of course, I never do indulge in this play for when I return the first image is past and with it the power to grasp with enthusiasm. I am a blundering image-seeker who thrives on the ironic tricks my thoughts find on every side. Bless a twisted thing—fuck the blessing, just forgive. Oh, baloney, I'm just sorry I can't write—to you SEE?

All pray for the men of Dingle Island. Soothe the sorry lot. Cast up naked on Dingle; they Dangle. Pushed into playing with themselves; their inner ear feeds only on Female Ells' (or is it Eels?) (yuno, they shock) tonsils. Their eyes are so constructed they see but from the corners. The Order of the Day for this nunnery of the Unsoiled Ulcers is to do Penance for these stricken men of all-flesh. The creatures have no bones nor any solid matter excepting the nose's bridge. The better to blow you with little Red Riding. Sit on the pot each night, retch with the rectum, gain the holy Dingle Beery.

Six minnows in the pond, with all around them tadpoles. Who will be selected? Hope it's me, hope it's me, hope it's me; not me; I can't peewee.

Did You Fossilize properly this season? Have your sessions in combat been authentic? I must impress on you all, the extreme urgency of full fossilization. This mission has top priority with the High Command. Pass on these Orders.

Wipe that smile off your face, this is murder, see? We're gonna catch that rat and you're gonna tell us where he is. Sam, bring the girl in here. All right, lady, this the guy?

Classification 3-A, Jazz-hounded C. has a sore butt. His wife gives daily injections of penicillin for his thumb, which produces hives; for he's allergic. He must take 60,000 units of Fleming's juice within a month. He must take one tablet every four hours for this month to combat the allergy produced from this juice. He must take Codeine Aspirin to relieve the pain in the thumb. He must have surgery on his leg for an inflamed cyst. He must rise next Monday at six A.M. to get his teeth cleaned. He must see a foot doctor twice a week for treatment. He must take cough syrup each night. He must blow and snort constantly to clear his nose, which has collapsed just under the bridge where an operation some years ago weakened it. He must lose his thumb on his throwing arm next month.

Carolyn is now five months pregnant with our second child. If it's a boy I shall name it Jack Allen Cassady. If it's a girl I shall name it Carolyn Jean.

Bill on the border, Allen in an institution, Huncke in jail, Jack in Denver, Neal in the land's end. The horizon here is the sea. I lay me down on the brink, the west end. Frantic Frisco, yes, frenzied Frisco, yes, Fateful Frisco. Frisco of frivolous folly; Frisco of fearful fights. Frisco of Fossilization. Frisco: Fully Fashioned Fate.

Your Book sold! I sit here thinking of my elation and how best to let you know. I come up with but one word: Glad, Glad, Glad, oh, so damn Glad, Gee, I feel so Glad. I'm Glad.

Allen; I conjure up things. I wonder; How and why? The details, the details I want. Wot Happened?

Bill I knew would end in Texas, Huncke too, no surprise once he was busted again. But, Allen? How, why, where, etc.

Two things threw reality into sham relief: Your successful sale and Allen's commitment. The whole bugaboo of external forces I've evaded so purposefully for 3 years is brought close once again. This has much bearing to me, not directly, but, as a point of Philosophy, if you will. Your book selling means success you see, or, in competition with the world of big boys, recognition. This bears on the whole idea of constructive involvement and the like. You understand; star on the forehead, etc. Now, Allen's internment means the force that so painfully involved Lucien, and yourself to some degree. This is the force I've evaded with success for three years, almost four. As a preamble to getting to the point, however, I will say I fear you can't feel the deep involvement I have had in this negative fashion. All the struggle for your book, all your constructive involvement has been the prime thing with you. Even thru your period in the nuthouse with Big Slim,[6] your part in Lucien's business,[7] etc. your deep anchor has been this involvement with writing, which, unerringly threw you into the other camp. The camp of involvement had your mother, father, and other factors. To be blunt, you were never in jail so many

6. Kerouac underwent psychiatric examination in the sick bay of the U.S. Naval Training Station at Newport, Rhode Island, in the spring of 1943, after finding it difficult to endure naval discipline. A fellow detainee was William Holmes "Big Slim" Hubbard, a former Louisiana State University football player.

7. Kerouac was also interned in the Bronx jail as an accessory to Lucien Carr's knifing of David Kammerer in August 1944.

goddamn times you had nightmares of future arrests. You were never actually obsessed with the year-by-year more-and-more apparent fact that you couldn't escape the law's stranglehold. You, in short, were never where Huncke is now. I was not where H. is now, not for the first few years anyway. I stole over five hundred cars in the period from 1940 to 1944. I was caught but three times for cars. Good average you see, no cause for obsession. My first arrest was for license plates. Wait, forget for a moment the above paragraph, I feel like a remembering of things past. If I don't get back to all the points above etc. forget it. So, here's a brief history of arrests. A case history.

My first job was on a bike delivery around Denver. I met a lad named Ben Gowen with whom I used to steal anything we saw as we cruised in the early A.M. in his 27 Buick. One of the things we did was smash the high school principal's car, another was steal chickens from a man he disliked, another was strip cars and sell the parts. I bought the Buick from him for $20. My first car; it couldn't pass the brake and light inspection, so I decided I needed an out of state license to operate the car without arrest. I went to Wichita, Kansas to get the plates. As I was hitchhiking home with the plates concealed under my coat I passed thru Russell, Kansas. Walking down the main drag I was accosted by a nosey sheriff who must have thought I was pretty young to be hiking. He found the plates and threw me in the two cell jail with a county delinquent who should have been in the home for the old since he couldn't feed himself (The sheriff's wife fed him) and sat thru the day drooling and slobbering. After investigation, which included corny things like a fatherly quiz, then an abrupt turnabout to frighten me with threats, a comparison of my handwriting etc. I was released and hiked back to Denver. As I think back, I can recall much of my crimes and little of my next arrest, but, I believe this was my second arrest. I had been to Indianapolis for the 39 Auto Classic and to South Bend to see Notre Dame and to Calif. to live in L.A. and so all this hitchhiking on my own had made me see the wisdom of hiking in the day and stealing a car when nite fell to make good time. Well, when I returned to Denver this became a habit and every nite I'd sleep in some apt. house bathtub and get up and find some friend's place to eat then steal a car to pick up girls at school when they got out. I might change cars in midafternoon but at any rate I'd get some girl and spend the night in the mountains, returning at daybreak to my bathtub. I got tired of this and decided to go back to Calif. I knew a fellow named Bill Smith and he wanted to come along. One day in the spring of 41, I was just 15, we stole a Plymouth on Stout and 16th Sts. We ran out of gas just as we pulled into Colo. Springs. I walked a block or so and saw a 38 Buick at the curb, got in, picked up Bill on the corner and we were off again. Passing thru Pueblo I saw a cop's car behind and suggested we cut and run, but Bill was adamant. Sure enough they stopped us, disbelieved our story, and took us down. At the police station I found they had caught us so quickly because it happened I'd picked up the D.A.'s car. An hour later the C. Springs D.A. came to regain his car and take us back to be tried. They wouldn't believe Bill's name was really Bill Smith for it sounded so like an alias. They wouldn't believe he was a hitchhiker too, as I told them. I had some Vaseline for my chapped lips and the desk copper leered and asked if we punked each other. We were confined in the Springs County jail for thirty days, then taken to trial. Smith's father was there and got us off. Again, I returned to Denver.

The next arrest was a year later. During that time I'd returned to my brother's to sleep, but didn't work and kept up the car stealing routine with the girls each nite. I left Jack,[8] lived with one Bill Mackley (I had before). We started to Calif. again. This time Mackley and I had no trouble until we got to Albuquerque. We were washed out in a really disastrous flood (knocked out water supply, etc). We were stranded for two days, getting no rides and finding no cars to steal. We spent the night in a RR roundhouse. Bill wanted to return, me too. I finally saw a doctor park his Buick for a minute in front of the hospital. I dashed up, got in and picked up Bill and we were off for Denver. After a 100 miles or so we were drunk from the pint we'd found on the floor and Bill wanted to drive. He did, at 80 MPH he skidded in the still raining weather and we hit the ditch. We walked and etc. to get back. I was flirting with Brierly that fall of 41 and living at his Aunt & Uncle's. I was stealing cars with Ben Gowen again and stripping them. One night, we were cruising about and just happened to drive by a lot where I'd parked a hot car some months before, in the summer. I glanced at the spot and, believe it or not, my eyes saw the same car. We couldn't believe it and creep warily up to it. As you know, Jack, a hot car, if left on a lot in the lower downtown section was sure to be found in a few days. (The lot was, since you're in Denver, on Lawrence St. between 19th & 20th.) Well, somehow this car had been sitting there for 5 months and still wasn't found. We were elated. This meant the car was cool by now and we could disguise it and keep it for our own.

8. Jack Kenneth Daly (1912–1992), Neal's half brother, with whom he lived, 1936–39.

The local kids had played in it and pulled it apart some, damaged the radio etc. but we got it going, put air in the tires at a station and were—

Just paused to reread the last page—too hastily done, silly: I stop. I've been arrested 10 times and served an aggravated total of 15 months on six convictions.

Sun. P.M.—17th

Sitting on a sore ass in my kitchen with the ball game, gurgling daughter, grass-watering wife, full belly from two dollar steak. A new book, "Escape from Reality" by Norman Taylor[9] is fairly interesting and deals with all forms of junk, stuff, coke, etc. I bought it and gave it to [Jim] Holmes (who is quite a tea-head, now) as a going away present. Glad you and Hal together again; hope he does something tremendous in his field. Suppose Brierly snuck in on the Aspen festival somehow; manager in charge of all underdone men who provide transportation for overdone women. I've always liked the old guy. How's Central City this year? Ed White still in Paris? What else new?

Sat., Mid. 23rd.

I tried to call you by phone last week, but the operator said the phone listed under name Davidson had been disconnected. So guess I'd better mail this. Come to think of it, I've written you 4 letters now since you've left SF. One particularly good one was about St. Patrick's day and also dealt with the Ides of March. Another one consumed in flames was a travelogue I planned before I broke my hand. The last was bits of paper and like scrap I got together for mailing. After I'd compose a letter I would allow it to lay around for a few days then discard it as outmoded, so, thus you didn't hear from me.

Ain't gonna give nobody my jellyroll, got no jelly in it anyhow. Bass, drums, piano, guitar, tenor, alto, (doubles on good clarinet), trombone.

9. Norman Taylor, *Flight from Reality: The Marvelous History of Hashish, Marihuana, Opium and Opiates, Peyote, the Cocoa Leaf, Alcohol, Tobacco, Coffee, and Other Drugs and Stimulants* (1949). A decade ahead of its time, an intelligent and well-written treatment of what have come to be known as recreational drugs. Neal's having read this book underscores his erudition in such matters.

May as well say it; started a book—again. News is a bit late, I wrote what I've done on it last May. The prologue[10] is wee bit under-way—4 pages. Haven't touched it since I started to work June 1. Very dull anyhow: family history, got as far as 1910 when my pop was 17.

You know, you and I've never tossed the ole pigskin around; played catch etc, so I could show you my magnificent arm. 70 yards in football, and an unmeasured distance with a baseball, many times I've awed the opponent with the distance I'd get with a special "hop" I've got when we'd peg rocks and the like. Too bad, like most southpaws, I'm slightly erratic in accuracy.

Tues. 26th.

Just started reading "Dr. Faustus" by T. Mann; despite the reviews I find it the best thing I've ever read by him, except, possibly the "Magic Mountain" (which I read when young and influenced me a lot). Strange to discover his latest work starts much as mine.

Yesterday I had a new cast put on. The thumb looks better and although there'll always be just mush and no bone in its tip, it may be saved; we'll know when this latest (and sixth cast over my folly) cast comes off.

Last night got an illiterate letter from Holmes and Hinkle, who are now in Portland, Maine. They ask about Allen and you. Send them the word, huh? Their address: James T. Holmes, 223 High St., Portland, Maine.

Got to go to work now. Love you; write again please, I'm lonely. Tell your Mother if she really wants to work out here I'll look into it with accurate reporting to you at once. You know how things change and perhaps by now the shoe factory and Union news isn't necessary. I want her to know the speeding ticket in Washington isn't forgotten. God Bless her; honest, Jack, I feel so fond of her when I think of the day I caught her alone and working on that rag rug, waiting for you to come home from Frisco a couple of years ago. Goodbye now, must rush.

NEAL

10. The prologue to Neal's autobiography deals mainly with the history of his father and mother, up to 1932. Not included in the first edition of *The First Third,* City Lights Press, 1971, it was published as part of the second edition in 1981.

On July 28 Kerouac quickly replied to Neal,[11] telling him that he was expecting another $1,000 advance from Harcourt Brace that Christmas, and asking Neal if he'd like to travel to Italy with him. Neal invited Jack to leave Denver and spend some time with him and Carolyn at their new home in Russell Street, San Francisco.

TO JACK KEROUAC

[Late July 1949
29 Russell St.
San Francisco]

DEAR JACK;

Just got your letter; understand everything and in this moment of finishing it I know I must decide. I think of the different possibilities of you going East, Detroit, NY etc. I know I should let you go, I know I have nothing for you, I know I have no valid reason for calling you to me. Yet, if you're free for a few weeks, if you would like to help your brother, if you could stand the hardship of coming to me and be disappointed when you arrived—then please come. I am so excited as I punch out this plea to you. I—, well, I don't know what the hell to say; my mind isn't coherent, I just want you to be here. I want you to come live in my house, I want you to be here so we can hear everything together, music, street sounds, etc.

Now, seriously, I have this big little five room house, there's plenty of room and beds and food and radios and washing machine and back yard and refrigerator, etc. I am *not* going to work for at least two weeks; you see the thumb, after three more weeks in the cast, failed to respond to treatment and last Thursday they decided to cut it off—just the first joint. So, Mon, A.M. I get operated on. Carolyn will be working all day including Saturday and we will have the house to ourselves. We can play music, talk; etc., etc., and in the evenings, bop, mad nigger joints, etc. Now is the perfect time, Jack, now, while I'm free of work and routine, now, while I can't shy off decision by escaping into routine, etc. You must come to me now, at once, every day counts. I'll be free at least those two weeks and we can make the most of them. I make no promises, I don't know what the result will be, I

11. Letter published in *SL,* pp. 211–17.

don't know my own mind or anything, yet, you must come to me, *now* is when I need you (not flirting, not as the one being helped) I mean only this; I want to have a perfect two weeks vacation with you, a vacation wherein you and I decide what can be done; I want a vacation of talk and beer, cigars and smutty jokes, nights of crazy happenings, etc. I want mostly to decide.

I can't say more, you must come. Please come, I insist; the weather is perfect, the whole idea of anything ever having a perfect time in a perfect place is here exemplified. This is really the moment, come now, no hesitancy, rush to SF, see the business as our last try (or first, really) or anything you like, just please come.

In reading parts of your letter, I can clearly see how poorly I write and leave undone many things, so that everything I want to convey is completely reversed. I will be able to tell you when you arrive so I stop.

Hear that? When you arrive, I said. So, you must arrive, you gotta come on out here. Please count on a place to stay, food to eat, things to do.

I know this is all a bit too much to force on you, I don't mean to try and force; I know you can see my sense of urgency without using that form. If you can make it Jack, please come. I have no money to send you, damn it. I'll get some money the 8th, but, you'll be here by then. (I hope)

I rush to mail this; I only repeat: think of all the reasons for coming here, then multiply by ten, and think of my joy, and, then, you old fickle fucker, get "On The Road."

Until about the sixth, when you'll get off the bus at Seventh and Market, walk over and catch the O'Farrell St. cable car, and get off at Hyde and Union Sts., walk back 40 paces, turn right down an alleyway called Russell, stop at 29, on your left, and knock.

NEAL

In August, Kerouac duly arrived at the Cassady home in San Francisco. Carolyn, four months pregnant with her second child, soon tired of Jack and Neal's nocturnal activities and demanded that they both leave.[12] *Accordingly, in a series of driveaway cars, Neal drove with Jack to New York, via Denver, Chicago, and Detroit, as described in Part Three of* On the Road. *Because of his broken thumb, Neal dictated a farewell note for Carolyn to Helen Hinkle before he left. It would be almost a year until he returned to California.*

12. See Carolyn Cassady, *Off the Road,* chapter 20.

TO CAROLYN CASSADY

August 1949
[San Francisco]

CAROLYN

Am leaving today—won't ever bother you again. I won't come back in a month to make you start it all over again—shudder shudder!

Here is a few dollars that I can give you. You won't receive any more until Sept.

The things of mine still at the house—do what you want with.

I am going to Denver, Detroit, and New York City and won't ever come back to Frisco.

Incidentally, I'm *not* going to see LuAnne—don't know where she is.

NEAL

Writ by Helen Hinkle

Arriving in New York that September, Neal stayed with Jack for a few days in his mother's new apartment in Richmond Hill. Shortly afterward, at a party, Neal met fashion model and writer Diana Hansen[13] *and moved into her East Seventy-fifth Street apartment. Diana had graduated from Barnard College, New York, majoring in philosophy and aesthetics, and had married her English-literature professor, Ted Hoffman.*

13. Diana Hansen (1923–1974) is portrayed as Inez in Part Four of *On the Road,* and as Diane and Diana Pomeray in *Visions of Cody*.

1950

On January 26, Carolyn, alone in San Francisco, gave birth to her second daughter, Jamie. In February, Diana became pregnant with Neal's child and telephoned Carolyn to request that she divorce Neal so that they could marry. Carolyn eventually filed for divorce and appeared in court in June. With the separation not becoming final for another year, Neal decided to travel to Mexico for a "quickie" divorce. He drove to Denver, where Kerouac was staying, and picking up Jack and Frank Jeffries,[1] *traveled to Mexico, as described in Part Four of* On the Road. *Leaving a sick Kerouac with William Burroughs in Mexico City, Neal returned to marry Diana at City Hall, Newark, New Jersey, on July 10. The witnesses were Allen Ginsberg, Alan Harrington, and John Clellon Holmes, who described the Mexican divorce papers as comprising twenty pages of foolscap studded with red seals. It later transpired that the divorce was invalid, and hence the marriage to Diana bigamous. Within two hours, Neal boarded a train for California, with a pass provided by the Southern Pacific railroad, to resume his brakeman's work.*

TO DIANA HANSEN CASSADY

July 13 [1950]
San Francisco, Calif

DEAREST WIFE,

It's very hard to write. All across the country I've thought of sentences, parts of paragraphs, etc., which would go in my first letter. Instead, this—what can I say? I know one thing, I miss you so much I wonder, in odd moments, what it would be like to touch you once

1. Frank Jeffries was a friend of Kerouac's in Denver. Portrayed as Stan Shephard in *On the Road,* Dave Sherman in *Visions of Cody* and *Book of Dreams,* and Jim Cochan in William Burroughs's novel *Queer.*

again. I want to begin at your hairline—both hairlines, and just get lost diving into your body to get that kernel of juice my mouth would need to come up with.

It's stranger than you can imagine, my thoughts and how they revolve around you and take your face and ways of your mind—no, what I mean is, in those times when I see anything (mother & child etc.) that makes my emotions respond to the present & this turn of thoughts of you.

Now darling, you remember I said I will have trouble writing to you—why? Because I only have one attitude toward you, anything that's everything about you in itself returns to its structure & is the *one* way I think of you. The only thoughts are ones of love. Must catch train.

More love,

N.

When Neal arrived back in San Francisco, Carolyn refused to take him in again. For a few days he stayed at a hotel but still spent most of his time at 29 Russell Street when not working.

TO DIANA HANSEN CASSADY

July 19 [1950]
[San Francisco]

DEAREST WIFE;

I was called before I had a chance to write you. I just got back from my first trip—where a fellow brakeman & myself were between two trains & I only escaped injury by steady nerves (ha ha). He was taken to the croakers with his head bashed in. Life's tough.

It looks like Henry Funderfuck[2] has slipped his gears—anyway I may not move in tomorrow or 21st. Don't worry about the mail if you've sent the check—I'll get it—somehow, I hope. The 90 days you're doing now are all much rougher than any I've done—but you're free to do as you wish; I wasn't.

2. Henry Funderbuck was living at 230 Divisadero Street, San Francisco, where the Hinkles had a three-room apartment. Neal's mail was forwarded there, and he moved in for a month in September-October, when the Hinkles were in San Luis Obispo. Longer term plans for Diana to live there with Neal did not materialize.

If you can stick—come here on vacation—go back to have the baby—then we'll settle. We'll have money, my first trip over, I get $29.00, see? Send my two jackets & those black shoes by Regal, when I send you a permanent address. I may stay at this hotel, don't know, for a couple of days. Listen, there's no need for you to suffer—come to me & forget all your pressure to get fucked by me. If you can stay until vacation time, good. Then you'll be free from that shit, I'll have money by then.

We penetrate each other sufficiently well to retain the prerequisite of living together. Those prerequesits—son of a bitch, letters, Bah!—prerequisites, goddamn, pre-necessities—bah fuck. Anyhow, come here & struggle with me, that's all I can ask—you must trust I can, I can effect the planning of our lives so they not only come out strongly enough to raise our family & still gain further strength to do so or to conquer the horror of our mutual systems—but, also, you'll come here so we can together plan how our future life is to be so engaged that we can conduct ourselves into those channels where—guess you know—where we will be together. That's what must be gathered first; living together to answer to our Gods & get on with the business of life & find ourselves to the task of help master. Jesus, we've got to be together first, starting under our handicaps.

Still (dear Diana, sweet woman, I love you), we will make it—believe it or not. I have yet faith & yet some strength; come here the 20th or before & save me & the world, it is ours yet.

Love, N.

Neal wrote to Kerouac in Mexico City, to bring him up-to-date after leaving him there the previous month. Jack had arrived back in Richmond Hill, New York, by July 24.

TO JACK KEROUAC

July 20, '50
[San Francisco]

DEAR JACK;

At last—Read to listen.

First, chronological sequence:

Early A.M. ride from Mex.City. Heat of day & recollections of our southward trip keep me musing. Incidents of difference from being with you & Frank [Jeffries] & being alone, particular emphasis on digging the young Mex. men I meet; in relation to my knowledge of U.S. guys. Was cheated once, I'm sure, on gasoline charge—only 1 or 2 pesos tho.

Long ride thru the pass of those great mountains; stop for disinfection at lowest altitude (hottest with humidity). Slight worry over cargo[3]—Car begins to show pronounced effects of trip, enters into the period when there is no longer any chance for me to imagine it is alright.

The approach to C. Victoria, with my mind carefully cataloguing the process I'll use to find Gregorio G.[4] was intolerably long. I drove so as to assure arrival just at dusk. Coasted down the grade on the hill, with its monastery, south of town.

Since I had been asleep when we had stopped before, I had to reconstruct the memory of the particular architectural structure of the service station he was to be found.

I have everything cautiously tucked away in my consciousness, but realize I have hardly begun the story, besides, altho I am guaranteeing the ability to write it—I shan't, for a reason: mails are sometimes exposed to the eyes of fools whose method of livelihood is perhaps only once removed from those of U.S. detectives.

Therefore,—one sentence style. Long solitary kicks before chance gives me Gregory at moment I was to give up hunt & leave.

5 particular, different, levels of things done that night, including: teaching English to 2 boys before another whose education was to enable him to watch over & handle his father's gone fruitstand. Visit to Wakikii Bar, greatest of all—Whew! 2 separate & more prolonged, in time, hallucinations. Pick up on Elitch Garden[5] with new Victoria, greatest shit the world has ever shown. Other incidents: car generator made for 2 hours of complete hang up with owner of gas station. I skip rest & best & continue: after, for reasons later I shall tell when I see you, Victoria, I pushed into the jungle over roads which broke my rear springs, & slept nude. More hallucinations & insect bites—off at dawn. Hours of bumps before I reach Linares, where we stopped to exchange fan belt & fix carburetor, same garage. 12 hours, while 2

3. Neal was bringing marijuana back with him.

4. In *On the Road* (Part Five), Kerouac reverses these names, with Dean meeting Victor in Gregoria.

5. Code word for marijuana, named after the Elitch Gardens amusement park in Denver, where Neal and Kerouac would go to smoke it.

Mex. kids 12 yrs. old try & lift spring into place—at last fixed it. Large fee.

Drove police chief & sheriff's deputy from Linares to Monterrey. Left Monterrey at dark & last 150 miles to N. Laredo was without lights & couldn't stop car engine or it wouldn't start again.

At last thru customs & into hotel & long rest. Continue after fix generator. Thru long Texas all day, Houston at nite, dawn found me having troubles with car I couldn't diagnose—neither could mechanics—at last realized what it was outside Lake Charles, La. The rear end fell from out of axle. Sold car for $32.00 & flew to NY on 4-engine Constellation, after 14 hours in New Orleans. Great trip & good life.

21 days of solitude in NY except Di at night, during which 2 full ozs disappeared. Long hassle to decide futures—then, finally, 4 day & nite trip across country on Streamliners from passes SPRR gave me via telegram to return to work here in SF.

Spent 4 hours with brother Jim[6] in KC & 24 hrs with Beverly Burford[7] & Ed White in Denver, Colo.

Ed & I understand each other. He tells me he knows E. Gardens since you & I & Frank left, he & Beverly pick up heavy in that period. We tell fortunes & exchange understanding for its worth until I leave. Beverly fucks me out of a good all-night fuck—after she & Ed arranged it—as soon as Ed left she chased me upstairs to bed, she & the goddamn girl slept together. She's malicious that way.

On my first RR trip another brakeman I knew well & myself were standing between a moving freight & a passenger we were to board.

As the end of the freight passed, an over-wide boxcar approached us, (as the engine of the stopping passenger arrived) & seeing how really close it was I extended my nerves & put all my effort into facing the wide car & turning my body sideways; my nose grazed the car door but I escaped—He didn't; when I turned around as the caboose passed, he was lying under the passenger kicking & twitching like a dying rabbit. I lifted him to a bench 2 tracks away & told the passenger conductor to get an ambulance & doctor.

His head was bashed in, the area from the back of the neck to the midpoint of the skull, & from ear almost to ear, was flattened. Blood

6. James Robert Daly (b. April 1921), Neal's half brother, was living in Kansas City.

7. Beverly Burford (1926–1994) was the sister of Bob Burford. Portrayed as Babe Rawlins in *On the Road* and Vera Buferd in *Book of Dreams*.

was matted; in his hand he held the hat; he refused to part his fingers. It took me at least 10 minutes to fall asleep, after I had boarded the passenger train, I was so affected. You gotta watch your step in the West.

Hinkle's in San Luis Obispo. Carolyn & babies impossible! Diana prostrate. I tell her to come here, but she's undecided. Things fine, however.

How's Frank? Bill, Joan, children? Read your letter to Allen & J. Holmes as I was getting married to Diana in Newark, just 2 hours before I boarded the train for St. Louis & the West. Saw Alan Harrington[8] & had fair talk. Understand him better.

N.

Neal continued to implore Diana to come and stay with him in California and was also making more extensive plans for their future together. This included the proposal that Neal spend six months with Diana, followed by six months with Carolyn, to help him decide with whom to settle in the longer term.

TO DIANA HANSEN CASSADY

July 27 [1950]
c/o Hinkle
230 Divisadero St.
SF Calif

Please read slow—good God, do understand I love you and can't write

DEAR DI, THE WIFE—

Come here and help me. The enormous difficulty of getting my life and your life into the necessary groove—in the light of circumstance—is such a long tough pull for both of us that if you don't arrive soon I shall start my hives again. (Felt them on my upper right thigh while realizing life, & you—& what must be done.) Come here by

8. Alan Harrington (1919–1997) was a friend of John Clellon Holmes's whom Kerouac first met in 1948. He was a writer whose novels included *The Revelations of Dr. Modesto* (1955) and *The Secret Swinger* (1966), in which most of the characters are modeled on Beat acquaintances. His nonfiction work *Psychopaths* (1972) includes a section on Neal Cassady. Harrington features in Kerouac's *On the Road* as Hal Hingham, and in *Book of Dreams* as Early Wallington. Alan Harrington was one of the witnesses at Neal's marriage to Diana Hansen.

the 20th at the latest. You said you'd leave all the decisions to me, the horrible hardness of decisions make it important to me you get here without delay.

I can hardly function either. Most assuredly, without you here to continue the planning of our life, & thus allowing me to continue planning my life, I will remain in the dilemma you are so aware of, & the one in which there shall be shattered against the walls of the nerve-ends that pack my skeleton, with its flesh that has been the bane of all the existence I can recall, & in the light of the capacity; I shudder at this capacity, my neck is bowed with it, the capacity of everyone I know in the world possesses,—for suffering etc.

You must understand my theories refute so many other things—look, my mind, you see, has to find words to select, any words, to put down. These words therefore first come out through (filtered thru) my mind, so, of necessity, refute any other structure of logic. I'm hung up, hooked with my mind, please come here & vacation yours. I've got to have you to talk to, play with, & push into where I am. But that takes so much effort, the only solution of a man's soul is (you know, go to heaven), only achieved by the exact mathematical percent of effort he puts into living. i.e.—this earth, our reservoir of sustenance, our home, gives off all the chemical pulsations for our life. The sun acts thus: it bombards the human (as the spark in an internal combustion engine: the auto) man. These two interactions are to be responded to—must be, & the image of a valve, human valve (find out what a rod is) (ask Robert[9]) responding to life & gaining heaven by jumping straighter & more honestly than human valves that jump in other directions—evil, etc. Working harder thus, you gain death and disease—insanity, etc., you live.

Paragraphs resulting from this process cut the stream, the thought continually changes, changing the image into words are, by their nature, (of time—images pound themselves into one another continually, & time to develop any accurate sketch of what is passing the fore-brain—stamping with feet which are so strong as to flatten one), impossible. Life is so demanding, the capacity of responding to it is the Criteria of God's Creed. That response cannot be denied & for all humans the only thing that happens to them—sanity, insanity, nerves, belly, cock, is true, i.e. becomes the soul of that individual, his medical history, etc., etc.

9. Robert Tappan was Diana's cousin, a brother figure to her, who lived with the family in North Tarrytown, New York.

Where is New York? Where, in my mind, can I find how to select words which show things I know? How is Diana? Really, how is she? Who knows better the quality of her cunt—I know the butter also in her belly. But how, indeed, is anyone to know anyone but themselves. Enuf—(wholly bastardized is that word—enuf. Too reminiscent of a style of words selected to cut & bounce the paragraphs—indication of the mind's refusal to continue the arduous process of changing images gathered in each moment of consciousness to words. Too like my last two years—can't write—Proust can.)

Things can't ever be said without misunderstanding; it's not a question of intelligence, but one of sensation; the sensation that which one chooses (we can choose in smaller escalating orbit,—those remaining capacities for dreams, on the strength of grasping a means into a larger orbit. Of those things our nature demands & those demands passing into other demands that, when made, cannot be found in our inner idea of self—& thru hardness to decide wherein lies the way) & having made choice, in previous years & in each moment, now, of the stuff of our dreams that the reflection of previous choices when those reflections bounce off the arduous business of maintaining those dreams within the realm of hard success in life, & gathering of those fruits which lie in our respective bellies. Then, the whole understanding passes into a larger process of preoccupation with you that has made me suffer with frustration, frustration of all sorts, just the sort that are your conditional patterns which in your knowledge of mine, make it difficult to make you see one thing—your knowledge of me must change into the state of understanding I'm in (not a good one to live with) as you change to me & me to you.

The new switch in plans back to Tarrytown now is OK but not quite the thing just now. Here's the way it is—exactly as possible & because of circumstances of job,—will take place this way: There are 3 alternatives, here is what we'll do in order of 1, 2, 3:

1. I will be in SLO [San Luis Obispo] anywhere from Nov. 15 on. When I do get cut-off anytime in Dec. I'll go directly to San Rafael & try for NWP.[10] If get it I'll stay there as long as possible, probably until next June—But maybe not. They are very strict over there, don't like young brakemen & also the business might fall off at any time. But if I do get NWP will look for house for us if I'm making plenty, otherwise, on March 1st at latest you'll use pass I send

10. Northwestern Pacific Railroad.

you in Dec. (good for 90 days & will expire around March 15th) & come West & you and I'll live in 230 D[ivisadero] for as long as you want to. Eventually, when you're tired of 230 D., we'll get a house for you.

So, that's plan 1, it all depends on NWP & your coming here—will be anytime after Jan. you want to come, but, since you'll be nursing & to give Baby further strength & because I'll get passes on RR made out to N.L. Cassady & wife, so Jack can come with you if he wants to cross country for free. I suggest you wait until late Feb or March 1st because Helen Hinkle won't be out of 230 D. until then & we would just have to find a place, probably, for a month or so, unless of course I got money & am lucky enuf to find good cheap house at once. Thus OK to come sooner anyway, that's Plan 1 & most likely I hope.

Plan 2: I get cut-off, no NWP possible, & so go to El Paso (or near there somewhere) & work until March 1st when I'll get cut off. At that time you & possibly Jack, come across country & go to 230 D. & move in. While you're there you don't work, you just continue breast feeding and caring for kid in best fashion & fix up place & line up work you'll want, & look for house if you want. March 1st I go to Phoenix & work for good money until May 1st, I get cut off & if Jack's around somewhere we'll go to Mex. City & I'll be in SF late May for us to begin 6 months.

Plan 3: If no good RR (unthinkable) or RR only in cold part of country (Salt Lake, Portland, etc.) or for some other reason (like miss you so, or accident of some kind, or get fired, or can't make good money, or, am spending too much living & sending to you and Carolyn, or some such shit) I can't make good connections out West or down South, then I'll come to Tarrytown for remainder of winter & we'll live there until May, then back to SF & SP—there is the possibility I might work on RR in West until get cut off in Phoenix in late April & immediately I'll come East, where you stay until I arrive. I'll get there by May 1st & help you pack & get ready to cross country & then when I've helped you get all ready I'll get Jack & we'll go to Mex. City in car & meet you in SF in late May. The only possible reason this last alternative may not be so good is chance of RR pass expiring, but I can always get an extension of pass or another one, so that's not much worry. The thing is, if you can stay put in Tarrytown until I get there on May 1st, of course, 230 D. would be going to pot for March & April since the Hinkles aren't there & we might be paying rent on the place for no reason. Actually, no one can know anything about future until I'm cut off, so it's not much good to plan except to know definitely that I'll do one of these things, depending on which job I get and how much I am OK:

1. Try NWP.
2. Try South West, El Paso, Tucson, Douglas, Tucumcari, T. & N.O. in any part of Texas, etc.
3. If nothing gained, moneywise, I come East in Jan. or so.
4. Might come East anyhow in May 1st 'cause no work anywhere that month & could get you all ready for SF move & pick up Jack.

But I figure, no matter what I do, working, you'll see, will be in SF March 1 at 230 D. & be there as long as you want. So, get the picture? I'll see you in Jan. maybe, somehow, March, or, latest May 1st or so, that's it. You could come West, possibly earliest, in Jan. most likely, March 1st, maybe not until May 1st. That's it. 6 months begin moment we get together. This, of course, puts a hell of a strain on Carolyn. No one can expect her to wait anywhere from next July to next Jan 52. So, even if we did split & I wanted to go back to her, the way circumstances of guarantee and work life are, I have managed to effectively split her & I up forever. That's OK by me, if only she could make it by herself or find a man. But, no shit, just as you were in bad shape & she was in pretty good spirits now, you two have switched & done such a turnabout in your attitudes about life that you're strong as hell compared to the big hole she's dug for herself again. When I saw her last she was in a hell of a depression, not just because of me, or because I was leaving, but she can't even get up any of the old gumption to do anything. I fear for her. She talks of deserting kids but can't, going home, but can't, giving kids to us, but can't, working, but can't, finding man, but can't, sticking it out, but can't. Loving me, but can't. (The 10 days, or 7, I was there we had not one moment's peace, or understanding, or love, or any pleasure.) She realizes she now is at fault & can't manage, no matter how hard she tries, to feel at ease with me or love me so that she can stop nagging & bitching at me. Even if we were together forever & there was no Diana, she feels we can't make it anyhow, especially if she has to wait 7 or 12 months for me. She can't live with or without me, with or without kids, with or without friends. She's in a bad way. Apart from everything else, she's so blind, she refuses to see anything good about you & so anything you could write her would just be misconstrued & would be no good. So I advise: don't, & so it goes. Jesus I feel badly about her, I was as nice as possible to her, but, I would still get so hot under the collar I'd get incoherent at the impossible reasoning her mind formulates about life. Horrors! So, how can I tell her we are thru—her & I—after just so recently holding out hope that her & I would perhaps be again together—forever, too. If she could make it alone, so as to be of any use to the kids, I'd feel OK about it. But, those kids! Damn, she's running them & herself & me & you—I can't expect her to be strong enough to make a good life for herself & kids. Not after how I myself fluctuate. But, she is so convinced I have absolutely no consideration for her & kids, & worse I put everyone ahead of her & am just the shits all around; but, when I am OK to her & everything's fine, really fine, just at that point she begins to get unbearably bitchy, becomes unhappy as hell & begins to drive me away, then, since she has enough sense to see what she's doing & what it means psychologically & proves we can't make it no matter how good I am because of her attitude & so on, then, everything falls in so that it's plain we should part & I begin to feel: at all the cost to everyone, at last a decision! But, no, the next minute, a renewed diving into the whole morass. So on & on & on & on, ugh.

Will write you in hospital. Good luck lovely. I realize your worth more than you know or I can show, it's just I am afraid to speak because I am so inconsistent in my manifestations of emotion that declarations of love mean nothing but hurt to most females.

Love, anyhow.

N.

On August 10, Neal moved to Watsonville, on the southern end of his regular freight run, some one hundred miles from San Francisco, and lived at the railroad dormitories there. Arrangements were made for Diana to join him there for two weeks commencing August 20, when they would take an apartment uptown. Neal's long-term plans appear to have centered around having each of his two wives based at either end of the railroad track.

TO DIANA HANSEN CASSADY

Aug. 12, 1950
Pajaro Dorms
410 Salinas Rd
Watsonville, Calif.

DEAR DI;

At last, my god, at last! I've finally landed. The absolute B.S. I've been going through is finally over. Here are your final instructions to reach the place. I've at last been able to decide (& be RR allowed) to make money. A tough fight, glad it's over.

First: Send all my things Railway Express (the office here is near) to brakeman N.L. Cassady, Pajaro Dorms, Watsonville Junct., Calif. Try and send the trunk—you pay, if you have the money. You see, the wonderful landlady here is so kind I'd hate to have her have to pay the expressman & also, by the time it arrives, you'll be here & we'll be living uptown somewhere & the landlady would be further inconvenienced if I'm not living here, as I won't be at that time. However, if you haven't the money, don't worry, just send the things collect.

Second: Pack all your & baby things—just in case. But make it—just in case. Who knows the dark future; Al Hinkle was robbed tonight. But, do have your things ready to send for them if we see I can make more money here (on RRNWP or etc. RR) after Nov or Dec or so. If not, then we might return to Tarrytown for the kid & your Ma & G'Ma & for me & you & for God almighty.

Three: Hop on a plane, take limo service from airport to SF. Once in SF go immediately to 3rd & Townsend Sts., SF & get on train number 78 (the Del Monte) which leaves at 3:00 P.M. RR (Pacific Standard time); 4:00 P.M. SF Daylight Saving Time. However, if you arrive in SF more than an hour before train time, just go to the greyhound bus depot at 7th & Market & get on next bus (leaves every hour or so) for Watsonville. When you get off the bus catch any city bus in Watsonville that goes to RR Ave. (near the RR depot; ask the driver) & get off at the dorms. If you catch the train, walk two blocks to the Pajaro Dorms. When you get here—men only allowed—just walk in & you'll see my name on the blackboard & go to my room if there is no one in the lobby. If there is someone there, ask for Sarah Howard, the landlady, & tell her you're my wife, & wait for me to come in from RR. This sounds complicated, but isn't. Just go to train or bus, ride 100 fast miles & go to dorms & wait for me.

I'll probably be in from my railroad run when you arrive anyhow. The reason I can't meet you is because of staying here to catch every call & so make more money, which we need so desperately (also don't know your expected arrival time). Anyhow, you now have my permanent address so you can write and call in emergency. As soon as you arrive, I'll move out of here, and we'll get a room or apt. uptown & stay here as long as the money rolls in (or until you hate it & I find I can make almost as much money in SLO or SF, but doubt that the way conditions are now on RR). Later on we could move elsewhere.

Now I don't want to plan for baby here, etc., but if you stay (in the light of how awful I am) I know baby can be taken care of here (not Watsonville, but SF Hospital). So, don't worry if you're here when baby arrives, we'll go to SF & I'll work off that board while it's being born. The month or so after it's born (since we probably want to find apt. or good place in SF & so I'm worried on that score) I'll go to SLO & get us place for baby & finish the RR season there. All this involves a hell of a lot of moving & neither you nor I want that. So, since there's so much vagueness & difficulty to the whole business, let the matter stand so that you can go back to NY & have baby there & I'll follow in month or so. (This means you stay here with me until October 15 or so & we can live anywhere.) Got everything straight now? Send all my things, bring only your necessary things. Come out here & see what you think of the place & me. Bring a coat, it gets a little chilly at night; beautiful weather. I'll go back to Tarrytown if only to get some good meals (home cooked). I hate these cafés so; I've been eating in them a month & more now & am about to choke. How's G'Ma? & Ma & yourself? I gotta catch a train (really) must run for it. So don't worry, don't plan anymore just get out here at once, we've still got time to spend the whole night in b.s. planning.

N.

While staying with Neal at Watsonville, Diana wrote him a testimonial.

August 27, 1950

TO WHOM IT MAY CONCERN:

I hereby certify to all and sundry females to whom on occasion it may be necessary this certificate be presented that the following are the terms of the "penal" code enacted on this date & are true & valid under the agreement of pact #7013. This voids all previous treaties per se & in the event subsequent rules are applied by this council it is understood there are to be no modifications of this agreement #7013, nor are there to be any rules made that conflict directly with the provisions & terms of charter #7013.

The articles of law #7013 stand correct as amended & certify that:

1) It is my wish and command that the following conditions be acted upon with all the frequency & vigor that can be mustered by my husband Neal L. Cassady, to whom the right is granted to:
   a. Meet all women possible & without restraint, conscious or emotional, attempt to seduce them without delay, personal involvement or inhibition.
   b. Further, it is granted to him that all such affairs be carried to complete physical extremes & there is to be no limitations on the number or type of sexual penetration.
   c. He is to feel no guilt, self-abasement & shame, nor is there to be any mental conflict whatsoever.
   d. The attributes of each and every woman's body are to be fully catalogued & appreciated by him without hindrance or without fear of any result of compassion with mine.
   e. It is further stated that he is to have a totally free hand in his selection, and statements about any & all women, including female children.
   f. Finally, he is granted all imaginable freedoms not included in the above that pertain to women & all those freedoms pursuant to his personality & mind on this subject.

It is fully understood by me that he must cater to the emotions of his soul.

Being of sound mind (legally) & in possession of all my faculties I affix my signature to this document the expiration date of which is to be the date our relationship of marriage is severed.

DIANA H. CASSADY

P.S. With the authority gained through 27 years of life as a highly sexual personality—unsatisfied in love to the point of neurotic illness (which demanded 6 years of intensive psychiatric treatment) & with my mind & emotions thus conditioned, I am better qualified than most to judge Neal's sexual powers. I therefore testify that he is a veritable Mecca of sexual satisfaction & pleasure. His ability to create sexual delights in others is evident in the sworn statements of all those I know to whom he has made love. Without exception they state fervently that he is "the best lay in the U.S.A."

Diana left Watsonville on Saturday, September 2, but, her flight out of Oakland being delayed, arrived in San Francisco to stay the night with Carolyn. Neal was surprised, when visiting Russell Street on Sunday morning, to find her cases in the house and was unprepared for the conflict that ensued. Meanwhile, Neal was making plans to return to San Francisco.

TO DIANA HANSEN CASSADY

Sept. 10, 1950
[Watsonville, California]

DEAR DI;

Enclosed find $50.00. I would have been able to send it sooner, but I had trouble getting my check again & yesterday & today the money order window at the P.O. is closed, so actually I'm mailing this on the 11th.

I am *definitely not* moving back into Carolyn's. We have decided that for sure. But here's another move I'm making: The dorms are the shits—I would have to go to the city (SF) anyhow occasionally to clean my clothes & see the kids etc., and there's no way for me to get there except using expensive bus part of the way, also, phone calls, also, no meals down here, also no home life like radios etc., etc., anyway—Hinkle has gone to San Luis Obispo & Wed. (13th) Helen, his wife, leaves to accompany him & stay in the city (SLO). With near RR cutoff time, there's an outside chance she may move back for a month or two in Dec or Jan. Anyhow these will help with the rent which is only $32.50 a month for 3 big rooms, refrigerator & other furnishings. So I'm leaving Watsonville Wed. & moving in there by myself, & will stay at that address permanently (230 Divisadero St #4).

I am still on that job I had when you were here—there was no "bids" for the job & I will have it until the 12th anyway (maybe longer, so that's why I stay here till the job is taken by someone else).

See that Joe Killian & hurry send me some shorts, I've only 3 or 4 beat pair. Send all my stuff to 230 Divisadero St., R.W. Express. I presume you've sent shorts already which I need like mad. No—wait a minute—I was just thinking & realize I might be out of town on a RR run (more likely than not) when the RR Expressman comes with my gear—so, send all my stuff to Russell St. because Carolyn'll be home, & I can pick them up there. I'm not (of course) absolutely sure of getting Divisadero Street yet anyway (for example, might catch 15 day job down here before I leave, or once in SF, on first day might catch 15 day holddown job in San Jose—anything can happen).

I saw your bags in the bedroom last Sunday A.M., & sat on steps next door for hour debating, but, expecting to have it out 3-way I entered to face the music & found that both of you unable to sit down for a 3-way conference about future. The validation that both of you were acting entirely crazy & my surprise at seeing you as such a mass of nerves & Carolyn as the opposite, etc., blunted my ability to respond to either of you straight & allowed me to ignore once again an overnight journey into the nerve-jangling hell of emotion I am forced to feel when I think of you & watch you crying & feel you suffer & know so intimate the pangs you suffer. What could I do but retreat into the same "care-not" you spoke of when you first arrived in Watsonville? May all God's children rest in peace.

Carolyn has found a big lover boy who satisfies her completely, so, I've only got my foot in the door as the man who supplies the money & reminds her of her conquest of days gone by. Strangely enough perhaps, I feel happy she's got a good cock to play with & feel no jealousy, unless he makes it inconvenient for me to see the kids off & on or for me to get a little (like he has this Sunday, I hope). All my clothes dirty again & intended to go up to SF this A.M. & wash them & come back late P.M. or early A.M. to get here for work, but I overslept & about 10 Carolyn called to check & see if I was coming (she didn't know because that prick was due at noon & she didn't want me to walk in on them). (They don't go out much, she likes to just fuck in the kitchen). Ah well, life is so interesting; a look into the future would be nice occasionally.

I'm just beginning to learn to live alone again. I had forgotten how philosophical it makes one. I am currently engaged in a horrible overconcern with time—minutes & hours. My mind is occupied much too fully with what to do in the next 10 minutes & how to handle each day & what the necessary things to be done in the near future are & how to handle them numerically—(I say to myself—

now, Monday you must call the trainman's timekeeper about a mistake in your check & also go to depot & ask for time voucher for $5.91 & see crew clerk about foot doctor, etc.). What a mad life, I wish I could be of more help to you, sweet Di, my Lorelei Lee[11] from the Eastern Sea. Page 7 is for the folks, thank you, (8 too).

Love, N.

Now Grandma, despite the habits you've accumulated in the last 80-odd, you ought to know it's not nice to read other's mail. In fact, I must say it's horrid of you to add to the bad taste by also going to the extreme presumption of taking upon your own fallible & faulty meaningless mental processes attempts to grasp the letter's content & in connecting it with your 80 yr old brains, gray & gray-tinted cells, with its black & charcoal-like linear arrangement—so that this mass can then assume the right to screech to the very life blood that feeds it—the young girl called Diana & her fellow misanthrope, lonely Robert Tappan & beyond screech.

Oh horrors, you also rant with such heavy intension you force the eardrums of young Diana to accept the ill-sounding tones your voice chooses to use & the words issuing forth produce in her an effect that long years of custom have caused to give & yield, a sensitive soul, to give you a victim to sustain you. My goodness?! You don't want that. Come on ole gal, be a little kinder & see if the desires of the little girl can yet be obtained; namely to make your old age a little happier & other emotional desires of love for you. I stop. Besides you've had plenty of life—don't hold on to it so hard—ease up a little. You won't collapse. Do please advise your daughter Bessie to try a little of the same. You two will never find your Bed of Roses anyway. Remember old Scrooge in the Dickens "Xmas story"!

11. Lorelei Lee was the infamous creation of writer Anita Loos (1888–1981) in her book *Gentlemen Prefer Blondes: The Illuminating Diary of a Professional Lady* (1925). It was launched as a successful Broadway show in December 1949, and a film version, starring Marilyn Monroe, appeared in 1953.

TO DIANA HANSEN CASSADY

Personal—supposedly

Sept. 11 [1950]
Pajaro Dorms
410 Salinas Road
Watsonville, Calif.

DEAR WIFE:

Disregard enclosed letter about your family—just a good obstinate bit of orneriness which is only a sample of rearing up my hind legs over two or three things that occasionally get my goat—this one was opening letters by people to whom they are not addressed.

I am taking 230 Divisadero from now until December, Apt 4, so write me there.

1) Get 2 or 3 (better 3) pairs of plastic pants (snap buttons)
2) Get two pair sleepers (no nighties)
3) Wide blanket for kid: 1) Jennifer Jo - 2) Jennifer - 3) I prefer Ned & Tom.

Don't buy but ½ doz bottles at most (& then only if kid not satisfied with your milk or needs more). Send radio immediately for 230 Divisadero (better send all things to Carolyn's—I'll pick them up there—the SF board is turning so fast I may not be in town for days on end).

Must rush to get train. Love to you—relax—I can't.

N.

TO JACK KEROUAC

Sept. 10th [1950]
[Watsonville, California]

DEAR JACK; (Writing on engine of train).

My great wonderful friend. I have done you the justice of reading your letter from Richmond Hill high and gone to inner-inner land.[12]

12. Kerouac had written to Neal on August 19, expressing his tiredness of sophistication and his desire for a new, simpler life.

I must say you are M'Boy, you beauty—well, dammit, listen. I'm going to begin from the moment I left you & Frank & go to Now. This is such a gigantic task, I feel like Proust[13] & you must indulge me.

First, understand the agony of my writing—I shall enclose coupla notes made while conked out in lonely dorm bed on subject of writing.

(Going around RR curve now.)

Left M. City, "tightening my belt" for long drive ahead. Became more engrossed in landscape & noting people as I drove. Being alone, I was not called upon to make summaries to any other mind & since I was not responding to other voices calling (big curve; engine jumps) my attention to other views of countryside or otherwise, did not notice what I may have missed seeing as I drove, because there was no one to call my attention to it & thus having only my own mad thoughts to contend with, I responded to each emotion perfectly as it came.

The arduous climb thru the mountain passes with the extreme beauty of handling the car so as to function perfectly on the road's surface while my mind was thinking such thoughts that soon I actually thought of how at last I could tell you on paper perhaps the knowledge of action—But later—anyway I must emphasize how wonderful it was.

[Two pages of original letter missing]

Now, eyeball kicks are among the world's greatest, second to none actually in terms of abstract thought, because it is thru the way you handle these kicks that is what determines your particular conclusion (in abstraction with mind) to each moment's outlook. Remembrance of your life & your eyeball view are actually the only 2 immediate first hand things your mind can carry instantly.

One's mind carries at all times the pressure of its own existence, & remembers previous eyeball views to recall what its previous life has been & feeding on this stuff, carries a heavy understanding of things it is capable of knowing & this knowing is blocked from coming out, because while one's mind carries one's life's past constantly, it also carries before it all day the world which comes in thru the eyeball.

I became so engrossed in my eyeballs & what they brought me over each ridge & thru each town that I looked out into the world as one looks into a picture. My field of vision then became like the can-

13. Marcel Proust (1871–1922). French author of the huge work *Remembrance of Things Past* (1913–27).

vas, and as I looked, I saw the 4 corners of the frame which held the picture. Since then, at any moment when I feel the slightest ennui, I simply look up from what I'm doing & note carefully the particular scene before my eyes. (Right now—to my left the fat greasy neck of the blubbery fireman carefully picking his nose. Near the center of the picture the hot fire box with the yellow . . .)

Carolyn & I get hi & her kicks are crazy—she sees everything in the mystic way. But with her logic of art she attempts to explain the whole business & she is weird especially when she gets hi on Benzedrine & fucks. Wow! Can she blow—Wow! She's pretty too.

TO NEAL CASSADY FROM DIANA HANSEN CASSADY

Friday A.M. [September 15, 1950]
(on train)
[190 Courtland St.
North Tarrytown, New York]

MY DEAR OLD MAN,

Your letter arrived yesterday (Thurs.)—hurray—& makes me feel ashamed of my insomnia & incipient morbidity of the day before. I'd figured you'd mail it Mon.—& that it would arrive Wed., but it obviously takes longer sometimes.

The money order (thank you—poor "money bags" Cass) was promptly endorsed & handed over to Mother & Gram, who must now manifest confidence in you. (By the way, I'm enclosing the letter Mother immediately sat down & wrote you. Try the athlete's foot suggestion. *Really* cured hers.)

Your "Personal—supposedly" had its effect. I got a call about the letter & she said, "It says 'Personal—supposedly'—what does he mean?—Shall I open it?" Don't think any more will be opened.

Payday today & we're on our own after I get those 2 last 319 bills paid off.[14] Then hand over board money to Mother & get the few essential baby things (will follow your advice here). I'm almost finished with the white sweater—Gram is doing a yellow one—& promises a third, in blue. Bed will be the wicker laundry basket

14. Diana had an apartment at 319 East Seventy-fifth Street, New York City, where Neal had lived with her earlier that year.

Mother insists on, but I've talked her out of the pillows in it—I think.

So the list now reads: 2 pr. sleepers, 2–3 pr. plastic pants, 2 belly bands & the bedding, diapers & assorted bath materials. No feeding equipment except the couple of bottles necessary for water & orange juice. I'm determined to make the breast feeding a success.

I dropped a note to Carolyn last week thanking her for putting me up Sat. night, apologizing for my "breakdown" & asking her about what kind of diapers best & the meaning of all those "pads" in the "essentials" list. She hasn't answered—so I guess she wants to discontinue the communication. Just as well—I feel wretched about that awful Sun. A.M. As for the practical questions—I'm getting bird's-eye diapers (sound stronger) & I've at last found out that the pads are bedding (not Kotex). (Did you say I was intelligent?)

As for the Sun. A.M.—we don't have to discuss it because I think I understood. It was just so painful & unpleasant—& I for one was completely worn out from the battle with the airlines (you don't know the half of it—in the end it only cost me about $25 extra—no more airplanes for me. They'd also neglected to make a reservation for me *out of* L.A.—so I had to stay the extra day. Good enough because I needed the rest.

Mysterious though how all sorts of "accidents" seemed to be trying to keep me in SF & close to you—the big grass fire sweeping down the hillside in San Bruno, the airplane business in Oakland, & then Sun. noon my plane to L.A. blew a tire when just about to take off & we were stranded out in the field for over an hour while they made the change. The whole thing & the sadness threw me in a sort of trance. I don't remember the trip down to L.A.

You do sound a little rejected over Carolyn's being interested in someone else. Please don't feel badly—I know about the need for "home life"—laundry etc. but we'll have that soon. Really it's good that Carolyn's life is "looking up." And you'll always be able to see her & the kids.

By the way, "Jennifer Jo" it will be (I'm trying to prepare myself for the possibility of a girl). The name I know you know is a little tribute to Cathy whom I am quite in love with (I'd rather have a little boy & a Cathy-like big sister.) She's so full of silent real conversation & understands so much & is so brave when she doesn't (a very mature acceptance of things). I still have the vision of her being raped by the cocker spaniel & the gentle way she handled the attack.

Anytime Carolyn doesn't want her—I'll bid. But I'd ruin her, I'm afraid. Better my own offspring in this order: 1) cat; 2) dog; 3) boy; 4) girl.

The Divisadero St. move for you sounds just right, provided you don't get too lonely. I'll ship the radio pronto. Also your things (all to Russell St.) By *all* your stuff I assume you mean *everything* you left here. Let me know if I'm wrong.

Would the Divisadero St. apt. be any place for you, me & baby to stay till we find our own apt.? Please let me know all about the prospects of the Jan.–June in SF rather than here. Work angle, etc. I have to do something about the 319 "possessions" as soon as I quit Tobé Oct. 1st.[15]

My darling—these are hard months but we'll make it . . . & we both know our jobs. Right now I'm following my diet carefully (no meat, eggs, salt, etc.) & trying not to be scared about the delivery. As for the breech position—the baby may turn around yet & anyway lots of kids are born that way—it just takes longer. I think it's rather appropriate *my* contribution should be born ass-first.

I'll write more tomorrow—must quit now & get to work.

Love,

DI

P.S. Be sure & put your name on Divisadero St. mailbox. I'm still getting an occasional letter back & addressed to you there before. Also please tell me what streets No. 230 lies between (my guess is—either Greenwich & Filbert or Fulton & Grove. I don't know which way the street nos. run). I want to mark your exact spot in SF on my wonderful map.

Neal began making plans for Diana to travel to San Francisco in December so that they could spend their six-month trial period together at the Divisadero Street apartment.

15. Diana worked as publicity/editorial assistant for the fashion retail consultants Tobé Associates of Fifth Avenue, New York (established 1927).

TO DIANA HANSEN CASSADY

Sept. 16 [1950]
[Watsonville, California]

DEAR DI;

I have received all your wonderful letters, from the L.A. library postcard (very funny I love your humor) right up to the note with your hospital diagnosis which I got yesterday. I say your letters are wonderful mostly because they have subtly changed from a morose form of suffering (in the first letter) to actual and beautiful statements about yourself and the situation. Also your letters have come to mean much more to me than they ever have. Each day when I awake in this cell #10 I look on the floor near the door & there lies another envelope containing another poignant missive from the wife. I love you very tenderly when I read each line (& between them), in fact, to make it last longer I usually fold the letter paper in such a way that the sheet can be read only one line at a time. I do hope you make the most of my letters in like manner. Which reminds me—I must admit a bit of uneasiness & shame over my first Sunday to you. Not only was the letter ill-written & inconsiderate by nature, but since most of its subject matter was vile & off-key it follows that the unthought-out inappropriate tenor of the thing, with the surly tone of a child defensively yelping over a trivial, made for a most unenjoyable "first Sunday" for you—& after you had looked forward to a real letter too. I'm very sorry & apologize to you, sweet Di. Of course the things I said to Ma & G'Ma still go. I realize how foolish to create issues with them (foolish because what they see, or can't see, is no concern of mine; also why needlessly antagonize poor old women just because they are bitches) but, goodness gracious, they've done such a poor & badly-underestimated job of being your parents that they have forfeited forever the right to say anything of a governing nature to you. Let alone yell their stupid heads off so self-righteously.

I've already mentioned the lovely humor of the L.A. postcard; onto a summary short answer of each of your letters:

1) Sept. 6 Wed A.M.:
I'll hold up my conception of my "end of bargain"; it does no good to fret over that anyway. When possible get on the

ball with the big fashion wheel in SF. Tell your family that they are the "darnedest mess"; forget doing the housework for their "taking you in."

2) Sept. 8 Thurs. night:[16]
I've answered this letter; about baby things & apts in SF & job etc. What I haven't answered will be taken care of at the end of this letter.

3) Sept. 9 Fri. night:
Good joke about "waistline." No more phone calls, agreed. (Incidentally I gave Carolyn an extra $20.00 this month for her phone calls—only did so because she is really broke. Don't worry I'm not going to give her another extra cent—so don't bitch at me.) (That move left me 30 to live on till 26th. Can't quite make it, I think.) I believe it's very healthy that you have unburdened your soul to no one. Don't forget you've been doing that for years & it's about time you learned to stop. I'm sorry it took such emotional blows as you've received from me to finally make you stop such shit, but remember that much of the reason no one is [listening is] just because you're always unburdening your soul to them & usually from their viewpoint didn't have very much to unburden, or worry about. Jet Black, not reddish.

4) September 12 Sunday:
Tell your goddamn mother to leave you alone, not to bother you, ogle you, feel your belly, or talk to you in such tone. You must quit catering to her, Di; put her in her place & tell her to moan alone, or in unison with G'Ma.

5) Sept. 12 Mon.:
You and I won't have to put any ads in SF paper—we got our home here.

16. In this and subsequent dates given here by Neal, he appears to be referring to Diana's letters by using the day of the week on which they were written—Diana's only indication of date—preceded by the date given in the postmark on the envelope, which was usually a day or two later.

6) Sept. 13 Tues. & Wed. A.M.
Tell your mother to sterilize her soul & prepare for God; you'll take care of baby. Don't let 319 stampede you. Take it slow & tell them you're thru & don't want any part of the whole mess; be bitchy enough to impress on the bastards that you gave them the goddamn place & in return you want some consideration. And without outside help etc., you have them, & Robert, to help you get all our shit, books (& most important, radio, which you send at once to me at 29 Russell) etc., & ship only best books West—Céline,[17] Proust, etc. Books are sent by mail at 1¢ a lb. if plainly marked—Books. In other words, get out of 319 everything then forget about the place entirely. Think what a relief to get that over.

Now, down to the specifics, facts, etc. I have the keys to 230 Divisadero & am not there already only because I'm still on the job I had when you left & getting off it before Monday isn't possible. But Tuesday I'll be in SF, our home. Let me describe: 2 doors from fast bus service in all directions. Good neighborhood. (Explain, but to do just would take too long & my left thumb hurts from writing.) One unpleasant sign as one enters outside door—it reminds one to turn off lights in large letters. Up one fairly long flight of stairs (18 or 20) 2 feet right to miss corner, 5 feet to rear of attractive door with glazed glass upper half & varnish pencil in bottom. Enter apt. 4—largeness of rooms amazing (10 ft high), pleasant walls, large bookshelfs straight ahead, (but bit to the left) & bit to right is fireplace, pretty, & the fireplace is quite useable. On same wall as door one enters & to left is a large closet 10 feet deep with shelves 10 feet high. Closet has door & is not noticeable. On right is beautiful couch & table lamp & other things (I forget, only saw the place for 10 minutes & didn't memorize). Living room quite acceptable anyhow. One goes across room & to right is entrance to kitchen—with large good stove, refrigerator, cabinits cabanats (can't spell, strangely enuf) flush with wall all around more closets—sink, dishes, (a few needed, frying pan etc.) etc., etc., for kitchen. As one entered kitchen there was a door just to the right; open that & one is on back porch all glass enclosed & with

17. Louis-Ferdinand Céline (pseudonym of Louis-Ferdinand Destouches, 1894–1961). French doctor and author of *Journey to the End of the Night* (1932) and *Death on the Installment Plan* (1936).

chute with cover you lift & slide all garbage & things you don't burn in fireplace (if desire).

Well, there you have faint picture of your new home. There is laundry, grocery, drug and other stores at hand. All in all, OK. Rent is 32.50, all utilities paid by landlord who does not live in building—make all noise baby can take. Helen without malice but to safeguard herself is keeping place in her name. Al & she are now in S. Luis Obispo & will be until Dec. or Jan. then Al goes to school in Denver Jan. (late) to June. Helen stays at 230 Divisadero (maybe) from Jan. to Feb., has kid in Feb in SF & goes to Denver to be with Albert. [. . .] So we won't be stuck with Helen any longer than a month, or longest 6 weeks, then 230 is ours permanently & as long as we want it. I had 2 talks with my boy Al (& remember he's the master & has Helen really under his thumb) & he said not only is the place ours while they are in Denver, but, when they return next June he would like to be the last guy in the world to kick me out. We're dealing with friends, honey.

I haven't time to reread for mistakes or illegibility. You must struggle thru on your own with my letters. I gotta run & catch a train again. I was SF brakeman again. Although the last 2 weeks they worked like mad, wow, with guys from other divisions making the board long as hell, they aren't making much again. Woe is me.

Love, N.

On September 19, Neal moved back from Watsonville, into the apartment at 230 Divisadero Street, San Francisco, and began seeing Carolyn more regularly. He wrote to Kerouac, enclosing drawings by Carolyn of his second daughter, Jamie.

TO JACK KEROUAC

Sept. 22 [1950]
[San Francisco]

DEAR JACK,

I am going to my death. It seems to happen every autumn, more particularly, each September of late. The realization of the things that go to make up one's death is such a personal thing, with so heavy a pressure on the intelligence, that it becomes unbearable agony to put word to paper. Each one with their privacy contained in mind has within their reach a seed of death which becomes the thing to be aware of & its use is not to be escaped so, . . .

Your letter was perfect; a real gem and so clear & I dig you & I know you could dash off a hundred like it (have done so) & I thrill & think of life again & by golly I gotta tell you how hi I get. Wow. Yet I'm on new sane kick. Analytical, no less.

My thumb too, the one I bashed on Windsor door,[18] the knuckle is 2 times bigger than my mutilated left thumb. Also eyes burn so. Need glasses.

I've already bought the car which will take us to Mexico next spring. It's a tight nice little '33 Ford Coupe with a fine clean seat covered interior. Plenty of room in trunk for luggage, spare tire, et al. Now the brakeman who sold me car for $75.00 is a mechanical wizard who will not only perfect the car mechanically for the trip—it's already almost perfect—but, if I want he will put in brand new motor he's got for it. The present motor is last 4-cylinder job Ford made.

N.

[Drawings of Jamie Cassady, by Carolyn Cassady]

Venus de Russell St., Céline Jane Cassady.[19] Named her after Louis Ferdinand,

N.

TO DIANA HANSEN CASSADY

Sept. 24 [1950]
[230 Divisadero St. #4
San Francisco, California]

DEAR DI;

Received all your letters, enjoyed some, but cannot remember one from the other, so repetitious. Railroading is liable to cause one the sweats. Just before I left Watsonville I committed a mistake with a switch & only the providence of the god I cater to prevented 15 or so

18. In addition to his broken left-hand thumb, Neal also damaged the thumb of his right hand when he tried to break down the men's room door of the Windsor Hotel, Denver, that previous June, as described by Kerouac in *On the Road* (Part Four, chapter 3). (As a child Neal had lived for a time at the Windsor Hotel with his father.)

19. Carolyn and Neal's second daughter was originally named Céline Jane, but they thought that this sounded too much like *saline*, so it was changed to Melany Jane, or Jamie. She now spells her name as Jami, to avoid confusion with her brother John's son Jamie.

boxcars going all over the ground, so wasn't fired. The next night the whole crew overlooked the train order & in another 20 seconds (if we'd kept going) we would have had a "main line meet" & all of us fired for sure. Ah well.

Thank goodness my gloves & black ties are on the way. I am buying a uniform tomorrow & need the ties & shirt before can use. Lost my army hat & my gloves in rags. I wear heavy army coat now. This SF board is awful—I haven't made $100 yet & want to get out again until Monday nite so the check I get on the 10th couldn't get to 150, probably 125 or so (clear). Speaking of money—listen:

Right now I have rent money left from last check & that only by skimping—rent is 35.50. Tomorrow get paid & get almost 200: 100 to Carolyn; 73.50 uniform; 27.50 to live on till 10th. (or less). Goddamn it; when will I get ahead enuf to save? Each month—C. 100; Rent 35.50; expenses 100 & I'm only making 275–300 at best. Fuck the whole business.

Bright side: can work in El Paso, Texas this winter & make gobs of $. Also Phoenix, Arizona.

Divisadero—you win. No need to put c/o Hinkle on letters. Pack up books & whatever Robert can carry—tell the 319 tenants they are bastards & to go to hell & go see your junk man down the block & get what you can & let him cart the furniture in his junk pile & forget it. I think you're in for a hell of a bad way & I'm not much better, so, will tell you something helpful when possible—maybe can find words to write later this week. Can't think of a thing to say now. Sunday deadline.

My toes are falling off. I decided to go to SF Hospital—went & waited hours so to hell with it—I'll try Ma's advice. Thanks to her. The main thing—send the radio quick—need music.

Honestly, I'll be able to write you a serious letter soon perhaps. But don't stay on your bum kicks if you can help it. I don't know how to advise you—or me—just now. Besides, advice does no good, even when good, so don't hanker so damn much. I really think you're impossible to please on any subject wherein frustration is inherent. Try not to long for so much; it does no good & after you get what you hanker for, your appetite just increases.

Love, N.

Visiting Carolyn at Russell Street, Neal typed a long letter to Kerouac with an account of his recent railroading exploits.

TO JACK KEROUAC

Sept. 25, 1950
[San Francisco]

DEAR JOHN;[20]

I moved from Carolyn's to Watsonville to live in the RR men's dorms and work there on the local freights. I spent a month and more just working each day and getting hi before and after each trip. During these hi's I was more amazed than usual by the whole panorama of life I saw daily. There are countless things I should tell you about, for example: One day as I looked the train over for brakes sticking etc., I happened to climb up on the top to check the indicators of a passing train (our pride, the Daylight, number 99) and on top of the reefer was a bum. I see at least 10 or 20 bums each day, however I was really stoned, the sun was so warm, and I had almost an hour to wait before my train pulled, so I sat beside this guy and we talked. Suddenly he began telling of his hallucinations. These were a collection of semi-ordinary bum ideas, like the one about when he arrived in SF. He walked along Mission and when he saw the patrol car he thought he heard the policeman announcing over the car's loudspeaker, as his fellow policeman drove slowly by, these words over and over: "The time has come, everybody lie down so you won't get hurt when the sun bursts." His mind heard these words, but his emotions felt they were actually driving toward him to arrest him because his fly was open (zipper broke and no pins to hold it closed) so he ran to hide in an alley but they drove by there too; so he left SF and caught a freight to Watsonville.

This is the simplest and most believable of his images. It all began after he had had sour wine and actually not eaten for four days. He was in the Sacramento freight yards, and he boards a flatcar to lie down. The world seemed normal and there was no indication anything unusual was to happen. It began slowly and normally also—the common thing of one's mind taking up the sound of a big steam engine as it passes slowly, and arranging its bark into a rhythm and then putting a short phrase to the rhythm. The particular accentuation of a steam engine is well known (like—*He's* a nigger, *he's* a nigger, on and on with the accent on the first word. Of course if one stays

20. Kerouac's first novel, *The Town and the City*, had been published in March 1950 under the name of John Kerouac.

with it long enough you can place your accents anywhere because the exhaust of the engine changes with the amount of pull—like shifting gears) that most people if they do fall into creating a phrase to match the engine's sound, so get bored with the project and stop soon. This bum began that way, his phrase—"What's my name?" As he got stuck with those words while the engine was passing he didn't attempt to answer himself because it was unnecessary. Once the engine was gone he idly asked himself what's my name and with a shock found he didn't know. He thought he'd just forgotten for a second and his mind confidently began to wrestle out the answer. He kept trying to wrest the words that were his name from his memory. Not succeeding he tried sounds that might be similar to it: John, Juan, etc., then he tried different words: John, Peter, etc. He finally exhausted himself lying there on the flatcar. He figured he'd go to sleep and it would come to him when he awoke. This failed too, so he got panicky. He said he felt an overpowering desire to jump down and run as fast and far as possible, but he felt an equaling overpowering inability to move. Then the train beside him began to move so he struggled to it and not caring where he was going laid there trying to remember his name by recalling his past including what he'd been doing recently. He remembered little about his early life, but easily recalled what had happened recently. He had been out in no man's land in the San Joaquin Valley heat picking fruit. Once he'd gotten a stake he'd gone to Sacramento and got hung up and friendly with a barkeep. A few days later someone snuck into his room and stole his money and shoes. The barkeep got him some old shoes and got him drunk on the house. Then he went to the yards to get a train to Salinas (south of W'Ville), etc., etc.

I found so gone a whorehouse in W'Ville that for days after I couldn't believe what I saw and almost came to doubt its existence. I got loaded and went to dig it on a Sat nite; they were so busy that the line outside stretched from the door along a 50 foot strip of alley to the street. You sit in a beautifully furnished room on couches with magazines to read, etc., while the absolutely amazingly beautiful girls march in singly or in pairs and you look them over in their wonderful costumes which are so revealing. Finally one comes along that is what you want, like picking out one movie star from among others, and you go off with them to their room and have your ball. The girls are all 16 or 18 and so stunning you can't believe they are there being whores instead of in the movies or modeling or something unbelievable.

I've got a great bachelor 3 big room apt. with everything, refrigerator etc., and I only pay 35 a month and I go to Carolyn's and we understand each other and things in general are fine, except worry over Diana and her coming child and what to do about it.

In Dec. late or early Jan. I get cut off and will go to El Paso and make gobs of loot there (which I'm not making here; I'm really broke despite working so hard. I give Carolyn 100 or more, and rent and buying 75 dollar passenger uniform, and my minimum expenses are 100, and Di needs money, etc., etc., and Di expects to come out here and she would need at least 150 for that plus her kid expenses, etc., bah!

I'll be in El Paso until April then to Phoenix, Arizona for a month or so then back to SF and work the rest of year here on SP again. Now regarding annual trip to Mex City, you come to me in El Paso or Phoenix any time in Spring and we'll take off and stay there until May or June when I got to come back here to hold seniority on SP. I think April a good month 'cause you and me don't need time to dig things together, we crowd more into a month than we can assimilate in a year. Besides, my families thruout the land need so much money I can't blow my wad more than a month a year. Let me know lover.

Carolyn was so impressed with your book[21] so almost wrote you a big "forgive me" letter, but thought better not—we all understand each other anyhow—I mean everybody. Hinkle in the Southland with his wife and kid problems similar to mine (we see each other), Holmes in NY and Harrington and Fitzgerald and on and on, it makes one feel like we're all together in the same beautiful boat of life and one can't help gushing warm come over the whole works and feeling well and relaxed—I feel like a romantic old maid with her Ideal—all this so juvinal juvenile and not what I mean to say at all, but you can tell by my very carelessness in typing and spelling I feel OK about everything and know even tho I'm so unable to write my big thoughts (which are changed, as are yours) and I trust my intuitive self so much I assume you got yours in there too, and as I don't regret too hard the things which are so important that you and I can't get across I expect you're the same. Like your new acceptance of being alone with all that implies (Hal-like) and the real peace of knowing the things one does know, etc., etc.

I have no t left and in the knowledge I have that come Dec I will send you some from El Paso I ask for a pittance of the small amount you've left. Make your return address a phoney and send it to Cassady

21. *The Town and the City.*

SP cigar store Watsonville Junction Calif. Wrap it in small prescription cardboard box (aspirin or like) and send parcel post. If they open it will look like tobacco for cigar store.

Love, will write again soon,

N.

The following day, September 26, Carolyn made the first payment on a Webster Electric model 109WE Ekotape recorder for Neal to use as an aid to his writing. Meanwhile, Diana, in New York, was having to deal with the censure of her family as well as her worries about the future.

TO NEAL CASSADY FROM DIANA HANSEN CASSADY

Tuesday night [October 3, 1950
190 Courtland St.
North Tarrytown, New York]

DEAR NEAL,

Must admit I'm shedding a tear . . . in fact, a whole lapful. Reasons sundry, I suppose . . . or rather just the same old ones which have slambanged themselves into undeniable reality during the past few months.

You don't love me . . . in particular; you don't feel any sense of responsibility toward me . . . in particular; ditto the child . . . in particular. My coming out to San Francisco is not because you want me to be with you . . . in particular. You would, in fact, be just as happy if I and even more the child did not exist in your life . . . unnecessary appendages, troublesome in fact, but you are used to trouble and so a little more fits into your stride. Take it or leave it. This I know, and it is my secret. I am harder than ever putting up my good front to the world. What else can I do? Should I crack up, "jump in the river," lead my army over the cliff, fall on my sword, lock myself in an old New England house and write poems about my marriage to Eternity? That would be pointless, and besides I am really a peasant (thank God) as well as a misanthropic Child of Darkness.

The tide of luck has turned against me right now. Your fault? Yes, I dare blame you a lot . . . my fault though for wanting, trying, trusting, planning, dreaming, hoping (or as Allen said and says—"Don't go into the water if you don't want to get wet.")

If it weren't for the baby coming, I doubt if I would be writing. By now our relationship would be silence; you would have "done me wrong" and I would be mending a mere broken heart in an insignificant cloud of friends, business—social activities, everyday's little conquests, a new hat or bit of junk jewelry to make me feel good. As 'tis the tragedy goes on, and the poor unsuspecting child will be in for it too . . . unless I can continue the "good front" for it as well. I know I shall treat it extra-tenderly . . . with fiendish determination (or as I heard my mother comment to my grandmother the other day, "I can see Diana plans to take care of the baby *herself*. A good thing . . . we certainly don't have the strength.")

What brings on all this? Again the usual. I am always covering things up with assumed peace only to have the chaos crop out again like a recurring fever . . . Home tonight. Your this week's letter hadn't arrived; it will tomorrow, but I was a little disappointed. (Actually I am more satisfied here, knowing you *will* write me once a week. But still it would be nicer if you wrote me more. I know your difficulties there though . . . both physical and spiritually.) Instead of your letter I got my bill from the income tax people requesting my payment of the $125.43 I owe them, payable within 10 days to avoid further interest. (Memo to myself: I must write them, send them five dollars and tell them I have no job, no money, my husband cannot support me because he is already supporting two other children under divorce agreement, I am expecting a baby next month, then I plan to return to work as soon as I can get a job, I will send them five a month regularly, then when I get my refund on this year's tax what I still owe will easily be covered because the addition of the baby will give me 2 dependents for 1950 whereas in my withholding I have only been claiming myself as one, etc., etc.)

I eat supper—small pleasure. Your packages I note are *still* here, and I am informed by family that postage on just one of them will be about $6 parcel post, $8 Railway Express . . . the others are quite a lot lighter. The paper they're wrapped in costs 20¢ a sheet, the cord who knows what, the stickers ditto. I say confidently that I've written to you for the money to cover the postage (I don't mention the underwear which will come to about $3). They say, well you'd better send it. Mother—sick in bed with swollen foot—carries on mournfully about why couldn't you play fair, why do I have to be married so slipshod to someone who doesn't care for me and apparently doesn't *care* for me . . . why, why, why . . . Grandmother asks her if they should send the packages before receiving the money. Mother says Yes—

adds with passion, "I'll be glad to get the damned stuff out of the house—and the Cassady baby too!" I ask her if she really means that, remind her it's a Hansen baby too, and that anyway children should never be blamed for their parents no matter what or have things flung up at them. She brushes off a noncommittal answer. I repeat for the millionth time you didn't leave stuff here just to burden them, you hadn't known you were going to stay in San Francisco and you only took the things you really needed. Robert in the meantime who has been tying up one of the packages mutters something and walks out of the house slamming the door. I ask my grandmother what's the matter with him. She hesitates . . . "He's disgusted with Neal and the whole business . . . He doesn't think Neal had any right living with you and getting you 'in a family way' and marrying you and deserting you." I say "I want to have the baby. I could be in California with Neal. I'm just here to have the baby at Lying-In. He hasn't deserted me. He wants me to be with him and we're planning on it. The money and the marriage business are just things he can't help." She'd rather drop the subject. Everybody decides to go to bed and I am left to weep or not. I weep since no one's looking.

What should I do? Fact is—I'm stuck. Should I be drastic—have baby adopted and tell everyone it died, go through appropriate breakdown etc. What—that wonderful baby, that sweet innocent goodness who gives me such gentle little kicks so's not to hurt, for whom I have the lousy old clothes all nicely washed and folded in its bureau drawers (and trying not to care that they're not the pretty soft blue new clothes it deserves—that's life), for whom I have the little sleeping corner all laid out and the powder all in place next to the baby oil—even the laundry bag hanging.

No, I will stick with baby no matter what and try not to disappoint him. Where do I live? What do I do? What do I live on? Oh, I am looking at the realities tonight and they are very hard.

The things I know about you I don't dare admit even to myself . . . and what you did to me so unbelievably contrary to vows and protestations . . . and your trying to say, goodbye to me on the flimsy ground "it's kinder to be cruel now" at a time when as a point of honor you would take your responsibility for better or worse . . . and what I saw and heard with my own senses.

But I'm stuck and I'm defenseless. I have no place to live except with the family for this while; no job until I can find one wherever I go and it will have to be out of New York; also I must arrange for someone to care for baby. I use "I" because you see I really know about you.

So I move to San Francisco and we have a "marriage of convenience" . . . Can't think anymore. Must go to bed. Perhaps tomorrow's letter will be more cheerful.

DI

Neal contacted his older half sister Betty,[22] in Los Angeles, about the fate of his younger sister, Shirley Jean, offering her the opportunity to stay with him in San Francisco.

TO BETTY DALY COOPER

Oct. 5, 1950
[San Francisco]

DEAR BETTY;

Since I am now in San Francisco for good, it may be possible for me to be of some help to Shirley Jean. I understand from Jim (who received me most graciously on two separate visits I was able to pay him and his fine family this year) that Shirley was in Oakland some months ago and the possibility she may still be in that city prompts me to ask you for her address. You see, I now live in a nice and large 3 room apt. in SF and in the next few months before my wife comes from the east to join me perhaps Shirley would find it convenient to share the place with me because the rent is so cheap and with the wonderful kitchen the place has (refrigerator etc) she could inexpensively whip up a few dinners for her brother and herself. All this is just a thought and if she did find it suitable to her plans (a place to live etc.) I would be only too happy to have her; if, however, she might find it too difficult to commute to Oakland each day (or whatever) tell her to give no more thought to the above suggestion. It's just that I've a place for her to hang her hat if she needs it, that's all. Since I don't know what she or you or most of the family are doing I am breaking the long silence in this fashion. If you (or anyone) happen to find the time or feel the inclination, do please drop a line. Of course, you know me—no answer guaranteed.

Love to All,
N.L. CASSADY

22. Betty Louise Daly Cooper (b. May 1919).

In early October Neal was concerned that Carolyn may have become pregnant again. He shared his anxieties with Diana and continued with plans for her to move to San Francisco in December, after the birth of her baby.

TO DIANA HANSEN CASSADY

[October 1950
230 Divisadero St. #4
San Francisco, California]

DEAR DIANA;

Received your letter re. phone calls to Carolyn. Thank you. Carolyn spoke of some, but only in monosyllables. Anyway, from now on try Underhill 1-5699. No more phone calls tho. You wouldn't need them. You see, I've definitely decided only I know the torments of all the past few weeks, but I ain't talkin'. I hereby & unequivocally certify I shall be your husband under Man & God until the date June 1 of the year 1951 of the present Christian era. Thank you. So help me God. Amen.

Do relax the pressures & worries a little. I've come up with a sickness of life which, at last, approaches true exhaustion. Thank you. Love the baby & all it means to us. If you come out with anything under 7 pounds, or a girl, I might be forced to renege & change the date to May 31, 1951. Thank you.

230 Apt here OK, Hinkle & otherwise—heat may be small problem for child occasionally—all SF Apts. No central heating, don't need it. We got fireplace (Dandy) & good stove. Don't worry, slow up a little & give kid a chance. I want healthy yells out of him. It's lonely here.

The present situation makes it not for us to question but to act out God's will, the only reason for Dates indicating periods of husbandship is due to the overwhelming odds of 3 children to 1. If Carolyn has another it will arrive June 1st—I know none of us want it, so send abortion information soon. Sterility then? Perhaps, only after my eyes, teeth, throat, bronchial tubes, chest, asshole, hernias, prostate gland, feet, thumbs & brain are examined and exterminated however.

Seriously. All my best wishes for an easy confinement. May the good doctors excel themselves—including admission—& make the little bastard pop right out. It's not too easy a thing to be the father of bastards, but, since it's much harder to be the mother of one, I take this opportunity to tell you my regrets, sympathies & apologies are in order & proffered with an enthusiastic promise to try once again to lift this dreary weary old fart up by the bootstraps & make a most honest effort to help you live happier in the days ahead.

Godspeed, my sweet, I'll send fare Dec. 10th. (Hope, pray)

N.

TO DIANA HANSEN CASSADY

Oct. 10 [1950]
[230 Divisadero St. #4
San Francisco, California]

DEAR DI;

Hold the presses! Carolyn has come sick! Forget all consecrations for evil doctors and all the fears and money spent; the suffering inherent in all that business. Thank God that's over!

Now all you have to worry about is if I'll have enough money by Dec. 10 (payday) for you to come with ease and if I shall be able to find a good rail job in this area. Believe it, I'm damn near sure (despite my recent incurable pessimism) I can find good money across the bay on NWP. Anyhow, now you got home, husband, and bbbbabby (I stutter). The recent fluidity of all the soul involved in this has settled into a fixed plan for another half year and more.

There are no guarantees, of course, because the things which you women bitch about so are as yet apparently still in some state of flux and by their nature are not understood properly even by me, but I come the closest, as does each individual in his own soul. However, who knows what the dark future holds? That life immediately before us makes one quack (most women) and quake (me) with fear. By June 1st '51 maybe all would be happiness between us. But, again, remember that there is complete freedom of action on both our parts. I know how horrible that sounds; things are that way because I'm the horror existing as an ogre for all my children, etc., etc.

I'm tired and about to get called again so must stop. This letter is meant mostly as a Flash release to have you more able to enter the hospital properly.

I hereby consider this formal notice that upon the date (June 1, 51) the terms of the contract end, I shall have fulfilled all obligations (romantic etc., not, of course, monetarily to our child) and commitments, and shall be free to flee to the hinterlands in sackcloth and ashes to ponder the whole shittin' mess.

Amen. N.

Carolyn says "she won't like it that you used my envelope"—to hell with that—time & speed in dispatch of this letter more important than any of those kind of considerations, & will be so in the future. Horseshit.

Amen. Thank you. N.

TO JACK KEROUAC

Oct. 15, '50
[San Francisco]

JACK: THE GREATEST;

Unbelievable! You write me *exact* a description of what I've been doing, and *how* I've been doing it![23] Gene Kelly[24] correct; I dug him that way too (I mean, lying there, stoned, digging the difference between him and Mel Allen; Don't forget old boy I hipped you to Marty Glickman[25] last basketball season, etc., man, etc.).

And let me tell you how I've discovered similarly the eye sockets of *all* brakemen. Sunken in so from the long hours of staring with the focus on a distant point (a mile or more away) like cattlemen and old time farthandlers of Indian juice.

I dig you about Wolfe. I am so amazed (as usual) how *really* alike our kicks (everything, I mean, thoughts everything, not happy kicks of self-satisfied life) like, listen, Important.

Look here I enumerate; 1st, VOICES:

I have done and gone done the gonest thing: I BOUGHT A WIRE RECORDER! not a *wire* recorder, but, better, a tape recorder, a gone instrument which reproduces so flawlessly (you can hear a clock ticking from way over in next room when you play back recording) and so cheaply, and so *effortlessly,* and the tapes last *forever,* don't break, can save any part or all of anything recorded, etc., etc., etc. The hour tape for example is only about 5 inches in diameter and weighs only few ounces and can be filled on *both* sides, so is really 2 hour tape (I got 2 half-hour rolls too) and simply record, go to nearby postoffice and mail to *ME* A LETTER, better, 2 hours of our VOICES talking to

23. Kerouac wrote to Neal on October 6. The letter is published in *SL,* pp. 230–34.
24. Not the dancer, but a sports commentator from Philadelphia of the same name.
25. Mel Allen and Marty Glickman were also famous sports commentators.

each other; Save all labor of letters for writing (SO HORRIBLY HORRIBLY SHITPOT HARD FOR ME) until such time as have written, then maybe, I too could reel off a 5000 page letter every day to you. Gawd, I sho (don't know dialect yet) does admire any of the fellers can write them books an' all Geezus Christ! Get it now? buy an EKOTAPE tape recorder small portable size, look in telephone directory it has EKOTAPE dealers, buy on time (costs no more) and get at once, cost 150.00 dollars, down payment, say 60 or so, don't know. GET AT ONCE. (184 with tape.)

YESTERDAY, believe it, yesterday, I picked up, for the first time in *years* TOM WOLFE and recorded his gone poem prose prologue introduction preface dedication page beginning of "Time and the River" which is so old to me in years of past knowledge of it and etc. Of course I was hi and I've also recorded all kinds of such, like recent "Hi Hour with Proust" and of course a Major Hoople (me as W.C. Fields) of a little thing I tossed off on "The Repeating Rifle in the Bulgarian Army" (All bullshit, "Repeating Rifle" believe it, comes from *Proust*! Etc., Etc.).

I got lots of *Mexican* Indian Mambo from gone old *Mexican,* Watsonville, Calif. (record girls tell me have nothing but real Mexican Mambo (all Spanish gone gibberish) 'cause *hundreds* of Mex. cats cut in and that's all they'll buy, no Dave Barbour,[26] etc., etc.

I know what voices mean and since I was so stymied in writing and sweating so, and thinking of *everything* I could to begin and finally decided I had to write from beginning in *words* of each character (begin with my old man telling of moving to Denver etc. on down the line), I thinking, actually thinking on sandbox and dormitory cot of *what* to write about voices and you write me about voices, I buy recorder and for the first time in lifetime I dug my own voice hi and otherwise, sniffle wise, fucking and blowing wise, and you write me about Voices—World series (which I dug) to Gawd.

Now I know you've always seen my flaw of being so damned amazed at any little coincidence or am so quick to point out as we walk down street any time the two minds touch and so on, but damit, your letter is so vital to me because it showed me, once again, I wasn't alone in my mental world, and again, served as another kick in the pants to get going and trust yourself and no matter how well you know you'll never put any single thing in *words* as they come from the voice in your head, just try like hell and don't regret each failure so

26. Dave Barbour (1912–1965). Jazz guitarist married to singer Peggy Lee.

much. (Incidentally, man, if thought there was anything at all in my letter—there ani't (missplell ain't, and misspell misspell)—you should see the crazy shit I tore out of myself when I first went to Watsonville for 5 lonely weeks in the RR dorms, I got so complicated I fell into the cookie jar all by myself.) You're going into the deepest parts of the mind until they are like sunlit corners because one recognizes them so well because of the repetition and emotional strength of the deeper images is so common to me that all my jump goes into probing instead of percolating with the mind, and sameness of thoughts not coming out in writing, make for such staleness that the soul withers in terror at being trapped, so that any thought no matter how gone becomes so binded and cramped that the vegetation entangles itself endlessly and rots in jungle fashion of rot, and while no outlet for *accumulated* thoughts which are so gone like Victoria P.M. there is still occurring each minute other thoughts which so weigh one down with the burden of memory that when one begins to record the whole fuckin shop closes on wildcat strike and the light goes out and the fuckin mind struggles in the morass until it give up with a lick and promise and turns itself to more ass. I masturbate every day at least 3 times and have done so for years no matter how much I'm fuckin and blowing at the same time. Years ago I had all day orgies where lying there all by myself I think of a woman (thousands of images, remember 9 years old, 4 foot mex cunt in Denver night of carnival, and she and fellow school chum phoned) and come 11 and more times in 6 or 7 hours. Now it's a daily habit before going to sleep, (or can't sleep until do masturbate) and a brakie sleeps never more than 4 or 5 hours until called, when business good, and must catnap anywhere and so on. I didn't begin masturbating until the very late age of 17; I had fucked for almost 5 years before started masturbating (it began heavy and has since stayed that way from the time I did 11 months and 10 days in Colo. State Reformatory, etc., etc.).

You won't believe this if you've any sense left, but I *Heard* you call me F.D.R.[27] that afternoon and just before you spoke Franklin D., with such amazement I knew it at once and purposely put on more exaggerated gestures for your benefit because (that is, I felt that way) you had picked up on what I called you (just after yelling into the backseat how hi we really were), but now I've forgotten what I called you, you remembered what I was called by you, damnit; there you see how I've vegetated in this west land where the problems are like the

27. Franklin D. Roosevelt.

redwood trees and the lovely moon of the midwest has changed, like the NY moon is so damn cold and bright and the warm ripeness, believe it, of the moon I dug crossing the country driving all night in a race from NY to Indianapolis—and on to Denver at night; the SF moon is a wet pale thing hardly noticeable.

I have just completed the greatest feat of the last 5 years, perhaps even longer; since I escaped from Calif. Reformatory or talked, unbelievable now, out of jail again once I was caught for escape (due for San Quentin): I have just written you a complete letter hi! this whole thing from first to this word (I CAN'T TYPE: kid on lap) is a product of me sitting down and forcing myself to cover these two pages with semi-sense. Unbelievable, and so heartening, bah.

Now the Shadow, he knows, don't say he don't man, why I read him for 3 years straight from 11 to 14.

Etc., Etc.—Eastward with this.

N.

Neal breaks the news to Diana that their plan of spending six months at the Divisadero Street apartment in San Francisco has fallen through, and that he intends instead to join her in New York in January.

TO DIANA HANSEN CASSADY

October 17, 1950
[230 Divisadero St. #4
San Francisco, California]

DEAR DI:

It is only justice that we, who are always planning and planning, should get our comeuppance just when it was all settled, more or less, exactly opposite to the way it's going to turn out:

This straw breaks the rhinoceros's sacroiliac completely. The horror has happened. No I'm not fired; worse, as far as you're concerned . . . Helen Hinkle has pulled the pin on all the plans we've wallowed in, perhaps for the best. With finality she has refused us the apt. It was clearly understood that I was just using the place until Dec. After that she doesn't want you or me anywhere near, definitely. Understand? 230 is out, non-existent, blotto; forget it. So, forget it; so, now what? now this:

Description of what I do and what you do until June 51: no

change in these plans no matter what (except small matter of exact dates). What I do in Oct., Nov., Dec.: Move from 230 Oct 21 when rent due. Live with Carolyn from then to cut-off. That existence goes this way: I spend all time on RR, rest of time waiting long, long, long, etc. hours sitting in SP hospital fixing 1, feet; 2, eyes; 3, throat; 4, lungs; 5, cough; 6, hernias; 7, prostate gland; 8, thumbs; etc. Rest of time spend in 29 Russell attic beginning book. Rest of time spent fucking and such. (All this in order of importance and time spent on each task.) So my life all ordered until cut-off. After cut-off: leave SF in auto that mechanical wizard fellow brakie will sell me for 75. This car is old, of course, but, in perfect condition, with new motor he and I to put in it next month. Now, I really know the true awfulness of the ice and snow that mars this fair land in Jan. The car has no heater and I've frozen before too much to care for it now, so, even if there is no valid reason for me to do so, I would still come to you in NY to escape such weather. I will go East by way of southern route to escape such weather so that if, for any reason, I'm short, too short, of money at that time to meet all expenses, including of course the money you'll need and C's money and trip money (very cheap, I should easily cross country on 40 dollars at most). If I don't have at least 100 to arrive in New York with (for Ma and all our expenses until I am working at Chevrolet plant, or otherwise) I shall work a week or so to make that hundred. If I can't make a pretty big stake within 2 weeks at the longest, I would still have other chances as I go thru Texas (On SP-owned T. and N.O. RR) etc. Anyhow, I'll be in NY in early January with enough money for all baby needs et al. Don't think I'll get hung up down South working to see if I could make a lot of money in a short week or two, you see I'll know almost exactly what I'd make before I begin RR there, so, if I couldn't make enough would continue on across until I found lots of money, or, (unthinkable) arrive in NY without having worked and so see you sooner. Once in Tarrytown, I submit to the horror of the climate and work the best job available until June 1st, late May, or even middle May. At that time I'll be called back to SP in SF and will take Jack with me and return via Mexico. Of course, if we are to stay together, I will get crosscountry train pass for you and kid when I get called back. Before I leave NY your transportation will be in your hand (like mine this year) so, you'd be set up in SF (we'd have guarantee of a good six months of money; this year we only had 4 months and money spent unconstructively). Naturally, you'd be about six months late getting your home in the West, but, you see, if you did come out next June, everything would be settled anyway at last, whereas, now, if you came it would be a horrible mistake.

Although I know your heart's set on coming out now, let me just take a few lines to show how impossible that is. It almost looks now that I'd barely have fare for you and kid (Joan Adams' fare from Huntsville, Texas to NYC with 3 month old Willie in roomette on train was 106 dollars) let alone you arrive with me no job and no place to live for us and having to set up a place for kid, with all the stuff we'd have to buy. Besides which there is the obvious doubt; if we did split up, you'd be here with kid and etc., etc.

I know what a drag for you to stay in Tarrytown an extra six months, but, we must consider the kid will be taken care of and that comes first, otherwise, well, consider the fact that tho life there is a tough deal for you, think of me. Say for example there was no kid or I had not guaranteed six months to you. Think how wonderfully I'd be set up. When I got cut off I'd just drive my little buggy to El Paso and work a couple of months, go to Phoenix and buggy to El Paso and work a couple of months, (the money there is terrific in March and April, only 16 hours a day). Then May first Jack and I'd go to Mexico City in my little car and in June I'd return to SP here and live with Carolyn and kids until next year when I'd do the same thing. Carolyn thinks all this would be wonderful and I'd have no trouble there. But, all this supposing is, unhappily, not the way things stand because I make a promise to you and intend to keep it, no matter how poorly, and how sick at heart you must feel about this whole upsetting way of life.

Well, what further can I say? I'm convinced you can't come out here now, that one thing is sure even if it kills you to stay with MAMA. But, what if we split up? There is much likelihood to that possibility altho I'm coming East with all the love I can muster and will try my goddamnest to pull my oar (the thought of other work than RRing kills me; it probably will with my awkward and unskilled thumbs). I say if we do break for good I'll still help in any way possible and that's about all there is to say now.

So, altho I know how awful this all is to you; how you'll rebel, there's really nothing you can do about it, so may as well relax and spend your free time fixing up for baby and working on your ideas for business which is equivalent to me trying to write and Carolyn trying to draw even while living through this period.

Where are my shorts? If you've got them from Joe, just keep them and I'll have to come to NY just to get some underpants. Better write me at 29 Russell from now on, no more lovely 230. Maybe next year a better 230, huh? Jesus, I'm sorry.

Love, N.

P.S. Enclosed are one of Helen's letters; she's written others to back this one—3 in two days. I thought I had it all fixed up with Hinkle. He assured & reassured me all was OK. But, Helen owns the place & she even said she'd split with Al if he let me take advantage of him one more time.

P.P.S. They all think I'm taking advantage all the time & my having done so has caught me & you.

With his mind evidently on the escalation of the Korean War, which had begun that summer, Neal wrote to Jack to inform him of his new plan to visit New York in January, to be followed by a trip to Mexico in May.

TO JACK KEROUAC

Oct. 22, 1950
[San Francisco]

DEAR JACK;

Stop the presses, hold that headline; insert this: Keroassady to fuse in east within 10 weeks.

The importance of the recent Truearthur meeting in the Pacific led to renewed speculation by usually reliable sources in this city of rumors that to balance the effects and offset the advantage gained by Dugout Doug[28] and Tess Trueheart's[29] erstwhile sugar daddy Harry, Big Dick Cass and slept with the best of 'em, semi longish John would meet in the east just north of Horseshit Harry's Hideaway. This may lead to war. Of course, the initial preparation necessary by the dark duo would perhaps delay the beginning of any feasible festivities until hostilities, which commence only after agreements decided

28. Nickname of General Douglas MacArthur (1880–1964), a veteran of World War II in the Pacific, who had been placed in charge of the United Nations forces in Korea.

29. Girlfriend of comic strip police detective Dick Tracy.

upon in Jan. unless sooner, are declared and then whambo, give it to 'em Charlie, Cannastra is Dead.[30]

Unkle Jack Diggerback was never without his pissgun of snortin' tobacco; this led to war. He had all the other guns for miles around fartin in their leadbelly. This led to war. They were bleedin' thru the snotmouth before he was thru, true blue I say, always give it to them boys, we're in this thing to the end and I say, give it to 'em boys, never fart till you see the banks of the stix, unless you're eatin beans. I planted some, or rather, unless because black too.

I'll see you in ten weeks when I arrive NY with new Mexico car which will take us in mid-May; please, if you can possibly, try to arrange yourself so that mid-May is ideal for our month So. of Border. The car will hold you and I and luggage.

I wish Allen would write; maybe if I had his address, I would. I am going to, immediately (soon as I finish this letter) record my entire Cassaynovel up to now.

Write me at 29 Russell instead of 230 Div. I'm here till Jan. Then 190 Courtland with Diana till May then Mexico with you till late June then SP RR again till next Jan.

Long yellow pissbarrels are the pinch, unless we can get the war relations board to persuade all the constituents to write to our holy American slopjaws, there is no hope to gain an ordinary $100,000,000,000,000,000,000,000,000,000,000, (while I was doing the 0001, oops, mistake, the 000, I didn't Inted, oops, *intend* to, I was just hungup on the physical kick of moving my right forefinger from letter to letter and quit when I fumbled.)

Where *Is* Cannastra?

Oh boy, I'm so happy, doggone. (It just occurred to me while, for entirely different reasons, I was writing oh boy, etc., it looked as tho, because it followed so soon after Cannastra question, which was so important and so strongly felt, that it looked as tho I was glad Cannastra was dead; not so, by all the degrees of love that exist.)

I wrote oh boy, etc., because I was knocked out thinking of Thomas Wolfe, that son of a bitch. Jesus, here it is again.

We rushed thru the Mexican towns too fast. This time, not rush,

30. William Cannastra (1921–1950) was a Harvard Law School graduate who mixed in the W. H. Auden circle as well as with the Beats. He was killed in a freak subway accident on October 12, 1950. Cannastra appears in Kerouac's books as Finistra *(Visions of Cody* and *Book of Dreams),* as Agatson in John Clellon Holmes's *Go,* and as Genovese in Alan Harrington's *The Secret Swinger.*

and besides digging underneath visions, the careful pleasure of a *slow* easing thru the country will bring again to mind the small remembrances that unbeknown to us will always retain the sum of the experience.

What happened to Frank? (the guy who went to MexCity with us). The Nash automobile is strangely constructed, not just weird new design, but, looking at one out this broken window I see a strange contour which replaces simple executive concern with style. The guys who made it are crazy, pure slashbacks, yellow and purple.

I'll come to NY by way of L.A., Tucson, El Paso, Texas, Houston, New Orleans, and up thru the deep then upper then silly south, Washington, Baltimore, NY. We'll go to MexCity your way, either via Denver, Detroit, or black southbergengurabeningtonabergstienslob.

Love to all,

N.

On October 20, Diana wrote a twenty-two-page letter to Neal, expressing intense disappointment that her intended six-month stay in San Francisco was not to happen, and claiming that Carolyn was to blame. Diana expressed doubt that their "test period" in Tarrytown would be a success, since they would have to live with her mother and grandmother, and suggested moving to El Paso or Phoenix as alternatives. Meanwhile, on October 27, Neal was called to work at San Luis Obispo, some 180 miles south of San Francisco, for several weeks, lodging there with Al and Helen Hinkle.

TO DIANA HANSEN CASSADY

Oct. 30, 1950
[San Luis Obispo, California]

DEAR DIANA;

Your big letter, with the suggested alternatives to Tarrytown was a very nice intelligent healthy letter. The follow up to it, sent to 29 R., was also a beauty. Thank you. The same day I received the last letter of yours (on yellow paper) I was called by the crew clerk to deadhead from SF to SLO. He said I would be here in San Luis Obispo anywhere from a week to any number of months. At that I packed 6 socks, 4 shirts, 2 pants, toothbrush, 1 book, beauty pictures of Diana.

Here I am, sitting & sleeping on a couch that slants so badly I prop my elbows on my suitcase to prevent the shame of falling off the couch & exposing my little fleshy ass to Al and Helen Hinkle at whose residence I spend the 12–24 hours I am in SLO. I go to Watsonville & Santa Barbara on my runs & may make some good money after all, but, it's too late in the season for me to come up with any extensive pot-o'-gold.

Carolyn has a sick girl to handle. Cathy has such bad tonsils they must come out. Expensive operation; at least $100 or more. Bah!

N.

While Neal was working in San Luis Obispo, he and Carolyn exchanged letters that attempted to clarify their plans of a future together.

TO NEAL CASSADY FROM CAROLYN CASSADY

[Late October 1950
San Francisco]

DEAR NEAL;

First, know that I love you all I want in life is to be your wife & the mother of your children—but I want all that this implies. Foremost it means I want you as a husband and father—and all that this implies.

I had begun to feel that slowly we were achieving this; you said just live along & things would work out thru the living. I now realize vividly that we are not achieving this, in actuality we get farther from this and are growing increasingly distant from each other. The facts now stand that you are more unhappy than ever, yet you seem to want to create the impression that everything is ideal. Naturally such a deception, no matter how well intended, not only falls short of its aim, but is dangerous as well & thereby no help in any way as I believe you mean it to be. I cannot comprehend such action; why anyone tries to live, or look as tho he were living in a way opposed to his desires or needs. I firmly believe it is not possible to maintain. You have attempted this before; and tho you say you are incapable of any more explosions—this is not true—and this type of thinking leads to more sudden & unpredicted explosion, tho probably of a different nature. Still, such an occurrence *must* be prevented this time—or at least I must be prepared. My primary concern at present is to help you or make you find what it is that's lacking to your well-being & do anything possible to remedy it forever this time. No cost is too great. If you & I cannot work it out together, (I assume you can't alone) then you must find who or what can, or *if* it is impossible, then work out some liveable compromise. This evasion of the issue, this refusal to be serious regarding it must cease. Too much is now at stake.

My awareness of your problems comes thru the frustrations of what you tell me & what is carried out—or not—in actions. I cannot function thus. You call me wife; you say you love me, yet I cannot see the evidence & cannot act accordingly either. From the objective view I can find *no* place at all where I fit in your scheme of things—other than housekeeper. I *can* function as such, but not contentedly & I couldn't guarantee how long. Since I can offer no "or else" now, the only alternative is my ceasing to try for "wife" & to do whatever I can to further my independence. I would much prefer (see opening axiom) to work with you for your happiness, believing that mine would follow. There is some evidence to support the view that you would still choose to support me & the girls, were you "adjusted"—but even if you didn't, the price is not only worth your happiness—but as I say—no cost is too great—& it must be found. (Now, now—don't jump on the word "happiness"—I can't keep mustering a synonym.) At any rate—the present mode is out.

As to examples of my end—why I know—since you don't tell me—well, *there's* one. When you returned last summer, I felt you had matured & learned some lessons because for the first time you could talk to me "straight" and as a friend regarding your problems, which you also seemed at last willing to face & be able to admit without shame that your usual actions weren't so hot. That was one of the few ego builders you've ever given me—yet this respect is surely due a wife—you made me feel you felt I was intelligent enough to grasp your meaning—& mature enough to "understand"—perhaps even to offer a worthy suggestion. Not so since. You still have not learned that the hurt resulting from whatever your expressed feelings is nothing compared to that of learning them otherwise & to feel so little regarded as to be unworthy of sharing them or assisting with them. Besides, the pleasant results you hope to achieve by withholding them are never there either. Especially if you are unsuccessful solving them alone.

We all have love affairs, & are more or less shaken or affected deeply by persons &/or events in our lives. However, when & if we find out what we really want, those things lose their psychic significance & emotional pulls. Hence, knowing you are who I want, & a marriage with you what I want, I no longer am influenced or affected by past-occurrences—all energies are directed to the fulfilment of the requirements here involved & in *living* this chosen life. In my case it means managing a home & raising children for & with you—primarily. Other interests & activities are there & to be encouraged, but *none* of them in any way are separate entirely; none can detract, but all must add to the furthering & enhancing of the primary aims & chosen way of life—either by improving those conditions directly or by building the individual person so as to be of more value to the work as a whole.

Therefore, I do not consider you as a husband & father, or me as considered a wife or that such conditions the answers to your desires when two other women can still draw responses of influence or emotion from you as a result of past experiences with them. I realize that when you returned to me you did not profess (in the end) that this was a solution in the way it is for me; you distinctly said "I can live with anyone." However, since then you have given me the impression that you wanted me to feel that we were "married" & that that was what you wanted most (or rather, second to incidental possessions, i.e.—sax, etc.) I have said—if it is still "I can live with anyone" to you—then this is how you must act—I can find a way to live the compromise—but not the pretense.

The sex problem has suddenly struck me too. I know I fail as "wife" to you there—but know that it is because I am not considered as one otherwise. I feel sure were the other conditions corrected, I could remedy my failure there. But I saw in a shuddering flash how out of proportion this phase of your life has become! When I perused the latest addition to your library, I was really appalled—not by that alone, but the total picture. I say frankly I'm frightened of & for you again. Anyone who saturates his mind with that sort of thing so constantly is bound to come up with a pretty gruesome effect someday. Many things (& many in your own past, sexual or no) begin innocently enough or with no malice aforethought, but with such influences to work with—end disastrously—right?

I have no definite act in mind—I am only afraid & feel it highly probable that one will occur. As I've told you, I think one of your major difficulties is this whole attitude of "let it ride, it will work out." You should see by now such is rarely the case—most things must be faced & hard work is required, at least at first, to correct or overcome—& in this case as in the others—to avoid tragedy. I repeat (some more) *I* intend to do all I can to prevent—to look ahead—to anticipate, to face every danger sign I see in order to prevent any further damage to you—to me or to our children. Hence my resentment is growing toward your escape mechanisms too. I feel if you directed as much energy to correct basic causes as you do toward getting T or losing yourself in other ways—we'd all benefit & you could win. At any rate, *I* am no longer willing to by-pass or let ride—I'm satisfied I know *my* answers—so now I shall direct every effort toward yours. If you won't cooperate—then my only choice, my only "or else," is to do as I said, work toward freezing my love for you & gaining independence. But the big moves must come from *you*. (This most imp't—no paper)

TO CAROLYN CASSADY

Nov. 1, '50
[San Luis Obispo, California]

DEAR CAROLYN;

There are so many things not ever to be understood: certain specific differences between us which are really unimportant, but, which, under the stress each of our respective personalities put on our minds, cannot be reconciled emotionally. The particular flaws I present your mind with are now stretched from original vices to abstract notions of me, which, thru so many modifications are no longer true. Not true because the inner workings which have, for so long, been so dormant & weakened that for a long time now I've not held, for example, any *real* opinions & so on. But, since all individuals become, after any period of time, merely a collection of ideas about the individual which the person observing & judging who cannot have the wherewithal to keep abreast of the changes inherent in life's process cannot, then, stay objective & pushing the frontiers of imagination into understanding forms a set picture which cannot be materially altered & so becomes, in time, untrue ideas.

Love has nothing to do with it, for all processes are, by nature, intellectualizations about abstracts which are conveyed by words whose meanings are lost to the mind, but on the strength of recurring emotional reactions, the mind forms convictions which are, as it were, the basis of love's continuing although the usual convictions formed are anti-love, anti–being loved, because of perversity on the part of the heart & because the words spoken intend to convey another thing altogether, etc.

For the first time in years, I'm returning to an intellectual snobbery, altho, of course, I have no right to, being incoherent as ever &

more unable to be understood by anyone on questions of life. Perhaps this is because I'm here with Al and Helen and realize, once again, and more fully than either you or Diana can see, how essentially I am far in the lead of any one of us. This means nothing. Especially in the light of the horrible position I've gotten us all into, but still, I must be, cannot help being governed by these things I know.

No matter how difficult for everyone—no one of us really understands the real & inner terrors of the other, & cannot expect to do so—the thing has now gone so far & is now beyond the realm of ordinary problems of the mind dealing with what is "best," that, now—no matter what the urge to "decision" & belief, so foolhardy, of individual "freedom" to decide & live correspondingly, etc.,—there is, truly, nothing to be done. Nothing to be done, that is, as far as the realm of "decision" is concerned, for the next ½ year or so.

This means circumstances are now so developed that, no matter how we each suffer, there is nothing left but to go through with it (the plan). Not in any sense of "truth" am I writing; there is none actually that can be recognized, & "truth" is a matter of the understanding process *only*—read Spengler, Vol. 1,[31] near middle somewhere—& since each of us can not really understand each other—in the sense that time defeats ability to understand anew & afresh each instant—& that quality is impossible, yet is just what is needed to remain abreast of each original shift & by sifting thru comprehension allows one to see the essentials thru the trivial, not as jewels in mud, but the trivia plastering the walls of the house containing the essentials. The interest of the paperhanger is intent on his job & since he knows the tabernacle is intact & has the chalice safely inside there is only periodic checks on the limits of how he can get lost in trivia & those come in those interruptions that not attending to business consistently bring about.

Now is a period of interruption. The present is such an iron-clad pressure on the soul that being so weakened by lazy coasting, I can now do nothing but barely summon the strength to keep the process going—just as one doesn't realize how weak he's grown until he attempts to chin himself & finds instead of being able to go up & down 70 times in succession as of yore, he can do it but once, & then with such difficulty that he realizes the *best* he can now hope for is that once, but to do that once daily & so gradually regain the lost strength, at least he's truly doing his best. However, in my case no one is sure

31. *The Decline of the West* (1922), Oswald Spengler's apocalyptic interpretation of the cyclical rise and fall of civilizations.

that I ever had the "lost" strength. It's worse than that. I know the strength that was there is gone forever, *because* it was illusion. This calls for strict measures. The effort to gain peace has passed, then, into an obnoxious struggle to show people something. This I cannot do; it's not there, no matter how I attempt to manufacture. So let things be; help everyone with kindness, help them to win out, since that's what they want, but, for yourself (me) suffer your peculiar hurts in silence and hope for nothing—except to be able to not regret too much and to forget.

I've just gotten called & have to shave, eat & dress so must stop since I want to get this off.

Has Bill fixed the car? Get him to, please. I am really sorry you're stuck with Cathy—2 more weeks & maybe we can operate. I got to be there, so if I can I'll do everything to get released down here. Sheer Hell.

Love, N.

TO NEAL CASSADY FROM CAROLYN CASSADY

Sunday [November 5, 1950]
29 Russell St.,
San Francisco

DEAREST NEAL:

I'll not attempt an *answer* to your very nice letter as yet. Just a note to superimpose on the funeral dirge of the other day . . . that was a bit of play . . . play like the danse macabre . . . but allowed only in view of Bible stories etc. I was very flattered by your thoughtful long letter.

All you say is true . . . everything is true, nothing is true. Any argument of logic can be valid or invalid, etc., etc. I'm reading Vol. 1 [of Spengler's *Decline of the West*] avidly and will have more to say to *you* latah! I think you've every right to be an intellectual snob, at least I have faith in your intellect and greatness even if you are the only one who *knows* it. I don't even think it has to show . . . I think of the guy on the mountain . . . but S[pengler] says we Westerners can't be Oriental in the sense of "being" but must "become" all time. Anyway, I think your greatness would be readily accessible to all if it weren't so twisted and thwarted by your life . . . wherein in there *is* the element of "decision" and choice but only here.

I'd thought the 6 months was over long ago. At least it had not appeared to me as a problem for some time, and its original problematical nature as far as I ever saw it was only in its relation to your taking immediate and constant action to begin to clear away the rotting underbrush . . . small as well as major actions count . . . here was a place to start or to add more unnecessary thorns. All this you should know, but as you say, we've gone so far, we can hardly talk together and doubt our ability to make the most obvious statements understood. I sense that you and Diana both still think I'm perturbed about the 6 months for other reasons, even tho I told you as long ago as Santa Cruz that any choices to do with your women would take care of themselves, there was no rush, if you became uninvolved with yourself first, become satisfied with your own actions, "decide" how best to live with yourself and not let others dictate, even me. Yet I suppose you both think it's simply that I want to "win" you, take you away from her, get you back, or foil her plans somehow and the other things I'm continually accused of. But it's my own doing too, for the sloppy way I make myself known and the petty emotional behavior clouds the purer motives. So to hell with it . . . it is of no consequence anyway.

As far as you and me . . . I too think there are just too many conditioned responses et al to ever alter the present relationship significantly. But who cares about that! The only important thing in the whole web is you. I wish you could be completely selfish not just half-assed so, then polite. You won't make it doing as you propose . . . or at least not for awhile, but no other way is possible perhaps for the next 6 months except in little ways and by taking care that way.

As for me alone . . . that is apparently the best way. I feel great and jubilant. I can be that and purely objective (or very nearly so) if treated fairly. I don't want to bother you in any way except from however I can be of help to you (not used for evil gain) at your request from now on. I KNOW I don't want anything from you, I don't NEED you, I can't get emotional about it any more unless you force it; I refuse to suffer in any event over it further. Don't use your "kind" ideas on *me*. If you're interested in helping me "win out," the *only* way you can do so is by respecting me as a friend whenever contact is necessary or desirable. I am no keeper of your conscience or thoughts, I don't think I should know anything you don't want me to, unless it involves some contradiction of action expected of me from other presuppositions. If you ever want to forget the whole thing . . . PLEASE do so and with no apologies. I won't be "hurt" nor pester or "blame" you. It's like the facial tension . . . "don't smile if you don't feel it," so I say, don't be dutiful or kind NO MORE!

When you are away and when you write as you did, I am left with the feeling only of pride to have been a Mrs. Cassady, even such a one, to have been accepted briefly for whatever reason, and to have two precious lives as a result. You have not destroyed me and you have given me many a priceless treasure. I know this positively when I've spent evenings with these "mature" people who are still on a college level and the only requisite of one is to be "clever" with the small small talk. I have lots of "fun," but I love you or the remembrances with a great joy and pride, asking nothing further than to have known you. This is the way it *must* remain, and I shall do everything in *my* power to see that it does.

It was sweet of you to feel you'd left us in the lurch; I appreciate the thought. But don't feel badly. Cathy and I are making it fine since I stopped worrying about it. Whenever advisable I take her for walks and we're teaching the puppy too. The noses still drip altho $6 worth of sulpha has been so far administered. The Dr. is a bit unhappy about the length of time. She'll have her operation as soon as the cold goes. No further word from Bill . . . I'll call again if nothing soon.

I feel for you where you are. If *you* would rather be here then I hope you can make it. Just know that all is well here, no problems, no complaints to be taken for "blame," it's all set and solved. Please check this party off your list. Of anxieties that is, otherwise if you wish, not if you don't.

If your strength was an illusion as you say, I believe you'd have been in some institution with the incurable fire bugs or the like long since. I have faith that you have much strength and it will win out . . . otherwise . . . the danse macabre. It's all yours to find a way. Just prove it to *yourself*.

You allow misunderstanding thru obscurity, whether intentional or not. Also by keeping your hurts to yourself, which is what you've always done as far as I know, you can't accuse others of not understanding, when you don't even try to be understood. This all . . . if it matters to you . . . but don't feel so badly about it, if you do, is all I'm saying. One has to try and hurt you just to see what does, if you won't tell. Here's your transparent mind you spoke of . . . who's ta know?

Anyhow, to hell with other people for awhile, eh? Inside—don't be blue . . .

Love from CAROLYN, CATHY AND CÉLINE CASSADY

High on marijuana, Neal wrote a rambling thirty-six-page letter to Kerouac.

TO JACK KEROUAC

Nov. 5, '50
[San Luis Obispo, California]

DEAR BUDDY,

Did I have a dream last night? Yess, O yes!

This dream after masturbating 6 times straight. Not unusually hard to do nowadays.

I shan't, can't describe it. No need to anyhow for only one; no, two emotions stand out.

I discovered I love LuAnne but bigger and stronger; I passed into another world; really another—all colored in shades of black & so perfect a bliss I passed out further than ever—when at last I made her come with such sweet red skin did her inner cunt kiss, no suck my whole face, except for top forehead & tips of ears as I slid headup into my hole. Such a perfect gem. But enuf—don't think I don't dream gone sex dreams, & otherwise nightly—it's just that this beautiful dream left such emotion for so long I got horribly sick at heart—it just made me sick.

Had to whittle down pencil with damn ole bread knife. Don't think I'm not hi, can't even form letters to words & no control over way fingers press to guide. I am hi on *real* last residue of fine powered mist of dust left of 6ozs before first manicure, remember? in Mex City A.M. before I left you.

This Dusty[32] & the other girl Madrene[33] or something, both from Lusk WYO are well known by Bill Tomson & Al Hinkle et al, small world, ain't it? Bill had big false story for me about them (or boyfriend) when I hit Denver last.

Then, of course, there's a good chance I may not get to NY before March 1st or more likely May 1st (at latest)—it depends on job or maybe me, anyhow, when I wrote I was about set for NY, but Diana wrote with alternate suggestions because of money etc. so now set for

32. Dusty Moreland, a young painter from Wyoming, was one of Allen Ginsberg's first girlfriends in New York, in the autumn of 1950. She's the Josephine of *Visions of Cody, Desolation Angels,* and *Book of Dreams,* and the Arlene Wohlstetter of *The Subterraneans.*

33. Mardean, one of Kerouac's girlfriends, is the Nardine of *Visions of Cody.*

El Paso until March & Phoenix maybe until May. But, when I read your letter I gotta go to NY in January as I said, but so cold to work there if I could find job & *gotta* work, Carolyn & kids & Di & kid need money so badly can't stop work.

So you write about how to live, so see enclosed advice from Carolyn on how I should.[34] But wait, since for first time I'm bothering to enclose words of another, I'll send it to Diana instead. Honest Jack, I'm so hi—listen; when I began this page I thought I was writing to Diana altho my mind also was aware it was you to whom I was writing yet *trying* to think of something to say in the vein of trivia & not to miss anything that came to mind. I wrote what I intend for Di to you. Clear?

Each page different. What about Cannastra? Is he dead? *Where* is he? Allen says "end of an era" so tempting a proclamation at once would present itself to mind if Cannastra killed himself. It would be suspect just because it does seem so appropriate an epitaph.

God save the King.
Who has his art?
" " " soul?
" " " cock?
" " " cunt?
" " " money?
" " " ".

Yes indeed, will push beyond Mex City, beyond end of panamerican pavement at Guatemala onto dirt panam hiway until end of Highway in Panama or so,
then Indian heat &
" " cunt "
" " heads "
" " & so on.

in 52 or 53 I'll bring new auto trailer home to match new Chev. station wagon & live in trailer around country as I "boom"[35] from one RR job to another & yearly Diana & me you & cunt will go to *Peru* where her folks live (rich) & we'll dig Indians gone on coca leaves.

You gotta find me a flute, I aint got one & need one made of wood not plastic or tin. Woodwind. On May first we leave NY go to Key West & cross water to Cuba etc & then back to car & on to Burroughs

34. Carolyn's letter to Neal of late October.
35. *Boom:* to travel around the country to other railroads in the hope that they need labor.

& Central America & man let me tell you the greatest, yes O yes, I been absolutely killed reading Oswald Spengler Vol 1 & 2 of Decline hi. I been so hi that when I dig his Indian classical Faustian & Magian soul & their culture & relationship & cities & philosophy & etc., etc. & law & etc. I'm stoned, & besides Spengler reread Céline, dug him in different way, he's so down, French & not as really hip as you & me. Of course, I can't put a word together like him. Damnit.

You writing so fine to me, it affects me & I get sloppy & don't give a damn 'cause I know you know & so I allow myself to just put down any old thing in any old way & soon I get so abstract in mind & try to counteract it by simple thoughts, repetitious & lazy, that my letters are tripe or abalone; unless they are swordfish playing leapfrog with sailfishes in your all contradburgerfriedyesterbumstieving.

I'll blow that flute until it falls from my fingers thru sweat & hot breath.

My recorder is complete. What a gem! Oh hum. Fine life.

No, I get my mind properly out of gear & reread your letter, it was your advice about living to defeat death that brought to mind my unconscious act on page 5; Carolyn wrote of death & dire predictions of mine & why I tried to help in her way & so altho so different I brought them together 'cause I got your letter & hers at same moment & so on. We'll go to Lowell, so as I get there. Can't wait.

On to Nov. 5 P.M.

I'm not hi, not low; just waiting, actually I've been just waiting since I got back to the RR July 15th. I've been in San Luis Obispo for 10 days now & will be here at least 5 days more, then back to SF until cut-off time. Continue to write me at 29 Russell. Rereading Karamazov[36] again. How in hell can he keep on the subject so long. God damn what funny scenes! I laugh like a sonofabitch at some of them; one where Mitya is going wild & rushing over the whole countryside trying to find a certain realtor & a drunk forester hangs him up for 2 days by getting drunk & incoherent just at the wrong time, 3 times.

Hinkle can sit for days & not get up except for RR work. I'm the same way now, just sit, can't write or read for long etc. but, it's not half as bad as it was so don't worry about me none old pal.

36. Fyodor Dostoyevsky's novel *The Brothers Karamazov*.

This picture is one of the mind that America can't fathom; just what do these Indians think & feel as they walk all day loaded with heavy gear up & down 18,000 ft. mountains not eating nor having to because they are hi—get it—hi on cocoa leaves that give strength & hallucinations to body & mind. What's their kick?

Talking of Koreans—see everything you write now to me is just as I said in my last letter—the same things I'm doing. The only show I've seen since last we met had a couple minutes of Korean pictures as they were "liberated" when US crossed the 38th parallel[37] & one shot seen for less than 10 seconds showed a celebration dance & the characters! One guy I just caught a glimpse of—gone hi—out of this world—in a trance as his limp body jolted about, eyes closed & disjointed mannikin steps. Where was he? Where are we? I just dig the other side of the Peru Indian picture damn good too.

Moby Dick is here too.

Have you got a conga drum? Buy one & a flute for me (or find where a flute can be bought).

I dig what you mean about Reanna (she's same girl Allen raved about NY eve). I dug her. I was hi & she was *nice* to me instead of being antagonistic as per most cunts, & she looks fine, what tits & slim body. I bet her cunt is juicy & ripe, huh?

You lucky dog, I ain't had a fuck in ages & no new girl (except whores) since 1945. In fact, pal, if you love me, you'll do all in your power to find a girl, any girl (like 'em skinny) (for fuckin' that is, you see, skinny girls are all *cunt*) & tell her I can fuck all night & blow them till their belly falls out & get their cunt inside out so I can fuck them to the real bottom, not that I can't anyhow, with a little cooperation, but get a cunt & your cunt & us'll have a *real* orgy unless you want to go "lonely fucker." I am expected in NY in Jan, March or May, unless long prongs are no longer acceptable.

The beginning of my book is: "For a long time I held a unique position," etc., etc.[38] I really go into it a bit more than usual—the token fatherhood of bums on Larimer & me as their unnatural son, etc.

Music is the only thing good that's not dependent on the eyeball. What a nice thought to make one unafraid of eyeball-falling. I have

37. In Korea, U.N. forces crossed the thirty-eighth parallel dividing the north and south of the country on October 9.

38. This is the beginning of chapter 1 of Neal's autobiography, published as *The First Third* in 1971.

other means of retaining patience with my body & its demands. I can think of no better than a cunt tho, I love a pure & sweet cunt, one whose power is such as to prevent the owner of same from falling into any mistaken idea about what it's for. A cunt that makes the girl & thus creates a woman to take my cock everywhicholeway.

I've got much more sense than anything I do indicates—just as in your case, Jack—But when it comes to letters I show up most badly.

How does one *meet* a girl? I got no troubles once I get alone with them. To get into position to fuck by all the simple sensations that make my heart beat so rapidly that I sometimes fear I'll faint; not now but soon, in a few years, when I get a girl.

Listen to this—Most Important:

I met my true love *twice*! One girl then another—one by eye & one by ear. Agnes Millar & LuAnne Bullard Henderson Cassady Murphy.

On March 31st, '48, I got accepted by SPRR to make a date and start my seniority going. Al Hinkle & I got on a streetcar on Geary Blvd. in SF to go to SP depot & go to Watsonville on April 7th, *1948*. As we rode down Geary & passed Van Ness & approached the true tenderloin of SF I looked out the window avidly searching for any pretty skirt to feast my eyes & remember for that night alone in Watsonville dorm bed & knowing I would *see* no girl for weeks. The streetcar was at top speed in mid-block when my glance took in a redhead that looked—was!!!—my old flame from Denver of '43—Agnes Millar, a true love, a whore like LuAnne, but *more*—things you don't know, Jack, things only I remember & feel. But by the time I reached the next corner I was sure it wasn't Agnes but simply a similar looker & a wish look on my part, so instead of jumping off & catching her, I continued streetcar ride.

Was late for train ("short time") & also not to spend dime, etc. I *let her go*. But in next 6 weeks of lonely Watsonville hell—had many similar hard-life Watsonville weeks since—I thought of Agnes & all she had meant to me, etc. To continue:

On Oct 13 (Friday) 1950, 2½ years later, I went downtown to buy necessary RR hat. On way home, since I had just blasted & was really gone digging SF & people, I stopped in drug store to indulge in soft drink on that hot day. I sat perhaps 2 & ¾ minutes anticipating large coke I had ordered to remember summer of 47 & Burroughs & Huncke, et al, in Texas & 1 case a day of coke—drank by us, I look down counter to dig any women & *look*—Agnes Millar!! my love, LuAnne's sole predecessor. But keeping cool I compose my features consciously while my mind races—"It's Agnes Millar, it's Agnes Millar!" Then I look closely & see her dyed hair & see at once she's a *real* whore now.

She sees me—"Why, Neal! Come over & say 'hello.'" I'm all smiles, but hi, understand Jack, Hi, & with this suddenly can't speak, even harder too than usually is the case. I stumble to a stool beside her, I sense she's known in this drug store so near the whore hotels & where I'd seen her in '48; so I try & underplay to suit her unexpressed wish. My heart!! It won't stop pounding!!

I think of death & how one wants to explode all his soul out thru his cock into these lovely creatures & how they make you do it, but, still you can't get started. She asks what you're doing now, as casually as tho you'd met just yesterday & you are thinking of the *terrific* orgies you & her had had, her tears & cocksucking!! You're conscious of your ugly unshaven pimply face & the new weird Harley sunglass hat & instead of impressing, as it seems she needs to be impressed, you catch yourself saying over & over until you don't know how many times you said it or when you began saying it, after you sat beside her & as she finished her drink:

"I'm so glad to see you!!!"

" " " " " , "

" " " " " " etc.

& as she ups & leaves, she just smiles & promises to call on Friday next & refuses to see the agony in your eyeballs.

So, altho I lived in a gone bachelor apt. last month alone & had Ekotape & tea & wanted her so, she never came or called or anything & daily when I came in from RR I'd sit & wait for phone to ring or door to knock & so never saw her again & realized again about the girl—What a fuck she was, wooee! & how I truly loved her in '43 while I was in jail & it was to see her that I gained courage to make that glorious escape that only 4 before me had accomplished & in face of the tortures of those caught, so I knew I loved her. I dashed to Denver; I had left her loving me so wholly that I'd felt so guilty of leaving her crying as I went to Calif. earlier that I advised her to marry & forget me—a line not usually spoken by me.

But when I returned after escape & waited hours outside her restaurant (waitress) & saw her figure & knew the dreams I'd had in prison wherein I got Agnes & we found a shack alone on the sea & never stopped fucking, etc. What dreams, asleep & awake—could still come true!

I rushed to her as she exited the cafe. She played with me as a cat will a mouse, only not so maliciously; she was, I noticed at once, a bit broader of beam & when I touched her it was not as in my recent dreams & not so absolutely passionate as before, but I attributed this to the fact we had only been together a half hour or so & were still self-conscious as we walked from her cafe to (strangely) my old schoolhouse at 23rd & Fremont (grammar).

At last she said "Aren't you going to hold me?" I started to & just then the cops drove by the bushes & flashing light said, "move along there" & so we walked clear across town to another spot I knew & Jack, I confessed to her my dreams; I gathered her into an imaginary world of us & the future of fucking & life spent one for the other in bed & pure.

We had a quickie; I didn't come & was only telling of the future where there was better *bed* fucks & us living contentedly as we walked slowly across town again to her home. 3 blocks from 30th & Downing St. she told me! She had just done what I'd said & was in love with me & so sorry she had believed what I'd advised was the thing to do. Yes, she had *married* while I was gone—a sailor.

What emotion as I staggered to the nearby steps of the Negro Holy-Roller church, deserted at this hour—I *almost* cried. Anyhow, I had the weirdest relationship—simply gone—with her the next 3 or 4 yrs. always unexpected & *really* strange. So strong & genuine an emotion I felt, these three or 4 separate & distinct crazy gone periods we had & I won't tell them & *look*! yet, yet, she is here in SF & alive to me & never will I see her again. Oh, Love!

When I realized this after weeks of waiting, on Oct. 25th I turned, once again, to LuAnne. Remember Jack, I hadn't seen her since May 31st at 5 P.M. in 1949. So I was, at last, going to call her. After almost 18 months of daily knowledge of her I was to phone her number; I'd known it for weeks (in SF Phone Book—R.T. Murphy—428 Stanyan St.) I dialed & it rang! A voice I knew was her: "Hello!"

I stammered out the exact months, weeks, days & hours since I'd seen her & said I felt I had the right, because of the past, to once again hear her voice. "Yes, I'd known she was 7 months pregnant." "Yes, she had known I was married again." Then she began a detailed description of how difficult to get her & Murphy's marriage confirmed in the Catholic church 'cause they had trouble finding *any* Baptism or Confirmation papers in Denver. She asked if she should confirm their marriage. I told her to do so. Asking of all of us, she made my cock hard, sitting there as I thought of her mouth & what it could do. I spoke of Jeffries; she casually *dis*-remembered him. She then asked if I'd called before; *someone* was always calling her. Surely, I thought, she can handle all the cocks that punch at her, then I got so heartsick I let her beg off meeting me & so lost her again, as I had done last on May 31, '49.

What is there to say? I'll tell you. I am going to write a book, yessir, before I die & before I lose anything else, i.e. mind, cock, cunt, etc.

So until you & me get together to kill old NY by us knocking out ourselves on it, just by using the eye & hand, I don't want any foolish nonsense falling from my sloppy lips anymore. I know to have a cunt to love & suck, one that is so perfect you can't resist raising your tired body above it to spend all the pure feeling you've left into the hole that matters. Of course, any girl has it; just to get my hands on one & spread my filthy fingers all over the body so's I'll know it forever.

Love, N.

TO DIANA HANSEN CASSADY

Nov. 7, 1950
[San Luis Obispo, California]

DEAR DIANA;

I am casting a vote for that man of iron will & sterling character, that champion of coxmen & great sucker of cute little pink skinned juicy black-haired cuntwomen. Yessir, I nominate myself to the post of honorary "best man" who will not, would not, could not, & should not be underestimated anymore. I've played my last "Bullshit" role. Barrymore & myself, I always say. I've been pretending deafness & other mis-functions on myself for so long that, once again, I've decided to pull up by the old bootstraps for awhile. I usually do this every 5 yrs or so by doing the following:

1. Stop smoking; 2. Masturbating; 3. Other excesses; 4. Drinking; etc. Character is the way of the pig. This, of course, is not a silly sticking to vow. I'll smoke a little when I feel I don't need it & same for other excesses. Masturbating is a bit different; I get so hot I can hardly sit still & when that happens I gotta, 'cause I ain't got no girl. All this is just a little way of keeping on the ground & is used in despair & yet, discretion—something to play with.

Enclosed please find recent letter from Carolyn. Gives you an idea of how things are laid out in her mind. After I answered her "funeral dirge" with the points that even you don't know, Di,

(Spengler & logic & truth etc.) she promptly wrote letter number 2 the "good one" enclosed here also.[39] Keep letters, at least number 2 because I have seldom received such a clear allowance to "do as I want" from her. You need not write to her about anything anymore it seems, she's in pretty good shape too. Thank the Lord & on to Di!

I really don't know what's happening. I shouldn't go back to SF 'cause there's about $200 a half month here & only about $125 or so there. On the other hand Helen & Al want to kick me out. Helen hasn't enuf to do here so bitches she is never alone with Al, altho he & I are never here together—he's on road or I am, & hates me & bitches 'cause I don't buy all the food etc. Al has no backbone & just whispers that she gives him a bad time because of me & so, fuck 'em. If I stay here in SLO to work where money is I'll have to now put out $1 a day for another room & at least 1, 2 or $3 a day for eats, so where do I gain? Besides, am beside myself down here & can't get untracked concerning anything. Of course, I'm always hung up, but it seems harder here 'cause of no cunt, etc. Who was it that said "an educated person is one who can sit in a room and not perish"? I am slowly getting my education together—i.e. I am going to live up to my ego & my opinions. If you'll notice I've allowed myself to fall into a system of unopinionated "oh well" nonsense, but here, living with Al & Helen, I realize more strongly than ever the stupid life of U.S.A. people & literature.

You've got your intelligence & I got mine & I think, with your wonderful attitude & understanding, even after the horrors I put you thru for no reason at all—you didn't do anything wrong; you were always so good to me, I was just unable to get straight for you, and still am anyhow. I think we are OK in the head 'cause you're not hung up on so many sheer intellectual stupidities as most, & won't force your own truths, "psychology," on me unnecessarily & I won't make you feel any emotional "visions" that are not necessary for an understanding between us about "how we made"—as people of horseshit.

Helen asks "Is it in the North or where, that there's long days, or is it nights, huh Al?" & Al is just smart enuf to know & then Helen hears corny Turkish music Americanized & comments about the guy at the 7 Seas who has a Chinese veil dance & Al corrects her that it's really a Tibetan, Burmese-like dance, etc., etc., & that's their level. I can't mind it because I know all that so well I hardly listen, but, when

39. Carolyn's letters to Neal of late October and November 5.

I gotta have their presumptuous optimism of me manifested in snide little remarks & horseshit antics, I give up.

Every page different—almost. Election night in the U.S.A. I sit here, about to be called to RR, & listen to all the tense voices giving returns that, actually, mean nothing. Republican, Democrat, bah, the only difference is whether the particular man is poor or terrible. Our System is set & so damn ingrained with stupid ideas—war monger on foreign policy & help the nab with money on the home front—look at SP: it controls the whole damn state in regards transportation & is fucking us brakemen at every turn & the damn politicians don't do a thing & refuse all our poor union's restrictions.

Alternative plan: so I can be with you sooner & still elude weather a bit and avoid getting mired for a long stretch in poor NY job: I try NWP. Don't get it, then "boom" South & get money in a week or two weeks around L.A. train, El Paso or parts of Tyler. After big bundle of quick money, be in NY in late Jan. at latest. Work in TT & be with you until March when you use train pass to go to SF and 239D while I go to Phoenix & get in 6 weeks of Big Money & then South & then SF & you in May. You'd be alone for about 2 months & could settle yourself to what you want & how best to get it & so on. This is only to be considered because of big $$$.

I'm borrowing $2 off Al to last (that's all he has 'cause bitch Helen who knew I needed money, refused to draw enuf from bank) & to see us thru until payday in 48 hrs. I can't make it if I'm called to go East so damn her hide, the peasant. I have got all debts paid when I give Carolyn $150 out of this check for month of Dec., & for buying car for me. On Nov 15 I'll have enuf made to pay for all expenses in car & so, except for living expenses, I shall, at last, be caught up & in the clear until Jan 1st '51. Except for Cathy's operation & any money I send you—whatever you need. I didn't tell C. I sent you 60 a month. What bullshit; I love both of you for it.

Listen, I really know how wonderfully you're standing up under the pressure of waiting for terrifying birth. I wish I were there with you, at last. I'll try to show you how much I've been missing your big body & what I intend to do to you will be so violent that you'd better soundproof our bedroom or send the folks to a show—or we'll give them one.

Are you sure you want me? I don't want you to need someone so badly that you're just fooling yourself that "I'm the one." I want you to feel free as hell & I'll help you anyway I can. If you find I've destroyed your love by my awful blundering & you can't feel it again as you once did, then it's up to me to make you again in such a way as to remove your doubts. Unless I find that too hard & just fuck you good & long & hard.

You had better have a big baby & sit back & nurse it fine with those big beautiful tits of yours until I get there & push "it" over to get ahold of them myself. We'll have regular hours for each of us, I demand first choice & of course, first claim to the rest of you.

I just read "1984" by that damn Englishman[40] who follows in the footsteps of all the others who are hung up on that kick, Wells[41] & Huxley,[42] etc. They are the only guys who get their gun that way & it's better than other ways I know. I liked "1984" better than the reviews—which don't matter a damn in any case. Had more than think it would.

I'm listening to radio program of '20s music & sure digging you fine. You know, you're a weirdie. I've just thought of some of the things you've done & said & think & you're a real weirdie, but such a one that I've got sowed to, that whenever I see cats—I ran over one in a gig Diesel engine pulling 100 cars last trip—or see little girls, daily—or see anything or feel any emotion that even indirectly reminds me of you, I realize I've developed a real affection, in a perverse way perhaps, & I'm sure you're a lovely cunt that I respect more and more. So when that kid finally pops out I'll get him all the beer he can drink & all the girls he likes. If it's a girl I'll restrain myself from any indecent overtures 'cause she'll be so pretty I'm sure.

In other words I'm not worried if it's a boy—despite you & Ma & G'Ma's influence—'cause I feel any boy of mine would be a bum anyhow & so if he's a fag it'd at least be different & perhaps an improvement. A girl worries me 'cause I'd have to spend 21 yrs keeping my hands off her & I have no feeling for females except sexual ones & I'm afraid I couldn't bring her around in a healthy enuf way. A Canadian father arrested for fucking etc. all 7 of his girls, daughters from age 12 to 21—they testified he beat them & made each sleep

40. *1984* by George Orwell (1903–1950), a political satire published in 1949.

41. Herbert George Wells (1866–1946), an English novelist best remembered for his scientific romances including *The Time Machine* (1895) and *The War of the Worlds* (1898).

42. Aldous Huxley (1894–1963), author of *Brave New World* (1923), whose experiments with mescaline and LSD were described in *The Doors of Perception* (1954) and *Heaven and Hell* (1956).

with him in rotation & together after & before mother died, of being over-fucked, I'm sure.

Actually I don't care for my own daughters & so I guess won't any other girls I have, but, when they are older? This shows how hard up I am nowadays, my tail's bothering me & all I think about are girls' cunts. A fine thing to write you while you're about to suffer the agonies of a woman doomed & at this time, if any, I should be all consideration, says the books, so here goes:

I really want your precious womb product & it'll be in a class all its own 'cause they grow 'em different in the East, I hear. I'm sure if it's a boy he'll be OK no matter what, & if a girl—girls don't starve, dig Lorelei Lee,—so don't worry, sweet. U.S.A. is all for mothers.

There are so many things I would love to write to you, to talk to you about, just now, after 2 hours of battling for sleep & trying not to think because each idea brought out my weaknesses so clearly. I got called to go West & turned on radio for gone classical music & other things—anyway must rush now. All I can say is I feel so remorseful I'm not with you in your crisis when you need me most & the pangs of guilt penetrate my selfishness. I love you. You're not the only poor fish in this ocean! I got company too in my misery. We're all up the creek together; small consolation I'm sure. Tell Ma, G'Ma & Robert love. Slowly, but so sure, the waning flesh overrides the best in us & soon that's all we have—& memories. Till Death.

Love, N.

On November 7, Diana's baby, which had been expected since late October, finally arrived. Called Neal Jr. at first, he was eventually named Curtis Neal.

TO DIANA HANSEN CASSADY

A.M., Nov. 13, 1950
[San Luis Obispo, California]

DEAR DIANA; MOTHER & PUSSYCAT,

What a fine mess! You send me note of Nov. 6, 3:15 A.M. telling of water & hospital. I don't want to miss telegram so stay here in SLO to get word. I return from trip to Santa Barbara on Nov. 11th late in P.M. & here's letter from Carolyn, been here since night after I went on trip Nov. 9th. In it is your letter describing little Neal. Why did you send it to 29 R.? & where is telegram? I stayed here in SLO for 5 days unnecessarily & didn't hear a word from your Nov. 6 note until late Saturday. I went to town to send you telegram in hospital & couldn't find open telegraph office & was on short call & was all hung up, so rushed to train & just *now* is first chance I have to write you. I'm sorry I didn't get word in time for hospital note, so you'll get this at home with N. How is he? How are you? I know how long 30 hours can be & I only hope you didn't suffer too much & are recovering nicely. There's not much else one can say about childbirth, it's just one of those things no one but women feel & even they forget the pain soon & when it comes time for another they are really unable to recall the sensation as it was (American Medical Journal circa 1949) & so do it all over again, etc. Well, at last it's over & your belly is empty & you can relax once again. I do much wish I had done something to make it easier for you, but it's too late for that & so will try to help the kid right from the start.

Enclosed find picture of your puppets, small world & few Japanese, I guess. I'm returning to SF tomorrow, so write to me at 29 R again.

On the fatal day I knew everything with my infallible intuition. I knew Warren,[43] etc., would win, I knew you were having kid, but placed it in A.M. instead of P.M.; I knew the horrible letter I was writing, that I carefully headed November 7th & spoke of Nov. 7 in, was a thing I feel shame for, a really awful letter, full of just the things that shouldn't be there, etc. I knew as I wrote you would not want that type of trash on the same day as your son's birth & oh yes, I knew absolutely it was a boy, so wrote some ideas I had in letter about boys. I apologize for letter & I am sorry if talk of girls' cunts bothered you; if it didn't then forget all this & I'll stop worrying about my thoughts.

How's the family taking the blow of the little bastard? Tell them I've no respect for him, and call him bastard just to try & get a raise out of them, goad 'em a little for kicks & see what reaction you get from such minor shockers. Pastime. Let us hope they aren't suffering as much as Carolyn from the birth. A boy! Ugh! She had sworn that it was really the end if you came up with a male & so I enclose little note she enclosed in letter she sent to me at 29 R, talking of birth. Your triumph is well deserved considering your suffering.

43. Earl Warren, governor of California, won reelection on November 7.

Nov. 13, '50 P.M.

Enroute to SF on slow train with 2 sheets of paper & no cigarettes; but book tho. One takes care of little boys by feeding them, *leaving them alone* when awake & letting them sleep as long as possible. When you feed him love & hold him & at other times, like diaper changing, love him, otherwise, leave him alone & don't love him just to be doing so & you'll find out when he's older he'll be much less of a problem to handle. i.e. Cathy was always fondled & is a problem, Jamie was never held & is a doll. Let's hope he doesn't get colic, but I'll probably be there to help soothe him by the time he may contract it. Find out from Doc. how to best handle wetting problems of boys.

I left SLO just before Mon. mail delivery so probably had letter or two from you & missed it. Helen will forward, but mailman is once a day and so delay. I know mother must be fed up with giving you money, so since, at least, I'll be clear on Nov. 26 check, will send you some then. You pay mother what you owe her, if she demands it, & altho, of course, you won't need much & will go slow on it, don't feel you're broke anymore & thereby escape fret over money & let me worry about it. I've got many things to do in SF & so will be definitely busy with RR & Hospital & teeth & long days working on car, & fixing sandbox & backyard for Cathy & all the time trying to write a novel—it begins: "For a long time I held a unique position" etc., as it tells of bums and their token fatherhood to me, etc.

When I get cut-off I get RR pass for you and see about NWP or other RR work near SF, then try Western Division, L.A. Div., Tucson Div., Bakersfield Div., Rio Grande Div., card end North line, Tucson card (doubtful, too cold, that's why I eliminate sure jobs in Portland, Salt Lake, & 800 to 1100 a month in Alaska), El Paso, T. & N.O. from there to New Orleans—anywhere in Texas, then Florida East Coast lines (game job, great I hear), Seaboard, Atlantic, or Southern, & then NY & NYC, out of Tarrytown. Now listen, I'm determined never to work at anything but RR so, despite the weather I'm working on closest RR job near Tarrytown & so I advise in Jan., or so, when I arrive we contact Davenport if necessary (I doubt if winter is busy time in East, summer in West). So I can work on highest paying run available near TT, on best available RR I'll boom across country as fast as possible. It's raining here badly & I know it'll slow up business & I'll make poor money in last 30 days (which I'm in) & may cause sooner cut-off. Ah, well, will see you and Neal that much sooner. I'm not sure about Neal, too late of course, but should have named him John (after Jack) Allen (after Allen). I knew you'd clear 7 lbs handily, he'll lose a few ounces at first, tho. Are there any small abnormalities? besides pointed ears, etc. you mentioned. Be damn thankful he's not in bad shape. I just saw a pitiful little 5 or 6 yr old girl with ugly forearms, about 4 inches long & badly bowed legs altogether horrible as I was walking to depot to board train.

Last page, no more paper dammit. Had 4 separate train wrecks I was on, all small variety except one that tied up RR for 16 hours. I was not at fault in any of them & enjoyed it. Little girl of 5 on this one coach local to SF singing "Moonlight Bay" unselfconsciously. All adults so solemnly silent & stare at each other while refrain after refrain of songs in childish style fills coach, then, after tension is sensed they talk to each other more freely & their self-consciousness passes away & patronizing small pinched smiles change to gentle grins. Passing camp Roberts I see large segment of men drilling, target shooting etc. in this heavy rain. Ugh! Just think of what they are doing & why & the type of man that goes for war & those that don't etc., etc. (I know type who make soldier & no one else does. It's not the class of men one realizes except abstractly & so no one's got the clue but me and the men themselves, who, strangely know they are it, but only individually & not collectively). Wish I could write of things to make you happy—all I say is—Love.

Love,

N.

Returning from San Luis Obispo and settling back with Carolyn in San Francisco, Neal typed Allen Ginsberg an eight-page letter detailing some events during his train journey from New York back to California the previous July. He also mentioned completing the three-part prologue to his autobiography, eventually published as The First Third, *but confessed that his tape recorder had not assisted his writing.*

TO ALLEN GINSBERG

Nov. 15, '50
29 Russell Street
San Francisco

DEAR ALLEN;

I would have written much sooner, but I've been in San Luis Obispo for some weeks and had no facilities.

There's not much that I can say, altho there are more things in my mind than ever. Since I can't think of any particulars that are simple enough for me to make clear, I'll just ramble.

When I left NY, so long ago, I got on a streamliner of the Pennsy that was crowded as hell. I didn't want to get hungup looking for my car so asked a young semi-hipster who seemed in the same difficulty. We joined forces informally and managed to get settled side by side in a car that was going thru to St. Louis. I went to the head and blasted after going under the Hudson. I came back to my seat in that peculiar way that I've developed whenever I've got to traverse a distance under the eyes of others. The heightened sensibility that one experiences after a good bomber is so delightful that it is absolutely imperative for one to really take it slow. The actual process of placing the feet, swinging the arms and otherwise maintaining balance so as to float thru a crowded RR car was my concern. I slid into my seat without the usual sign of recognition to this sharpie beside me. It's not only a flying mind that's the characteristic of fine t; the whole body responds without restraint if given the command, however, if one "goes," the big exertion—eventually—eliminates that type of kick. Again too, the opportunity to "go" seldom presents itself often in the manner one wishes; fuck and blow. So, one takes advantage of available kicks and makes the most of them—without regret. I decided, after a short 10 minutes of musing on what I was leaving and the trip and future, to allow myself to dig this guy.

He had been straining at the bit anyhow, a young blood without relaxation; one who had never heard of tensions. By God tho, he sure had plenty of other points of interest about which to have opinions. Never, in recent years, had I so consciously drawn out and controlled a piece of talk. Not that this poor fool was not unbridled, that was just the flaw; how he could spout horseshit. Worse, his catalogue of trash was encyclopedic. Now being hi, this huge dose of stupidity was doubly obnoxious; but, I had vowed patience. The length of the trip was designed to be the nemesis of any such firm resolve and defeated my tolerance. Of course, at once I was sorry I'd opened the gates for such a flow. One doesn't mind anything another says, no matter how poorly put together, if the words imply that "tick" that all of us are tuned to—Dig that colored cat in Fitzgerald's Poughkeepsie; the one with the gospel. It all began casually enuf, murders he'd seen, taken part in; cops he'd helped waylay; toughies (Brooklyn style—it all took place there, under the shadow of the great bridges) he'd known; gang-fights etc. From this collection of James Cagney (he even looked like him) ideas, we passed on, with me still able to get in an agreeing word or two, to the broader fields. To him, this was Science. We all know about that (I have happened to further rehash this field and am in possession of all the facts, any specific you might worry over, consult me) but, I was more than generous in giving full allowance for his youth (20, I guess) and mind and was prepared to hear everything I'd heard many times and not cringe or puke and just dig all the world thru him and the rest of the car as I listened to the drone. The possibilities of imagery when one has decided to open up the mind completely are without number. I have perfected this technique to the point of art. The one thing I've accomplished these last years. Naturally, crushed to the plush of a RR car, surrounded by the Fellaheen, I surrender with more grace, wit and pure self-knowledge; I had blasted again by now.

From his fascinating thesis on the great wonders of science and his wholehearted support of its value, he carried over into our next subject the self-confident enthusiasm this one had kindled. Yessir, by golly, no stopping him now. While he'd been shooting off his mouth about the way things are to him, the student of holy science, so loudly the rest of the car had fallen into embarrassed silence and even old women without a grain of brain had sensed his foolish statements (he knew no facts even, not the simplest second-hand "Popular Mechanic" or Public School texts) I had been evolving a little plan which I liked the more as I mulled it over. It was in self-defense; every man for himself now, and I needed sleep. Carefully, to prevent any premature oration too far afield, I mentioned books. This warmed his ego like nothing else I could have brought up would. He was about to reach out and hug me he was so happy. His eyes sparkled, one could feel his brain pulsating orgasms of ecstasy, I had hit his subject. He caught his breath, literally restraining a torrent of babble. He switched to the casual. Why yes, he knew books, literature was his real interest. "In fact," he leaned close to confide, "I've done a couple of little things myself—pretty good too, in their way of course." And here he popped out with the one thing *I* could have wished; that which made the initial plan crystal clear and its fulfilment so easy that I couldn't resist the first ego gloat I've had for some time. (There are many gloats; the one I must needs use constantly to keep within everything without flagging and to retain a grip on the rock in the belly of the mind is the gloat of knowledge: looking out anxiously on the whole of all that's before me each moment as tho I was about to die every minute and therefore straining all ways to feel the experience fully and hunger to store it all and save everything in the mind so that when I feel any similar emotion it will recall the scene and conversely, when I see any object or hear any sound that had the aspects of an object or sound that was seen or heard in one of the moments when I gathered in a strong emotion, I can then, whenever it's necessary, release some of the hoarded memory to think on it and when I do the resultant emotion becomes one of gloat; a gloat of knowledge, self-knowledge to be sure, but one that bolsters with a poignancy that renders me truly inarticulate and the flood of sure truth saturates my brain and I reel under the meaning of life and I wonder that it is there and the sheer beautiful bliss of being allowed one more precious minute of consciousness, so as to feel these things, overcomes me and I thank God unreservedly).

So, this young fool said he'd done a few little pieces, but, the best thing he'd written was: "an objective, clinical scientific study" called, "The Confessions of a Dope Addict." I think you'll agree my ego gloat was justified. I slowed my pace even more and it was my turn to have considerable difficulty in restraining a pop of the gut. My happiness was offset by concern that I wouldn't be able to pull this off properly and to flub, or even booble such a perfect chance to squelch this overextended slicker; show even blind and cocksure him what a bumpkin and dupe he actually was. In a sudden flash I saw I could throw a pure scare into him both ways: awaken his shallow mind to fear for itself—if only a transitory fright—and make his yellowbelly flip over enough that he'll be afraid to peep and I can get some sleep. Weeellll, I asked for a little description of the noble work. A vague general statement, a couple of "you know's" and after that, blank. I pressed him harder, in ratio to my insistence did his silence grow. I wasn't overbearing at all, just simple little questions: "How does one begin to go about finding out what a dope addict feels, thinks, or would want to confess, objectively?"—i.e. how does his clinical scientific method peer into the addict's being? How can one begin to know, let alone write about, the convictions that precede any confession; how they came about, what they mean inwardly, to the mind and soul of the addict? Then I began to get hot. "What!" I yelled, "you mean you didn't even preface the work with any clue, statement or otherwise, as to specifically what type of Dope he was addicted to?" Then, naturally, I raved a bit about the different types and their different effects. I also pointed out that in the end each man speaks for himself and even if one shared every iota of dope exactly with a fellow one could never know exactly what was up with the guy. Worse, indeed truly impossible, if one attempted to *deduce* by scientific method of objective external measurement such an essentially mystical thing as a confession of a dope addict would be—unless, of course, the confession was a catalogue of incidents leading up to, or while in, addiction. Even an intelligent man, carefully attempting to accurately confess to the lay world the kernel of something the addiction produced that changed him from what he was before, as well as what makes him different from them now, would only be able to come up with an abstraction, further modified by writing, of the "it." So how in hell can the laboratory, with or without the addict's aid, help to bring a single grand logic out of any confession, etc. Now, about this time I felt I'd better put a good cap on the whole business while I had him floundering in, "I'd not meant that," "Oh, I didn't intend to write it that way," "I didn't want to get close to the addict, I just wanted an objective clinical study, I wasn't concerned with the soul." So, I suggested we adjourn to the club car to quench our thirst and I could there get him really alone to nail him thoroughly; he bucked and squirmed to get away, but had no reason at hand, so accompanied me.

In the luxurious surroundings I held his eye and said, "You know, I'm an addict." He had been expecting it, but, when I said it he still wasn't prepared enough and there came a big slack in his jaw which was instantly covered with a blustering, "I knew it all the time, why I even knew it *before* you got on the train, in Penn. station I looked at you and said to myself; now there is an addict that's under the influence right now." I told him I'd not been hi getting on the train and asked him to guess what I was on. He surmised I had been smoking opium "or something" and in his ignorance wanted to know if I knew where I was, what I was doing or if I would pass out. I had him scared alright and decided to pour it on because he really was malicious as well as dumb and truly deserved it. I talked quietly but practiced a seething-seeming self-control which I easily made to seem just under the surface and about to bust loose at any moment. I told him how the powerful Marijuana I was feeling caused a murderous surge of hatred for anyone who crossed me, how strong the stuff made one,—bending a heavy silver spoon quickly—and how hard it was to control myself whenever I thought of anyone's neck; I got hungup on the neck, I elaborated fully on the urge to throttle all necks, especially feminine and skinny ones; I explained I wanted to squeeze until I was exhausted, press my palms together, with a neck between until the exertion made for collapse. I boasted about what I could do to a neck; oh, I really warmed up to the subject, began to image new things as I progressed, what heaven to possess a neck, etc. I had his old Adam's apple twitching by golly; he didn't finish his beer, got up in the middle of one of my words and left the dining car. Oops, dammit, I've done it now, I went too far; he'll tell the conductor, call the cops, or just plain blab the whole thing to all the train in general and our car in particular. I sat there stunned for a few minutes, deciding never to fuck with squares again since there's never any real pleasure anyhow, then, went back to my car to face them.

There was no trouble, he was sitting mute as I slid past him to my seat next to the window. We never spoke again, he was afraid to and perhaps ashamed; I put him out of my mind in a few minutes and soon was digging the Pennsylvania countryside until I fell asleep. As I dozed throughout the night I occasionally came to and noticed everyone in the car was asleep except him. I observed him closely from lowered lids; he was sitting there like a ramrod, refusing to sleep and eyeing me now and again with tense worry in his expression. I farted and returned to sleep. The next A.M. the car thinned out and he took another seat. That P.M. as we approached St. Louis I saw he'd hooked up with a dimwit soldier just like himself; more so, even louder. They began pacing the train, leering at girls, giving out with where they'd been, what they'd done, what everything in the U.S.A. and the rest of the world was about, particularly pertaining to War. I noticed them finally settled in a standing position in the vestibule near my end of the car, some 3 seats away. They began looking at me and whispering; I knew the fool had told all with relish and distortion; I was happy. The journey was over and these boys were wondering and clucking to themselves. For any provocation there might be violence but I knew they would start nothing themselves. Altogether, I came off so well that when I found in the St. Louis station my pass was all fucked up, I had the old drive and dashed downtown to the Wabash offices, got the RR pass to Denver and further got it fixed to be good on a train just leaving and not usually free for Brakies and was on the train and gone again in less than one hour and still found time for two innings of All-Star Major League baseball. So, the end of the "scientific clinical objective" story.

Since I'm returning Cannastra[44] without delay I presume to ask for Jim Holmes' scribbled (I'm sure) letter to you; I would like to see the old boy's Hi. Thank you. How's Carl,[45] Lucien, your girl etc. I got a nice PC from John Holmes, I shall write him. I think we all know intuitively what you generalize about tragedy and chance and death; I, for one, have always felt that way. I will be in NY in Jan., March or May, if not then maybe sooner, later or never. I've had several fairly exciting RR wrecks, two that I might have gotten fired for, one that tied up the RR for about 16 hours, 3 or 4 that stopped first class streamliners and the first trip I made when I got back was just finished and I was coming home with a few other guys when myself, my conductor and Stiengasser stepped between moving trains. When it was over the conductor was pale as hell, I was nervous and gulping and Stiengasser is still in the hospital with a smashed skull and paralyzed limbs. I had a fine little note I wrote to you which was the beginnings of a letter I wrote in longhand with pencil but leaving SLO I forgot it so this is all I can come up with. I have finished (tentatively) the prologue in 3 parts, begun the book only in that I've created my opening page of the manuscript. The tape recorder I have helps not one whit, don't ever think you can write by using a recorder of any kind; a fantasy for sure. I'm broke as hell, this fucking RR hasn't got it like the parking lot had, however, I'm never going to work at anything but RRing again, not that I like it, or that it's easy, but it's the closest to eliminating the job hangup and the way conditions are I shall have to "boom" across the country every year to get work and so shall get to travel. Of course, even after 20 years one can get fired at any time, so I can lose SP job but still work on other roads—unless they find out I'm color blind; a test of each RR's physical is a color test and luck has to be with me to fool them. Every new

44. Ginsberg had written to Neal on October 31 (*As Ever,* pp. 70–74) describing William Cannastra's fatal accident, and enclosing a newspaper clipping.

45 Carl Solomon (1928–1993), a writer whom Allen Ginsberg had met when they were fellow inmates at the Psychiatric Institute of Columbia Presbyterian Hospital in 1949. Represented by Carl Rappaport in Kerouac's *Visions of Cody*. Ginsberg originally titled his famous 1955 poem *Howl for Carl Solomon*.

thing I discover or come to believe I keep like a secret, so am getting my mind back and having convictions after so long without them.

Love,

N.

Having read an essay coauthored by John Clellon Holmes on the western movie and its heroes, Neal wrote to him, quoting from Spengler, and also detailing some of his teenage exploits in Denver.

TO JOHN CLELLON HOLMES

Nov. 20, 1950
29 Russell St.
SF, Calif.

DEAR JOHN, AND I KNOW YOU ARE;

What a pleasure to get your great little card! You see, I went to San Luis Obispo on Oct. 27 and didn't return until Nov. 15; at that time, altho I live with Carolyn here, I went to 230 Divisadero to see if there was mail—and there it was; the ole garbage-pickers pennypound worth of type. I hope you receive some degree of the cheer I felt at yours when you get this. Down goobering with the meatheads the RR possesses as brakemen on the south end of this division, I was badly in need of a note from the eastern front.

I read your Myth of the Western Hero in 7 of Neurotica[46] and got a real boot out of it; even tho you write such stuff to eat (and so whenever one begins to praise any of it you depreciate it all and so belittle yourself that one is tempted to accept your deprecation and not deal with it seriously), I only wish I could come up with anything that can approach your "trash."

In the beginning, when the Faustian land was still without cities, it was the nobility that represented, in the highest sense, the nation.[47] The peasantry, everlasting and historyless, was a people before the

46. "The Myth of the Western Hero" was published in *Neurotica* #7, autumn 1950, under the pseudonym of Alfred Towne, and was a collaboration between John Clellon Holmes and the editor Jay Landesman. Carolyn Cassady subscribed to the magazine.

47. This and the following three paragraphs are quotations slightly edited by Neal from Oswald Spengler's *Decline of the West* (1928), vol. 2, chap. 6, sec. 5, pp. 184–86.

dawn of the culture and survives when the form of the nation has passed away. The Nation, like every other grand symbol of the culture, is intimately the cherished possession of a few: those who have it are born to it, like men are born to art or philosophy. When a nation rises up ardent to fight for its freedom and honor, it is always a minority that fires the multitude. The people "awakens" is more than a figure of speech, for only thus and then does the waking-consciousness of the whole become manifested. All these individuals whose "we" feeling yesterday went content with a horizon of family and job and perhaps home-town are suddenly today men of nothing less than the people. Their thought and feeling, their Ego, and therewith the "it" in them has been transformed to the depths. It has become historic. Then even the unhistorical peasant becomes a member of the nation; a day dawns for him in which he experiences history and not merely lets it pass him by.

But now, in the world cities, besides a minority which has history and livingly experiences, feels, and seeks to lead the nation, there arises another minority of timeless, a-historic, literary men; men not of destiny, but of reasons and causes, men who are inwardly detached from the pulse of blood and being, wide-awake thinking consciousness, they can no longer find any "reasonable" connotation for the nation-idea. Cosmopolitanism is a mere waking-conscious association of intelligentsias. In it there is hatred of Destiny and history as the expression of Destiny. Everything national belongs to race—so much so that it is incapable of finding language for itself, clumsy in all that demands thought, and shiftless to the point of fatalism. Cosmopolitanism is literature and remains literature, very strong in reasons, very weak in defending them otherwise than with more reasons; not blood. All the more then, this minority of far superior intellect chooses the intellectual weapon, and all the more is it able to do so as the world cities are pure intellect, rootless, and by very hypothesis the common property of the civilization. The born world-citizens, world-pacifists, and world-reconcilers—alike in the China of the "contending states," in Buddhist India, in the Hellenistic age, and in the western world today—are the spiritual leaders of decay. In the history of all cultures we find this anti-national element. Pure self-directed thinking was ever alien to life; alien, then, to history—unwarlike, raceless. Consider our humanism and classicism, the Sophists of Athens, Buddha and Lao-Tze—not to mention the passionate contempt of all nationalisms displayed by the great champions of the ecclesiastical and the philosophical world-view. The world-feeling for race (which is not what you believe, but is *expression*!; explain some other year unless forced sooner) has to retreat and make room for a tendency of which the standard-bearers are most often men without original impulse, but all the more set upon their logic, men at home in a world of truths, ideals, and Utopias; bookmen who believe that they can replace the actual by the logical, the might of facts by an abstract justice, Destiny by reason. It begins with the everlastingly fearful who withdraw themselves out of actuality into cells and study-chambers and spiritual communities where they proclaim the nullity of the world's doings; it ends in every culture with the apostles of world-peace. Every people (historically speaking) has such waste-products. Even their heads constitute physiognomically a group by themselves. In the history of intellect they stand high with many illustrious names numbered among them; but, regarded from the point of view of actual history, they are inefficients.

The Destiny of a nation plunged in the events of its world depends upon how far its race-quality is successful in making these events historically ineffective against it.

A nation is humanity brought into living form. The practical result of world-improving theories is consistently a formless and therefore history-less mass. All world-improvers and world-citizens stand for "finished" ideals, whether they know it or not. Their success means the historical abdication of the nation in favor, not of everlasting peace, but of another nation. World-peace is always a one-sided resolve. With it is the one practical significance that it makes a formless population the mere object of the willed power of warrior groups. The Babylonian, Chinese, Indian, Egyptian worlds pass from one conqueror's hands to another's and it is their own blood that pays for the contest. That is their—peace. From the intellectual point of view, no doubt, the extinction of the nations puts a world above history that is civilized at last and forever. But in the realm of facts it all reverts to a state of nature, in which it alternates between long submissiveness and brief angers that for all the bloodshed—world-peace never diminishes that—alter nothing. Of old they shed their blood for themselves, now they must shed it for others, often enough for the mere entertainment of others, that is the difference. More better Spenglerian riffs anytime you want.

I brought to my first job a product whose use gave me such an advantage as to outearn all the other punks. Denver's Dime Delivery Co. was similar to Western Union in that we delivered messages; but also small packages. The system was different also in that the amount of money one could earn depended exclusively on how fast one was.

This is where I shone; you see, I had a magnificent French racing bicycle. Whereas the other bums made from 8 to 12 dollars a week, with my beautiful machine (with the rear wheel almost directly under the seat post and the shorter chain thus needed was further added to speed by a large 32 prong front sprocket and a 7 pronged rear sprocket; a single that could do 50 MPH!) I always cleared some sum in the teens and often 20 a week. So, with ease I led the field except for one Ben Gowen. The fellow was about the same age as most of us employees; 13 to 16. He was also a full-blooded Indian from Neelyville, Mo. who was noticeably laconic. He had other qualities; a pair of striking grey eyes, hawk nose, slim Ginsbergian body and a strange voice. His passions were women, cars, whiskey and twist chewing tobacco. His family consisted of a drunken old chief who'd left the reservation long ago to become a skilled autobody mechanic, a humpbacked mother who spoke little English, one sister I never saw and an older and younger brother who were exactly like Ben, *exactly*!, except one was 3 or 4 yrs. older in mind and body and showed what Ben would become, and one was 3 or 4 yrs. younger and showed what he had been. All were fabulously hungup on autos, buying truck bodies at 10 bucks, interchanging motors etc., and creating whole fleets of bastardized crates which cluttered the back yard of the horrid shack on the outskirts of southeastern Denver which had been their home since leaving Neelyville several yrs. before. At payday I watched the sum noted on each pay envelope as it was passed out, just to see who came closest to me so I could gloat and earn more next week. I had been doing this for some weeks and knew no one would ever catch me or even come close to making as much dough as I did, when this Ben Gowen came to work for D.D. At the end of the week he was less than a dollar from me! The next week he made *more* than I did! Each week thereafter it was a tossup between us for the distinction of racing around the city faster than anyone else during that hard hard cold cold cold winter of 1940. I was doubly amazed that Ben could compete with me because his bike was a real junker, a flimsy nothing for speed. I admired this; told him no one had approached me before he came there and with open wonder asked how he did it. This was the first time I'd talked to him and suspected his taciturnity of answer, "Just keep going," was because he didn't know me; not so. Anyway I didn't press him, just worked like hell that week to beat his ass. Along about the middle of the week I noticed he had another bike which I figured he'd gotten to try and make more money, but, that reasoning didn't make sense because his new bike was even worse than the old one. I don't remember who won that week's race, altho I do recall it was as nip and tuck as all our week's pay were to be while we were at D.D. together. I really came to love the guy along about then; he was not full of loud bullshit like the others, etc., and besides, I secretly knew he was faster than I because with his bikes (which were changing weekly or oftener now and I realized must be stolen) I couldn't have made 10 bucks a week. So, we formed one of those intimate friendships which my life has been indelibly stamped with and whose depth of emotional union makes up fully for the few and comparably infrequent friendships I do manage to attain. Ben and I became inseparable during waking hours, working and thieving around the clock. Ben's large capacity for larceny blended well with my own undeveloped vein and so we spent full nights touring the city for any loot that struck our eyes. Auto accessories; including seats, radios, spotlights etc., likely articles in store fronts on secluded streets—a simple matter to bash in the window and run, etc., etc.; we'd always end the night snitching bottles of freshly delivered milk from doorsteps etc. We finally quit our jobs and took to selling auto parts we'd stolen, then, vacuum cleaners from hallways of the many apt. houses I knew my way around in. Finally we took to stealing poultry, yessir, big fat hens in the revealing light of day. We got a good price and were never quizzed (possibly because the crooked owners of the fowl houses would immediately dunk the birds in scalding water and skin their feathers in 20 seconds; who could identify their own lousy chickens then?) so, we decided to make a steady business out of it for a while. At first we'd barge about in the henhouse, floundering in the stinking shit, lunging after the birds with squawks and fearful cackles in our ears and chicken feathers and droppings plastered to our sweating clothes. Later on, with experience, we got a fine hunk of baling wire, bent the end to fit their legs and plucked them off with ease; two or three every minute stuffed in the loot sack of burlap.

Goddamn my soul, John, I just stopped for the first time to reread this letter. What a bunch of blabbermouth junk, poorly thought out, worse in construction and pretentious as hell. I began to tell a little story about Ben Gowen, didn't even get started before I feebly fell apart and wandered elsewhere for no good reason. Shove the whole business please.

Just where is Alan Harrington? What did he write; is he finished; how is he? Re. Jay Landesman:[48] did he go to Europe, come back, any new hangups?

Nov. 23, late

So, being a bum I let this lazy farce lie on the table for a week. I just got small note saying Jack K. married![49] Diana was newsbearer. Now to get Allen in a female for good, then Ansen,[50] ha!

I'm sure I must be as broke as yourself; I busted my ass all year and will finish up still without even 50 bucks to cross country, bah.

Happy thanksgiving, without any t or prospects of any; double bah.

Happy thanksgiving etc. to your mother, wife, younger and (woooeee!) older sister. See you in a few months maybe; so long old pal. Goodnight.

P.S. Altho I can't write a letter, or seem to get anything else done—about to get fired because for 5 months I've not gotten around to filling out a simple form, I shore does appreciate receiving letters. Any little line from you about any little thing would certainly help me get my pants on; to get out in the cold world & over the hump

Thanks,

N.

Also, of course, one must watch out for horseturds in the clover.

There are 17 varieties of eastern clover, which, combined with the

48. Jay Landesman (b. 1919) was the editor of *Neurotica* magazine for its first eight issues, before handing it over to Gershon Legman. Landesman wrote and produced the Beat-influenced musical *The Nervous Set,* which appeared on Broadway in 1959. In 1964 he moved to London with his wife, Fran. The first part of Landesman's autobiography, *Rebel Without Applause,* was published in 1987. He makes a brief appearance in Kerouac's *Visions of Cody* as Jay Chapman.

49. On November 17, Jack Kerouac married for the second time, to Joan Haverty, William Cannastra's last girlfriend. Allen Ginsberg and Lucien Carr were his best men. Joan Haverty (1930–1990) is called Laura in the final chapter of *On the Road,* and June Ogilvie in *Book of Dreams*. Her book, *Nobody's Wife,* appeared in 2000.

50. Alan Ansen (b. 1922) became W.H. Auden's secretary in 1947. Through William Cannastra he met Ginsberg and Kerouac. Ansen wrote the novel fragment *The Vigilantes* in 1952 and has produced many poetic works, collected in *Contact Highs* (1989). Ansen is depicted as Rollo Greb in *On the Road,* Austin Bromberg in *The Subterraneans,* and Irwin Swenson in *Vision of Cody* and *Book of Dreams.*

47 possible shades of thorobred Indian juice, makes for a grand total 437 hundred brand new purple pasture pastes. While they retail without result there is only one pissable hope—to be given away free, unless determined by the tariff, then, of course, to be taken away free—to all.

Indeed, a joyous thought on these happy holidays. I trust.

*Allen Ginsberg wrote to Neal on November 18 (*As Ever*, pp. 81–85) with news of Kerouac's marriage the day before. Neal replied with his thoughts on the matter, with a character analysis of their friend. He also told Allen that he found it difficult to write to Diana, describing what appear to be symptoms of depression.*

TO ALLEN GINSBERG

Nov. 25, 1950
[San Francisco]

DEAR ALLEN;

It is not an easy task to write to you, or anyone; in fact I can't bring myself to write at all. In regard to this vacuum wherein I can find nothing to say to anyone, Diana has the worst of it. Accordingly, if you see her at any time please tell her I just can't write or do anything else and that's the end of it. I have many beautiful instances of my inability to function at hand, and could recite them for you, but need not since I really haven't the strength. I can't overemphasize too strongly how ugly my life has become, simply because of this "do nothingness," and how low I've gotten by realizing emotionally *every* damn moment what a really disgusting fish I am. Honestly it's awful, not only am I unable to do the ordinary things necessary (brush teeth, see doctors, do important RR things, sleep) but also, can't do absolutely imperative things. i.e. my car's broke down, needs easy to fix spark plugs; do you think I'm able to walk two blocks to get them and take ten minutes to fix it, no, no, I've been riding streetcar to work for weeks, etc., etc. Things even worse, but suffice to say I just eat every 12 hours, sleep every 20 hours, masturbate every 8 hours and otherwise just sit on the train and stare ahead without a thought in it. One thing I do is think every 5 seconds of the things I have to do, I keep reciting them over and over again in my mind: "fix car, fix feet, fix teeth, fix eyes, fix nose, fix thumbs, fix bronchial tubes, fix asshole, get new RR lantern, get pass for trip back here in March for Hairy Jack and Harassed Diana, (if they want it) get started on book, get lined up for RR jobs on way east, get dog (I got thorobred cocker for Cathy) rabies shot, get backyard fixed for Cathy to play in, get this read and that written, etc." The net result of all this is my belly is sick all the time, it's loose, I eat and I feel sick after, I smoke and get mad for not stopping, etc., etc. I wish I had a toadstool to crawl under and die.

To attempt to get an exact fix on the ever-mysterious soul is futile.[51] But nowadays one must needs have abstract thinking and it forces the physicist of the inner world to elucidate a fictitious world for oneself by fictions piled on fictions, notions on more notions. He transmutes the non-extended into the extended, builds up a system of cause for something that is only manifested physiognomically, and comes to believe that in this system he has the structure of the soul before his eyes. But the very words that he selects, to notify to others the results of his intellectual labors, betray him. The word as utterance, as poetic element, may establish a link, but the word as notion, as element of scientific prose, never. Easier to break up a theme of Beethoven with a knife than break up the soul by methods of abstract thought. Images—likenesses, are the only way for spiritual intercourse yet discovered. Rembrandt can reveal something of his soul, to those who are in inward kinship with him, by way of a self-portrait or landscape. Certain ineffable stirrings of soul can be imparted by one man to the sensibility of another man through a look, two bars of melody; an almost imperceptible movement. That is the real language of souls—it remains incomprehensible to the outsider.

"Soul" for the man who has advanced from mere living and feeling to the alert and observant state, is an image derived from quite primary experiences of life and death. It is as old as thought, i.e., the articulate separation of thinking (thinking-over) from seeing. We see the world around us, and since every free-moving being must, for its own safety, understand the world, the accumulating daily detail of technical and empirical experience becomes a stock of permanent data which man, as soon as he is proficient in speech, collects into an *image* of what *he understands*. This is world of nature; what is not environment we do not see, but we do divine "its" presence in ourselves and others, and by virtue of "its" physiognomic impressive power it

51. In this and the following two paragraphs, Neal presents edited extracts from Oswald Spengler's *Decline of the West* (1928), vol. 1, chap. 9, pp. 300–304.

invokes in us the anxiety and desire to know; thus arises the meditated or pondered image of a counterworld which is our mode of visualizing that which remains eternally alien to the physical eye. The image of the soul is mythic and remains objective in the field of spiritual religion. Scientific psychology has worked out for itself a complete system of images, in which it moves with entire conviction. The individual pronouncements of every individual psychologist proves on examination to be merely a variation of this system conformable to the style of the world science of the day. At any particular time, therefore, the current image of the soul is a function of the current language and its inner symbolism. Scientific psychology and the psychology of the same kind that we all unconsciously practice when we try to figure to ourselves the stirrings of our own or other's souls is unable to discover or even approach the essence of the soul. Like everything else that is no longer becoming but become, it has put a mechanism in the place of an organism. Everything our present day psychologist has to tell us relates to the present condition of the western soul; not to the human soul at large.

The imaginary soul-body is never anything but the exact mirror-image of the form in which the matured culture-man looks on his outerworld. A soul-image is never anything but the image of *one* quite definite soul. No observer can ever step outside the conditions and the limitations of his time and circle, whatever it may be that he "knows" in itself involves in all cases choice, direction and inner form; is therefore an expression of his proper soul. And the soul remains what it was, something that can neither be thought or represented; *the* Secret, *the* ever-becoming, *the* pure experience. When one convinces oneself that one knows the soul of an alien culture, or man, from its, or his, workings in actuality, the soul-image underlying the knowledge is really one's own soul-image. In this wise experiences are readily assimilated into the system that's already there, and it is not surprising that in the end one comes to believe that one has discovered forms of eternal validity.

Since you are being the victim of a big fucked out of your Spengler,[52] because Carolyn refuses to part with it until I buy her another, I'll give you these quotes until I buy you a copy to replace my pricky theft.

There is not one, not one, thought in my head. I've sat here 20

52. Allen Ginsberg had given his two-volume edition of Spengler's *Decline of the West* to Neal in New York, 1948.

minutes trying to come up with an idea and there is none. Anyway, I'll give out with some bullshit; just anything to get on with this nonsense—

The particular mexican t that Jack and I have been blasting (I ran out almost a month ago and if you lovely boys would take pity and just send me any small amount available I'd surely swoon) was different than any other t because I've noticed that anyone who uses it has a tendency to think the same strange things as do others who have it. I know t has similar effects on all of us, but this stuff was moreso; even Al Hinkle entered completely into the same pattern of kicks once he'd blasted. In the light of this, and letters Jack has written me, I suspect the brooding alone on Richmond Hill for what it was: a final and most disheartening realization of himself. This is not to say he was not happy, it was that itself which showed him the truth of the matter. Under its (t) influence he was really stoned consistently for long periods; and alone. When one is alone on this stuff the sheer ecstasy of utterly realizing each moment makes it more clear to one than ever how impossibly far one is from the others. Not different from them or intolerant; one is more close than ever to people and the world, but, in the end alone, for no one can ever follow the complexities that make up the mind that is so t conditioned. One, then, cannot make one's self clear to others: the difficulties of yourself tracing the trail of inner feeling and conviction are so insurmountable that not only in writing, but even speech and action, one is completely misunderstood—because all that comes out of one is a caricature of what one is thinking & that is so distorted from the actual thought that people pick up on this caricature as your action or thought about the matter at hand, whereas really one *had meant* it for a caricature (realizing inwardly the incapability of even beginning to speak or show action about what one is experiencing) and once beginning this trait is unable to stop and so, actually, becomes artificial. A horrible fate to be artificial, no genuine feeling left; all is bemused thought that means nothing to anyone else but one's self. This artificiality is not too readily observed if there is no one at hand to point it out to one. The mind, when alone, is usually hungup playing with one theme and then another; hop, skip and jump. Trying to make pleasure one discovers tricks, then forgets them. When hi one is stunned at the fullness of the perception experienced; they mean so much one feels there'll never be doubt (of comprehension) again. And so it goes. (Too obtuse to continue.) At any rate, Jack has had this and despite saying he's writing the greatest stuff ever; he knows he is not. This may not be so in Jack's mind, there's no telling that; but, the reasons behind the marriage can be attested to this t; so much so that I say without the t and its effects Jack would not now be married. This can lead to trouble because it's just so much horseshit, but, you know I had to come up with sumpin! Then, of course, there's my poor dead mother's chinese wedding dress; if it had only been hung properly the tail might not have ended so flat. In truth, tho, as you well show in your letter, no one can say the reason for the marriage. There are no reasons for so many actions of this type, in fact, I have perhaps more insight into this matter than any of the rest of us, you see, I can clearly recall all my three marriages and the emotions and reasons that led into them. Knowing Jack and suspecting his recent life while remembering how he'd stated for so long that he'd marry, I can put the memory of my past and my feeling about Jack together and sense there is as little inner as there is outer reason for the marriage. All this means nothing; reasons *for* marriage mean less than you believe, Allen, you I think are so firmly pursuant of making marriage *last* that you can't feel properly the mere whims that led to marriage. That is to say, realizing permanence so well you do not sufficiently give credit to those whims inside yourself to justify action on them. A marriage such as I am inclined to believe Jack's is, and know mine were, is a combination of willful blindness, a perverted sense of wanting to help the girl and just plain what the hell. Besides, there are no good reasons why two people shouldn't be together, excepting children, no matter what the distance between. As for children, what can one say?, it all depends on the attitude of each partner toward the other as that attitude has been conditioned by the various actions and ideas that have influenced each person's particular personality. The many compromises, even tho intellectually not begrudged, push the limits of love and soon each person affects a static comprehension of the other and there is no changing this viewpoint. If one is convinced of the other's integrity all is OK usually, but, if this is gone there['s] no hope. Then it becomes a matter of remaining together for the children, if this too cannot be achieved because of emotional (true) dislike, one can only hope the best one for raising them gets the kids. I could go on indefinitely from experience. There are always things in a marriage no outsider sees, this can't help from being so, also there are many things in a marriage outsiders see and the married one cannot, but, this is a moot point and matters not to the person involved. All in all each marriage is only what the partners make of it and what becomes of it depends solely on what they want it to be. The conflicting ideas of same are the crux which combined with the emotional habits of each make for the strain that, once ruptured, needs an external responsibility to save the marriage—church, family, pride, children or some such absolute. My god! I sound like the ladies home journal or worse and never having done this before give that excuse. I stop altho I haven't even warmed to the subject yet, or gotten halfway to the place where I could begin to make my points about Jack and his wife. It does not matter anyway, Jack will cater to her mind's shallowness, in return for her body's fullness, until such time as he breaks under the complete awareness of one female's demands and his inability to meet them, besides which he'll tire of staying on her level; she would, but can't, get on his, so mutual frustration—which they'll (Jack will) combat by vague retreats from understanding. This is a pretty good system and works almost as well as any I can now think of; whenever a point that looks as tho it might matter comes up one just quickly and magnanimously agrees, forgets, or says it doesn't matter anyhow since everyone is different, so as to hide the whole business more readily and slip into another backwash of thought less dangerous. It all depends on how much she'll leave Jack alone; I fear she won't be bright enough to see this, or strong enough to do it, when he wants (needs, as habit) it, this sure can become a big sore point if she's inclined to goad. Then, also, there is her whole unknown world of emotion (from what you say of making vulgar Cannastra shrine, I'll wager she at least has a big, foolish, and feminine one) which cannot help but be a pleasure for Jack to discover, *if,* he can find peace from other things to be able to indulge in that greatest of all gone kicks of finding out a woman from the soul (soles) up. As time passes he'll lose the strength to be consistent in this (as he knows more) and will hanker elsewhere even if there is great love and they are welded solid, for the actual task of rising to the game is too difficult, unbeknown to us all, and, unless by that time there are other things, that new elixir, Jack will fall prey to this inherent weakness (no hardon) and fuck big only in imagination. But, that's another problem. So where do we stand? nowhere, yet; I haven't said anything valid about Jack's marriage. Where does one begin? I prefer China since it's furthest away, but, being practical, Ha, how about starting with looking at Jack objectively, Ha, Ha. More shit; I'm dashing it off now—

The intense drives that affect Jack's actions are extremely varied and strong; this is of prime importance and I must continually orient to one and then another of these multitudinous forces to escape oversimplification, and so will seem quite contradictory—as he himself is. Ah! but to properly etch in the exact shades of his personality, so that the degrees of conflict can be approximated and his whole upright self stand firmly, sharp and clear. A delineation of his mind seems in order, but, his emotions are so pronounced! Ach, bah, anyway—But, by god, Allen, what a man he is, just stop and think of it. Certain traits stand out so as to make him a true peasant, as he says, "like a potato" and, again, what wisdom he can flash! He lets people bully him, intellectually and otherwise, he shows always a shy diffidence, a gentle nature; witness, tho, his claws as he rants for pages on end and sometimes, at parties, raises up in anger at wrongs (usually social) he imagines inwardly or witnesses; yet, he'll be the first to wither under any real hint of sweetness on the part of the other person. He has a morbid dread of hassles (he will attempt mightily to escape even the suggestion of one in his marriage) but when it comes down to it won't knuckle under. He has consideration, but a manly selfishness, boyishness, but a certain poise, etc., etc. Damn it, I don't want to, and can't be presumptuous enough to, give you any of this simple trash. You know him a hellofalot better than I do, longer than I have and probably love him the more. You see, when I began this I was just struck by the thought of the actual difference between you and Jack. (What if you had married and I was writing Jack your traits?) I realized you have only a few definite drives. Several instincts so strong as to be ineffaceable, your mold is as that of cast-iron; stiff and so set with its properties that there is no bending allowed; you came from the forge doomed to splinter, you must crack under the blows of the hammer of life, but, aha!, as long as there are any remains of you, no matter the number or size of the cleavages that rend you thruout, the stuff of which you are made remains the same; there is no altering your shape, always recognizable you are, never any distortions of the kind possible with the pliable nature of Jack's chemical; tempered steel. I, of course, retain exclusive rights to the grandeur of the black mold; ingredients of the rose-scent, the apple-blossom, all the pasture's products and finely-spun old lace combined with green lumps of eyeballs, louse-infected chicken liver, purple pastes of puke, grey miles of intestine, red-ringed assholes and brown bunches of bullshit which created the chemical of my soul; low-grade slag, destined for the pits of Hades, where I will quickly be found unburnable and so tossed on His slagpits to wallow forever.

But the Springtime is gone, it has passed in character, with rush and upheaval. The Summer, too, in heat and humid longing, has fled I fear. Far into the shortness of Indian Summer am I, but before me still lies the plump Autumn; season of understanding! I trust the Winter, cold passionless rage are its most powerful storms; no heat involved. The present Indian Summer provokes the memory storehouse into Proust-like recollection wherein the egg-seeds generated by the past are carefully gathered in the brain's basket so as to hibernate until nursed into bloom at Autumntime. Etc., old boy.

Being as how you nasty easterners think this western fart can care for himself, I done went out last night and with beautiful struggles that could make a better story than any "Pennsy RR," I managed to fall into the most wonderful joint of t that it has been my pleasure to come across in months. Not only that, with my last few bucks, come Monday, I'll pick up an oz of same. How do you like them apples, huh? Great, great shit I tell you—Carolyn was so hi, (stoned mind you, as I was on just this one stick between us) she actually fell on her ass when she attempted to walk across the floor; her equilibrium was so poor the floor just wasn't there when she stepped.

Love to everyone of you silly jerks who spent half their life suffering the cold, snow, wind and attendant hazards of the adverse NY weather; fools.

Neal sent Diana some money and continued with plans to visit her and his new son in New York in January.

TO DIANA HANSEN CASSADY

Dec. 1, 1950
[San Francisco, California]

Enclosed find fifty (50). You might not get more until I arrive in NY next month. See you in about 40 days.

TO DIANA HANSEN CASSADY

Dec. 3, 1950
[San Francisco, California]

DEAR DIANA;

I came in from a job at 7 A.M. on the last Tues in Nov., did not get out again until Dec. 1st at noon, now it looks as tho the soonest I can get out again is next Tues., so, one week and I make 12.70, less than 2 dollars a day. These bastards won't cut the board and yet no one can say the work will pick up again, and all of us would rather be cutoff than waiting 4 days to get out. For this, and other reasons I am truly broke, so much so that I left myself only 8 bucks to live on till the 10th when I sent you the 50. I honestly doubt that I can send anymore until I'm working at another job elsewhere. If I get cut this week I'll try for a job around here to get enough money to go clear East in one shot. If I'm not cut until after the 15th (doubt) I will probably have enough dough to go East without stopping, however, if must I'll stop and boom as I go. The car still has not been fixed, I just can't get the damn brakie at home and there's a lot of work to do. I should wait until Jan. 2 for license plates. Calif. has not issued new plates in 4 years and mine are falling off and disintegrating, and there are so many things I ought to do before I leave here. I can't get RR pass from NY to here until next May when they call me back, then I'll get one just as happened this year, except I'll get pass for me and wife, so don't worry about this. I'll get pass from here to there, just in case the car does break down. At any rate, I'll get to you as soon as I possibly can and the latest will be second week in January. We will stay in TT until May and since I'll arrive with little money and because I've inquired about and hear the RR Eastern situation is not so good for jobs, so, without delay, I do believe it necessary to take advantage of Davenport connection. Ask him to please look into the whole business thoroughly and preferably to get me a job switching (awful torture in winter) as near as possible to TT, that way I will work 8 hours a day and will know exactly when I'll be home and can almost live like a white man, otherwise, on the road, I'd be gone at all hours you know, anyway get me any kind of RR job available. If there are no openings I would prefer Chevy plant drive-away, but, since auto production is to be dropped 35% this month etc., there may be no openings there either, so I'll look for an indoor job of any kind just to get through winter. This rough line-up you know already so, since it would help (almost imperative) if I went to work same day I arrive, please look around as best you can without making undue difficulties for yourself and N. and family, etc., etc.

I will get less than 100 dollars on Dec. 10th and the car plus trip will entirely consume that, in fact, to get there without stop I must have a few bucks more, and all in all it'll be pretty tight. If, however, you need (I know you need, but I mean must have) more money now just say so and I'll send and will then boom home to you. As for money for the next six months, all I make will go to you and family so, except for 100, you will have my paycheck and ought to be able to get everything you mention as necessary before too long. Of course, Dec. you'll still be broke and most of Jan., but after that I believe you can catch up good. Since I'll be (hope) making enough to support us perhaps you need not work this winter. Naturally if you would like to it would surely give us enough to be able to travel in May, otherwise I doubt if, come May, there will be any money saved to allow us to cross country (and surely none for my Mexico). This blow is alright with me only because I feel I've fucked you out of at least 500 bucks, actually yours and potentially yours that I've denied you these last months, so I do want to make everything possible up to you and if I support us and give you all my money until May I'll imagine I've somewhat equalized the difference, and if I'm going to Mexico, Jack will have to have enough to take us, which he hasn't, but no matter, I want you to do exactly what will make you happy and personally I think you would be better off at home caring for N. and working on your projects. If you do this, tho, I doubt you should get a substantial wardrobe at this time and should wait until May for Summer wear to cross country, if you want to then, or clothes to work then, or whatever.

I wrote you long letter (bigger than this) but it was all a jumble of words (even more so than this) and without doubt not worth sending. Carolyn, also, has written 2 long ones, but didn't send because she knows there's no reason to and I think your correspondence is over. It's better that way and I am sure it's advisable you don't write her too. I don't care, but you and her only get upset, etc.

It certainly has been a long time for you and I know you've done wonderfully; which I admire and respect you for. It has not been easy on C. either, but, at last I'm pretty sure it's OK to leave her because emotionally she feels very little about the whole thing and has, in her own way, done an admirable job to attain detachment, so when I get East don't you feel any need to get hungup on her again. Limping along without money is a horrible drag and my big wish is that we could all bust out of its confines soon. Maybe in late 51. There isn't much to say until I see you; I'm so sick of how poorly I've handled this year's RRing and the constant daily planning and change in plans etc., that I now feel very little emotional worry over what is to happen now that I am at last in position to do some of the hassled plans. I'll just get East as best I can, save all I can, work where I am at this time (TT I hope), do the very best I can to please you this winter etc., etc. Actually I've reached a lack-of-emotion state where I'm unable to be pried out and as safe as in the womb. There is no necessity for you to worry over me or try to work out any of your latest ideas to save me. I know, when you see me, you'll realize there is really no need for any of that sort of thing and since I've got my type of peace you will feel it enough that you should find your peace (elsewhere being another personality) and won't have to work me over in the belief it'll help me and thus help you to be happy. The relaxed way we'll live is unavoidable, you'll see, I don't want nothing and I'm sure I can meet your demands, anything will be OK with me; just please no issues of abstraction (being in common, ideals this way or that, etc.) I got my mind and explore it my way, no one affects it by setting out to do so, you are right "in there" in your own right, be satisfied with that and we'll make it fine. Believe it, I'm the most considerate guy you could ever want, don't fear I will make you cater to me, just the opposite. I want to do everything I can to please you and you'll see how easy I am to live with, I'm just a wishy-washy about any old household thing, and will beat the rugs, wash the dishes, and out-Robert Robert while I'm there—if it's necessary. I'll just work and be a Major Hoople around the house while still trying to write a book, take you to NY for social nights once in a while—you always come with me when I go to NY whenever necessary (3 times a month) to see the boys and get my kicks blowing my top on a flute and any that's around. You see, Di, you'll come to know me and find there's nothing to fear from any visions I can find to keep me on the ball; it's not a frantic thing anymore (not that I won't be frantic at parties) and my actions when hi are all my own private little affair and do in no way affect you, it's just the personal mental life of a man, etc. I want to see everybody happy and if you can find any pleasure in being with me while I'm indulging in caricatures that usually make me out a fool in your eyes I would be most happy. It all doesn't make any difference, however, if you just don't make an issue of it; if you give in perhaps you might find yourself laughing like hell and enjoying yourself thoroughly. There's no need for a hassle, tho, any way you choose to look at it, because I'll compromise all over the place if you're fair in any specific demand, otherwise, I'll just keep my opinions to myself (have to mostly anyhow; can't talk really) and suffer in silence. The fact is I won't try to force understanding on you (you'd have to smoke t and form your own system) if you'll just let me keep the type of ideas I like to play with; you can't change them substantially anyway. I appear to be making a full-fledged point of all this, but, not so. I'll stop this rambling by saying there is absolutely not one valid thought in this messy letter.

So, don't worry yourself, I'll go along in anything you wish,

Love, N.

Neal's first letter to the newly married Kerouac began with a long description of a dream sequence. The pair had been exchanging details of their dreams for several years, and this may have inspired Kerouac to record his dreams in some detail, which he began to do in 1952.[53]

TO JACK KEROUAC

[Envelope addressed to] Now Honorable Married Mman.

*FORWARD*ing best wishes
*PERSONAL*ly, I'm glad and
*RUSH*ing out to celebrate in
FRAGILE auto—come January 1951

DEAR POSTMAN;

Interesing? Too obvious, huh? Oh well, thanks for delivering.

Dec. 3, 1950
29 Russell St.
San Francisco

DEAR JACK; for the first time truly a man of marriage and family.

The hot sun of early afternoon lit up the bare interior of my New York RR flat. I had several hours to wait so was in the bedroom trying

53. Kerouac's *Book of Dreams,* first published in 1961 in heavily edited form, with the complete version following in 2001, presented a transcription of his dreams between 1952 and 1962.

to get some rest. Suddenly, through the apartment's shadeless windows the sound of approaching merrymakers floated up from the street to disturb me. Slowly I came awake; then sat upright as my hazy doze was fully penetrated by the nearing noise fast becoming a bedlam of carnival hysteria. The tenor of the multitude's voice changed further into a sustained roar like the ocean's surf which now and again was punctured with shrieks and loud shouts as occasional rifle fire rang out. At first I did not deign to stir myself from the comfortable bed; I realized the revolution had come, but since I was in no way involved, I just laid back on the pillows, smoking and listening. There was no doubt I was surrounded completely by thousands of screaming people gripped in the destiny of that day, yet I still felt no concern, although I do remember feebly attempting to visualize some of the scenes I knew must be happening below. Also, I memorized the date so as to recall it later. The gun-play, which had been unmistakably sharp and loud single rifle shots, now increased its tempo to a continuous round of fire, so fast that I was sure machine guns had been brought into action. I decided to go to the toilet and left my bed. Listlessly I began crossing the kitchen to reach the bathroom. Immediately I experienced intense fear . . . my God! . . . I'd been lying there for hours while countless bullets, surely tens of thousands, had been flying every which way and like a pure fool I now intended to calmly walk past open windows and flimsy walls just to take a piss. I dropped to the floor wondering that I had not been shot already, but I did continue to the bathroom on my stomach. I sat on the bowl to urinate and pondered in amazement why I'd felt so secure in the bedroom and soon decided I'd just not thought of the possibility of being hit because, after all, I had nothing to do with it and had no desire to join in what was going on outside. Then I came to feel even more secure in the bathroom and thought I was pretty safe in this small windowless room, although I realized the danger fully now and knew I'd have to face the crowd sometime—even if it was only that their actions would disrupt community service, and I would have trouble getting food or gas for my car—there was no escaping them indefinitely, still one does not rush into the arms of a lynching mob, so I decided to stay where I was. As I sat on the toilet seat, I looked around me and was thankful the walls here were thick enough to stop most any bullet, but—the door! Damn! The door was only one thickness of plywood! There was no bathtub or other place to hide, and I was sure, sitting there facing it, that any shot fired through the door would be bound to get me. This discovery really shattered any sense of safety and put me in a big sweat of indecision whether to stay or go. Finally, however, I left the bathroom—partly because I just couldn't sit there any longer, but mostly because I told myself nothing had happened to me yet, and the brave thing to do was to go back to bed; so I did. Now the gunfire, which had been a bit muffled to me in the toilet, was even more rapid, and every shot I heard was from a machine gun blasting away at top speed. The crowd, I judged from its noise, was even denser and more frightened than ever. Nothing else now entered my head, abed, except the thought that I must get through all this without a bullet touching my body. I felt sheer terror at this repulsive idea, and lay there listening intently, shivering with cold and nearing the breaking point.

Jack K. entered the apartment grinning and completely at ease. With him was a negro dwarf he had helped smuggle off a Portuguese steamer.

"Say, boy," I yelped with worry, "ain't all that gunfire outside dangerous?"

"Why sure it is," he grinned even wider, "but as soon as the messenger boy comes we got to go, right?"

"I suppose so. I guess I'll dress then," I said, and started to do so.

I was about to begin questioning him as to why in hell he was so nonchalant when all this nonsense was busting loose outside and how he got there, why he hadn't been shot, etc. Then I decided all that could wait and was just opening my mouth to speak of the troubles I'd been going through when something dawned on me. In the beginning I was not sure what it was; I hesitated in the gesture of speech and strained to listen more acutely so that I might grasp the subtle change I sensed was happening. Into my head came a slight difference in the ear-pulse and slowly it was there—jackhammers! The machine guns had become huge air-driven chisels men were using to tear up street pavement.

So that was the revolution—an industrial one—and the workers bucking the drills were out to set a record. The crowd was cheering them for ripping up the boulevard all the way from the square to the pier under my building in just a few hours. I now knew why Jack had been so gay when he'd bounced in on me—he had just left a festive throng of people breaking through colored banners and carrying big whoopee signs. I realized he thought I was making joke when I'd asked about the dangerous gunfire, so left it at that, for it made me a wit in his eyes.

Just then a knock interrupted my reasoning, and I looked up to see a small head peering over the transom; I looked down and saw a pair of big feet under the door, and, although the door remained closed, the visitor managed to thrust his hairy arms, one on each side, through the cracks between door and jamb.

"Aha! The message!" Jack exploded, and rushed for the paper the freak held in his hand. Then, stepping back, he waved, and the head, feet and arms disappeared. "Now we can go."

Jack, the nigger dwarf and myself were walking the sandy beach near a green ocean. Soon I noticed offshore a few yards, about two feet deep in the water, a sort of anchor, the purpose of which, I knew, was only so that the surf would just graze the top of it as it came in. Then, as we walked on, I saw another anchor-like object which was, in weight and in distance from the first anchor, exactly in multiplication ratio of 2, 4, 8, 16, etc. This I sensed just by looking. Also, I realized the depth of the water increased at each anchor in the same ratio, although the distance of the object from shore was only half as much each time. Thus, the first anchor was the size of a beer barrel, the next, like an outhouse, the next a semi-trailer, cab up, etc. Always, they were scientifically adjusted in their respective depths so that the water just barely, but always did, clear the object by only a cunt-hair with each wave's stroke. This continued until we had walked miles, but when I commented to Jack about the strange objects offshore, he said he didn't see anything. I was really excited, however, and insisted we push on faster.

Meantime, Jack was telling the nigger where we were, the places inland at this point, what they were like, and seemed to be conducting a personal Cook's Tour.

At last we came to my final sea-thing. I knew there were no more, because I had multiplied well over 100,000, and there could be nothing twice the size of this last one. It was something that looked like a flat iron, circa 1900. The bottom of its massive base rested on the ocean floor in depths unbelievable. The water's surface, as usual, was just breaking over the top of this base. It was a few miles out, and I was overjoyed to have far-sighted eyes, because I could distinguish its handle too! Parallel to the shore, it towered to enormous height; the end pillars curved majestically, and the miles-long top consisted of a series of railroad locomotive diesel engines. I could hear their roar, and I knew this was the last and biggest thing ever to be built by man.

At that moment, we came upon a new Pontiac station-wagon with two very young hipsters in the leather-covered back seat. The car was stuck in thick mud, and they ware waiting for a freeze to harden the ground so they could drive away. I told them, "Fools!", and got everyone to pull on the front bumper until the motor started. I drove; everyone got in the back seat except the nigger. Immediately ahead I saw an impossible curve, yet I attempted to negotiate it. We slid left and turned over into the side of a barn. While we fell I was speculating why I had driven off the road; I knew I couldn't make the curve, yet I never missed any turns. By the time the car stopped, I was confused, but couldn't articulate to the boys about it because the farm animals were putting up a hell-of-a racket and we all had to run away.

Then, seeing Jack's house in the distance, we slowed to a tired walk and plodded along over plowed fields toward his HOME.

P.S. Later I found out the hipsters had been waiting there to trap us; the reason the car turned over was that they had a gadget in the back seat with which they could drive the car. They were so stoned, they didn't care to tell me that I was not in control.

I left Brierly standing in the loud light of the lush theater's marquee. He had the newspaper's final edition with the latest election returns in his hand and had taken over the doorman's platform to pass them out to all who entered or left. Occasionally someone would pause and quickly he would overwhelm them with bursts of oratory. If they stayed on to listen further he really outdid himself to please their ears, working up a tremor in his smooth voice and ending his pitch by manufacturing a tear in each eye. Oh, he was sure shining; I got the impression that with each person he came on in just the style their personality called for, however, to me whichever way he spoke the words came out exactly the same. I wondered how he could keep repeating the same silly statements over and over with such emotion. This got me very tired, and exhausted I drove from the Denver theater to Burroughs, a short distance away on Reforma. There was Joan, the same as ever, but Bill wouldn't be home for an hour or more because it wasn't noon yet and that was his lunch hour. He had been working across town for the last few months, with a construction outfit. While I waited I decided to work on the front spring of the Ford. I had two sets of wheels under double fenders, one directly behind the other, and what with the weak spring too I could hardly steer. Lying under my car, with my legs draped over the curb, I was the butt of jokes and scorn from all the Mexican women and children crowding about. I couldn't understand their words and could only see their feet and brown bare legs from my prone position, yet I knew they thought I was a fool for having such a car and dumber yet for trying to fix it.

By golly, I was having a hellofa time fixing it too; I just wasn't able to get the nuts off the bolts, figure out what came next and what went where or anything else. I had taken everything apart by the time Bill showed up, but had botched it so that I knew I couldn't get it all back together. Bill came out to the street in his work overalls, watched what I was doing and talked with me about the most commonplace things. I realized Bill had reformed completely and was so changed he didn't even remember his past. Just then the Mexican plainclothes men arrived; Bill saw them before I did and scurried into the house, altho there was no stuff in his possession. I just kept fussing around the car as tho I wasn't aware of their presence. They interrupted my activities with tender questions about my business here in the narrow street, blocking traffic and creating a nuisance and hazard to the public by drawing a crowd with my nonsensical car repairs. At the same time they stuck their noses into my upholstery sniffing for contraband, obsequiously snuck up my hood to search the motor but didn't mention it or quiz me about anything else. I told them I had no money for a mechanic, was having trouble putting the spring back in and asked their help. This scared them away; they wouldn't soil their handsome suits and so left me there working under the car and cussing like hell to pretend anger and hurry to cover my emotional relief and to successfully hide my thankfulness at their departure. I felt that Bill's rushing into the safety of his home was not to desert me or because he recalled ever having been a victim of the police, but simply the crowd had made him nervous and when some forgotten sense had warned him there was to be trouble he'd avoided any bothersome explanation since it might have made him late for the afternoon's work.

P.S. Later I found Bill was dead (not sadly, but gone off gently to Africa) and Joan's partner had been the man I now tell you about.

On August 17th at noon I was called from the Watsonville extra brakeman's board to work on the Salinas Classifier, local run no. 353, which goes on duty daily except Sunday at 2:50 P.M. I had been living in Watsonville for over a week at this time and about 2:30 or so I sauntered from the dorms to the yard-office all ready for a hard night's work and carrying my light, hat, gloves, coat; wearing my levis, army shirt and heavy hi-top shoes. I recall that afternoon I had really blasted just before being called, and, Jack, I can't overemphasize how completely stoned I would get in those Watsonville dormitories alone. That day wonderful sensations of feeling each action I made, every little movement was divine; I slowly shut my dorm door and clicked my heels down the long hard linoleum corridor. I felt again the strong tunnel sensation of this hallway, with the rose color my dark glasses gave to the harsh sunlight coming into the building from its front door. Once on the street I strode with precision and grace and came to think of the above-noted clothes. I turned up the tracks from the depot to go the few hundred yards to the place where the traincrews always meet, the crossing shanty hard by the yard-office. I saw the watchman, who I knew, sitting inside his cubbyhole. On the stool outside sat Bill Burroughs in overalls, checkered plaid wool shirt, similar jacket and—my eyes bulged—the same, exact same, black felt hat that Bill wears. The hat was the same, but the rest of the clothes different; except for these clothes, HERE WAS BILL BURROUGHS! I looked him over real careful believe you me. Everything I say here is *EXACT*. With t-heightened perception I compared him with Bill. The same sandy hair, same shape head, ears, forehead, cheeks, chin, mouth, nose, eyes and exact same style glasses. Now slowly reread last sentence, IMAGINE! Nose exact length, eyes same watery blue, (most important, these eyes gave out pure replica of look Bill sends out on world; you know the usual look that a certain pair of eyes present; Bill's is calm, slightly smug because the eyes know what its owner is doing all the time; somewhat bland since the eyes are not due to be surprised; patient eyes that learned there's no good in emotion and eyeball straining and rolling; eyes that look out carefully and do not bore into others; open, but always hiding behind an almost imperceptible shade which allows no one to plumb their depths; eyes that show there is a cool mind working inside that head; they don't impress, belabor or make a point of themselves; intelligent and calm, going overboard not to express emotion, they never give away what's happening inside, but one glance into them shows one there is instant awareness of each moment's occurrence; yet coupled to this a noncommittal attitude of detachment and one realizes these eyes will always stay this way; one will never be confronted with a sudden startling expression passing thru them; set in their business of just looking out to observe and not playing the game of showing what's inside, they are a likeable organ for there never is the need to meet them with one's own eyes. When Bill realizes any eyeball intercourse is in the offing he throws the bland covering over his iris to break contact and withdraws just in sufficient degree to discourage pursuit. Elimination of penetration makes it impossible to ever attain the pleasure (knowing one's eye is receiving wholly and completely another eye's intention and mutually that eye receiving to its very toes the meaning one's own eye gives) or the pressure (fear, combat, embarrassment, anger, disgust, etc.) of the eyeball-game, etc., etc.); this man sitting there had on Bill's modern rimless glasses too. The whole head, I repeat, was perfect in all dimensions, coloring and texture. The neck was Bill's thin one. Looking at the body I knew the secret of this amazing reproduction: he had Bill's exact build, same type of structure. Combine this with his height, 6 ft. and a cunt-hair, weight, around 160, and you got Bill B. Slim B. ambling along with his head slightly forward and down, as he got up and walked across the tracks for his daily ritual of an ice cream cone before work. But, wait, he comes back; I see he has B's same long thin hands as he gracefully curls his tapering fingers about the cone. I see again B's long legged bent-knee stride as he walks to the yard-office to get the freight bills, I realized this guy would fool any of us, perhaps Joan even, if he was in B's perennial sharkskin suit; he had his hat as it was. Then I was sad; I knew when this fellow opened his mouth to speak his voice and choice of words would not be in such duplication as was his looks, mannerisms and walk. He came out then and asked if I was Cassady; I actually shivered with joy; he did have the same style of speech, so matter-of-fact and somewhat lip-pursing. I thought, by god, if he'll just give me one little snort thru the nose I'll demand some t. So, we sat down to wait; this job hardly ever got out of the yards on time, or even within a couple of hours of being on time. This gave me plenty of time to dig the old boy. His name is Hubbard[54] (he has a perfectly crazy first and middle name that I love, but I've suddenly forgotten it and here in SF I can't call him or anyone to get it; will tell you later) and he's been a brakie on SP 14 years, the last 10 of them out of Watsonville. He has wife, 13 and about 7 yr. old boys, house west of town and 37 Chev. Loves to hunt and fish (every damn RR man does) and in off season, until recently, used to run a grocery store. He doesn't talk much, but is always right in there when you mention anything and will carry it along. We finally left town and got to Salinas to do our work of switching out 2 complete 100 car trains of reefers, one for another job, then we'd eat, and one for us to bring back to Watsonville. I outdid myself to do a

54. No doubt inspired by Neal's letter, Kerouac was later to use the pseudonym Hubbard for the William Burroughs character in his books *Visions of Cody, Dr. Sax, Desolation Angels, Book of Dreams,* and *Vanity of Duluoz.*

good job of pin-pulling etc., since he was the tagman who ran the job and he was perfect at it (more examples later of why he's about the best rail I know) and I wanted everything to go smooth so we'd click. We made a good team and he liked to work with me and came to sound more like, instead of less, B every minute. We'd get the switchlist and he'd say, "Well, Neal, let's get 2 behind 3 off 1, then double to 4 to set out the east cars, spot the express reefer, pull 5 and kick 7 down the lead, then it'll be a trey, deuce, 4, another deuce, 5 aces, and a trey, hang the head car and come to 15 to shove that rail, then get the caboose (crummy) off the limey and we'll cross over to tie up 8." That does sound like Bill, huh? But, honestly, aside from any rail talk Hubb (called him) sounds just like Bill when he's telling a story. I'd make some crack and laugh and lead him into any subject at hand about which to make snide remarks; usually this was the trainmaster, a new one, little jerk named Payne. When he got onto Payne's path he would wring it dry, like Bill, and further his imagination pleased him, as B's does him, and beginning with: "Pain is right," or "Painful Payne," he'd build up a story about Payne's blunders in handling the RR as B makes a story of Charlie Ellisore[55] running amuck in a schoolbus and not controlling his penis, (but handling it good) and soon Hubb *would* be snickering down his nose just like B; no genuine snorts tho.

Dec. 5

More and more, Hubb is a subject I've decided to save until I see you.

The motherfuckinbrakeman who is to fix my car has been unavailable for over six weeks now and all I get is promises. Horseshit.

I'm so broke I haven't enuf to come east in one shot; I'm afraid I'll be "booming" all over the country fore I get to NY, however, I've already written Diana I'll be there around Jan. 10, so, in one of the first weeks of the next year I will pop in on you and your family at Richmond Hill. If your mother and wife can't make you behave tell them I can fix your old red wagon up brown and make you grovel all over the place by just hinting that this fine old Ekotape is broken or that we wouldn't let you use it unless you're a good boy and make lots of money for fur coats and beerbottles. Then too, of course, there's

55. Charlie Ellisore was Burroughs's farming neighbor in New Waverly, Texas. He appears as Jimmy Low at the beginning of the tape section of *Visions of Cody*.

the national guard with its black and yellow pigeon-toes; if that doesn't give you a hardon nothing will, unless you happen to prefer a more expensive model with an extra wheelbase, but those things are likely to occur only on Palm Sundays.

I'm sure happy to hear you got married; naturally I was as surprised as all git out, but I knew you had to do it sometime. When a man approaches 30 (ugh) without being well on the way to having little kiddillies it begins to become a teensy bit too late and soon all he can do is write books. It'd be fine, then, if your "impregnated on the 18?"[56] is right and there is a-building in the mixer a miniature K, with big ears and a bigger thingajigger. Since you're poor as me nowadays we shouldn't mind too much if he's postponed for a short time. You tell that wonderful girl you picked out of that whole big city to just relax and not get into the silly habit of worry. That old bugaboo is one thing girls shouldn't bother themselves with, all they gotta do is leave everything up to the old man, cater to a couple of whims, play along like a Pollyanna whenever it seems he can't be reached at the moment and by not making with the emotional upset game so clear the air that it'll brace up both of them. Beyond this bunk tho, Jack, with all your fooleries, you can never escape your serious and overconcerned nature nor the destiny of your blood and your inclination, to the Home (what the hell has your wonderful mother and father taught you all these last 25 years and what else but this is your great book full of?) and all the times you've spoken about, and otherwise revealed, to me the hankering for family. If there is ever any fear on this score by Joan, you tell her not to be blinded and misled in the glow produced by the sparks and flame created with the hot friction of the mass of things in collision on your heated mind's surface, that the germ of your emotional need of family is unalterable and her cross to bear (if so) is having the unusual distinction of being married to a man so rare that there is contained in his soul a paradox that few attain. Because I better keep a few things to myself, Jack, I shore ain't gonna tell you what the hell the fragile beauty of the flower in your soul is, and I won't come out with any fancy names for you to play around with; if Joan, at any time, wants to find out the real lowdown on you, or what nonsense I'm putting out about paradox and all that junk, you just tell

56. Kerouac wrote to Neal on November 21 (*SL,* pp. 235–36) that he had possibly impregnated Joan on November 18. This appears to have been incorrect, since their only child, Janet Michelle, was born on February 16, 1952, and was therefore conceived around May 1951.

her to get me a joint of honest nigger weed (or price of same) and I'll tell her what makes you tick in exactly no time at all. Incidentally, I wrote a letter to Allen (in which I shot off my mouth about a lot of stuff I don't know a thing about and struggled thru just because I've never written, actually put down the words, nor (I discovered as I wrote) thought of that kind of trash before) and rejoiced over a prospective oz of great shit; connection fell through, damdam-damdam.

Love to that fine little gal you got—Lucky stiff—ahem, uh—is it?

N.

While Carolyn painted his portrait, Neal wrote to John Clellon Holmes with more reminiscences of his teenage years in Denver.

TO JOHN CLELLON HOLMES

Dec. 7, 1950
[San Francisco]

DEAR JOHN, THE RAMBLER OF ST. IVES;

Woooooooooooooooooooooooooooooooooooooooooooooooooo oooooo-EEEE! A real whiz of a letter, a whoop-de-do that you may not have overextended yourself too much to rip off, but, for me, the hard work involved—with 20 man-hours of sweat—WOULD make a similar feat impossible. I don't know where to begin and certainly can't answer your 10 single-spaced pages of monumental thought.

I'm typing this blind and with one finger since Carolyn has me in an impossible pose (with my eyes on the ceiling) for another of her innumerable portraits of me, so please excuse all the mistakes—tho I'm writing at rate of 2 words a minute to avoid them.

Denver, in the magnificent Spring of 1940, was a pretty joyous place for me. I was living with the family of one Bill Mackley, with whom, years before, I'd sold papers in friendly rivalry on opposing street corners. Previously we had stayed with his bro-in-law, only sister, and their two kids in a runt of a shack smack in the middle of the city dump at 53rd and Columbine Sts. We were to live with them again—come 1941—in a tenement apt. on 36th and Gilpin where they had moved after truly just barely escaping with their lives the winter night their self-built dumpy home poofed up in flame created by the drunken sister's dropped still lit cigarette. This sister of Bill's

(Dorothy) was a real rounder and there's a lot to be said about her, but I'm not concerned with her here because at this time Bill and I were living off the begrudged generosity of his parents. Bill Sr., and his wife, Dorothy Sr., were typical of countless poverty-ridden couples on Denver's lower eastside. The fine life before the depression rankled their memory, but they knew it was gone forever. The old jane was always comparing her present struggles with the easy existence of past decades and yearned after it so that she constantly bitched at her husband, and Bill and myself too. Bill's father tempered his hankering after the old days with a fatalism conditioned by long years of being the victim of his wife's tongue. Besides which, the difference in their respective attitudes toward this mutually important "remembrance of things past" that hung over them was further accentuated by the many years of hard drinking they had done together. Whereas Dorothy was always raving against everything, drunk or sober, in her shrill sharp style, Bill Sr. only mentioned bygone times when he had a jag on, and then always in the form of stories told to us boys in a beautiful soft tone. He used to sit for hours, on these occasions, curled on the end of the couch of the living room in their beatup three room 2nd floor apt. at 31st and Stout Sts. With his long thin legs crossed, and his hand on the outer thigh of the upper leg, he would give out wry tales of happenings that were mostly imagined, but the hesitant sweet way he caressed each word (sometimes several minutes would pass between each word and from the beginning of a sentence to its completion took 15 minutes) and the bland smile forever on his toothless mouth would raise itself to a gentle chortle at those moments when his sly mind reached out especially far to recall some potent wit. He never wore a serious mien, even when sober, and broad humor spiced with pure pointlessness was his dish. Despite his efforts I knew he was a sad old boy and loved him for it. He was a painter and paperhanger and the men of this trade are notorious drunkards. Because of this man I was to improve my living, immensely enlarge my outlook, and to change altogether the course of my life. Thru him I met Brierly and everything subsequent follows—.

The days I spent bicycling and the nights I devoted to the gang. I was about the only one of us who had a job, so they treated me with respect. Most of the others had access to a car though and this equalizer sure had its effect on me. The story of the social life I luxuriated in that season must await another day, but I did have some fine flurries of fucking.

Late P.M.

This whole damn thing must await another day; I just got called and told I was cut-off from the RR in SF; I've got to go to San Luis Obispo for a last trip or two before I'm released entirely until next May. So, since I will see you and Marian in a month or so (if things go right) and I have a lot to do before I catch my train tonight, hope to continue this verbally soon.

Love to all,
N.

With Neal sent back to work in San Luis Obispo, Carolyn kept him up-to-date with domestic news, quoting from Dr. Spock's book on child care.

TO NEAL CASSADY FROM CAROLYN CASSADY

Saturday [December 9, 1950
San Francisco]

DEAR HONEY-BUN;

Aha, I can write another letter at you . . . The enclosed came yesterday. If you like I can just jot off a check and you can pay me when you get it and get here. Check book should come today . . . Probably also the landlord's since the rent is overdue.

May as well fill this up with Diana chit-chat about the wife and kiddies. Oi.

Called Louise about watching Jamie. She said no she had to clean out the basement. I said OK, I'll have to manage when you're gone anyway. Then she said no, she had decided to work upstairs so I must leave her. So comes the last minute, I push the doorbell 5 minutes, no answer. So I come back in, deposit kids again, run around back, and there is Louise in the basement. Too late now, so I just give Jamie to her. Cathy and I made such good time, altho soaked, we were out of the doctors by 10:40. He said she could start school Monday. Having this time, I trotted C down and got her shoes too. Got back at noon as I'd planned. Went to collect Jamie, and there she was, lying on a mat in the basement covered with some old cloth of some kind. She really looked like an orphan. She had cried for me and then gone asleep. (I had assured L that she wouldn't because she didn't wake till 8:30, but I think it was one of her escape sleeps . . . which she does when she gets mad, cries and gets no attention.) Anyway, her pants were full, but L had had no time for her. That's all very well, since it was best anyway for me, but I wonder what happened to her vehement decision to work upstairs. Oh well, it didn't feel too cold and J is none the worse, but that's the last time I can go anywhere without her, evidently. I called the school and they almost said no they were too full. But then they decided Cathy could go if I get her promptly at 3. They cut off an hour every time, and that will be hard to manage, cutting the afternoon square in two. I'll have to start training J to nap at this time, but I think I can leave her OK in the mornings until she is really walking. Then I'll think of something else. (I know, you offered the car . . . I wish I could risk it too, but still feel too nervous about it, and am sure I'd never make it back up the hill. It would save 20 cents a day too.)

We settle back in the old routine as soon as the door shuts behind you. This time it's lonelier somehow, but not depressive. Cathy is better, and sleeping better too. (The night you left, she was a wreck and I had to let her sleep with me all night.) I think all this goes to show what the authorities point out and the nursery school maintains rigidly . . . that 2 year olds must have a regular schedule every day in order to feel "secure." But I don't see how people in big families manage it . . . certainly then there is a lot of coming and going and rushing about. I suppose the mealtime and bedtimes can be organized and settled. Still with a job like yours it's difficult too. Anyway, I'd hate to end up saying that C is better off with just me and Jamie . . . I just think the answer is that her day isn't full enough as is, and that she senses my unrest and more so yours. I also believe it is either city living . . . no immediate access to outside roving, or else my inability to manage it in the city. A large part of it in the final analysis is that I worry about her too much and haven't a purpose and plan to my own life to sweep her along with, right? Anyhoo, the point here being, that we'll get along just as well without a father for the next few months as you generously offered, and I think unless she has one permanently and for keeps she shouldn't have temporary ones every now and again at any age. She's now playing here very nicely with Jamie and the toys as she did yesterday. School should help, and as I see it, this is the best I can do until either I get a settled life or she is old enough so it's either too late or doesn't matter. At least I see no reason for me to be emotionally upset any more to the extent I have been so that should be important to her. Doncha think so. I look at them now and see that they're both babies, two little helpless trusting beings looking at ME!

So, poppie, you just work on your own troubles, but we're here if you want us to help. I only wish I knew a way. I feel that when you do try and express your anxieties, and I try and show you I'm sympathetic by giving you "reasons" for your feelings which are never real causes and don't hit your sore spot, that you then feel I don't understand and no one does and you have to just bury it deeper. Then you are less and less inclined to try and express them . . . . . then I complain you don't confide in me on and on ad nauseam. Yet all the time, I try and say *something* to show I care or am feeling around for you or to help draw you out. But nothing helps. I'm still stuck with my old theory of "security," but since you've never had it, it's impossible to guess where you'd find it. I, having had it once, can better find ways to find at least temporary contentments by picking up old habits and actions. But of course these don't do anything for you. Oh fob!

Why can't we just love each other simply and directly. Absolutely too much introspection and analysis. Such as another thing I noted the other day. There's a way of looking at members of the opposite sex which you and I never do. The other evening I looked up at you when you were kissing me and saw such a look (tho I think it was the angle and my interpretation, not you looking so.) My old heart bounced on my diaphragm. I can never look at you that way, since I can only use it on guys whom I think want me and who are "in my power" so to speak. You have only looked at me that way when jealous . . . like the night Bud[57] was here and you outside. That's the passion stuff and that which makes for good sex and more lasting excitement in the love (you and Lu have this all the time, but this exclusively which doesn't work either). Still, we need more of this, but apparently, since we didn't have it to start with as do most couples, we can only reach it thru conflict. Otherwise we know each other too well or something. Interesting thing . . . I keep dreaming about you as Chuck and when talking to myself around here, often speak of you but say Chuck instead of Neal. Maybe the only male relationship I can know of, permanently at any rate, is that of a brother . . . or maybe our "buddy" solution is the only one. I guess we're both misfits even to ourselves.

Forwarded a letter from JK and Mrs.[58] I'll bet Jack has all his kids

57. A friend of Carolyn's brother, Chuck Robinson.

58. Kerouac wrote to Neal on December 3, in a letter published in edited form in *SL*, pp. 237–41.

by one wife . . . at least by one at a time. These things. Your son. My daughters. Too many people. Too little and too much love. What's up. WHAT DOES THE FUTURE HOLD? Aha . . . exciting any way. What what what what

I want you for Christmas. Don't stay away too long. Try and find what will lift the rock, snap the shackles and we'll all do our best to get it for you.

Isn't this a nice wifey letter? Aren't you sick up to here with em? Well write me something, do your agonizing on paper. Don't let Helen pick on you and come back home soon.

Love

CI

No mail yet from your lover, probably today. Nope, just got the mail. Well! I leave you as the radio sings "I'll miss you, but I won't be lonely; I'll remember April and I'll smile." That's like I always say, I'm so glad I got married in April, there are so many tender sentiments to rely on . . . ain't that right Gertrude? Now it's "I get along without you very well." So you see?[59]

P.S. Cathy eats all her meals fine again now . . . and she measures 35 inches.

Tell Helen I'm mad she didn't write & that I miss her while wrapping packages & that I'll have a lot of stuff left if she needs any.

TO NEAL CASSADY FROM CAROLYN CASSADY

Monday [December 11, 1950
San Francisco]

DEAR POPPIE;

Well, here I am again, with the daily newsletter from the wife in the West . . . in the little gray home in the. I trust you like mail there.

I have a new little girl. Her name is Cathy. WOW what a relief! She chirped off to school merrily this A.M. and felt so free I dug right into all the clutter, dirt and mildew. The back porch is livable again,

59. "I'll Remember April," music by Gene DePaul, lyrics by Don Raye and Patricia Johnston, from the 1942 western musical comedy *Ride 'em Cowboy*. "I Get Along Without You Very Well," words by Jane Brown Thompson, music by Hoagy Carmichael (1938).

and I even restrung all that clothesline overhead (tho all the wash isn't hung *yet*). Worked like a little beaver but have only made a dent. Hope I can get everything shipshape by the time you return, and also get it organized for when Annette appears. Apparently my poor old mind can only function on one thing at a time, so when there is anyone else around I get so confused I can't see what's going on. Amazing to be so. Anyway, I got Cathy at 3, they say she was fine and she was so happy and sweet the rest of the afternoon we were both in ecstasy. She missed Jamie evidently 'cause she talked about her all the way going and coming back and loved her up all evening. She has gotten color in her face again and what with her bangs cut and in her bright red suit, she looked so breathtakingly beautiful, I couldn't believe she's mine. But the laughter and agreeableness made a big difference. We just had fun all the time. She got a few fears back by bedtime, and we had a little difficulty there, but most of it was just because she was so manic and couldn't settle down to solemn sleep. Finally she kept saying "Poppie's bringing re-cream" tho she is apparently resigned that Poppie is working in 'bispo on a choo choo tain. She only waked twice last night and once a legit request for toilet, so we'll see how goes it tonight. Jamie was a cross patch much of the day, probably missing Cathy too, and in the evening couldn't quite see why Cathy was so suddenly affectionate so took it not in the spirit of things. But I put some bubble in her bath tonight (to hide the stopper so she'd leave the water in a minute) and was she funny! She was fascinated by the bubbles, would splosh so hard it would all fly in her face and then she'd look up giggling and gulping suds. You know how she sits down . . . plopping her fanny a foot away from home plate . . . well when she'd do that in the tub, she'd hit the side and the curve would give her a push and she'd skate on her tail sideways down the length of the tub. She kept floundering around slipping and sliding and I was laughing so hard it was all I could do to rescue her in dangerous moments. She stood up once after a big duck and looked like this: (if I can get it . . . sort of French poodle). Well, much funnier to see . . . plus her expressions. I think we should call her Tullu . . . because of her long brown bob and mugging. (The shading is just to show white soap contrast, not colored.) Which reminds me too, that when alone, I bathe them both every night and have fun, whereas otherwise it's a big chore. Ohmygosh . . . what's the matter with me. Yesterday, per se, regarding Cathy, I decided to let her do whatever she'd like just to see how awful it would be or to prove to myself that nothing so chaotic would happen. But even while the resolve was forming, I was already "don't"ing and *could not* stop it. As each one added more guilt, by the end of the day I was shrieking at her in the old style. I know no worse agony or frustration than not to be able to control oneself even when one knows and desires desperately to do otherwise. I could have torn down a wall. The same way with you . . . when I'm alone here, I think of all the bossy and bitchy things I've said to you and wonder why on earth I ever felt that way and how I could do it. I wish I wish I knew a way to get along with you and with the kids and with myself. I am so sick of battling myself . . . of being a slave to my inner compulsions and neuroses yet ardently desiring the opposite of what I am doing or can do. How can I just resign myself to being what I seem to have become or what is showing I am when I don't really feel that way, and want so badly to be otherwise. What a life.

Last night after beating myself about Cathy's horrible day, I reread Spock[60] and saw some things I'd forgotten or which hadn't applied till now. He mentions about all her current problems, so I guess it's normal, and he finally says just hold tight, there's clearer sailing ahead. One thing I thought interesting in the light of her behavior when you were here and which had us baffled . . . maybe this is it: "Sometimes a child around two and a half can get along with either parent alone, but when the other one appears, he flies into a rage. It may be partly jealousy, but at an age when he's sensitive about being bossed (ouch!), and trying to do a little bossing himself, I imagine he feels outnumbered when he has to take on two important people at once. It is more often the father who has to take the abuse at this period, and he sometimes gets the feeling he's pure poison. He shouldn't take it seriously. If he will learn when not to barge in and how to let the child come to him when he feels like it, he can keep the explosions to a minimum. He can feel confident that the child loves him underneath. By 3 or so it will probably all be different." This last doesn't exactly fit you as the father, but I put it in just in case you felt like poison at times. (I had almost drawn that conclusion in my last, no?) Also about the bedtime thing, he says that since they are dependent at this age on the parents, they want to keep track of them and hence want to come out of the room for various reasons. I've noticed that Cathy does look around when I take her to the toilet, I suppose to see if you are about. Sometimes she asks, or rather guesses, or just says aloud where you are and waits for confirmation. It now appears

60. Dr. Benjamin Spock (1903–1998), *The Common Sense Book of Baby and Child Care* (1946).

that it is age 3 when they need fathers the most, tho naturally no age is excluded, but at 2 there should be few changes, take everything slow etc., but at 3 they reach the stage in their emotional development when they feel their fathers and mothers are wonderful people, identify themselves with them, etc. The automatic balkiness, the hostility that was just below the surface at 2½ seems to disappear after 3. The feelings toward the parents aren't just friendly; they are warm and tender. Here are some tid bits about fatherless children . . . I pass them on just to give you some reading matter in your present dilemma, to impress them on myself, and because I never remember to read them with you tho we discuss the subject a lot:

"It would be foolish to say that his father's absence or death makes no difference to a child, or that it's easy for a mother to make it up to him in other ways. But if the job is well handled, the child, either boy or girl, can continue to grow up normal and well adjusted.

"The mother's spirit is most important. She may feel lonely or anxious or cross at times, and she will sometimes take it out on the child. This is all natural and won't hurt him too much. The important thing is for her to go on being a normal human being, keeping up her friendships, her recreations, her outside activities as far as she can. (Hmm) This will be hard if she has a baby or child to take care of and no one to help her. But she can ask people in, and take the baby to a friend's house etc. (ha). It is more valuable to him to have his mother stay cheerful and outgoing than to have his routine stay perfect.

"A child, whether he's young or old, boy or girl, needs to be friendly with other men if the father is not there. With the baby up to the age of a year or two, a good deal is accomplished if he can just be reminded frequently that there are such creatures as agreeable men, with lower voices, different clothes and manners than women." (Milkman, grocer or something.)

"As a child grows on toward 3 and over, the kind of companionship with men is increasingly important. Whether he is boy or girl, he needs chances to be with and feel close to other men and older boys." This next sort of hits: "ANY CHILD of 3 or over will build up an image of his father which will be his IDEAL AND INSPIRATION, whether he remembers him or not. The other friendly men that he sees and plays with will give substance to the image, will influence his conception of his father, will make his father mean more to him." "The boy without a father particularly needs opportunity to play with other boys, every day if possible by the age of 2, and to be mainly occupied with boyish pursuits. The temptation of the mother who has no other equally strong ties is to make him her closest spiritual companion, getting him interested in . . ." (lists feminine interests).

"It is easy to see that a boy needs a father to pattern himself after, but many people don't realize that a friendly father plays a different but equally important part in the development of a girl. She won't exactly pattern herself after him, but she gains confidence in herself as a girl and a woman from feeling his approval. I'm thinking of little things . . ." (lists dress, hair-do, cookies) "When she is older, he can show her that he's interested in her opinions and let her in on some of his. Later, when she has boy friends, it's important for him to welcome them, even if he secretly doesn't think they are quite good enough for her . . . She, by learning to enjoy the qualities in him that are particularly masculine, is getting ready for her adult life in a world that is half made up of men. The way she makes friendships with boys and men later, the kind of man she eventually falls in love with, the kind of married life she makes, will all be influenced strongly by the kind of relationship she has with her father throughout her childhood." *Mine,* for instance!

Enuf about fathers. He also says first children have it tougher. Also, I just glanced thru the part about jealousy, and he says it's not possible that there be none . . . that even when the older child appears affectionate, his feelings are mixed, when he squeezes the baby too hard in hugging it, it isn't accidental, and that the jealousy comes out in all sorts of ways. Yipes, maybe this is her trouble! No doubt her concern today was partly because she realized Jamie was home with me, and she out. She did keep saying "Jamie home." Also she hugged her a lot too hard and 'kissed' her with her teeth. So now I better watch that too, tho I thought I'd done pretty well there. It seems this might be the clue. Incidentally, she has gotten up 4 times in the last 25 minutes. Worse than ever. Boy oh boy. Blissful afternoon blasted. Patience . . . .

I wish to hell I could live, love and *enjoy* life! You, the kids, and everything, and stop being so damned anxious, fearful and bitchy. How, where, when, who. WHY. All this probing . . . I yi yi. I was never so. The father business made me wonder if it would be better for C never to know one, to acquire one suddenly at a later age, or to switch them suddenly. I think the middle choice is the worst . . . Imagine what that would do to a child beyond the age 3 period, not having allowed for such a relationship and being so much closer to mother. I think just friendly men would almost be better, not one . . . unless at a still later age she liked one enough. Oh jesus, I don't know, nor do I see much point in my deciding. All those alternatives are not at hand and anyway I don't know how to run a normal household, so why worry about the abnormal ones yet. Last night I had a whole new angle worked out whereby I could see a sort of a life for you and me . . . an agreement sort of thing if there were no Diana. Even with her distantly I could almost see then, since I should be used to such threats and not afraid any more . . . but this A.M. I figured oh what the hell, leave well enough alone. Anyway, besides being tired of the particular struggle, why should I be bothered with Dianas and LuAnnes. They tell me I have all the necessary traits of looks, brains, talent and "Goood background" so I should be able to pass it off on some joe who thinks those things are desirable, and doesn't realize the myth. Besides a *highschool* boy whistled at me *two* different times, so I'm so damned cocky . . . HA! On top of all which the fact remains that when you're here all is not as I feel it to be when you're away tho I don't understand it and know I'm to blame and thus doubt seriously I'll ever be able to be easygoing with anyone. And further and beyond all else, there is no decision pending anyway, all is as it is, and why keep on with it only except I guess because I have nothing else to think on and I think about you as a result fairly often. Finally, I'm hopeless.

But nevertheless, Duckie, you are being missed, and we are eagerly anticipating Christmas so you *must* be here. I'm trying, albeit, not to make a lot of plans etc. so as to get my recurring disappointments, but just to enjoy you, it and the kiddies as much as possible, and hope most of all that it will be some kind of fun for you, since I suspect it will be like most of yours . . . nothing so much as just watching somebody else's. I wish I could think of some way to make you feel more a part of it and something to take your mind off your anxieties and the horrid immediate future you will be facing . . . all alone. I repeat, I'm hopeless.

You should see the tree now. Who said no packages. And they are only half here. I hope you'll enjoy the kids, even tho it isn't as important to them this year, it should be funny too. Some of their things, which are of course, really mine as far as enjoyment and the fun of it goes, weren't wrapped, so I had to see some. I wrapped them tho and they'll be a surprise to you then. One of Cathy's is a dream, and I think we'll love it as much as she or more. I'll have to put it out of reach after the initial inspection I think. Anyway, there is also lots of food I'm sure, and that you can share . . . besides I can't eat all those plum puddings alone. Helen and I had the last ones till Easter. Anyway, the packages are stacked now, and as I say, more on the way. I can't believe mine are all wrapped and all but two sent, which I'll do tomorrow. Whew. (Cathy opened a book too.)

Speaking of futures . . . I sent the papers to Dr. H. re the disability and she said she'd extend it but I don't know yet how long.

Dad got the dog but not until FRIDAY! Should have been Wednesday. And that small crate and not much food. Dad said he was very gaunt and ate a full meal and drank a whole bottle of milk at the office. Mom came in while he was writing and he says she was in raptures, so I guess all is well there. He also sent a check for all, so relax.

Cathy has to have her picture taken yet, and I'll TRY and do it Saturday., but if Louise is busy I may have to wait for you. I think the new book is made up soon, so it should be done.

I'm anxious to get back at the back yard too. It was a beautiful Spring day Saturday (we all went walking) but the rain is back. Everything reeks of mildew and oozes. No rain forecast for the next day or so, so maybe, maybe. The silly lilies are about to bloom and it's only Christmas . . . not Easter.

I think about your writing all the time and what fun it is.

Well, this should help you get to sleep. Be careful how you handle that thingajigger.

God, having just mailed you a letter from D, I think of you swamped with details of your children all over the country and how desperately you must wish you were free of the whole lot. What on earth are *you* doing in this situation, Neal Cassady? Life is a bag of tricks.

Hurry home Santy, and you *might* drop me a line . . . I worry about your feelings at present. Nite nite poppie.

Love,

CAROLYN

CATHLEEN

CÉLINE

CASSADY

Tuesday A.M.—Cathy had to sleep with me finally—guess it isn't just you or men the cause. She woke up, looked at your side of the bed & kept saying "Poppie, Poppie, Poppie," etc.

On his return from San Luis Obispo, Neal typed Kerouac a long letter of reminiscences of his life in Denver following his release from the Colorado State Reformatory in 1945. Known as the "Joan Anderson" letter, it had a free-flowing conversational approach that was much praised by Kerouac, who later claimed that it directly inspired the style he adopted in his April 1951 scroll typescript of On the Road. *The original letter is lost, and the fragment that follows is estimated to be less than half of the total.*[61]

TO JACK KEROUAC

PERSONAL: For Security Reasons

[December 17, 1950]
29 Russell St.,
San Francisco, Calif.

. . . To have seen a specter isn't everything, and there are deathmasks piled, one atop the other, clear to heaven. Commoner still are the wan

61. In early 1955 Ginsberg loaned Neal's letter, together with work by himself and Kerouac, to Gerd Stern, a poet who was the West Coast representative of A. A. Wyn's Ace Books, in the hope of getting them published. (Ace had published William Burroughs's *Junkie* in 1953.) Kerouac later claimed, in interviews, that the Joan Anderson letter was lost by Stern over the side of the houseboat in which he lived in Sausalito, California. Stern strongly denies this, maintaining that he returned all materials, including Neal's letter, to Allen Ginsberg when they were rejected by Ace.

Estimates of the size of the complete letter have ranged from 13,000 to 40,000 words. The surviving extract is 5,100 words long. The original envelope of the letter, and the double-sided handwritten addendum of December 22, are preserved in the Ginsberg archives at Columbia University. From the amount of postage used it is possible to estimate the size of the letter as twelve to twenty pages (10,000 to 16,000 words). In recent communication with Gerd Stern, he clearly recalls that the letter comprised seventeen typed pages. Given Neal's average rate of eight hundred words per page at that time, this would amount to around 13,600 words for seventeen complete pages, closely matching Kerouac's original estimate, in his December 27 reply to Neal, of 13,000 words. It would appear that a portion of the letter had been copied, probably by Kerouac, before it was lost. In 1964 John Bryan published the surviving extract in his magazine *Notes from Underground* #1, calling it "The First Third." Bryan claims that Neal came along to his 1303 Rhode Island Street, San Francisco, basement and helped him print it. The title used is confusing, but it may be that by that date Neal was considering the Joan Anderson extract as part of his ongoing autobiography. The same extract was published by City Lights in 1971 as an addendum to Neal's book *The First Third* and was later to form the basis of the 1997 movie *The Last Time I Committed Suicide,* directed by Stephen T. Kay, and starring Thomas Jane and Keanu Reeves.

visages of those returning from the shadow of the valley. This means little to those who have not lifted the veil.

The ward nurse cautioned me not to excite her (how can one prevent that?) and I was allowed only a few minutes. The head-nurse also stopped me to say I was permitted to see her just because she always called my name and I must cheer her. She had had a very near brush and was not rallying properly, actually was in marked decline, and still much in danger. Quite impressed to my duties, I entered and gazed down on her slender form resting so quietly on the high white bed. Her pale face was whiter; like chalk. It was pathetically clear how utterly weak she was, there seemed absolutely no blood left in her body. I stared and stared, she didn't breathe, didn't move; I would never have recognized her, she was a waxed mummy. White is the absence of all color, she was white; all white, unless beneath the covers, whose top caressed her breasts, was still hidden a speck of pink. The thin ivory arms tapered inward until they reached the slight outward bulge of narrow palms, and the hands in turn bent inward with a more sharp taper only to quickly end in long fingers curled to a point. These things, and her head, with its completely matted hair so black and contrasting with all the whiteness, were the only parts of her visible. Quite normal, I know, but I just couldn't get over how awfully dead she looked. I had so arranged my head above hers that when her eyes opened, after about ten minutes, they were in direct line with mine; they showed no surprise, nor changed their position in the slightest. The faintest of smiles, the merest of voices, "hello." I placed my hand on her arm, it was all I could do to restrain myself from jumping on the bed to hold her. I saw she was too weak to talk and told her not to, I, however, rambled on at a great rate.

There was no doubt she was over-joyed to see me, her eyes said so. It was as though the gesture of self-destruction had, in her mind, equalized all the guilt. The courage of committing the act seemed to have justified her to herself. This action on her conviction, no matter how neurotic, had called for all her strength and she was now released. Free from the urge, since the will-for-death needs a strong concentration of pressure to fulfill itself and once accomplished via attempt, is defeated until another period of buildup is gone through; unless, of course, one succeeds in reaching death the first shot, or is really mad. Gazing down on her, with a grin of artificial buoyancy, I sensed this and felt an instant flood of envy. She had escaped, at least for some time, and I knew I had yet to make my move. Being a coward I had postponed too long and I realized I was further away from commitment than ever. Would hesitancy never end? She shifted her cramped hand, I look-down and for the first time noticed the tight sheet covering a flat belly. It was empty, sunken; she had lost her baby. For a moment I wondered if she knew it, then thought she must know—even now she was almost touching her stomach, and she'd been in the hospital ten days—surely a stupid idea. I resolved to think better. The nurse glided up and said I'd better go; promising to return the next visiting day, I leaned over and kissed Joan's clear forehead and left.

Off to the poolhall, back to the old grind; I seemed to have a mania. From the way I loafed there all day one would scarcely believe I'd never been in a poolhall two short years before; why, less than six months ago I still couldn't bear to play more than one game at a time. Well, what is one to say about things he has done? I never again went back to the hospital to bless Joan, oh, that's what I felt like; blessing her. Each day I lacerated myself thinking on her, but I didn't go back. "Sometimes I sits and thinks. Other times I sits and drinks, but mostly I just sits." I must have been in a pretty bad way.

Anyhow, two more weeks went by in this fashion, my inability to stir from my poolhall prison became a joke, even to me. It was the night before Christmas, about five P.M., when a handsome woman near forty came inside the gambling gaol's gates and asked for me. I went up front to meet her, as I came closer I saw she was better than handsome, a real good-looker and despite her age, making quite a stir among the boys. She introduced herself, said she was a friend of Joan and invited me to dinner. My heart bounced with guilty joy, I accepted and we walked the five blocks to this fine-though-forty lady's apartment without talking. The fatherly taxidriver opened the door, my hostess said it was her husband and that Joan would be out in a minute. Preparations for a huge dinner were in the making, I sat on the sofa and waited. The bathroom—ugly word—door swung out and before my eyes was once again the gorgeous Joan, "second" of Jennifer Jones. Fresh from the shower, mirror-primped, stepped my heroine resplendent in her new friend's housecoat. Just when you think you've learned your lesson and swear to watch your step, a single moment offguard will pop up and hope springs high as ever. One startled look and I knew I was right back where I started; I felt again that choking surge flooding me as when first I'd seen her. I started talking to myself, determined to whip the poolhall rut and drag my stinking ass out of the hole.

Over the prosperous supper on which we soon pounced hung an

air of excitement. Joan and I were leaping with lovelooks across the roastbeef, while cabby and wife beamed on us. And we planned, yessir, all four of us, and right out loud too. I was kinda embarrassed at first when the host began without preamble, "Alright, you kids have wasted enough time, I see you love each other and you're going to settle down right now. In the morning Joan is starting at St. Luke's as a student nurse, she's told me that's what she would like to do. As for you, Neal, if you're serious I'll get up a little early tomorrow and before I go to work we'll see if my boss will give you a job. If you can't get away with telling them you're 21—the law says you gotta be 21, you're not that old yet are you? (I said no) so that you can drive taxi, you can probably get a job servicing the cabs. That okay with you?" I said certainly it was and thanked him; and everybody laughed and was happy. It was further decided that Joan and I stay with them until we got our first paycheck; we would sleep on the couch that opened out into a bed. Gorged with the big meal, I retired to the bathroom as the women did the dishes and the old man read the paper. (By golly, it seems everything I write about happens in a bathroom, don't think I'm hungup that way, it's just the incidents exactly as they occurred, and here is another one because—) A knock on the toilet door and I rose to let in my resurrected beauty. She was as coy as ever, but removed was much fear and embarrassment. We did a bit of smooching, then, seated on the edge of the tub she asked if I wanted to see her scar. I kneeled before her to observe better as she parted the bathrobe to reveal an ugly red wound, livid against her buttermilk belly, stretching nearly from navel to the clitoris. She was worried I wouldn't think her as beautiful, or love her as much now that her body had been marred by the surgeon's knife performing a Caesarean. There might have been a partial hysterectomy too and she fretted that the production of more babies—"when we get the money"—would prove difficult. I reassured her on all counts, swore my love (and meant it) and finally we returned to the livingroom.

Oh, unhappy mind; trickster! O fatal practicality! I was wearing really filthy clothes but had a change promised me by a friend who lived at 12th and Ogden Sts. So as not to hangup my dwarf cabbie savior when we went to see his buddyboss next A.M., my foolish head thought to make a speedrun and get the necessary clean impediments now. Acting on this obvious need—if I was to impress my hoped-for employer into hiring me—I promised to hurry back, and left. Where is wisdom? Joan offered to walk with me, and I turned down the suggestion reasoning it was very cold and I could make better time alone, besides, she was still pretty weak, and if she was to work tomorrow the strain of the fairly long walk might prove too much,—no sense jeopardizing her health. Would that I'd made her walk with me, would that she'd collapsed rather than let me go alone, would anything instead of what happened! Not only did the new promise for happiness go down the drain, and I lost Joan forever, but her peace was to evaporate once and for all, and she herself was to sink into the iniquity reserved for a certain type of beaten women!

I rushed my trip to the clothes depot, made good connections and was quickly on my way back to the warm apartment and my Joan. The route from 12th and Ogden to 16th and Lincoln Sts. lies for the most part, if one so desires, along East Colfax Ave. Horrible mistake, stupid moment; I chose that path just to dig people on the crowded thoroughfare as I hustled by them. At midblock between Pennsylvania and Pearl Sts. is a tavern whose plateglass front ill-conceals the patrons of its booths. I was almost past this bar when I glanced up to see my younger blood-brother inside drinking beer alone. I had made good time and the hard habit of lushing that I was then addicted to pushed me through the door to bum a quickie off him. Surprise, surprise, he was loaded with loot and, more surprising, gushed all over me. He ordered as fast as I could drink, and I didn't let the waitress stop, finishing the glass in a gulp; one draught for the first few, then two for the next several and so on until I was sipping normally by the time an hour had fled. First off he wanted a phone number—the reason for his generosity I suspect—and I was the only one who could give it to him. He claimed to have been sitting there actually brooding over the very girl on the other end of this phone number, and I believed him; had to take it true, because for the last five months it had become increasingly clear that he was hot-as-hell for this chick—who was my girl. I gave him the number and he dashed from one booth to the other. I had cautioned him not to mention my name, nor to tell her I was there, and he said he wouldn't. But he did, although he denied it later. The reason for his disloyalty, despite the fact it cost me Joan, was justifiable since as one might when about to be denied a date of importance while drinking, he had used my whereabouts as a lastditch lure to tempt her out. He came back to the booth from the phonebooth crestfallen, she had said she couldn't leave the house just now, but to call her back in a half-hour or so; this didn't cheer him as it would have me, he's richer and less easily satisfied. He called her again, about forty five minutes after I had first been pulled into the dive by my powerful thirst, and she said for him to wait at this joint and she'd be down within an hour. This length of time didn't seem unreasonable, she lived quite a ways further out in East Denver. I thought everything was going perfectly. Bill got the Girl, I got my drinks and still had a short period of grace in which to slop up more before she showed (I certainly didn't intend to be there when she arrived) and I'd only be a little late returning to Joan where I'd plead hassle in getting the clothes. O sad shock, O unpleasant time; had I just not guzzled that last beer all the following would not be written and I could end this story with "And they lived happily ever after."

Whoa, read slowly for a bit and have patience with my verbosity. There are two things I've got to say here, one is a sidepoint and it'll come second, the first is essential to the understanding of this story; so, I gotta give you one of my Hollywood flashbacks.

I'll leave out the most of it and be as brief as possible to make it tight, although, by the nature of it, this'll be hard—especially since I'm tired.

Number 1: On June 23, 1945 I was released from Colorado State Reformatory, after doing eleven months and 10 days (know the song?)[62] of hard labor. Soon after returning to Denver I had the rare luck to meet a 16-year-old East Hi beauty who had well-to-do parents; a mother and pretty older sister to be exact. Cherry Mary (Mary Ann Freeland) was her name because she lived on Cherry Street and was a cherry when I met her. That condition didn't last long. I ripped into her like a maniac and she loved it. A tremendous affair, countless things to be said about it—I can hardly help from blurting out twenty or thirty statements right now despite resolution to condense. I'm firm (ha) and won't tell the story of our five months' intercourse—with its many incidents that are percolating this moment in my brain; about carnival-night we met (Elitch's), the hundreds of mountain trips in her new Mercury, rented trucks with the mattress in back, at her cabin, cabins I broke into, day I got her to bang Hal Chase, time I gave her clap after momentous meeting between her and mother of my second child (only boy before Diana's), time I knocked her up; and knocked it, mad nights and early A.M.'s at Goodyear factory I worked alone in from 4 P.M. to anytime I wanted to go home, doing it on golfcourses, roofs, parks, cemeteries (you know, dead people's homes), snowbanks, schools and schoolyards, hotel bathrooms, her

62. "In eleven months and ten more days, I'll be out of the calaboose . . . ," a song by Arthur Fields and Fred Hall, from 1930.

mother's vacant houses (she was a realtor), doing it every way we could think of any-old-place we happened to be, in fact, we did it in so many places that Denver was covered with our peckertracks; so many different ones that I can't possibly remember, often we'd trek clear from one side of town to another just to find a spot to drop to it, on ordinary occasions, however, I'd just pull it out and shove—to her bottom if we were secluded, to her mouth if not, the greatest most humorous incident of the lot: to please her mother she'd often babysit for some of their socially prominent and wealthy friends several times a week, I drove out to that particular evening's assignment, after she called to give the address and say the coast was clear, (funny English joke; man and wife in livingroom, phone rings, man answers and says he wouldn't know, better call the coast guard, and hangs up, wife says, "Who was it, dear?" and man says, "I don't know, some damn fool who wanted to know if the coast was clear," har-har-har) and we quickly tear-off several goodies, then, I go back to work; in Goodyear truck, don't you know. We'd done this numerous times when the "most humorous" evening came up. It was a Sunday night, so no work, I waited outside 16th and High Street apartment till parents left and then went in and fell to it. I had all my clothes off and in livingroom as she was washing my cock in bathroom, (let this be a lesson to you, men, never become separated from your clothes, at least keep your trousers handy, when doing this sort of thing in a strange house—oops, my goodness, I forgot for a second that some of you are out of circulation and certainly not in any need of "Lord Chesterfield's" counseling[63]—don't show this to your wives, or tell them that I only offer this advice to pass on to your sons, or, if that's too harsh, to your dilettante friends, whew!, got out of that) there's a rattling of the apartment door and into the front room walks the mother of one of the parents of the baby Cherry Mary is watching, so fast did this old bat come in that we barely had time to shut the bathroom door before she saw us. Here I was, nude, no clothes, and all exits blocked. I couldn't stay there for what if the old gal wanted to pee, and most old women's bladders and kidneys are not the best in the world. There was no place in the bathroom to hide, nor could I sneak out due to the layout of the apartment. Worse, Mary suddenly remembered the fact that this intruder was expected to stay the night. We consulted in

63. Philip Dormer Stanhope (1694–1773), the fourth earl of Chesterfield, remembered for his daily letters to his son, instructing him in etiquette and the worldly arts, including approaches to women.

whispers, laughing and giggling despite all, and it was decided Mary would leave the bathroom and keep the old lady busy while suggesting a walk or coffee down the street and still try to collect my clothes and get them to me; no mean feat. My task was to, as quietly as a mouse, remove all the years-long collection of rich peoples' bath knick-knacks that blocked the room's only window, then, impossible though it looked, I must climb up the tub to it and with a fingernail file pry loose the outside screen. Now, look at this window, it had four panes of glass 6" long and 4" wide, it formed a rectangle of about 12 or 13" high and 8 or 9" across, difficult to squeeze through at best, but, being modern as hell, the way it was hooked to its frame was by a single metal bar in direct center! which when opened split the panes of glass down the middle and made two windows.

I could hardly reach outside to work on the screen—since the window opened outward—but I pushed and making a hellova noise, split the screen enough to open the window. Now the impossible compressing of my frame for the squeeze. I thought if I could get my head through I could make it; I just was able to, by bending the tough metal bar the slightest cunthair (in those days I cleaned and jerked 220 lbs.) and of course, I almost tore off my pride-and-joy as I wiggled out into the cold November air. I was damn glad I was only on the second floor, if I'd been higher I would have been hungup in space for sure. So I dropped into the bushes bordering the walk along the side of the building, and hid there shivering and gloating with glee. There was a film of snow on the ground, but this didn't bother anything except my feet until some man parked his car in the alley garage and came walking past my hideaway, then, much of my naked body got wet as I pressed against the icy ground so he wouldn't see me. This made me seek better shelter since it was about 9 P.M.—I'd been in the cold an hour—and a whole string of rich bastards with cars might start putting them away. I waited until no one was in sight then dashed down the walk to the alley and leaped up and grabbed the handy drainpipe of a garage and pulled myself up. The window I'd broken out of overlooked my new refuge and if anyone went in that bathroom they'd see the havoc wrought the place and be looking out to see me. This fear had just formed—I was too cold to be jolly now—when I saw Mary at last come into view. She had my pants, shoes and coat, but not my T-shirt and socks, having skipped these small items as she bustled about in front of the cause of my predicament "straightening up." The woman had only noticed my belt and Mary had said she had a leather class at school and was engraving it.

When I'd bashed out the window Mary had heard the crashing about, (the old lady must have been deaf; while I was escaping kept talking about Thanksgiving turkey!) and had come in the bathroom to clean up, close the window and otherwise coverup. I put on my clothes and chattering uncontrollably from my freezeout walked with Mary to the Oasis Cafe for some hot coffee. And so it goes, tale after tale revolving around this Cherry Mary period; here's just a couple more:

At first the mother of this frantic fucking filly confided in me and, to get me on her side, asked me to take care of Mary, watch her and so forth. After awhile, as Mary got wilder, the old bitch decided to give me a dressing down, (I can't remember the exact little thing that led up to this, offhand anyhow) and since she wasn't the type to do it herself—and to impress me, I guess—she got the pastor of the parish to give me a lecture. Now, her home was in one of the elite parishes and so she got the monseigneur—it was a Catholic church—to come over for dinner the same evening she invited me. I arrived a little before him and could at once smell something was cooking. The slut just couldn't hold back her little scheme, told Mary to listen closely and began preaching a little of her own gospel to warm me up for the main event. The doorbell rang and her eyes sparkled with anticipation as she sallied forth from the kitchen to answer it. The priest was a middlesized middleaged pink featured man with extremely thick glasses covering such poor eyes he couldn't see me until our noses almost touched. Coming toward me across the palatial living-room he had his handshake extended and was in the midst of a normal greeting, the mother escorting him by elbow all the while and gushing introduction. Then it happened, he saw me; what an expression! I've never seen a chin drop so far so fast, it literally banged his breastbone. "Neal!! Neal!, my boy!, at last I've found my boy!", his voice broke as he said the last word and his Adam's apple refused to articulate further because all it gave out was a strangled blubber. Choked with emotion, he violently clasped me to him and flung his eyes to heaven fervently thanking his God. Tremendous tears rolled down his cheeks, poured over his upthrust jaw, and disappeared inside his tight clerical collar. I had trouble deciding whether to leave my arms hanging limp or throw them around him and try to return the depth of his goodness by turning to it. Golly and whoooooeee!, what a sight!! The priest's emotion had been one of incredulous joyous recognition, Mary's mother's emotion was a gem of frustrated surprise; startled wonder at such an unimaginable happening left her gaping at us with the most foolish looking face I've ever seen. She didn't know whether to faint or flee, never had she been so taken aback, and, I'm sure, didn't think she ever would be, it was really a perfect farce. Mary and her sister—who was there to lend dignity to her mother's idea—were as slack-jawed as any of us. Depend on sweet Mary to recover first, she did, with a giggle; which her sister took as a cue to frown upon, thereby regaining her senses. The mother's composure came with a gasp of artificial goo, "Well! what a pleasant surprise!!" she gurgled with strained smile, feeling lucky that she'd snuck out from under so easily. Oho!, but wait, aha!, she'd made a mistake! Her tension was so unbearable—and she had succeeded so well with her first words—that she decided to speak again, "Let's all go into supper, shall we?" she said in a high-pitched nervous urge. The false earnestness of her tone struck us all as a most incongruous concern and she'd given herself away by being too quick—since her guest was still holding me tightly.

The ecstatic priest was Harley Schmitt, my Godfather when I was baptized at age 10 in 1936. He had also taught me Latin for some months and saw me occasionally during the following three years I served at Holy Ghost Church as altar boy. At our last meeting I was engrossed in the lives of the Saints and determined to become a priest or Christian brother, then, I abruptly disappear down the pleasanter path of evil. Now, six and a half years later, he met me again in Mary's house as a youth he'd come to lecture. Well, he didn't get around to the lecture, it never seemed to enter his head because it was too full of blissful joy at finding his lost son. He told me how he'd never had another Godson—it just so happened that way—and how he'd prayed night and day for my soul and to see me again. He could hardly contain himself at the dinner-table, fidgeted and twittered and didn't touch his food. He dragged the whole story of the long wait for this moment out into the open and before the sullen-hearted (she gave me piercing glances of pure hate when Father Schmitt wasn't looking) mother actually waxed moistly eloquent. When the meal was over the dirty old bitch knew her sweet little scheme had backfired completely for Schmitt at once excused himself, saying he was sure everyone understood, because he wanted to talk to me alone, and we left. We drove to his church and then sat in his car for two hours before I got out and walked away, never to see him to this very day, now five years since. He started in with the old stuff, and I, knowing there could be no agreement and not wanting to use him unfairly, came down right away and for once I didn't hesitate as I told him not to bother; I was sorry for it, but we were worlds apart and it would now do no good for him to try and come closer. Oh we did a lot of talking, it wasn't quite that short and simple, but as I say, I finally left him when he realized there was nothing more to be said, and that was that.

The other incident I wanted to tell you about can wait, I must cut this to the bone from here on out because I haven't the money for paper. Anyhow, the reason for this little glimpse into the months just prior to meeting Joan was to show there was some cause for what happened to me in the bar with my younger blood brother. Mind you, I hadn't seen Mary's mother for at least a month before this night in the bar, although I'd seen Mary about two weeks earlier. Ah, what's another few lines, I gotta break in here and tell you that other funny little thing about C. Mary. It is this; she was such a hypochondriac that she often played at Blindness. Now wait a minute, this was unusual, because she never complained of illness or anything else, in fact, she didn't complain about her eyes either, just the opposite, she played at having a true martyr complex toward them. Often we'd spend 12–16 hours in a hotel room while she was "blind." I'd wait on her hand and foot (and cock) during these times. They'd begin casually enough, she'd simply announce that she couldn't see and that would go on until she'd just as quietly say she could see again. This happened while she was driving—I'd grab the wheel—while we were walking—I'd lead her—while we were loving—I'd finish anyhow—in fact, this happened any old place she felt like it happening. It was a great little game, she didn't have to worry if she smacked up the car, or anything, the old lady would come to the rescue with lots of dough, wouldn't she? Oh enough!

Continuing then, from about 1,500 words ago, as to why Joan and I didn't live Happily Ever After; Very simple, we were given no chance.

You see, as I drank the last Blood-Brother beer—I remember deciding in all seriousness that it was definitely the last one—2 plainclothesmen approached, asked if I was Neal C. and promptly hauled me away! It seems Cherry Mary's Mother, listening on the phone extension to my friend give my whereabouts, had called the police—and she was politically powerful! Why, why, after release on statutory rape with testifying flatly refused by panicky Mary and not a shred of evidence otherwise—flatly panicky, I continued to be held in jail charged with suspicion of Burglary! Of my poolhall hangout yet. Because the charge had a superficial plausibility, since I racked balls there a couple of times and knew the layout—I knew a lot of fearful moments before Capt. of Dicks admitted he knew I was clear all along, released me finally weeks later.

Joan had disappeared completely!

. . .

Dec. 22, '50—P.M.

Just finished this insufferably egotistical letter. Few notes on it I hadn't time to include; enclosed J. Jones press clipping[64] was discovered by me on Dec 19th, 2 days after I began letter & 1 day after it was published in SF News. You always chide me on my "coincidence" hangup—you know, every time any two people happen to draw breath together, I bust out with "amazing"—But, if my novel is ever put up for sale the editor's preface will be: "Seldom has there been a story of a man so balled up. No doubt many readers will not believe the veracity of the author, but, assure these 'doubting Thomases' that every incident, as such is true."

Excuse me, that'll be part of the jacket blurb. I know it's the style to create a fiction of a bunch of characters thrown together in a composite—like Wolfe or Proust did. But how for one as just straight case-history? I know none of the characters would stand up—no living one person has all the necessary attributes to hold water in a novel.

I'll see you Jan. 10–20. I might not have car, still don't know. Tell John Holmes and Allen G. Hello. Mexico trip in Spring off unless big money comes from somewhere.

Rushing for train now. Hope you can read this, but having read other letters from me I've no doubt you'll manage to decipher.

Sincere Xmas joy to my sincere Buddy. N.

After the birth of her son Curtis, Diana notified Neal's father, c/o Zaza's barbershop, Larimer Street, Denver, giving Neal's return address on the envelope. Neal Sr., who was in the county jail at the time, eventually replied to Neal.

64. The enclosed clipping from the *San Francisco News* of December 18, 1950, reported a miscarriage by Jennifer Jones, the actress wife of movie producer David O. Selznick.

TO NEAL CASSADY FROM NEAL CASSADY SR.

[December 1950]
1523 Market St.,
Denver, Colorado

HELLO NEAL,

Rec'd your letter today, was sure glad to hear from you. I hope your wife is feeling well & that big boy is getting along fine. Sure would like to see him & hold him in my arms like I did with you Neal. I know just how you feel, like I did when you were just borned. I thought nobody could hold you just right even your own mother would laugh & say it will soon get old. I bought a new baby bugay & when we went to a show I would say I'll carry him, somebody might steal the baby carage. I hope you are well along. Neal, when I get to work I will help you along & send you some money. Awful sorry I didn't have any money but will send you the first I get. Am in the Co jail lieu a $3 hundred fine. Will be out 15 Feb. Excuse pencil.

From your father
NEAL

On December 20, Diana wrote to Neal telling him that her Christmas gift to him was a reduction of her demand that he spend six months with her to "two weeks or so." She claimed that he had killed their relationship by neglecting her and suggested that they do something legal about dissolving their marriage. Neal continued to make plans for his New York trip, telling Kerouac that he hoped to set off in early January. The railroad pass he had obtained for Diana to accompany him back West he now offered to Jack and Joan so that they could return to San Francisco with him.

TO JACK KEROUAC

Dec. 30, 1950's last gasp
[San Francisco]

DEAR JACK; THE ONE AND ONLY, THE GREAT JOHN L.,

Here comes the most sadistic blow ever struck by man, the most evil of all renigs, a most immoral stab-in-the-back, from the most ungentlemanly wound I create you shall suffer the stings of maddened wasps, your life-blood shall flow unchecked, impotent rage will clutch your guts, joy will lose its bloom, saturated with despair you will fall to the floor cursing your fate, unrelished your love, unaware your mind, unsatisfied your senses, uncaring your eyes, unfulfilled your ambitions, unhinged your brain, unappreciated your talents, unlamented your future, unknown your life, ununderstandable (that's a goodie) your underwear, unbuttoned your shoes (you vulgar square), untied your necktie, uncombed your hair, unzipped your fly (you vulgar modern), unapplied your applepolish, headpolish, toothpolish, bootpolish, fingernailpolishamburger, unexcelled your anguish, unparalleled your weeping, wailing, wallowing, groaning, griping, (etc.; to do that one properly takes too long) (in fact, etc., etc., to this whole paragraph, on thinking over a finish for a moment or two I find I'm too lazy from the big supper I just ate to attempt to round this out.)

Of all the extraordinary bastards this earth supports, I am undoubtedly the most extreme of the no-goodnessgraciousmelandsakesalivever to lie in his teeth, thatsrightthatsright, you guessed it, go ahead beat me, scream your loudest, demand my scalp, pull my trolley, pound your head to the wall, push my face in, get me fired, put clothespins to your nose when I pass, heap me with dung and ashes, boil my balls in bubblebath, (etc., etc.; I'm too relaxed for any thinking.)

I AM NOT BRINGING MY TAPERECORDER—EKOTAPE, YOU KNOW—TO NEW YORK CITY.

There is little else to say, after the raw deal you've suffered no words can convey an excuse, there is none—there ought to be a law, huh? Enuf of this.

Leaving SF Jan. 3rd, I go to either Tucson, El Paso or Tucumcari to boom for two weeks, then, on to N. Orleans, Montgomery, Atlanta, Washington, New Y. Return to SF same route on Feb. 3rd; might detour to Denver to dig my old man (just got sweet letter—borned for born, carage for carriage, babby for baby—written in laborious pencil on bunk of his county jail cell) when he gets out of the jug second week in February. I plan for him to live with Carolyn and me. Car and money has fallen thru completely, so have Diana and I, so has U.S.A. But, wait a minute, you lucky devil, don't think I've done you entirely wrong. Instead of taking return RR pass to SF via Denver I purposely had my return fixed via south. Further, I done went way out of my way and hassled around with trainmaster and got pass for me and Wife!! Know why?, well, you silly fool, realizing my poor simple buddy has taken a real hosing from those fag bookbinders and allied abnormal bitches (you get the twist there, old pal) I got my greasy mind to slip over a few rusty cogs and lubricated up an idea, for whatever worth it might have to you and Joan. Here 'tis: My pass is good until March 14th, and I can easily get a 90 day extension, so you and wife can use it to go to the point in Texas closest to Mexico for a small sum (altogether free transportation from New Orleans clear to SF. From NY to N. Orleans is over foreign lines—not SP rail—so, costs half-fare, i.e., $20) and then dive across border to continue jaunt to MexCity on your own. Naturally, this is only if you're going there. But wait again, old boy, I don't want you to go until we can all go and do it up right, or else you can go but come back to—SF, yes indeedy, SF, not NY. What if you put off Mexico trip; why then you just use my pass all the way to SF and get a little job here and stay here until Jan. 1st, 52, when I get cutoff again and we can travel. This is all very loose, but it's tighter than it looks. Carolyn thinks you're it and all the old nonsense is finished, also I, ahem, have gone attic to work in, gone Alto Saxophone to play, gone Ekotape to blow to, will always have car for you to use (new car next year, 61, OK, OK, 51 Chevrolet station wagon, doubt huh, wait and see, you bum) etc., etc.; will talk it all over with you when I arrive. Point is, you and lovely have transport from NY to SF for 20 bucks or so apiece. Bus fare, as you and I well know, would cost about 100 at least for both of you, and here you get streamliners. Now, let's get down to brassballs; if you and wife and I travel together, on train, you and she use pass and I can almost certainly get conductors to carry me for free most of way across country, if I have to pay here and there, at least it's quite plain that this is by far the cheapest way for 3 people to cross country, right? Money being as important as it is right now, this can't be overlooked if you plan to travel soon. Difficulty of course is you most probably won't want to leave NY first week in Feb., if not, but do want to use pass later, you gotta advance me an amount of money to insure that I get home; if I have good luck with bumming rides off various conductors, I must be trusted to return to you all money not actually used for fare. Is this clear? I'm typing at a recordbreaking (for me) clip of three words a minute. All this is just a thought and if it's any good we'll figure out details when I see you; nothing lost anyway. The pass I now have in possession is for me only from SF to NY and return; I went down yesterday and jumped pass bureau for them to forward a single trip pass on to me at North Tarrytown for the use of my wife. So if you cast (that's supposed to be cats) don't want, can't use, aren't in need of, etc., this wife pass from NY to SF, I'll cut around the village or someplace and try to find a girl that wants to go west for a couple of sawbucks and let her use the pass for, ahem, ahem, and whoopee, a certain fee I have in mind, gosh, shucks and the like. I hope you two find you don't need the pass, so I can maybe be lucky enough to get a little strange nookie. If you're not going to use pass, keep your eyes open, or have your friends do so, for a skinny chick wanting a cheap ride over the rails for a nominal price that most any girl can afford, I trust.

About my soon to be had saxophone: a fine old conductor I know got to talking to me about music and mentioned how he used to play cello, violin, trombone (slide), trumpet, clarinet, saxophone and most any instrument. He last played a few years ago, just for kicks with his wife on piano around home of an evening; well, the horn he blew was a gold-plated bell and gold-plated keys etc. melody saxophone. That is a sax in the natural key, like a piano, its tone is just under the alto, but higher pitched than a tenor. He bought the best horn money (he's got piles) could buy, around 200 bucks. Now it's just gathering dust in its beautiful leather case lying on closet shelf. He's a fine old boy and doesn't care one way or another if he sells it, but he promised me to not sell it to anyone else (the thought of selling it didn't enter his head until I asked him to sell to me) until summer when I'm back to work and can buy it. If I don't want it that's OK, the price is a low 65 dollars. He will teach me some tricks on it, but I must get some nigger cat to teach me music reading (or even cheap teacher) yet the reason this particular sax is so good for me (and us, Jack) is that it is not in E flat or some other goddamn key that one must transpose as he plays; it takes a musician to transpose music and all horns except this C melody horn calls for that, but with this in an evening or two (he really knows music and assured me) I can play a recognizable tune, of course, months of practice for good tone, but fingering will come pretty easy, tone's the thing to try for, by holding a sustained note for 15 seconds or so, etc. Even if I fail on this horn, I can easily sell it for 65, besides, if I do get good I can then trade it for a solo horn like a B flat tenor, etc., etc. Well, nice wife Carolyn insists I get it at once, so when I get back, for my birthday Feb. 8th, even if we starve, I get wonderful saxophone to blow my head off with. You better get to SF, old man, the world is passing you by, heh, heh, I got everything I'll ever need or want: 1, typewriter to write novel; 2, terrific work room in attic (not in use until I get back); 3, sax to learn music on; 4, recorder to save notes otherwise lost to thin air; 5, a car. Those are my three chief desires: writing, music and driving. Most of my mind is taken up with these activities, and except for 24 hours of sex a day I don't give a damn for anything else. I repeat, heh, heh. Oh yeah, I got a bugle (regulation army, made in Japan) and another toy flute.

Go ahead and write to me if you've got time or can come up with anything without drag or too much effort; Carolyn will forward any mail I get to spot in south that I happen to be working, up till Jan. 20th, then, expect me to sneak up to your door with an embarrassed face for not having dragged the 55 lb. (I weighed it) extremely fragile, sensitive to cold and damp, ruined by slightest jar and expensive to repair Ekotape recorder across US to you. Forgive me, besides, it's a lure to get you to SF; chortle, chuckle, snort.

N.

1951

Neal did not leave on January 3, as planned, since there was no promise of the expected railroad work along his intended southern route to New York. Instead he found work in Oakland and decided to postpone his trip East until the end of the month.

TO JACK AND JOAN KEROUAC

Jan. 8, '51
[San Francisco]

DEAR J. AND J.K.;

Unfold the blasted blanket, unhinge the bloody gates, disperse the billowed drifts, make bellows blow piled coals, pour laden ladles, launch leviathans, roaring ranges rake the pale paste of pallid pals, dispelled is Eastern gloom, nullified is accursed weather, belittled is frost-bitten feet, frozen fingers, frigid face, chilblained children of chance, cripples caste, chosen chum commutes, travelers of twisted trails, tasters of tempting trips, tantalized tipplers trooping to triumphant trash, truck tour thru tanktowns, torn tits toddlers to tough thugs they tumble toward their torturous trials, totaling the take, the trying tribulations, the tepid tops, the terrible tomfoolery, the tendency to torrid trembling, twitches, tricks, troubles, troubles, troubles, troubles, troubles, troubles, troubles, troubles, troubles, dollarless drips dropping dimpled dingleberries deep down dipping dolleyseats madden monologues made, modern madcaps mocking money, milady makes me messy.

Ugh, bah, fap, grr, ick, ump, pah, awk, urg, eek, wok, fud, poo, etc. I've wasted 19¾ minutes on above paragraph for no reason, whatsamatterme? I gotta get going on plain facts and plans, I gottum all figured out, really pay no attention to this junk, I just can't get started on struggle to make clear how things are to be, altho I've spent every day and night thinking of every angle to simplify matters for us, prepare for loose rambling whose very blabbering along will indicate paradox, I actually dream of details and have everything ironed out, so don't suspect I Meerschaumpipesmoke, listen—

Immediately, immediately, immediately, immediately, not tomorrow, you hear, you lazy lout, but right now, YOU GET A JOB! You hear me, you sluggard, loafer, bum, scamp, wastrel, for a measly three weeks you gotta suffer sickly work for 8 hours per, no, better yet, (ha) get two jobs, yes that's it, wash dishes or mop floors all night and jerk sodas all day, 16 hours a day and in your spare time get a part time job delivering papers every early A.M. Pick out the toughest tasks and do penance, you old fart, grovel in the shit of daily horror necessary for a lousy few bucks. I am sick, I shudder at the thought, how can one be expected to do it? Oh well, however best you can make it, do so by my birthday. Amethyst for sincerity, Violet for modesty, that's February; Boy Scouts founded 1910, Cassady born 1926, that's the eighth. By Feb. 8 at absolute latest you must have a very minimum of 150 dollars. I am purposely holding off going to NY until last second so as to give you enough time to get the necessary loot.

There is no RR work down south and by sheer luck I got a good job switching boxcars in Oakland. This job is from midnight to 8 A.M., usually, and best of all I think it will hold out until Spring, when I go back to Coast division of SP. Anyhow, I'm broke and must work until last of month to get 100 bucks to give Diana and balance for trip. I can get a business leave from job and go back to work minute I get home again. So: Feb. 1, leave SF on freight "Zipper" at 7:40 P.M.; 2nd, arrive L.A. at 6:50 A.M., go to Inglewood and Compton to visit sisters, Aunt, brothers, cousins, niece, nephew; leave L.A. at 11:59 P.M.; 3rd, travel into Arizona; 4th, El Paso and Texas; 5th, New Orleans; 6th, Montgomery, Ala., Atlanta, Ga; 7th, Washington D.C. and NYC; 8th, celebrate birthday and anniversary by busting in on you kiddies; 9th, I spend entire day with you two and other experts to search out a suitable truck and on this day also get license etc. and at nightfall start loading your gear, sewing machine etc.; 10th, clear up last things and this night have final fling, a party for everyone; 11th, leave NYC and Sunday tour thru Penna; 12th, Ohio, Indiana, Illinois; 13th, Mo, Kan. City, get good feed at my brother's,[1] you dig; 14th, arrive Denver, see Ed White etc.; 15th, my old father released from county jail, I see for better and unknown details of my early child-

1. Neal's half brother Jim Daly was living in Kansas City.

hood etc., if he's available he might come to SF; on 16th, we leave Denver, get to my birthplace Salt Lake City; 17th, Nevada and California; 18th, I mark up on RR workboard as we go thru Oakland; arrive my home, 19th. If you two don't move in next door, (good chance I get you fine 30 a month apt. in house with backyard etc., next to 29 Russell), you stay with us and sleep in my precious attic while Bennington Girl we have with us (since Jan. 1) sleeps in front room, as she does now. 20th–28th, find you job, easy to do, get everything lined up for you two lovelies, etc., etc., etc., etc., etc.

March 1, Helen Hinkle leave SF and you take her 35 a month good apt., if necessary, 2nd, etc., until—?

My expenses mount. My putt-putt Ford fell apart and I spent last of my money for downpayment on really necessary car (Carolyn needs too, take kid to school, use for getting about town etc., for pictures and art work etc.), for me to commute across bay for job which might be anywhere from Berkeley or Richmond to a point 35 miles south at Chevrolet Plant we switch. It is a 1941 Packard blue club coupe, new 6 cylinder motor, radio, *HEATER,* defroster, new tires, seat covers, overdrive (not connected), new springs, etc. I fear rear end is falling out, however, and don't dare take it across U.S.A. The car will stand up OK for city use and Carolyn must have, so I leave it here, besides, we couldn't pack all your stuff in small coupe and I know car would break down and would be no good for what I intend doing with it and your truck come summer. We'll drive easy and I'm sure truck (being a truck) will make trip without mishap. I'll have only about 50 dollars at most and that for our expenses, so it's up to you, Jack, to get 100 or so to buy truck. As soon as we are in SF we get you driver's license, easy, and you use it and my Packard too; come April or so, I give you some loot (I warn you now, you skinflint, I'm an old horsetrader, no relation to ED, (you might not get that sidesplitting joke, explain later) and when it comes to dickering for a beatup old truck I'll slicker you out of your eyeballs if you don't watch out) for your truck and with some good luck I might find an auto dealer that will accept Packard and truck together as the downpayment on a new station-wagon. So, you see truck is necessary for trip and can come in handy to drive around SF after, and I stand on my policy, (if it wasn't for my other pardners in the corporation I'd give my cars away) I'll pay top prices and beat any other dealer's offer, yessir, "No Nonsense Neal," the truck owner's friend, come in and see me for a R-E-A-L deal, I don't turn down nobody, nosir, the working man's friend, that's me, yessir.

I ain't got no more to say to you sweet sillies, Carolyn is bursting with impatience to have you here and says it's about time youall came to your blarsted senses and left that frosty fagtown to live in foggy Frisco. I'm liable to show in NY a couple of days, or hours, early. I gotta make a run to Tarrytown and Diana, and if we figure got a few extra bucks we can all go and (in truck) dig J. Fitzgerald and wife and kids (what's latest, girl, boy?) and gone nigger cat Cleo and continue to Lowell, Mass if we can so arrange to get to Denver by 15th that I can rescue pop from stir before he gets lost in drunken Denver desert. I got further plans up my sleeve.

I have received your magnificent first instalment,[2] can't speak of it now, don't think I didn't have an experience over it (vision dozing on cab of engine). I don't think you got my dream letter, the one about bullets and Burroughs etc.,[3] and if Allen got my Nov. letter, why he no write? 60 days gone. And don't give me (you better, you bastard) any more wonderful bullshit, you giggling cuntlapper, about my letter attempts, I know I can't even write my name without getting stuck. I wish I could believe you tho, better, I wish everyone else did; the beautiful page you wrote comparing me with other writers will, above all the hundreds of gone pages you've sent me, be tucked away in my treasured file and there remain in solitary splendor.[4] Secretly, it was just to receive such a thing from you that I found the strength to do the damn tribute. Now, lookiethere, that proves I'm no writer, my mind is so dull that in that last sentence I put the word "thing" where tribute should be and the word "tribute" where thing should be, heh, heh. And so it goes, up the lazy river—

Just re-read crummy letter, with its opening alliterations, closing dim-wittedness and all the misspellings between. Enclosed page from SF Chronicle and J.H. Jackson, not jumping Joe, but rather Jerky Joe Jackson. Dig that "unanimous" opinion of all who "discovered" T. and C., so right.[5]

2. After Kerouac received Neal's "Joan Anderson" letter, he began writing similarly long letters about his own childhood and sending them to Neal. (See *SL,* pp. 246–306.)

3. Jack replied that he had received Neal's dream letter (of December 3) and had read it aloud to Allen, wife Joan, and Seymour Wyse at Christmastime, and that he considered Neal a great wild genius as a writer.

4. Kerouac also wrote congratulating Neal on his Joan Anderson letter on December 27 (see *SL,* pp. 242–45), stating that it employed the best styles of Joyce, Céline, Dostoyevsky, and Proust, and describing it as among the best of American writing, comparing it favorably with the work of Dreiser, Wolfe and Melville, Hemingway and Fitzgerald.

5. Joseph Henry Jackson reviewed Kerouac's first published novel, *The Town and the City,* under the heading "Breakup of a Family" in the *San Francisco Chronicle* of March 10, 1950.

Carolyn insists Joan become pregnant, to have kids, of course, and catch up (impossible) with us, but, to also live next door and we can swap them, tossing the little wigglies over the backyard fence. I'm mailing this weak crap at once, forgive—I can't seem to think much the last few days. Thank you.

Got Joan's fine letter to me, tell her Carolyn feels same way as she about Pickup, Kickup and Shackup. See youse in less than a month, positive.

Love to Mama, little Joan & you, you big bum.

N.

Jesus Christ, Jesus H. Christ, goddamn it man, Carolyn reread this letter & said "Neal, you silly ass, you forgot the most important thing, what about the T?" I almost shit my pants & rushed to pen this little note. Let me tell you MAN, SF's so hot every single connection has fled or is busted, NO T anywhere. Carolyn, but mostly me, are, or is, in real starved condition & the only reason I come east is to pick up on your promise of some T. So, have it ready, old boy, I'm dyin' (gasp) (choke) as says Lil' Abner.

Carolyn is really truly disturbed over mistakes of old & insists you & Joan (she loves her already) (I'm not shittin' my old buddy) come to SF so we'll have some friends & she can make amends if necessary, which it ain't. We know no one here, boo-hoo. You gotta have a kid too, she says. See you soon,

N. & C.

After telling Kerouac to expect him to arrive in New York in early February, news of a forthcoming ten-day lull in his railroad job led Neal to start his journey right away, and he left San Francisco on January 10.

TO NEAL CASSADY FROM CAROLYN CASSADY

Thursday, January 11, 1951
29 Russell St.
San Francisco

DEAREST NEAL;

Don't you ever ever ever go away again!!!

I looked back and saw your silhouette against the train light, striding across the tracks carrying that big suitcase, and could hardly push on the gas. You looked so little and lonely, and it just didn't make sense all of a sudden. But I think I believe it's best, provided you get back all right, and am glad we plunged so. So please please be extra careful this time! I have awful superstitious feelings that now that you've changed to doing the right thing, your so-far-good luck will change too. Just when everything's about to be all right, etc. I worried half the night that since D. was so cold she might be capable now of carrying out her threat, and almost wrote Jack to ask him to go with you and watch over you. She called this A.M., and tho I didn't talk to her since I wouldn't accept the charges, I felt she wasn't in quite that state yet, tho now maybe she's madder? I wanted to talk to her and it was hard not to, but I realized she could buy her crib and more for the phone bills. I wrote her airmail-special to show her how fast and that 21 cents is different from $21. So I hope they won't harm you, but in all respects PLEASE take care of you!

I didn't have anything to say to her but suggested things about the crib, such as borrowing or even Robert making something and then she'd only have to get the mattress. I also don't see why those two old women couldn't care for a tiny baby even if they had to crawl on their stomachs just long enough for D. to get a job and guaranteed income. I didn't put it like that to her . . . just asked her to write not call, and told her something of our dire circumstances at present (not car tho), and why I was such a pig about the calls.

I'll try and send off the baby and your clothes this afternoon . . . I notice I forgot the envelopes. I hope you'll get a chance to write, tho I know it will be hard, but I'm on tenterhooks till you get back safe and sound, and would like occasional reassurances. I hope to keep busy busy busy so the time will fly. Oh do be careful.

We love you very much and miss you all day. And night. I'm going around in a fog today and feel tired . . . but I'll get on it. When you get back we'll show you how much we love you and not how we can do without as has been the habit formed. We certainly cannot do without ever again. There's so much to be done, and the second quarter century must be as rich as the first was wanton. We're very humble and honored that you want to spend it with us . . . truly . . . so please hurry hurry hurry.

As Cathy says "Be careful"
Neyew Cassasy

All our love,
CAROLYN, CATHY, CÉLINE

I spilled the beans with this letter preceding you? Hope I didn't spoil anything.

TO NEAL CASSADY FROM CAROLYN CASSADY

Saturday [January 13, 1951]
29 Russell St.
San Francisco

DEAREST NEAL:

Just a note to report about your job. They called you two nights after & finally an old fuddy like Joe talked. Said he had no notice of your leave—did you have a letter? I thot you did, but come to think of it, don't remember an actual letter. He looked to see that you had not been one of the cut loaners & said he'd put you on the leave board to protect you. Said too bad you left now because you could have worked every day. I told him what you'd heard re the 10 days slow, & he said "Well, they must have something up their sleeves because they're still hiring men," but he was loaded with them. So apparently he doesn't know all. Anyway, gave me his name & said you should call him as soon as you return & soon. Hope all is well, honey.

It is with us tho I feel sort of funny & unreal & nowhere. Hurry home, please Neal—but don't worry & have fun too.

All my love, CAROLYN

Car OK.

Reaching New Orleans, Neal scribbled a quick message to Carolyn on a post-card showing the Huey P. Long Bridge.

TO CAROLYN CASSADY

[Postmarked January 13, 1951
Washington, D.C.]

DEAREST WIFE,

Train-wiggled writing—so far on time—should leave N.O. noon Sun. NY Tues. Won 10 bucks, poker. Texas snow. Now La. rain. Long trip. Tired; still sane. No pick-ups. I love you more each minute.

Proust-crazy. Will write letters henceforth. No more PCs. I'm hungry. Love, N.

Writing to Neal in New York, Carolyn broke the news that she might be pregnant again.

TO NEAL CASSADY FROM CAROLYN CASSADY

Wednesday Jan. 17, 1951
[San Francisco]

DEAREST NEAL;

I'm finding it hard to write you for the first time . . . largely because I don't know if you'll get any more letters, not knowing where you'll be. But I'll make a stab at it anyway to keep you posted. Got your card; you're very sweet.

Business: The car: It has been a gem, no complaints at all. However . . . bringing Cathy back yesterday afternoon, it ran out of gas j-u-s-t a ---- hair the other side of Leavenworth. In other words, if it had just gotten the back wheels over the top, I could have coasted either home or to a gas station. But no. Fortunately there was room to park albeit nose up which I realized no good, but couldn't help. Walked Cathy home and then went to the Pontiac garage (aha . . . an excuse!) and told my sad tale. A *very* attractive guy found a can and carried it dripping to the car for me. It wouldn't pump it up hill, so he managed to back it over the curb and around and go down hill. It started at last and he drove back to the garage. There he put in 5 gallons of Chevron Supreme. He said he couldn't charge me for it since he had no permit to sell it . . . I wept buckets, thanked him and tootled off home. Incidently, with that good gas the car acts like those Shell ads . . . It nearly shot across the street and this A.M. started like a rabbit without the usual 15 tries and much pumping. But I got it filled with old poop again so it's as bad as new. Anyway, I think that is half its trouble, but I know your sentiments on your 23¢ stuff. Now then, the mileage. You said to fill it around 41575, right? Well, it ran out at 41400. Hmmm. No doubt it's just running right out the tank, but I'll be darned if I can find the place to soap it or how you reach it anyway. I'll try harder dear, but hurry up back and fix it. It took 13 gallons this A.M. The oil and water OK. I haven't driven it too excessively. Saturday I drove down around Fisherman's Wharf looking for bricks, boards or junk and I've been over to Helen's a couple times. That is all . . . oh once to UC . . . other than Cathy. Jamie does fine and when they're together, C holds J up so all is well. The insurance papers came as well as the thing from the bank re payments . . . it looks like we only have 200 something to pay, yet the repayments are 34 something 12 months which doesn't come out right, I don't believe. I notice it is in your name with NO EXCEPTIONS, but so what for this one, eh? The station wagon can be MINE? Nix, always "ours" from now on, OK? Think that covers the car. I love it, and you for getting it for me.

The girls both have colds, but not too bad and C goes to school anyway. She has wet the bed twice in a row now tho, and I don't know what, if anything, it means 'cause she seems happy enough. She doesn't appear as anxious about you as she was on previous absences, tho still mentions you, but confidently and as tho she understands, which is good. It helps in that either Pat[6] or Helen are here when she is so there are no long lonely spots. That Pat . . . well, I'll tell you all the little things . . . nothing important and she doesn't bother me seriously for which I'm relieved and think maybe there's hope for me. She has been pretty nasty with Cathy till one night she shouted NO at her and looked pure hatred. Cathy came over to me with the biggest look of bewilderment I've ever seen and searching my face for explanation. I was very tender and reassured her. Pat felt like 2¢ as she should. I explained a little to her about babies again and she's been better since. Of course it's my fault to begin with because I do that, but C seems to understand about crabby mommie tho it's different with other people. But all in all all is well. She sleeps all right tho comes to bed with me every night about 3:30 A.M. I let her because it's cold and I'm too sleepy to do anything else. I don't think it will hurt her too much and feel she'll stop when she feels happy etc. eventually and when you are back to stay.

I've been writing mental letters ever since you've gone so when I finally get down to it, it's hard to think of things and how and loses some of the verve . . . as we have discussed. I've been wondering about your state of mind, how you feel in general and about us, etc. Wondering if you're feeling any of what I am or if mine is largely physical. I have no doubts or any real depression, it isn't that. But I've never felt just this way before that I can remember and it's hard to describe since I don't understand the cause. Nothing is very defined.

6. A Bennington student who was staying with the Cassadys for her nonresident term at college.

No real drag about things, but no drive, or rather it's difficult to sustain one. I'm so disappointed because always before I've been able to go like a houseafire when you're away and this time I've so much I want to do and things for you. But it is with the most extreme effort that I can get started on anything, and if I pause at all or am interrupted, I can't get back to it. One thing, as I say, I feel rotten physically . . . again a new feeling. Sort of all nervous and fluttery in the viscera (look it up) and every bone and muscle sore and achy and heavy. No actual mental depression goes with it, as I said, tho no particular anything upstairs . . . pretty blank and no emotions . . . unreality. Damn. Now then . . . the probable cause . . . hold tight. I still haven't menstruated! It was a week late last Sunday and that was about my last hope since I've never been later than that. Well, I just won't accept it, it really burns me up, and believe me, dear, I'm going to do everything I can at all think of to do something about it. I've been stewing for days at how unfair it is, and realizing the cruel stupidity of present day laws. The Catholic Church being far more sinful by setting itself up as God and making a universal judgement that you cannot destroy life at that point when the result is far far worse for all lives concerned etc., etc., etc., and all these people who don't believe in the CC anyway abiding by such stuff. That is they abide by it if it suits their fancy to. Also the hopeless economics of it and truly the survival of the fittest . . . the richest that is. Just to find out if I am it costs money . . . to take care of it, it costs money to have it, it costs money. These smug characters you have to go and grovel before, baring your intimate relations and personal habits which we've always been taught are so sacred and private . . . become a topic of public discussion and a thing to be commercialized and capitalized on by some bunch of rich bastards in the driver's seat. If you catch them in a good mood and a full stomach, they might be "charitable" . . . if they had a fight with their spouse or a bad lunch they are all righteous and must obey the "laws." Oh well, just to realize how hog-tied we all are by such things, how dependent on others and their fancies makes me boil. What I hope to try is this: I'll go to Dr. Railton on Friday when I take Helen out there. (She incidently is due any minute.) I'll tell her the whole story (here I go again) about us, point out the financial problem, the fact that next fall I would be just beginning to achieve the first bit of freedom in 4 years and ability to help with the income which the arrival of no. 3 would postpone another 3 years. That you and I have enough against us and if we're to succeed at all we need that freedom, that money and the relief of a few burdens rather than any addition all of which is worth it for the present girls' sakes. Also that emotionally, I don't think I could take it. I'm hoping that since I've got this proof of having a post-partum depression from the last one, that she can get some surgeon to do a job on me on the grounds it would endanger my mental health to have another child now . . . which is quite possible in fact anyway, eh? I shall also bear heavy on how careful we've been . . . something else that makes me so mad . . . how miserable it is, and what the hell else can we ever do and must we look for this every year. I envision all these slimy people in conspiracies . . . selling us contraptions they know won't work, rubbing their hands and chuckling as they give me faulty directions, so they can clean up one way or another when I get pregnant. If we'd been careless I might feel differently, but Jesus Christ, pardon me, I just don't see what more we can do! Just because you got a hard on (you just ate) or we laid down together, or my monthly period didn't happen, all sorts of people have to know all about it and calmly take every cent we've got every year and sentence several individuals to hard labor the rest of their lives because somebody sets themselves up to judge others and it's the "law." There isn't even a fair trial. You know me on babies being accidents, "knocked up," etc., etc., and I'm still there . . . if one is promiscuous, callous, or careless. But I repeat, what more could we do? and in such cases, and there must be millions, there should be some fairer means of judging. Well, you get the gist. If she suggests adoption . . . which I don't think she will . . . I think I can convince her how impossible that is having two already plus my original feelings. They can fool Helen by keeping her under all the time, but they can't me. On and on . . . I fume about it all day and night. She really is our one big hope and I cling to it . . . since we proved in Helen's case you can't knock it if it's really there and determined as mine are too. I'll try Dr. Caldwell too, the best in the business, but don't know the password to make him call back tho I'll try and find it. Do you realize that I have never before gotten pregnant when I wasn't willing to, and that each time we have decided to be married, bingo. Anyway, poppie, don't fret . . . we'll do the best we can, and be assured I'll leave no stone unturned to avoid it. I wasn't going to tell you for fear you'd worry when there's really nothing you can do, but thot maybe you should know the score . . . but please don't worry since I'll do all I can and only will call on you to share the horror and comfort me if I fail. So maybe this, then, is what makes me feel so dragged.

Just got your N.O. card, sweety pie, tho the last word escaped deciphering. Hope you will have time to write. Also got a letter from Diana who's putting up a brave fight but I fear will be disappointed in your lack of time. Take more there and less elsewhere if there's a choice I suggest. The better you do there now, the better it will be later. I'm afraid she counts too much on your visit for solution, and really don't see what you can do to help. Better not tell her I'm pregnant. Not now anyway. *Wish* I could think of something helpful!

Also got a letter from an old school chum . . . Joanne Sokol, of whom I've told you but you probably forgot. Anyway: lots of money, lots of beaus, married and divorced once, every man falls for her and she for them. She now lives in her own apt and tells me she still works where she has 2 years . . . HARCOURT, BRACE AND CO.! I'll write her and ask about her job, she'll know of Jack, see if she has any influence (doubt it) and just see if she can be any help. Or in future. If you want to look her up, say hello from me, or see for yourself (see how I trust you?) her address is: Apt. 6H, 161 West 16th Street. Whatever you think. I also got a very sweet letter from the landlady wishing us all sorts of luck and being very pleased and saying nice things about our girls. So good.

Jack's 2 letters have arrived, and I took the liberty of reading them.[7] He had a lot of plans worked out, but I guess they'll go thru many changes since he didn't know. Hope it can be arranged happily for all. I got a kick out of the second one about SF in February. His mention of hassles with me made me sigh. We sure got all messed up and hardly a word ever has passed between us. I fear it will be a long time before I can feel at ease with him. It was bad enough to start since I always admired him so much and was so in awe I act like an adolescent tongue-tied girl in his presence and feel as stupid as some awkward farmer. Silly I know, but that's how it was. I always wished so hard I could talk to him and especially about you and me but was afraid to put him on the spot, he was always so loyal to you and your excuses and I couldn't feel him an ally. I remember one day at Liberty Street when he was very sweet and tried to help me by saying how you wanted everything and hadn't learned you couldn't have it that way, going on to explain his guilt at the moment about his own mother. As usual I was too shy to say anything. I think that is part of the reason I relished his book so much; I felt I could "talk" to him

7. Kerouac wrote to Neal on January 10, with plans for his and Joan's trip to San Francisco (*SL,* pp. 307–8), and also on January 8, where he mentions previous hassles with Carolyn at Liberty Street in early 1949 (*SL,* p. 277).

without the necessity of self-conscious reply. Then to have him think he had any part in all my hysterics and I couldn't explain that he didn't or that I didn't hold him responsible in any way. In fact he was the only friend you had I approved of without reservation. My lack of control in his presence allowed because I felt he was a "part of the family" or so close he'd either understand or know I felt we had nothing to hide from him. Ha, well, that's life. I hope it can be cleared up and guess it will thru you. I've also never forgotten his wonderful letters when we were first married, his anxiety for my approval, and your only acquaintance who took it seriously and made me feel married to you and not just the current "bed with a girl in it." So it goes. Sorry to hear about Allen, and Diana said he was there during a big scene so he will probably not be making you too happy. Diana did say if she were the last and if one was resurrected it was worth it, which is very noble of her to even say whether she can feel it or not at present. So keep that in mind and remember we need you. Tho now I feel so awful to be always just adding to your burdens instead of helping lighten them at all. You poor dear guy! With which thought I'll try and get Dr. R on the phone now so I can give you more news instead of waiting till Fri. Wait a minute.

Well, I talked to her. She says it must be fate in my case and that something wonderful must be going to happen to me; that "we'll all have to pitch in" and help out, that I'll get thru it somehow, etc., etc. However, I got more frantic at this point, explained all our situation, how 2 more years would be, etc., and finally she said we'd ask Dr. Binkley (obstetrician friend taking care of Helen) since he was smart and see what he'd say. I know her policy is always to try and talk you into keeping babies first, which is OK, but I think if I'm anxious enough she may help. So now I feel I have to wait for you and really weigh it, she got me confused, and I do want to be convinced. But I still feel you need a light dose of family to become a family man slowly and not overdo your difficult role, especially so near the beginning. So your reaction will help me a lot and we will work it out, won't we honey, some way or another? Right? Please don't be discouraged, tho that's a big order, and I'm so very very sorry to be the bearer in all senses of more burdens for you. I asked her where it would end; just one more forever. So there's still hope, but now I do feel I need you. Poor kid . . . be Scarlett O'Hara and think about it here with me; forget it in the meantime, please Neal, don't let it spoil that dubious vacation any more. Hope to hear from you tomorrow, and look for the date I may expect you, and about the

Kerouacs. (C. looks at his picture all the time since I told her he was with poppie and you were bringing him home.)

Also I want things for *you,* not put everything into kids—you *need* personal achievement and reward—not continual setbacks & hard work, right?

All is really OK, Neal, no rush—I feel awful for this—but you just be careful.

Arriving in New York, Neal visited Diana and his baby son, Curtis, to make plans for their future apart, before starting his return trip home on January 22. Kerouac writes about Neal's brief time in New York in the final pages of On the Road, *and Joan Haverty Kerouac describes Neal's arrival in chapter 17 of* Nobody's Wife.

TO CAROLYN CASSADY

Jan. 19, '51
[New York City]

DEAR WIFE; MY ONLY ONE;

Writing a quickie to you while bouncing along on commute from Tarrytown to NYC. I have just left Diana after 48 hours of talk & tears. I am pleased, happy, amazed, proud, overjoyed & impatient to report to you that everything, yes, every little thing is completely & perfectly & absolutely OK—i.e. we have come to an understanding. Oh, it was touch & go for awhile, tears flowed & feelings hurt. She's showed a mind of comprehension, tho, little gems popped out & lo! agreement!! Failure I would not accept, tho the night before thought it seemed inevitable. Actually, she made all the final decisions & to gratify her is simple enough as it consists of phantasy worlds. I again repeat, in all that counts, on every level, the trip has been miraculously converted into a glowing success.

The long trek home to you & my loved children commences on Sun., the 21st & if I have the luck I had going East, I may catch Thurs. nite's SP "Zipper" & waken you Fri. the 26th at 7 A.M. That is the absolute earliest I could arrive. Really I'll be lucky to catch 72 in L.A. at midnite & get home Fri. at 5 P.M. If I miss that I should surely get it, 72, next day & be home Sat. at 5 P.M. at latest. I can again visit my family in L.A. so time not entirely wasted if must lay over in impatience.

I reiterate, everything perfect, you need not worry over Diana.

You understand, I mean don't fret your mind over her. I feel a great weight is lifted off my poor harassed brow; she is OK enough & now you & I can get on with our life. Remember, she is (altho similar in agony) a different personality than you, my sweet, & she is now satisfied, see? She knows now she really *doesn't* want me & we are, in practical aspects as well as phantasies, totally unsuited. We both want different things & feel no respect for the other's ideals, or desires—i.e. she thinks my writing a joke, or at best a poor hobby. That's OK; you & I feel much the same but, somehow, are serious about it, huh?

There are other things, but, success, success; I'm happy she is going to stick to it on her own & has already a peace. So, you little blonde bundle of nerves, cease your fears, your frets; your unfulfilled desires may not be so hot, anyhow, so better be wise & be content with just me as a husband who tries to please you as best he can.

Approaching NYC & a night of talk with Allen & Jack & reading of Holmes' novel[8] & other readings & etc. I am whole, happy & for the first time rushing unreservedly to my one & only family. My sweet Carolyn, I love you. You'd better treat me with respect, I'm smart now.

Love, Love, N.

P.S. Jack & Joan not coming with me. May follow in month. Don't worry about them or anyone. N.

TO CAROLYN CASSADY

Jan. 25, P.M. [1951
Washington, D.C.]

MY BLONDEST BABY,

On way home from Chinese Gardens—at last. Delayed 24 hours extra to dig Mad Kat—P.V.M.[9]—also to make deal. The whole thing was necessary, believe me. Now I can write book! Dying for you,

8. John Clellon Holmes's first published novel, *Go* (1952), was written between August 1949 and September 1951 and dealt with events that included Neal's visit to New York in early 1949, the arrest of Ginsberg and Huncke, and the death of William Cannastra. In the novel, Neal is portrayed as Hart Kennedy, Kerouac as Gene Pasternak, and Ginsberg as David Stofsky.

9. Peter van Meter, a hipster friend of Kerouac's and Ginsberg's in New York. Portrayed as Paddy Cordavan in *The Subterraneans,* and Buddy van Buder in *Visions of Cody* and *Book of Dreams.*

nonetheless, so staying over until Mon. P.M. was struggle for me. Got waylaid 5 hours in Wash. D.C. & if I can't make conductor on L&N[10] in Montgomery & another conductor in Mobile, Ala., will just pay fare anyway & have to lay in N. Orleans & leave Thurs. (today) noon (I hope). Then 65 long hours to L.A., if miss SP train #71 leaving L.A. Sat. midnite, there's no "Zipper" on Sun. so, since can't DH[11] on "Daylight" or "Starlite"[12] there is no other train until #71 again at mid. Sun. It takes 16 hours to SF & arrives at P.M. 5, Mon., so *latest* I can be home is Monday at P.M. o'clock 5.

I miss you; I have everything perfectly straight & for you to worry one little ---- hair is nonsense, for not only would it tend to give me a grey nest to satisfy & cling to, it might also do a harm to your love—even the slightest—& so make the wonderful absolute joy I know & feel at thoughts of next quarter century with you (rich, not wanton, is right) be dwarfed, infringed upon, cheated, & the pure husband you now have would be cramped in displaying in *all* ways the love he possesses for you alone. This calls for action, harrumph!!

I've learned how to treat possessions!!—especially *material* ones. I know also, many other things! Most of all—I'm, at last, ready for you, & C&C, & life. I'm a happy man, believe this. Harm it not by any foolish fears. I love you & know what to do with us—all. We just follow the plans we made, positively the gonest, they are too. I write in attic & blow sax & you. You paint pictures in front room & me in back, don't get it, huh? But that's not all; you'll see when I get there, *never* to leave you & never again travel anywhere except Watsonville etc., unless Mommie & Cathy & Jerky (I love her so) are holding down back seat of 1951 Chevrolet st. wagon with their beautiful little asses, (you too) while their faces shine on me.

Got your 3 gone great letters to me at Jack's house. *Worry about nothing*—included is third child, if can't kick it without any physical or psychological harm to you. You come first, first, first, in everything—kids next—never fear, at any rate, when I get home we'll discuss, & love (wow).

Money very short; if I can't bum conductor in Mobile & spend $4.90 to N.O. will arrive home near broke. Save monnies. Jesus, I love you, can't wait, forever & each moment real & gone. Perfect just to watch you, work for you, & I'm *not* hung-up on lazy kicks any

10. The Louisville and Nashville railroad.

11. Deadhead. To take a train as a passenger in order to pick up a work train.

12. The morning and nighttime passenger trains between San Francisco and Los Angeles.

more!! I've got secret of perpetual energy!! I'm in there with you at last too. Please be happy. If this writing seems weird it's just I'm trying too hard to make love to you & be with you and I'm hi on life & you & everything. Hi forever. I know how now. Still sane & ahead of you. Trust the joy you face.

N.

Back home in San Francisco, Neal resumed his switchman's work at Oakland and wrote to Kerouac describing his return trip and urging caution if Jack and Joan still intended to use Neal's railroad pass to travel West.

TO JACK KEROUAC

Feb. 6, '51
[San Francisco]

DEAR JACK;

Absolutely impossible to write, just as I found we couldn't talk. We are collapsing, so is everyone, we must keep the strength we've left and you and I both feel so for the other fellow as a crutch, but can't make it in talk, so what—kill the pity in yourself, for yourself; broken holes we cling to, torn, tough.

None can hold a candle to you tho, still, and more so than ever, really. Henri Cru, taboo, frightened Allen fiddles, I stink.

Gibbly-goop, hippidy-hoppedy Cassady, I hurt my left knee switching Streamliners, "cut, bruised and swollen" on my 2611 injured on duty report. Myself and an old switch foreman named Bill Mast are the only two men who are working out of the 809, eight hundred and nine, switchmen who are out on strike at Oakland, Calif. I work 16 hours a day, 2 eight hour shifts, all the federal law allows, I rest eight hours—spending 2 of these eight driving to and fro, then back to more labor. Kicks tho, I do get hi, the miseries are paid all the same.

Money, money, I'm broke, can't pay car, can't even eat, beans, from 10th to 25th have 25 dollars to feed kids, C. and me. Whew!

Helen Hinkle gave up 230, lives here until strike over and she can use pass on now cancelled train to Denver and Al; Bennington girl here too, see letter from my wife to yours for dope on apts. for youse.*

Ekotape broke.

Music greater than ever.

I get fractured hi on real Hash (you ask Allen for Peter Van Meter). I talk to myself in phrases. I'll be hi driving and say a line aloud, (anything personal) then repeat it until another line comes, sometimes there is twenty minutes between lines. Mysterious.

Train trip back to SF crazy; one night in Texas I had whole washroom playing my toy musical instruments (3, three, different flutes, toy harmonica, wooden sweetpotato, borrowed banjo from Hungarian refugee) including mad Texas soldier who raved "escape" all night, Hollander on third day in states, spent 3 years in Dutch navy in D. East Indies where sailors are instantly killed by torture by insane natives in jungle, even armed parties in daylight are attacked. He says the two peoples can't understand each other; dig this in sense of Mexican guys, I did—being hi and watching a Roanoke Va, folly, a foolish flyboy in his new uniform telling my Dutchie about U.S.A., poor Dutchman, so earnest and innocent.

Other things, but bah, dreams are best, I knock myself out daily, no, more often, two at least, more likely three, different sleeps I get in naps from 5 to 8:30 A.M. (get up take Cathy to school; when I got in bed at 5 or so it was after 16 hrs. work) then sleep from (after breakfast) 9:45 or ten to 3:00, get up, dress, run for Cathy at school, drive fast to work at 3:59 P.M., usually a 10 to 30 minute catnap somewhere in the 16 hours (at beantime) then home again. Rugged tensions. Whew!

Packard no brakes, rearend, leaky gastank (can't fix) and I spent my last 42 dollars for necessary (since driveshaft about to tear up thru floorboard and kill kiddies) universal joints.

Be very careful about wife RR pass; if anything happens let me know at once, so I can immediately notify SP pass has been lost otherwise I'm fired and fined for misdemeanor, all I could salvage for you is halfrate from NYC to Washington and from there on to Atlanta, Ga; you are on your own from there dammit, I flubbed again.

I got different things on my mind, women.

*Carolyn didn't mail letter; kids tore it up. Apts. OK. Helen Hinkle now gone, Bennington girl will leave when Jack arrives. (She better, huh Joan?)

Still urging Kerouac to visit him in San Francisco, Neal wrote with more dream descriptions and enclosed another piece of writing, about an early trip from Denver to Los Angeles, that he'd dashed off the previous month, before leaving for New York.

TO JACK KEROUAC

Feb. 13, 1951
[San Francisco]

DEAR JACK;

Under the spreading horseshit banner "Come Save the Westerners" you must get on your hihorse and gallop o'er hill and vale to the secluded nook with a 41 Packard at its door (with initial C, in gold, for knocker) and be treated with infamous hospitality.

Seriously, you old bum, please hurry here. Get Carolyn's cooking and cleaning until your old lady gets here to get some too. Things are in a horribly bad way for us re people, if you two don't get here soon to get hi with us and dig every damn old thing we can find we parents will just shrivel into even dryer prunes.

Enclosed poor remnants of RR half rate orders, hope they can help.

My mind is utterly blank, can't think of a thing to say, it's really a form of exhaustion brought on by the steady use of t, which, with its enormous number of images contents the brain with just thoughts—terrifying tho they now are—so, no can write.

I'm not talking just bullshit; everything I look out upon fills me with a tenderness, a nostalgia for life. The state I've been reduced to consists now of living only for my dreams. Not dreams loosely, I mean actual dreams. Now that I've been on the 16 hours schedule for a week (just ended, back on graveyard shift) I have had the privilege of having the most extensive and unusual series of nightmares I've ever had. I am hungup on new weirdies; Blood, diving off incredibly high places, a frantic chase that excels in spit-second [*sic*] eluding of pursuers—I'm always caught tho—who question me and I summon up all forms of amazing complex logic for defense, which deters their vengeance and we all stand around together in an indecisive group—waiting. Other things; (I here intended a long thing on cunts, but so new and involved I desist). I dreamt I shared flight, after drinking red wine in high-ceilinged vault over long rough log tables, with St. Francis of Assisi. We rushed thru large warehouse buildings, thru corridors in shadow, with alleyways between. He had grey burlap robe, mine was brown and tripped me as I ran, I thought him incongruous as he revealed skinny legs with no hair when he held up the front of his robe to run. We got thru a door into a cobblestone cellar—from which I saw at once that there was no escape—just as our enemies, a group of real Roman Soldiers, reached it. Francis didn't hesitate tho, and seemed to know right where he was leading me because he dived for a depression in the floor which was a sort of drain and tugged at the bricks to reveal a trapdoor. I followed him, but was just a cunthair too late in closing it over my head and the leading Roman—with big beautiful helmet, you know, with the topnotch of clipped feathers and the wonderful scroll-like piece that covers the ears—saw the crack between the floor and the edge of the door as I closed it. Instantly they jumped in after us and at once I became as tho invisible, that is, I didn't have to participate in the dream from here on and was just an observer and the clattering mass of soldiers disappeared and all that was there was an oriental in white and St. Francis, also in white and half changed into an oriental too. No words were spoken between them. Francis kneeled on a wooden block that appeared and prayed or otherwise meditated while the newcomer oriental whetted an enormous long curved blade on his thumbnail, much as a barber tests a razor. Then he smoothly slit Francis' forehead so that a piece of skin hung down and covered his eyes, he lifted this skin and cut the eyelids and I remember I was mad as I watched and thought him purposely careless as he nicked the eyeball; I knew he was more skilled than that. Then bright bright red blood, red on the white garment of Francis, but no more mutilating, they just stayed in their positions as I watched and waited; after a long time the scene faded to L.A. Other things of a more frantic emotional nature; driving over roads in an open touring car with hills so steep that even worse than being straight up and down they bent inwards! Understand? Overhanging they were, a perpendicular cliff which at the bottom curved in at the base. Naturally I knew all the time I couldn't make it, but always was compelled to drive on. The boys in the back seat always fell out and really scratched the hell out of themselves and they were angry with me for being able to save myself by holding desperately to the wheel. So I said fuckit, someone else can drive and I'll take the back seat. And I did, and didn't fall out and saved myself from getting hurt by a series of impossible physical contortions at the exact second when we'd hit the danger spot at the end of each hill on the roller coaster road. Then the big mad one where I was the hoghead (engineer) on a hotshot train of passengers out of Grand Central. This dream is really too big tho, I'll just give snatches: it changed from Grand Central to Los Angeles tunnels and I was just hired and on first trip in hotshot interurban streetcar with three coaches of people; anyhow I can't see red light for stop or yellow for slow and being afraid was running late and cursing myself. I sat as on a windowsill with my legs dangling over front of first car. I didn't brake or accelerate properly. Now get this: I came into open stretch and determined to go fast as hell no matter what; I came quickly to another tunnel very long and I knew if didn't keep my speed I'd be much too late when I got to other end. Here's what I want you to see: as I started in tunnel the train went thru but I went over top, still sitting on ledge and steering and it didn't seem strange to me that tunnel-top separated train and me. Some dirty bastard put a portable derail (device purposely placed on rail to protect mainline from any car rolling into it) on track and we had big wreck which flung me into space and I sailed thru air about (accurate) 300 feet above ground level. Now, this is not a strange thing to my dreams, I either fall out airplane or off hi building or something so that I sail along for a distance of about a half mile and all the time I fly I'm preparing myself for the shock of landing. This time in train wreck I chose soft sand bank and slid thirty feet and was unhurt. In the air tho I became just the head brakeman and the regular engineer was flying along right beside me. As we whished by we saw a train in the siding and the engineer smiled at the train crew watching us and he raised both thumbs and gave them a "spot" sign. A "spot" sign is what one passes whenever the immediate work is done and there is nothing to be switched for a few minutes so everyone can go on the "spot." It's just like "take ten," or time out for coffee, except the usual case is the brakeman sits on the sandbox or the top of a boxcar or someplace to rest his feet, and the engine crew read the paper or stretch their legs over the throttle and go to sleep. Well, in the fury and fear of flight and landing I caught this engineer giving a "spot" sign as he sailed to certain death. The humor of this, and this evidence of his philosophy, gave me a hell of a boost and I wasn't as afraid anymore.

Other things, other things, but enough of this, it reminds me too much of the period that Allen was in at the time he lived on 74th and First Ave. His season next to the church, the time he was approaching the saints, the lull before Huncke and downfall.

Goddamn my ass, how in hell can you whip up thousands of words then be so goddamn cruel to your pal as to say "do you want to see them?"[13] Don't you dig what a horribly frustrated fucker I am? Why, I get a letter from you and put off reading it for several hours, just anticipating. When I finally get settled and start to read it I do it in parts, a page at a time. So too with everything I do. Proust has nothing on me. Please send your latest on to me if you will, I'm most careful with your letters and have all you've sent (not years ago tho, damit, damit).

I enclose here a real quickie I whipped off in just a couple of hours. Actually I wrote this poor little start of a thing around the first of January before I came east for visit. I don't feel badly as to its weak qualities because I just dashed it off without a pause.

I better see you soon, or else I'm even further up the creek. I want a lot of serious things to be done by us yet. Expect more action and come down to facts and exchange between us etc., etc., when you arrive. We still got time and it's not too late. Bunk. Love to Joan, sweet thing that she is.

N.

My second trip from Denver to Los Angeles was not the starved struggle the first one had been. I established a pattern used in later years when hitchhiking south from my home town, that is, I always afterward left the city in the fashion I did this time. The policy was to be on Denver's southern outskirts at dawn and by not leaving the road for an instant, hope to gain Raton, New Mexico by nightfall. I never failed to achieve this goal. It seems I possessed the inordinary luck to conquer this 250-odd mile distance by catching quick rides that often got me into New Mexico in the early P.M. Conversely, once on Raton's highway junction—the right hand leg went to Texas and southeast, the left to the southwest and California—some blocks beyond the railroad underpass where the hotshot freights begin to pick up speed, I could never get a lift until I'd waited many hours. My first trip had switched its mode of travel at this point, when at midnight, after thumbing cars for eight full hours, I'd caught one of these hiball reefer trains and continued the balance of the journey by rail. A couple of years later I was to wait 2 days in this spot without being

13. In a February 8 letter to Neal, Kerouac remarked that he had written six thousand more words of "confession," the continuing story of his childhood that he'd been working on since receiving Neal's "Joan Anderson" letter in late December. He asked Neal if he wanted them.

picked up by a friendly motorist. Now, however, I had the good fortune to make connections right away with one of the infrequently passing cars. He took me to Taos and when I got out it was not yet dusk. I was cheered; this was making the fastest time ever and just escaping from the Raton Rut buoyed me no end. I was confident, I was happy.

I bounced along the narrow blacktop with eager strides, breathing deep of the clean mountain air, marveling at the luxuriant vermilion gold of the sunset. Adobe buildings lined the way; every tenth structure housed a bar. From out their opened doors came loud Mexican music and the aroma of spiced food. Drunken Indians, their long black hair braided under strange hats used the center of the hiway as a path upon which to stagger. Some were singsonging to themselves, none talked, and most passed me in dark silence with cold eyes. Ahead, half up a slight hill, I saw a white rancher leave one of these taverns and make for a pickup truck; he was finishing a bottle of beer as he slowly walked to the machine. I hurried to catch him and bum a ride. He sensed my intention before I had a chance to voice it, and looking me over for a second, he said, "Get in." He didn't take me far, but I soon caught another ride which took me into Santa Fe near middlenight.

I sauntered thru this city in a fine state of hunger; fine, I say, because I hadn't eaten since morning, and in my pockets was the money for a good feed. Knowing the unlikelihood of an auto stopping for me after nightfall, I anticipated taking in the sights I could of this State Capital while hiking leisurely across it, then, settle in a cozy restaurant for a lengthy meal. I figured this program to get me "On The Road" and in position still in good time before dawn, so I followed it. I recall as I passed the State Police barracks two stern troopers left its well-lit interior and crunched their swank boots on the gravel driveway for brief seconds before they piled into their radio-dispatched police car with automatic motions of tough efficiency. This flashing glimpse of their hard gestures and unslack jaws, clamped so tightly against the grim upper lip, and their faces immobile as steel emphasizing the sheen of their merciless eyes glittering with zeal to perform their duty made me shudder as I thought of the short shrift they gave their prey. They spun the wheels and roared away while I was pitying any quarry they nabbed that night. Their ruthless tactics I well knew and couldn't escape a twinge of relief that I wasn't their intended victim. I went by crowded tourist cafes serving well-to-do travelers Mexican and American dishes, catering to their every wish, as their slick automobiles, parked to the rough street's high curb at an angle, patiently waited in quiet splendor to carry them away—escorted in magnificent style—when it was their whim to leave. The downtown area was packed with throngs of humanity, altho it was a late hour, and I don't think it was a Saturday night. The congested glob was heightened by the streets of alley width (20 ft., or so) along which cars crawled with exasperated honking. The sidewalks were overflowing with people; men in cowboy apparel and otherwise, Indians, solemn and otherwise, Mexicans, chattering and otherwise, whites, drunk and otherwise, women everywhere, beautiful and otherwise, Indian girls encased in moccasins, Indian squaws encased in fat, Mexican chicks in tight skirts and provocative stride, old Mexican women in more fat and burdened with unwashed infants, white women of all kinds, waitresses, heiresses, etc., and kids, kids every place imaginable, leaping and yelling, lunging between cars in mid-block, many quiet and morose, scuffling along with head down. Above all this mass of activity glared the lights. Edison's greatest invention hung over the gathered heads in astonishing profusion. These wonderous dissipators of darkness were in every color and all shapes. Countless thousands of lights squeezed into a square mile displayed a garish brilliancy that plunged the surrounding parts of town into seeming blackness. They blazed from every wall, shone down from every ceiling, illuminated every storefront from row upon row of arrayed bulbs. Gigantic markers jutted sharp fingers of flame beyond the rooftops. Enormous signs thrust out their bulk from the building face and drew the eye to multicolored letters proclaiming announcements with electric gleam. Long billboards in continuous circle covered the second-storeys with emblazoned script. Big single ones popped from the wall over every dazzled doorway. Smaller ones, controlled by hand chains, had been flicked on inside every building. The tiny ones were obliviated in this steady stream of lights aiding the streetlamps to rival the sun. Under a theater marquee engaged in combat with night by flashing bright blasts of garbled glare at regular intervals, I paused in mid-step, struck with the size of this small city's electric bill. Most of their overhead must be electricity, paying sums I couldn't guess for the privilege of this crazy glow. Were two thirds of the lights switched off, the remainder would still outshine Times Square with its artificial daylight. I envied the owners of the utilities company that supplied Sante Fe.

My supper was consumed in a gaudy restaurant decorated with a Mexican motif. I lingered over a second coffee until 3 A.M., then, stepped to the hiway. Instant luck, amazing luck!! A 1941 Packard cream convertible (this in 1942) screeched to a halt some hundred feet past me. I raced forward and got in beside a lone man. He was going (believe this) to Los Angeles!!! What a trip! I've never had it so good. He raced at 80 per for several hundred miles, then, pulled over and slept for a few hours in the front seat; I had the back one. We stopped here and there as whim dictated: Grand Canyon, wayside pottery stands, etc., etc. He bought all the meals. It was, all in all, a dream come true, save he didn't suggest I drive, and not to risk antagonizing him, I wouldn't ask.

We approached L.A. from the south, on hiway 101. Once in Venice, Calif., (actually a part of sprawling L.A.'s 444 square miles) I thanked him profusely and got out, within five blocks of the place I had traveled 1300 miles to reach.

Neal continued sending money to Diana each month, but asked her to stop telephoning, effectively terminating their contact at this time.

TO DIANA HANSEN CASSADY

Feb. 27, 1951
[San Francisco, California]

DEAR DI;

I apologize, I grovel, I'm a bastard. I mean a bastard, a selfish bastard, a fool, a prick. I want you to know that for *once* your phone calling did some good. Be that as it may, I can only send you $50.00 believe me. Whatever happens, don't go anywhere near Southern Pacific, especially Mr. Mace; nobody'll get anything if I lose SP job, and that's for sure. Your previous call (2 months or so) was paid for by me, which deducted from your $50.00 leaves $43.37 since it was cheap, only $6.63. This is serious only because C. & I have fought bitter battles for weeks over this damn $6.63. But, naturally, I won't—too low a trick—deduct it, altho she thinks I will.

I can cover up $6.63, but your last phone call would be impossible to hide, so, if fucking phone Co. tries to collect I must deduct it from next 50, which, incidently, you will receive the 1st of every month. Try to stay alive if you can. Please don't write, because I can't and there's nothing to say.

N.

In March, Allen Ginsberg wrote to Neal,[14] *praising his "Joan Anderson" letter, which he'd just read, telling him that he was impressed and astonished at its magnitude, and suggesting that he could get it published for money with very little change. Allen also told Neal that he'd be interested to see how he wrote poetry, and so Neal obliged.*

TO ALLEN GINSBERG

March 17, 1951
[San Francisco]

HELLO DEAR ALLEN;

Once again we try to speak to each other, and it's harder to do than it ever was. I can't piss a drop, there's not a word in my head, I'm leaky as hell. (is).

All the crazy falderal you two boys make over my Big Letter[15] just thrills the gurgles out of me, but we still know I'm a whiff and a dream. Nonetheless, tho I blush over its inadequacies, I want you to realize the damn thing took up the better part of three straight Benzedrine afternoons and evenings. So I did work hard at it and managed to burn a little of the juice out of me and if the fucking thing is worth any money that's great. For the same half-conscious impulse that made me not do any Neurotica Automobilestuff (I'm bidin' my time) I hesitate to try and force that letter into anybody's hands and tell them I'm serious about it. I pretend I would blow my little plastic flute all day if the letter fell into print, but I can't really feel it, so unless they'd give 50 cents or more for it; thank you and forget any effort on its behalf. As for finishing it, a snap, a breeze, I think to myself, but I won't do it because I can't even spare any attempts at a letter to you or Jack since all the little writing I do is on the novel. And that stupid novel is a horrible stinker, really a fart.

The real reason I don't write is because there is so much to say and if I begin I get hung detailing everything, and that's just too goddam much work. That is the truth and is why I fuck the dog about letters. Knowing how important a pleasure they are I will crowd the shit out of my busy day (and I mean it, you don't know) and fret out one or two or throo or foo or foodedo a month to you, and that's a vow.

14. Letter published in *As Ever*, pp. 92–104.
15. Neal's "Joan Anderson" letter of December 17, 1950.

While I'm at it, about my alliterations with words: why shit man, I know all about that old stuff you went to all the trouble to lay down to me, and I appreciate it and realize you know all about everything I could possibly ever put to you, but I like their naivete and play with them as one will a vice that is passing for good and one gentle blow can absent it forever anytime one so desires; example: Doc Savage and the Shadow; I stayed with them until Julian J. Frierby[16] frowned at such rot and instantly they dwindled so that I even lost the kick of smirkreading them. And on, blah, blah. I think I'll name him Julian Koalters Frierbee. Anyhow, your criticism of my letter was right as rain, esp. about sentences forced out of natural context; my main trouble for sure. Enuf on this stuff. And Lyric is supported on bubbles and what is too foolish to be said is sung.

March 20, 1951

Going thru old papers happened to see this beginning of a letter to you on St. Pat's of two years ago.[17] We were both pretty well at the bottom of our fucking barrel at that time and my few paragraphs certainly show it. On other side of page is 50 sentence excerpt from 50,000 word appeal of Commander in Merchant Marine, Mike Walton, to his insane Communist wife, Lorna. He begged for reconciliation to this dumpy bitch, but she tossed him over and made off with a really dumb nigger Buck and all Walton's money. All very goopily felt by me.

In your lovely letter of a few days ago you talk of poetry, as usual, a productive pastime I have not formalized for myself yet. Because you asked for a few lines I devoted exactly 7 minutes to the following ones and did it in the same sense of careless freedom I used to make "Joan's Letter," but, of course, the below is so awfully poor I must try and explain it away by telling you I'm as destitute for things to write to you as you are in things to send me; (incidently, I didn't change a word and used the first one that came into my head):

I'm off on the wings of Tangierian Swells,
For flowing from Fable on Fable comes the pattern of Belles,
That pressure the mind and weaken the bowels, tis true,

16. Justin W. Brierly.
17. Neal's letter to Allen of March 15/17, 1949.

But not as other things do.
So, I long to lick the Lymph Glands larder
of bubblely juices, and harder tarter,
And make amends with a woman's Tits; and farter,
and stick my neck in the noose of her garter,
A plaything's above it to which I'm a martyr.

Love,
N.

At home, after his short trip to New York in January, Neal found it difficult to concentrate on his writing. Kerouac had no such problem and, inspired by Neal's "Joan Anderson" letter and others of the previous fall, produced the scroll version of On the Road *in just three weeks that April.*

TO JACK KEROUAC

April Fool
[April 1, 1951
San Francisco]

DEAR JACK;

I've tried to write and can't. I love you and love you, but am so bothered by other things that each letter I begin ends at the first paragraph. I can send these on if you wish. I even have funny little things torn from magazines for you. This card to let you know I'm alive and have your latest confessions and PO card hid away and highly prized in secret chamber near new upstairs fire extinguisher. First 10 torturous sheets of doublespace done on novel. Life hard with no tea to swallow or money for anything. Wish, but think fearfully not, that NY could forward rare Ceylon import. C. [Carolyn] and D. [Diana] having tremendous long distant roaring match this very minute, been yelling in frustrated rage for halfhour. I'm sick to my stomach with sorrow. Want to emphasize how great I think all you've written is, really most beautiful.

Neal told Allen Ginsberg of his efforts at writing, coherently explaining, in great detail, the problems he was experiencing, and the difference between his approach to his novel and letter writing.

TO ALLEN GINSBERG

May 15, 1951
[San Francisco]

DEAR ALLEN;

I have not written anything for a month. This is not particularly bad, that is, I didn't quit in the habitual doubt and depression. There is a dissatisfaction; a basic deeply disgusting impatience and feeling of overwhelming inadequacy with words. Especially acute is the awareness of my lack of ability, an almost entire lack I fear, to delineate any character literarily. Yet, as I say, this last stopping was not too frustrating since it was actuated by a rational slackening-off (altho I'm the last person recommendable to slow down; Time and my personality makes that inadvisable; in my 25 years I've written only a rambling prologue, an even weaker first 20 pages and pitifully few letters) to escape the mediocre monotone of what I'm writing by assimilating "Tender is the Night"—F. Scott Fitzgerald,[18] and a little poetry to freshen my outlook, now that my oolong is gone and to substitute for too powerful Dexedrine. Again, too, the RR program makes writing difficult because I'm seldom in SF more than 8 hrs. at a time. To compensate I carry a note pad and write a sentence or two as I think of it, but these caboose-lines are always, of necessity, the next ones of the book and have accumulated into a number of illegible longhand pages. Being not at home long enough to work these into a typewritten reality, I simply quit writing until such time as I can catch up. So I do have an inflexible body of swollen adjectives to attack and shall do it, tho the slowness of the labor quells my spirit. I may as well tell you why. It happens this way in my untalented case: Of course, I have in mind a rough outline which consists only of an attempt to recall my befuddled memories. To put down these happenings gives me the original impetus for each line—at best I write only from sentence to sentence and can't construct beyond this—and I begin to write. After the first statement is out, and often before, I get hopelessly involved in words to contain the increasing number of ideas. As I progress this morass becomes larger and my head more and more deeply engulfed in recurrent themes which are enfolded in sickening profusion. While on the paper, in attempting to snatch all I can before I forget, I

18. F. Scott Fitzgerald (1896–1940). American novelist and short-story writer best known for *The Great Gatsby* (1925) and *Tender Is the Night* (1934).

am soon so overextended—stretched grammatically and logically to the point where any semblance of clarity is lost—that I am forced to stop. These bunched ideas cannot long be consciously retained as I write and are lost by being momentarily thrust back into the mind, each as they come except the immediate one pinpointed, and the sensitive things, once rejected for a second, shyly vanish in an unrelenting march of steady retreat into their Limbo while I'm floundering at sloppy deliberation in the choice of every new word, and thus damned up my soul is left to rot. The limit of my foremind to tap and drain onto paper any flow from my residue of self-saturated thoughts is usually half a page at any one sitting. Naturally, the shorter the space of time between each diving-in the less satisfaction I could weave for myself and each continuing made more oppressive the friction generated by rubbing so familiarly against my blocks. When confronted with these boundaries I had once either often changed the subject upon which to think or didn't write at all, mostly the latter. Now, in my still inconsistent and inconstant fashion, I've burst thru somewhat (¿) so face bigger things. These are more of the straitjacket variety and perhaps approach your own problems of poetic thought, but that is no help and might be something else entirely. Be as it may, the way it happens is simply that a particular word one knows pops out for use. But we quickly learn not to be content with just any word and look for a second, or third, or fourth choice. (Incidently, when I first began typing, if I accidentally hit the wrong letter to start a word I would, rather than erase, think up a word to suit the letter and as another and then another mistake came up I had soon altered completely both the meaning of what I said and the things which I was saying—with all the accompanying change in chain of thought.) At last I come to the core of my writing faults, flaws in reasoning, windiness or too tight style, grammar troubles, triteness, etc., so shall put off for a minute any delving into our straitjacket problems per se, altho all is tied together, I give you detailed example to show that most of my inability to get on with the book lies in my slowness in selecting words, more properly I mean my slowness in fitting into a sensible sentence the words that select themselves. My primary weakness is that I try to crowd too much in; once a word has come to me, no matter how obviously poor, I am loath to leave it out of that sentence. Seeing it won't fit I set out to manufacture another sentence for it; in doing so I create more, etc. Let us look at this a little more closely. Right away I've got a surplus of cheap old common words. In the interval it takes to make the sentence structure a few more hit me and they force the sentence into a ridiculous bulge which I must prune pronto. To load each sentence with all it can carry takes time and the longer I linger the more abstract possibilities flit across my mind. Then I'm really in for it because I start switching words about like an over-zealous brakeman with poor savvy. A compromise must be reached and the slow decision on each one is what puts me in the hole so muchoftenfardeeply. See what I mean, those four words just popped and I had to choose. To continue this asinine level of elementary writing frustration you are to turn back to the upside down question mark on last page. I was about to modify "somewhat" by using these words—to adapt an attitude by attempting to be attuned for each topic in a subject matter—but when I began arranging the words I realized I was doing typical writing in one of my normal sentences and tho they didn't mean too much, even if poor (and they are not good words, as can be easily seen) I was about to use them because each one had just popped out in rapid order and because they had come I felt it necessary to try and put them in after "somewhat." Instead I left them out, and it's most unusual for me to leave anything out just because it's stinking and that's why the ordinary level of my writing is so trite and shallow, and put in the question mark to call your attention to the space and put the words here for you instead of where they were intended to be placed when I wrote them. Enuf. Back to the straitjacket problem of control. For me to cultivate adequate management of ideas so as to keep them and to be able to put them down clearly is an ever-present difficulty to my stumbling mind. Incidently, it was along this line of trying to save something for writing until I could learn to make it all one process of just thinking and putting down that thought, that I rationalized into the decision to buy my Ekotape recorder. The experiment has proved somewhat disappointing so was abandoned in its infancy a few months ago, but when I again get 10 bucks to get it out of the repair shop (magnetized by sitting next to a radio in long disusement) I will begin a new attempt with it. Now, if I'm on the novel I write longhand and type it up with a bit of changing as I go along; if I'm writing a letter I just type word for word as I think of them, unless I get particularly involved, then I write that sentence or two in longhand before typing. In this letter, except for the majority of lines 25 to 40 on the first page and one or two other single lines, I typed right along at my average (a little better than average, I think) speed of—well, figure it up if you've the patience; I've taken exactly four (4) hours of sitting here, with a couple of times-out to piss and quiet kids, to reach this sentence, anyhow, it must surely be at least several words a minute, I guess, huh? Right now my book stands much in relationship to the above words I gave you that were supposed to follow "somewhat" on page one. That is, I have a lot of longhand junk that has each sentence in it crammed full of stupid words that make faulty reasoning and poor flow because of the jampacked verbs and adjectives. This makes for a whole stretch of pages that are not only poorer than usual, but also has no uplifting line or two to compensate. In other words, one Sunday a month or so ago I wrote all of this weak part in the sunshine of the backyard (sitting on a piles-making square of concrete) and got horribly involved in my nemesis of too many poor words. So there I'm stuck because I can't throw it all away and can't satisfactorily patch it up. All I can do is finish this part and try to do better on the following pages, and if I ever accumulate a great many pages I can either throw this part out or graft it on elsewhere. So it's really not too bad, as I said in the beginning, it just happens to be where I am right now. Ugh, OK, I stop for the sake of intelligence and apologize that the reasoning of this whole letter would give discredit to a retarded ten-year-old. But I must say this as it seems apropos: I find, and for the first time, that when I read F.S. Fitzgerald I'm dealing with a writer that I'm about equal to. Not yet, of course, and maybe never in terms of word-use, but I know I'm in there already almost as far as he ever was. I was amazed to discover that his writing reasoning was nearly exactly paralleled by me. Not that I can approach his style, nor do I much care to, in fact, strangely enough, it seems somehow beneath me. What I perhaps mean is that I feel he and I both try with about equal intensity. If I can't come to eventually write as good as he did I fear I'll honestly be pretty much of a failure; ego? no, truth. I realize he's not much and only extolled as American (at least a dozen, including our pal Jack K. are better) and I see him as a baby compared to Proust or Céline.

I halt these digressions so that I may begin the next page clean.

(I'm cheating with a smaller second sheet because you didn't finish your single page, you bum.)

Now to answer what I can of your letter, and I must keep it shaved down into short bursts otherwise I'll get hung with expressing full feelings on each matter, or come up with something good enough to make me use another page, besides, I've got things to tell you of my external life that I save for next time; this to make you answer soon.

Your poem fine as usual, but an illiterate like me can say nothing about it, so, I'm reminded instead to ask you if you've ever written a little takeoff on Hope's poem that begins "When first I Loved"? If you have I'd appreciate a forwarding.

Great news that Jack's finished On The Road; I trust in his writing, but fear for it because the theme of On The Road is too trivial for him, as his dissatisfaction shows. He must either forget it or enlarge it into a mighty thing that merely uses what he's written as a Book 1; since what he's done doesn't lend itself to stuffing he should create another and another work (like Proust) and then we'll have the Great American Novel. I think he would profit by starting a Book 2 with the recollections of his early life as they were sent to me and then blend that into his prophetic Dr. Sax. Of course, I'm sure I don't know what I'm talking about, but I do worry for him and want him happy.

Children, children, the pox of freedom and demander of money that siphons off luxury, but an enormous sponge to absorb your love and a bottomless pleasure pit into which I throw myself sometimes.

What does cryptic line of your letter mean, the one that reads "And Jack said 2 nites ago he went back to the woman that wanted him most"? Ma, Pauline,[19] Edie,[20] or just imagination figment, huh?[21]

Next year or two we might all go to Mexico together in my (then) station wagon. Tell Van Meter I began letter to him and had passes (RR) for him, but decided RR just too awful for anyone, still not too late tho, I think. Also you asshole, if you loved me even a little you'd get me some t from him or Brandenberg,[22] or somewhere; I haven't written to ask because I've no money to pay, but in few weeks could manage same. Please, if possible without too much hassle. Also tell

19. Pauline was a girlfriend of Kerouac's whom he met in 1948. Represented by Lucille in *On the Road,* and Christine in Holmes's *Go*.

20. Edie Parker (1922–1993), Kerouac's first wife. They married in 1944; annulled in 1946. Edie is Elly in *Visions of Cody,* and Edna in *Book of Dreams* and *Vanity of Duluoz*.

21. In his letter to Neal of May 7, 1951 (*As Ever,* pp. 106–8), Allen Ginsberg had written: "And Jack said 2 nights ago, 'he went back to the woman that wanted him most.'" In his reply of May 20, 1951 (*As Ever,* pp. 61–64), Ginsberg clarified that Jack was talking of Neal (returning to Carolyn) rather than himself, although the quote has been misinterpreted as referring to Kerouac returning to his mother after leaving his wife Joan.

22. Bob Brandenberg, a small-time crook operating around New York, 1940s to 1950s. Portrayed as Bob Hindenburg in Kerouac's *Visions of Cody* and *Book of Dreams,* and as Jack in William Burroughs's *Junkie*.

Van great stuff he gave me and thank him. Is he writing? He fuck Dusty much?[23]

Re. Joan Letter; can do same anytime, not now tho.

I know of Chase and Bill[24] from Al Hinkle who is back on RR and lives 5 blocks away. Helen (wife) has got him over barrel (I mean he's sucker) and he refused several (more than 4) thousand dollars from rich people whom she allowed to adopt their child and he's in big debt for lawyer fight which got Helen back her whim (kid). Besides, she found he fucked old girlfriend in San Bernardino on his way home from Mexico and latest is that he's kissing her ass in a big way; foolish, I say knock her on her bighugeenormouslyfat ass. There's your SF gossip for this time. More and better anytime, OK?

Got latest Neurotica, (tell you of coincidence sometime) since Carolyn subscribed years ago, and dug Solomon and Chris Maclaine;[25] both off their frantic side nowadays, well aren't we all?

I have $200 C melody saxophone can buy for 65; old conductor owner will save for me (has since last Nov.) yet, since am about to lose car for lack of 35 buck payments will be at least fall before I start blowing on a sax. I'll learn tho.

"Gashouse McGinty" has fair Joyceian center part, but J. Farrell[26] only farts, and too loud.

Give me plenty NY gossip if you can please. Tell Jack I become ulcerated old color-blind RR conductor who never writes anything good and dies a painful lingering death from prostate gland trouble (cancer from excessive masturbation) at 45. Unless I get sent to San Quentin for rape of teenager and drown after slipping into slimy cesspool that workgang is unclogging. Of course, I might fall under freight train, but that's too good since Carolyn would get around 40 or 50 thousand settlement from RR (god's truth, maybe more—only reason I keep job instead of driving Greyhound bus with gals to sniff at). One thing sure, I'll just keep withering away emotionally at about same rate as have last 3 years, so unlikely that I can become insane or kill myself because there can be no further explosions except cap-

23. Dusty Moreland, Ginsberg's ex-girlfriend, was now seeing Peter van Meter.

24. William Burroughs had been attempting to seduce Hal Chase in Mexico City.

25. *Neurotica* #8 (spring 1951) included a short story by Christopher Maclaine, "The Sea Is Red," and an article by Carl Solomon, under the pseudonym of Carl Goy, entitled "Further Afterthoughts of a Shock Patient."

26. James T. Farrell (1904–1979). Chicago-born naturalist novelist, best known for his *Studs Lonigan* trilogy (1932–35), and *Gas-House McGinty* (1933).

pistol blowoffs. Have attained a run-of-the-mill schizophrenia brought on by past dwelling on loss of love and guilt of actions, but it is still a petty watery blue-green and can't fade into a real greyness until another 10 years of steady Proustian recollection of life. There is hope for some unhealthy blast sooner tho because my frustrations are at a near-record high. I'm afraid I've irrevocably slipped however and in my mediocrity have become precisely what Jack long ago feared was my fate: I am blank and getting more so.

Tho I'm tempted, no more pages, esp. since called for train; also can boast letter mailed same day writ.

N.

Carolyn has varicose veins of the pussy; Cathy & little one have measles & I am going slowly blind in left eye from little black & grey spots that have multiplied from single 1950 one.

In early June, Jack and his wife, Joan, had parted. In an attempt to cheer him, Neal wrote, inviting Jack to spend time with him and Carolyn in San Francisco, with the opportunity of making money by working on the railroad there.

TO JACK KEROUAC

June 19, 1951
San Francisco

[Telegram]

Wait. No foolish moves. This serious. Unparalleled opportunity. You come here. Orders. You must obey. We mean it. You need it. Carolyn agrees. Hurry. Letter follows.

NEAL

TO JACK KEROUAC

June 20, 1951
[San Francisco]

DEAR JACK;

Alright now listen you, let's get serious. You going to write another book, huh? I'm trying to write one, right? You love me, don't you? I love you, don't I? If we're so all-fired good, then think of the funny times historians of future will have in digging up period in last half of 51 when K. lived with C., much like Gauguin and Van Gogh, or Nietzsche and Wagner, or anybody and how, during this time of hard work and reorientation C. learned while K. perfected his art and how under the tutoring of the young master K., C. ironed out much of his word difficulties and in the magnificent attic K. did his best work and etc., etc., etc. No, but listen now; you'd have perfect freedom, great place in which to write, car to cut around in, satisfaction of knowing you're helping me when I need it most. No bother, great books to read, music to hear, life to see, up at any hour, to bed at same, free rent, best of all, a real period wherein instead of, when you're actually at a weak point as now, going thru hassle and money spending of setting up own pad—as you just got thru doing—you come to me for rest and relaxation and find a spot with absolutely everything you could need already set up for you. All you have to do is take advantage of my hospitality, like a weekend that stretches into months in an English countryside estate, and say to yourself that you need a quiet place of freedom in which to write a new book and bone up on those few things you might hanker to know while you've got the chance to just lie around doing so, a time in which to gather your strength and your thoughts, a period of recuperation wherein you solidify your soul; everything is not jazz, cunt and kicks as you know so well, and before you indulge in same by taking off for some far-away place before you're really ready, you must come here to listen to me and make cement the liquid putty of our life. I have absolutely greatest bed in the world on the floor of my extraordinary attic; I got books and shelves, great huge desk that's bigger than any desk could possibly be, since Carolyn made it out of 6 ft. by 6 ft. piece of plywood, with immense dictionary of 30 lbs, and foot thick proportions, and fine lamps, and good radio (one downstairs too) and wondrous tape recorder made for not only endless kicks on sound but for dictaphone type writing and recording of thoughts, hi and otherwise, and golf clubs, and baseballs and (soon) tennis racquets with nearby court and all the socks, handkerchiefs and dirty pictures one could want, and perfect weather, no heat, no cold, and world famous town to dig, and beaches and zoos (great on t) and art galleries and railroad you must dig, and Al Hinkle and maybe Bill Tomson and whorehouses, if you've the money, and freedom, man, freedom, no bull, Carolyn loves you, be like your mama without you having any need to cater like to her, and coffee, gobs of expensive coffee, I steal it from store, and clothes washed free, and your portrait painted, and front parlor for smooching with anything handy (before you go upstairs for complete privacy) and good typewriter and ribbon, and the greatest of subtle thinking drugs, and so soft and easy to take: Dexedrine, it's perfect and mellow and is such a mental wonder that on it I write poetry (after a fashion). I got lots of it and journals and paper and if you don't come home for days or stay in your room for days or sleep forever or stay up all night or growl or cuss or dig my gone little chicks who are positively no bother even to a child-hater like Dillinger (much less than even Julie or master Bill, Jr.) until I think you're lecherous, or if you want to get serious again like an idealistic youth and want to really get in there on some subject, whether by yourself or with me, or if you want to go to pot so as to be further prepared for a tropical clime, or if you want analyst at free clinic (50 cents a visit) or if you want to work on RR, or any damn old thing that strikes your fancy, do all of it, it's OK, more than you can possibly realize, for you don't know what easy living is till you dig old man C's brand at 29 Russell. As soon as you get tired of us you may, if you are prepared in your own mind, leave at once for your shangri-la, or else, if you succeed in finding a bit of peace, or in doing a work that can't be quickly abandoned, you will stay here until December, at which time we will all pile into my station wagon with all its roominess and very slowly dig everything as we drive to Mex City where we will stay until short money completely fades and then the wife, little kiddies and I will bid you fond goodbye and leave you to your own devices in that city of magic. All this with less tension and anxieties than one might experience with even Mr. B's family, for Carolyn and I, at last, are a smooth running little team, that tho we sputter and snort a bit, are compatible as hell.

The main thing, of course, is the saxophone. A 200 and more dollar C melody Alto that I am almost owner of, i.e. definitely, definitely the conductor owner has promised to keep it for me indefinitely and since he is a most conscientious man I am guaranteed the instrument the moment I have $65. Now, you remember my boy?, the colored cat of 37 or so who blows the Alto?, the guy we took over to Richmond one night, name of Ed Sousiox?[27] well, I am to see him tomor-

27. Ed Sousiox is the real name of the alto sax player called Ed Fournier in Part Three of *On the Road,* and Ed Laurier in *Visions of Cody.*

row or so and since he's been going to music school for 3 years he will be a very good and adequate teacher for a nominal fee because he's so damn broke and has nothing but the best t.

Naturally, in the back of your mind must be the remembrance of the rough receptions you've received at 29 Russell in the past, in fact, less than 2 years ago, but you must concede it was not as difficult for you as a murder or suicide might have made such a brief visit. Carolyn wants to try and make it up to you by a few group orgies or whatever, altho this might sensibly be postponed until after Oct. because she's as big as our house and the bed is only four feet across. You understand that if you don't come here now it will curse my new son forever, since you won't be here to be his Godfather, and because you will have deserted him, I would be forced to not name him John Allen Cassady as is my present intent. And be sure and bring your Bongo drum, or you'll have to go down on O'Farrell and see the gone drums there.

I spent the buck twenty for telegram to you so that you might be impressed enough to come west and make the third time a charm, otherwise you're just a big bum who's afraid to sleep under my roof and have a good time with my equipment.

Early A.M.

Just got back from daily passenger run—I'm a big passenger brakie now, with a pretty monkeysuit that looks like a tux from the rear—and can't think of much more to say that might entice you to cover the long trail to this end of the world for no good reason, except that it's too hot in NY or Mex (we'll be south of the border at right time of winter season, eh?) and too European in France and too trite in Great Neck and too early for Siberia or Africa. Incidentally, when all is lost you and I will go to Morocco and build railroad for thousand a month. All we do is ride while African coolies dump ballast over roadbed. They'll be a-building for years so whenever you want to be a brakie I'll teach you and together we'll make our fortune on our ass and spend it on Black same.

Night I left you at Henri Cru's while Seymour[28] and I went up to

28. Seymour Wyse (b. 1923), an Englishman, was a schoolfriend of Kerouac's at Horace Mann, 1939–40. Later, in New York, Wyse helped to introduce Kerouac to the emerging sounds of bebop. Portrayed as Lionel Smart in *Visions of Cody, Maggie Cassidy, Vanity of Duluoz,* and *Book of Dreams*.

J. Newman's[29] to hear his end-all music and blast his t and some of mine etc., is when I really dug your pal Jerry, so for old times' sake make him lay a joint on you for me. As for Mezz Mezzrow, ha, you don't know, I suppose, that while under the influence of really really stuff at B's ranch in Texas 47, I read, over a course of 2 or 3 weeks of daily hi, Mezzrow's little ghost-written gem "Really The Blues,"[30] which lays down all the shit he picked up on from early reform school days of Tinny Alto and sneaked butts thru Lush Chi and Weeded Harlem to eating balls of straight opium at ballgames as tho was popcorn and blasting the pipe with old Chinamen buddies in Harlem janitor's very gone basement while janitor was always having to rise off his weary ass to go upstairs and chase the nigger whores out of upper floor's bathroom which they brought clients into in absence of any other place, and Al Capone and brother's gang, and whore Mezz saved from same, to marry, but she liked cock too well, and all Chi gang of musicians, all of them, and first nigger wife and their kids and Satchmo[31] helping him to kick the habit and Satchmo making a roach of a bomber joint in two mighty drags and Satchmo this and Satchmo that, and hundred other things including very sensible defense of t, and book ends, as I remember, with him going straight and getting job as salesman or clerk or something for NY business firm. I recall ole Bull snorting and twanging to me "that Mezzrow sho is an ole nigger lover, ain't he?" Later in SF I saw innocent little schoolgirl on streetcar digging book with big eyes of excitement and disbelief while her straight little legs were just a-twitchin' from the way her wet wee thing of slime squirmed her tiny hot bottom. I'd like to see that old jew's wife, by golly. Tell Allen hello and please send on Ouspensky book[32] and I promise return. And tell everyone you see hello for me. And don't worry about nothing. And you needn't bring Proust 'cause

29. Jerry Newman (1920–1970) was a friend of Kerouac's who had a record shop in New York, in partnership with Seymour Wyse. They founded the record label Esoteric, issuing recordings that Newman had made in the Harlem clubs in the early 1940s, including some by Dizzy Gillespie and Charlie Christian. Jerry Newman is represented by Danny Richman in Kerouac's *Visions of Cody* and *Book of Dreams,* and by Larry O'Hara in *The Subterraneans.*

30. *Really the Blues* (1946), by Mezz Mezzrow and Bernard Wolfe, the biography of a jazz clarinetist from Chicago. Neal talks about reading this book during his visit to Texas, 1947, in the tape section of *Visions of Cody.*

31. I.e., jazz trumpeter and entertainer Louis Armstrong (1900–1971).

32. Ginsberg had been reading the occult novel *The Strange Life of Ivan Osokin* (1947) by Russian journalist, philosopher, and follower of Gurdjieff P. D. Ouspensky (1878–1947).

I got all of him here. And dying to read "On The Road" so better have it published quick, or have spare ms. And if don't come because of intellectual reasons or because you just feel you can't make it, I will understand just as I think I do about poor Joan, and if I pine and die away as she without you: just meant to be.

N.

*Kerouac replied on June 24 (*SL*, pp. 320–21), thanking Neal for his offer but explaining that he could not afford to travel to California and was going with his mother to visit his sister, Caroline, in North Carolina.*

TO JACK KEROUAC

July 2, 1951
[San Francisco]

DEAR JACK;

Can't write, not just to you, but can't write at all. So send this instead to tell you I hear every word and understand yours of June 24. You must send me ms. of "O.T.R."; I guarantee its rushed return. I'm a desperate man, much like yourself, but have fossilized into the blank brakeman limbo, whereas you're still alive somewhat. There is the sax anyhow, I get it next week, and Ed the alto man will teach me; altho he's now threatening to retreat to Chi., Ill. Can also get station wagon now, since car (Packard) is paid for, but hate to take on the added debt so might wait month or so. Now have greatest elitch; one gives; no half a one, after-effects that linger for three days! And music, wow! And reading, but no writing, woe. And sad sickness makes me yank 4, 7, 11 times everyday, tho Confucius say "Better use old hen than pullet," and I say, I love coffee, I love tea, and that's what ails me, thinks she.[33] But kiddies hold me always.

N.

Writing from North Carolina on July 10, Kerouac responded more positively to Neal's earlier invitation to visit him and Carolyn in San Francisco.

33. "I love coffee, I love tea, I love the Java Jive and it loves me"—"The Java Jive," recorded by The Ink Spots, 1940.

TO JACK KEROUAC

July 16, 1951
[San Francisco]

DEAR JACK;

I knew you'd wake up, old pardner. Don't wait too long to get here; sooner you come more chance to be RR brakies at 400 a month. They are making student brakies now, but might have all they need by middle of Aug., hurry. I am now proud owner of the most perfect greatest station wagon in town, real gem, gone. Also got my saxophone today, yes indeedie, at last a great big horn to blow on, and I can make big sounds already, easy as pie; in two, three months we'll blow Little Harlem out. So, everything's here: car, sax, typewriter, paper, journals, ekotape, baby-drums, regulation US army bugle, made in Japan and bent a little to give it flair. Happy wife, beautiful kids, good job, mellow climate, whorehouses, bum elitchs (stuck with) and me and you learning to write and play music together; what else? Send me more exact plans of trip as it unfolds; hurry and don't forget your ms, of "OTR." Bring your drums please, and Balzac/Stendhal/others. Goal Aug., sooner?

N.

After arriving back in New York, Kerouac replied to Neal on July 23 (letter reproduced in the Kerouac ROMnibus*) but was still undecided about how or when he could travel to California. Neal continued urging him to hurry.*

TO JACK KEROUAC

August 10, '51
[San Francisco]

DEAR JACK;

Og jooseie poopoohoed azujackeracsonenburgerphapemsteinersaxianiojustin; My brain waves on this stuff must form a very pretty picture; i.e., I feel I have most surely squared the circle, tho so jazzed are the jagged lines as they return to the starting point that it makes me tired.

My uncle's uncle was an uncle, that's so silly.

Sunday I dropped into the Little Harlem and when the B-Girl

approached me I recognized her as the fat slob who insisted she was the wife of Freddy Strong[34] and so to avoid having her ask for a drink I casually asked if she'd heard from Freddy lately. She laughed and asked if I was kidding her, and seeing I was serious said, "That's Freddy right next to the phone there." He heard his name called and so came over with a big grin and handshake and taking off his hat (cap) to expose a burr haircut and say that I must not have recognized him because of a new haircut. I said, "Why hell man, I didn't even see you and what's your haircut got to do with it when all the time your hat was on?" So then he started laughing and shaking my hand and saying that it must have been Chicago where we'd met and I said no, and he said it must have been NY then, or anyhow someplace East, and I said no, no. At last he remembered the Hudson and you and me and that evening exactly two years ago. Aug. 9th to be accurate. I told him how I'd heard about his going big-time with Dizzy Gillespie, etc., and he said yea everything was fine and would I like to hear one of his records. So Hinkle, Freddy and me cut around to *crazy* café and there on big juke box was number 16, "Slick Cat Blues" by Freddy Strong. We listened to his loud jumbo voice while he sent a moron in a beat old army jacket—which I could see he wore as dress on a Sunday because of that desire that vague minds have sometimes for uniforms—to cut around corner and get three joints. And the pictures, you know, like Cleo in Poughkeepsie, all the nigger cats do on Sunday is go around to everybody's place and show off the snapshots made last week with Charlie or some other Joe. That held up our blasting for an hour or so. Then he had to take our picture, and my new station wagon, and his buddy's '30 Chevrolet, and all the guys who happened to pass draped over its fenders. After the snapshots and blasting we retired to the L Harlem and Freddy and his buddy Kemp scat sang for an hour straight and during intermission Fred sat at piano and goofed in most hi fashion. I could see he was local boy

34. Freddy Strong was a jazz singer whom Neal and Jack had seen performing at the Little Harlem bar, Third and Folsom, San Francisco in August 1949, as described by Kerouac in Part Three of *On the Road*. In that book the singer is combined with a tenor saxophone player to become "the tenorman." In "Jazz of the Beat Generation," a merging of material from *On the Road* and *Visions of Cody*, published in 1955, the identities of the two musicians are kept separate, and the singer is called Freddy. In *Visions of Cody* he's Freddy Strange. Freddy Strong recorded with Dizzy Gillespie in March 1951, with John Coltrane on tenor saxophone.

come home with a recording tucked under his arm to show his success and acting with that mixture of coyness and cockiness which is so typical. I dug him alright and will see him again.

I forgot to mention; for christsake don't ride any train up from Mex City to the border, it would take two or three days, without food or drink, too.

Carolyn and I have never gotten along so well, her whole attitude has completely changed, at last. No shit, she is really nice as hell all the time now, I can hardly understand it. And she lives only for the mailman and a goddamn letter from you; why in hell don't you write? If you pop in on us that would be great, but the suspense in no letters is killing all of us, including Cathy with her "Unca Jack." Hurry up please, it's time.[35]

The C-melody sax is so unpopular that I can't find an instruction book and there is almost no music written for it, looks like I'm stuck with another white elephant, huh? We'll learn tho, it's a kick and so easy.

The 11th,

Carolyn and I have never gotten along so, well, her whole attitude has completely changed me, at last. No shit, she is really hell all the time now, I can hardly understand it. Your eagerly anticipated letter depressed her and when I gave Cathy a sip (whole glass!—C.C.) of beer—I've money enough for a quart a month—the depraved action shocked her into a prompt scream of horror, but since we no longer bother to dicker or work up any emotional sweat, she gave up quickly and at the next pass of my chair she stooped and with a kiss ruined all the thought of this paragraph and my viperous ideas were nipped temporarily.

Carolyn and I have never gotten along so well, etc., etc.

Dear Jack; the Cat
from east of the slat,
and all old stuff like that.

35. "Hurry up please its time" is from T. S. Eliot, *The Waste Land* (1922); Section II, "A Game of Chess."

I have, somewhere in my messy papers, a couple of Benzedrine poems written as apology for no letters to you, I think. I would send them on, but even if I found them they would be mostly undecipherable. It doesn't matter, all I want to say is that I knew, while driving hi with Al H. [Hinkle] the other nite, that probably the real value of our early acquaintanceship was that, unlike myself and Al, we took each other seriously. What we said to each other meant something. Later, when I used to get hung you would urge that I continue to try and reach an ending, whether it satisfied logic or not. Now, what with further T and wives and all that, we've reached another plane, but both of us are so wedged into our final cracks that neither have the strength for rescue, save perhaps in vague ideas that make more imperceptible additions to our intangible structure of love. To come off the queer kick, too bad I could never get on it, I just am trying to say thanks for all your great letters to me, tho they don't quite save my soul they'll surely grace yours. I lay all this shit on you cause I want you to lay some shit on me. I have wasted over thirty bucks buying oz's of bum shit in this town. Honest, there is none to be had, no good stuff here, I swear. PLEASE, please, if only a couple of joints, ask Jerry [Newman] or, better, plead or tell him somehow that as a favor you want some shit for me. If worse comes to worse, I'll even pay. But soon. And some seeds too, I got a fine backyard and good window boxes and will send Jerry a percentage—preferable to paying since I'M really broke, really broke.

Aug. 25;

DEAR JACK;

Here's an immediate order, if you've got the hankering for money with no work you'll follow it. In the face of even the most attractive other things that might occupy your time, this offer should be attractive enuf for you to drop everything and come a-running. First off, the offer might expire about when August does; it might continue, but even so each day's delay means something like a 20 buck bill to you. The SP is advertising, actual newspaper advertising, for brakemen in big type ads. I teach you and it's easy, falling off log, and after two week student trips which only pays 50 a week, you go on extra board with me and make 500 a month with a little luck, but with income tax, RR tax, hospital tax, etc., taken out you will only make about 425–450 a month take home pay. This ain't hay for just sitting on your lard ass in a caboose or deadheading on a passenger train or watching an engineer operate while you doze off in the seat beside him. I guarantee, I mean no horseshit guarantee, or vague wishie-washee promise, but I swear that if you come here now, NOW, *now,* now you will make at least 350 to 400 for Sept., 450 to 500 for Oct., and maybe more in Nov. and about the same in Dec. as in Sept., so at a conservative figure you'll absolutely easy make 1700 to 2000 bucks before Xmas comes. Honest and no shit. Completely simple I show you how and all I ask in return is you take me to gonest whorehouse in Watsonville—and they might close for election time, so hurry—for 5 bucks a throw. You lay out for the whores 'cause I've not had 5 bucks or fucks since god knows when. Or we can go to whorehouse in city, but they are not as good. I don't give a shit, if you're so damn dumb you don't come here for 90 days to pick up easy 1500 dollars, you are nuts. Nothing else as important; pretend doing 90 days in jail or something, but come on fast. OH yes, you got to buy a joint or two of the greatest shit, I can't afford and each payday say I will, but don't get a can, or else bring some of Newman's and save yourself money for whores. I got one track mind, money, t and women, in fact going to Psych doc now to cure.

Job waiting you can work same day arrive, little red tape, only requirement is hi school and ability to see colors and wall at 10 paces. They are desperate for men and will hire a flock of em right now so come on and learn to be old rail and you'll establish seniority date for next year when you can work anytime and all thru April to Dec. What the hell's 90 days to you, compared to a grand and a half. Come here you simple ass, don't think, pack your two pairs of socks and lay out a borrowed 49.50 for immediate bus fare and jump on in t daze and dig country relaxed and you'll be here before Sept. 1st, no waiting or bullshit ideas about book or Mexico first—dig Mex in best, winter season when it's cold in U.S.A.—just immediately make your editor or horseshit [Lucien] Carr or even [Jerry] Newman give you 50 bucks for bus—which is only two trips to Watsonville and which you would not even notice repaying come the 25th of Sept. Paydays are 10th and 25th of month. Don't worry over unfinished business in NY, you can go back and finish in winter, I expect you to leave the day you get this.

Seriously, after long thought, I *know* best thing for you to do is come here at once and make easy money. Hurry and do like I say, old buddies don't steer wrong.

N.

Might ask Allen to see if Peter Van Meter wants to come. He's crazy goof t-head, handsome, writes s. stories, funny.

*Suffering another attack of phlebitis in his legs, Kerouac spent three weeks in the Veterans Hospital in the Bronx, from where he wrote to Neal on August 31 (*SL, *pp. 323–25), explaining his plight.*

TO JACK KEROUAC FROM NEAL AND CAROLYN CASSADY

Sept. 7, 1951
29 Russell St.
[San Francisco]

DEAR JACK;

I wrote you three times in one letter, Aug. 9, Aug. 20, and Aug. 25, I mailed it about the 27th, its advice was for you to rush here to make lots of money as brakie; in view of your condition I presume that's out, damn. My mind is entirely empty and I've nothing to say and that's too bad 'cause the only reason I'm attempting to struggle out a letter is to let you know how very worried I am over your serious illness. And more especially, its consequences, no smoking, now no brakie job—or most any work—no t, nothing but rest, on or off a cunt. I don't know what to say to you nor can I think of anything practical to do, for you, myself or anyone; there's just one thing: man, I admire you. I respect every fucking thing about the difficulties you've got. And you can take it like nobody else I know; I don't think I could, so I'm catching a train and rushing this off or never will; can't write, sorry.

Got all your letters;
Love you,
N.

DEAR JACK;

We're shocked to hear of your trouble! And disappointed you couldn't come out—still hoping you'll make it—I need your help in making life worth living for Neal—I can't make it by myself I guess. Can't you convalesce with us? Even tho I don't know what we're offering & probably plenty of domestic yappings—But we can try to make it pleasant for you anyway. N's mind truly a blank—(he said: verify it). Wait till that psychiatrist gets going on him! Comona my house,[36]

CAROLYN C.

On September 6, William Burroughs shot his common-law wife, Joan, in Mexico City. Neal wrote to Kerouac, telling him how he heard the news and also announcing the birth of his son John Allen on September 9.

TO JACK KEROUAC

Sept 13, '51 12:01 A.M.
[San Francisco]

DEAR JACK,

At 4:00 A.M. Sat, the 8th, I was called to deadhead from SF to San Jose to await a freight train's arrival & then take it to Watsonville. This is ordinary procedure for thru frt. service. I got off the passenger at Sta Clara & walked to the Newhall St. yard office to take my call. The "Blue Room" is where we brakemen sit & read & bullshit until our train is ready to leave. I had read all the A.M. papers, but idly picked up the Oakland Tribune to study its different format & type. Then I saw the "William Tell" article, but since, in my youth, I seldom read the names in the news, I overlooked Bill's name. After reading it then I happened to see the woman's name, Joan, & then the "Mexico City (AP)—Sept. 7," & only then got an inkling & saw Bill's name at the same instant I realized my hunch.

I went from restaurant to restaurant to collect different versions & from the News & Examiner got the largest clippings. Then, in as much of a wondermost daze as I ever get into nowadays, I moped into Watsonville. There I met the call boy Dean & took him roller skating. At 10:00 P.M. I was called to take a reefer train back to SF. I got home at 6:00 A.M. Sunday. There was Al Hinkle's car, & he & his wife in bed. "Carolyn's in the hospital, she called us at 3 A.M. & is having baby." I went to sleep for an hour. Helen woke me to say it was a boy,

36. "Come-on-a My House," sung by Rosemary Clooney and written by the American novelist and playwright William Saroyan and his cousin Ross Bagdasarian, was a million-selling record in 1951. Saroyan had used the song in his play *The Son* the previous year. Bagdasarian went on to further record-chart success under the name of David Seville in 1958 with his Chipmunk records.

delivered at 5:10 A.M. I went to see Carolyn & heard details, then because Helen wouldn't stay with my kids I hunted up sister Shirley in Oakland & so am busy as hell with problems of fatherhood.

I got letter from Allen in Galveston, Texas in which he gives short resume of happenings.[37] My boy is full term & healthy, tho seems a month early. He is amazing looking with *absolutely* white platinum blonde hair, like Jean Harlow's was, only more striking with it growing over his ears already. I have, of course, already named him, after you & Allen. John Allen Cassady, J.A.C. (Jack). Also, Jack Cassady when said properly sounds like Jackass, as I'm called Cass-assady & Kiss-my-assady & etc., etc. Diana has D.A. after me; so is selective service; no women tho. Love, N.

By October 1951, Kerouac had discovered a new writing technique he called sketching, introduced to him by his architect friend Ed White, who suggested that, just as an artist sketches with lines, a writer should be able to sketch with words. In this style, Kerouac eagerly began writing a new version of On the Road, *which would eventually be published as* Visions of Cody. *He was still intending to travel to San Francisco, but Neal warned him that it might now be difficult to find railroad work there.*

TO JACK KEROUAC

Nov. 28, '51
[San Francisco]

DEAR JACK, I SEE YOU THERE, BUDDY;

I have written to you, a real nothing it was, has been returned, if can find will send on, tho it's but a piece of empty-worded paper. That doesn't matter anyhow because I've got your Nov. 26, 3:30 P.M. letter[38] which shows you alive and stronger; must be for winter is setting in, and not in Persia or at the sea's bottom. And what a reunion with greatness!, a beautiful letter, only its beauty and the things you say, and show, in it has proved powerful enuf for me to again, the 1st,

37. While William Burroughs was away in Ecuador, looking for the hallucinogenic drug yage, Allen Ginsberg and Lucien Carr had spent a week with Joan in Mexico City, leaving there on September 1.

38. This is possibly the letter that appears at the end of Part One of Kerouac's *Visions of Cody*.

first, time in 7 months, attempt to even send you a letter, let alone any other writing. It's not as desperate, as say, the long time I didn't write before I finally struggled out a note from Pixley, Calif. on a local frt. hold-down of two weeks while I was on the extra brakeman's board on San Joaquin division in Bakersfield in 1948 in summer in June.

And I've found out a little more about Death and Life, too. It happened Saturday November 24 about 10:30 A.M. at the derail switch of the long drill track off the eastbound Mainline at Palo Alto. It was the day of the Big Game between California and Stanford and of the 92,000 who attended some 15,000 were coming by special train from SF and Oakland, and our crew was rushing for an early Sat. quit and if we didn't get out of Palo Alto before, say, 11, we would get stuck in the hole there until afternoon. This hurry had no direct bearing on the accident; I, as head brakeman, with fewer duties that were so plaguing our temperamental French conductor, Charlie Plomteau, or our tag, or swing, man, Charlie Peck, and the nervous rear man George Lansdale, was as relaxed as the proverbial dishrag when I brushed with Death. We were pulling out of the drill with a cut of about 13 cars and were slowing to a stop; I had my arm full out giving a big "easy" sign, and since I was hanging onto the short ladder over the rear trucks of the first car on the point, i.e. next to the engine, and the stop was about to be made, I didn't get off the car as the hogger was not quite over the main switch and tho around a three car curve could keep me in view, & if I hung far out from the car I could save 30 steps, thus I was passing an easy sign the lazy way. And I was HI, that is, had blasted a bomber roach, almost half a joint, about two hours before and tho that usually affects me somewhat stoned in the mind and the stunned watching of things as they pass before my eyes which my mind fully understands tho it remains immobile, and so under ordinary conditions I usually waste three or four seconds before understanding a fact so as to act on it, Miracle that it is, my nerve endings responded with lightning action in an emergency; I now know I am safe still because my body has always kept the quickness of immediate movement latent for any threatening moment, like a chipmunk with its mass of nerves I am, tho my attitude seems limp as a matter of self-discipline, I found I was actually as poised as a weasel ready to leap. I had my back to the engine and was watching intently for the expected stop sign, so as to relay it instantly, when also instantly I was struck powerfully in the exact center of the backbone and flung in corkscrew fashion to the rough gravel ballast and my head was lying across the rail and my left hipbone and asscheek hit the wooden tie and both knees scraped gravel as the leading trucks of the second boxcar, the wheel, nudged my left little toe. I knew what was happening even before I hit the ground, tho my mind as I say was miles away and I might be suspected of wasting the second or two reaction time that has cost so many men their life in this way, i.e. "going under" (the cars). I had not even the usual leeway of being on the ladder over the leading wheels of a car (that's the way to ride a boxcar, because if you do fall off and under you have the moment or two that it takes the next set of wheels, at the other end of the car, to reach where you have fallen). I had not that leeway; was riding on the wrong end of the box and the wheels were not three feet away when my fall began; but enough B.S. i.e. Brotherly slop.

Dec. 1, 9 P.M.

DEAR JACK O LANTERN;

I'd like to tell you a fairy tale, if I can think enough to do so. One night in the full summer of 1945 I was out with a fellow named Chase. He had been drinking and I was riding high on characteristic energy waves that emanate so beautifully from a strip of benzedrine, to which Haldon, his given name, had just introduced me:—Not that very evening, but some days earlier, on my poolhall bench . . .

A terrific explosion has just rocked Dallas, Texas. Tho the source of the bladder blast is still inconclusively exact, I will lose my brakie job this month most likely after Xmas, so, whether you know what's happening or not, your hitchhiking ideas count nought for you getting here because shut up. You'll use these tickets of free rail service cross-country for nothing almost. Can't get passes for you if cut-off and will be in week or more, so I'll apply for pass tomorrow, but takes two weeks and a day or two to get it. I'm allowed only two off-division passes a year, will make it just right for you to have free travel and leave right after holidays, right? Attic, everything here, only moreso than before; hurry to me. Jamie my second girl, fell down attic stairs and broke nose, we thought; last night x-ray and 4 hospital hours proves nose OK. And where are the French this wondrous night; what would they say; I hear they are intoxic.

Dec. 2, 69 P.M. [sic]

DEAR BROTHER JACKSON,

Of all the fine Knights of the Mystic Sea, this train is only going 45, I belong to the Josephine Antuar Linard ring, as in the third of August group. My brother Jack Daly, the soldier you met in Denver in 49 while you & I were there to drive Cadillac to Chicago is now stationed at Livermore, Calif. & I saw him & wife (German war bride) this day from 1:45 to 2:20 P.M. Will see him again. I showed him your book "Town & City" & he sat & read it like little boy in company. Grandfather Proust is very hard. *Let me tell you,* I get hi on t & *read you,* letters-like to me, it is—your Town & City—I read you in my attic. If I'm ever to mail this letter, meaning ever get it written, must do so now. Enclosed in this scrawny piece of paper is nothing but to let you know I'm alive still. Honest,

NEAL

Neal wrote to his father, offering to accommodate him at his San Francisco house.

TO NEAL CASSADY SR.

Dec. 4, 1951
29 Russell St.
San Francisco

DEAR FATHER;

You must write to me, I mean MUST, understand? Jack Daly is out here now, stationed some 50 miles away and the 1st thing he said when he saw me is, "Where's Neal? where is your father?" I didn't know, no one does. Therefore you must write to me, you must come out here, but only if you want to. I mean I want so terribly to see you after all these years. Please come out here and live with me and my wife and two girls and another boy child. I have a wonderful room for you to sleep in, you can get a job, and best of all, I have almost free transportation out here for you. Free railroad passes from Ogden to here in fast Southern Pacific train, since I'm SP brakeman, have been for four years now, can get free pass for you if you tell me to before Xmas. I'll get cut off for three months at first of year and can only get your pass and, also, a half-rate Order, it will cost you only eating expenses to make whole trip, if I put in for them before I'm cut off job last of month, so, write short note immediately accepting my offer to come here and see your lonely son, at once now, hear me and write.

Kerouac was hoping to ship out from New York to Los Angeles, but the plan fell through and instead he traveled by bus to San Francisco, arriving at Neal and Carolyn's house on December 17. He worked four days as a railroad baggage handler, then took a trip to San Pedro in an attempt to find work on a ship there, but this fell through due to union problems. Jack spent Christmas Day in San Pedro with Henri Cru before rejoining the Cassadys in San Francisco on December 26. Carl Solomon, Allen Ginsberg's friend, wrote to Jack there. Solomon was working as an editor for his uncle A.A. Wyn, who owned Ace Books. Ginsberg had submitted William Burroughs's novel Junkie *to Solomon for possible publication—it eventually appeared in 1953—and was also considering Ace as an outlet for work by his friends Kerouac and Cassady.*

TO NEAL CASSADY FROM CARL SOLOMON

December 14, 1951
[New York City]

DEAR NEAL,

Enclosed is a letter I wish you would give or forward to Jack K. in care of his ship. Thanks. And a merry Christmas to you and all your dear ones.

Christmas season evokes nostalgia and frightening reminiscence. In recent weeks I have had strange dealings with many strange people in connection with a strange packet of pages on which the strange name Dean Pomeray[39] is applied to a strange character who strangely resembles and does not resemble a strange apparition of my very commonplace post-hospital nightmare which was not a nightmare.[40]

39. Dean Pomeray was Kerouac's pseudonym for Neal Cassady in a twenty-three-page piece called "October in the Poolhall," written in the fall of 1950, which was one of the items sent to Solomon for consideration. It was later incorporated into *Visions of Cody* (pp. 47–70), where, in keeping with the rest of the book, the pseudonym was changed to Cody Pomeray.

40. In 1949 Carl Solomon had spent several months in the Psychiatric Institute of Columbia Presbyterian Hospital, where he first met fellow patient Allen Ginsberg. On his release, Carl held a New Year's Eve party, at which Neal was the star performer. See Carl Solomon's autobiographical miscellany, *Emergency Messages*, p. 41.

I remember you! During the same period I mentioned in the above paragraph I detected another suspicious similarity and unsimilarity between said Dean and a character called Hart[41] in a lengthy and tortured and untitled novel by a strange character and author named John Holmes who has used elsewhere the pseudonym Clellon and elsewhere the pseudonym (later borrowed by one Jay Irving Landesman and his ghost-writer, a negrofied Hollander named Ernest Van Den Haag) Alfred Towne. I pried from John the admission that he is a direct descendant of General McClellan, who was defeated for the presidency by A. Lincoln. Who, along the Holmes-McClellan line, decided to introduce the non-sequitur Clellon?

I remember you! Poor amnesia victim that I am, I remember you. In fact, my remembering you is so earth-shaking as to be worthy of being made into a movie!

Neal, isn't poverty terrible?

I am working in publishing now—for a piddling 56.25 a week. But I think that there is good reason to hope for future advancement. Olive, like Allen, is working at NORC.[42]

I have never committed a serious crime, one for a large sum of money. Do you think I should? If it pleases you, counsel me on its advisability. By mail.

Greetings,
CARL SOLOMON

41. Hart Kennedy is the Neal Cassady character in John Clellon Holmes's novel *Go*.

42. Olive, Carl's wife, worked for the National Opinion Research Center, a market research company. Ginsberg had been working there since December 1950.

1952

Neal and Carolyn had Jack as their houseguest in San Francisco for the first four months of 1952. Kerouac lived in the attic of the Cassadys' house at 29 Russell Street, where he completed work on Visions of Cody, *his definitive book about Neal. In the evenings they recorded long, rambling conversations on Neal's Ekotape machine. The following day Jack would transcribe them and they would eventually appear in the tape section of Jack's book. During this period, Jack and Carolyn began an affair.*

Diana forwarded a letter from Neal's father, to whom she had written with a photograph of Curtis and a request for details of his family history. Neal Sr. seemed unaware of the existence of Carolyn and the other three children.

TO NEAL AND DIANA CASSADY FROM NEAL CASSADY SR.[1]

[Jan. 5, 1952
Denver]

MY DEAR SON & DAURTER:-

Recd your most welcom & was sure glad to hear from you & often wandered where you and Neal was at. He sure is a nice looking boy you have & he sure looks helthy. Thank you for the picture you sent me & I'll sure will take care of it. Would like to see you & Neal & your son also. Tell Neal I took a trip back home last summer. I enjoyed my trip very much, but most of my sisters are dead. Only two of my sisters are living, sister Eva & Emma would like to see you & Neal very much. Might make a trip back some time. Neal will tell you we both took a box car father an that where he was 12 yr old. Tell Neal they all

1. This letter is discussed in detail in the tape section of *Visions of Cody* (pp. 171–76).

asked about him & wanted very much to see him. I told them that he was married & when he was at.

P.S. Tell Neal I havent heard from Shirley Jean so I dont know wher his sister is at. Think she is married now.

My mother name was Mildred Mullinex

Diana, my father name was Samuel, no middle name. Mother name Mildred. How are you getting along. Please write & tell me how you are all getting along. Would sure like to hear from you and about you & how you are getting along & about Neal & what he is doing now? if you will and tell me all the news & if you folks would like to see me I would make a trip back ther. I am not to old can still ride that old Box Car yet. Tell Neal I havent come to that Second Childhood yet, so I am still in my prime, ha ha. Only 59 this year.

Well sure was glad to hear from you & write often.

Yours truly NEAL CASSADY
c/o J.J. Green Co 1723 Market St or
c/o Za Za Barbers Shop Larimer St

*Kerouac had written to Carl Solomon on December 27 (*SL, *pp. 328–29), after returning to the Cassadys' home, enthusing about Neal's writing, and urging Carl to contact Neal and ask to see a sample for possible publication by Ace Books.*

TO NEAL CASSADY FROM CARL SOLOMON

[January 1952]
181 Prince St.
NYC

DEAR NEAL,

All joking aside, that rare person Mr. Kerouac has informed me that you're writing a book and, indeed, have already written 20,000 great and careful words. He also tells me that you're bashful about considering your writing literature. Bashfulness in such matters is easy to understand, is inevitable, and probably desirable. However, once experienced, it should promptly be over-ridden.

I've seen fragments of your prose and, in feeling considerable enthusiasm over the novel-in-progress he mentions, I don't think I'm being unduly influenced by Jack's opinions—or Allen's. Please understand that publishers' secretly felt feelings about the novels they themselves publish year after year are far more unfavorable than any unfavorable opinion you may entertain of your own work. Since Genet,[2] a short time ago, renounced literature the novel has been in a bad way. Now if only Mr. Kerouac does not join him in renouncing literature and if you overcome your timidity and send on your pages to me for perusal, we may be able to resuscitate the damned thing. Your subject, being your life, cannot possibly in any way duplicate Mr. Kerouac's (as his letter intimates he has discovered) since his subject is his life. I believe we can place you both.

I have just acquired Ansen's novel-in-progress[3] for Wyn and, though I feel no personal rapport with him or the way of life he describes (life in the Auden circle), I do feel that his book can represent a new approach to high tea-cup life if he has the stamina to finish it. We're still undecided about giving him an advance.

Our editor shortly will be superseded by a new "big" editor we've purchased from Doubleday.

Neal, please send it. Promptly. I'm quite serious. I expect many limitations. But I really feel it may mean pork-chops to me. Please. Thanks.

Warmest regards,
CARL SOLOMON

P.S. Tell Jack his letter confirms the faith I have in him. Also that Allen's shipping next week.[4]

2. Jean Genet (1910–1986). French novelist and dramatist. Author of *Our Lady of the Flowers* (1944) and the autobiographical *The Thief's Journal* (1949). Fellow protester with Allen Ginsberg and William Burroughs in Chicago, 1968.

3. Alan Ansen's novel-in-progress was about "a spectre of a party at Cannastra's." Ansen sent the first four chapters to Solomon, but insufficient interest was shown, and so no more was written. The four chapters were published as *The Vigilantes* by Water Row Press in 1987.

4. Allen Ginsberg registered with the National Maritime Union on January 7 and hoped to ship out as a yeoman. However, no such work was forthcoming and so he remained in New York.

TO NEAL CASSADY FROM CARL SOLOMON

February 13, 1952
New York City

DEAR NEAL—

Birthday greetings. Where is your manuscript? Send it on at once. If you can't make the postage, send it collect! I must have it!

P.S. We may publish a translation of the Marquis de Sade. Have you heard about Marlon Brando playing Van Gogh in a forthcoming film?

Regards to all,
CARL SOLOMON

Neal eventually sent Carl Solomon the prologue and first chapter of his autobiographical work-in-progress, The First Third. *Solomon replied with an unfavorable assessment.*

TO NEAL CASSADY FROM CARL SOLOMON

Thursday [c. March 1952
New York City]

DEAR NEAL,

Just finished reading 77 pp. and re-reading 2 letters about your plans. I don't know as yet what I ought to do about them. At the moment I feel the best course would probably be to hold on to these and sit tight waiting for you to send me further installments and gradually get the kinks out of your system (get used to writing, I mean, with further practice). Your case is quite different from Jack's—though I feel your potentiality is quite as great. Since "Town And City" he has been wrestling with a personality problem that has expressed itself in a confused tangle of literary forms and with what he would have appear to be (on the surface) a loss of novelistic control and mastery. It is an understandable and profitable (within limits) malingering act. On the theory that he will slowly find himself and then be left with even enhanced powers of expression, we have invested 1000 dollars.[5] We never doubted his technical (i.e. conventional) ability. In your case, clear vision, vital content, grasp of character and the concrete, seriousness of approach, etc. are all excitingly evident . . . and the shortcomings are technical. They are problems that can be overcome by work and work alone. Jack's must be overcome by mature insight. I could run to Wyn with 25 pages of Jack's "novel" and say, "Uncle Aaron,[6] this novelist will survive! Let's risk it and tide him over his present rootlessness if he is willing." With your 77 pages, I can only say, "Uncle Aaron, this man is a natural storyteller and if he decides to learn the rudiments of the Craft he will be worth having. Of course, he makes his living at present as a 16-hour a day railroad worker. So the probability is that he won't bother learning unless he finds a good and compelling reason to become a writer." I agree with you about the prologue. It's too self-conscious and is an old amateur's device to provide an excuse for writing at all. So you were born, so you had ancestors, so you have a reason for writing a book . . . The first chapter, though, frees itself of much of this awkwardness. It is a big advance and, in some ways, is even good. There are traces of the original weakness, though. You use complex words like a farmer wears store-bought clothes . . . as an excuse for being in the city . . . as an excuse for telling a story (which you get down to in this chapter after muffing the prologue, making it an excuse for sitting down and writing anything). As you get down, in future chapters, to the bare bones and language of your story you will discover the real reason for writing it. Then you will even realize that much of the good, bare-bones narrative is not part of the main story and you will cut it out (keep it for other books). You may find that this "autobiography" is really just a book-length (or maybe shorter) story of Zaza's, or even merely a story about a season spent with a Dago family—or maybe just a story of a one-night binge in a hotel room. Then, when you have isolated the part, the segment, that is the really meaningful story—then you will find that, bare-bone though it be,

5. Anxious to find a publisher for *On the Road,* Kerouac had offered it to Ace, who agreed to invest $1,000 in the project, advancing $250 as a first installment. Fearing that the complete book was too large for an Ace paperback, Jack extracted a 160-page section from the rewrite he had produced while at the Cassadys' and offered this to Ace for a paperback edition, but urged them to publish the complete work in hardback. Kerouac's contract with Ace eventually broke down, but the 160-page extract was posthumously published in *Visions of Cody* (beginning p. 338).

6. Aaron A. Wyn, the owner of Ace Books.

you haven't included the whole skeleton; you will remember and fill in with more minute details, with a mood and a rhythmic chronology, with the flow of barely perceptible facial expressions, etc.—until the Thing is so perfect that you won't let anybody change a word unless you feel it absolutely justified. Jack makes out he's not writing for an audience (his real audience is everyone who can read and he really wants to please them); You don't have to go thru that horseshit—but the danger for you is that you will go to the other extreme (oh, you won't) and feel that everybody in the US is waiting to jump on you because you had the presumption to think yourself a writer. You can avert that danger by a) spending hours at the typewriter, making it your crony, and reading your stuff and learning to recognize your weaknesses and b) reading, CAREFULLY and professionally, the books of the writers who are today most popular. Make their tricks, grammatical constructions, cliches, etc. second nature to you—so that you can scoff at their achievements with some assurance and proceed to surpass them in your own, inimitable way. Read, most of all, lots of pocket books. Read Mickey Spillane.[7] Read Gold Medal Original pocket books so you will know what the people are accustomed to, so you will acquire the few conventional skills that they insist upon before giving anyone a hearing. Those conventional skills are becoming less recondite every day (that's why I say, "Read pocket originals"). They are becoming more and more accessible to and tailored to the background of the common man. College education helps very little now and what's more it's easier to get. Grammar counts for less and less and is becoming less bookish anyway, though a writer must still respect some of old grammar. First-person autobiographical form is part of the great confession vogue (read "Mr. President," Truman's confessions just published by Farrar Strauss to get the essence of it). Watch a lot of TV. See a lot of Hollywood movies. Learn what those money-makers do. YOU CAN DO IT TOO. BUT BETTER AND MORE TRUTHFULLY. American puritanism has come full circle and is ready to be re-born as the most natural, rational, man-satisfying phenomenon ever seen on this earth. Pocket books will outdo the invention of the novel in a) opening up new subject-matter (like yours), b) creating, and creating a market for, new writers from new classes new groups, etc. (again like yourself), and c) creating new avid readers by the millions in places where books have never been

7. Mickey Spillane (b. 1918), a popular writer of crime thrillers. Best known for *I, the Jury* (1947) and *Kiss Me Deadly* (1952), which was filmed in 1955.

read and men have never tried to communicate with one another . . . THIS IS TV.

Little magazines are dying by the dozen. There won't be a one left in 10 years. Why? Because nobody but a few old evil snobs want or need them. Big, new-critic professors are going to be washed away by the flood of honest amateur writers on GI bills and in writing correspondence courses who, until now, have been frightened away from the delights of literary confession and self-justification by the likes of ALLEN TATE,[8] PARTISAN REVIEW, my penmanship teacher, and the whole apparatus of stinking capitalists. Writing will fall into its proper place. Watch the audience, not the writers (I said watch Spillane because he is a pretty good reflection of what the poor joes of the audience want and what they're soon going to write—but without the phony conventions—with conventions, but without the phony, inhuman ones). With this great new audience, bred on Woodford and Genet and Jane Russell, will come the final great battle against sex-censorship. It'll be won and then what use will we have for the phoney literary contrivances, puny mystical imaginings, erudition, lispings, too deep masturbatory metaphysics, euphonism, existentialism, boasting, alliteration, etc. of the bunch of sick pricks who write books for the "discriminating" nowadays? BOOM you dig. FACT, INTELLIGENCE, COURAGE, SYMPATHY, UNDERSTANDING, HARD WORK—are what I look for in books. Keep writing, keep sending—I'll keep reading and keep making suggestions, revisions, etc. until I think you're ready (which I'm sure you can be in 1½ years at most if you want to be—*there is lots of money in it you know*)—and when you and I are agreed you're ready, I'll go to Wyn and see he publishes you. It's a bit premature to try for an advance—I'll do that later. Your stuff is great, if haven't said so already and KEEP WRITING AND LEARNING AND *SENDING TO ME,* and write about SEX—that's the key.

Warmest,

CARL S.

P.S.: I feel you would profit greatly from taking and then transcending a creative writing course given by any reputable institution in the evening. (Don't listen to Kerouac, he knows nothing.) (He tries to confuse everybody—he is using your life as an excuse for not living.)

My only recent poem:

8. Allen Tate (1899–1979). American poet and critic.

LEFTY'S CREDO

If any man claims not to know the nature of Existence,
I say that he is a damned liar.

P.P.S. "Shorty" episode and "cat-book" episode are the very best.[9] Remember, Conrad[10] didn't even learn English until he was 26.

Seymour Wyse, Kerouac's English schoolfriend, had for a while shared an apartment with Neal in 1949 at Fifty-sixth Street, Eighth Avenue, New York. Wyse, who returned to England in May 1951, wrote to renew contact with Jack and Neal.

TO NEAL CASSADY FROM SEYMOUR WYSE

March 22, 1952
33 Kingsmill
St. Johns Wood
London, N.W.8
England

DEAR NEAL,

Now I realize that it's rather a strange kick my writing a letter and you dig I must have some specific purpose in mind in so doing and I do but I also want to hear from you because it's a long time since I saw you and we had some great kicks. Well, to straighten the first issue, I heard that Jack K was in California and I've written him a couple of letters to NY which I suppose he never got. And the first thing I can think of when Jack and California are mentioned is Neal Cassady, who, of course, must know his whereabouts. So that is the hype on the letter kick. But, naturally, I'm very curious about my boy Neal. And I dig, man, that you can straighten me out on a lot of issues, important and otherwise, which perhaps in your more reflective moments you would care to do.

9. Sections from chapter 1 of Neal's autobiographical *The First Third*.

10. Joseph Conrad (1857–1924). Polish mariner who moved to England and became a novelist and short-story writer, producing *Lord Jim* (1900), *Nostromo* (1904), *The Secret Agent* (1907), and *Under Western Eyes* (1911).

Perhaps this is vague and perhaps you have no wish to get hung up on writing a reply letter or perhaps you aren't even there, maybe in Mexico or Europe. Well, see, I'm fantastically hung up in England which believe me is a place where nothing ever happens except of course that you concentrate on keeping out of the cold and settling small things. To give you an example, I've put on about 25 lbs in weight since being here and not on food either. It's just that the lazy kick becomes more excusable here than in America because there are so many good reasons for *not* wanting to do things.

I do know one real cool cat here who's from NY and who shares this pad, a painter-musician cat. And we make it on most issues excepting the creative and destructive things. So that from that angle, I'm pretty well detached from real existence.

Now, man, what is your news? Let's like establish a thing, a precedent in exchanging matters. You do see that as a thing don't you man. And of course if Jack is within shouting distance tell him that I want very much to hear from him.

For now, then, goodbye and don't forget—write write write.

SEYMOUR WYSE

In April, when the Cassadys traveled East to visit Carolyn's parents in Tennessee, they took Jack with them as far as Nogales, Arizona, where he journeyed on to spend three months with William Burroughs in Mexico City. There he completed work on his novel Dr. Sax. *In a May letter (*As Ever, *p. 127), Allen Ginsberg informed Neal that he was trying to get his "Joan Anderson" letter published in Bob Burford's* New Story *magazine.*

TO ALLEN GINSBERG

May 20, 1952
[San Francisco]

DEAR ALLEN;

You're the same great wonderful guy and I'm more of a bum than ever so, tho I love to get your letters, I can't think of a damn thing.

I meant to tell you that I was struck that your reaction to something was exactly similar to mine about whatever the damn thing was; coincidence.

Just finished 7000 mile car trip SF, S. Barbara, Los Angeles, S. Diego, Nogales, El Paso, N. Orleans, Nashville, K. City, Denver, Albuquerque, SF.

Back on brakie grind until Dec.; will write on book if can get started. You can publish my Joan letter, I'll polish it if necessary.

Why don't you come out here? nice place if one likes it. Be brakie and make lots money. Or write in attic and make love to wife and me.

*Kerouac eventually wrote to the Cassadys from Mexico on May 27 (*SL, *pp. 358–61). Carolyn and Neal replied to tell Jack that they were thinking of moving out of Russell Street and finding a new home.*

TO JACK KEROUAC FROM CAROLYN AND NEAL CASSADY

June 4, 1952
[San Francisco]

DEAREST JACK:

We were relieved to hear from you; we've been haunting the mail box ever since we got to Tennessee and were greatly disappointed to get no word from you. After leaving you in that dismal morning at Nogales we had the more cause to wonder what became of you. Incidentally, *why* Nogales? We couldn't figure it when we got to El Paso and saw so many ads for all the handy ways of reaching MexCity from there. Ah well, you made it, and evidently with some worthwhile adventures besides. Nevertheless, we missed you dreadfully the rest of the trip. Neal and I lapsed to many of our old squabbles capped on the return trip by a really hellish time at Denver. We were OK at home and have been better still since our return to SF. The entire trip was pretty eventless including the brief stay at home where we did and saw nothing other than a few of the old friends of the family and my other sister from Michigan. Still it served its purpose, the children couldn't have been better and seemed to enjoy it. I learned a good deal I discovered when we returned, and it was good to get back.

Neal began work immediately on the RR and now holds a steady job on Maxey's local from noon to the early morning hours. Hence he asked me to write for us as he has no time, tho he had wanted to himself.

Me: What'll I tell him from you?

Neal: Ask him what happened to all that information he was going to get us about Mexico. Tell him to come back here and go to work on the RR and make a couple of thousand clear before Dec.

Me: I should think he'd prefer going to sea whereby he can have more adventures and get more writing done.

Neal: He can write all he wants to in Watsonville.

Me: You're very insistent. I guess he thinks you're not happy with him because he doesn't.

Neal: Tell him I'm mad at him because he won't work on the RR.

I say that whatever you decide please be assured you're very welcome here, and I hope you'll still consider this your home in San Francisco. I've done some rearranging here and there which makes the house seem more spacious and more comfortable and easier to manage. The change is good for the morale too. Also gives me lots of busy work.

Our future plans are not fossilized yet. We think we'll move somewhere when he gets cut off, will buy the new car this summer and try and save every penny. This last will be really difficult again; it gets moreso each year. We would like to investigate Mexico further too, and are thinking of a trip there when he's cut off at least. Everything depends on the money. I must be pessimistic tonight since I did a good hunk of shopping this A.M. Neal hopes not to have to work anyway next winter. We may have to rent something in San Jose and look around for buying or building, but intend giving Mexico an extensive investigation first and anyway. If it isn't practical now it still might be in a few years. We are anxious to talk to you about it more too.

Allen gave us our first word of you shortly before you wrote, and doubtless you've heard our queries from him since. From his last answer to me I gather he still resents me, willingly or no, and probably moreso now because of your kind remarks. As I think on it I'm pretty sure it must always be so. Tis a pity but cannot cause me much concern, as it would were it you. Tho I feel no need for defensiveness on my part, I know I'll never be in accord with his sexual desires and were he closer would probably feel a bit ruffled over such a pressure. But we'll cross that bridge, etc.

You got only one letter here from your sister which we returned to her. There was one from Allen to both of you, one from John Holmes and one from Al Sublette,[11] all of which Neal opened hoping to find a clue about you. If you wish we'll send them on . . . will anyway as you'll want to have them. Forgive the rifling.

The kiddies are all grraand and ask daily about Jack. Cathy repeatedly says she wants Jack to come home again and she wants to go to Mexico and see you. Jamie asks Where's Jack and remembers the blistered paint on the table which you'll never live down. She calls the baby Baby Jack. They play games of going to Mexico (the pronunciation is quaint) now supplanting "the big city." If they hear bop or drums on the radio they say it's Jack. When I wear your shirt it puzzles them and the whining for Jack starts in all over. We've lost our baby now and have a little Samson crawling and climbing all over everything. He learned to stand up in Tennessee and to get back down when we got home. Now he is up and down but constantly and should be walking in another month.

Allen says you planned to go south with Bill and that he might get killed. That's interesting. I hope your letter to us was a later issue? Leave us have many more. You must inspect our garden. It's especially green this year albeit we've but 12 new plants and they of every different size. The largest is as yet only less than a foot high. The window box was parched and the pot drowned. Next time we'll know better, but I'd say the climate was not altogether exceptional for experimental botany. San Jose should be perfect in that respect.

It's just too hard writing you; much better you should be telling us your latest adventures in person. I really miss having those glittering pages to read we were once honored with. We're reduced to reading spy thrillers aloud. I'm anxious to hear the reports from the East on the reception of the book.

How is your mother and did she take to the Mexican plan? If *I* ever moved there I'd feel a lot better having her near.

Now I'd best leave some space for Neal to add his 2 cents. So you don't have to know the language, eh? 12 cents, eh? Hmmm.

Love,
CAROLYN
AND THE OLD MAN

11. Al Sublette was a merchant seaman friend of Neal's and Jack's in San Francisco. Portrayed by Kerouac as Al/Mal Damlette in *Desolation Angels, Big Sur, Tristessa,* and *Book of Dreams.*

DEAR BROTHAH JACKSON,

We have won-ton. We had rare pleasure of meeting my half bro. in KC, Mo.[12] These are P.S.'s from Carolyn; I'm too high—hi; just discovered I have hair like Dick Tracy—oops, I now find it's my head, not hair. The great mental powers of my brain are feeling too overpowering overflowing my oversparking de luxe. Or else a Ford, Chev, or Plymouth 52 overdrive R & H. Jamie, drinking Cola, spews it out like a fire-eater. Here's to ya—Real r.j. (root juices) Ingredients: carbonated water, sugar, dextrose, caramel, plant extractives of birch, sassafras, licorice, vanilla, sassaparilla, hops, evergreen, whitegreen, ginger, pipscoseux, & flavors. Write right away. Write right away.

N.

How's Mombo Pat Henry shows?[13] Great vacation *he's* having.

*Allen Ginsberg wrote to Neal on July 3 (*As Ever, *pp. 129–32), referring to* Visions of Cody *as a "holy mess" and telling him there was a chance that New Directions might be interested in publishing the first chapter of Neal's autobiography in their annual anthology. Neal replied that he thought it would be better if the "Joan Anderson" letter were published first.*

TO ALLEN GINSBERG

July 10, 1952
[San Francisco]

DEAR ALLEN;

First, always, I'm struck by the intelligence in your letters; your reasoning in all their statements is usually sharply simple, due to the conciseness of focus, yet is often nearly 100% correct, esp. about people. In particular, your understanding of Jack and myself, when I think of it, coupled with the genuine interest your soul engenders for your letters, and indeed, operates the entire lever for your powerful wise attitude toward everything in general, makes me know and feel most pleased that you are the most sincere, close and best friend that we ever had.

12. Jim Daly.

13. Pat Henry (1926–1999) was a disc jockey who played jazz on radio station KROW, Oakland, in the 1950s, before founding KJAZ, Northern California's first all-jazz radio station, in Alameda, with a transmitter on San Francisco's Russian Hill, in 1959.

P.S. I have the Joan Anderson letter and before anyone would publish the beginning of my novel it would be easier to persuade them to publish it.

I'll deliver anything for you. You're right about Jack's and my book. We're moving to San Jose as soon as I can find a place. Jack's with the Indians permanent and said to send you any messages for him.

I wrecked the station wagon and must get a new one. Jack's for Taft, ugh, your Harriman's OK,[14] but it makes not one whit of difference who gets it, say I. Carolyn wouldn't trade me for anybody and the same goes for me.

In August, Neal and Carolyn and the children moved to a new home in San Jose. Neal wrote to Diana, suggesting a secret get-together that winter.

TO DIANA HANSEN CASSADY

Aug. 21, 1952
[San Jose]

DEAR DARLING DIANA,

Your letter came today, a sorry thing it was, I felt sweet & sad reading it. What an awful thing, really just think of it, for no good reason at all, absolutely no reason at all, I left you. You had done nothing wrong, you had always been loving & wonderful to me, your body was always mine whenever I wanted it. We got along fine, we made love fine, we understood each other, you were the best, and for no reason we parted. For good.

You were so beautiful in Penn RR station, we were truly Irene Dunne & Charles Boyer[15] (not Nelson Eddy, ugh!) & you loved me & I gave only reasons & bullshit in reply. Now, where are we? What to do? First, Carolyn confessed she had destroyed your turn-of-the-year letters. Jack was here screwing her & everybody was happy. She wanted no interruptions. I had been told you wrote last in Dec. & it was finished. Then Jack left, we moved to San Jose & went further in debt. I owe $2700.00 & don't break even on payday. Everything has

14. Robert Taft (Republican) and William Harriman (Democrat) were nominees for the 1952 presidential election.

15. Film stars who appeared together in several romantic movies, including *Love Affair* (1939) and *Together Again* (1944).

gone to hell, at best C. & I just endure each other. I get no loving & no understanding. Of course, I'm no angel myself & so Carolyn has a tough time, all work & kids & bitching & no sympathy or entertainment for her. We're all unhappy & full of fear & fight. Why? Only because I thought I was being noble & big, reasoning that it was better to take care of three kids than one. Happiness be damned, consideration of you be damned, the kids are the thing, bah!? Well, where are we now? up the creek, bored, & afraid, tired & mean, kids are beat too.

Do I love you? I know I miss you terribly, think of you, esp. when I see any tall dark-haired girl on the street. I think always how I did you dirt for no reason, you were really swell to me. Truth to tell, I miss your fucks like crazy, remembering all the nights in our back bedroom, mostly the way you let me get it all the way in & you say "Neal, oh Neal" etc. You were a great cunt, just my size. I get an erection every time I think of your great cunt. I want to be with you desperately. How? How long? Where? When? I've got to see you & fuck you again so badly that I'll gamble anything. I've come up with this:

I lose my job here Jan. 1st. I leave here to work on Florida East Coast line, I come to get you & Kurt & we go where you want to or stay in Tarrytown, any place, just so I can work for big money, since I must have 70 for car, 75 rent, 25 utilities & milk & 75 for food for C. & kids. $250.00 a month to them minimum. You and I need 150.00 anyhow. That['s] at least 400.00 a month, really more, so you see I've got to work constantly & hard to make that kind of dough. I get called back here in May & you & Curt in San Jose, Watsonville, or San Francisco. It is possible I can get away from Carolyn; I hope so, if not you'd have to wait until I can. But I would see you daily & be with you all I could. How does it sound? Willing to gamble again? Still want me? want my loving? my cock? Even if you don't you can come West with me & settle anew.

You've got four (4) months to make up your mind, I've made mine up, tho it will be almost impossible, sheer terror, out-of-the-question type of thing to leave Carolyn when I'm cut-off. She will surely die, she is frantic with fear even if I am a couple of hours late getting home. She doesn't trust me an inch. If she even knew I had sent you this letter I'm convinced she would murder me in my sleep, she's jealous & deathly afraid for herself & the kids, she hates my guts because I treat her like a thing instead of a person. She would be alright if I loved her, but she knows I don't. I'm a fool & a dog & all I think of is sex & sex & sex & sex etc. I'm no good for nobody or no thing but I want to fuck you.

Perhaps I shouldn't send this naughty letter to you, if you took in your head to mention it, or horrors! send it back to Carolyn, I would be dead, maybe that's why I flirt with suicide—a letter like this to you. If you ever did use this letter against me I would feel absolved of all my guilt toward you—another reason, perhaps, why I'm writing. But, seriously, burn this. You don't want Ma to find it & if Carolyn heard of this we'd all die & the kids would never be right again she'd treat them so meanly. She hates Cathy, endures Jamie & loves the boy. I love them all & that's why I'm here, the only reason. If you will contain yourself & not write any more to us, no matter how much you'd like to, to get Carolyn, or to help her, or anything, instead do this! Write to ME, everyday, & tell me you love me & want me & everything else you want to. Send me pictures of Kurt—I know it's Curt,—habit—& all the news of him & yourself. Send me your cunt hairs & pictures of yourself & write & write & write & dream, if only for the reasons I do—how many times we'll do it the first night—dream of the future again, I'll be with you again, I'm sure of that.

So write to me at Neal L. Cassady, General Delivery, San Jose, California. I'll get your mail there, never at the house, & answer every one of your letters & we'll plan & plan until I can get away to come & get you & make love to you. If you don't want to, just forget it & I'll send you money, every damn cent I can get ahold of—very little I'm sure. I know I can never make up to you for what I've done to you & I guess I won't even try, but I will love you & see you & best of all, be with you at least for 4 months from Jan. to May & I'll be with you & Curt every second, & we'll be happy for a little while—if you want to that is.

This is the end of this letter. Don't think it's neurotic or impulsive—it's cold & calculating. It's calculated to let me fuck you again & live with you & Curt this winter—even against all the enormous odds I'm facing. There's every reason why I should stay in San Jose when cut-off, but I'll get to you come hell or hi water if you want me to. For God's sake Diana don't let Carolyn know, I make you an offer even tho reason tells me you should, for revenge, get me by sending this to C. Don't, because I'm trusting you & I want you to know I love you.

Another page; I shouldn't send this, but I trust you because I know your heart & for old times' sake I tell you how I really feel. I haven't done that for 2 yrs because I thought it better to be a man of iron & suffer doing hurts to you in silence. Do not really think I could have been as mean to you as I have been if it wasn't that I was telling myself to be a goddamn bastard to you so as to hurt you so that there would never be a chance for me again & it would be all over, severed like the Gordian knot, between us. I hope you know my surgery has failed & I think of you constantly & this letter is to tell you I'm willing to let everything go to hell just to try & get you back again.

N.

This is an innocent gesture, most naive I'm sure, & not the work of a grown man. All I can say is if you can't treat it tenderly, then don't treat it at all. I'm trying tho, honest. I thought of writing you to make you promise to keep your silence & then I would forward this letter, but no, strange to say, I trust you to do as I say & write to me at General Delivery so that we can plan. OK? I know you're suffering; I want to stop it right away.

Returning to his mother at his sister's home in North Carolina in July, Kerouac sought work on the local railroad, giving Neal's name as a reference. Neal responded with gusto.

TO J. C. CLEMENTS

August 21, 1952
1047 East Santa Clara
San Jose 27, California

J.C. Clements
Captain of Police, ACL RR.
Rocky Mount, N.C.

DEAR SIR;

Mr. John Louis Kerouac has been my closest friend for many years. I met him while we were both attending Columbia University in New York City. His character is excellent attested to by the fact that he has never been in trouble with the law and is a God-fearing man, firm in his faith. Mr. Kerouac's reputation is unreproachable and must be so since he is an eminent author, having been published in the spring of 1950 by the firm of Harcourt, Brace and Co., a house that accepts no miscreants, but rather men like Sandburg, Eliot and Pound. John's habits are the moderate ones of a wise man and if I can accuse him of an excess it would be in his worklife. His education was cut short, at least formally, in his second year of college by the death of his father which necessitated procuring a job to support his mother and younger sister. Of all his attributes John's honesty is perhaps his outstanding characteristic. Hard as it may be to believe I tell you that once John, just like in the tales about Honest Abe Lincoln, walked halfway across the town of Denver, Colorado solely to repay a minor debt he had incurred from a comparative stranger on the day before. That's Honesty, right? Naturally, no man has all the superlative virtues I seem to be attributing to Mr. Kerouac, nonetheless, he is the only man I know into whose hands I could entrust the use of my saxophone, fountain pen or wife and would rest assured that they were honorably and properly taken care of.

I, myself, have worked for the Southern Pacific RR for five years as a brakeman and I am curious to know if John is entering your service as trainman. Also I would very much like to know his new address so that I might write to him and tell him mine. I would consider it a personal favor that would be most appreciated if you could find the time to send on to me Mr. Kerouac's home address in a reply by return mail. If this is possible I take the opportunity to thank you in advance, Mr. Clements.

Sincerely yours,
NEAL L. CASSADY

Learning Jack's address, Neal wrote to him, explaining why he could not send the money that Jack had requested from him in June for travel from Mexico back to New York. He invited Jack to come and stay with him in San Jose and get a job there working as a brakeman on the railroad.

TO JACK KEROUAC FROM NEAL AND CAROLYN CASSADY

Aug. 22, 1952
[San Jose]

DEAR JACK;

Damn you for being in Mexico without me. Why in hell not give up the Indians to come back and tell me about them and to still earn about 2000 bucks on RR before the year's out. You can easily live in our big 9 room house here in sunny San Jose and ride about in my new station wagon.

Don't think for a second that I've had even one damn dollar to send you. Since July my wages have been attached and I've bought necessary stove, refrigerator, wash machine and I'm 3000 bucks in debt. Sept 26th is the first paycheck I'll have enough clear to even buy the 3 dozen light bulbs that this house needs. But after you wrote me I couldn't bring myself together enuf to answer and tho I did in fact borrow money and go to the PO to send you 20 dollars, I didn't because it was Saturday P.M. and the joint was closed and I spent the money and then the attachment of my check and then borrowing again, from Hinkle, to pay rent, and then it was too late because you were with the Indians and surely mad as hell at me. And rightly so, and I started letters and never sent them and I told Carolyn, who wants you back so desperately, to write you, and everything went to hell and I'm fucked to death without even any help from Miss Green, and where in the hell are you? I'll send you fare to get back here on, only hurry up or there won't be much RRing left, or anything else either. Come on now; quit all your fucking; if you can't bring some back with you, get it here. Stay here until December then you'll have plenty to go east on and buy a trailer or what in hell you want.

DEAR JACK;

Neal got this far when the reference letter came from the RR indicating where you are. I'm sorry about that maudlin epistle to Mexico, if you got it—tho that was something like it then. I hope you aren't mad at us but suspect so if you aren't RRing on the SP. The kids still speak of you *daily* & I find myself watching the door—& of course the mail box.

Neal & I still not making it without you. He says to tell you he'll join you in Dec. & you'll both go booming on the Florida East Coast line—I shouldn't doubt it & I'll be saying just what Cathy did the other night: "Daddy & Jack both went off & left me."

Wish you could see our new house—Ah me—please write us anyway—eh?

Love,
CAROLYN

TO JACK KEROUAC FROM NEAL AND CAROLYN CASSADY

August 27, 1952
[San Jose]

DEAR BROTHER;

Of all the goddamn silly jerks; why, oh why in hell didn't we make you take your student trips in February or March? You see there has been a ruling made that there will be no more student brakemen made who have reached their thirtieth birthdate. So anyone who is 30 cannot hire out as a student. You are 30; was so in March? well, anyway, there is still a damn good chance. First I'll get Wally Lipford, Al Hinkle's uncle, an old head conductor, to get you hired anyhow, despite the rule. Now they are only going to hire for the next few weeks, 30 days or so at most, so you gotta get here in a hurry. You will be able to work until Dec. 1st anyhow, making at least 1200–1500 dollars. Figure a good solid thousand clear minimum. If Wally couldn't get you hired because of the ruling things will be alright anyhow if you will just make yourself use all your brains. Here's how: you go up and hire out as an *experienced* brakeman from some road back east. It will take them about 45 to 90 days to check up and everytime they notify you to come up to the personal record clerk you stall a couple of weeks and then give the fairy clerks some bullshit and get by a while longer. Actually all the above would not and will not be necessary, if you can just show them that you are 29 and won't be 30 until next year, or September 13, or something. So, if you can just say you're 29 you're in, it's simple, they don't ask for proof; just say you are 29 and if anything came up you simply missed a year somewhere. Saying you are experienced would be hard to do not only for personal records, but also because it would take all your intelligence to fool even the dumbest rail for any time at all. I have checked with the trainmaster and they definitely are hiring for about another 30 days, so that's sure. Also I've got a wonderful reputation with chief crew clerk Galen and if worse came to worse, as a personal favor to me I'm sure he would get you hired, and of course there's that head man of the baggage-room, remember? and there are a *lot* of other angles, so don't worry; the main thing is for you to get your ass out here immediately, right away, now, first week in Sept. I wish to god I had some money, my checks been attached over a sewing machine and I've got nothing to live on right now, instead I send you some (all I have) old trainmen receipts and button and two old 1949 passes from N.O. to SF; now this is a real money saver and serious and just because you're a shy sly old t head you not going to escape doing what I say, just this once please, for old times' sake, be sensible and do this: go to Rocky Mount depot and find data on train to New Orleans, *or* to next division point where conductors are changed. Don't try and ride Hummingbird or most other streamlined trains as they are usually restricted from employees riding. Show up ½ hour before train leaves and ask nearest *brakeman,* one that looks like he's going out on same train, what conductor's name is, also what he thinks are your chances of riding, etc.; then, go up to conductor *before* train leaves and ask politely and quietly if you might ride in restroom or on some jumpseat to place where he gets off. This, you tell him, you are being presumptuous enuf to ask for free ride because you've been member of trainmen (Brotherhood RR Trainmen) for 5 or 6 years; show your button and flash the receipts and say you've been laid up sick, ill all this year and so withdrew from BRT and also you withdrew because you heard of the new organization, United RR Operating Crafts, U.R.O.C., and are going to join them (this only if you see a UROC button on the conductor's uniform), anyhow you been sick, so no later receipts of BRT and are now going to SF to work as brakeman, etc. Now, follow this procedure all the time: ask the conductor first and in, (I swear, really) 99 out of 100 cases you will be allowed. Let me tell you the hardest part is getting from RM to New Orleans. If conductor says no can't ride, just go in station and buy ticket to next Division point *only*! Now, once in New Orleans get to SP dept about 9 A.M. and catch that train, there are only two, one is the Sunset Limited; *don't* catch that, catch the other one; I think it's called the Overland. Then ask conductor as outlined above, then if he hesitates pull out old 49 pass and say it's an old pass you had and didn't use and you are in a big hurry and didn't have the two-three weeks to wait that it takes to have them send a new pass to you and if cond. wants to he can come thru train and punch your pass as tho it was good one and that's OK because (this is important) you, and everyone does, keep pass until final conductor at L.A., Calif. punches it then he and he alone collects the pass, so you see it's simple; the conductor will *always* say sure you can ride, why? because he's in the clear; if anyone happens to notice, all they'd see is he was punching your pass as tho it was good one. So that the conductor won't think you're a stoolie of the SP Co. you must show him BRT button and receipts and then he'll know you just a rail like himself. Got all this now, here's the main thing, the best part of it all: when you get off at Los Angeles you will still have pass, DON'T use it, because conductor would pick it up and the General Office would call me up on carpet for misuse of transportation and Kaput, so, get on Zipper, remember, train number 373 overnite to SF and ride to San Jose and get off and call my house CYprus 7-0295 and we come get you. Now if it's Fri., Sat. or Sun. there's no Zipper so get on train number 71 mail and baggage and show conductor pass and say you using it only to come here and hire out as student brakeman, but under no circumstance let them pick up pass, OK? Division points between New Orleans and L.A. are Houston, San Antonio, Big Springs or Great Bend, or something, and El Paso, then it's Tucson and Yuma. Be sure and double check by asking each cond. where he gets off, and at that station get off with him and go up to entraining cond. and ask him; in 9 times out of 10 the old cond. will fix you up with the new one. If you did happen to find a prick don't lose any time but go into station and buy ticket to next division point only; there a new cond. will take over and let you ride. If you don't ever have time to go in depot and buy ticket it's OK because all conductors sell them on train and if one of them won't let you ride make a great show of telling him he's a prick and pull out your few pennies and count them out slowly in his chickenshit hand and then spit in his eye. All this is really much more simple than I'm making out, I'm just thinking of every possibility so there's no chance of you getting hung up; just pull out this letter and read until you come to the part that concerns whatever you're hung up on. The first time you ask is the hardest so make yourself do it and you'll find it a breeze, esp. on SP lines; if cond. does say no, don't get off train because you'd have to wait 24 hours for another one; just buy a ticket to next place where they change conductors. Remember all conductors are wishie washie type, even if they *start* to say no, just keep on talking and they will begin to worry themselves into saying yes, it's easy and sure. Just be nice and look clean; that's important, keep clean and talk quietly. If you don't do this I'll be mad as hell because I've done it and know how easy it is, and no matter how embarrassed you might think you'll get you got to do it because even in the course of everyday RRing here you will be called upon to talk to all kinds of conductors and dispatchers and the public, and you'll be on phones in the booths on siding and have to flag and stop streamlines and boxlines and hairlines all the time. Just do it as tho you didn't have a penny and your poor old mother was dying in a San Jose hospital of the gallopin consumption and all the kids were starving and naked, even, esp., 16 yr old Jeannie and Joanie. The house here is great, an old estate, made into rest and convalescent home; 8 big rooms, big rooms, and front and back yard and in town, and busses at front door and two cars to drive and all kinds of young stuff in filmy sheer no underclothes dresses, Santa Clara college few blocks away, new hi school just behind back yard fence, so all this fall you and I get hi and sit in easy chairs and look down on football field and watch all the day and nite games and cheerleaderesses and crowd like in your book. And living here we are home twice as much because we are not spending all our time deadheading from SF to SJ to pick up freight train to take to Watsonville, we just stay at home until train all set to go then he (crew clerk) calls us and we ride 1 hour and 25 minutes to Watsonville then come back and are home while other poor bastards are taking another two hours to ride home to SF.

Did you get my recent letter to R.M. [Rocky Mount]? Enclosed is picture of me & ma enduring each other until Daddy Jack returns. Take train & save money or I shoot you & hit you with new billy club I got lately for you.

Love,

NEAL

DEAR JACK;

Just to say I *really* need a man around *this* house! I warn you—you'll be just in time to help—& ole Neal wants to get to stay in the big city more.

Love,

C.

Before receiving Neal's instructions, Jack set off hitching to Denver. When Neal discovered Jack was there, he sent him a telegram urging him to hurry to San Jose within six days to secure a railroad job and wired him some money.

TO JACK KEROUAC

Sept. 2, 1952
San Jose, Calif.

Jack Kerouac
care E White
4801 South Ogden St.
Englewood
Colo.

Must arrive before Monday. Van can work student with me. $25.00 follows by wire sent only RR help to NC. Cant get pass. Love

NEAL

Kerouac arrived in San Jose in time to begin work as a trainee Southern Pacific railroad brakeman. Living with the Cassadys in their new home, he continued his relationship with Carolyn, as Neal related to Ginsberg.

TO ALLEN GINSBERG

Oct. 4, '52
[San Jose]

DEAR ALLEN;

I've never written a letter, or learned to type, epypupipwep even so; with my thunderbolt eye I see my children and me. We are convalescing my sweet Cathy from Osteomyelitis of the left leg. 200 plus doc and medicine and hospital, ugh, no insurance and I live in front of an insurance agent (whose son is beside Neal and John Allen and Jamie helping in the convalesce) from whom I wouldn't buy, but I got a whole closet full of weed that's grown for six months and is hanging its beautiful curly head medusa-like and downward but curled under since it's 6' and some inches length cannot come full unfurled beneath the 5 foot height of the shelf. Jack refuses to smoke (almost); Carolyn knows and satisfactorily proves to even me that it has surely made my mind fully blank, still I do get very very hi, still stoned and happy. Jack is, almost needless to say nowadays, not happy, perhaps is quite unhappy. I could fill up much copy with separate items of interest about bro jack, I am worrying about the boy, but I don't, can't quite, have never managed to tell him adequately. This and much else of trivia bothers him yet I'm not really guilty since everybody should know that all of us are usually trying to make it as easy as we can, I mean trying to get by in life and feel a little peace in the belly and it's hard as hell to do, at each moment, the actions and vocalizing that other people demand, deserve and need. Jack's the lonely fucker; of Carolyn, who blows him; he was almost capable of going 3 ways, but hope for that is about given up since he's so morose all he talks of now is moving from up here to way down there on skid row 3rd street, to be near work (he brakie now too) and write. It seems to be all my fault but why bother, it's nothing that one can explain, esp. a moron t head who locks his tongue while his heart pounds watching people, and the sound of their voices! like in these marvellous moments which are happily coming so often nowadays (despite the external pressures to deny my soul its precious privilege both those of job and home; keeping alive—falling under the wheels of the boxcars, staying unfired—ten demerits for derailing an engine which ended so much on the ground that it fouled the Eastbound main in the face of all the homeward bound commuters forcing me to flag to a stop trains number 78 to 148; the one wish, so strong that now it's become vital, of Carolyn that I could stop blasting, altho she gets hi with me and unlike Jack who goes to sleep or broods after being insulted, tho unintentionally, she's sensual and lazy tho) when I'm driving to 50 miles away Frisco and filling up all the weeded air my lungs will hold and just before and during release of the minute and some seconds held breath, which has been exhausted of its vegetable qualities by my eager sacs extended lips, at which instant the mystic spin develops at the head's peak and dives downward to the toes travelling along the nerves with a relaxing rush and the floodgates of amazement are open and every sight astounds and mystifies to manufacture a thought that startles one into exclaiming aloud a big soft "Oooooohhhh!"

Send me my "First Third" please, before thanksgiving maybe. I understand you bugged Jack in NYC, me too, I guess, in San Jose 27. We moved from SF in August, the 75 a month 9 room, well built house began as an estate, became a rest home before the Mexicans prior to Cassady got it. The landlord is the estate's lawyer in Boston, Mass.

HOW'S LIFE EAST//¿?¿?¿?¿?

I saw a priest as a personal favor for a religious brakie friend; I knocked him with my account to god for t, esp. since Father Schmitt is head of Catholic dept delving into dope (he accompanies government agent in old clothes once a week to "dopedens," talked for an hour to J. Edgar Hoover, witnessed gang murder on 106 and Madison below Malcolm's window). The church digs this stuff to know how to combat devil with youth clubs where they play pool, drink coffee and dance and coo in blue lit hall with great jukebox, I wish I were young enuf to join; the most are only 17 and watch you, with moist eyes under fluttering lids imply as good a piece is wanted as can, by them, be given; or is it only 69? I hope. Write soon & good. Thank you, buddy. Ship ahoy! Love, N.

A week later, jealousy between the two men had caused sufficient tension that Jack moved out of the Cassady home and into the cheap Cameo hotel at Harrison and Third in San Francisco's skid row. There he wrote about his railroad experiences in a piece to be known as "October in the Railroad Earth." In early November, Neal, finding Jack sleeping on an old couch by the side of the railroad, took pity on him and invited him back to San Jose. By December, the railroad began laying off men, and as a newcomer, Jack was one of the first to go. He decided to travel down to Mexico City to visit William Burroughs again, and Neal, anxious to obtain marijuana, drove him there in his new Nash Rambler station wagon.

TO CAROLYN CASSADY

Dec. 2 [1952], 10:00 P.M.
[Mexico City]

DEAR DEAR WIFE, CAROLYN DOLLY;

Sitting in the gray ghost Nash in front of B.B. [Burroughs's] house in which Jack & he are sleeping. I write by light of brakielanternfreightsize.

My heart is bleeding for you. From S.J. to Bakersfield—first stop for gas—my thoughts of you filled my mind so that I knew I was composing great love letters. Naturally I came by lovely things to say to you. Mostly it came out—I love *you*.

Stopped in L.A. at dawn at nonexistent share-the-ride places, & since it was right-on-way stopped at brother Ralph[16] & family for 2

16. Ralph Seaton Daly (b. February 1909) was Neal's half brother.

slices French toast, then drive down #101 to San Diego—I thought of you. Then San Diego to Yuma, Ariz. Now it was late, P.M. daylite & I had not yet given up the wheel, so let Jack drive for 8 miles, then drove because he couldn't[17]—I tell all this later; wait till I get home.

I have got to mail this now. Everything all OK. Be home Sat. P.M., leaving here Thurs. A.M. *This is truth:* I have not, & *will not,* touched any kind of any ole female; I am with B.B. & [Bill] Garver & Jack, talking only.

Love, N.

17. After his return to New York, Kerouac wrote to Neal and Carolyn on January 10, 1953 (*SL,* pp. 395–96), explaining that he could not properly control the clutch and did not really know how to drive, just typewrite.

1953

With no railroad work in the coastal area and none promised until March, money was becoming short. Neal heard of employment on the Southern Division as a freelance brakeman and left home to travel the five hundred miles to Indio, in south-central California, where he hoped to work for two weeks. He and Carolyn had grown closer together since Jack's departure, and the separation was difficult for them.

TO NEAL CASSADY FROM CAROLYN CASSADY

Thursday nite [January 29, 1953
San Jose]

DEAREST DADDY:

After you left I got desperately busy so as not to think too much of what thoughts would be coming to your mind as you faced that lonely long ride back to more loneliness and grind. I rearranged the bedroom first. Got lunch, then wrote a whole page plus some outline on the book. (Ha ha, but it serves its purpose sometimes.) Took the girls to the store, made the soup, took Johnny out in front while I watered. He sat on the steps in the sun mostly chewing on his carrot. I hid the trowel after I planted your six roses so he had to get that and bring it to me. (I could swear he didn't see me hide it.) Then Jamie joined us. The two of them stood on the porch side while I watered that bed and Johnny calmly took a step forward, spun gracefully and lit flop on his back in the flower-bed. He has no conception of height at all! It didn't hurt him and hardly surprised him. Cathy came around to show us some kites high overhead that boys somewhere, known only to her, were flying. An hour of that and yanking Johnny out of the water and off the "slide" and the soup was ready. It was good but can still stand some more cooking so it may last till you get back;

I'll just keep adding water every day. Everyone seems more calm and cheerful since your lovely presence, we're getting on smoothly, but each in his heart carries a poignant longing for daddy. A wistful remark escapes us each occasionally as to his return. I can't think of the place as anything but a house till you come live here and make it be a home. We've only scratched the surface. But you stay as long as you need in order to ease your mind about the money. I want to see that burden off your back so the sooner the better it's over and not dragged out. Do whatever will make you feel best in the long run and we'll all bear it somehow. I feel I must force myself to keep going or I'll dissolve or break somehow, and you must too; don't think, just do. If we must, we must and we will.

Rie[1] came over at this point, tho I was going to bed early. I got your most welcome phone call and am so relieved all went well and you got there safely. Sweet daddy, great thrills go through me just to think of you. It's like you were to me after Denver only much more so and no doubts to rationalize. I believe you're Christ more than ever and cannot believe I'm so lucky as to have you. But to realize now I really do, something I've never felt. The aspects of what this means unfold in new lovely ways as I think of you and especially when I see or feel you like last night. When I really realize past my conditioning that that beautiful thing is all mine, that I'll never even see any other ('cept Johnny's) that it will never be enjoyed or enjoy anyone but me, that it's mine to care for, my cherished responsibility to keep it happy and to let it make me happy etc., etc., all kinds of new aspects of life, love and the pursuit of happiness become apparent. Please daddy, make me know that this is so and never let me doubt again. A long time ago I had some such idea that such a thing would be heaven and knew the meaning of marriage bliss, believing of course the two went together automatically. I never knew how good that could be and have all that before me yet. I am positive beyond any possible need for further proof that that is the *only* way, certainly the only desirable or pleasurable way. I promise forever to do my very utmost to cast off the shell that fear and rejection have given me as soon as I can and to learn all the ways to make it ever more convincing to you that your present wonderful determinations are the best ones and you'll never need any more will power. You are becoming romantic to me too; I

1. Marie and Dick Woods, with their children, Chris and Cindy, were the Cassadys' neighbors in San Jose.

hope I can feel as such to you ere long and be a woman with you again. I'm so glad I never had oysters at midnight with anyone else,[2] and shudder with pleasure to think of all the things like that we've never done, have yet to do. Why, we'll still be honeymooning when our kids are. Where did they come from?

I must to bed now—I'm going to work hard on 1) unplugging the love for you I tried to stop & 2) giving Cathy more affection & losing my instant irritation & aggression.

To hear you say everything's even better is the most thrilling news of all—keep thinking that—think happy thoughts of the future & know above all that we'll always get along all right as long as we love each other & face it all together. We only *need* each other—nothing else—or rather all else will be taken care of—as it is now doing because of our love. But I must get you not to worry about the bills so much. Best way is not to make 'em, I guess, or to earn some money myself.

Good nite darling, I'll dream of you all night & love you all day. I'll try & write daily—you do only when it's necessary to you—but I won't worry if you don't—I'll think you're getting the rest I want you to. I mean this now—don't make yourself write when you should rest. Eat well, take care & rush the days away.

All my love forever—it seems so little, CAROLYN

I'll do all I can to be worthy of you!!

TO NEAL CASSADY FROM CAROLYN CASSADY

Friday [January 30, 1953
San Jose]

DEAR POPSIE:

I got some stamps at last so I can mail these when written.

I'm supposed to be baby sittin . . . and am, but came home for this as it's 11:30 and I'm tired. Not that I've done anything. Today was a toughie to get thru. Can't seem to make it alone so good again, can't get interested in anything. Maybe because it's so cold out for one thing; it's better when I like going outside more. Tried to work on

2. In a letter of December 9, 1952, Kerouac, in Mexico, wrote to Carolyn asking her to visit him there, and they would have oysters at midnight (*SL*, pp. 386–87).

page 2 but got stuck on what name to use for you. It's hard work, ain't it? And like everything *I've* ever started, it'll never be finished. Didn't know that, didja? Or didja? But who knows, if you love me all sorts of miracles may happen; I sure feel like I need it bad. It looks to me like the greatest and most desirable thing in all life to me. Is it really possible? I've never felt any real, close and lasting love, you know. I think perhaps not being close to my parents has made it hard for me to be close to Cathy or you as part of the dilemma. I've only given and accepted the illicit, temporary and "safe" (insofar as permanent responsibilities and demands are concerned) kinds. You too? The real stuff is constant test and a tough one. I want so much to make it a natural and desirable process. For all my preaching, you've gained the ability much sooner than I and against bigger obstacles. I've always looked to you as the master, and now that you've proven it, please, have you the patience to help a floundering soul? Can you save us all? Do you really want to? I can't believe I can be worth it to you. I'd love to be convinced. Tell me what you want me to do and how you want me to be and what sort of picture you have of the woman you love and why so I can try living up to it. You're altogether too uncritical, and, as I say, the times when *I* try being appealing or try to impress you I fail, so I've no idea what I do that you like or don't. Most times when you say I'm beautiful, I know better, and the times I think I am, you don't even see me. Gotta get the concept straight I guess.

Wow, am I sleepy. Where are they! Washed my hair at last and the warm bath helped some. (Will you quit telling Rie that I never take a bath? Now, is that nice, I ask you? Can you hear Dick saying that?) I'm joking you know, not seriously perturbed as it may sound. It's one of those cute ways of yours, one of those habits, eh? Darling just don't believe such things yourself, that's all that matters to me or worries me. Now why has this turned into complaining letter? I don't feel any such way . . . only wanting you and having nothing to say today trying to fill up a page to be closer to you. It's awful to have to postpone and wait for one's resurrection. Are you waiting for Easter?

I'm mad at you for not saving my old letters and sending that one to Diana. They'd have helped reconstruct some emotions and phases.

Saturday morning [January 31]

DEAR BABY:

Feel fine this A.M., all rarin to go again. (I know it all depends on Cathy . . . so far all well . . . hope every day to keep it.) Love you SO! We have great plans, but all depends on daddy. This year you'll probably have to work the Xtr board, eh what? to get ahead, but next year WE SHALL SEE ABOUT THAT! And the next and the next and the next and the next. Wheeeeeeee. Must dress Johnny now and clean the joint. Oh golly I love you, what a long week this will beeeeeeeeeeeeee.

All yours forevererevererever
LOVE unbounded
CAROLYN

What names are *you* giving me, LuAnne & Diana, or do you know yet?

TO CAROLYN CASSADY

Feb. 3, 1953
SP Club
Indio, California

DEAR SWEETHEART;

I sit in the car in 100% heat, no place but a cot in a dormitory room to go & no money to go even there so I wait until I'm sure to be called (within 12 hours) & then plonk down the dollar & sleep to dream of you & kids.

The worst part is not having a room of my own, no place to hang clothes etc. Since I must keep everything in car it smells of dirty socks already. But I like sitting here in back alley behind cabin dorms block from depot, ½ mile from yard office of work, & writing to you, mother of sweet Cathy & Jamie, one of whom is responsible for the pencil marks extemporaneous & irrelevant (not anthropied [*sic*]) that besmirch this page along right & center. Unless it was Johnnie, my own little pup, whom will, I pray, wright, write, right? Papa Neal a little letter of condolence for being so hard at work made doubly so by being far from the poignant place where he & my she is, 611 RR miles.

I may get a two week outside holddown in El Centro or Calexico on border (a water tank & work gang houses) where make 30 a day, every day, instead of just 20 a day, most every day, between here & Yuma. This is good for money, hard for health, heat & feet, only thing: holddown outside Indio means might be few days late home since can't quit while on holddown. But money yes!! That's why I'm here, suffering, & will come home with at least 300.00. But aim for more since need, & still no coast work till March 10.

The heat is getting me, ugh, still I carry on, oof!, goof, scaviroooofffffff. Busy RR men, called to work & walking by, are staring hard at me in car, sweating & writing. One old carp-head is looking particularly suspiciously at me, reminds me of Floyd Sisson, about-to-die coast conductor who never speaks.

There are other things, principally you & our mutual peace of mind, by any other name as sweet, but for today I'm carried away by yesterdays with you. This is the first moment I've had since leaving you. I drove to Yuma, 145 hiway miles beyond here, to hire as yard man making only 5 days a week at 16 a day, but thanks to old conductor who called & fixed it I became brakie here at 20 or more a day.

I'm getting so that I can look at passing women with*out* passion! Few attractive & those that do remind me of you, hardworking unselfish no-vacation mama, I'll be there to help you soon, just thought you'd like to know I ain't sopooke to anything resembling woman of female spieeceess. Thank you!

And, there are things ahead of, behind & between a letter, those are the things I wish you could receive on letters from me. But I'm not up to the task. Each word a writer's cramp of hurt left thumb, heat & you in my mindeye, eyeful aplenty, *best* of so many who, unlike you, never care for a chew or even blew a balloon to the moon so soon, as I arrive home triumphant & tired, but oh, so inspired to be wired to you.

Guess I will now partake of some nourishment, ah, good meat, liver, & onions too for only (ulp) a dollar a day for food except more for tiny breakfast. I'm starving, I'm broke, I'm happy to know that I have you I can send my love to, yoo-hoo you, I'll be thru, but till I do I'm blue for you. Love to all. Hinkle turn key in car off alright?

You may, if you're not abed already from having no help with problem kids, find a moment from housework & all the tremendous things you do daily, find time to write daddy. Enclosed find address on match cover; or else, Brakeman Cassady, SP Clubhouse, Indio. Either place, I'll get it. Listen, don't struggle to produce an MS, just a note to Poppy. I stop here so will have strength to write again tomorrow. It's so hard longhand, at best, without a desk to sit at & besides the rough edge of this upholstery is bruising my tender skin, unshirted. Love, N.

I'm so hi I could cry, I could die, I could buy a good why? So I'll try & I'll try but can say only goodbye. Not goodbye, but so long until tomorrow. Sunup & sundown I think of you & the brood & my stupidity of former years, when your tears filled my ears with the fears that my dears would be lost thru the years if my beers were but beers instead they were leers at my seers & my peers were forgivenst of my sneers & my jeers of their years, oh my dears!

Yes, my love, I've taken my first puff of cigar, only after work one a day. I still have the whole box which you so kindly gave me for Xmas, ha.

Feb. 4, 1953

Just now called for El Centro, means be there at least a week, maybe two, so *do not* write to me at either of the two addresses enclosed; I'll find out what's happening in El Centro & will write you at once. I go to work at 1 P.M., 2-4-53 & so will be off after midnight & will write you tomorrow A.M. (2-5-53) & I must emphasize one thing for you to remember: I love you truly, N.

TO NEAL CASSADY FROM CAROLYN CASSADY

Tuesday nite [February 3, 1953]
1047 East Santa Clara St.
San Jose, California

DEAREST DADDY:

It's now 10 P.M. so I'll put down my paints & spend this hour with you. I make myself start to bed by 11 anyway so I'll get up between 7 & 8—I seem to have more than ever to do & less time. I feel very fortunate when I think of what you have to do! I hope the change is invigorating in some ways anyway & you aren't too lonely. Try not to wear out the barber pole & keep a clear head at work. Stay away from Palm Springs unless I'm with you. We'll winter vacation there someday, promise? (Not the vacation, but the not doing it without me.) End of advice.

We are getting along better than I feared—the time *is* going by & I'm trying especially to be nice to Cathy & to replace your attention a little. The mornings are cold & foggy, but the girls are outside all of them anyway. I've tried to schedule my time to work in the A.M. & be free after their naps to cater to them. I take them to the store when they get up & before Johnny does. I let them look at toys in the hardware store & go in the Mayfair for television & more toys when I can. Today I got out their paints & they took turns painting at my easel & loving it. The one not doing it goes outside till her turn. They couldn't be better so far. The house is filthy & I could do jobs all day, but figure it's more important to let it go to be with them. Johnny cuts around as usual—no strain—*except* he has a renewed passion for the toilet. He sees them wash & get drinks of water at the sink, & since he can't reach it, substitutes the water he *can* reach—the toilet. He washes & drinks it yet, every chance he gets. I'm trying to lift him to the sink as often as I can instead. He has some diarrhea—either from the soapy bathwater or the more adult food. I'm trying to cut out both. Rie suggested Jamie's rash might be orange juice, so I'm trying that—It hasn't been getting better without the powder so that can't be it. We all got our hair washed tonite. Yesterday I got them some 25¢ books & today animal cookies.

The Hinkles left Sunday around 5 tho I could have used Al more. I guess Helen had had enough. I've been working on it since & it's almost done. Only costs $1.50 to have hers cut & mounted oval (not framed) & I wish I could get it done. No car, no daddy, no pioneering spirit. When you return.

Now don't go staying any month! Rie was telling me how they refinanced their car, getting the payments lowered & $250 in cash besides. If we get stuck we could probably do that too?

People are enquiring about pictures & tho the trade would probably be mostly children, I'll push it. This "studio" makes such a difference—tho I need help with the kids.

How can they call you if you sleep in the car? I trust you don't. It should be too tough—can't wash, can't write, can't relax. Surely you have a room. Do take care of yourself. Don't *worry* about your virtue—a splurge now & then does one good. I'm not so puritanical & specially now I get my share & more—so trust your own character—you have a very good one & an indulgence or two—honestly accepted as such, won't make you an addict again necessarily. I believe in you more than ever, am proud of you & love you. CAROLYN

Feb. 4, 1953, 2:00 P.M.
[El Centro, California]

DEAR WIFE;

I am on a cool bench before the El Centro depot waiting for 2:30 P when I go to work instead of 1:00 P, because the crew worked over 14 hours last nite so need 10 hours off—that means about 30 bucks a day. Hope I stay here in the heat & despite my feet until I drop exhausted into car & fly home to you 700 & some miles away. I read Proust slowly & realize I really can write like he does. Of course, he's better but I'm younger & while less brilliant still have a chance to learn how, with your help & patience. I am terribly interested in life & wish you were here to share my musings & comments about living and dead things that pass so abstractly before me.

I can't seem to find my writing—the last page of which was in longhand & I thought in a suitcase with me. If I need it & you happen to find it I'll let you know. Tonite after 14 hours work, about 4:00 A.M. I'll sleep in car, work tomorrow then rent room for bath, then sleep nite in car, then room, then car, etc. etc. Save a buck or more a day & might thus last until get to Indio for voucher money if necessary. Temporarily unworried; hope you're doing OK enuf to find yourself missing Poppy & yet able to handle kids.

It's about time to get coffee before work, will continue this after work & sleep & mail tomorrow A.M. (2-5-53). Hope I do OK & not put engine on ground or feel feet pain too much.

Back in Indio 2-5-53 2:00 P[.M.]

Well I worked 14 hours for 29.10 & was released (unusual) to DH to home terminal here. So let's see: 1 trip to Yuma on 2nd 19.00; 1 trip return Indio 17.00; I then DH on 4th to El Centro 9.15; 29.10 there, DH back 9.15. That's over 83 bucks in 3 days & I'll be called to Yuma again about 6 P.M. today (4 hours away) & that round trip is always worth 35 or more so by tomorrow (the 6th) I have over $120.00 & it's just starting. Realize mama, that's over 240 bucks a week. A fellow made 583.00 last half & most checks run over $400.00 a half, so Poppy's in the loot again. If I can hold out.

It's alright to write me, please do, but be sure & address it to me at

SP Clubhouse, Indio, Calif. Listen honey, I'm going to rush & mail this so it'll catch tonite's train, besides I can't wait to hear from you & last letter said don't write; well do write, so I'll know what new there is to talk about. Here's one thing; I've swore off my one-a-day vitamin cap. Yessir, thought you'd like to know. It's now one-a-few days & soon one-a-week. Thank you. Love, N.

TO NEAL CASSADY FROM CAROLYN CASSADY

Feb. 6 [1953]
1047 East Santa Clara St.
San Jose, California

DEAR DADDY,

I hope you got my letter & also that I hear from you tomorrow for an address for this. It's very late & I should be in bed, but think I'll have a hot bath as my back has been stiff for a couple of days (guess it's the wet weather—really getting old!) I just finished painting Cathy's stove I made at last from stuff around here & about a dollar's worth of gimmicks & paint. I must say *I* think it's cute & they seem to too.

It's so different this time—not that I don't miss you even *more,* but the peace of mind, the common cause, & the new purposefulness is making the wait much easier. The days pass rapidly—I've so much to do, yet seem to get little done—just play with things like this stove & plans. I've been interested in the food & have made them pudding or jello every day—some sort of special somethings each day. Rie has added pie & cake too. We've had some fun times & a few bad ones the past two days. I aim for improvement every day tho, & they are happier than I feared.

Jamie's rash is spreading now, so I guess it wasn't orange juice. Maybe Joy. I'll try, then call Dr.

Johnny still has diarrhea & I can't figure why. Chris fell off your car & cut his head, but otherwise nothing serious so far.

I also washed all their fuzzy animals & sewed eyes & ribbons on all—I feel so extremely lucky to be allowed this role. Doesn't seem fair & I intend to help you get more play too & not so much work. You're a dear sweet daddy & we love you so!

Yesterday Johnny got in the girls' paints & I flooded the back porch. Jamie had smashed her concertina with a hammer I discovered so it was a bit troubled. They've been great tho—I'm very happy—

will be in heaven when I really get along right with Cathy all the time & when you are here *never* to go away again!

They're going to start a big Ford plant at Milpitas (did you read?) & I wondered if that wouldn't boost the railroad some. Mostly WP [Western Pacific] I guess, but even so—eh?

I hated to think of you so lonely & hot (warm from sun, that is). Please don't delay any longer than this holddown! 300 is fine. I went over the bills to see about the income tax & boy, you're right, we're in the red. But this should do it enough. Not any extra tho yet, but we'll make it this year—I'm determined we'll get ahead. First tho, we must get some tricycles & that's all!

Do eat, honey! I've only spent 10 bucks, still have 20 & put the 70 in the bank today. But you must take care of yourself. Don't guzzle too much pop.

Say, when you write, how about half of it anyway not hi, OK? All very entertaining, but I'd also like to hear from YOU.

I am getting anxious for your return now! Sweet daddy, I'm so lucky to have you & I mean to treat you better too!

Our grass is coming up in some places. Need more sun now—had lots fog & 2 rainy days. Nuff.

I'm so filled with creative ideas & keep seeing things to paint—no time, but then again—lots of time. I feel much more easy going & that there *is* lots of life left yet. I'll stop for now in case I want to add if I hear from you. Nite nite—this cold big bed!!!!!!!!!!!!! xxxxxx

Saturday [February 7]

Got yours this A.M.—you don't seem to have gotten my letter—I sent it to crew dispatcher so check—I'm sorry you didn't.

Today the girls have bad coughs & Johnny's diarrhea is worse—he doesn't feel a bit good. I feel the signs too. I hope it won't be flu or something. Your letters make me long for you so—I do hope it'll be no longer than another week! Bless you for cutting down on the vitamins. Sure you can write—we've a lifetime ahead now & we're gonna squeeze it dry before we die! Hurry home! All our love—C, C, C & J

TO CAROLYN CASSADY

Feb. 8, '53 at 27 yrs.
Webb's Rooms
44-871 Towne Ave.
Indio, Calif.

DEAR WIFE;

It has finally happened; it took years to occur, but at last it's reached us: the first week apart. How arc you? I'm 27 & not so dumb. But how are you really? Do you love me? Me you?

Now I am official paid up until the 15th resident of room #6 at kindly old maid 90 & sister 89, Webb's Rooms at 44-871 Towne Ave. I think it's 44-871; oh well, I'll get any mail if it's addressed just Webb's Rooms, Towne Ave., Indio. It is a horrible place, raw cabin duplex shack partitioned off from old hacking cough brakie off another division, just room for bed & dresser, only place in town where you don't have to sleep in dorms, etc., etc.

This is letter #3 in less than 6 days, (Sunday last I drove & worked Mon. before could first write you) so I'm averaging letter every other day. Not bad. Long to hear from you, *wish you were here*!!

How's Lover-boy John (the younger, nach) & Converted Cathy & Jumpin Jamie?

The whole Coast Division xtras are down here & it's turning slowly. I've only made 150 bucks, clear in a week, they were & I yet will make 200 clear & more a week; every buck counts.

I was almost tempted to spend money for show, but thought of you not getting to even go, so I didn't. I read Proust; try unsuccessfully to avoid Old Lady Five-Fingers as some say, and Lady thumb & her four fingers, & will now recite a poem:

Rah-rah-rah, sis-boom-bah,
" " " " " "
" " " " " "

We want CAROLYN!!

Aren't I silly? Aren't I willy? Aren't I nilly? Yes, Nillyon Cassady, husband of great portraiture artist. Joe Smith here says yes to portrait next Summer if you want to.

Feb. 9, 5 A.M.

This shows ill & good luck; got called just now for Valley rt in El Centro 30 a day, but I just rented this room for week & so lose its 8.00 unless commute 80 miles daily after 14 hours labor. But, I want letter from you so will come back here in day or two for it. Listen, tell me when you get the 70 unemployment check & how's everything. Must fly south now.

Love & X's N.

TO NEAL CASSADY FROM CAROLYN CASSADY

Monday Feb. 9, 1953, 12:30 A.M.
1047 East Santa Clara St.
San Jose, California

DEAR DADDY,

Here I am again waiting for the hot bath (I'm froze). I'm ashamed of myself not having a letter to you sooner! It ain't that I don't think of you *constantly*! I do! I just keep so busy busy. Gosh, it seems you've been gone a month, not a week. Oh hurry, hurry home!

I thought of you so yesterday & vowed never again will we be apart on birthdays! Yours especially is gonna be important (not only to catch you up to me—mine we won't mention so much).

The girls & I had cake & sang you Happy Birthday anyway, but I get mad too, thinking of you down there alone—not being a birthday boy & letting us pet you. *Never again*.

Today I worked & washed—got all the wash done & put away (sun & wind), cleaned house, scrubbed the bath & kitchen floors, finished Cathy's stove, cleaned up the telephone nook & tonite—I uncrated the furniture—Yep, it's here already. It was never meant to be uncrated but I dood it with my little hammer. Tomorrow I'll scrub that room & have the fun of putting it in to surprise you.

The kids seem well again, thank goodness, tho Jamie still says she has cold. ("Mommie, I'm sure I'm cold," & feels her brow with very distressed face.) Cathy & I doing great in spite of her getting me to play sick, covering me up, shutting the door & taking Johnny in & giving him the paint. I rescued him in time & kept myself from too much anger. We made it OK & talked.

These crates will give me lots wood to make them more stuff—goody.

Vera called today—they've all been sick all winter—but have made progress on the house & Ray loves his new job.[3]

Dick & Rie were just here for coffee. Rie went to Mothercraft & ran out of gas so she siphoned from the car here—I couldn't start it the day after you left, so that's that.

How does all this sound in perspective? Not too bad I hope? No mail of interest since you left (a bill or two tho).

I'm completely happy except for one thing—it *all* hinges on YOU—& where are you? Sweating it out for us way down in the desert! Dear daddy—How can it be worth it to you?

We do love you so—Do quit when you hit 300—I has enuf! You've done more'n your share.

Be peaceful & careful & want us—(me too). Hope I get letter tomorrow.

All my love, CAROLYN

I've a new idea for my book. I can do anything if you love me.

Although originally intending to be away from home for only two weeks, Neal decided that the extra money he would earn by staying until the end of February would be extremely useful, and so he broke the news to Carolyn.

TO CAROLYN CASSADY

Feb. 11, '53, P.M.
[Indio, CA]

DEAR HEAVENLY LIFESAVER WIFE CAROLYN QUEEN;

Johnny's diarrhea must come from toilet; Jamie's rash must come from not calling Doc who doesn't know either. I love you so much it hurts me. I wish I long I pray I gotta see you.

I promise about Palm Springs. I promise about no fuckie anyone but you & that a lot when I return, right? Right! Your crass "splurge now & then" horrifies me. Don't you do any "splurging" & I won't 'cause I can't 'cause I love you & want you good & unsplurgie with

3. Vera was the landlady of the Cassadys' previous home at 29 Russell Street, San Francisco. Ray was her husband.

anyone but me & that, as I said above, is to be a lot upon my return home.

Feb. 12, '53, P.M.

DEAR SWEETIE PIE DELUXE DARLINGBUG:

I love you too, only more so, in another way perhaps, but enuf until I see you which will be?

There are hundred things to say & only a page to say them.

1st money: I now've made better than 235 but 15.00 for eating-books off that & 100 more that I'm drawing in couple days out of which I send you anything you need. Did you pay phone bill? Will you need any money before the 26th? If so, how much? I send to you because must stay here—ugh, hate it, but listen to this: on 26th *must* pay rent & part of bills balance of which *must* be paid March 10th which we'll be unable to do if quit now. Where would be March 10th check for car, living, etc. etc. You know besides 18.00 taken from 1st half Feb check plus hospt. etc., etc.—*None* such taken from 2nd period Feb check, so also this: no work on cast, balls must be cut,[4] we need vacation from work for while in March & only way is to work here until pay day, which must stay here for anyway because already sent in form that sends my 26th check to Indio, leave Indio 26th Feb. *Must* do this, tho hate to so much. *Miss you*. What you say about "alone" is right & sad & blue for you, esp. 'cause all you say in your letters (which you must number) is so true & right & just how I feel too. I love you & know you understand & need me & this: *I never go way again*.

What else can I do? Conscientiously looking at it, I must work last of Feb., also because is *last* of rush here & no work anyhow, anywhere after that until April.

Oh depression days! Not let them strike my home & kids because they reflect my love for Mommy who is hot lay, I say.

Here's the main thing, the reason we'd be worse off than before if I quit now: unemployment wouldn't be gotten & no other income. If I got my check of 26th now I'd get less, much less than 100. How? Eat-book deductions etc. & 100 I'm drawing for living until March 10th (both households), the other 100 or so (I've still 2 days left in

4. Neal was planning to have a vasectomy, but the operation was never performed.

half) for rent & few bills 26th *then,* if work last half Feb. on the 10th March get 400.00. Why 400.00 & this time only about 300.00? Deductions not in last half check, plus rush work & layoffs for big festival will probably put me in El Centro for 2 weeks at 30 a day & DH 20. So money March 10th pays all bills, gets Cathy's bike & Jamie's trike & Johnny's bloomers and your camera & my balls cut & live for 2 or 3 weeks on.

TO NEAL CASSADY FROM CAROLYN CASSADY

Thursday [February 12, 1953]
1047 East Santa Clara St.
San Jose, California

DEAR POPSIE,

I'll try again, tho it seems you haven't gotten my other 3 letters. (One to crew dispatcher & 2 to the clubhouse). You move about so I'll try this again on the nose.

We're really counting the days now—I expect to hear *tomorrow* when you'll be back. I figure Sunday nite earliest; Tuesday morning latest—rite?

I have still (or only) 4.50 left of the original. Haven't touched the $70, but I've bought a lot besides food I must admit. We've had good meals tho & something special every day. Yesterday I got the cheapest, yet what proved the most fun surprise so far. A 10¢ jar of bubble stuff apiece with blower. Boy, such fun—I like it too, and I played an extra hour last night, not even realizing it.

Ah me, you should see our living room—who'd a thunk it! Such a difference. The old joint is getting homey-er by the day. 'Course I have endless plans, for endless supply of money, but I'll take it slowly—I hope. I fear you'll have to get tricycles somehow—they're waiting for it tho I think they'll forgo the promised jungle-jim, slides, etc. I've got a mile long list of small needs, but imagine most will have to wait—that's okey dokey. I should iron or mend instead anyway. I've really done a lot since you've been gone & managed to keep the ants to a minimum tho Rie's house is crawling worse than I've ever seen.

I'm finally pooped tonite so not too interesting, eh? But I'm most happy & grateful, but miss you *so* much. I hope you truly feel as satisfied with your way of life, whether it was chosen or no, as I do. I feel now that we've really begun & I'm greedy & eager to jostle as much of life as possible, & with *you*. I thought of a dilly of an opening for my book & have renewed determination. All dreams—but such fun. I can't imagine what it's like to be depressed—if we both can reach that we'll never be since we do it to each other a lot, yeh?

Mom sent the wrong rug—I'm most disappointed, but not the way I used to be & will simply dye it & have fun & not complain.

Also you must tell me more what *you* want & how you want to live so I won't force you into this pattern I've made because you've been gone so much. I think of you so much as I do what *I* want &, since you're not here to object or have other ideas, I just assume when you are here it'll be the same. But I *want* to adjust to your wishes & I'd like to get real "cool" 'bout everything & take it *all* in. So long as you're *happy* doing it. So make a few more demands & be my master. Guess so far you haven't *asked me* to—just done it regardless—or something like that. We'll *live* & *learn,* eh Pop?

Cathy has said several times "We should have *another* little boy & little girl." Wonder what *that* means—but I think it's an improved attitude anyway. Lately she's been cutting Jamie out like mad & most things, as I see it, are an attempt to be a "Mommy." No doubt shows too much pressure from Mommy. I'm trying & trying—mostly to regain control of this trigger temper I never knew I had & still can't get used to. If you'll be my friend I'll make it.

Oh, do come home & live with me!

We probably are to get a thermostat control & a cleaned furnace. Greg came out today (60 bucks worth) Not OKed yet by Sunseri. We'll see.

Where's our Daddy??? I can hardly make these last few days, honey.

All our love, C.

I get curse Sunday (I hope).

For Valentine's Day, Neal sent Carolyn a dozen red roses and a card that read, "Double the days that 14 are, and that's the day that I'll be thar," implying that he would be home by February 28. However, Carolyn received his letter of February 11/12 before the Valentine gift arrived.

TO NEAL CASSADY FROM CAROLYN CASSADY

Feb. 14 [1953]
Be my Valentine?
1047 East Santa Clara St.
San Jose, California

DEAR N-,

You beast! Write me a letter I can't read except that you won't come home like you *promised*—I feared this would happen—but thot not *this* time! (Tone not as reads!)

Still we *do* have to have the do I can't deny. So if you can stand it I guess I can. I was so sure you'd be here tomorrow—hanging on desperately. I've worked myself out, wearing out this time, now tired. Ah, think of how tired *you* must be! I'm a selfish bitch! (Sound like Diana).

But I've been waiting to hear what to do with this 70 & when more & etc. Can't understand your letter well enough to know how many bills to pay & how long we have to live on this 70. I'll try to figure it out myself today & pay some. Do write sense & how you plan it. If you don't I'll have to spend *something* to work with to use up *another* two weeks.

Does the enclosed letter change anything? I wish I had the car, then. Haven't taken Jamie to Doc, waiting you & it. Some rides would help too. John's diarrhea OK—rash better.

I feel so sad, but I do understand, appreciate you & will be most happy with the money too. I *know* how lucky I am to have you & I love you—but when do I *get* you?

Well, I'll set up some more projects to do before you get back.

Cathy says: "Dick built us a new house & a bench—& I want to say to him—uh—uhm—what do *you* want to say to Daddy, Jamie?—& tell Daddy—we go to store by ourselves (with you) (me) & Johnny has Jamie's cowboy pants & we've got the living-room all fixed up—and—uh—" She's gone.

We'll stick it daddy, boo hoo—but rather than have you worry about money, & I've a lot of ways to use it, I must say—

Lou Wolfe[5] came by first time yesterday to get you go fishing. Says picking up on RR.

Save me from the Wolves—I want only you. WRITE.

Love, CAROLYN

5. Lou Wolfe was a freight conductor on the Southern Pacific railroad.

Tell me at once—new plans from call-back letter—I guess you'll stay where most money till have to change—so? Or what?

Tel bill 15.49, so send me money!! Two parking warrants $2 each. I pay also $5 in bank. Keeping 20 for myself.

Saturday aft., Feb. 14

DEAREST NEAL,

It's a good thing I couldn't get any stamps or I'd a sent this nasty note without knowing of your flowers. I've felt like crying all day & now I could just bawl! I can hardly believe it, I've never been so touched & pleased—Oh Neal! But, tho Rie says it should give me a big boost, I just long to see you more. I feel so lonesome today & it seems the kids have surpassed themselves with pranks. I'll sleep early & start again tomorrow—looking often at your lovely flowers & reading your poignant poetry. Oh gee, I don't deserve it.

I just called Hart's, to see if I could order some tricycles sent out & charged, but they don't have the right kind—damn. They really are getting wild for them & restless with all else. What do you mean *28* days more? Another *month*—no—that is *too long*. I'd rather starve. Please—please—It's the surprise element again that depresses. I thought we'd discussed & *decided*.

Bless you, poppy—do come home tho—we'll make it, huh?

All my love,
CAROLYN

TO CAROLYN CASSADY

Feb. 15, '53, P.M.
[Indio, California]

DEAREST ONE;

Today I am the loneliest yet; I mean lonely, alone & cut off from all but you; & it scares me; I realize how much I need you & how hopelessly helpless I am without & even with you.

Songs mean so much to me, would you sing to me alone in our bedroom I will depaper & repaint with you?, songs of love?

I feel like the talkative bull, every time he saw a heifer he wanted to jabber, 'course I ain't a fickle horse always switching his tail because I know what happened to the oversexed mouse; pussy got him.

Who's your everloving Daddy? Didn't he spend his last five foolishly to send a ½ dozen red roses to his own sweet Blue Lady. Will you be my Valentine?, every day? Will you hold my sad head & soothe the savage beasts, Pathos & Passion, that twirl toward my heart each time I think of you, who is all there is, all five ft. 2, between me & the gallows death I dread. Or am I morbidly insane to jumble up all the tender things you are & squash them into my tiny mind to bubble & hold me down from exploding.

And then there are the facts of life: 1. Better, henceforth, send all letters to SP Club, Indio, I might leave Webb's here if called for vacation holddown in A.M. of 16th. I made 300.00 alright, but barely, & out of that is 100 cash I got already (send for money if you must, but not until absolutely necessary) & 18.75 RR retirement, 4.75 hospt., 45 or so federal tax, so I get only 125 to, at most, 150 on 26th. 75 for rent & bills & we live on the hundred here in my pockets until March 10th; almost impossible, right? So hold off until March tenth when we get 350 or so clear if I hit the big half I expect to this 2nd period Feb. No deductions except 50 bucks or so federal & rest is bill, car, your camera, my nuts, kiddies' bikes & living until called back or something I hope.

I am called for DH SP to Yuma, will return here again tomorrow.

I love you, I miss you, I need you.

I can't do without you. You must tell me to stop worry about money.

I'll return & never leave.

I know you are all I need.

If you care, just say every day you do & I'll be happy.

Send me our landlord's address so I may mail rent to him & save you the trouble. S. Sunseri?

Tell Cathy & Jamie & Johnny that Daddy loves them almost as much as he does his girl, Mommy. True? I'll be home before you & they are even ready for me.

I see they had big blizzard over Canyon Pass & all cars were stuck. Good thing I got thru, huh? Luck of the Irish I got, I guess.

Love, N.

TO CAROLYN CASSADY

Feb. 20, '53, 10:00 P.M.
[Indio, California]

DEAREST CAROLYN;

I'm enormously pleased with life. Why? *You*. Oh yes, I'm a nervous wreck, or worry wart, a fearful father. There are other times tho when I see life so clearly & surely that I'm compensated for all.

Take wives for example, there's only one—you.

"	lovers "	"	"	"	"	"	
"	rivals "	"	"	"	"	him.	
"	writers"	"	"	"	"	him.	
"	books "	"	"	"	"	it.	
"	beer "	"	"	"	"	Schlitz.	

Feb. 24, 12:01 A.M.

This midnight I returned from 70 hours on the road, Indio to Yuma, Yuma to Dieguinos (in old Mexico) to bring in broken-down steam-engined train, Dieguinos to Yuma, Yuma to El Centro via old Mexico,[6] 3 hour release in El Centro to evade full-crew (lookie me I wrote "full-crew" just now & I meant "hog-law," i.e. work only 16 hours in any 24) hog-law. El Centro to Yuma, Yuma, at last, to Indio. Rush to SP Club & grab your blessed letters to Daddy & jump here into *cold* bed, really colder than outside, believe or not, & devour them, the great works of prose that they are, & them the works of *my* baby, & as I read I say aloud to myself & eavesdropping hacking-cough brakie the other side of partition, great phrases like "what understanding she has," "what a great soul," "a *perfect* woman, unbudded as yet," "why look, a hard-on comes of itself when I read her sex words." (Then a great huge natural erection untouched by my hand & set into action of enlarging only by the thought of your body, what's

6. The most direct railroad link between Yuma, Arizona, and El Centro, California, was on seventy miles of track constructed between 1905 and 1909, which dipped some ten miles below the Mexican border into Baja California. The track was leased to the Southern Pacific railroad from 1912 until 1959, when it was acquired by the Mexican federal government. Dieguinos was fifteen miles southwest of Yuma, along this track.

between the cunt-hairs, your tender skin I love to pluck, (oh no, I refuse to tempt myself into more rhymes like above to allow saying——), "a great page, surely the second one won't equal it." Imagine my surprise when I saw your 2nd Fri & Sat A.M. one, was even *better* than the 1st.

"I really *need* only her & she realizes the same about me, too," "I'm not tempted to stray, why I did I'll never know, & that's how she thinks too, now," "she has great self-knowledge," "I feel just like a kid again, I love her so all I want is to be beside her (preferably in bed) & know she knows I know that *you know,* ya know what I mean?" I can't even recall any letter to Diana & surely what fun she & I will have in our new living room & rearranged bedroom, how you rearrange it, huh?, & read again to each other all our love letters when I get home & how all too few they are & how we'll make up for it by telling each other mouth to ear all the things we feel, & are then feeling, together & those things we want to say, & have wanted to say forever, to each other.

Feb. 24, 8 A.M.

DEAR BABYDOLL;

Here I am called again, can't even write a letter to you before on the road again, just remember this; I've solved my sex problem, don't forget to remind me to tell you when I get home. Will write you soon as possible. Love, N.

TO NEAL CASSADY FROM CAROLYN CASSADY

Sunday nite [February 22, 1953
San Jose]

DEAREST NEAL,

Won't type 'cause I opened their door already. Ah, it's the evenings that are lonesome. The days seem to go fast, but the week slow. I can hardly remember you again, & I want you here so much like you are—how good you make me feel.

Last nite the Woods brought over dessert & we had a "party" all together. Dick made them boats yesterday afternoon (broken before bath time, but the bottoms still float a little), & a telephone of tin cans after supper. They returned & chatted in the evening. Today we all pulled vines in the morning & had a picnic lunch all together at noon. More exchanging of papers after naps. They have been an amazing help while you're gone. Don't think I could stand it otherwise. Cathy & I had a perfect day today also & I think I can make it with her sometimes—then I'd really be in heaven I know.

My eyes ache from sun & reading so this will be short tonite—add in the A.M. maybe. I think of you all the time but try not to talk too much—not to make the girls sad too. We would like a man around the house!

TO NEAL CASSADY FROM CAROLYN CASSADY

Tuesday nite [February 24, 1953
San Jose]

DEAR DADDY,

Whee—I got to cross 2 days off the calendar tonite 'cause I forgot to last nite. Only 4 more days—at least till *this* stint is up. Take 'em one at a time—just in case there're more. Hope to get a note from you tomorrow, but suppose you're awfully busy & tired so it's OK. Lou Wolfe is all for you staying there till your 30 days is up—hmm. He and Tommy somebody (fat with black curly hair—glasses—very nice) were here this afternoon "on the loose" & looped. Rie & I were tugging vines so made them help with the last big push. She & I have cleared all but a couple up by her house. The fig tree & shed are clear & a big hole to next door. Amazing—& Mr. S. thought it would take a bulldozer. "Never underestimate—," etc.—but I think we deserve some compensation. She says in time the two of us will probably rebuild that fence too at the rate we're going. If we get tired enough looking at it—who knows. It's fun tho, the exercise & the results are both needed & gratifying.

This morning I spent 10 bucks (I have $26.85 left)—I felt Cathy's shoes & her toes were pushing right thru the end—so I rushed her to the Mayfair (bless it) & got her some tennis shoes that fit. Poor kid, & the straps were cutting her feet. Whazza matter with me? Whew. I *had* to get Johnny some rubber pants too & a few sewing needs. I've tackled the mending the last 2 nights & we've lots more clothes now—(still not the ironing). I've some hard work to do & some "grippers" to put in but that's that. Johnny will have more pants than he can wear. Rie sat over here & sewed with me. What would I do without them! Things are getting done & the days wearing by—that's the main thing. That wind storm has filled the yard with junk so that needs raking & soaking. We could use some rain, but I really appreciate this sunny weather. I do a lot better—& today it was light till nearly 7 so we even went out a bit after supper while Dick burned under what we'd pulled. Johnny gazed at the moon & the 2 bright stars in wonder & then in the house stared at the light-bulb with such serious & awed look—"looking-at-life" look—I was all over come—er—that is—overcome.

Guess he'd never *seen* the moon & it was really bright as were the stars. Now he wonders, I guess—what wouldn't we give to know what went on in his head as he looked at the light-bulb after. He looked so long. He was horrid all day tho. Guess it's the 2 upper molars just breaking thru—sweet thing. (Yesterday he fell off the step "slide" *I tole you so*—only bit his tongue.)

Boy, on these warm days I really miss you. We've all been out playing. Dick makes gadgets for the kids all the time & all out together in the sun is so nice—& poor daddy—sweating it out like that! I just *can't* have you do this forever—we must find a way to get your burden lighter. It's nowhere you're giving us all this if you can't share it & we can't have you. Lou thinks I'm crazy to want you instead of the money—but I do—I feel *all* the time—I'm glad of the diversions, but that's what everything is—just something to hurry the day. I'm never really content without you near. If I didn't have you to think of & know we're together in our hearts at least, it would all be nothing.

There's a constant ache underneath & I *never* forget you for a moment—talk of you constantly & do *everything* with you in mind. I'm nil without you.

So to bed to dream & stroke some more tomorrow. Not even mail except ads & croc—oops—I do owe Mom one.

Guess I better take a hot bath tho it's so late, but I'll be stiff I fear else. What are you thinking?

I love you Neal—
CAROLYN

I think I shall call you Kieth in my book with Irish last name not yet set—Flannigan or similar. That not quite it—or is it Keith? They both look wrong now—you know the name.

Tryin to make a kiss print without lipstick which would smear.

TO NEAL CASSADY FROM CAROLYN CASSADY

Wednesday nite (3 more days!) [February 25, 1953
San Jose]

DEAREST SWEETEST LOVER-MAN:

The water's running—I must be brave—it's gonna hurt when I put all these scratches in hot water—but the vines are no more—all gone (except the digging of the roots). Amazing difference! Did it all with clippers with *1 inch* long blades. Hauled it all away too—no wheelbarrow, *more trash*.

I write this assuming you'll get it before you leave assuming you'll leave Sunday if you're coming at all. You asked for Sunseri's address so I risk it. It is: S. Sunseri, 67 Younger Ave. Good you get it there—he chewed out Rie for it being late—odd of him. But I've lots of favors to get from him so let's not give him the chance to complain of us.

Got your wonderful, clever, amusing, heart-warming, soul-stirring, happy, lovable sweet letter—now all I want is you. Please tho, as I say, we'll bear whatever you think best, daddy.

Chris collapsed tonite with a fever—the Doc suspects flu—so a couple days we'll probably have it too—damn—now that it's getting warm enough to open the house afternoons & the kids to be out all day. We've been too lucky I fear, but this is a hell of a time. Pray it doesn't develop, or only slightly, but everyone who's had it has been pretty sick.

The bedroom rearranging was not for looks but for convenience this time—looks worse, but I put the table by the bed & windows so I could see to type & sew & could have both shades up & look out windows—get nice afternoon light. Put the big chest back in 'cause it does have my clothes in & 'cause it's so ugly I don't want it to show as much as it did in dining room. This till we get what we want in here. Also the Ekotape is right by bed (give you any ideas? Did me.)

You are a great uncle—your nephew in SF, Murphy, had a boy. I'll save the announcement. So goo nite, great uncle Neal. I can't think of anything now but hearing whether you come or stay. This is the last I can write if you're coming home. I don't take *nothin* for granted with you! I love you madly & all you say is music to mine ears, I can't believe at last!

(Chris really sick this A.M.—damn!)

I have reserved 3 tickets to ballet March 9. Just *had* to ask Rie to go too, tho she insists on paying for her ticket—$1.80 each—not too good seat but as high as we can go & better than none, eh? I do hope you'll be here, but we can't get hi as we would by ourselves—no need—you make me feel hi anyway, rite?

When the time came for Neal's return home, he learned that he was required to stay for another two weeks, much to Carolyn's distress.

TO CAROLYN CASSADY

Feb. 27, '53, Noon
[Indio, California]

DEAR BABY;

Still waiting to be with you. It's gone from bad to worse. Hold yourself; they *won't* release me! Yet, business is about to fall off, & besides they must release me before March 13, since that's the time (end of 30 days) must be back on Coast Division. So lookie here, it's really for the best, why? You got not even enuf to last until March 10th ($26.00), I got only rest money (see enclosed check stub) & no bills can pay & on March 10th we have nothing, you out of money & so am I, what will we do when March 26th rolls around & no check coming in; oh, I long to be with you, I feel so fatigued guessing about you, & am sure you're as impatient as I to be together & I love you for trying to give me peace of mind by saying to me "don't worry, daddy, work as long as you must then hurry home."

I got all bills figured & all money facts at my fingertips, I know I'm lucky to work here until 10th (be home on 11th) because—then end here, no coast work yet, etc., etc. I paint, after unpapering, wall to bedroom & plant garden first thing & fix front yard, etc. I'm only sorry I'm not handy like Dick & could make toys for kids.

I've made over 225 already & will make about that clear on 10th, car & bills & living until 26th are in it, on 26th we get around 150–200 for the next 10 days (March 1–10) work, then will be on coast again.

I've been alone so much I sing songs aloud now, I also read Proust & am warning you to look out when I get home; I've not masturbated since the 26th & won't.

What can I say? What can I do? Must stay here in the hell away from you for 10 more days, only occasional music & Proust to keep me alive until I get to you. Around March 3rd I send you maximum of $20.00, minimum of 10–15 dollars to hold you until I get March 10th check & get my ass out of here & home to my sweet Blonde Baby & her sweet blonde kiddies

& " " " pussy
& " " " mind
& " " " pussy.

Must work 16 hours tonite going to Yuma, which is to say, wish I was home in bed with you tonite. Love, N.

Listen, don't fail to send me Sunseri's correct address so can mail him rent money order from here.

I've kept my promise, you kept yours? I know you have & you know I have, right?

I love you. You are really making me happy to know I have such a wife who makes such a fine home for her everloving Daddy.

I'm not sure of anything except I love you & I can write & I like life better daily if you only care for me.

Last page until I hear you & all the things you are.

TO NEAL CASSADY FROM CAROLYN CASSADY

Sunday [March 1, 1953]
1047 East Santa Clara St.
San Jose, California

DEAR NEAL,

Sunday is too awful—our peaceful living-room is fine for funnies & the concert & the almond tree almost thru blooming. I'm sick of telling you of things I enjoyed you are never here to share—We've had so *little* time "together." I fear again you've found other interests & that's no good an attitude. How *can* you stay away is the $65 question 'cause I know I couldn't for whatever reason.

I hope the call-back will enable you to compromise.

A big drunk just walked right in the front door—I'm still shaking—He *said* he wanted food—I gave him 50¢ 'cause I couldn't get him out—He grabbed Johnny & kissed him. Johnny screamed—The guy cried—(he has 3 of his own)—I called Sunseri for a lock—Think of all the times—especially nite I go to Woods for hours—Wish I had a husband at such times—fuck the money—if it means this—I guess

I'm incorrigibly selfish—Do as you think best—I'll try not be bitter again. Love, C.

TO NEAL CASSADY FROM CAROLYN CASSADY

Monday morn [March 2, 1953]
1047 East Santa Clara St.
San Jose, California

DEAR DADDY,

Good thing such a sweet letter that was. This has been a blue weekend & a worse morning. I got up feeling like something had been put over on me again, but I'm fighting the impulse. Last night I got panicky & felt I just couldn't stand another minute—5 years of this waiting, the last days of expecting being the hardest when I go around keeping everything straight, touching my hair, dressing me & the kids to look pretty for daddy & hearing every car all night within miles even tho I try not to listen. And all for naught, again & again. And now that it's all supposed to be right & we're just about to *begin*—why can't I begin—why can't I have it now? Everything is the same as ever on the surface.

But I can't fight the facts—we do need the money & I can't be so selfish—but I still feel bewildered by it all. I never could have made it if the Woods hadn't been such constant company. The worst times are the dinner hour & Sunday afternoons & evenings, or if they go out for a ride. They've been wonderful & included me most of the time, tho.

Now I'm sick 'cause you won't go to the ballet with me & that whole idea was as a new thing for us to do together. I don't even want to go now, but I guess Rie & I will. Seems too bad to spend the money—I don't care a thing about it without you. One more disappointment & WHY can't we do these things? There are so few things that interest us to go out to, but that damn RR rules everything. I hate playing second fiddle to that too. I've seen *no one* but I'm beginning to think I'm going to have to! Not banging of course & I'm not threatening as it sounds. I'm talking to my daddy & telling him I've *got* to have a daddy & I must be close to somebody. I can't do it any more alone—it's been so long marking time, waiting for you to be my daddy, and now you say you want to at last, but where are you? I'm terribly hungry for masculine attention—I guess that's why I strayed last year. I'm frantic to make up the ego I lost the last few years. Life's too short to wither away by myself. And the kids get it too if I get depressed—it's all wrong. You've got to love me—& poor you—I fear it'll take as strong & shocking a dose of the positive as it was of the negative to ever convince me you really do. All this delay & frustrations & loneliness aren't helping.

Now, I've blabbed it out—I can now say I know too you aren't really to blame & you're torn between all the demands I and we make on you & doing your best which is *the* best, & suffering it out to make it even better later—all the stuff I used to advocate. I think you're *terrific*!

Don't worry—I'll make it I know & try not to take it out on you any more. But this is almost a worse separation—I'm less prepared, I feel like there's less reason for it, yet here I am again. Down deep tho I have the warmth of your new words & I cling to them desperately & review the *facts* constantly. Oh why can't you come on the 8th? Another weekend & I'll die. I thought the letter was dated the 9th or 10th—surely you can think of an acceptable excuse? I can't believe they can do that—Al always gets around them. Now, now, that sounds awful. Thank God you don't do as he. I just mean 3 days *can't* be so important to them & it is to me. I keep getting afraid of what you want—feeling you'll do what you really want to do—except for money matters of course—but couldn't we manage without those 3 days? I can't see we've—well—I guess we would be starving now, but I thought you were going to have so *much* money. You've been gone a month already & only living expenses, eh? Damn, I must stop this—I don't want to discourage you—I'll cry to myself. I know you're doing the right thing & I'm just confused. Forgive me darling—it just all stems from wanting you so much & I hate myself as well as the situation that makes me feel & say such petty things.

The washing machine's busted & Johnny has a fever this A.M. I'll have to get medicine & the Woods' cost $5.69. I'll charge it on their account, but will have to pay them the cash from what you send—they're broke this week too, sold some books to live on. So I guess the money you're making is what I should be blessing & blessing you for persevering, instead of whining & complaining.

I wasn't going to write at all to avoid saying all these things. Now I have, maybe I can be better—so please don't be mad at me.

Jack just wrote a note asking you to write him a word about the RR.[7] He seems to be afraid the men don't like him & he'll have a bad time or something. I don't get it—such an affliction he has—what does he care what they think? As far as I can see nobody thinks much about anybody. But you tell him—I'm tongue-tied!

7. Letter from Kerouac to Carolyn Cassady, late February 1953, published in *Dear Carolyn* (p. 8).

Dear sweet Neal, you'd make me feel a lot better if you'd gripe more & tell me of your hardships! Part of my job you know & I want you to let me soothe you—be my baby too. That's why I'm overdoing it so—just to get petted, but if I could think of you more, I wouldn't so much. You're *too* nice to me.

It's cold as hell here now, snowed yesterday (about 1 minute) & real cold today. I planted some seeds so I guess they frizz. Jim Walters is preparing to build fence & remove shack since Rie & I cut vines. Everybody jumps when the Cassadys move in, eh what? New polish & wax outfit next door now (cars), just leasing it.

I love you—I'm afraid to think of it tho—I do. I love you, daddy, C.

B. Goodman on radio, "My Guy's Come Back." I thought I'd be singing that too—

TO CAROLYN CASSADY

[c. March 6, 1953
Indio, California]

DEAR CAROLYN,

It now looks as if I shall be stuck here until late Sunday A.M. at the earliest. There is a possibility I may not get away until Tuesday A.M. However, do please look for me Sunday; if I'm not there by noon you may notify your "Bill" you're free to indulge until Tuesday—at which time I hope to sneak in & catch you two in the act. Now dear, speaking of acts, I've got a couple of new ones to try & I'm saving up my Indian juice to make it good. N.

TO CAROLYN CASSADY

[Postmarked March 7, 1953
Indio, California]

DEAR LOVER;

Things still in uproar around here. One report says no releases definitely. Another says all loaners cut Monday. At any rate, job or no, be home Tues. A.M. There, no one else but you, ever.

Love, N.

Neal arrived back in San Jose on March 10 and resumed his brakeman's job on the coastal division of the Southern Pacific. A month later, on the night of Friday, April 10, Neal was accidentally knocked from a boxcar, breaking most of the bones in his ankle and foot. He was taken to the Southern Pacific hospital in San Francisco, where Carolyn visited him the next morning. In the following days they began considering claims against the railroad company for the accident.

TO NEAL CASSADY FROM CAROLYN CASSADY

Monday morning, April 13, 1953
1047 East Santa Clara Street
San Jose, California

DEAREST NEAL,

Looks like I can't get up for a couple days—Vera is coming in the hospital tomorrow & Wednesday while Kenny has his tonsils out. (Can we buy a new pen when our SP ship comes in?)

I feel as tho I didn't see you at all yesterday—nuts. Don't know what to say now—but talk to you to myself all the time. I have such a lovely feeling of peace about you & me. I feel like a new bride & want to talk all the time about my wonderful husband.

But here we go on another stint of building habits separately. We never get the chance to put our new feelings into practice—but I hang on to the hope you'll be home *all* the time, the rest of the year! or most of it anyway—at least all the warm summer. We'll have a great time & I'll try & see that you don't get bored & restless.

Johnny is being a beast. He climbs up the chairs by himself now & on the table. He turns on the kitchen light all the time. We're due for some falls I suspect.

I want to hear everything that happened to you—start to finish—I feel cheated again. It was so hard yesterday, & as you say, you'd told it already. But you can tell *me* how much it hurt & such as that. Why can't I be near you now! *Six* weeks again.

I called Corman[8]—got him up—said he'd only said on report he knew nothing because he wasn't there. No mention of G at all.

I'm praying for you, darling, but please don't get too anxious for the money—don't let *anything* bother you, daddy, will you?

8. A Southern Pacific railroad brakeman.

What a blessed relief it is not to have any more doubts or fears about us. I feel so confident, sure, safe & excited about you & at last feel free to love you like I want to. Look out.

Take it easy if you can tolerate stupid hospitals & nurses. Don't fall in love with any, will ya?

I'll probably be up Thursday or any day after. Won't be able to stand it. Saturday for sure. Friday I'm watching the Woods kids at dinnertime. Wish I could get all chores done so you & me could just play after you get back. Wonder how long it takes to get any claims.

I love you, love you forever, daddy

CAROLYN

P.S. Guess you lost Wayward Bus.[9] Wasn't it in your clothes? I'll get another.

DARLIN'—

This is what they gave me. In order for you to have Friday April 10th as day starting claim, you'll have to mail this by Thursday or Fri—so I'll mail it. It'll get there as soon as I, I think, maybe sooner.

Find out what that "I waive" means—tho I guess it's just to release the hosp. information. It's worded so funny you better make sure—as tho you wouldn't know. You fill left page, Dr. fills right.

Mr. Walters says a switchman he knows got $60,000—whee. Also another had to threaten to go to court before they'd raise the ante where he wanted it—so shoot high—get advice before moving. Let's do our best, yet stay in the job—right?

Miss you so much. The car helps a little but not to replace you. I love you—be happy, kip smilink.

See you soon—

CAROLYN

After a month in the hospital and several operations, Neal arrived home on crutches. Meanwhile, Kerouac had been recalled to the railroad and took a job at San Luis Obispo, although Neal wrote recommending that he try to arrange a transfer to San Francisco.

9. *The Wayward Bus,* a novel by John Steinbeck (1947).

May 6, 1953
[San Jose]

DEAR BROTHER JACKSON;

Well it's about time you wrote, I was fearing you farted out on top that mean mountain or slid under while pissing in Pismo, beach of flowers, food and foolishness, but I knew the fear was ill-founded for balancing it in my thoughts of you, much stronger and valid if you weren't dead, was a realization of the experiences you would be having down there, rail, home, and the most important, climate, by a remembrance of my own feelings and thoughts (former low, or more exactly, nostalgic and unreal; latter hi) as, for example, I too seemed to spend time looking out upper floor windows at sparse, especially nighttimes, traffic in females—old or young. And this knowledge, that you were sticking it out and in much the same fashion as I myself often had, made for a certain added feeling of similarity to you, which has been missing, more or less more as time passed, and now directs me to this duty of writing concurrent, that is, to a new concern for you, as far as self-centered me can muster, that is independent of personal or subjective relationship with you and hence I've double reason to write.

You must go immediately to crew clerk, ask for SF, if refused see trainmaster then as last hope write Galen crew clerk in SF; say something to them, like must go and settle mother in new home in SF, and must arrange nurse for her as crippled or something and stick to it, whatever you decide to say, and hurry since rushing up here now and I'd give a blind wager they are there too, or about to, anyhow get transfer, etc.

May 7

DEAR FATHER JOHNSON;

Your latest lesson in Freethinking shows Martin Luther had nothing on you and if Catholicism was so easily dented by him perhaps you could stagger Einstein as well or join forces with that writer in Amazing Stories whose Battle of The Brains flipped me enuf to go on and read. . . .

May 8

DEAR SON;

The usual thing, you can see, is happening. Each day I decide to get hi and write Jack, instead, I just get hi, so to get this off today I'm playin it straight, hairy and close to the vest by dictating to Carolyn. Naturally, your first month's board bill, including free car, gasoline, etc., is paid for (over and above) by the 56$. After that . . . cash on the barrelhead? or kitchen table? Better hurry and get here before Miss Green flees the coop.

Most sincerely,
BROTHER NEAL
AND SISTER C.

Neal spent some of his recovery time trying to work on his book but found it difficult. He wrote to Kerouac for help. Jack visited the Cassadys but moved once more to San Francisco's skid row. Lonely there, he wrote to Dusty Moreland in New York, inviting her to come West for a vacation.

TO JACK KEROUAC

[c. May 1953
San Jose]

. . . the real thing, Jack, is that I'm completely stuck with my book & unless you come out & stab me in the ass with just enuf to get me over this hump I'll be still stuck until D. Day.

If Dusty wants vacation tell her can send her RR pass good to SF & back for 90 days & cost $20.00. Or any girl you want.

Charley Mew, a merchant seaman friend of Neal's whose young daughter Linda the Cassadys sometimes looked after while he was away, brought news that Jack had quit his railroad job and shipped out to sea.

TO NEAL AND CAROLYN CASSADY FROM CHARLEY MEW

May 27, 1953
c/o Nel's Hotel
719 Ellis St.
SF, Calif.

DEAR FRIENDS,

I meant to get this in the mail a few days ago. How are you and all the kiddies? It goes without saying that I'm worried but in my case it's natural.

I have not been able to ship out yet, nor have I obtained a job. Seems that every place I apply they are laying men off or else I'm too short.[10] During the war my height was never questioned. Supply & demand in manpower makes a hell of a difference. They even offered a prospective employee a cigar & paid him a compliment at the least provocation. How times do change.

One great problem I have solved is that I have found a home for Linda when I ship out. They seem like very nice people. The lady is a girl-scout master. Has 31 girls or so. They live in Santa Cruz, on the outskirts.

I cannot thank you two enough for all you have done for me and Linda. When I return to sea I shall not forget you and if you won't take money then some gifts it will be. So think of what you would like and let me know. Should I make a (around the world) ship—and I feel certain I will—then you would have many places to choose a gift from. The Orient, France, India, etc. Or maybe you would like a surprise.

I'm really serious, so if there is something you have always wanted from overseas please don't hesitate to say so.

I saw Jack last night & he says he quit the RR and is going to sea. Says he managed to ship out through Seamen's International Union—a Lundeburge outfit. For shame! Oh, well Jack isn't acquainted with the labor movement.

10. Charley Mew is portrayed as Jimmy Low in *Desolation Angels*, where Kerouac describes him as just four feet two inches tall, although in *Some of the Dharma*, Charley Low is said to be four feet ten inches. Mew is also portrayed as Charley and Jimmy Low in *Visions of Cody* and *Book of Dreams*.

Jack got a bedroom steward's job and he will be making beds & changing linens. Can you feature that?

Jack told me my little Linda is fine and her being in your care I haven't worried too much. Although she is constantly on my mind. What worries me most is when she crosses streets. That reminds me of her shoes. I guess they are just about worn out.

I can thank that son of a bitch Lundeburge for all of this. It's amazing how a man like he can indirectly cause many people to suffer. I guess he is what is meant when the Bible mentions DEVIL. Of course I don't believe in the Bible but some of the characters it portrays are often descriptive and applicable to places and people.

Well friends, so long for now. Will probably see you Friday? Good luck and my best wishes always. As always,

CHARLES

P.S. Please read to Linda:

Hello Linda dear, this is your Daddy writing and hoping you are fine and having lots of fun.

Please obey Carolyn and Neal, and be nice to them and the children.

I love you very much Linda, and I hope you are happy.

Many kisses and all my love.

Your daddy, CHARLES

Neal relayed the news about Kerouac to Ginsberg and, missing Jack's presence, invited Allen to visit his San Jose home.

TO ALLEN GINSBERG

June 1st, 1953
[San Jose]

DEAR ALLEN;

Jack has quit the RR and got himself a job washing dishes on a ship bound for Alabama, maybe New York,[11] then Korea and—if he stays on, which I'm personally sure he won't—then a continued shuttle between SF and Korea. So that takes care of the wandering

11. Kerouac wrote about his maritime experiences of summer 1953 in a piece called "Slobs of the Kitchen Sea," published in *Lonesome Traveler*.

minstrel for a while, except that thru his own lack of schedule (not doing what one expects him to do) he missed the huge 18 cent letter you sent him and so he agreed to send an address to me and I will forward it, after reading it as he said I could; right now it's in a nigger hepcat's room and will be for two weeks more before I retrieve it.

I got a bone chip still unassimilated in my healing foot so will have another operation next month and tho I have a walking cast on now I can't walk because it's ill-fitting and the ankle itself isn't ready anyhow, etc.

I might here remark that your last letter to me[12] was a real fine one and I wish only that I could answer you in kind (good descriptions, intelligent questions, keen insight into me and life, interesting new kick, etc.) but I find it much too hard to even get out half a page a month on my book so you can see I'm really exerting myself, tho it's taken 3 weeks and more to complete it, to get this letter off to you and still make it more than just a one paragraph note, tho I realize it's not much more than that and not clear or pretty or anything—it might be moreso if I rewrote or thought it out as I went along but again that would make me work as hard as on the book and we both know that is taking too long, indeed threatens to stretch out another ten or 20 years and might better be called "The First Half" or "All Of It," so I ask again please excuse, understand and write to me oftener and anyhow, throwing yourself into a letter as only you can and despite the fact that I don't, as much as I should anyhow; the real fact is that I can think of nothing to say that matters for my mind is blank. Take heart, dear Allen, and write again.

NEAL (over)

I might come to NY next June, after a May 30th stop at Indianapolis, & tho I know it's much too far away for plans I hope to see you & regain again something of the spirit of old, if only over a bottle.

You really are a poet, you know, & as shown by your continued interest in same; who else but a poet could look for hours at mystical & metaphysical pictures & rhymes; not impatiently, except hi; tho you might discourage often and/or deeply, remember the thing, whatever it is, that makes it worth it; to me reading alone is almost enuf reason

12. Ginsberg had written to Neal on May 14 (*As Ever,* pp. 139–44).

for continuing the struggle, but perhaps that's due to the flat-on-back weeks in Hospital, where that was all one could do.

Chipper Cass they call me.

Love,

N.

Incidentally, you know, of course, that this big house I got is only for you to come & enjoy for as long as you wish. Why not visit me soon & get kicks of easy life—come on out, I dare you, there's nothing to it & there's everything here for fun, mind, culture etc. Come on, so says Carolyn & myself & real gone kiddies.

N.

Neal also attempted to get in touch again with his old friend Hal Chase.

TO PARENTS OF HAL CHASE

[c. June 1953
San Jose]

DEAR PARENTS;
(or Hal, I hope)

As an old acquaintance who has for far too many years (a full half dozen or more, at least) been denied any knowledge of Haldon, I am here humbly requesting his present address so that I may drop him a line. Allow yourself assurance, nervous parents, that my motivation in this is simply one of attempting to give Hal the momentary lift of diversion that any chatty letter might give him on a perhaps boring or depressing day.

I, myself, have for five years been a brakeman (now conductor) on the Southern Pacific out of San Francisco. I am blessed with a lovely wife and three wonderful children, two girls and a younger boy, and they so fill my time that if it were not for a recent industrial accident forcing me to the inactivity of hospital convalescence I probably would not, even now, be writing to you, despite that Hal has often been on my mind over the years. I do trust you will heed my genuine appeal (and cater to what might be called only a nostalgic whim if it were not that he has always meant so much to me, as a friend to be admired and—yes—envied) for word of his whereabouts when I tell you that, for my part, I have *never* known a finer, fairer, more interesting, or as intelligent a young man as was Haldon when I had the pleasure of his proximity at all-too-brief intervals during the mid-forties.

Thanking you most gratefully for soon using my self-addressed envelope for the purpose it's enclosed,

I remain,
Sincerely and respectfully,
[NEAL L. CASSADY]

The Cassadys received word from their friend the merchant seaman Al Sublette that he was also due to sail out.

TO CAROLYN CASSADY FROM AL SUBLETTE

June 17, 1953
[San Francisco]

DEAR CAROLYN,

Received your note Monday and was glad to hear from you. No, I haven't shipped out as yet but I expect to in the near future. How is everything at home? Hope you kids are making it this crazy month of June.

How are the children and San Jose? Hope Neal's leg is mending. Perhaps I'll come down some weekend before I sail. If not, I'll write and let you know which ship I'm on.

Concerning the Ginsberg letter, received word from Jack about a week after I last saw you, postmarked Long Beach. Forwarded letter to:

Jack Kerouac
c/o S.S. William Carruth
Transfuel Corp.
25 Broadway
The Apple (NYC)

If I'm not here the 22nd, you'll know I'm at my Union Hall trying to make the President Polk which is due in the 21st. And so—until later,

AL

*With a letter of June 23 (*As Ever, *pp. 146–50) Allen had sent Neal a book of "mystical pictures," thinking that his birthday was in late June. In his letter*

Allen brought news of their joint friends, noting that Jerry Newman was about to issue some recordings of Dizzy Gillespie that he had made in 1941, and that he'd thought of titling one of the tunes (an improvisation on "Exactly Like You") "Ginsberg," but had eventually decided to call it "Kerouac." Still feeling abandoned by his friends, Neal repeated his offer to accommodate Ginsberg at San Jose.

TO ALLEN GINSBERG

June 29, 1953
[San Jose]

DEAR ALLEN, ORIENTAL OGLER;

Thanks for oxherd pictures, I like much. My birthday Feb 8. Tape recorder is Ekotape. Your letter to Jack he has by now at: JLKerouac, care of S.S. William Carruth, Transfuel Corp. 25 Broadway, The Apple (NYC); letter not delayed by me but by it, I mean him, the thing from another world—of his own making, in which he'll allow only himself. Above unwanted marks of hand etc. made by son John Allen during moment typewriter untended. Haven't seen letter, so don't know of Green Auto, would like to. How does one investigate verbal seas? would like to myself if knew how, and not too much work.

Anytime you need great climate—winter average 55, summer 69—sunshine 364¾ days a year—beautiful country with ocean on right and mountains on left—rich people, of U.S.! 3003 counties mine, Santa Clara, ranks 19th in per capita wealth, produces ¼ billion lbs. of prunes a season, rich land with apricot, fig, almond and walnut trees in my back yard, blackberries too, nine room house ancient estate, then rest home, then Mexicans got it then Carolyn who clean up their mess and make great castle of it. Etc., then, come on out here to the west where men are men and the women are damn glad of it. Oh yes, and quince tree too, in front yard along with another almond tree and beautiful gigantic palm, roses etc., etc., even old tea-weeds in vacant lot next door. And there is great private room for you with great oversize desk, this machine, Ekotape, radio-clock, coffee table, etc., french windows, weird lights, you see, the next 90 days I have absolutely nothing to do; will be going to beach, driving up and down country, etc., and if you came now—esp. to escape NYC heat—we would have great vacation with no money worries, much time for everything; if you don't come out here now, on bus for 50 bucks, which in one month alone you will make up by having free rent, food, recreation, etc., you would not see me except about 4 or 5 hours in 36 or 48, because in about October I'll return for RR work for 2 or 3 months before being laid off, or very slow work, until the third month of 1954, begin gradually busier season until Xmas. So, if you aren't here this summer, come next winter, lowest temperature is low forties, between January and April or May. Do your best in this 'cause life so simple good and easy here that it's actually unreal seeming, like a joke or dream, no reason for worries, tho from old experience I try to, and all troubles of world like mirage one reads about only to keep abreast and pass time. If you want to suffer in frantic east, do; if want calm and midget auto races, do come; ball games to see, parades, archery, grammar school across street, jr. hi, block away, big new modernistic San Jose hi directly in back, so all year I watch from garage roof, sport, football, baseball, track, hi jump, broad and pole vault, etc.

No personal autographs on cast except Ike's and Joe Stal.[13] Very true what you say about you and Gotham Life; much sorry, please accept my apology, I knew what I said not true even as I wrote it for sake of faint and false fear I thought I should have, thank you. You always very accurate in appraisal of people and situations, your chief attribute, in fact. Glad to hear about John Hollander,[14] always knew he'd make it that way tho, funny, had no doubt of his success at all. This damn tiny paper, can't write since always tempt to chop up every thought by supposedly pithy sentences, do not work because instead one just feels free to be sloppy in ideas as well, so no thinking, no good letter, only thing put down in here is first word that arrives in head. Great telegram to Ike,[15] too bad, I agree with you, did so to everybody long before your letter came. My phone number in San Jose home here is: CYpress 7-0295; make it station to station since I'll always be home as long as there is anyone here to answer for (I mean phone, not that last for).

Enclosed find carbon of letter sent to Hal Chase at old Denver address. I doubt if anyone there anymore so wasted effort unless hap-

13. Neal jests. "Ike" was Dwight D. Eisenhower, president of the USA. Joseph Stalin was the Soviet leader.

14. John Hollander (b. 1929) was a poet friend of Ginsberg's and Kerouac's at Columbia. Allen had written to Neal to tell him that Hollander's work had been published in *Kenyon Review* and that he had become a scholarly instructor in Illinois.

15. Ginsberg had sent a telegram to President Eisenhower, pleading for a stay of execution of the convicted Soviet atom spies Julius and Ethel Rosenberg. They eventually died in the electric chair on June 19, 1953.

pen to have parents forwarding address. I understand Hal's father is dead, but I no mention in letter.

Took cast off this week; put ace bandage on, told me to walk, but can't since foot too far out of line and tendons unbendable, etc. Final removal-of-bone-chip operation yet to come. How's your brother, mother and father, W. Carlos Williams, Ezra P., T.S.E., W.H.A., D.T., C. Shapiro and C. Sol. and A. Gin?[16] Did you know flying saucers are Bees (honey, you know) from Mars? Did you know I have one dose of scopolamine (twilite sleep they give mothers in childbirth) from black Mandrake plant which even most ardent Hunckes say about that "Once is enuf"; have had for almost 2 years now and still haven't found the 36 to 48 hours of free time necessary to indulge. Save till you arrive to hold my head and direct my feet toward pisser. tytyui is Hello from Jamie (middle kid) after-reward making up for spank; she just spilled my beer but that not cause of spank which I don't know she (wife) did it outside just now. Yanks and Giants for pennants, war within 3 years, Ike win again in 56, 4 minute mile by Wes Santee of Kansas State, 60 foot shotput by O'Brien of USC, 200 foot discus by Innes of USC, finish of FIRST THIRD in 55 at Xmas, Death of Kerouac in 1970, Cassady 76, Ginsberg 2000, Carr before you are, B.B. [Burroughs] same year as Jack, and everybody rich before IT comes hard for JLK, NLC, Carr and Burroughs, easy for you, but take too long. John Allen Cassady is and will be the greatest thing to ever hit the world, and remember, like Drew Pearson,[17] I'm 83% accurate.

By the fall, Neal had recovered sufficiently to take a job in a local parking lot. Hoping to resume his railroad work early in the new year, he wrote offering the parking lot job to Allen and Jack.

TO ALLEN GINSBERG

Nov. 20, 1953
San Jose

DEAR ALLEN;

For reasons better left untold since they are so diverse and elaborate as to defy putting here, I am not forwarding the long 4

16. I.e., poets and writers Ezra Pound, T. S. Eliot, W. H. Auden, Dylan Thomas, Karl Shapiro, Carl Solomon, Allen Ginsberg.

17. Drew Pearson (1897–1969). Journalist and broadcaster.

page letter which I've spent the last two days writing to you and Jack; perhaps I'll save to show it to you and he when you arrive. I have a job for you or Jack or both of you if it would be too much of a drag for either of you to sit on your ass for 8 hours a day—one could sit here on parking lot in A.M., the other in P.M.—for I'm running a lot so slow all I do is sit and collect, the customers park their own cars. I think it will be a real kick to see you, a man who can't drive, a big important parking lot manager, ten bucks a day plus lunch money six days a week and all you do is sit and read or write and play with yourself; that's what I do anyhow. So there is your job.

Now fortunately you'll arrive after the xmas rush so I'll hold the job till you get here then I'll go back on RR; don't worry about it, an easier job you've never had; Cathy, my oldest kid, could run the lot except that she's not quite conquered sums yet, and, of course, the strict child labor laws.

Do not send me any money nor fear for living expenses nor feel you should in any way pay your way at my house because I've got plenty enuf for all of us including Jack and will have even more, much more than all of us put together have ever had, in the springtime, so I repeat you won't need a single penny when you get here, so I advise spending *all* your loot on a bus ticket and get here broke; now please do this one thing for me as well as persuade Jack of all the hundreds of reasons for accompanying you—whom I hold responsible for presenting to him in such a powerful fashion that it will be quite impossible to refuse us his warm companionship.

*Jack replied to Carolyn on December 3 (*SL*, pp. 403–4), saying that he was interested in working the parking lot and hoped to arrive in San Jose around December 29.*

TO JACK KEROUAC

Dec. 4 [1953] P.M.
[San Jose]

DEAR JACK;

Your plan of working parkinglot until Spring, RR Summer & Mexico Winter is most practical & just the thing. The first part—parkinglot—is already for you to take over, I work it daily & will do so rest of month & Jan 1st I begin breaking you in on job & when you feel good & ready to handle it, i.e. know all monthly parkers, how to set up lot each day, various ways of knocking down on boss & customers for at least lunch money, plus, etc., then you keep job until Spring RR rush—April—late March—& then give job to Brother Ginsberg who will be here then to learn job & hold it thru summer, or whatever. So that's about it till you get here. Be careful, forget God (no such thing) forget being farmer (far too late, or soon) say Hello to your mother for me, bring all your books, ideas of life & any amount of oolong tea you find to bolster stock at hand for New Year's Eve party.

Love, N.

Dec. 6

DEAR JACK;

Great! Let's make it a great New Year—I've the highest hopes & utmost confidence it must be so. A little bird done tole me.

Neal & I just got back from a racy game of tennis—we play every Sunday. We're pretty well matched—rotten.

Jamie had her tonsils out this week. A big experience for her & she came thru noble. She's sweeter than ever.

I've finally learned how to make good pies—name your brand.

We've no more cats (animals)—the last hit the dust yesterday.

Nuff chit chat crost the fence.

Hurry on down to my house—don't be late.[18]

Love,
CAROLYN

In fact, Jack was not able to leave as soon as he had hoped and did not arrive in San Jose until February 5, in time for Neal's twenty-eighth birthday.

18. "Hurry on down to my house, honey, ain't nobody home but me . . ." The million-selling 1947 record "Hurry on Down," written and sung by Nellie Lutcher.

1954

Kerouac lived with the Cassadys in February, working alongside Neal at the parking lot. On a car seat Neal found and read the book Many Mansions *by Gina Cerminara, the story of the mystic Edgar Cayce (1877–1945), and became fascinated by his theories of reincarnation. Meanwhile, Jack had taken an interest in Buddhism, and their discussions on the relative merits of each other's beliefs became lively. As there appeared to be no common meeting point, they agreed to differ, and when previous jealousies again threatened to erupt, Carolyn drove Jack back to the Cameo Hotel in San Francisco and stayed with him awhile. While there, Kerouac wrote his* San Francisco Blues *before returning home to Richmond Hill. Allen Ginsberg had left New York at the end of 1953, traveling to Florida, Cuba, and Mexico, and was hoping to join the Cassadys in San Jose. When they had not heard from him in months, Neal and Carolyn became worried.*

TO ALLEN GINSBERG

April 23, 1954
1047 East Santa Clara Street
San Jose 27
California

DEAR ALLEN;

Was notified this day by Western Union that you had not called for the money I sent you April 9th, so they have returned it to me, minus fee, 3.83. Naturally I'm very worried for your health and safety and wonder where the hell you are; here I was expecting you to show up hot on the heels of your last letter, but suddenly my money is returned and there's no, no Allen, no news, nothing. I'm writing a note to US Embassy, Mex City (the jerks returned all three letters I wrote you there) and one to Bill Burroughs in Tangiers and for godsake Allen write him; I get practically daily letters from him wailing over your desertion of him; he's desperate, believe me; you better write your father too, he's written here once long ago and if I don't hear from you before the 1st week of May I'm writing him to tell of your disappearance and at the same time, early May, I'm getting my lawyer to advise me on how best to find you, wire police at Salto De Aqua, embassy at Mex City, or what. So you better contact me or I'm scouring Mexico for you, in person if all else fails, tho I intend to return to work next week, and if I don't hear something soon I'll know you're in Jail or on the trail, dead that is, with buzzards long since digested your meat, if you they'd eat, who knows?!! . . . well I sure don't and that is why I write asking you to alleviate my condition.

Thank you.

Love,
N.

P.S. Jack suddenly decides to live away from here; goes to San Francisco to live in 3 dollar room for week then even more suddenly returns to New York via bus and is home with mama now. I lost parking lot job and was refused 300 bucks back pay which can't collect; but things here are rosy and will be even golden soon.

In May, as compensation for his railroad injury, Neal was awarded nearly $30,000. After payment of the attorney's fee and insurance deductions, this figure was reduced to $16,747. The Cassadys used some of the money to buy a car and were also looking for a new house. Neal sent $1,000 to Diana, with the suggestion that she should read about Edgar Cayce.

TO DIANA HANSEN CASSADY

May 23, 1954
[San Jose]

DEAR DIANA;

I have 1000 dollars for you; can send at once & will when I receive a little note from you c/o General Delivery, San Jose, Calif. Please answer in long hand & perhaps an intimate detail or exact fact from the time of our cohabitation would be helpful, as well as the exact name you want me to make out the cashier's check that you can cash at once in any bank & which I will send when you answer.

Love, NEAL

Thank you.

P.S. Naturally I wish you could use a hundred or 2 of the thousand for a quick 4 or 5 day trip to SF here & see me as you once did in 1950, late Sept., remember? True love & best wishes! Also, I know a book can change your life.

N.

TO DIANA HANSEN CASSADY

[c. May 1954
San Jose]

DEAR DIANA;

There is a stipulation: you must use several of these dollars to buy to read:

"There is a River" by Tom Sugrue. "Many Mansions" by Gina Cerminara.

Then write to Virginia Beach, Virginia & order "Edgard Cayce Readings" 1945 & 1947 & it will change your life, your Ma & Grandma too.

Love, NEAL

*With the compensation trial over, Neal was able to resume his railroad work. In a letter of May 12 (*As Ever, *pp. 179–82) the Cassadys heard at last from Ginsberg, who had been stranded in Xibalba, Mexico, but was now on his way to California.*

TO ALLEN GINSBERG

June 8, 1954
[San Jose]

DEAR ALLEN;

We countenance no further delay, so, if of bad thumb luck you are attacked, call us collect at CYpress 7-0295, San Jose, & I'll come for you in my new car. But, since I may be working when you call you might have to wait somewhere as long as 24 hours before I arrive; therefore, go to expensive hotel in town where you happen to get stuck & I'll pay bills or bail you out or whatever.

But, better, just thumb on up & do above only in emergency; of course if you get within a couple of hundred miles just call & if I'm not here Carolyn will come in car to get you.

Love,
N.

Ginsberg stayed with the Cassadys for two months, until Carolyn found him in bed with Neal. She asked Allen to leave and drove him to San Francisco a few days later. (Ginsberg writes about his stay in the Cassady household in his Journals: Mid-Fifties, 1954–1958, *edited by Gordon Ball, pp. 13–52.)*

Neal was also in trouble with his railroad work. Due possibly to his color blindness, which he had previously been able to bluff his way through, he was reprimanded for the use of a red rather than a green flag.

TO MR. BAYS

July 14, 1954
[San Jose]

DEAR MR. BAYS;

Regarding your question, "what is a red flag used for?" I find after careful checking that a red flag is to be used to display stop indication only, as rule 10 indicates.

Before answering your second question I beg your indulgence as I attempt to explain the cause of my ignorance on this point. I understand it is not clarified in the book of rules examination. What first led me to believe one could hiball[1] with a red flag was one day long ago when as head brakeman on a drag east I was so hiballed, and to be helpful I threw off a green flag to the flagman as we passed. He cursed and yelled and threw the green flag back. This convinced me the interpretation of the rules in this instance must be, that it is the sign given which counts, not the color indication, on the road that is, excepting herders of course.

1. *Hiball:* the signal the brakeman gave to the conductor to start the train going.

Subsequent red flag hiballings as recently as the current construction at Libby's in Sunnyvale only strengthened my erroneous belief. It may seem odd that I never asked anyone about this. However on all of my passenger runs (not many, it is true), from first to last, I have been acting on my misinterpretation of this rule, and no one has bothered to correct my misunderstanding, though they often stood beside me even as I improperly hiballed, and so the matter dropped from my mind.

So when you yelled, "What's a red flag for?" I couldn't comprehend your meaning. When I finally understood, once others had confirmed you, I must confess I was considerably embarrassed. Before that I felt indignant and the reason for this letter is to apologize for my presumption.

Question two: Why was I out of uniform? There was excess heat below Salinas, 104 degrees at San Miguel, and there were seven cars between me and any passengers—four deadheads and the two rear Pullmen full of half clothed soldiers who had been travelling for four days from Illinois. More especially I understood this to be common practice even on the very same car with 71's passengers.

Upon rereading, this whole thing sounds like childish rationalization and as far as that goes has nothing at all to do with the case. Strictly speaking I'm guilty on both counts. But the real value irrespective of what happens here is that your seemingly simple question about the flag and this attempt of mine to answer has brought out in me an awareness. As my student days receded an unconscious development of prima-donna-itis proceeded. Your chewing on me has made me aware of this tendency, and in closing I wish to thank you for calling me on it.

Sincerely,
NEAL L. CASSADY
Flagman on 71, 7-13-54

In August 1954 the Cassadys used some of their compensation money to purchase a house in Los Gatos, ten miles southwest of San Jose. They also invested $5,000, and this doubled within a year. Jack wrote a long letter on September 9, which he sent to Neal at the railroad yard office. He continued to praise Neal's writing and urged him to complete the work on The First Third.[2] *But Neal*

2. This letter is partially published in *SL,* pp. 471–75. In it, Kerouac mentions several episodes from the "Joan Anderson" letter that are not to be found in the surviving extract and were presumably in the section that was lost.

was writing virtually nothing at that time and did not even reply to Jack. With Neal established on a regular commuter run between San Jose and San Francisco, he was able to spend many hours in the city, where Ginsberg was now settled, and to mingle with his newfound friends. Toward the end of the year, Neal began having an affair with a tall redhead, Natalie Jackson.[3]

3. Natalie Jackson is portrayed as Rosie Buchanan in Kerouac's *Dharma Bums,* and as Rosemarie in *Desolation Angels, Big Sur,* and *Book of Dreams.*

1955

Carolyn became aware of Neal's affair with Natalie Jackson when she came across some notes while washing Neal's jeans.

TO NATALIE JACKSON

January 5, 1955, 5 A.M.

N TO NAT;

We both goofed, I feel, want to feel, such sympathy . . . thru having done it myself many times, over & in the bowl, like in youth a green or too strong cigar. . . . Beside which comes to mind the times of realizing fully the agony of other New Year party drunk friends. . . . Most particularly at the exact moment just before the actual regurgitating begins . . . for you, (the sympathy) as the pity one entity would have for another who is reaping similar karma as he himself must face, has faced.

TO NEAL CASSADY FROM NATALIE JACKSON

April 12, 1955, 11:10 P.M.
[San Francisco, California]

DEAR N.:

We're stimulated by pleasurable unexpected surprises. i.e. I love you more now, but better. In the everyday I haven't tried that yet or in another vein. The grass looks greener, etc.

I know your body—It's a mystery to me. I half forget about you then your body surprises mine; another awareness of a solution to the non-existent a moment before mystery disclosing itself.

I know every inch—mole, blemish, hair, scar, pore yet don't think of them really (except maybe a tenderness for a favorite or outstanding one) until I see them again—then the flash of memories, and have probably felt with my hands or touched and sensed and tasted all the feelings and your reactions to touch—and the different tastes of the various parts of your body yet it excites me more than someone or something that is as yet unexplored to me. I love you.

N.

At 5 A.M. this sounds like label on a bottle of English lice killer or care and treatment of scabies. Is best over absinthe.

TO NATALIE JACKSON

[Spring 1955]

How does one begin?, esp. after so long? Our moment was too brief; (as this train is too fast, the roadbed too rough, my penmanship too poor for good writing yet, my memory dwelling on those sweet brown eyes pouring out—into me for that instant—a need matching my own intensity, a lack simple & true of release of tension resultant from our "Human Condition."

I dreamt of you last nite; rather, it was 2 dreams, one night, one morning, among other things—including verification of validity of authentic vibration between us, as opposed to simple sex hunger, actually similar level of mind. I met your San Jose girl friend in the train yard & suggested I take her to you just so I could see you again. That was the main part of the dream, the desire to find you again.

Thinking back I find I've written almost no letters for maybe 5 yrs., a love letter for twice that; to begin again then—

I believe it quite possible, but rare, to feel a perfect lover, one with whom you are one because each match, as radios attuned perhaps . . . [ends]

Following Carolyn's discovery, Neal moved out of their Los Gatos home for a while, and into an apartment with Ginsberg and his new lover, Peter Orlovsky,[1] in San Francisco.

1. Peter Orlovsky (b. 1933) became the longtime partner of Allen Ginsberg after they met in San Francisco, in December 1954. A poet best known for his collection *Clean Asshole Poems & Smiling Vegetable Songs* (1978), he is represented in Kerouac's work by George *(The Dharma Bums)* and Simon Darlovsky *(Desolation Angels)*.

TO CAROLYN CASSADY

[May 10, 1955
Los Gatos, California]

DEAR MA;

I hate myself & you know it, but, I looked long & hard at my son last nite & I fully realize my responsibilities, plus, I am in full fear of my feeling that once a man starts down he never comes back—never,

N.

Neal had begun gambling on horse races, using a system of his own that he considered foolproof. Certain of winning, he persuaded Natalie to impersonate Carolyn, and the two of them withdrew $2,500 of the Cassadys' investment from the bank to use as stake money. Unfortunately, most of the sum was lost, and worse still, Carolyn was alerted to the fraud by a suspicious banker in Cupertino.

TO NEAL CASSADY FROM CAROLYN CASSADY

Wednesday [autumn 1955
Los Gatos, California]

DEAR NEAL,

In case I'm too sleepy to keep you awake tonight, I'll talk at you by this less painful method.

What did we say about getting greater tests when stronger? It sure happens fast. The good Lord decided I should know about your other deal in Cupertino, too. I keep wondering why and am going on the assumption it's to give me an "opportunity" to overcome rather than one to get even. This time it seems Mr. Scoville neglected to get you to sign the receipt. So he got your LG address from the SJ 1st Natl and called me. It was pretty funny because the first time he called I said no, we hadn't gone east nor had my mother died. I really thought he had the wrong Cassady, because of the Cupertino origin. *Cupertino?* Anyway, you clever boy you, when he persisted and I had to admit ignorance of the deal (why must you make it so complicated?) he was going to sell the stock immediately and swear out a warrant for Natalie's arrest. I thereby dashed over there and countersigned the whole thing and said for him to hold it. He is at least more human than some and seemed to understand better. He wasn't eager to prosecute as I suspect the fellow at LG would have been. (I meet more bankers thru you!) But he feels pretty foolish and would be happy to have the thing paid off. I said to let it go along, but he assured me he'll be standing by if I ever want to give the word to bring the guilty party to justice and to get the remains of the investment money in my hot little fist. I did my best to explain that you thrive on punishment and retribution so nothing to do but try something different and hope the horses come in. It's my private unsolicited opinion you'll not be having any 2500, but not to sell the stock till you've had your fun. No *wonder* your parties were so renowned. WOW! By the way, is the identification card of mine she had something I'll miss? She did very well, I must say, but could use a bit more practice on the "C"s.

Like you say: I ain't dead yet.

Guess I've said all I can't keep from. Wake me if I won today. C.

Natalie's guilt was so strong that, on November 30, she committed suicide by jumping from the top of a three-story house on San Francisco's Franklin Street, an incident included in Kerouac's novel The Dharma Bums. *The following day, Neal moved back home to Los Gatos.*

Kerouac was in California again, staying with West Coast poet Gary Snyder in Berkeley, and meeting occasionally with Neal. Jack and Neal began making plans to visit Mexico together in the New Year. With Bill Burroughs now in Tangier, they sought accommodation with Bill Garver in Mexico City.

TO JACK KEROUAC AND NEAL CASSADY FROM BILL GARVER

[Postmarked December 15, 1955
Mexico City]

DEAR JACK & NEAL

Just received your card. Write & tell me more of your plans. Will be glad to see Neal when he comes in January. If I should move you can always get my address at the First National City Bank of New York (Mexico Branch), Ave. Isabel la Catolica y Uruguay, Mexico City. Ask to talk to Miss De la Vega or Mr. Nunez-Mora. They always have my address. Write airmail at once c/o the Bank so I know you receive this letter.

Love,
BILL & ESPERANZA[2]

2. Esperanza Villanueva was a heroin addict in Mexico City, the subject of Kerouac's novel *Tristessa*.

1956

Neal and Jack did not visit Mexico in January, as contemplated. Instead, Kerouac returned to spend Christmas with his sister's family in Rocky Mount, North Carolina, where he wrote Visions of Gerard *and meditated in the woods. Meanwhile, Viking had agreed to publish* On the Road, *and Kerouac was to work with his editor, Malcolm Cowley, at Stanford University before taking up his fire-watch duties in the Cascade mountains of Washington State that summer. Neal left a note for Carolyn before going to bring Jack home.*

TO CAROLYN CASSADY

[March 1956
Los Gatos, California]

DEAR MA;

I've gone to pick up Jack at Stanford, then on to the races, if my courage holds, anyway—home at dark.

P.S. Behind commute fleet,

P.P.S. Hide the wine,

P.P.P.S. (Save this note for information on back)

No further letters of Neal's have been found for the rest of 1956 or the following year. His writing talent appears to have dried up during this period. On October 30 Neal badly cut his foot while working on the railroad and was forced to rest for a while. Carolyn wrote to inform Ginsberg, who was currently in Los Angeles with Gregory Corso, en route to Mexico City and a meeting there with Kerouac, with whom they were to plan a trip to Europe.

TO ALLEN GINSBERG FROM CAROLYN CASSADY

Thursday, November 1, 1956
[Los Gatos, California]

DEAR ALLEN,

I just got your card from the mailbox. I shall take it to Neal Saturday. He is in the SP Hospital, Ward D, having cut his ankle getting off the train Tuesday night. I don't know the full details myself yet but so far they assume he'll be there still Saturday & won't work again for a long time. If Al Hinkle calls here I'll try & get him to phone Peter & give him your number. Best I can do for you. Give Jack my love & say goodbye if he goes with you. God be with you all & and forgive me, etc.

Love,
CAROLYN

Upon recovery, Neal continued working on the railroad and living with Carolyn and the children in Los Gatos, with occasional forays into San Francisco for kicks.

During this period Allen Ginsberg had success with his epic poem Howl *when it was published by Lawrence Ferlinghetti's City Lights press in August 1956 and was subsequently the subject of an obscenity trial, which it won. Jack Kerouac also found fame overnight when* On the Road *was published in September 1957, placing Neal's alter ego, Dean Moriarty, as well as the Beat generation, firmly into the public consciousness.*

1958

When in San Francisco, Neal sometimes stayed at the Victorian house at 1403 Gough Street where he had hung out with Natalie Jackson in 1955, and where the painter Robert LaVigne had a large apartment.

TO ROBERT LAVIGNE[1]

[Monday, March 24, 1958
San Francisco]

DEAR BOB;

Please be home, or leave door unlocked (I'll lock it) from 11:35 A to 12:30 P. Tue.

NEAL

In February 1958, Neal had unwittingly passed three marijuana cigarettes to a couple of undercover narcotics agents in North Beach, San Francisco. In April he was arrested, then tried, and sentenced to five years imprisonment, of which he served two years, first at the San Bruno county jail, then at Vacaville, before being transferred to San Quentin state prison in October 1958. Neal also permanently lost his railroad job. A collection of Neal's letters from the period between May 1958 and May 1960 has been published in Grace Beats Karma: Letters from Prison *(1993), comprising fifty-six letters to Carolyn, and six to his godfather, Father Harley Schmitt.*

Carolyn had written to Allen Ginsberg about the situation. Allen was traveling in Europe and staying at the "Beat Hotel" in Paris, with William Bur-

1. Robert LaVigne (b. 1928). The artist and theatrical designer who introduced Allen Ginsberg to his longtime partner Peter Orlovsky in San Francisco, 1954. In Kerouac's *Desolation Angels*, LaVigne is represented by Guy Levesque.

roughs and Gregory Corso. Allen replied, offering his help, with a brief note from Burroughs.

TO NEAL CASSADY FROM ALLEN GINSBERG AND WILLIAM BURROUGHS

July 7, 1958
9 Rue Git Le Coeur
Paris 6, France

DEAR NEAL:

I hear you're in San Bruno County Jail, so taking a chance with this note in hope it will reach you—I'd have written before but had lost your Los Gatos address—how are you—what's happened—I got letter from LaVigne telling me news of you and N Beach—Neal, Neal hello—write me—I leave here in 10 days and return home to join Peter in New York—everything's OK here, Bill's with me in same hotel—we met young 24 year old genius millionaire,[2] digs Bill, same kicks as Bill, anthropology & Harvard & horses you know—they'll go to India, this young Frenchman & Bill (he's married a beauty & has kid)—he's crippled & thin angel, polio—a Rothschild—writes—and he'll set up a big house for us to join them, outside Calcutta—study Yoga & meet the Sages of India at last (he been there 14 months a year ago)—so next year after a year home I will head Far East with Peter I hope. But only fragmentary news of your difficulties reached here—tell Carolyn to write me if you can't, with details, & what future looks like & what family situation is, & what arrangements have been made for house, etc.—Is there anything I can do—I mean get together any character references or witnesses—Witt-Diamant[3] from State College or whoever I can arrange for, I don't know if that's any help—I will be in NY around the 25th of this month—if there's anything I can do on the spot tell me & I'll come out there & be what help I can—I have no idea of the situation. I wrote Gary Snyder, he's the only one with strong sense (he's in hosp

2. Jacques Stern, author of "The Fluke" (unpublished prose). Moved to New York in late 1970s.

3. Ruth Witt-Diamant was the director of the Poetry Center at San Francisco State College and had met Neal there, as described in Kerouac's *Desolation Angels,* where she appears as Rose Wise Lazuli.

for operation right now) to find out the score & find what need be done—If he can help you can reach him 340 Corte Madera, Corte Madera—I think he'd pitch in. If you can write me right back to reach here before the 15th of July do so—if not, answer me at 416 East 34 Street Paterson NJ, I'll get letters there when I get back. Have you been in touch with Jack? His address c/o Joyce Glassman 338 E. 13 Street Apt C-1, NYC. Bill sends his love, Gregory sends his—he left yesterday for trip to Bullfight fiesta in Pamplona, Hemingway backwater—he's glowing nowadays & very funny—We made an English trip together, read in Oxford, explored Soho head area. I guess you're OK, hah? Bill you know lay alone in Tangiers for half a year 1957 & finally, meditating all afternoon alone in darkened room, for months, received his first perfect bliss, that is he says, he felt, after loud despair, a new sense of "indifferent benevolent sentience at the center of things"—his first real faith—so came here to Paris to clear up early tangles in a last mop-up psychoanalysis—he's changed a lot—very balanced, kind & gentle—now even tender—his whole hang up with me completely disappeared, miraculously, it was only a last ditch grab at some connection before godliness, now he's alone with the Alone—me, I have got too hung up with my identity as poet-power & after yearlong hassles with publicity & pulling wires of beat behind scenes to get poetries published, got to give up again, & go be nobody again & regain my god calm prophecy feelings—life here been frantic & second rate, everybody in my room all the time, I never get alone enough—but I've seen Tangiers, Spain, Italy, Vienna, Munich, Paris, Amsterdam, London—tomorrow night Bill and I go make visit to Céline—I spoke to him on phone, he has shy reticent young voice, almost quavering—very delicate voice & hesitates—no ogre—I said "How lovely to hear your voice"—he said "anytime Tuesday after 4." But I never got to Warsaw & Moscow, tho I tried.

What have you been doing all this time? I hardly could get news of you & asked everyone I wrote in SF—write me a note at least—here or to Paterson—when will we see each other again? Come fly over ocean at night and meet me in mid Atlantic sky in a dream—or I'll arrive & hover in clouds over San Bruno shedding prayers in the moonbeams. Keep Neal—I'll keep Allen as ever—write me—

Love

ALLEN

DEAR NEAL,

Sorry to hear of your situation.

Good luck—I can't say more.

Love, BILL

TO ALLEN GINSBERG FROM CAROLYN CASSADY

July 20, 1958
[Los Gatos, California]

DEAR ALLEN:

It was so very nice to hear from you directly again. I or we enjoyed Peter's communiques early in your trip and I would have liked to answer so's we could hear more, but I kept trying to get Neal to do it. He started to a couple times and we certainly all thought and spoke of you often. I've been delighted to hear how thoroughly and eagerly you've devoured everything possible over there and how I envy your art inspections! I'll look forward to the day we can hear more and more in person. We've all (Hinkles) been anxious to hear about Céline. Also wondering how all this publicity has affected you and how you can resist not being here to receive it. I started out trying to save clippings and things for you, but it got too much and I've only seen a fraction of it. You've probably seen more yourself. I have your letter to Neal too, and I gather by that it has not been too profitable. Seems to me you could make something just in personal appearances around here, but I'm not learned in how this all works.

Now then to us and our new situation. I'll enclose the news articles and Neal's last letter to give you a better idea of what's happening. I can't help but feel it is the best thing that's happened to us yet, but I have to be careful in expressing this publicly. Even in this letter I sound *glad* it happened. I'm not yet at *that* point, but all this helps deal with it & not get panicky. I started to once, & *never* want to look down that pit again. Neal was arrested April 8 on two counts of selling narcotics. They kept him in the city dungeons for a week, then the grand jury met, found insufficient evidence and released him. The next morning he was rearrested on 4 counts plus everything else they could think of. The two inspectors responsible got furious at him in the city jail because he wouldn't tell them about all the people he knew, and threatened to send him to San Quentin. So they got more furious when they found him sprung and rassled up a lot of stuff, called a special session of the grand jury and had him indicted and bound over to the superior court on the spot. He spent a week or so in the county in SF then out to San Bruno. The first time he got a great PD, but the second and last time got a bum. His bail was set at 28,000. He had this reduced and tried to get me to put up the house to get him out. I must have lost my mind maybe, but I didn't. I didn't because he was so wild. The first time he had been real calm about it all and had been a savior in the jail. The second time he got violent and kept yelling about some mysterious 100,000 dollars he had to get out and get. If he hadn't said that I'd not have been so worried about him and have done it. He sounded so unlike himself, I was a sissy and feared he'd do something worse and we would have lost the house, the only thing the kids had left. I was probably wrong, and I don't blame him for being mad; since which time I have seen some of the things that maddened him and I'm even madder. Anyway, he has forgiven me and understands my stupidity. He didn't tell me about the trial and I couldn't get his PD to talk to me, so I missed it. I must now get a transcript and find out what happened. He did tell me about the sentencing and I got to that. From it I gathered he had had to defend himself at the trial and the general result was that everyone disliked him and disapproved of his attitude as he still refuses to "cooperate." The judge as much as said they have no proof of his selling any, only know of 3 cigarettes he gave to the inspectors for a ride and evidently tried to talk them out of arresting him. All this infuriated the judge and he called Neal every name in the book, said he was the city's major supplier and got red in the face and sputtered because since Neal "was not a user he had done it all for purely monetary gain!" Well, the whole thing was amazing, especially since Ferguson[4] is right there being treated like a king and getting the same sentence tho he was caught with a car full of marijuana and a pocket full of money. But he "cooperated." I was real proud of Neal; they couldn't make him crawl. Connie's murderer[5] was sitting next to Neal and *he* was the pitiful one . . . never saw such an innocent guy, and so pathetically doomed. Anyway, Neal was sentenced to 5 to life twice but to run

4. Doug Ferguson and his wife, Margaret (Peggy), were friends of Neal's in San Francisco and arrested at the same time.

5. Connie, the girlfriend of Al Sublette, was raped and murdered in San Francisco by another merchant seaman. Portrayed in *Desolation Angels* as Baby.

concurrently. I shall get busy and see what can be done about the obvious injustices. The opinions around here are that he'll only have to do a year, but I'm now filling in forms for Vacaville, where he now is, and from all their psychiatric studies they decide where and how long. He can receive letters only from approved persons. I'll give him your address and if there's time he can put you on the list. You'll get a form to turn in before he can receive your letters. So I'll have to write him what you said in this one.

I say it was a good thing from his standpoint, and he agrees, because he was really rushing at it pell mell. He didn't tell me much, but did say wistfully once that he was allowing people to use him. Of course the day he was arrested he broke all ties, got a job here in SJ, we had a wonderful day and all was well until that evening. Still, he needs the rest, the contemplation, the renewal, and possibly the chance to learn something he can do that will use more of his abilities. He was devastated to lose the railroad job, but I have since learned the SP, amazing enough, have not put anything on his record about his being arrested or convicted. Only that he was dismissed for failing to show for an investigation, which is nothing, and he can have the job back, without seniority, tho with union help even that could conceivably be restored. I'm glad for him, but I also hope he can do something else.

As for us, after the awful initial shock, one miracle after another has been happening. From the time the paper came out I wasn't left alone for two weeks solid. Either I was on the phone or someone was here or both. Groceries and money flooded us, from everyone I'd ever heard of around here as well as many I never had. It is still coming in now and then. People came over and cut grass, fixed fences, etc., some local stores canceled the bills, portrait orders, job suggestions and offers, baby sitters, anything . . . people couldn't do enough, begged me to tell them what and when. Groups got together to pay for the house if need be. Everyone still brings canning products, fruit from trees, I just put a fresh caught salmon in the oven, Monte Sereno birthday party remains of sugar and coffee, etc., etc., etc. I was so busy with the recital[6] when it happened I couldn't think of or do much else until the middle of June. At that time an envelope was passed around and I came home with 55 dollars. Bud[7] paid me as well 50 for doing it.

6. The annual spring production by the Los Gatos Academy of Dance, for which Carolyn did the costumes, makeup, and some scenery.

7. Bud Curtis was Jamie's dancing master, whose father was a well-known insurance broker in Los Gatos.

Now I'm painting portraits every afternoon, painting signs, keeping the books still at the dance school, am supposed to be tinting photographs, painting mannikins, and in the fall start drafting for a landscape architect. I just did the costumes and make-up for another show which is on every weekend this summer and am supposed to do the designs for Lillian Fontaine's "Midsummer Night's Dream," but have too much else. To think of all the years I tried to get any kind of art job! I'm painting better and hope to make a go of it just with portraits someday. They exhibit them all over town and when I get enough will have a show at Montalvo and join the local art associations. So I feel one purpose to this event was to jolt me out of my procrastinations and get me active in art again. At first I was denied welfare because the car was worth more than their ceiling on personal property, but friends of friends got busy and now I've got it . . . ANC.[8] With this goes free monthly rations of govt surplus butter, cheese, dry milk, flour, corn meal and rice. I had one blow when one of Neal's creditors came out and took the car. That about finished me, but again friends to the rescue. Bud's dad bought it back from both the loan Co and the bank so he is the legal owner and we switched the registration to the Hinkles' name. So now no one can take it away. I'll have to either sell it and buy another or buy it back from Mr. Curtis, but in either case the welfare will make the payments. We get all kinds of things we could not afford before: Cathy will be sent to scout camp for two weeks free, Jamie gets free swimming lessons, we get dental bills paid, eye exams free, free school lunches. The church has even given the children bibles and "keys to the scripts." I got the house homesteaded so no liens can be made against it for debts and a friend furnished the lawyer. Now friends of DA insist I see the DA personally to straighten out the oddities of Neal's case. My conclusion is it is important whom you know and either money or position plays a part. Mostly tho I'm amazed at all the good hearts and the eagerness all these "successful" people show to be of service to someone. Even the banker paid my back taxes to the tune of 100. I'm still only a hair away from foreclosure on the house and we eat sporadically, but no matter how little I have, somehow the meal materializes. Talk about manna. I've had only bits of earned income for over 3 months, yet we're still here. I've decided it's better without much money, any food tastes delicious and there are no choices between all the millions of beckoning goodies or the worry about what to do with it. I would like enough to cover

8. The welfare organization Aid to Needy Children.

some vital repairs, necessary clothing, etc., but it's been kind of a relief not to have it. I realize more and more too how faith in God has helped us all. It sometimes looks as tho all this has been planned and timed. I was a good deal worried about Neal this past year as even pay checks began to go to the track. I worked 3 days and 2 nights a week and kept us in food, but he was really getting desperate. He had even started an affair with another girl, (why did I say "even") who, from all reports, was much worse off than Natalie, whom he himself tried to get committed to an institution. He'd been doing well resisting women up to then. I saw Hugh Lynn Cayce[9] soon after his [Neal's] arrest, and his opinion was an interesting theory I thought. He said maybe these people (and he had talked to Natalie) were Atlantean souls that Neal had done in back then and for whom he felt responsible to save on the one hand and still yet repeated some of the sadistic acts as well. His intense efforts to sell them Cayce sure sound like it. Natalie told Hugh Lynn she never had the foggiest notion what Neal was talking about and had to come and see Hugh Lynn for herself to be sure he existed or something. Anyway, be that as it may. It was a timely occurrence in many ways. Now if I had pulled the pin as I so often was tempted it would have been a sorry road to travel for me. But this way the children can't resent me for it and I got this tremendous boost I'd not have had otherwise. Funny how fast one gets accustomed to things. I would like him out, but I hope mostly this will help him find himself and if it is this sort of life he seeks or a compromise of some sort, we'll have at last some real hope of achieving some harmony and a life for the children. I realize mostly what a huge job *I* must do and wonder if even a year would be enough. My attitude had improved I think in the past year so that I stopped condemning and nagging him and we had real good times when rarely together. Not 100 per cent of course, but I was gaining on it. I no longer feel everything he does is a personal affront to me. I learned to love him more and more as I concentrated on the good parts and not the bad. But I've a long way to go yet to be a help to him when he starts out again. It won't be easy to act as tho everything were all right, yet I think I should, and not be always expecting him to fail. So there's much to do, but at least we've a better idea what it is.

The first time he was arrested I had to tell the children because everyone at school knew. But when he returned in a week the black

9. The son of Edgar Cayce, who continued his father's teachings.

cloud lifted and they were so relieved I didn't have the heart to tell them again. So they think he's off working someplace and repaying some debts. People have helped protect them and they have had little effect from it considering. Johnny stopped doing anything in school for the rest of the year, but picked up a little near the end. He had a wonderfully helpful and understanding teacher. They miss him of course. I tried not to have any big changes occur so as to cut down the trauma, and was fairly successful. They're very good about the low funds, my working or leaving them alone, and help do the work. Pat Donovan[10] returned from Canada after his wife had him evicted and tho he's consumed with ways to either get even or get her back, he now comes down weekends often (with a chaperon) and cuts the grass and fills in the male role to the children very kindly. I've become more stubbornly faithful since Neal must do so.

We've been quite disappointed not to have heard from Jack and not to be able to share his success. No doubt he has adequate reasons for dropping us. I wrote him a big letter to Mexico which I gather he never received and hence has probably never forgiven me for my regrettable outburst previously. I thought he knew me better than to take that seriously, but he was always prone to think he was being condemned forever. Neal didn't answer his letters either, I believe, so the Cassadys could be considered to have let him down. On the other hand he just may have moved on to new and different attachments, and isn't concerned one way or the other. Anyway we've followed his publicity with delight, tho I personally didn't think much of The Subterraneans except as a commercial venture. I probably am a rotten critic, but I much prefer some of his other things. But it seems to have scored if what we read re the movies et al is true. It is sad not to see him any more. I hope all this has made him more content. One of our columns printed something about him having been knifed in Greenwich Village under mysterious circumstances.[11] We wondered what that was all about. Anyway, thanks for his address. I'll send it on to Neal so that he can add it to his list if he likes.

This should keep you busy for awhile and give you an idea of the situation. None of our families knows about it yet. We are actually

10. A disc jockey friend whom Neal had introduced to Carolyn when he'd moved to San Francisco to live with Natalie Jackson in 1955.

11. In March 1958, Jack Kerouac was beaten up by three men outside the San Remo bar. He was taken to the hospital with a concussion, although the incident was reported as a knifing by Dorothy Kilgallen in her gossip column in the *New York Journal-American*.

happier than we've been in years tho of course it is a big job, I miss him terribly, yet do feel at last there's hope for us.

Thanks so much for your kind words and concern and offers. I see no necessity for you to come out if you aren't planning to. Bob LaVigne has been very sympathetic and I knew he could reach you if needed. I hope to get up to see his show, but I've a busy schedule for awhile. I hope I can pare it down soon and have a moment to myself. The Hinkles just happened to move back down to SJ for the summer . . . another lucky break for me. They went with me to all the jails etc. and helped me thru the shaky part. Everything has been so amazingly clicking into places. I think even the Cayce was part of the preparation; without it I never could have made it and I'm sure it has helped him make a good thing of this and ease what would have been intense suffering.

I hope your year in NY will be what you wish it; India plans sound marvelous. Say hello and love to Peter. Pat wants to be remembered to you also. I'll keep you posted on Neal's situation if you can't write him, but I'm sure he'll give them your address . . . unless they think you a dangerous associate . . . do you think it possible? I've seen stranger ideas in action lately. How oddly these authorities we must respect behave. Well, I'll see what I can do.

Love from us all,
CAROLYN

Please send enclosures back & do write when you can—give Jack our love too. (Over)

Just reread Neal's letter. Tell Jack not to think I feel he *owes* us *anything*—you know Neal—but really no one has any designs on his money. I'm sure he can use it & besides he *doesn't* have any obligations in this direction. I hope he'll not withdraw further because of this erroneous idea. I'm not a bit interested in his money.

Our local paper sent their star hero out the instant the SJ paper hit the streets. I've known the editor & publisher from sewer conflicts[12] so they decided, since they had to print something, to try a different

12. A battle waged, successfully, by Carolyn and her neighbors, to obtain a sewer connection to Los Gatos, although outside the city limits.

angle. He talked to me for hours & I babbled on inanely. I'd just been read the S.J. News & was so shaky & confused I wasn't too coherent. He did fairly well editing the junk, but anyway wrote a very dramatic & sympathetic 2 page story which appeared that evening. I'm too embarrassed to have you read it—you & I know the real story—but it impressed the area favorably & packed a wallop. I was overwhelmed at their effort & help & it was probably the biggest boost I got. A newspaper yet. I felt the connection with you "poets" was a good one as people are more tolerant of "artists" than plain "bums" or "dope addicts." Anyway I kept it on that subject, but the remarks he picked to print are dopey & slanted to those who'd read it.

1959

With Allen Ginsberg back in New York after his European trip, Carolyn kept him updated on Neal's situation in prison.

TO ALLEN GINSBERG FROM CAROLYN CASSADY

January 7, 1959
[Los Gatos, California]

DEAR ALLEN:

Boy am I ever a lousy correspondent. My poor family finally had to telephone they hadn't heard in so long. I remember you asked about publishing something of Neal's, but presume by now you've made your own decision anyway. He said he'd rather you didn't, and he'd like to become completely anonymous forever, but, as I say, I was so long in answering you may have already done it. Naturally, where he is, he is regretting his past entirely, consumed with remorse, bitterness and guilt much of the time, and longs for just the opposite of what he's ever done. But no doubt he will strike a happy medium and forgive and understand better in time, I pray. He's in the worst possible place to learn self-acceptance or the like, but sooner or later he must. Poor guy . . . I see him every other week or so; I'd go every week and hope to, but either have a portrait or no tires. At the moment the car has quit altogether or I'd have gone today. He's on maximum security at San Quentin and considered one of the most desperate of criminals and treated accordingly because of the California hysteria about narcotics. He won't know till at least next fall and possibly not until 1960 how long he has to serve. I went to a lawyer, but he said everything was legal and nothing to do from that angle. He admitted it was all pretty hard and unfair, but the judge was within his rights. He's just a speck among 5,800 some other sad men and I'm at a loss to know what to do to help. It takes them at least an hour to find him when I go to visit, and there are probably hundreds of other unjust cases. I could get real excited about the penal system, but what's the use, and of course, according to Cayce, there's no real injustice, or it's all for a purpose. I take it out on my social worker I'm afraid tho, since there's just about as much stupidity in that agency.

The Hinkles and Al Sublette were here for Christmas day and Al stayed thru the weekend. We're all curious about yours and Jack's plans as we hear all kinds of rumors. It would be real good to see you both. An actor in one of my theatre groups came up to me the other night and said if you were coming out he had a couple friends that were interested in you and would like to put you up for a week each. This sounds like studying a specimen or something, eh? But I imagine both of you could live for nothing for sometime out here with all the young fans you've got. This boy has borrowed all Jack's books to study the style since he's trying to write something too. It seems so odd not to have seen either of you since all this fame; I don't know if I'd know how to approach you. Anyway I hope you will visit sometime, and it would be nice to hear something straight from the horse's mouth too.

Well, it seems I've told you nothing. Let's see. You can't write Neal nor send him anything. Supposedly what would help his record are letters from "nice" people but he isn't interested in it yet and won't send out any forms. You wouldn't be able to visit him either, but can if you get an address here to which he can send that sort of form first. If and when you do come out, if you can let me know if you know where you'll be, or if you come here, we could get that process under way. At least it's possible to go any day of the week and anytime bet[ween] 9–4.

Here comes my "customer." I must go draw. Write if you can, give my love to Jack and I love you too.

CAROLYN

On January 10, Allen and Peter Orlovsky wrote a reply (published in As Ever, *pp. 193–96) in which they asked for more information on how to correspond with Neal. They told Carolyn about the experimental movie they were making with Robert Frank, and Allen informed her of his plans to visit San Francisco in May. A letter from Gregory Corso was also enclosed.*

TO CAROLYN CASSADY FROM GREGORY CORSO[1]

[January 10, 1959
New York]

DEAR CAROLINE,

It's been a long time since we last saw each other, Allen and myself on our way to L.A. 1956, yet I'll never forget not wanting to eat those sunnyside-up eggs that morning because the night before I dreamed I broke eggs, all kinds of eggs, chicken eggs, sparrow eggs, penguin eggs, and got much matted with sweat when I dreamed a snake egg nightmare; when I woke that morning I wanted no part of eggs. But I couldn't tell you or Neal that, so I just kept quiet and nibbled the eggs. That's the last impression I have of your good child-rampaged house; a funny one, yet enduring. I don't know you and Neal as well as Allen or Jack, yet I feel a closeness that perhaps equals their knowing. My closeness goes to Neal in many ways; first the few vital goddamn trips to the track with him, and the certainty of his car flights, and the beauty of his speech and idea, and love.

This is hard to say yet I feel I have the earthly journey that in miles and miles of vision and sorrow and awakening to say: Neal's walk in life has always been pyloned by roses; and, if a great old sick rose blocks his walk, he'd certainly not sidestep. That's what is so true and lovely in man. When you see him please tell him for me that I well know that all things render themselves; I never knew this before because when I used to come upon that obstructive rose I'd not sidestep, yet would I continue on, venture on, but stand there, and complain; well I learned enough this last year in Europe to dispense with the complaints; how absurd I realized to complain that which is life. I hope this makes sense. I want it to, because I am very unhappy about what has happened to Neal. I'm almost apt to say, Poor God, and not, Poor Neal.

My love,
GREGORY

1. Gregory Corso (1930–2001). Poet friend of Ginsberg's and Kerouac's. His best-known poems are to be found in the collections *Gasoline* (1958) and *The Happy Birthday of Death* (1960), and he was also the author of a single novel, *The American Express* (1961). Portrayed by Kerouac as Yuri Gligoric in *The Subterraneans,* and Raphael Urso in *The Dharma Bums* and *Desolation Angels,* the latter book including descriptions of his visits to the racetrack with Neal, and his stay at the Cassady home in Los Gatos.

TO ALLEN GINSBERG ET AL.
FROM CAROLYN CASSADY

January 28, 1959
18231 Bancroft Avenue
Los Gatos, California

DEAR ALLEN, PETER, GREGORY—

I was greatly cheered by your nice notes—thanks you-all. I shall read them to Neal—who is much better—less bitter & more cheerful. "Getting settled" I expect. He also has a ray of hope in that they *may* let him learn the printing trade—if they do it will be the first time they've ever allowed a "narco" to do so. "Narcos" aren't allowed to work at any of the good jobs—just the menial labor things. But I'm encouraged too, because if they're doing *him* any favors, his attitude *must* be better. He bases all his hope on being considered by the parole board next October & being released in April 1960. I doubt anything can be done to expedite an earlier consideration but if Jake Erlich[2] could do anything or even make the Oct. consideration a certainty, it would be wonderful. Neal said he wasn't writing me often because he's "so *busy.*" He's writing a lot of book reports for an English class which is good practice, yes? If you'll give me Jack's address I'll give both to Neal & he can start forms going.

I'm a little anxious about our reporter friend.[3] We had quite a session. He came to see me and talked 5 hours, taping it. I was most dissatisfied or dubious after that, but fortunately got to spend another day with him as he took me along to go see Henry Miller.[4] I'm not sure at all what he now has in mind to write about us, but I wish you'd do what you can to steer him into a more perceptive understanding—if possible. What I mean is—he kept saying "All this mystic and spiritual side I just don't get—I just turn my back on that," which

2. A volunteer lawyer with whom Carolyn had discussed Neal's case.

3. Alfred G. Aronowitz, a journalist, was researching for a documentary series on the Beat generation. He visited Neal in San Quentin in January 1959 and also interviewed Carolyn. The articles were published in twelve parts by the *New York Post*, with the Neal Cassady story appearing on March 11, 1959.

4. Henry Miller (1891–1980). American bohemian novelist and essayist who lived for many years in Paris, France. His adventures there are described in *Tropic of Cancer* (1934) and *Tropic of Capricorn* (1939), while *Air-Conditioned Nightmare* (1945) tells of his return to America, where he settled in Big Sur, California. Miller was an early supporter of Kerouac's work and wrote a glowing preface to a 1959 edition of *The Subterraneans*.

seems to me will just cause him to miss the whole boat—as well as produce just one more sensational-type report done so often already. If anybody's going to bother to write more on the subject, looks like they oughta get another point of view—which he himself said, but I don't think he's interested in anything but the effects & surface manifestations. Neal said they reached *no* rapport in the entire 3 hours they talked 'cause Al just wanted to hear about his women & wouldn't let him talk about anything else.

I ended up convinced he's entirely materialistic also, which fine except I don't think the "beat generation" is at all. Anyway, I'll spare you my theories—but Al Hinkle suggested Aronowitz let you, Allen, proof-read the darn thing. Good idea—& I gather you've had enough shoddy publicity too.

It was fun to meet Miller & to hear him say how marvelous he thought Jack was. He said "spontaneous" writing was only as great as the personality of the man writing it—& he thinks Jack's writing tremendous, so there you are. Tell old grouch I verified this theory for Miller in respect to Jack. It makes me very sad tho that he does so much drinking & bellowing now—Jack, that is—when I remember all the fun things he used to think up to do & how he enjoyed life & living. Ah well—these geniuses.

I'm hoping to see that movie,[5] find it hard to imagine, especially without the angelic Bishop. If it ever does get out here we'll have to send him a ticket—Ha. What's it called? Did you leave out big Pat Donovan?

Rereading your letters: Explanation of forms: The prison sends you a questionnaire to fill out. You fill it out. If they approve of you as a visitor you never hear from them. If not, in about 2 weeks they tell you—no. One of the questions is if you've ever been convicted of a felony & I think there's a bit about using narcotics. I *presume* you *can write* even if above is true, but it all goes on his record. The practice is

5. In January 1959, Robert Frank was making the short movie *Pull My Daisy* based upon the third act of a play, *The Beat Generation,* that Kerouac had written in October 1957 for possible production on Broadway. The play itself derived from events at the Cassady house in the fall of 1955 when a bishop of the Liberal Catholic Church was invited there to talk to Neal and Carolyn, with Kerouac, Ginsberg, Orlovsky, and Pat Donovan also in attendance. In the movie the action was moved to the Bowery, New York. The part of Neal was played by the painter Larry Rivers, while Gregory Corso took the Kerouac role, and musician David Amram that of Pat Donovan (called Pat Mezz McGillicuddy in the movie). Allen and Peter played themselves, and the actress Beltiane (Delphine Seyrig) took the part of Carolyn. Jack Kerouac provided the sound-track narration.

to determine how the man will be rehabilitated when he is paroled. If all his friends are shady characters they won't be so eager to let him out. If dozens of dear sweet solid citizens are pining away without him, they'll hurry him out. See? It's difficult to follow their concepts but I think the above is fairly correct. The fact they are contributing to the delinquency of 3 minors & creating an old homicidal bitch doesn't worry them in the least—*and* using the taxpayers' money to do it!

I hope you will stay a while with us, Allen, you know of course you're part of the family. It will be great to see you and I wish you'd all come. I've been so grateful for your letters & cards, Peter, & would so like to talk to you like we never have been able to. Of course, I recall Gregory's visit well, but feel so sorry he couldn't just say "to hell with eggs, throw 'em out!" Next time I trust I won't appear so fearsome.

Just to clear up my situation—No I don't work—that is out. I paint or draw portraits of kind people—so far mostly the $35 variety. The "theatre" group I do costuming & make-up for—sometimes for pay. I do designing for a ballet school in exchange for the girls' lessons. The welfare has us on the list & we get some benefits, such as govt. surplus butter & free school lunches, but the matron social worker I've had resents this & has been crossing me up on the allotment, so I never know how much money I'm getting from them. So finances are practically non-existent but thanks to all the great people in the community we are making it somehow. They've given us money, groceries, clothes, well—everything. Christmastime I should have opened a store—we had a turkey & 3 chickens, not to mention the loads of canned goods—2 trees & presents by the car-load. Then just last night a friend gave Jamie a birthday party which I couldn't manage. Such a lot of loot. So we're very well cared for miraculously & I attribute some of it to the fact I never worry about anything—sure enough, every time I get down to buttons, something comes along. One man paid the loan & attachment on my car for me, the guy at the bank pays the taxes, etc., etc. I can't possibly list it all, but we sure have been blessed. The children still don't know where Neal is and neither do any of my family (till the dear old Post articles come out—maybe it'll stay in NY papers only). My sister has been hospitalized for suicidal mania all fall & is now living with my parents, so I figured they had enough anyway.

I know everything is going to be just great & I'm real glad to be painting again & anxious to learn more. Bob LaVigne came down once & I think he's wonderful—wish I could see him more & learn from him. I'm just a babe in the woods & 10 years out of practice. But so far everybody's happy with the commercial type portraits they buy & I like the money. I did do one oil for $100—I think it will build into something & I can help Neal catch up & relieve some of the strain for him.

Please write, Peter, even if you're well. Give Jack my love—what was all that about moving to Florida?

Love to all
CAROLYN

In April, Kerouac made an application to correspond with Neal in San Quentin, but it was refused by the prison authorities. He did, however, provide some money so that a typewriter could be purchased for Neal to continue his writing. In June, Neal managed to send a card to Jack.

TO JACK KEROUAC

June 12, 1959
San Quentin

DEAR BRO. JACKSON;

With ears forever flapping faster than Stan's[6] once did, can only pin them back, applying the emotion causing their wiggle towards creating the opposite one aroused when watching him do it, on this Glorious Flag Day but one year after conviction in that marsupial Court where also heard orations honoring the 1st Law Day wise Ike inaugurated to offset Vile Red Mayday, refuting usual Man OFF Street agreeing with News Item: Making gifts to cops soliciting them is wrong, by saying, in such happy gratitude that less than 340 of the 430 days now spent behind bars count on the nearly 2,000 it's my privilege to pay Society, that giving those 3 offbrand cigarettes to that cop who asked for them so pleadingly proper did finally free me from that ludicrous lifetime job & the even funnier family it supported so could concentrate entirely on really important things like at which wall to stare in the 4½ × 7½ × 9½ ft cell I share with a gunman.

Thanks for your kindness; written in exactly 12 minutes.

Too slow?

N.

6. Stan Laurel, of Laurel and Hardy comedy fame.

Ginsberg, visiting San Francisco, had been instrumental in obtaining testimonies for Neal from prominent literary figures such as Lawrence Ferlinghetti, Ruth Witt-Diamant, and James Laughlin and produced the following fact sheet for the use of lawyers, journalists, and others preparing an appeal to the parole board on Neal's behalf.

July 1, 1959
Allen Ginsberg
c/o City Lights Bookstore
261 Columbus
[San Francisco]

NEAL CASSADY

A47667 San Quentin—been in jail since April 16, '58, sentenced July 3, '58

5–Life 2 counts possession & sale of marijuana—Judge Carpaneti.

Public Defenders for him: Robert Nicco first, & sympathetic, (charge dropped). A Mr. McNamara second, & sluggish.

Probation report made by Wallace Takeguchi with minimal examination of Neal Cassady & no information about his literary character & career.

Convicted on sale; but tho he used marijuana quite a bit was in no sense a professional pusher, probably gave it out socially. Refused to talk about connections, so cops were annoyed with him. Not out on bail for months before trial & didn't have lawyer. Probation report was ugly & Judge Carpaneti denounced him as a double-life monster on stand before sentencing.

Married—Mrs. Carolyn Cassady, 18231 Bancroft, Los Gatos. Has ranch style house, 3 children. Wife presently on Welfare (Santa Clara County A.N.C.—Aid to Needy Children). She's sympathetic & wants him out.

Worked around 10 years steadily as Brakeman & Conductor on Southern Pacific Railroad. SP Union voted him his seniority back whenever he gets out & can come back to work. SP management probably hire him, with union assent. His friend Albert Hinkle (an SP conductor who doubles as Geography instructor at SP State College) knows this scene—Andrews 6-7695 (San Jose).

Letters recommending early parole already in from James Laughlin 333 6th Ave NYC (Laughlin runs New Directions and offered to publish Cassady writings); Ruth Witt-Diamant, San Francisco State College Poetry Center Directress (affirming his literary reputation & value to community etc.); and Larry Ferlinghetti of City Lights, offering to publish a book of Cassady's & also offering a job at City Lights. More letters due in from Grove Press in NY & various professors at U.C.

He's an old friend of Jack Kerouac & Ginsberg (known him since 1945) & fellow writer. Howl is dedicated to Cassady, Kerouac & Burroughs. Kerouac's On The Road had Cassady as the main heroic character, so an early picture of him can be got there. He's since settled down & has wife family house steady job etc. New Kerouac book called Visions of Neal (titled Visions of Cody) will be published in Dec. by New Directions—consists of adventures and tape recorded literal conversations together.

Kerouac credits Cassady with having done the first advanced spontaneous prose style narrative which put Kerouac on to his own literary style, & taught him how to write modern prose modeled on natural speech, in certain Western rhythms.

None of Cassady's mss. have been published, most consisted of long letters (up to 40,000 words) of autobiographical narrative. Some of these have been lost. A selection of early letters by Cassady is being prepared by Kerouac for publication in an anthology of modern prose & poetry that Kerouac's been assembling for paperback publication later this year—Avon Press, NY.

Cassady is writing in San Quentin (with typewriter sent by Kerouac) but since his subject matter is intimate & personal-confessional Dostoyevskian autobiography, in detailed & (Proustian) style, it would be unwise for him to pass his mss. thru official hands. Probably be censored there for subject matter might get him in trouble re parole considerations. Outside of smuggling mss. out, therefore, there's no way of getting new material from him while he's in the can.

Cassady has already a considerable literary reputation in SF among local writers, since his identity as Dean Moriarty in the Kerouac book is well known. He was the subject of a study by the NY Post, as a literary hero; and his name is mentioned & discussed in respectable literary magazines in Germany, France, Denmark etc. A month ago there was an article & discussion of his literary role in the Paris Express, with a large picture of him & Kerouac. He's taken quite seriously & is well known as a U.S. literary figure in Europe. Which adds poignance to his obscurity & imprisonment here.

At the time of his arrest he was considerably depressed & made no attempt to get a lawyer & defend himself adequately—told his wife not to try raise his bail, so was not out before trial at all. As far as I can tell, he did not at the time think that the sentence would be so lengthy & serious, & so was negligent in securing his rights & outside aid.

Unless some reasonable intervention is made, or representations of the situation to the Parole people, his parole, which comes up in October will be mechanically passed over for another year. When Parole board does finally reconsider his file, it will be Oct 1960 and even then there is no security against their setting a lengthy sentence. Depending as they are on an inadequate & lurid Probation report, he may be in San Quentin for years.

Gavin Arthur,[7] who teaches a Saturday morning Comparative Religion course at San Quentin, knows him & is sympathetic & would help; as presumably would Eichelman, the Protestant Religious Chaplain at S.Q., who is acquainted with him.

Cassady has a long interest in oriental religious devotions & is quite Faithful, in an original fashion; it's his main interest.

He has a beautiful soul, & is a great & secret author; his family life is getting balled up; his job is waiting for him; continued incarceration is completely meaningless & quite horrible.

TO CAROLYN CASSADY FROM ALLEN GINSBERG

August 25, 1959
170 E 2 Street
NYC 9, NY

DEAR CAROLYN:

Back in NYC now, been busy making BBC TV shorts, beating off people & writing. I have not heard anything on Neal's case since I left, do you know what's happened? Has the letter from the Super been got? That seemed crucial, among other things. Jack & I wrote Neal a postcard yesterday, we were in Northport. Jack's mother moved down to Fla. with all the furniture & then decided she didn't like it there, tho Jack had sold house, so she's returning this weekend. He bought a different smaller modern more cozy one for her hoping she'll like that. What a hassle he has. Peter & I wandering round

7. Gavin Arthur (1901–1972). Astrologer and gay liberation foreleader. Grandson of the twenty-first U.S. president, Chester A. Arthur.

NYC in bathingsuits. Hello to Al & Helen, say. Let me know about Neal.

As ever
ALLEN

A few weeks later, Neal was able to write to Ginsberg with the good news that the appeal to the parole board had been successful.

TO ALLEN GINSBERG

October 12, 1959
[San Quentin]

DEAREST FRIENDS, ALLEN, ET AL.;

Well, old buddy, illustrious poet, mutual Mother mitfordiser, and your companions in ritualistic retroperistalsis, the "good news tonight," a la Gabby Heatter,[8] this Columbus Day card surely cheers you to receive as much as it does me to write, is that I shall be without Wainright or White (that blubber bellied colonel whose asst. you so well belabored, remember?) having helped, released next Summer, and, even better, at least one full month sooner than I'd ever dared hope, i.e., *JUNE 3, 1960*! Yes, it has at last been officially decreed that my own D- (departure) Day shall also be the first week in June, when, after finishing over 26 straight months behind bars, will be allowed to begin that relatively easier and far freer stint of a three (3) year, one (1) month parole, during which time of course I must remain in some one California county so, if we all are ever to see each other before this restriction expires in July '63, you, after India I assume, will have to visit me, not I you.

Perhaps Caroway [9] can drop seeds instead of you, *thanks*. Bev Burford *sick*; write her.

Love,
N.

8. Gabriel Heatter (1890–1972). Popular network radio commentator who opened his nightly news reports with the words "There's good news tonight."

9. I.e., Kerouac.

TO ALLEN GINSBERG

October 25, 1959
[San Quentin]

DEAR FRIEND ALLEN;

Since I'm already well past 90, and not just emotionally either, any trade you intend taking out must necessarily be retroactive and, as you perhaps gathered by my "Caraway dropping seeds instead of (poverty-happy) you" hint, it best be in pins; but quickly, else this, being my very last card, may well be the only time you will hear from me, until Eastertide at least; so remind as I thank you, all Postal Money Orders are c/o F.P. Dickson, Warden. Nice to know about H. Huncke,[10] isn't that 1933 Side Show piece the very one he spoke about doing while in 1947 Texas Bayou Bath? or did the distraction of nibbling fish nipping flesh fool my hearing then, or cause exact memory to fail now? Is Big Bill B. having any new work published? Tell poor women-starved me the inside on Arly Francis & Margie Mead—or, fearing the older one is really R. Benedict's lover, just Arly.[11] Always thought Greg needed something, maybe the Hydra Hap. is it, may it prove lasting—& what did he use? Disagreeing with Varda.[12] "Gin, so decadent, is Magnif." I remain,

N.

Both Allen Ginsberg and Gary Snyder had visited San Quentin and read before the comparative-religions class that Neal was attending, with Allen performing his long poem "Kaddish" to a group of prisoners. A similar offer to visit was extended to Kerouac, but never taken up.

10. Herbert Huncke had been released from a four-year spell in prison in 1959 and had begun writing, including a piece about a side-show performer, "Tattooed Man," published in *The Evening Sun Turned Crimson* (1980).

11. Margaret Mead (1901–1978) and Ruth Benedict (1887–1948) were renowned anthropologists, and lesbian lovers. Arlene Francis (1908–2001) was a popular American actress and TV personality.

12. Jean "Yanko" Varda, a celebrated artist who lived on a houseboat in Sausalito.

TO JACK KEROUAC

October 27, 1959
San Quentin

DEAR BRO. JACKSON;

On the night of the 20th, Herr Beat Brendan Behan Balzac, better not guzzle too much wine because the next 9 A.M. you'll be following the lead of G. Snyder & A. Sinsberg—ask him about the scene—by addressing our class studying COMPARATIVE RELIGIONS; in which, forum-style, anything from the Big Table—in the Chapel library here, thanks to Allen & a Pastor from Texas—on up is religiously compared with life, as guessed at by we two dozen students so separated from it—tho the room, indeed the entire building, would be overpacked to fire hazard proportion if I dared let out that YOU were coming, why they'd stampede! honestly, I'm sick of overhearing your nigh notorious name being always mispronounced in "Big Yard" conversations EVERYDAY. At first I was very much shocked, judging by your choosing to publish me, that you presumed to be an editor of anthologies, then your parenthesis well explained it: you're just getting even with Hearst Jr. for his senior's own horrible editorial policies by trying to match them in the literary field with "works" such as mine; shame.

Bev Burford *sick; write* her, OK?

N.

1960

With Neal due to be released from prison on June 3, with three years' parole, his father wrote to Carolyn, enclosing a photograph.

TO CAROLYN CASSADY FROM NEAL CASSADY SR.

[c. April 1960]

DEAR CAROLYN

Hope you are feeling fine. I am feeling fine. Well Carolyn it wont be long now untill we will meet again I hope so. It seems like it has been ages dosent it to you. I got a letter from Neal a few days ago he think he will be released on June 3. I hope so. I dont know if you have seen my mug if not am sending you one it might help keep the mice & rats *ha ha*. I wrote to Neal that I thought you were mad at me & he said he dident think so. I *hope not*. Do you make trips to see Neal? If so that helps for him a whole lot for him to pass time away. How is the children healthy I hope. Well Carolyn dont wait as long to write to me. With love you & Neal & the children.

New address 1433 17 St, St Elmo Hotel

Well Carolyn here they are, I went to the Depot & got them, so I dont think you will be bothered with rats. Arent they *cute* ha ha.

TO ALLEN GINSBERG

[June 2, 1960
San Quentin]

DEAR ALLEN, ET AL;

The lights have failed in the cell-block so am writing this last S.Q. line in semi-darkness, making my scribble excusable for once. Assuming I get thru this 787th straight nite behind bars, just as I assume you missed the Chile—got your great letter from there—Earthquakes—& are still alive, I shall leave here in the morning & go to a job at Con. Lithograph Corp & my home at 18231 Bancroft Ave., Los Gatos to begin a 3 yr. parole.

Love to all—Write,
NEAL

Herbert Huncke, whom Neal had last seen in 1947, when they spent time together with William Burroughs in East Texas, wrote to welcome Neal on his release from prison.

TO NEAL CASSADY FROM HERBERT HUNCKE

Saturday June 18, 1960
[New York City]

NEIL;

Peter [Orlovsky]—just fell in a few minutes ago—mentioning his intention writing to you—also with a great scroll he unrolled before me. I have been somewhat solitary—the past couple of months—having lost touch with the great happenings of recent and though I knew you were due on the scene—it was but a short while ago I heard of your release. Welcome back—and—after these many years—hello!

I have been kept informed to some extent of what has been happening with you—thru Allen and Peter and of course—Jack. It would have been more to my liking had my contact with you been of a more direct nature. It seems so long ago—we spoke—drove up from Texas—smoked pot—and I listened to and felt—that tremendous flow of enthusiasm—so much—then—a part of your personality.

I have been doing a little writing—the last few months—assured by Allen—it is worth the effort. Frankly—I am not convinced—but it is an outlet. Did have a short story accepted by 'Escapade'[1] but as for the rest of my stuff—it is accumulating in a pile near my bed.

I am working—also on parole until next June—when I am planning to do some traveling. Might cut back out West. Have a hankering to see California again—after low—these many years. With your permission—will look you up.

Will enclose this with Peter's letter.

Drop me a line—direct—next time you feel an urge to write letters.

Keep cool—man.

HUNCKE

With a prison record, Neal found it difficult to obtain work. He was eventually employed as a tire recapper, first in San Jose, then by the Los Gatos Tire Service. At this time, Neal briefly continued an affair with Jacqueline Gibson, whom he'd met shortly before going to prison, passing her on to Kerouac when he visited during his stay at Big Sur that summer. Kerouac was later to write about these events in his novel Big Sur.

1. Herbert Huncke's short story "Elsie" was published in *Escapade* magazine, vol. 5, no. 5, August 1960, and reprinted in *The Evening Sun Turned Crimson* (1980).

1961

After working all week at Los Gatos, living with Carolyn and the children, Neal would take off most weekends on extended visits to San Francisco. During one of these, in February 1961, he met Anne Murphy, who was to become Neal's regular girlfriend over the next six years. In June, Neal's father wrote to inform Neal of his health problems—he had suffered some minor strokes.

TO NEAL CASSADY FROM NEAL CASSADY SR.

17 June 1961
c/o St Elmo Hotel,
1433 17 St.
Denver
Colorado

MY DEAR SON NEAL

How you feeling & your wife & children feeling fine I hope I feel pretty good. Neal are you living with your wife & children at home you only have to report at your fulher [*sic*] place once a mo dont you? Neal I had planned to go & visit & stay a year or so with you but on account those strokes I havent had one since Dec but of course I take tablets three times a day. My Dr advises me to stay close in case I did have one so I cant even go back & visit with my folks but Neal there isn't no pain only I don't go very far alone when I run out of tablets I go back to the Denver General Hospital they give me enough to last a month there isnt no charge on account of my age.

Neal I am shure dissapointed that we cant be together I get awful lonesome for you O well as long as we have got our health I guess we are luckey & not in bed all the time thank god for that

My sister Emma died three mo ago she was the only mother I even had & my 3 brothers died so that out of 7 of us there is only 1 left the one that fixed us fried chickens for us & we eat on the way back on a box car Neal I never forget the time you was teasing in front of them bums & eating chicken in front of them ha ha do you remember?

Neal when when will your parole be out? Well Neal tell your wife & children I said Hello.

B B and I always love to hear from you.

From your father & my son ans p.

P.S. Barba said tell you hello

She is home at present poor kid spend a lot of time you know where.

In August, Neal took a two-week vacation and visited his father in Denver. He carried a notebook with him, to record his impressions of some of the scenes he planned to write about in his book. On October 25, Neal appeared in the Westinghouse TV series PM West, *hosted by Terrence O'Flaherty from San Francisco. In this episode, titled "The Beatnik Poets," Neal was featured with Pierre DeLattre, Eileen Kaufman, and Shig Murao, receiving a fee of $24.*

That fall Neal began mixing and partying with young students from nearby Stanford University, meeting them in Perry Lane, the bohemian area of Palo Alto. In February 1962, One Flew Over the Cuckoo's Nest, *a novel by the writer Ken Kesey, was published. Neal met him and his friends when Kesey, an ex–Stanford student, returned to Perry Lane from Oregon that summer. Kesey had long wanted to meet the hero of* On the Road, *and the two discovered that they had a common interest in sports, literature, and drugs.*

1963

*With Neal's parole period about to expire, and no evidence of his mending his errant ways, Carolyn decided to divorce him, and this was finalized by July 1964. Neal initially appeared to spend more time than ever at home with his family, but when his father became seriously ill that summer of 1963, Neal took a vacation from his work at the Los Gatos Tire Service and traveled to Denver to be with him. However, Neal Sr. died on July 17, the day that Neal left home, and he stayed in Denver to arrange the funeral. Since his parole was now over, he was able to drive on with his friends Anne Murphy and Bradley Hodgman, a tennis star at Stanford University, to New York, where they met up with Kerouac at his home in Judyann Court, Northport. After their visit, Jack complained to Carolyn, in a letter of August 16 (*Jack Kerouac: Selected Letters, 1957–1969, *p. 370), about the rudeness of Neal's friends.*

TO CAROLYN CASSADY

July 21 [1963], Noon
[Postmarked Denver, Colorado]

DEAREST ONES:

Well, my father died the same afternoon I left to go see him, but the trip was necessary—to get him buried, et al. He left no money, so I had to sign papers & all to get him buried in the Holy Catholic Church. The priest will say a mass for his soul on Tues. I'm driving east to take Brad to NY. Will write soon.

Love to all.
NEAL

TO CAROLYN CASSADY

July 24 [1963], Noon
From Mama's birthplace
[Postmarked East Lansing, Michigan]

DEAREST ONES;

From Denver to Kalamazoo non-stop, no flats, tickets or trouble of any kind. Leaving Lansing at once & will be in New York in A.M. Probably stay there thru the week-end then right back home via New Orleans, Arkansas, Denver, Salt Lake.

Love,
NEAL

TO CAROLYN CASSADY

July 26 [1963], Dark
[Postmarked New York]

DEAREST ONES:

After safe arrival New York City, seeing Jack Kerouac—nutty as ever—$10 donation; acct. $9.50 phone bill owed—hearing about old friends, etc. Am leaving Sunday nite: see ya all that week?!!

Love,
NEAL

P.S. Tell Roy Tannehill (L.G. Tire)[1] I'll be back next Sat.—Aug. 3—(*hope* to)—so he can go hunting.

That August, Neal and Anne moved into the house on Gough Street, San Francisco, where he had previously stayed, and Neal started a new job at a tire service near Van Ness Avenue. At the Gough Street house, Neal would dictate from his First Third *manuscript while Anne typed. Allen Ginsberg and Peter Orlovsky, who had returned from a tour of Asia and were staying with Lawrence Ferlinghetti, moved into the house with Neal and Anne.*

1. Roy Tannehill owned the Los Gatos Tire Service, where Neal worked.

TO ALLEN GINSBERG

8 P.[M.]
[September 1963]

DEAR ALLEN,

My car broke down completely—so no way to see you until, say, Sat. P.M. or perhaps Wed. noon or so when I go pay tickets in San Mateo, Calif. Anyhow, Love; & remember work (writing type) starts in 2 wccks or so—right.

TO ALLEN GINSBERG

3 P.[M.]
[September 1963]

DEAR ALLEN,

Well, say, move in here, maybe—anyhow, work (writing) each A.M. starting Wed. Otherwise, most likely, going to Mexico—have you got any money?—until broke; return early Oct. to then start above described procedure.

OK? Artistically.

Love,
NEAL

At home if calls needed.

Although now living apart from Carolyn and the children, Neal continued to send them money whenever he could, sometimes with the help of Allen Ginsberg.

TO NEAL CASSADY FROM CAROLYN CASSADY

December 12, 1963
Los Gatos, California

God bless you and your new life.

Thanks so much for the $10 . . . and did you thank Allen for me for the donations he has been so very kind to pass on? All very much appreciated. We may have Christmas yet. How about you?

Come hear Jamie's tape sometime, I think she wants you to care.[2]

Love always,

C.C.

2. A tape of Jamie's past lives given by Dr. Neva Dell Hunter, a channel for a higher-plane master.

1964

In San Francisco, Neal met the literary editor John Bryan, who, in early 1964, published the surviving portion of Neal's "Joan Anderson" letter in his magazine, Notes from Underground, *with Neal helping him to run off copies.*

With the success of One Flew Over the Cuckoo's Nest, *Ken Kesey and his family had recently moved from Perry Lane to a cabin on a sprawling estate at La Honda, in the hills overlooking Palo Alto. With him came his band of followers, the Merry Pranksters, and Neal and Anne were regular visitors. Neal wrote to an anonymous friend with instructions on how to find Kesey's new home:*

Down Freeway to Redwood, then RT to Woodside then thru same to uphill that continually bears right—got it. Rear right at all points until at top of hill where #35 crosses #84 (the route you're on) then down hill to La Honda & thru same to "Boots & Saddle" after which turn left—that's left—at next bridge (¼ mile). Good luck. Love, NEAL

Kesey and the Pranksters had bought an old school bus, painted it in Day-Glo psychedelic colors, and wired it with sound equipment. On June 14, the bus, loaded with Pranksters, and with Neal at the wheel, set off for New York, the World's Fair, and the publication of Kesey's second novel, Sometimes a Great Notion, *filming as they went. They traveled through Arizona and Texas, calling on Kesey's novelist friend Larry McMurtry in Houston, and were in New Orleans for Father's Day, June 21. Continuing through Mississippi, Alabama, and Georgia, they reached New York City on June 25 and quickly hooked up with Ginsberg and Kerouac, who was not overly impressed by Neal's newfound friends. The bus traveled on to Millbrook for a meeting with Timothy Leary at his Castalia Foundation and some sampling of LSD and DMT, before Neal picked up his car from Brad Hodgman and drove back to the West Coast with*

Prankster photographer Ron Bevirt, leaving the bus and the remaining passengers to find their own way back via Canada. Neal overshot his two-week vacation by four days and lost his job at the tire service. However, Bevirt, who had a bookstore in Santa Cruz, offered him a job there, which Neal gladly accepted.

TO DAVE HASELWOOD[1]

NOON [c. June 1964]

DEAR DAVE,

Sorry missed Justin's birthday party.[2] Going to NYC Sat. & be back here 1st week July—see you then if not before—

Love, NEAL CASSADY

P.S. We're making color movie at NYC Fair.

1. Dave Haselwood was a book publisher and founder of the Auerhahn Press. He lived at the house on San Francisco's Gough Street.

2. Justin Hein was a gallery owner in San Francisco who also lived at the Gough Street house.

1965

In March, Neal, who had been given the name "Sir Speed Limit" by the Pranksters, was arrested for a driving offense. From jail he wrote to Carolyn to tell her that he might be further imprisoned for related transgressions, for which he could not pay the fine, and to reassert his love for her.

TO CAROLYN CASSADY

March 24, 1965 P.M.
Santa Rita Center
P.O. Box 787
Pleasanton, California

DEAR, DEAR CAROLYN—MY TRUE HEART;

Gee, writing this seems almost like old times, doesn't it? & tho I'm still writing to the sweetest girl in the whole world there's a big big difference from last time we communed under these conditions, rite? First things first however & "Seek ye first" etc. *is* now my goal—yes, hard as it's been on both of us, I've postponed writing more because I wanted to be *sure* that *He* was at last first on my list than because I didn't have an envelope until today—Gee, I love you!

Anyhoo, I'll get out Saturday P.M. unless there's a hold on me from Santa Cruz for doing 60 mph in a 50 mph & a #12,500, which is simply not having a valid driver's license in possession; in that case they'll keep me here Sat. & Sun., then Mon. or so they'll take me to Santa Cruz, which, you understand & thank the Lord, is the last offense that's outstanding.

So if I *don't* contact you before Sunday School the 28th, you'll know I'm staying on in jail until everything is cleared up—probably about Easter or so, I guess.

But it doesn't matter—except in money matters, you must be terribly broke by now—because I'm on the right (mission) path at last.

You'll notice I'm not asking any of the questions I'm burning to know—how's Johnny, at school & otherwise; are the girls OK, & most close to my heart, how are you? Love—& that is because I *don't* want you to write me here since I'd never get it. So tell me Sunday instead, OK? But enuf sentimental stuff (sob).

I trust your weekly meetings are going OK, I'll be thinking & praying from 8 to 10 tonite. I work in the potato (spud) locker here & am stuffing the food in so much I now weigh more than I ever have—165 lbs+ !

If I'm *not* held here I'll have only 24 hours to spend with you before I go to jail in Santa Cruz—from Sun. P.M. to Mon. at 2 P.M. when I appear for the judge to sentence me—but it'll be all I need to inspire me to do good & profitable jail time until I'm out once & for all & *at last* marching firmly in step in Christ's Army. Whether in L.A. or elsewhere (I pray each nite that *we* might find our way clear to remarry & still live up to our missions—mutual or otherwise) I'm just about ready to go forth as a real man; not thinking of self first anymore, or just "meeting the need" but truly inspiring & helping as I know I can—& must!

Have so much to tell you!

Love, NEAL

P.S. Didya know I make the final version of my "Drive" record?[1]

P.P.S. Please, Love, search your heart; is there still room for me?

In April, Kesey's cabin at La Honda was raided. He and thirteen others, including Neal, were charged with possession of marijuana and released on bail. The charges against Neal and most of the others were later dropped. At Kesey's, Neal had been living out of his white Plymouth car with his belongings, including some of his writings, on the backseat. The car was stolen and Neal's articles never recovered.

1. Ken Kesey and the Pranksters had made a series of recordings of Neal talking while at the wheel of a stationary Buick in La Honda. They planned to release a 45 rpm single of the monologues, backed by a group of local musicians called Robin and the Hoods playing a *Batman*-like theme tune. The single was never issued at the time, but several versions of "Drive" have been released in recent years.

TO CAROLYN CASSADY

July 7, 1965, 11 A.[M.]
Corridor, SF Hosp.

DEAR CAROLYN; DEAREST;

This $15 will be for kickoff on me beginning to send you money regularly again. No job yet—putt putt. Hug.

Note from Anne Murphy
11:11 A.[M.]

DEAR CAROLYN,

I'm sorry about Jonny. Neal & Sharon[2] & her brother Mike and me (again), are all sitting here and I'm explaining it all. I started to write you but couldn't because I promised Neal not to. Hope you are OK & that the money Neal (& Sharon) sends helps. Still trying (to get him). Love him still.

I've been reading Desolation Angels and the Dream Book—all about Evelyn & Cody—Neal's reading Big Sur, now.

I wanted to tell you, just simply, how devastating it was to know, beyond all doubt, what, if you don't mind being called "sweet," what a sweet woman you are. Because secretly I thought the opposite, just because I wanted to, I guess (a *long* time ago). I just wanted to tell you.

He's reading the part about the golden old-fashioned family on the Big Sur front porch & Jack's birthday, etc.

Love, ANNE

Noon 7-7-65

DEAR JAMI (STAGE NAME, NATCH) & CATHY;

Well, I hear your Sunday School's slipped some. Yes, I'd like to conduct some more soon; help your mother by being less nervous. OK?

All love, DAD

If I don't get strictly business bus trip to Idaho underway tomorrow or so, may not go—so—hip hip hurray!

2. Sharon McLaughlin, from Los Angeles, was one of Neal's girlfriends.

P.S. Work—work—if we, my soul & me, can have lasted till today 7-7 in the hell of 365 *times not* going to unemployment for your $200 a month. We can *also* reverse. (See you if got car.)

Love, N.

On July 18, Neal and Anne Murphy appeared with Ginsberg in a documentary film shot inside the City Lights bookstore in San Francisco. Neal sent Carolyn the fee he'd received and also talked of raising money by selling his letters.

TO CAROLYN CASSADY

July 18, 1965
c/o Kesey
Star Rt. #1
La Honda, California

DEAR, DEAR CAROLYN:

Made a T.V. show with Allen & here's my 1/3 of the $250.00 he got for it. Great huh?

How's everyone? esp you sweet thing.

Might get at least $1,000 maybe $5,000 for my old letters; anyway, they've been shipped east. Will get an old '50 Pontiac free from Geo. Walker,[3] who is one of the Kesey group, so shall see you soon, soon, soon,

Love to everyone; Hold tight,
Love again, NEAL

On Saturday, August 7, the local chapter of Hell's Angels took up an invitation from the Merry Pranksters to party at La Honda. There they sampled LSD for the first time and introduced the Pranksters to some of their own rituals, during which Anne Murphy was "joyously gang-banged" by a troupe of Angels while Neal looked on. The following evening, Neal took off on another trip East with his friend Don Snyder (aka Gypsy), leaving a note behind for Anne.

3. George Walker, aka Merry Prankster "Hardly Visible."

TO NEAL CASSADY FROM ANNE MURPHY

[August 1965]

DEAR NEAL,

Just read your letter, which brought tears and pleasure. I didn't think you'd really gone, and now I'll just wait and see what happens. I'm glad you didn't take me with you as I am having a great time here, trying to seduce, unsuccessfully, every male member of the gang. Ginger is here making things merry and everyone misses you, especially me, but I think everyone wishes you were back. And I never had such a gorgeous time as we spent together at the Lishes.[4] There's lots of things I want to say like if you love me why did you leave etc., but to understand my own paranoia, it's necessary to believe yours too. Faye[5] is trying to help me to endure, and be clean, if you'd only believe how hard I'm trying, and I love you so very much, and I think I've been hurt too much to right now have faith that we will be married which is my dearest wish in the whole world, but married or not I need to be with you. I love you, and your love is the nourishment of my life. Oh, won't we be happy when we're together?

I'm helping paint the bus, washing and cleaning for Faye, it's a beautiful morning, the Hermit[6] gave me some white powder he thinks is ground up aspirin, but in your spirit (and mine), I gobbled it up, and I must admit that I haven't got a headache, it might have been a little LSD, whoopee. Oh, I missed you that night when you left—Lee[7] brought your clothes and I put them on the bus, and I tried to get to Berkeley, and oh, I love you. I kept thinking you were coming back, and Oh, my darling, I love you.

Ken wrote a story about the bus trip, which I typed, and June[8] helped too, it's good. The part about you was very revealing, and showed how others look at you, again, which is not at all the way I see you, for I see you as my love not as a character, running wild. I'll copy it out for you. He loves you too.

4. Gordon and Barbara Lish. Friends of Ken Kesey's at Stanford, who lived in Burlingame. Gordon Lish has become an acknowledged writer.

5. Faye Kesey, wife of Ken Kesey.

6. "The Hermit," real name Anthony Dean Wells, Merry Prankster associate.

7. Lee Quarnstrom, aka Minister of Information. Later a journalist for the *San Jose Mercury News*.

8. "June the Goon," a blonde who, together with redhead Sharon McLaughlin and Anne Murphy, composed the trio of Neal's girlfriends during this period.

"Cassady and crew have arrived, barging in the gate and he didn't go to sleep last night with his mind on freedom. 'Been up for four days, Chief, since we were out here last, in fact in great shape and look here *three* to bring, now what do you think of that?' Anne and Sharon on each side and to this usual twosome (eek!) (me) he indicates that he may have added the blonde Swede, trying burlesquely to put his arms around all three. 'Oh, no, no, no' admonishing himself, breaking away, becoming confidential about a score, or two bucks for some minor repair on some ailing vehicle somewhere, making my refusal somehow inevitable by the tone of his asking, always skilled at wheedling a no from me, as one of the orneriest old farts to ever draw breath, as well as being one of the most phenomenal testimonies of the hidden human potential, talking, talking and moving while doom cracks under his feet, a ball of burning time." (My, my, shame and a pox on your harem.)

I wish we were married—the ring is on my right hand now, where it belongs for now. This typewriter is labeled "Neal Printing Co.," and they're playing "I can't get no satisfaction"—that's true alright!

They just had the last of the IT 290 and I tried to follow Babbs[9] & Hermit to see if I could get any, but was sidetracked by that foxy Mt. Girl,[10] and Sandy[11] sends his love, as he eats a sandwich made of Jewish rye bread and guess what, peanut butter and jelly. I made some cookies yesterday, and put Scotch lemon curd on them, and we had venison one night; they just played "I got you, Babe."

We should stop believing all the unhealthy things that seem to be. After all we're still alive. The hard thing is to please everyone, especially if you forget yourself, but without you there is no pleasing me, so I try to be a good sport but everyone wants me to want them without getting into trouble, and I make such a fool of myself. That's life, though.

Well, I'll get some answers to some questions finished, and send them to the lawyers—I was informed that I am suing that cat who drove the Volks for $25,000. Good luck, Anne! I love you. Please

9. Ken Babbs, aka the Intrepid Traveler. Ex–marine helicopter pilot who saw action in Vietnam. Back in California he became Kesey's virtual second-in-command as Merry Prankster leader.

10. Mountain Girl, real name Carolyn Adams. Had daughter, Sunshine, by Ken Kesey, in April 1966, before marrying Grateful Dead leader Jerry Garcia.

11. Sandy Lehman-Haupt, aka Dis-Mount. Sound-system technician with the Merry Pranksters.

come back or tell me to come to you and how. I'll try to be with you and thank you for the reassurances in the letter. Boy, did I need that. Forgive & forget, and the casual attitude to Sharon. I still can't believe it, my love, and how I love you. And I need you. And I want you. My c. drips when I think of you coming and being together. I love you. Hurry.

Love my Cassady,
and everybody's Cassady,
ANNE

Neal included a reply to Anne Murphy in a twenty-two-page letter to Ken Kesey while on his way to New York.

TO KEN KESEY

August 30, 1965 (5 P.M.)
[Wakeman, Ohio]

DEAR KEN, ET AL: ESP. YOU *GIRLS*!

This letter may not get mailed for some time, since I'm sitting here in Wakeman, Ohio without a dime. Still, having jacked off in the toilet, feeling rested & tonite's sleep (not to spoil it) being a long one, will write anyhow. Perhaps a rundown on the trip is first in order—*Never* have I seen one of such disorder!—it's been a Dietrip—O Mean! But a ball-drive! If it is to continue remains to be seen: acct. mechanic is busy & can't tear down engine until tomorrow & if this 1940 flat-head Cadillac 8 banger (not Bangor, that's another Maine; not the one I fear is busted by this King of the Road, if that has any bearing)[12] (Maybe I cracked the Cam too, woo!) can't be fixed I'll truly feel sorrow.

Let me tell you about this machine, a real dream; whether or not turned nitemare—the best truck I ever fucked up. A 1947 ¾ ton, with overload springs, International (yep, it's got an electric fuel pump, too—it must be characteristic of the stock ones to easily go out) pick-up that's got a 1962 *6* speed G.M.C. gear box—never use compound Low so really a 5 speed—a 1957 Metro van rear end, 2 fuel tanks

12. A reference to Roger Miller's hit song "King of the Road," which entered the U.S. record charts in February 1965: "Third boxcar midnight train, destination Bangor, Maine . . ."

holding about 26½ or 7⅞ gallons, the strongest truck type (like your bus) wheels sporting 2 brand new 8-ply Nylon 750 × 16 (cost $90) on the rear & a new 750 × 16 8-ply rayon on R.F. & a 6-ply 750 × 16 on L.F. that's got more tread than it'll ever use since the 6 inch gash in its center that I've been fretfully watching must sometime go, tho after 2,500 miles there's still no show that this is so. Plus another tire with over half-tread left—it gave me the one flat I had, in Utah—besides the smooth spare, another 750 × 16, as are all 6.

This long wheel base—about 145 inches, I guess—green colored (dark) gasser also has wonderful twin-pipes with chrome mufflers topped by a rakish cut that extend along each side of the cab—like a big diesel rig—& burble in one's ear so one can really hear the big cubic inch Caddy engine. There's also a new rear U-joint, a repacked recently front, new plugs, points, condenser, coil, fan belt, fan (only 4 bladed instead of 6, tho), radiator—a Ford truck one—the one it had, a 1932 Cad V-16, 4 inch thick one holding 32 quarts, was repaired in Ely, Nevada & replaced in Denver. New left rear brake kit, no vacuum assist tho—it was full of water, so took it off—so must pump brakes a coupla times before they take. A Tacks Meter that needs a cable to work & a broken bell housing a steel strap holds.

But enuf truck: & only one day—in Denver—did I get enuf fuck (or any); one was a truly sweet, small, dark-haired 19 yr. old Grinnell, Iowa college girl, whose defenses—I somehow "just evaporated" (was it to drive her new Buick?) & the other—both within hours, in the same apt., mind you; this one got in bed after the college girl left to be home when her parents got up—was, you guessed it, just like Sharon, a tall, white-skinned Red-head with green eyes from Big Sur Country now working in an aged Rest Home after flipping; (was I playing doctor again?) without drugs, yet! I could've had others of course, but no time of course, or their old man was present of course, or they were Black of course, or some other damn thing of course. Anyhow, the above was my only sex; so maybe not show this page to girls. Har, Har.

Oh yes, the trip; well, chronologically then: (for over an hour now Gypsy has been "meditating" under the pup-tent he's erected in the back of the pickup using aforementioned twin-stacks—they are actually made of 2" plumbing pipe; by the mad Piute Indian from Carson City who put this wild runner together—one must pass 60 before slipping it into 6th or it'll lug, altho 5th is so versatile one may lug along at 25 or so before winding up to the 60 MPH shift point—I've learned each and every shift point by the clatter the (by 5" steel that took over 5 minutes to bore a hole thru, that holds up to 5,000 lbs per sq. inch) reinforced bell housing the gears sets up—even neutral has its own discernable chatter from this bell as uniquely cracked tho certainly not as uniquely important, as that famed liberty of "meditating," I say by "plunking the twanger" (his guitar) as I sit in the cab trying to write—only he & I are left of the 5 that began—but now he's stopped & gone to sleep so maybe I can now concentrate, but doubt it, since "music hath charms." Oh yes, the trip; well, chronologically then: (Oh yes, the trip; like I say, never make the same one) (Oh yes, the trip; like I say, one's image can be remade in 21 days & since I've been on the road longer than that this time already; it's become a way of life.) Chronologically then: after leaving your place about this time of day that Sunday over 3 weeks ago—there goes a motorbike now—it was an unusually sad trip over the hill & to SF then cross-bay, only undoubtedly, ahem, because the owner of the '55 Olds—just like the one of Dale's[13] I tore up—Chan, his name, wouldn't let me drive; altho I did get to do so leaving the city because he stayed there at your friend Margo's overnite while Gypsy & his old lady, Jenny, (after we'd stopped at Frenchie's, the snag-toothed, open-faced thin, dark-haired Hell's Angel (after being rejected by them several times), who got badly burned lately (hospitalized) from too slowly retreating after pouring gas into a carburetor to see if the coat Chan wanted & Gypsy's got on now was his) & myself went on to Berkeley & for myself a solitary sleep.

The next day, Monday, Aug. 9th, I slept (alone!) The next day, Tuesday, Aug. 10th, I left before dawn, &, after helping Gypsy in a vain search over the streets on foot for a car part that'd fallen off, drove to the closing-too-fast auto wreckers for a fruitless attempt in a similar vein; so the 1951 Hudson Jet we were to make the trip in became instead the auto first left behind; the second one eventually also left behind was the car used to search for parts, a 1951 fucked-up gearshift Chev. with a cracked block & bald tires belonging to a fellow as new to me as was the car—which I drove, after Gypsy worked all Monday to get it running, exclusively until leaving it in Virginia City, Nevada—one Pete Libby, who, with his friend Doug Samuels, we took to Chicago after Doug Samuels' car, a 1957 MG sports car which I drove only around Carson City to try out, broke down in Ely, Nev. where it now is; altho I pulled it a 100 miles further before the first of 3 fans-into-radiator of truck curtailed that.

13. Dale Kesey (aka Highly Charged), cousin of Ken Kesey.

Now, since it appeared we'd have only the '51 Chev. to get us to NYC, albeit in tandem with Pete & Doug in the '57 M.G. as far as Chi, Gypsy, Jenny (his girl) & I spent the rest of the nite relentlessly pressuring the little girl who, (Faye might remember, she asked to meet you, Ken, just before I left that day) along with a couple others that day arrived with Gypsy; hopelessly pressuring, I say, her, altho she gave us $50, & $25 later, to loan for the trip her '64 Saab: yet she did let me, this Mon. midnite, along with Gypsy & Jenny (Pete & Doug, all packed in the M.G., stayed behind on this so as to sleep) drive the Saab back over to SF to get money from Ginsberg—I'd already driven it to get $5 from Pete Orlovsky in Berkeley—& say Goodbye to others, etc.

I forgot to mention that Sunday night, after seeing Hell's Angel Frenchie, we, despite my protestations of fatigue, went to see a R. & R. group that Chan insisted on observing—well, who was it? that's rite—Signe & The HiWires or the Sextones or the Jefferson Hi Bandits,[14] our pals, ya know; & they sounded great, esp. on one about a Hi Flyin' Bird;[15] Of course, Jerry Anderson was there, the first time I'd seen him since his hasty departure in Ukiah & he dashed over all greetings, put on a U.S. flag as a cape & in general showed he was swinging again—besides getting me a beer or two. So here we are now, back to Mon. mid., actually Tues. A.M., I've gone around looking for Bradley & anything else—Paul[16] of the HiWires gave me a leaper, as did Beth Young, so finally Gypsy, Jenny & I in the Saab end up in North Beach at a bar just down from Mr. Otis's as they were closing.

Who should be at the very end of the bar, all-sloppy-lips nuzzling a big floozy Blonde bar fly, but Allen Ginsberg! who at once turned to nuzzling me in between, introducing me to the few poets all gathered there whom I didn't already know—Charles Olsen, Bob Duncan[17]—to shorten this, suffice that no less etc., than 30 or more young D. Moriarty admirers, old queens, serious poets from Ireland, County Cork, drunk poets from the local gentry & others all staggered down Grant to Francisco Street & carrying a full case of beer, went to a

14. The band better known as Jefferson Airplane was formed in August 1965 with Signe Toly, an ex-folksinger as lead vocalist. In September 1965, Signe married ex–Merry Prankster Jerry Anderson, the band's lighting director. When Signe gave birth to a daughter in May 1966, she was replaced by Grace Slick.

15. "High Flyin' Bird" was sung by Signe at one of the band's first recording sessions.

16. Paul Kantner, guitarist and vocalist with Jefferson Airplane.

17. Charles Olsen (1910–1970) and Robert Duncan (1919–1988); two poets associated with the Black Mountain College in Asheville, North Carolina, whose journal, *The Black Mountain Review,* also published work by the Beats.

party as I regaled them from front to back of the block in two long columns with stories, homilies, introductions, warnings & other assorted Cassady Crap until by party-time we were *all* swinging up a storm. I asked everyone for a car to go to NYC in & the aforementioned Blonde Barfly led me to believe she had one, but didn't. Other happenings, more fun occurred & all had a great party, so it was about 5 A.M. before I finally left for NYC.

Gypsy, Jenny & myself—I driving—in the '51 Chev., Pete & Doug closely following in the '57 M.G., got thru Sacramento just ahead of the commute fleet that Tues. Aug. 10th A.M. & promptly had—about 20 miles further the first (& I might try counting them as I write this letter) of countless delays—a flat L.R. on the Chev. so, no spare, but a spare car. I took it off, threw it in the M.G. went back & on the Shell credit card belonging to Doug's mother—poor soul; even if a millionairess, she'll faint when she gets her August bill—at least 350 or 400 dollars!—fixed it. Whoo—flash, flash (not that kind, nothing to produce it with, sob, sob) word just reached my ear & I was right, as usually am—heh, heh, it was the main bearing, front, & worse, the damn cam or crankshaft I mean, torqued itself right off its slat in the block—so *no can fix*—here we are broke, 39 miles S.W. of Cleveland (the Babbs moved just yesterday!!) with tons of gear to hitchhike east with. Gulp, grrr!

8-31; 5P.[M.]

A night of really vicious raining having passed; everything (but me) in the truck having gotten wet; Gypsy didn't erect a tent designed to stop a flood; we set out to look for someone to trade a motorless truck for practically anything that runs—& after all day looking (including as near misses a 1949 Black Chev., a 1953 green one with smooth tires & a 1938 ton & ½ flatbed Dodge truck) we've come up with a 1955 Studebaker yellow station wagon with 49,000 miles, but no spare wheel or tire, radio, heater & such a badly leaking muffler that not only must all the windows be left down, but one must take aspirins ½ hourly for the headaches produced; also right smarting is the eye irritation; anyhow, it runs, altho burning so much oil the hiway behind is festooned with smoke & fumes. I know all this from having ridden in it as the war-injured man with eight (8) kids—He wears a brace like Babbs had—who traded us, drove me to the station to steer the truck as he pushed it home.

Understand, I'm continuing this letter here in the truck cab since the flies in the house—yes, house flies—are just too much (& because the oldest of the 8 urchins, a good-looking blonde about 17 or so has discontinued the goo-goo eyes & has gone to the show with boy friend, Billie, in his '55 Chev. that has a slight miss) instead of getting on the road because we have to wait until tomorrow to go to the courthouse here in Milan, Ohio—birthplace of Tom A. Edison, ya know—to get the car title transferred to us. So it was about this time of day & raining too as it is here now that after fixing the flat & pushing it as hard as I could over the mountains we wheeled the '51 Chev. into Virginia City, Nev. where Chan, Gypsy & Jenny jumped into Chan's '55 Olds (he had gone on ahead the day before) & drove out to Dave Melville's place in the desert to pick up the 6 months deserted truck I'm now sitting in. (Tell Anne Murphy her ex-lover wasn't there, "gone North to Alaska.")

Pete, Doug & I stayed on a knoll outside town sleeping in & under the '51 Chev. while they went for the truck—finally returning toward midnite & as Tues. 8-10 ended we were all huddled in the truck—save Pete & Doug behind in the M.G.—as we barreled it into Carson City where the Piute Indian who'd 1st put it together—he ran a junkyard—was to spend all of Wed—8-11 just getting it ready for the road again. We mostly stood around the garage as he worked, but I did take the M.G. for a spin & visited the gambling spots for a while till, about 10 P. word came that all was ready &, again with Pete & Doug behind in the M.G., we finally started east in earnest (mind you, we left the '51 Chev. & two lids with Chan in exchange for the truck—that's all it cost!)

9-2, 5P.[M.]

9-1 at 5 P.M. I was starting thru *all* of Pittsburgh, Pa's commute fleet in the noxious '55 Studebaker & despite having no power relative to the other machines I didn't let a damn one of them get past me in the long run & by adroitly switching lanes very few, one or two a mile, I'd say, got by me in the short haul; so there! But back to recounting Cassady's torpid trip East: 50 miles west of Ely, Nev., the truck ran out of gas—altho holding 27 or 8 gallons it got only 7 or 8 miles per same—so about daylight on 8-12, a Thursday, we sent Doug & Pete ahead in the M.G. to fill our 5 gallon can with gas. Well, hours later a tow truck came with the gas 'cause Doug's M.G. broke down about 25 mi. out of Ely—which itself is 200 from *anywhere*—& they'd hitchhiked. So, as I was pushing the M.G. into Ely at about 50 M.P.H. he decided to try starting it again—after numerous failures—& the subsequent bump put the truck fan into the radiator—the 1st of several times this was to happen—so the tow truck pulled both cars to Ely. We were there over 24 hours, until late afternoon on Friday the 13th, acct. several reasons: 1, the $50 Gypsy's parents sent arrived before the 5 P. W.U. closing time but we didn't pick it up before then. 2, The truck bell-house was to be fixed the next day—& was—by a RR brakeman we fell in with who let us stay overnite at his house of wife & 2 kids. 3, The M.G. decision was dependent on a generator arriving the next day—it didn't—so, after towing it 100 miles north toward Wendover, the truck fan hit the radiator again—it was a loose fan bolt, not motor mounts as we thought & we left the M.G. behind for good.

Bumming water & a crescent wrench from passing cars to get us to the next station, leaking like a sieve, we finally made Wendover after dark . . . Utah. At last, a pen provided by Jenny whose house we are at present staying—here in Bridgeton, New Jersey—some 40 miles south of Wilmington, Delaware & Philadelphia & will be for a day or so; her Daddy is the Methodist minister for this town of 25,000 & when he arrives from NYC—where I'll be going in due time this weekend—tonite I'm anticipating a spirited homily oration. Anyway, we left Wendover after using mud, tar, flaxseed, clay & spit to cover hole in radiator & got into Salt Lake City at 12:01 A.M. Sat. 8-14. I called Anne Gilhool's mother & she said it was much too late an hour & if I'd call at a respectable 8 A.M. she'd give me Anne's phone number—so I did & Anne's Daddy answered & said Mama was gone already & *he* didn't know his daughter's phone number, so that was that & I never did see Anne Gilhool. So no pussy, no money (Gypsy had spent it buying a shotgun in Ely, Nev.) no leapers, etc, etc., but we limped along—5 of us; 3 of us in the cab, 2 in back of the pickup—filling the radiator every few miles until, approaching daylight, we finally pulled into my hometown—& Gypsy's—of Denver on Sun 8-15.

Going directly to an Art Gallery owned by a nice little Toulouse-Lautrec named Phil, whose sister married Gypsy's handsome, blond younger brother, we all slept till late afternoon then went to Gypsy's parents in extreme So. Denver, then to Jenny's friends in Boulder, Colorado where we spent the night. Returning to Denver that Mon. the 16th about noon, I had the brakes suddenly go out as I was approaching toll-plaza so I had to coast thru, missing everything & no horn, shouting for all to watch out, pull over & fiddle around an hour or so before again we could go. That afternoon they sold all the pot & we've had none since, save a little weak Indiana Green in Chicago & some about as poor in Detroit. That nite Gypsy's irate father took a swing at me!!—held in check by a browbeaten mother—so Gypsy called the aforementioned Iowa College girl I got tight with & she (I) drove us all back to Boulder—No, wait, it was Gypsy's brother that took us to Boulder this Monday nite & Jenny's ex–old man who drove us back about noon on Tues. the 17th & I went directly to the Post Office & got Anne Murphy's letter which I will now take the time to answer, OK?

Dear Anne: Glad you got some "satisfaction (I can't get no)" from the reassurances in my letter & that you've proved unsuccessful in your seduction attempts. I don't want my old lady to be fucked by everybody; just almost every body—& that two weeks at the Lishes *was* a ball, but could have been so much better; for one reason or another, right? "To endure, & be clean"—how difficult! & I *do* believe you are trying, tho on the surface you've very little reason to & if you sometimes fail, don't worry about it, for I love you anyhow whether you try or not, succeed or not, altho just trying is mainly what I need to know you are doing—if only for my weakened ego. "Your love is the nourishment of my life"—would that my life were the nourishment of your love—or at least more so. Thanks for the quote from Ken you sent, I don't think it'll ever be that way again (all those girls, I mean). "After all we are still alive"—that's Rite!! & you damn well better keep it that way or I'll spank your bottom good in the astral plane too. Hoping to see you again, Love Always, NEAL

So it was Tuesday nite, the 17th that the college girl let me drive her new Buick & all of us back to Boulder, Colo., & Wed. the 18th that we all returned to Denver, save Jenny who had some things to get done there in Boulder; so Gypsy could stay at home a day or so where the truck was all this time & get things straight there, so Doug & Pete could stay at the Art Gallery complex & so I could—heh, heh—get a little as I mentioned on page 4 of this soon-to-be book. Thursday nite, the 19th & half of Fri.—20th, we all got hi on various goodies & I wailed for about 20 people at the Art Gallery & at the Red-head's apt. whose regular boyfriend is, I believe, Sid Wertz, remember him? I stayed at the red-head's as did Doug & Pete too, by now the Art Gallery crowd was tired of us I guess. Fri. nite—altho having to sleep alone since she worked the graveyard shift at the nursing home &,

after calling Justin Brierly—he really wants to see me on the way back West—if I go back West—& a few other things, including reading a couple J. Updike books, Gypsy, having gotten Jenny from Boulder, Doug & Pete & myself left Denver, the truck having been all fixed finally—we thought!!—with a new radiator, clutch rod extension, new L.R. brake, etc. Just after dark on Saturday Aug 21st we barreled directly to Akron, Colo., where Jenny loaded down the truck with a lot of wedding presents she'd left there & charged straight on—myself driving all the way, of course—to a town just short of Omaha, Neb. called Wahoo; it was at Wahoo, last year, that I let Bob Mills & Joe Riker drive their only time in my '55 Ply. I left NYC in after the bus trip, remember?—they drove from Wahoo to Lodgepole, Neb.—when, suddenly, whang—the blade of the fan tore loose (the same thing cut short Sterling Moss's great drive in a GT Ferrari in the 1961 Le Mans 24 hr) ripped a hole in the hood & sob, sob, tore another hole in the radiator!! Here we were, on a Sunday afternoon with no fan, 2 blades had flown off, not opposing ones either, no money again, & worse, no Shell station to save our necks. Gypsy had a distant friend in Omaha, who came out, took one look at us & drove right away again! So we fucked around Wahoo until dark—getting the local punks to help us—offering to steal fans etc.—when we drove off minus a fan & with the motor backfiring very loudly, *very loudly*.

Once in Omaha, after going to the friend's (?) house & being turned down for a flop, we spent the night sleeping beside a Sinclair station man, who said he'd pull the left bank and grind the valves for us—it wasn't the fucking valves at all; instead the kids in Wahoo had put the plug wires back wrong & two or more were firing in opposition. Of course, we didn't find this out until Des Moines, IA, & so drove hundreds of miles making a truly terrible racket—but he didn't & so we spent Monday morning, Aug. 23, going back & forth between Omaha and Council Bluffs trying to find a Shell garage that would take us. None would since it took a deep-seat grinder, the valves being in the block on the '40 Caddy engine; but we did find how to plug the leak in the radiator—a raw egg!!—permanently, so no more trouble on that score & we ended up sitting for hours in front of the Western Union in Downtown Omaha—a lot of pretty girls there—waiting for the money that Jenny had wired her folks for before we finally took off for Chicago still minus a fan.

We fucked around Drake University in Des Moines looking for a prof. that Jenny knew; never found him; fixed the plug fuck-up there & roared—much less loudly now—into Chicago just before daylight

Tuesday, Aug. 24, two weeks to the hour after we'd left Berkeley, Calif.—It seemed more like 2 months! My timing proving as good as ever, we pulled up in front of Pete's Japanese buddy's house just as he arrived from an all-nite binge & so we went immediately to bed & slept all of the 24th then got up late that night, got loaded on acid & went bar-hopping to hear some great Rock & Roll, finally ending up just before dawn running up & down the great sea wall guarding Lake Michigan's Chi yacht harbor. We were taken over to a gone chick's house where Doug, Gypsy & I were to sleep the rest of our time there; Jenny had flown home to New Jersey earlier, & where, altho I could have had some nookie from several assorted ones, I failed to follow thru & get any ass. But I'll be back there! Ha, ha. Last nite we went to see Moll Flanders & Lord Jim: Fair film fare.

9-3. 5P.[M.]

Today I spent mostly eating & sleeping; Gypsy went to Camden, but failed to fix the muffler, Jenny went shopping while the rest of the household, including her 19 yr. old brother who is majoring in radio & TV—he's told me some informative things in that field, i.e., it takes only $100,000 to buy or build a TV station, a little less for an FM station, etc.—went on their usual ways. I haven't discussed theology yet with Jenny's father—& doubt I will since they say he doesn't like to, but we *are* having fish for supper this Friday nite because I mentioned I was Catholic—their bugaboo.

Wednesday, the 25th in Chi we got up late, socialized around a little, turned on, heard more live music, went to Pete Libby's partner-to-be & got a tape recorder for Gypsy to play some guitar on & goofed in general. Thursday, the 26th, we finally got a fan in the truck, they being hard to find, decided to leave the hood of the truck off permanently; we'd had it off since Iowa, and tuned the truck up. Early Fri. 27th A.M. was spent making a talking tape with a guy—artist—who defended Hitler vehemently, both as a guy who was great & as a fellow German; the artist being one. "But look at all the ass he kicked," he kept saying of Hitler, UGH. Late Fri. P.M. we took in a spade party that was just too much; drinking, dancing & of the 100 or so there 90 percent of them was hustling something; the girls their ass & the boys their shit. Which reminds me—I can get all the straight old white cross bennies you want at $85 a thousand. I'll let you know from Chicago when I go there next week if the deal's still firm, tho I'm sure it is. Anyhow, I had a few & they are certainly OK, as well as the guy who's got them, & he digs me very much as well—another Irishman. Anyhoo, late Saturday, Aug. 28th with only a $5 bill & Doug's poor Shell credit card—Doug & Pete stayed behind of course, Chicago being their destination—Gypsy & I took off for NYC via Canada because he knew a girl in Toronto who supposedly would give us money. Sunday the 29th at 2 A.M. we tried to cross the border at Windsor, Ont., & they kicked us back to Detroit acct. insufficient funds, so we went to a buddy of Gypsy's—also a RR brakeman—& spent the rest of Sunday there, finally leaving just before dark that nite & continued non-stop to go around Lake Erie on the U.S.A. side & enter Canada closer to Toronto—to the point where we broke down completely & this letter began—Wakeman, Ohio, on the same day your trial began, 8-30-65.

Now, Ken & all of you dear hearts, esp. Anne, Sharon & June—are any or all of them still around? If I was there they'd damn well know it; from putting my arms & legs around any or all of them, singly or collectively—My schedule is this: Tomorrow A.M. we drive, Gypsy, Jenny & I, after I mail this, at last, so you'll get it Tuesday, Sept. 7th, to Pemberton, N.J. for some art frames, then Beach Haven, N.J. for a bikini beach party—pant, pant, ogle, ogle,—then finally to NYC in the late P.M., a full 28 days after leaving SF—could've made as good a time on a racing bike or a good go kart, huh?—where I'll go rite to the Village for some leapers, acid, grass or what have you on a Saturday nite; then after see Bill Burroughs at 803 10th Street—you can write me there, but since I don't anticipate being around to get any letters, why not write me at Chicago General Delivery since I'll be there about Wed. at earliest or Fri. at latest next week; anyway I'll tell Bill Burroughs to forward any & all mail to Chicago Gen. Delivery & that way you have an excuse to write him on your own if you want—slick, huh? & Ed Sanders[18] at the Peace Eye bookstore at 210 8th street, etc. I'll check on Al Aronowitz, the NY Post feature writer & Lucien Carr, the UPI Nite desk chief editor before taking off for North Port, Long Island & Jack Kerouac at #7 Judy Ann Court there; anyway Sun. &

18. Ed Sanders, poet and author of *The Family: The Story of Charles Manson's Dune Buggy Attack Battalion* (1971) and *Tales of Beatnik Glory* (1975). Founded the Peace Eye Bookstore on New York's Lower East Side in 1964 and was also an original member of The Fugs rock band. Sanders appeared with Jack Kerouac to discuss "hippies" on William F. Buckley Jr.'s *Firing Line* TV show in September 1968.

Mon. in NYC & environs then back here Mon. nite & if we put rings in the '55 Studebaker on Tuesday we'll leave that night, if not, we'll leave Tuesday A.M. the 7th about the time you get this.[19]

Once in Chicago I might very well stay there until Halloween or Thanksgiving cold weather drives me out. Not that I want to—I sincerely don't, believe me; I dislike the place, as I do all the east—but acct. I've been offered a hundred & a quarter a week truckdriving job there, tho the boss himself has not seen me yet, & ya know damn well how much back child support I owe—almost $1,600 now—incidentally my oldest girl is 17 on Sept 7th & the youngest boy is 14 on Sept. 9th—so I figure to work a couple of months—sending my ex-wife $100 a week—& then return to the West Coast for the winter; in Los Angeles probably. If I don't get the job, but I'm pretty sure I will, I very well might return as far as Ely, Nev. to pick up Doug's MG for him & drive it back to Chicago; if so you may be sure I'll continue on to your place to pick up my clothes & maybe a girl (or two, or 3, or 4 or more! ha) altho that red-head in Denver needs a vacation & is already half-promised same by both Gypsy & me, i.e., I'm sure she'd dig the drive. Anyway, if I get the job, collecting things for the Disabled American Veterans, I'll see you all in Nov. sometime, early or late. If I don't I'll see ya in Mid-Sept., with or without the red-head (she'll just go back as far as Denver anyway) & if Anne Murphy, who still has first call on my heart (what's left of it)—still wants me I'll take her, at least, off your hands—if not, or if I don't have to drive Doug's car back to Chicago for him, he may come with me to pick it up—I'll take Sharon (if she'll still have me) & go directly to L.A. for the winter. If neither girl is available, June (if she'll still have me) & I will take off together & be very happy I'm sure! I mean it all 100%. Otherwise in strict seniority order, I'll take the Denver red-head & be very happy, I'm sure! I mean it all 100%.

Love,
NEAL

Arriving in New York, Neal inscribed messages to bookstore owner Ted Wilentz, in copies of Kerouac's books Desolation Angels *and* On the Road.

19. Neal would have been unsuccessful in finding Kerouac, who was then living in St. Petersburg, Florida, having moved there from his Judyann Court address in 1964.

TO TED WILENTZ

September 9, 1965
[New York]

(Writ by Al Capp, I mean left hand of Cody (herein) at Ted's 8th St. bookshop)

FOR TED,

Since I've not really known you before, altho Ginnsy speaks—softhearted, ya know—well, OK your way—& besides not having read this book yet; what am I getting into here? (In more ways than one obviously); all I can say is, thanks indeed for the copy of Desolation Angels you've given me this day & love,

NEAL CASSADY (CODY)

TO TED WILENTZ

September 9, 1965
at his store on 8th St.
[New York]

FOR TED—

Who led me to believe that all bookmen don't resent giving themselves away in their entirety, nay, in their heart, aye!

With love,
NEAL CASSADY,
(Himself, I think)
DEAN MORIARTY

Back in California that fall, Neal was involved in a series of Acid Tests. At these events, which Kesey and the Merry Pranksters had inaugurated on Ken Babbs's ranch at Soquel, near Santa Cruz, in November 1965, the then legal LSD was dispensed to the audience in cups of Kool-Aid drink, and everyone got high, usually to the musical accompaniment of The Warlocks (who, a few months later, changed their name to The Grateful Dead) and a psychedelic light show, while Neal extemporized his hip monologues over the sound system.

1966

In January, Ken Kesey was sentenced to six months in prison and three years' probation. He faked a suicide note and fled to Mexico. Meanwhile, Carolyn reprimanded Neal for flaunting his lifestyle before the children, fearful of the bad influence it might have on them.

TO NEAL CASSADY FROM CAROLYN CASSADY

January 18, 1966
18231 Bancroft Avenue
Monte Sereno, California

DEAREST NEAL—

Once more I'm back in my old role—reprimanding you. Now that finances have eased for a time, I can give more attention to the real problem—John. (Just like you said—always something.)

Some time ago I told you the main thing he needed was not to be talked at but listened to. You did not heed. Now & for the past year—each time you "drop in"—(and you were asked to call always or not come) you have never ceased a constant expose of the thrilling life you lead & the *important* activities you're engaged in. No doubt, in the back of your mind you think you're telling him his old man is not so bad after all. What you have actually accomplished is to show him without a shadow of doubt that the life here that you rejected is for the birds—that any discipline, school work, self improvement, efforts for the future, respect for rules, me or the law is asinine—as you so clearly demonstrate. Obviously they never believe me when I tell them you're the most miserable of men—Ha—just look at you. They never see a particularly uninhibited & jovial guy on TV they don't say "just like Dad."

Well, your son is right in your footsteps already. I had a session with a counselor—more positive minded than most—who has branded him as "infantile." This will go with him throughout his future schooling—no matter how I contend all the areas of responsibility he does demonstrate. No matter—that's it. I have it on the authority of other counselors & teachers. We are paying another tutor to bring him up to the present work of the math class. He has been shown graphically that he tests out as high as the tests go—who knows how much higher his score might be—but he could care less. Besides, I can't get him to stop smoking—& why *should* he listen to me? After all, look at *you*—a delighted 6 year old having a ball in his colored wagon—no responsibilities are important—no mind power, no rules, no laws—only what "I want."

If you could just come into this house & be interested in *US*—not in glorifying yourself—if you'd been as intensely interested in HIM & what he might accomplish—& what we're trying to help him develop of his own tremendous potential! But no, you couldn't listen—only jabber.

I miss you too; I'd like to see you occasionally—but not at this expense. I can look at you objectively & be interested in *your* potential, but they can only see someone they love that chose between this life, them & what you're doing now. I gave you (well, not *gave*) freedom so you could be unhampered—but now it's worse without *any* desire to promote his good or appreciate my efforts—& only showing them you chose *that* life.

It's a heartbreaking losing battle, & if John doesn't see the light soon—within the next 6 months, his whole educational future is in the balance.

You're quite right—I am no influence—you are—I see it now. I don't know how I can stand to watch him go the way you have & be powerless to prevent it.

Well, I don't know what to do now. But even tho the damage is done, if you don't keep adding to it, maybe someday—I don't see how. So, once more I have to ask you to stay away completely if you can't help. There are many ways you could serve—so many times you could have inspired Jamie & John to appreciate their gifts if you only had. Jamie may come out of it—she may believe some in her own talent—tho not as much as she should—or she'd be thin not fatter & fatter—but John was too little to know about his before the dream of eternal childhood took over—coupled with smart big shot stuff like smoking.

You didn't need to be successful—just give of yourself—your ear alone would do it—just that. Will you sacrifice him again on your ego?

Don't know if you even care to read this, you haven't wanted to listen to me for a long time either.

Anyway—I ask again—*please* don't "drop in"—call, or not at all. Not that it's what *"I want"*—I think it best—feeble but best.

Love always
CAROLYN

P.S. If you're going to keep giving this address to police, you'd better check now & then. Since court, address has been changed. You'll go to the wrong one.

Carolyn wrote to Ginsberg about old tape recordings she had discovered of Neal, Jack, and Allen.

TO ALLEN GINSBERG FROM CAROLYN CASSADY

May 27, 1966
[Monte Sereno, California]

DEAREST ALLEN: (Hello Peter and Julie)

It was fun reading about some of the rest of your trip in Life . . . I wondered how you liked the write-up, since as I recall, you've never been too sympathetic with the Time-Life monster. I thought it a step up from the usual.[1]

I was sorry not to see you all one mo time before you embarked, but I cherish the memory of the fun time we did have. Also I've learned of your further generosity in my behalf and as you must know, am very very grateful. You're a most noble and generous fellow. I certainly hope I'll not be in this limited position much longer, and you'll be one of the first to hear. So far our organization is making

1. Allen Ginsberg had left San Francisco in his Volkswagen van in December 1965 on a trip across America, accompanied by Peter Orlovsky and his brother Julius. When they reached Kansas in February 1966, reporter Barry Farrell followed Ginsberg around and produced a long article, "Guru Comes to Kansas," in *Life* magazine, May 27, 1966.

good strides ahead.[2] We did a pavilion in the World Trade Fair, selling 2 lines of Italian fashions, Spanish wigs and German soaps, the latter retail. We got a lot of unexpected breaks in the form of contacts with the manufacturers of the other countries there and also a well-known SF photographer took an interest in our project and made dozens of free gorgeous publicity pictures. One day you'll hear of Communications Fashions International. Meantime, say a prayer for us. We still plan to go to Europe in the fall to sell American fashions over there, but the exact ways and means have not yet materialized. They will.

Now then, I want your advice and opinion. I was cleaning up all the odd tapes we have around and discovered the one you made in 1953 in San Jose. It's priceless. You read poetry at the start, sing a darling ditty called Green Valentine, remember? as well as an hilarious version of When the Saints. . . . On the other side is more poems, most notable the Green Automobile rendered twice in different modulations.[3] Your voice is so young and clipped. So I wanted to ask you what you think I should do with it. If Andy Brown[4] wants it, should I sell it to him, and if so, how much? Naturally, I'd have him make a copy. He has promised me copies of all the letters too. I regret the whole transaction was so unbusinesslike, but I was pressured from all sides and felt it was Neal's decision to make. Anyway, I hope they're all in the right hands and will be used wisely for the best good of you.

There's another delightful but short episode where Neal and Jack are reading, the former, Proust, and Jack reading Dr. Sax with Neal adding the "yeaaahs" in the background. The kids and I got a charge out of the ones of them that Christmas, the funniest part being Neal laying one of his stories on me in the background to get out with the car for a couple days. He's fantastic with the children though, and

2. A friend of Carolyn's had formed a venture called Communications Fashions International, hoping to market midpriced clothing. Carolyn was artistic director and won first prize for the pavilion she designed for exhibiting their goods at the World Trade Fair in San Francisco.

3. Allen Ginsberg's recordings, made on Neal's tape recorder while he was staying with the Cassadys in San Jose in the summer of 1954, included readings of his poems "Green Automobile" and "Green Valentine Blues" as well as "Walking at Night in Key West," sung to the tune of "When the Saints Go Marching In." All three were included in the 4-CD set of Ginsberg's recordings, *Holy Soul Jelly Roll*, issued in 1994.

4. Neal's old letters were sold to Andreas Brown, of the Gotham Book Mart, New York, who sold some to the Humanities Research Center at the University of Texas at Austin and others to the Rare Book and Manuscript Library, Columbia University, New York.

when I listen to that compared to him now, it breaks your heart. I fear his mind is turning to mush. Poor guy, how I wish there was something that would help, and now he won't leave this area . . . he says it's us, but I wish it were for the pending jail commitments. If that were so there'd be hope he could go somewhere more productive or with you.

Gotta get back to work. Let me know what you think.

Much love,
CAROLYN

In March, Ken Babbs had driven the other Pranksters to Mexico in the bus to meet up with Ken Kesey. That September, Neal and George Walker drove south together in Neal's 1955 Chrysler, meeting up with the others and staging further Acid Tests there.

TO CAROLYN CASSADY

August 2, 1966
1313 Univ. Ave.,
San Jose,
California

DEAR HEART & KIDDIES,

Here's that $20. Hope I *don't* see you all until Sept 7th: If you don't hear from me first—make no sense? Guess; or not.

Love,
NEAL (DAD)

P.S. Love

P.P.S. " Neal

TO CAROLYN CASSADY

[September 1966]
c/o [George] Walker
Lista de Correos
Manzanillo, Colima, Mexico

Manzanillo, Colima, Mex. shall see our show Sept. 10, Guadalajara Sept. 17, Mex. City Sept. 24—yet, aha, home before the 1st Oct. Until then may God in Him watch over you. Amen.

Got your letter, ones to our birthday twins following.

Love,
All fine but still smokin! NEAL

P.S. Please advise sell letters, OK?

Back in San Francisco that October, Neal forwarded a birthday message that he'd written in Mexico to his daughter Cathy.

TO CAROLYN CASSADY

Saturday [October 29, 1966] P.M.
268 6th St.
San Francisco

DEAREST ALL;

Hi Love, here's $30.00 & more, I think, this next week.

Love to all & I'll call soon.

P.S. Here's a little memo of Cathy's 18th I failed to mail from Mexico.

Love,
DADDY
NEAL

P.P.S. See you all very soon

To my oldest daughter on her 18th *September 7, 1966*

CATHLEEN JOANNE CASSADY

The only one of our three, 2 girls, who had colic also eczema & mother's milk.

Who used to be wheeled, at 109 Liberty St., into the large park behind Galileo High on Dolores St. so her 3 week-to-month old being could daily take air & sun; not the baseballs or footballs I still enjoy remembering forestalling by the artful angling of fine, new carriage behind tree.

Who loved to be held & walked, more perhaps than any other of my children; who always, eating, of my children in infancy, least perhaps, certainly least well, at least burped best!!!

Hi sweets!! Do you realize as I just did going on in the drivel on reverse to denote your maturity, that this is the first letter I've written you separately? So I'll stop poetizing & celebrate your grown state by quoting verbatim from mother's letters to me here. OK? Here goes:

"Cathy got the job at the Hospital & works 4 hrs daily, all day Sat., or 28 hours a week. I told her to keep all over $100 & save for car. She's over at W.V.[5] now figuring classes to take in only hours she has available from work. So now Cathy is both (& I'm proud of you for it!!) Breadwinner & taxpayer!!"

So you got your first traffic ticket last month, heh? Now you know what I've been foolish enuf to go thru for more years than you are old, rite?

Heh, heh.

Ken Kesey had reentered the USA in October, staging more Acid Tests around San Francisco. LSD was made illegal in California on October 6; on October 20, Kesey was arrested and faced trial on November 30, the result of which was a six-month sentence on a county work farm, which he began the following June. The final Acid Test took place in a San Francisco warehouse on Halloween night, with Neal in attendance as usual.

5. West Valley College, Saratoga, California.

1967

In early January, Neal drove back to Mexico with George Walker in George's Lotus Elan. Steven "Zonker" Lambrecht, Gloria Quarnstrom, and Anne Murphy accompanied them in a Ford belonging to Steve's parents. On their arrival, they rented a house in Puerto Vallarta for two months. Neal sent a postcard to his daughter Jamie on her seventeenth birthday.

TO JAMIE CASSADY

January 22, 1967 A.M.
[Puerto Vallarta, Mexico]

DEAR JAMIE;

A truly happy birthday, fellow Aquarian!

Love,
DADDY

P.S. All fine here—wish y'all were,

NEAL

TO CAROLYN CASSADY

February 8, 1967
[Puerto Vallarta, Mexico]

DEAREST;

Starting my 41st at place marked X on reverse. To Guadalajara today. Back here 2 or 3 days.

Love,
N.

Lista de Correos is my address. N.

On the way to Guadalajara, the Ford, with Neal at the wheel, lost its transmission and was abandoned and later sold for $100.

TO CAROLYN CASSADY

February 10, 1967
[Guadalajara, Mexico]

DEAREST ONE;

Finally saw Orozco's mad picture here.[1] Very little else. Am going back to P.V. on plane since dropped transmission on Ford near Tepic. Write me Lista de Correo, Puerto Vallarta, Jal, Mex.

Love, believe it or not,
NEAL

TO CAROLYN CASSADY

February 20, 1967
Lista de Correos
Puerto Vallarta
Jal, Mexico

DEAR LOVE,

Here's 48 bucks.
More soon, we pray

Love, NEAL

While in Puerto Vallarta, Neal and the others met the American postgraduate art students Kathy Van Leeuwen and her sister Anne, who were living in San Miguel, and were invited to stay with them at their apartment in the Palomar building. Anne Murphy, meanwhile, returned to the USA by plane.

1. Fernando Orozco directed the movie *El Hombre de la Furia* (1966).

TO CAROLYN CASSADY

March 15, 1967—7 P.M.
The Ides!
Lista de Correos
Puerto Vallarta
Jal, Mexico

DEAREST EVER & REST OF HEARTS;

Here's 50 from Ginzy.

A card today say Anne Murphy OK—after jet-planed away—& living in L.A. (Not SF!) So, now, & per last words uttered in your lovely presence:

"I shall return & satisfy you after cleared her up" Rite?

So don't write here.

Love always,
NEAL

P.S. See me in (1) March 13, Newsweek?[2]

(2) March Ramparts?[3]

(3) New York Herald Trib., Jan. 29 (Sun. Mag., by Tom Wolfe)?—pictures too.[4]

P.P.S. When's C.'s lying in?[5]

2. *Newsweek,* vol. 69, no. 11 (March 13, 1967), carried a review by S. K. Oberbeck of John Clellon Holmes's collection of essays *Nothing More to Declare.* The review mentions Holmes's 1952 novel, *Go,* in which the character Hart Kennedy was based upon Neal Cassady, "now a central figure in Ken Kesey's LSD-oriented Merry Pranksters."

3. Warren Hinckle, "A Social History of the Hippies," in *Ramparts* (Berkeley, California), vol. 5, no. 9 (March 1967). The article describes Neal Cassady as "the Tristram Shandy of the Beat Generation . . . signed up as the driver of Kesey's fun and games bus, which is rumored to run on LSD," and includes a photograph of Neal standing with others alongside the bus during a January 1966 Acid Test.

4. *World Journal Tribune* (New York), vol. 1, no. 137 (January 29, 1967), included a magazine with an article by Tom Wolfe, "The Chief and His Merry Pranksters Take a Trip with Electric Kool-Aid," as the first in a three-part series, "The World of LSD." All three parts of the illustrated series featured Neal Cassady and were later reworked into Wolfe's book *The Electric Kool-Aid Acid Test,* published in 1968, after Neal's death.

5. Neal's daughter Cathy was expecting her first baby in September 1967.

P.P.S. Mucho kisses

More money soon, N.
Hope home by our 19th ole thing.
Mucho mucho love, N.

By the end of March, Neal and George had moved on to San Miguel de Allende, where they stayed with the Van Leeuwens. From Mexico, Neal sent Allen Ginsberg a series of increasingly desperate postcards.

TO ALLEN GINSBERG

March 31, 1967, 6 P.M.
San Miguel 'Allende, GTO—MEX

I know it looks like my mind's gone—rite? But no—still, I'll recapitulate. But first—Bro. against Bro., almost, in USA. (Bloodless for most part) Civil War as Rite Rite cleans up for year or more—i.e. R. Reagan as governor has already appointed Big Business/man as Labor Commissioner, Welfare Chief is lawyer opposing welfare, State Conservator (redwoods) is a big lumberman, real estate czar an anti-fair housing crusader, as Clemency Sect., an ex-D.A. favoring capital punishment—get the idea?—then, late '68—not slow, but fast adjustment as new awakening spreads throughout our culture—meantime, watch out, fishes coming to the surface are to be caught—hooked if your beard's more than 3 inches or hair more than 7", say. All emotion, no reason, etc. etc.

S.W.A.K.

TO CAROLYN CASSADY

April 1, 1967
[San Miguel de Allende, Mexico]

DEAREST & CHILDREN;

Happy anniversary! Just found out, leaving for San Antonio, Texas before 4-14, then will hitchhike home that week so see you before your 44th! Miss you all *every hour*! Ginsberg sending another $50–100 at once. Left P.V. before you could have written, so trust you got his 1st $50.

Love, NEAL

P.S. Hi John, Jamie, Cath. Miss you so! Terribly really. N.

TO ALLEN GINSBERG

April 12, 1967
[c/o] Kathy Van Leeuwen
San Francisco 49
San Miguel De Allende
Gto. Mexico

DEAR ALLEN; COMRADE!

SERIOUS—TOP SECRET—DO THIS!

After 28th in New Mexico, (Invite: if in Phone book or at your Lecture there—ask audience—Bob Adams—Ask if he's friend of me & Justin Brierly) Take bus to Dallas (Dallas, Tex.) on 29th, be in Dallas Tex. 30th late or early 1st May so can, *you must* meet me. (May 1, noon) at JFK Ass. site (by bookstore).[6] Write at once.

Love,
NEAL

Neal's plans to return to California for Carolyn's forty-fourth birthday on April 28 came to nothing. When George Walker and the others returned to the States, Neal remained in San Miguel, staying with Diane Sward and her boyfriend and small child. Neal told Ginsberg that he might be remaining in Mexico for some months and asked him to visit and bring financial aid.

6. President John F. Kennedy was assassinated on November 22, 1963, near the Texas School Book Depository, on Elm Street, Dallas.

TO ALLEN GINSBERG

[April 1967]
c/o Diane Sward
Lista de Correos
San Miguel de Allende
Gto. Mexico

DEAR POOPSIE—COMRADE—ETC.

Again a change—decided against Dallas. Get on the plane or train and come down to San Miguel de Allende. There's a train that leaves El Paso every day around seven at night and takes thirty hours and leaves you at a town called Celaya at some incredible hour in the morning. If you come by train let us know when so we can meet it. If we don't meet the train just take a cab from Celaya—it will cost about 60 pesos ($5) to San Miguel.

Or you can take the plane to Mexico City and take a bus from there to here (4½ hours).

You can find me at Diane's house at 4 Murillo—and stay here too.

Then we can figure out what to do from there. But it's better than that. I got big plans—just stick with me—and really want to see you—

No need to make it immediately after the 28th—I can wait another week or so—but I'm going to stay here until you get here even if it's June because you've got to save me—if not mentally and physically—at least financially—

Really I'll stay until you get here—won't take no for an answer—

Enclosed is a card so you can let me know what's happening. Will be in Vera Cruz for a week—then back here by around the 26th—

I'm counting on you, Al—we'll talk when you get here . . .

Love & Hurry on Down Allen.

NEAL
(Himself)

P.S. I wrote Jack a card.
P.P.S. Don't get rioted & get your hairless head bumped, heh, heh.

N.

Ginsberg, on tour giving poetry readings, did not receive Neal's messages. Meanwhile, Neal had met the twenty-three-year-old Janice Brown (known as J.B.), an American who had been living in San Miguel for several years, work-

ing at the theater of the Instituto Allende. They lived together for a time, before Neal returned to the States in early May. There, he met up again with Kesey, staying at his newly purchased farm near Eugene, Oregon. When Ginsberg visited, they took off together in the psychedelic bus to attend a writers' conference at Western Washington State College in Bellingham, where Allen and Neal also appeared onstage with Jefferson Airplane in the Carver Gym on May 26.

When Neal returned to San Francisco, Janice Brown joined him there, and together they took off on a trip across country, calling on Ed White in Denver and revisiting Ted Wilentz and his wife, Joan, in New York. When J.B. returned to Mexico, Neal remained in the States for a while, but fearful that he would be arrested for nonpayment of the many traffic fines he had incurred, he decided to head for Mexico once more. Finding himself at the border crossing near San Antonio, Texas, he was able to visit the hospital where his daughter Cathy had given birth to her son William on September 6 and hold his grandson in his arms. Later that month, impoverished again in Mexico, Neal wrote requesting money from his old friend Lucien Carr.

TO LUCIEN CARR

September 15, 1967
Quebrada Norte #16
San Miguel de Allende
Gto. Mexico

DEAR LU;

Hi, you old fuck, how about sending me a few bucks to eat on down here?

How's Mardene[7] & everyone with you? . . .

TO CAROLYN CASSADY

October 4, 1967—11 A.M.
[Puerto Vallarta, Mexico]

DEAR MOMMIE,

It's true, I will bring home something *you'll know!* is good.

DAD

P.S. Caught a glimmer

7. In the 1960s Lucien Carr was living with Alene Lee, Kerouac's girlfriend in 1953, the "Mardou" of *The Subterraneans.* Possibly *Mardene* is a contraction of *Mardou* and *Alene*.

TO JOHN CASSADY

October 4, 1967
P. Vallarta, Mexico

DEAR SON;

As promised long—but not too—ago—long ago, I say—I'll write ya daily.

Love, DAD

P.S. Love to Jamie

TO JOHN CASSADY

October 23, 1967
[Puerto Vallarta, Mexico]

DEAR SON;

Here I am writing every day as promised—when was my last card, a month ago? Seems like a year; believe me: huh!

Anyhoo, as usual, expect one occasionally—if you don't see me first. O yes, I plan returning home before the month is out, or soon thereafter & I *mean* it!!!

I see Jim Clark won the Mexico Grand Prix yesterday—No I didn't see it—just read it.

P.S. (The heart of the letter) How are you?

Love,
DAD

TO CAROLYN CASSADY

October 23, 1967
[Puerto Vallarta, Mexico]

DEAR MOMMIE;

Napoleon had his 100 days too & since ole Speed Limit moves more (moron) on thoughts of you than his reasons I'll be back—or as Dugout Doug (MacArthur) had it: I shall return.

How's Jamie, John & Pat?[8] Has she published her book yet? I hope it sells well.

Love, N.

P.S. Please follow the advice of our old Sing Sing Sing record[9]—& swing too!! OK?

TO JANICE BROWN

[November 15, 1967]

DEAR JAN,

You're late. I thought you'd be here waiting—*it's time*
I love you, hurry up I can't wait much longer.

Second page More Same

Don't call, don't write—hurry on to me here

You better ditch those gigolos & get home to daddy Neal—lil Neal C.

Or call Gavin [Arthur] (346-?878) only if you aren't coming at once—otherwise just Roll on to PAPA.

Love, NEAL
Boo Hoo

P.S. Don't you miss me AT All Jan?

By the end of the year Neal had returned from Mexico and was staying at Ken Kesey's farm in Oregon. He visited Carolyn in Los Gatos on New Year's Eve, and a few weeks later arrived in Los Angeles, where he stayed with editor John Bryan, helping him with his current magazine, Open City. *He left on January 28 to travel to Mexico with an experimental filmmaker from UCLA and to meet up again with his current girlfriend, Janice Brown, in San Miguel de Allende. On February 3, Neal left J.B.'s house to walk to the railroad depot to pick up his belongings. On the way he came across a*

8. Pat McIntyre, one of the directors of Communications Fashions International, was living with Carolyn at this time and had written a romance, which remains unpublished.

9. "Sing, Sing, Sing," recorded by Benny Goodman at Carnegie Hall, 1938.

Mexican wedding party and drank alcohol with them, on top of the barbiturates he'd previously taken. He walked on toward the depot and was found unconscious the following morning beside the railroad track. Taken to the local hospital, he did not recover but died four days before his forty-second birthday. His body was cremated in Mexico.

Permissions

Excerpt from "I'll Remember April" by Don Raye, Gene DePaul, and Pat Johnston. Copyright © 1941 by MCA Music Publishing (ASCAP). International copyright secured. All rights reserved. Used by permission of Universal Music Publishing Group and Hub Music Company.

Except from "Java Jive," words and music by Milton Drake and Ben Oakland. © 1940 Warner Bros. Inc. © renewed 1968 Warner Bros. Inc. and Sony Tunes Inc. All rights outside the U.S.A. controlled by Warner Bros. Inc. All rights reserved. Used by permission. Warner Bros. Publications U.S. Inc., Miami, Florida 33014.

For permission to reprint letters acknowledgment is made to Sheri Baird; Elaine Friedman; Estate of Carl Solomon; James Grauerholz; Curtis Hansen; Ann Murphy; Jerome Poynton, Executor, Estate of Herbert Huncke; Bob Rosenthal, Trustee, Allen Ginsberg Trust (© Allen Ginsberg Trust); and Seymour Wyse.

Notes

Some of Neal's punctuation has been edited, in the interest of readability. His spelling and grammar were generally good, although some errors including misspelled proper names have been corrected. The spelling of Neal Sr. has been left intact in order that it might be compared with the descriptions of his letters given by Kerouac in *Visions of Cody* and *On the Road*. The removal of a single sentence from one of the letters in this collection (for reasons of sensibility) is indicated by [. . .].

Many of Neal Cassady's letters form part of an exchange of correspondence with Jack Kerouac, most of whose letters to Neal are published in *Jack Kerouac: Selected Letters, 1940–1956,* edited by Ann Charters. References are made to the appropriate pages of this volume (denoted by the abbreviation *SL*) in the notes. Similarly, Allen Ginsberg's letter exchanges with Neal can be found in *As Ever: The Collected Correspondence of Allen Ginsberg & Neal Cassady,* edited by Barry Gifford, and have also been referenced where appropriate.

Readers are directed to Carolyn Cassady's memoir *Off the Road: Twenty Years with Cassady, Kerouac and Ginsberg* for further details concerning many of the events mentioned in Neal's letters, as well as to Kerouac's novels, in particular *On the Road* and *Visions of Cody,* for a somewhat fictionalized treatment of the same.

MAIN SOURCES

Carolyn Cassady
Neal Cassady Estate
Berkshire, England

Carolyn and Neal Cassady Papers
Harry Ransom Humanities Research Center
The University of Texas at Austin

Allen Ginsberg Papers
Rare Book and Manuscript Room
Butler Library
Columbia University
New York, New York

Allen Ginsberg Collection
Department of Special Collections and University Archives
Green Library
Stanford University
Stanford, California

Neal Cassady Collection
The Bancroft Library
University of California
Berkeley, California

SOURCES OF INDIVIDUAL LETTERS

Abbreviations

AL	autograph letter	TL	typed letter
ALS	autograph letter, signed	TLS	typed letter, signed
APCS	autograph postcard, signed	TPC	typed postcard
TG	telegram	TPCS	typed postcard, signed

1944

October 8	To Justin Brierly. ALS. Edward White.
October	To Justin Brierly. ALS. Edward White.
October 23	To Justin Brierly. ALS. Edward White.
October 30	To Justin Brierly. TL. Edward White.
November	To Justin Brierly. ALS. Edward White.

1945

January 8	To Justin Brierly. ALS. Edward White.
February 5	To Justin Brierly. ALS. Edward White.
March 26	To Justin Brierly. TL. Edward White.

1947

January 17	To Allen Ginsberg. ALS. Columbia University.
March 6	To Allen Ginsberg. ALS. Columbia University.
March 7	To Jack Kerouac. ALS. University of Texas.
March 10	To Allen Ginsberg. ALS. Columbia University.
March 13	To Jack Kerouac. TLS. University of Texas.
March 14	To Allen Ginsberg. TLS. Columbia University.
March 20	To Allen Ginsberg. TLS. Columbia University.
March 27	To Jack Kerouac. TLS. University of Texas.
March 30	To Allen Ginsberg. TLS. Columbia University.
April 1	To Allen Ginsberg. TLS. Columbia University.

April 10	To Allen Ginsberg. TLS. Columbia University.
April 15	To Allen Ginsberg. TLS. Columbia University.
April 15	To Jack Kerouac. TLS. University of Texas.
May 8	To Allen Ginsberg. TL. Columbia University.
May 15	To Allen Ginsberg. TLS. Columbia University.
May 20	To Jack Kerouac. TLS. University of Texas.
June	To Allen Ginsberg. TLS. Columbia University.
July	To LuAnne Cassady. Allen Ginsberg notebook. Stanford University.
August 22	To Jack Kerouac. TLS. University of Texas.
August 31	To Jack Kerouac. ALS. University of Texas.
September 10	To Allen Ginsberg. ALS. Columbia University.
September 20	To Jack Kerouac. ALS. University of Texas.
October	To Jack Kerouac. ALS. University of Texas.
November 5	To Jack Kerouac. TLS. Columbia University of Texas.
November 18	To Allen Ginsberg. TL. Columbia University.
November 21	To Jack Kerouac. TLS. University of Texas.
December 25	To Jack Kerouac. TLS. University of Texas.
December 30	To Allen Ginsberg. TLS. Columbia University.

1948

January 7	To Jack Kerouac. TLS. University of Texas.
June 16	To Jack Kerouac. ALS. University of Texas.
June	To Neal Cassady from Allen Ginsberg. ALS. Columbia University.
July 5	To Jack Kerouac. TLS. University of Texas.
July 23	To Jack Kerouac. TLS. University of Texas.
July	To Allen Ginsberg. TLS. Columbia University.
August 3	To Allen Ginsberg. TLS. Columbia University.
August 10	To Bill Tomson. TLS (incomplete). Tamar Kotoski.
August 20	To Allen Ginsberg. AL. Columbia University.
September 7	To Allen Ginsberg. ALS. Columbia University.
September 10	To Jack Kerouac. ALS. University of Texas.
October 7	To Jack Kerouac. AL. University of Texas.

1949

January 10	To Helen Hinkle. AL. Columbia University.
January 10	To William Burroughs. AL. Columbia University.
January 11	To Carolyn Cassady. ALS. Columbia University.
February 3	To Allen Ginsberg. TL. Columbia University.
March 15	To Allen Ginsberg. TL. Columbia University.
July 3	To Jack Kerouac. TL. University of Texas.
July	To Jack Kerouac. TL. University of Texas.
August	To Carolyn Cassady. ALS. Carolyn Cassady.

1950

July 13	To Diana Hansen Cassady. ALS. Private collection.
July 19	To Diana Hansen Cassady. ALS. Private collection.
July 20	To Jack Kerouac. ALS. University of Texas.
July 27	To Diana Hansen Cassady. ALS. Private collection.
August 12	To Diana Hansen Cassady. ALS. Private collection.
September 10	To Diana Hansen Cassady. ALS. Private collection.
September 11	To Diana Hansen Cassady. ALS. Private collection.
September 10	To Jack Kerouac. AL. (incomplete). University of Texas.
September 15	To Neal Cassady from Diana Hansen Cassady. ALS. Carolyn Cassady.
September 16	To Diana Hansen Cassady. ALS. Private collection.
September 22	To Jack Kerouac. ALS. University of Texas.
September 24	To Diana Hansen Cassady. ALS. Private collection.
September 25	To Jack Kerouac. TLS. University of Texas.
October 3	To Neal Cassady from Diana Hansen Cassady. TL. University of Texas.
October 5	To Betty Daly Cooper. TLS. University of Texas.
October	To Diana Hansen Cassady. ALS. Private collection.
October 10	To Diana Hansen Cassady. TLS. Private collection.
October 15	To Jack Kerouac. TLS. University of Texas.
October 17	To Diana Hansen Cassady. TLS. Private collection.
October 22	To Jack Kerouac. TLS. University of Texas.
October 30	To Diana Hansen Cassady. ALS. Private collection.
October	To Neal Cassady from Carolyn Cassady. AL. University of Texas.
November 1	To Carolyn Cassady. ALS. University of Texas.
November 5	To Neal Cassady from Carolyn Cassady. TL. Carolyn Cassady.
November 5	To Jack Kerouac. ALS. University of Texas.
November 7	To Diana Hansen Cassady. ALS. Private collection.
November 13	To Diana Hansen Cassady. ALS. Private collection.
November 15	To Allen Ginsberg. TLS. Columbia University.
November 20	To John Clellon Holmes. TL. Private collection.
November 25	To Allen Ginsberg. TL. Columbia University.
December 1	To Diana Hansen Cassady. TLS. Private collection.
December 3	To Diana Hansen Cassady. TLS. Private collection.
December 3	To Jack Kerouac. TLS. University of Texas.
December 7	To John Clellon Holmes. TLS. Private collection.
December 9	To Neal Cassady from Carolyn Cassady. TL. University of Texas.
December 11	To Neal Cassady from Carolyn Cassady. TL. University of Texas.
December 17	To Jack Kerouac. *Notes from Underground* #1, 1964.
December 22	To Jack Kerouac. ALS. Columbia University.
December	To Neal Cassady from Neal Cassady Sr. ALS. University of Texas.
December 30	To Jack Kerouac. TLS. University of Texas.

1951

January 8	To Jack and Joan Kerouac. TLS. University of Texas.
January 11	To Neal Cassady from Carolyn Cassady. TL. University of Texas.
January 13	To Neal Cassady from Carolyn Cassady. ALS. University of Texas.
January 13	To Carolyn Cassady. APCS. University of Texas.
January 17	To Neal Cassady from Carolyn Cassady. TL. University of Texas.
January 19	To Carolyn Cassady. ALS. University of Texas.
January 25	To Carolyn Cassady. ALS. University of Texas.
February 6	To Jack Kerouac. TL. University of Texas.
February 13	To Jack Kerouac. TLS. University of Texas.
February 27	To Diana Hansen Cassady. ALS. Private collection.
March 17	To Allen Ginsberg. TLS. Columbia University.
April 1	To Jack Kerouac. TPC. University of Texas.
May 15	To Allen Ginsberg. TLS. Columbia University.
June 19	To Jack Kerouac. TG. University of Texas.
June 20	To Jack Kerouac. TLS. University of Texas.
July 2	To Jack Kerouac. TPCS. University of Texas.
July 16	To Jack Kerouac. TPCS. University of Texas.
August 10	To Jack Kerouac. TLS. University of Texas.
September 7	To Jack Kerouac from Neal and Carolyn Cassady. TLS. University of Texas.
September 13	To Jack Kerouac. ALS. University of Texas.
November 28	To Jack Kerouac. TLS. University of Texas.
December 4	To Neal Cassady Sr. TL. University of Texas.
December 14	To Neal Cassady from Carl Solomon. TL. University of Texas.

1952

January 5	To Neal and Diana Cassady from Neal Cassady Sr. ALS. University of Texas.
January	To Neal Cassady from Carl Solomon. TL. University of Texas.
February 13	To Neal Cassady from Carl Solomon. APCS. University of Texas.
March	To Neal Cassady from Carl Solomon. TL. University of Texas.
March 22	To Neal Cassady from Seymour Wyse. TLS. University of Texas.
May 20	To Allen Ginsberg. TPC. Columbia University.
June 4	To Jack Kerouac from Carolyn and Neal Cassady. TLS. Private collection.
July 10	To Allen Ginsberg. TL. Columbia University.
August 21	To Diana Hansen Cassady. ALS. Private collection.
August 21	To J. C. Clements. TLS. University of Texas.
August 22	To Jack Kerouac from Neal and Carolyn Cassady. TL. University of Texas.
August 27	To Jack Kerouac from Neal and Carolyn Cassady. TLS. University of Texas.
September 2	To Jack Kerouac. TG. University of Texas.
October 4	To Allen Ginsberg. TLS. Columbia University.
December 2	To Carolyn Cassady. ALS. University of Texas.

1953

January 29	To Neal Cassady from Carolyn Cassady. TLS. University of Texas.
January 30	To Neal Cassady from Carolyn Cassady. TLS. University of Texas.
February 3	To Carolyn Cassady. ALS. University of Texas.
February 3	To Neal Cassady from Carolyn Cassady. ALS. University of Texas.
February 4	To Carolyn Cassady. ALS. University of Texas.
February 6	To Neal Cassady from Carolyn Cassady. ALS. University of Texas.
February 8	To Carolyn Cassady. ALS. University of Texas.
February 9	To Neal Cassady from Carolyn Cassady. ALS. University of Texas.
February 11	To Carolyn Cassady. AL. University of Texas.
February 12	To Neal Cassady from Carolyn Cassady. ALS. University of Texas.
February 14	To Neal Cassady from Carolyn Cassady. ALS. University of Texas.
February 15	To Carolyn Cassady. ALS. University of Texas.
February 20	To Carolyn Cassady. ALS. University of Texas.
February 22	To Neal Cassady from Carolyn Cassady. AL. University of Texas.
February 24	To Neal Cassady from Carolyn Cassady. ALS. University of Texas.
February 25	To Neal Cassady from Carolyn Cassady. AL. University of Texas.
February 27	To Carolyn Cassady. ALS. University of Texas.
March 1	To Neal Cassady from Carolyn Cassady. ALS. University of Texas.
March 2	To Neal Cassady from Carolyn Cassady. ALS. University of Texas.
March 6	To Carolyn Cassady. APCS. University of Texas.
March 7	To Carolyn Cassady. APCS. University of Texas.
April 13	To Neal Cassady from Carolyn Cassady. ALS. Carolyn Cassady.
May 6	To Jack Kerouac. TL. University of Texas.
May	To Jack Kerouac. AL. University of Texas.
May 27	To Neal and Carolyn Cassady from Charley Mew. ALS. University of Texas.
June 1	To Allen Ginsberg. TLS. Columbia University.
June	To Parents of Hal Chase. TL. Columbia University.
June 17	To Carolyn Cassady from Al Sublette. ALS. University of Texas.
June 29	To Allen Ginsberg. TL. Columbia University.
November 20	To Allen Ginsberg. TL. Columbia University.
December 4	To Jack Kerouac. ALS. University of Texas.

1954

April 23	To Allen Ginsberg. TLS. Columbia University.
May 23	To Diana Hansen Cassady. ALS. Private collection.
May	To Diana Hansen Cassady. ALS. Private collection.
June 8	To Allen Ginsberg. ALS. Columbia University.
July 14	To Mr. Bays. TL. University of Texas.

1955

January 5	To Natalie Jackson. AL. Carolyn Cassady.
April 12	To Neal Cassady from Natalie Jackson. ALS. Carolyn Cassady.

Spring	To Natalie Jackson. AL. Carolyn Cassady.
May 10	To Carolyn Cassady. ALS. Carolyn Cassady.
Autumn	To Neal Cassady from Carolyn Cassady. ALS. Carolyn Cassady.
December 15	To Jack Kerouac and Neal Cassady from Bill Garver. APCS. Carolyn Cassady.

1956

March	To Carolyn Cassady. AL. University of Texas.
November 1	To Allen Ginsberg from Carolyn Cassady. APCS. Columbia University.

1958

March 24	To Robert LaVigne. ALS. Columbia University.
July 7	To Neal Cassady from Allen Ginsberg and William Burroughs. TLS. Columbia University.
July 20	To Allen Ginsberg from Carolyn Cassady. TLS. Columbia University.

1959

January 7	To Allen Ginsberg from Carolyn Cassady. TLS. Columbia University.
January 10	To Carolyn Cassady from Gregory Corso. TL. Columbia University.
January 28	To Allen Ginsberg et al. from Carolyn Cassady. ALS. Columbia University.
June 12	To Jack Kerouac. TPCS. University of Texas.
August 25	To Carolyn Cassady from Allen Ginsberg. TPC. University of Texas.
October 12	To Allen Ginsberg. TPCS. Columbia University.
October 25	To Allen Ginsberg. TPCS. Columbia University.
October 27	To Jack Kerouac. TPCS. University of Texas.

1960

April	To Carolyn Cassady from Neal Cassady Sr. AL. University of Texas.
June	To Allen Ginsberg. APCS. Columbia University.
June 18	To Neal Cassady from Herbert Huncke. ALS. University of Texas.

1961

June 17	To Neal Cassady from Neal Cassady Sr. AL. Carolyn Cassady.

1963

July 21	To Carolyn Cassady. APCS. Carolyn Cassady.
July 24	To Carolyn Cassady. APCS. Carolyn Cassady.
July 26	To Carolyn Cassady. APCS. Carolyn Cassady.
September	To Allen Ginsberg. AL. University of Texas.
September	To Allen Ginsberg. ALS. University of Texas.
December 12	To Neal Cassady from Carolyn Cassady. TL. Carolyn Cassady.

1964

June	To Dave Haselwood. ALS. Stanford University.

1965

March 24	To Carolyn Cassady. ALS. University of Texas.
July 7	To Carolyn Cassady. ALS. University of Texas.
July 18	To Carolyn Cassady. ALS. University of Texas.
August	To Neal Cassady from Anne Murphy. TL. Columbia University.
August 30	To Ken Kesey. ALS. Columbia University.
September 9	To Ted Wilentz. ALS. Private collection.
September 9	To Ted Wilentz. ALS. Private collection.

1966

January 18	To Neal Cassady from Carolyn Cassady. ALS. Carolyn Cassady.
May 27	To Allen Ginsberg from Carolyn Cassady. TLS. Columbia University.
August 2	To Carolyn Cassady. ALS. Carolyn Cassady.
September	To Carolyn Cassady. APCS. Carolyn Cassady.
October 29	To Carolyn Cassady. ALS. Carolyn Cassady.

1967

January 22	To Jamie Cassady. APCS. Carolyn Cassady.
February 8	To Carolyn Cassady. APCS. Carolyn Cassady.
February 10	To Carolyn Cassady. APCS. Carolyn Cassady.
February 20	To Carolyn Cassady. ALS. Carolyn Cassady.
March 15	To Carolyn Cassady. ALS. Carolyn Cassady.
March 31	To Allen Ginsberg. AL. *Communication Company Broadside* #CC037.
April 1	To Carolyn Cassady. APCS. Carolyn Cassady.
April 12	To Allen Ginsberg. APCS. Columbia University.
April	To Allen Ginsberg. TLS. Columbia University.
September 15	To Lucien Carr. AL. Private collection.
October 4	To Carolyn Cassady. APCS. Carolyn Cassady.
October 4	To John Cassady. APCS. Carolyn Cassady.
October 23	To John Cassady. APCS. Carolyn Cassady.
October 23	To Carolyn Cassady. APCS. Carolyn Cassady.
November 15	To Janice Brown. ALS. Bancroft Library.

Index